FRANCHISE OPPORTUNITIES

22nd EDITION

A business of your own!

Sterling Publishing Co., Inc.   New York

TABLE OF CONTENTS

Published 1991 by Sterling Publishing Company, Inc.
387 Park Avenue South, New York, N.Y. 10016
Distributed in Canada by Sterling Publishing
c/o Canadian Manda Group, P.O.Box 920, Station U
Toronto, Ontario, Canada M8Z 5P9
Reprint of the 22nd edition of *Franchise Opportunities Handbook*
issued in 1991 by the United States Government Printing Office

INTRODUCTION

Franchising is both an old and new concept. The term from the French originally meant to be free from servitude. Its meaning in the context of present-day promotions is the opportunity for an individual to own his or her own business, even if he or she is inexperienced and lacking adequate capital. During recent years, franchising, as a type of business operation, has been expanding rapidly and entering into new areas of application. Statistical evidence of such expansion is contained in the study entitled *Franchising in the Economy*, published by the International Franchise Association, Education Foundation, and Horwath International. The latest study, covering the period 1988-90, reveals that franchised businesses accounted for $716 billion in annual sales in 1990. Retail franchising, amounting to $615 billion, is equal to 34 percent of total U.S. retail sales.

What Is Franchising?

Franchising is a form of licensing by which the owner (the franchisor) of a product, service, or method obtains distribution through affiliated dealers (the franchisees). The holder of the right is often given exclusive access to a defined geographical area.

The product, method, or service being marketed is identified by a brand name, and the franchisor maintains control over the marketing methods employed.

In many cases the operation resembles that of a large chain with trademarks, uniform symbols, equipment, storefronts, and standardized services or products and maintains uniform practices as outlined in the franchise agreement.

The International Franchise Association, the major trade association in the field, defines franchising as "a continuing relationship in which the franchisor provides a licensed privilege to do business, plus assistance in organizing, training, merchandising, and management in return for a consideration from the franchise."

A former president of the International Franchise Association described franchising as "a convenient and economic means for the filling of a drive or desire (for independence) with a minimum of risk and investment and maximum opportunities for success through the utilization of a proven product or service and marketing method." However, the owner of a franchised business must give up some options and freedom of action in business decisions that would be open to the owner of a non-franchised business.

In a way, the franchisee is not his own boss, because in order to maintain the distinctiveness and uniformity of the service to insure that the operations of each outlet will reflect favorably on the organization as a whole and to protect and build its goodwill, the franchisor usually exercises some degree of continuing control over the operations of franchisees and requires them to meet stipulated standards of quality. The extent of such control varies. In some cases, franchisees are required to conduct every step of their operation in strict conformity with a manual furnished by the franchisor—and this may be desirable.

In return, the individual franchisee can share in the goodwill built up by all other outlets, which bear the same name.

A company that depends upon the successful operation of franchise outlets needs individuals who are willing to learn the business and have the energy for a considerable amount of effort. It can supply the other essentials for successful operation of the outlet. Among the services franchisors may provide to the franchise operators are: (1) location analysis and counsel; (2) store development aid, including lease negotiation; (3) store design and equipment purchasing; (4) initial employee and management training, and continuing management counseling; (5) advertising and merchandising counsel and assistance; (6) standardized procedures and operations; (7) centralized purchasing with consequent savings; and (8) financial assistance in the establishment of the business.

Investing in a Franchise

Be Aware of Risks

Everyone knows that there is some risk in investing money in the stock market. Investing in a franchise is not much different. In some ways, the risks are even greater than the risks of buying stock. After all, if you buy a franchise you usually expect to invest not only your time, but a good part of your working life.

Some franchises carry a greater degree of risk than others. There are "blue-chip" franchises which, like "blue-chip" stocks, are offered by companies with a track record of successful operation. There are also high-risk franchises that are offered, like speculative stocks, by new companies without a proven track record, or by some fly-by-night operators.

The risk of buying a franchise is usually greater than the risk of buying a stock for another reason. When you buy stock, you are relying only on the business skills of the company that issued the stock.

When you buy a franchise, you are relying not only on the business skills of the franchisor, but also on your own business aptitude and experience. If you give up a good job to purchase and operate a franchise, you will obviously have a lot more to lose than your financial investment if the franchise does not work out.

Protect Yourself by Self-Evaluation

How can you protect youself against making a mistake in buying a franchise? No answer to that question is 100 percent reliable. But, there are some important steps you can take before you make a commitment to buy a franchise that may help to reduce the risk.

The first step, and often the most difficult, is to take a hard look at yourself. Ask yourself whether you are really willing to make the personal sacrifices—long hours at the franchise, hard work, financial uncertainty—that are often necessary for a successful business. Do you enjoy working with others? Are you a good supervisor? Are you an organized person? Or are you simply attracted by the potential profits?

Some franchisors will help you to take this careful look at yourself. A reputable franchisor, after all, is investing in you because the franchisor will profit from your continued success. Others may only check to be sure that you have the necessary money or credit to invest. In that case, you will have to do your best to ask these questions yourself. Your family and friends can make an important contribution to your self-evaluation, and their answers will probably be more objective than the answers of a franchise salesman.

Protect Yourself by Investigating
the Franchise

The second step is to investigate the franchisor and the franchise business as thoroughly as you can. The best way to proceed is to do what most people do when they buy a new car or a new home. Do some comparison shopping, look at more than one franchise, just as you would look at more than one car or house before deciding to buy.

If you have talked with only one franchisor about its franchise, the most important step you can take to protect yourself is to look at other similar franchises in the same line of business. This *Franchise Opportunities Handbook* will help you get started, since the first part of the index categorizes franchisors by the type of franchise they offer.

Look at the brief descriptions in this handbook of the franchises offered and the type you are considering. However, don't stop your investigation there. Call or write to at least a few of the franchisors listed in the same category for more detailed information. You may discover that some of them offer benefits not available with the franchise you have been considering.

Protect Yourself by Studying Disclosure Statements

If the initial information you receive from a franchisor does not include a disclosure statement (sometimes called an "offering circular" or "prospectus"), be sure to ask for one. It will be a great help in comparing one franchise with another, understanding the risks involved, and learning what to expect and what not to expect from the franchise in which you finally decide to invest. You should study the disclosure statement carefully before making an investment decision.

A trade regulation rule issued by the Federal Trade Commission requires the nationwide use of disclosure statements. Franchisors are also required by state law in 15 states to provide disclosure statements to prospective franchisees.

The disclosure statement will contain detailed information on some 20 different subjects that may influence your decision to invest or not to invest:

1. Information identifying the franchisor and its affiliates and describing their business experience.
2. Information identifying and describing the business experience of each of the franchisor's officers, directors, and management personnel responsible for franchise services, training, and other aspects of the franchise program.
3. A description of the lawsuits in which the franchisor and its officers, directors, and management personnel have been involved.
4. Information about any previous bankruptcies in which the franchisor and its officers, directors, and management personnel have been involved.
5. Information about the initial franchise fee and other initial payments that are required to obtain the franchise.
6. A description of the continuing payments franchisees are required to make after the franchise opens.
7. Information about any restrictions on the quality of goods and services used in the franchise and where they may be purchased, including restrictions requiring purchases from the franchisor or its affiliates.
8. A description of any assistance available from the franchisor or its affiliates in financing the purchase of the franchise.
9. A description of restrictions on the goods or services franchisees are permitted to sell.
10. A description of any restrictions on the customers with whom franchisees may deal.
11. A description of any territorial protection that will be granted to the franchisee.
12. A description of the conditions under which the franchise may be repurchased or refused renewal by the franchisor, transferred to a third party by the franchisee, and terminated or modified by either party.
13. A description of the training programs provided to franchisees.
14. A description of the involvement of any celebrities or public figures in the franchise.

15. A description of any assistance in selecting a site for the franchise that will be provided by the franchisor.

16. Statistical information about the present number of franchises, the number of franchises projected for the future, the number of franchises terminated, the number the franchisor has decided not to renew, and the number repurchased in the past.

17. The financial statements of the franchisors.

18. A description of the extent to which franchisees must personally participate in the operation of the franchise.

19. A complete statement of the basis for any earnings claims made to the franchisee, including the percentage of existing franchises that have actually achieved the results that are claimed.

20. A list of the names and addresses of other franchisees.

Protect Yourself by Checking Out the Disclosures

After you have read the disclosure statement carefully and have compared it to other disclosure statements, you should check the accuracy of the information disclosed. A good way to start is to contact several of the franchisees listed in the disclosure statement and ask them about their experience in the business. They can tell you whether the information provided, and any other claims that are made by the franchisor, accurately reflect their experience in the business.

Be sure to talk to more than one franchisee. No single franchisee can ever be a very adequate representative of a franchise program. He is likely to be either better than the average franchisee or below average. If the franchise is worth considering at all, it should be worth your time to talk to three or more franchisees. While you may wish to talk to franchisees recommended by the franchisor, you should also make a point of talking to franchisees who have not been recommended.

Look for franchisees who have been in the business for at least a year. If none has been in business that long because the franchise is a new one, the risks you will run by investing in the franchise will obviously be higher than those you would face if you invested, instead, in a well-established franchise with an established track record in your area.

You should also talk to franchisees who have been in business for only a few years. They are the ones who will be able to give you the best advice about what to expect during your first year of operation. That is important because the first year of operation is often the period during which the success or failure of a new franchise is determined.

Protect Yourself by Questioning Earnings Claims

If the franchisor or its representative makes any claims about the sales, income, or profits you can expect from the franchise, you should examine these earnings claims carefully and demand written sub-

stantiation for them. Remember: earnings claims are only estimates and there is absolutely no assurance that you will do as well.

Franchisors are now required by law in 15 states to provide to prospective franchisees detailed substantiation of any earnings claims they make. A trade regulation rule issued by the Federal Trade Commision extends that protection to prospective franchisees in every state.

This documentation of earnings claims, which will appear either in the disclosure statement or in a separate document, is required whenever an earnings claims is made—whether it is presented orally, in writing, or in advertising or other promotional materials. It is required regardless of whether the earnings claim is based on actual or projected results or on average figures for all franchisees as opposed to arbitrary figures met by a small number of franchisees.

You should examine the documentation carefully and be certain that you understand the basis for the earnings claim and the assumptions that were made in preparing it. Ask yourself what would happen if an assumption proved to be wrong. For example, what if the wages you must pay employees turn out to be higher than predicted or if you must pay a higher than usual rate of interest for any financing you need in order to obtain the franchise?

If you do nothing else, be sure to note what percentage of the franchisor's present franchisees have actually had sales, profits, or income that equalled or exceeded the amount claimed. Then find out how many franchisees did that well during their first-year of operation, when their operating results may not have been as good. Your own first-year operating results are more likely to be like those of other first-year franchisees than those of franchisees who have been in business for several years.

Protect Yourself by Obtaining Professional Advice

You would be well advised to obtain independent professional assistance in reviewing and evaluating any franchise you are considering. Such assistance is particularly important in reviewing the financial statements of the franchise and the franchise agreement to be signed.

The reason state and federal law requires franchisors to include their financial statements in the disclosure statement is to permit you to determine whether the franchisor has adequate financial resources to fulfill its commitments to you. The financial statements will reveal to a professional accountant, banker, or other experienced business advisor whether a franchisor's financial condition is sound, or whether there is a risk that it will not be able to meet its financial and other obligations.

Unless you have had considerable business experience, you may need professional assistance in reviewing the franchisor's financial statements to determine whether special precautions should be taken to insure that you receive the services and assistance that have been promised in return for your investment. The cost of securing this advice before you invest will be a small price to pay if it saves you from getting involved with a franchisor that cannot meet its obligations.

The advice of a lawyer is unquestionably the most important professional assistance to obtain before investing in a franchise. Do not make the mistake of assuming that the disclosure statement tells all that you need to know about the consequences of signing a franchise agreement and related contracts. The disclosure statement is not designed to serve that purpose.

A lawyer can advise fully about your legal rights if you enter a franchise agreement and the obligations that will be legally binding on you as a result. In addition, a lawyer may be able to suggest important changes in the contracts you are asked to sign so that they will provide better protection for your interests.

A lawyer will be able to advise you about any requirements of state and local law that will affect the franchised business and to assist with the taxation and personal liablity questions which must be considered in establishing any new business.

The cost of obtaining legal advice will be relatively small in comparison to the total initial investment for a franchise. Moreover, the cost of legal advice at the outset is invariably less than the cost of later representation to solve legal problems that could have been avoided in the first place.

At the very least, you should be certain that every promise you consider important made by the franchisor and its representative is stated clearly in writing in the franchise agreement. If such promises do not clearly appear in the contracts you sign, you may be legally obligated to comply with your own continuing obligations under the franchise agreement.

Protect Yourself by Knowing Your Legal Rights

The trade regulation rule issued by the Federal Trade Commission will give you and other prospective franchisees a number of important legal rights under federal law:

1. The right to receive a disclosure statement at your first personal meeting with a representative of the franchisor to discuss the purchase of a franchise, but in no event less than 10 business days before you sign a franchise or related agreement or pay any money in connection with purchase of a franchise.

2. The right to receive documentation stating the basis and assumptions for any earnings claims that are made at the time the claims are made, but in no event less than 10 business days before you sign a franchise or related agreement or pay any money in connection with the purchase of a franchise. If an earnings claim is made in advertising, you have the right to receive the required documentation at your first personal meeting with a representative of the franchisor.

3. The right to receive sample copies of the franchisor's standard franchise and related agreements at the same time as you receive the disclosure statement, and the right to receive the final agreements you are to sign at least 5 business days before you sign them.

4. The right to receive any refunds promised by the franchisor, subject to any conditions or limitations on that right which have been disclosed by the franchisor.

5. The right not to be misled by oral or written representations made by the franchisor or its representatives that are inconsistent with the disclosures made in the disclosure statement.

No federal agency will have reviewed the disclosure statements and other documents you receive from franchisors before you obtain them. If you think they are inaccurate or that you have been denied any of your other rights under federal law, you should send a letter describing the violation to John M. Tifford, Program Advisor, Franchise and Business Oportunities Program, Federal Trade Commission, Washington, DC 20580.

If a violation of federal law has occurred, the Federal Trade Commission is authorized to obtain civil penalties against the franchisor of up to $10,000 for each violation. If you and other prospective franchisees have been injured by a violation, the Commission may also be able to obtain a court order that will remedy the injury you suffered. Such remedies may include compensation for any money you lost and relief from your future contractual obligations, where appropriate.

You should be aware that the Federal Trade Commission may not be able to act on your behalf in every case. In that event, you will need to consult a lawyer about your other legal rights, which may include the right to obtain relief in a private lawsuit for the violation of any of your rights under federal law.

You may have additional rights under state law if you are a resident of a state with a franchise disclosure law, or if the franchise you are considering is to be located in such a state. The 14 states which now have such laws are California, Hawaii, Illinois, Indiana, Maryland, Minnesota, North Dakota, Oregon, Rhode Island, South Dakota, Virginia, Washington, Wisconsin, and New York. You should contact the state agency, usually the state securities commission, which administers the applicable state law, to obtain information about your rights and to report any violations.

The best protection, in the long run, is to know your legal rights, candidly evaluate your own abilities, and thoroughly investigate a franchise before you make a commitment to invest. To do this will take some time and effort at the outset, but you may save yourself a great deal of time and money later on—the time and money you could lose if the franchise does not work out.

One final word of caution is important. Do not make the mistake of thinking that an investment in a franchise is risk-free, or virtually risk-free, just because federal or state law may provide you with some protection. That protection is subject to a limitation and may not be able to remedy every case.

As a result, investing in a franchise will always involve a certain degree of risk, which you can ignore only at your peril. It is always better to do everything you can to protect yourself than to be forced to rely on your legal rights and potential remedies.

In addition, you should investigate the territory you are considering and the market potential for the product or service you will handle.

For each of these factors there are questions to be asked and many facts to be secured. A list of 25 questions was devised which should be helpful in evaluating a franchise opportunity. These questions are incorporated in this booklet under the heading "Checklist for Evaluating a Franchise."

To assist you in acquiring the necessary background, we have included with this publication an annotated bibliography of current franchise reading material which should be reviewed prior to investing. In addition, the prospective franchisee should consult the *Readers Guide to Periodical Literature* at the local library. The local librarians can be of assistance to those unfamiliar with library procedures.

There also are many local special business career counseling services that can help an individual determine his or her own qualifications by organizing the facts about himself and by surveying franchise opportunities in depth. Such counseling usually increases a franchisee's chances for success.

The obligations of a franchisor to the franchisee are in the Code of Ethics adopted by the International Franchise Association. A study of this code will help the franchisee evaluate the franchisor under consideration before making his or her final commitment.

Code of Ethics
(International
Franchise Association)

Each member company pledges:

1. In the advertisement and grant of franchises or dealerships, a member shall comply with all applicable laws and regulations and the member's offering circulars shall be complete, accurate, and not misleading with respect to the franchisee's or dealer's investment, the obligations of the member, the franchise or dealer under the franchise or dealership, and all material facts relating to the franchise or dealership.

2. All matters material to the member's franchise or dealership shall be contained in one or more written agreements, which shall clearly set forth the terms of the relationship and the respective rights and obligations of the parties.

3. A member shall select and accept only those franchisees or dealers who, upon reasonable investigation, appear to possess the basic skills, educa-

tion, experience, personal characteristics, and financial resources requisite to conduct the franchised business or dealership and meet the obligations of the franchise or dealer under the franchise and other agreements. There shall be no discrimination in the granting of franchises based solely on race, color, religion, national origin, or sex. However, this in no way prohibits a franchisor from granting franchises to prospective franchisees as part of a program to make franchises available to persons lacking the capital, training, business experience, or other qualifications ordinarily required of franchisees or any other affirmative action program adopted by the franchisor.

4. A member shall provided reasonable guidance to its franchisees or dealers in a manner consistent with its franchise agreement.

5. Fairness shall characterize all dealings between a member and its franchisees or dealers. A member shall make every good faith effort to resolve complaints by and disputes with its franchisees or dealers through direct communication and negotiation. To the extent reasonably appropriate in the circumstances, a member shall give its franchisee or dealer notice of, and a reasonable opportunity to cure, a breach of their contractual relationship.

6. No member shall engage in the pyramid system of distribution. A pyramid is a system wherein a buyer's future compensation is expected to be based primarily upon recruitment of new participants, rather than upon the sale of products or services.

Checklist for Evaluating
a Franchise

The Franchise

1. Did your lawyer approve the franchise contract you are considering after he or she studied it paragraph by paragraph?

2. Does the franchise call upon you to take any steps which are, according to your lawyer, unwise or illegal in your state, county, or city?

3. Does the franchise give you an exclusive territory for the length of the franchise or can the franchisor sell a second or third franchise in your territory?

4. Is the franchisor connected in any way with any other franchise company handling similar merchandise or services?

5. If the answer to the last question is "yes," what is your protection against this second franchisor organization?

6. Under what circumstances can you terminate the franchise contract and at what cost to you, if you decide for any reason at all that you wish to cancel it?

7. If you sell your franchise, will you be compensated for your goodwill or will the goodwill you have built into the business be lost by you?

The Franchisor

1. How many years has the firm offering you a franchise been in operation?

2. Has it a reputation for honesty and fair dealing among the local firms holding its franchise?

3. Has the franchisor shown you any certified figures indicating exact net profits of one or more going firms which you personally checked yourself with the franchisee?

4. Will the firm assist you with:

(a) A management training program?
(b) An employee training program?
(c) A public relations program?
(d) Capital?
(e) Credit?
(f) Merchandising ideas?

5. Will the firm help you find a good location for your new business?

6. Is the franchising firm adequately financed so that it can carry out its stated plan of financial assistance and expansion?

7. Is the franchisor a one-person company or a corporation with an experienced management trained in depth (so that there would always be an experienced person at its head)?

8. Exactly what can the franchisor do for you that you cannot do for youself?

9. Has the franchisor investigated you carefully enough to assure itself that you can successfully operate one of its franchises at a profit both to it and to you?

10. Does your state have a law regulating the sale of franchises and has the franchisor complied with that law?

You—the Franchisee

1. How much equity capital will you have to have to purchase the franchise and operate it until your income equals your expenses? Where are you going to get it?

2. Are you prepared to give up some independence of action to secure the advantages offered by the franchise?

3. Do YOU really believe you have the innate ability, training, and experience to work smoothly and profitably with the franchisor, your employees, and your customers?

4. Are you ready to spend much or all of the remainder of your business life with this franchisor, offering his product or service to your public?

Your Market

1. Have you made any study to determine whether the product or service which you propose to sell under franchise has a market in your territory at the prices you will have to charge?

2. Will the population in the territory given you increase, remain static, or decrease over the next 5 years?

3. Will the product or service you are considering be in greater demand, about the same, or less demand 5 years from now than today?

4. What competition already exists in your territory for the product or service you contemplate selling?

(a) Non-franchise firms?
(b) Franchise firms?

GOVERNMENT ASSISTANCE PROGRAMS

Minority Business Development Agency

Expansion of minority-owned businesses contributed to the creation of jobs and the introduction of innovative goods and services in the U.S. economy. Recognizing this, the Federal Government has established policies and programs to ensure continued growth of minority enterprise.

The major agency that implements federal policies benefiting minority entrepreneurship is the Minority Business Development Agency (MBDA), established within the Department of Commerce by Executive Order 11625. Among the functions MBDA performs are the following:

- Funds 100 **Minority Business Development Centers (MBDC)** in areas across the country with the largest minority populations. MBDCs provide management, marketing, and technical assistance at the local level aimed at increasing sales opportunities in both U.S. and foreign markets for minority firms.

- Awards **grants and cooperative agreements** to organizations such as state and local government agencies and trade associations, to assist minority entrepreneurs.

- Maintains an **Information Clearinghouse** to answer inquiries concerning minority business development, make referrals, provide information kits, and disseminate reports, statistics, and research on minority business.

- Operates the **Minority Vendor PROFILE System,** a computerized database listing some 26,000 minority firms. PROFILE is designed to match minority entrepreneurs with marketing opportunities.

- Conducts, funds, and promotes **research** on various aspects of minority business in the United States.

- Works with **other federal agencies and departments** that have programs of value to minority firms.

MBDA has six Regional and four District Offices. If you operate a minority business enterprise or plan to start one and need information or assistance, contact one of the MBDA Regional or District Offices listed below. Its staff can refer you to the MBDC nearest you.

ATLANTA REGIONAL OFFICE

Carlton Eccles
MBDA Regional Director
1371 Peachtree St., N.W., Suite 505
Atlanta, Georgia 30309
Tel: (404) 347-4091

Rudy Suarez
MBDA District Officer
51 S.W. First Avenue, Room 928
Miami, Florida 33130
Tel: (305) 350-5054

CHICAGO REGIONAL OFFICE

David Vega
MBDA Regional Director
55 E. Monroe St., Room 1440
Chicago, Illinois 60603
Tel: (312) 353-0182

DALLAS REGIONAL OFFICE

Melda Cabrera
MBDA Acting Regional Director
1100 Commerce, Room 7B23
Dallas, Texas 75242
Tel: (214) 767-8001

NEW YORK REGIONAL OFFICE

John Iglehart
MBDA Regional Director
26 Federal Plaza, Suite 37-20
New York, New York 10278
Tel: (212) 264-3262

R. K. Schwartz
MBDA District Officer
10 Causeway Street, Room 418
Boston, Massachusetts 02222-1041
Tel: (617) 565-6850

SAN FRANCISCO REGIONAL OFFICE

Xavier Mena
MBDA Regional Director
221 Main Street, Room 1280
San Francisco, California 94105
Tel: (415) 744-3001

Rudy Guerra
MBDA District Officer
977 North Broadway, Suite 210
Los Angeles, California 90012
Tel: (213) 984-7157

WASHINGTON REGIONAL OFFICE

Regional Director
14th & Constitution Avenue, N.W., Room 6711
Washington, DC 20230
Tel: (202) 377-8275

Alphonso Jackson
MBDA District Officer
600 Arch Street, Room 10128
Philadelphia, Pennsylvania 19106
Tel: (215) 597-9236

International Trade Administration
District Office Directory

ALABAMA

Birmingham—Suite 2015, 2nd Avenue N., 3rd Floor, Berry Building 35203, Tel: (205) 254-1331

ALASKA

Anchorage—222 W. 7th Avenue, P.O. Box 32, 99513, Tel: (907) 271-5041

ARIZONA

Phoenix—Federal Building and U.S. Courthouse, 230 North 1st Avenue, Room 3412, 85025, Tel: (602) 379-3285

ARKANSAS

Little Rock—Suite 811, Savers Federal Building, 320 W. Capitol Avenue, 72201, Tel: (501) 378-5794

CALIFORNIA

Los Angeles—Room 9200, 11000 Wilshire Blvd., 90024, Tel: (213) 209-7104

San Diego—Suite 145, 6363 Greenwich Drive, 92122, Tel: (619) 557-5395

San Francisco—Federal Building, Box 36013, 450 Golden Gate Avenue, 94102, Tel: (415) 556-5860

COLORADO

Denver—Room 600, 1625 Broadway, 80202, Tel: (303) 844-3246

CONNECTICUT

Hartford—Room 610-B, Federal Office Building, 450 Main Street, 06103, Tel: (203) 240-3530

FLORIDA

Miami—Suite 224, Federal Building, 51 S.W. First Avenue, 33130, Tel: (305) 536-5267

GEORGIA

Atlanta—Suite 504, 1365 Peachtree Street, N.E., 30309, Tel: (404) 881-7000

Savannah—120 Barnard Street, A-107, 31401, Tel: (912) 944-4204

HAWAII

Honolulu—4106 Federal Building, P.O. Box 50026, 300 Ala Moana Boulevard, 96850, Tel: (808) 541-1782

ILLINOIS

Chicago—1406 Mid Continental Plaza Building, 55 East Monroe Street, 60603, Tel: (312) 353-4450

INDIANA

Indianapolis—Suite 520, One North Capitol, 46204, Tel: (317) 226-6214

IOWA

Des Moines—817 Federal Building, 210 Walnut Street, 50309, Tel: (515) 284-4222

KENTUCKY

Louisville—Room 636B, U.S. Post Office and Courthouse Building, 40202, Tel: (502) 582-5066

LOUISIANA

New Orleans—432 International Trade Mart, No. 2 Canal Street, 70130, Tel: (504) 589-6546

MARYLAND

Baltimore—415 U.S. Customhouse, Gay and Lombard Streets, 21202, Tel: (301) 962-3560

MASSACHUSETTS

Boston—World Trade Center, S-307, Commonwealth Pier Area, 02210, Tel: (617) 565-8563

MICHIGAN

Detroit—1140 McNamara Building, 477 Michigan Avenue, 48226, Tel: (313) 226-3650

MINNESOTA

Minneapolis—108 Federal Building, 110 South Fourth Street, 55401, Tel: (612) 348-1638

MISSISSIPPI

Jackson—Jackson Mall Office Center, Suite 328, 300 Woodrow Wilson Boulevard, 39213, Tel: (601) 965-4388

MISSOURI

St. Louis—D7911 Forsyth Boulevard, Suite 610, 63106, Tel: (314) 425-3302-4

Kansas City—Room 635, 601 East 12th Street, 64106, Tel: (816) 426-3141

NEBRASKA

Omaha—Empire State Building, 11133 "O" Street, 68137, Tel: (402) 221-3664

NEVADA

Reno—1755 E. Plumb Lane, #152, 89502, Tel: (702) 784-5203

NEW JERSEY

Trenton—3131 Princeton Pike Building, Suite 100, 08648, Tel: (609) 989-2100

NEW YORK

Buffalo—1312 Federal Building, 111 West Huron Street, 14202, Tel: (716) 846-4191

New York—Room 3718, Federal Office Building, 26 Federal Plaza, Foley Square, 10278, Tel: (212) 264-0634

NORTH CAROLINA

Greensboro—203 Federal Building, West Market Street, P.O. Box 1950, 27402, Tel: (919) 333-5345

OHIO

Cincinnati—9504 Federal Office Building, 550 Main Street, 45202, Tel: (513) 684-2944

Cleveland—Room 600, 668 Euclid Avenue, 44114, Tel: (216) 522-4750

OKLAHOMA

Oklahoma City—5 Broadway Executive Park, S-200, 6601 Broadway Extension, 73116, Tel: (405) 231-5302

OREGON

Portland—Room 618, 1220 S.W. 3rd Avenue, 97204, Tel: (503) 221-3001

PENNSYLVANIA

Philadelphia—Suite 202, 475 Allendale Road, King of Prussia, 19406, Tel: (215) 962-4980

Pittsburgh—2002 Federal Building, 1000 Liberty Avenue, 15222, Tel: (412) 644-2850

PUERTO RICO

San Juan (Hato Rey)—Room 55, Federal Building, 00918, Tel: (809) 766-5555, Ext. 555

SOUTH CAROLINA

Columbia—Strom Thurmond Federal Building, Suite 172, 1835 Assembly Street, 29201, Tel: (803) 765-5345

TENNESSEE

Nashville—Suite 1114, 404 James Robinson Parkway, 37219, Tel: (615) 736-5161

TEXAS

Austin—Suite 1200, 816 Congress Avenue, 78711, Tel: (512) 482-5939

Dallas—Room 7A5, 1100 Commerce Street, 75242, Tel: (214) 767-0542

Houston—2625 Federal Building Courthouse, 515 Rusk Street, 77002, Tel: (713) 229-2578

UTAH

Salt Lake City—Director, U.S. Courthouse, 350 S. Main Street, 84101, Tel: (801) 524-5116

VIRGINIA

Richmond—8010 Federal Building, 400 North 8th Street, 23240, Tel: (804) 771-2246

WASHINGTON

Seattle—3131 Elliot Avenue, Suite 290, 98121, Tel: (206) 442-5616

WEST VIRGINIA

Charleston—3402 New Federal Building, 500 Quarrier Street, 25301, Tel: (304) 347-5123

WISCONSIN

Milwaukee—Federal Building, U.S. Courthouse, 517 East Wisconsin Avenue, 53202, Tel: (414) 291-3473

Small Business Administration

The Small Business Administration aids those planning to enter business, as well as those already in business. This assistance includes counseling and possible financial aid.

Counseling may be by SBA specialists or retired executives under the Service Corps of Retired Executives (SCORE) program and could include various seminars or courses, or a combination of services including reference publications.

Financial assistance may take the form of loans or the participation in, or guaranty of, loans made by financial institutions. Such assistance can be given only to those eligible applicants who are unable to provide the money from their own resources and cannot obtain it on reasonable terms from banks, franchisors, or other usual business sources.

The Small Business Administration can guarantee loans up to $750,000—7 years for working capital and up to 25 years for fixed assets (real estate, fixtures, and equipment).

A list follows of Small Business Administration field offices as of September 1, 1990, where more detailed information regarding the various services available can be obtained.

REGIONAL OFFICES

Region 1
(Connecticut, Maine, Massachusetts, New Hampshire, Rhode Island, Vermont)

60 Batterymarch Street, Boston, MA 02110, Tel: (617) 451-2023

Region 2
(New Jersey, New York, Puerto Rico, Virgin Islands)

26 Federal Plaza, Room 31-08, New York, NY 10278, Tel: (212) 264-7772

Region 3
(Delaware, District of Columbia, Maryland, Pennsylvania, Virginia, West Virginia)

475 Allendale Road, King of Prussia, PA 19406, Tel: (215) 962-3750

Region 4
(Alabama, Florida, Georgia, Kentucky, Mississippi, North Carolina, South Carolina, Tennessee)

1375 Peachtree Street, N.E., Atlanta, GA 30367, Tel: (404) 347-2797

Region 5
(Illinois, Indiana, Michigan, Minnesota, Ohio, Wisconsin)

230 South Dearborn Street, Room 510, Chicago, IL 60604, Tel: (312) 353-0359

Region 6
(Arkansas, Louisiana, New Mexico, Oklahoma, Texas)

8625 King George Drive, Dallas, TX 75235, Tel: (214) 767-7643

Region 7
(Iowa, Kansas, Missouri, Nebraska)

911 Walnut Street, 13rd Floor, Kansas City, MO 64106, Tel: (816) 426-2989

Region 8
(Colorado, Montana, North Dakota, South Dakota, Utah, Wyoming)

999 18th Street, Denver, CO 80202, Tel: (303) 294-7001

Region 9
(Arizona, California, Hawaii, Nevada, Pacific Islands)

Federal Building, 450 Golden Gate Avenue, Room 15307, San Francisco, CA 94102, Tel: (415) 556-7489

Region 10
(Alaska, Idaho, Oregon, Washington)

2615 4th Avenue, Room 440, Seattle, WA 98104 Tel: (206) 442-5676

DISTRICT OFFICES

Region 1

10 Causeway Street, Boston, MA 02222, Tel: (617) 565-5590

Federal Building, 40 Western Avenue, Room 512, Augusta, ME 04330, Tel: (207) 622-8242

55 Pleasant Street, Room 209, Concord, NH 03301, Tel: (603) 225-1400

330 Main Street, Hartford, CT 06106, Tel: (203) 240-7400

Federal Building, 87 State Street, Room 205, Montpelier, VT 05602, Tel: (802) 828-4474

380 Westminister Mall, Providence, RI 02903, Tel: (401) 528-4586

Region 2

Carlos Chardon Avenue, Hato Rey, PR 00918, Tel: (809) 753-4002

60 Park Place, Newark, NJ 07102, Tel: (201) 645-2434

100 State Street, Room 601, Rochester, NY 14614, Tel: (716) 263-6700

Federal Building, Room 1071, 100 South Clinton Street, Syracuse, NY 13202, Tel: (315) 423-5383

111 West Huron Street, Room 1311, Federal Building, Buffalo, NY 14202, Tel: (716) 846-4301

333 E. Water Street, Elmira, NY 14901, Tel: (607) 734-8130

445 Broadway, Albany, NY 12207, Tel: (518) 472-6300

Region 3

168 W. Main Street, Clarksburg, WV 26301, Tel: (304) 623-5361

960 Penn Avenue, Pittsburgh, PA 15222, Tel: (412) 644-2780

Federal Building, 400 North 8th Street, Room 3015, Richmond, VA 23240, Tel: (804) 771-2617

1111 18th Street, N.W., Washington, DC 20417, Tel: (202) 634-4950

100 Chestnut Street, Harrisburg, PA 17101, Tel: (717) 782-3840

20 N. Pennsylvania Avenue, Wilkes-Barre, PA 18702, Tel: (717) 826-6497

920 N. King Street, Room 412, Wilmington, DE 19801, Tel: (302) 573-6294

10 N. Calvert Street, Baltimore, MD 21202, Tel: (301) 962-2235

Region 4

2121 8th Avenue, N., Suite 200, Birmingham, AL 35203, Tel: (205) 731-1344

222 S. Church Street, Room 300, Charlotte, NC 29202, Tel: (704) 371-6563

1835 Assembly Street, Columbia, SC 29202, Tel: (803) 765-5376

100 West Capitol Street, Jackson, MS 39201, Tel: (601) 965-4378

Federal Building, 400 West Bay Street, Room 261, Jacksonville, FL 32202, Tel: (904) 791-3782

5601 Corporate Way, W. Palm Beach, FL 33407, Tel: (407) 689-3922

50 Vantage Way, Nashville, TN 37228, Tel: (615) 736-6850

501 E. Polk Street, Tampa, FL 33602, Tel: (813) 228-2594

1720 Peachtree Road, N.W., 6th Floor, Atlanta, GA 30309, Tel: (404) 347-2441

Region 5

511 W. Capital Street, Springfield, IL 62704, Tel: (217) 492-4416

1240 East 9th Street, Room 317, Cleveland, OH 44199, Tel: (216) 522-4180

85 Marconi Boulevard, Columbus, OH 43215, Tel: (614) 469-6860

Federal Building, 550 Main Street, Cincinnati, OH 45202, Tel: (513) 684-2814

477 Michigan Avenue, McNamara Building, Detroit, MI 48226, Tel: (313) 226-6075

575 N. Pennsylvania Avenue, Century Building, Indianapolis, IN 46204, Tel: (317) 269-7272

212 East Washington Avenue, Room 213, Madison, WI 53703, Tel: (608) 264-5261

100 North 6th Street, Minneapolis, MN 55403, Tel: (612) 370-2324

300 S. Front Street, Marquette, MI 49855, Tel: (906) 225-1108

310 W. Wisconsin Avenue, Room 400, Milwaukee, WI 53203, Tel: (414) 291-3941

500 South Barstow Street, Room 16, Federal Office Building and U.S. Courthouse, Eau Claire, WI 54701, Tel: (715) 834-9012

Region 6

625 Silver S.W., Albuquerque, NM 87102, Tel: (505) 766-1879

2525 Murworth, Houston, TX 77054, Tel: (713) 660-4401

320 West Capitol Avenue, Little Rock, AR 72201, Tel: (501) 378-5871

1611 Tenth Street, Lubbock, TX 79401, Tel: (806) 743-7462

222 East Van Buren Street, Harlingen, TX 78550, Tel: (512) 427-8533

505 E. Travis, Marshall, TX 75670, Tel: (214) 935-5257

1661 Canal Street, New Orleans, LA 70113, Tel: (504) 589-2354

200 N.W. 5th Street, Suite 670, Oklahoma City, OK 73102, Tel: (405) 231-4301

7400 Blanco Road, San Antonio, TX 78216, Tel: (512) 229-4535

1100 Commerce Street, Dallas, TX 75242, Tel: (214) 767-0605

10737 Gateway W., Suite 320, El Paso, TX 79902, Tel: (915) 541-7586

400 Main Street, Corpus Christi, TX 78401, Tel: (512) 888-3331

Region 7

New Federal Building, 210 Walnut Street, Room 749, Des Moines, IA 50309, Tel: (515) 284-4422

11145 Mill Valley Road, Omaha, NE 68154, Tel: (402) 221-3604

815 Olive Street, St. Louis, MO 63101, Tel: (314) 425-6600

110 East Waterman, Wichita, KS 67202, Tel: (316) 269-6571

Region 8

Room 4001, Federal Building, 100 East B Street, Casper, WY 82601, Tel: (307) 261-5761

301 S. Park, Room 528, Helena, MT 59626, Tel: (406) 449-5381

Federal Building, 657 2nd Avenue, North, Room 218, Fargo, ND 58102, Tel: (701) 239-5131

Federal Building, 125 South State Street, Room 2237, Salt Lake City, UT 84138, Tel: (801) 524-5800

101 South Main Avenue, Sioux Falls, SD 57102, Tel: (605) 336-2980

Region 9

300 Ala Moana Boulevard, Honolulu, HI 96850, Tel: (808) 541-2990

211 Main Street, San Francisco, CA 94105, Tel: (415) 744-6823

2005 N. Central Avenue, Phoenix, AZ 85004, Tel: (602) 379-3737

880 Front Street, San Diego, CA 92101, Tel: (619) 557-5440

301 E. Stewart, Las Vegas, NV 89121, Tel: (702) 388-6611

6477 Telephone Road, Ventura, CA 93003, Tel: (805) 642-1866

901 W. Civic Center Drive, Santa Ana, CA 92703, Tel: (714) 836-2494

660 J Street, Sacramento, CA 95814, Tel: (916) 551-1426

300 W. Congress Street, Tucson, AZ 85701, Tel: (602) 629-6715

Region 10

1020 Main Street, Boise, ID 83702, Tel: (208) 334-1696

222 S.W. Columbia, Portland, OR 97201, Tel: (503) 326-2682

W. 601 First Avenue, Spokane, WA 99204, Tel: (509) 353-2807

701 C Street, Anchorage, AK 99513, Tel: (907) 271-4022

Internal Revenue Service, Department of the Treasury

The Internal Revenue Service offers a number of services to assist new business executives in understanding and meeting their Federal tax obligations.

For example, a *Mr. Businessman's Kit* (Publication 454), which contains informational publications, forms, instructions, and samples of notices that the IRS issues to business concerns, is available free.

The kit is a convenient place for storing retained copies of tax returns and employee information. It also contains a checklist of tax returns and a tax calendar of due dates for filing returns and paying taxes identified on the folder. Copies of the kit may be obtained from local offices of the Internal Revenue Service. Employees of the IRS are available to explain items in the kit and answer questions about the tax forms, how to complete them, requirements for withholding, depositing, reporting Federal income and social security taxes, and the Federal unemployment tax. Copies of the kit may also be obtained by writing to the District Director who will have it delivered and explained at a mutually convenient time.

The Tax Guide for Small Business (Publication 334) may also be obtained at local office of the IRS, the District Director, or the Superintendent of Documents, U.S. Government Printing Office, Washington, DC 20402. Free.

NON-GOVERNMENTAL ASSISTANCE PROGRAMS AND INFORMATION

Better Business Bureaus

Files on many firms that distribute through the franchise method are maintained by Better Business Bureaus. A summary report for a specific company on which a Bureau has a record can be obtained free of charge from the BBB in the area where the franchising company is headquartered.

If the address of the local Bureau is not known, send a postage paid, self-addressed envelope with the complete name and address of the company on which information is desired to the Council of Better Business Bureaus, Inc., 1515 Wilson Blvd., Arlington, VA, 22209. The Council will either refer your request to, or provide the address of, the appropriate Bureau.

International Franchise Association

The International Franchise Association (IFA) is a non-profit trade association representing more than 550 franchising companies in the U.S. and around the world. It is recognized as the spokesman for responsible franchising.

The IFA was founded in 1960 by a group of franchising executives who saw the need for an organization that would speak on behalf of franchising, provide services to member companies and those interested in franchising, set standards of business practice, serve as a medium for the exchange of experience and expertise, and offer educational programs for top executives and managers.

The IFA is highly selective in its membership. The Association's Executive Committee approves all memberships. Not all companies applying for membership are accepted.

A full member must have a satisfactory financial condition; have been in business for at least 2 years; have at least 10 franchisees, one of which must have been in business at least 2 years; have complied with all applicable state and federal full disclosure requirements; and have satisfactory business and personal references. Full members are granted the use of the IFA seal in their advertising.

The Associate membership category is reserved for those companies who are new in franchising, considering franchising, or who cannot meet all of the requirements of full membership. Associate members may not use the IFA seal. They are admitted so that they can be guided by more experienced franchising companies. Like full members, their membership is contingent upon continuing adherence to the IFA Code of Ethics.

IFA also offers international memberships on an information exchange basis to franchising organizations in other countries. Educational memberships are offered at low cost to business and law departments of colleges and universities.

IFA historically has supported the principle of full disclosure of all pertinent information to potential franchisees. It annually distributes thousands of copies of its booklet, "Investigate Before Investing," which provides guidance for potential franchisees, and its Code of Ethics and Ethical Advertising Code are widely respected. The Small Business Administration, in its booklet, "Franchise Index/Profile," reprints the Codes and the IFA's membership requirements and suggests: "It is worth a letter to the IFA requesting a copy of the International Franchise Association Membership Directory to determine whether or not the franchise you are interested in is a member. The codes themselves are reassuring."

The Association traditionally has been an advocate of reasonable legislation and has actively supported legislation which would assure greater protection to potential investors. It has many thousands of communications yearly with persons and organizations seeking franchise information and has cooperated with the Midwest Securities Administrators Association (now the North American Securities Administrators Association) to develop a Uniform Franchise Offering Circular to further uniformity in legislation and regulation throughout the states. IFA believes such uniformity benefits the states, franchising companies, and potential franchisees.

One of IFA's main functions is to keep members alert to changes in franchising law and regulation. The Association holds an annual legal symposium which covers franchise issues in-depth, and a series of regional legal roundtable discussions covering specific legal aspects of franchising. The IFA closely monitors legislation affecting franchising and works with legislators and agencies to develop laws and regulations that benefit franchising.

IFA carries out an extensive educational program dealing with all phases of franchise management and operations. Educational meetings are held regularly throughout the year, both on a regional and national basis. One of IFA's new ventures is the establishment of an educational foundation to promote franchising courses in the nation's universities and business schools. The foundation will also provide research on franchising and act as a resource center.

The International Franchise Association is unique in its status as the foremost medium for information about franchising. A quarterly newsletter, "Franchising World," is distributed to members and contains the most recent information about developing trends in franchising. Also circulated to IFA members is the "Current Legal Digest," which contains updated information on the status of franchise legislation as well as summaries and analyses of the most recent decisions from the courts and administrative agencies relating to franchising.

Of great importance to the Association and its members is its effort to make IFA membership connotative of the highest standards of business ethics and conduct.

Further information on its services and membership requirements may be obtained from the Association's executive offices at 1350 New York Avenue, N.W., Suite 900, Washington, DC 20005. IFA's telephone number is (202) 628-8000.

SOURCES OF FRANCHISING INFORMATION
Books, Pamphlets, Periodicals, Directories, Etc.

A Woman's Guide to Her Own Franchised Business. Anne Small. Pilot Industries, Inc., 103 Cooper St., Babylon, NY 11702. 47 pp. $3.50.

Explains the opportunities that have been created for women and how to take advantage of them. Includes a listing of over 150 franchise opportunities.

Business Building Ideas for Franchises and Small Business. Med Serif. Pilot Industries, Inc., 347 Fifth Ave., New York, NY 10016. 48 pp. $3.50.

Presents helpful ideas and suggestions on the promotional aspects of establishing a new business.

Business Franchise Guide. Commerce Clearing House, Inc., 4025 W. Peterson Ave., Chicago, Il 60646. Monthly or more as required. For price contact CCH, Inc.

Contains laws, rules, regulations, and reports of current developments involving state and federal franchising controls.

Checklist for Going into Business. Small Business Administration, Washington, DC 20416. Small Marketers Aids No. 71, 12 pp., Free.

Checklist designed to help the prospective franchisee decide whether he is qualified or has considered the various phases of going into business for himself.

The Complete Handbook of Franchising. David D. Seltz. Addison-Wesley, Gen. Books Div., Reading, MA 01867. 1981, 247 pp. $49.95.

For both franchisors and franchisees, this definitive handbook takes a step-by-step approach through the entire process—from planning and feasibility determination right through setup and daily operation.

Continental Franchise Review. 5000 S. Quebec, Suite 450, Denver, CO 80237. Bi-weekly, $155 annual subscription. Six-month trial subscription available for $77.50.

Eight-page analytical newsletter to keep both franchisors and franchisees informed and current on important topics.

Directory of Franchise Business Opportunities. Franchise Business Opportunities Publishing Co., Suite 205, 1725 Washington Rd., Pittsburgh, PA 15241 Published yearly, $23.95 plus postage.

Includes over 1,000 franchise and business opportunities with pertinent data and home office and/or business address.

Directory of Franchising Organizations. Revised annually. Pilot Industries, Inc., 103 Cooper St., Babylon, NY 11702. $5.00.

A comprehensive listing of the nation's top moneymaking franchises with concise description and approximate investment. Includes important facts about franchising and evaluation checklist.

Evaluation and Buying a Franchise. James A. Meaney. Pilot Industries, Inc., 103 Cooper Street, Babylon, NY 11702. 1988. $3.95.

Financial Security and Independence Through a Small Business Franchise. Donald J. Scherer. Pilot Industries, Inc., 103 Cooper St., Babylon, NY 11702. Revised 1976. 48 pp. $3.95.

Guide describing the management requirements, basic record-keeping methods, proper financial arrangements, and income potential to be derived from the establishment and operation of a franchise business with limited investment.

The Franchise Annual. Info Press, 736 Center St., Lewiston, NY 14092. Annual, $34.95 plus $3.00 postage.

Includes over 5,000 franchise headquarters with description and investment requirements. Handbook section details pertinent franchise information and how to enter a franchise agreement.

Franchise Encyclopedia. Dr. Alfred J. Modica. Published by ADA Publishing, 28 Sandrock Avenue, Dobbs Ferry, NY 10522. 1986, 300 pp. $75.00 including mailing.

Includes articles on franchising and articles relevant to franchising as a means for economic growth. Graphs and charts included.

The Franchise Game. (Rules and Players.) Harold Nedell. Olempco, Dept. C., P.O. Box 27963, Houston, TX 77027. $8.

Deals with emotional, physical, and mental traumas experienced by franchisees and provides insight from the point of view of franchisors as well as franchisees.

Franchise Investigation: A Contract Negotiation. Harry Gross and Robert S. Levy. Pilot Industries, Inc., 103 Cooper St., Babylon, NY 11702. 40 pp. $2.50.

Explains how to select, analyze, and investigate a franchise and then what to look for when negotiating the franchise contract.

Franchise Law Bibliography. American Bar Association, 750 N. Lake Shore Dr., Chicago, IL 60611. $20.

Contains over 350 annotated entries dealing with the law of franchising covering the years 1966 through mid-1982.

Franchise Manual. Dr. Alfred J. Modica and Dr. Anthony F. Libertella. Published by The National/International Institute for Franchise Research and Development, 3 Barker Avenue, White Plains, NY 10601. 1986, two volumes, 450 pp. $85.00 including mailing.

Provides step-by-step direction on how to franchise your business from concept to design, proving out your program before selling a franchise, go or no-go decision, testing evaluation cash flow, legal ramifications, marketing techniques. Examples of case studies, legal franchise agreements, and how to capitalize your franchise program from blueprint to opening your pilot operation.

Franchise Opportunities Guide. International Franchise Association, 1350 New York Ave., Suite 900, Washington, DC 20005. Summer 1990.

Comprehensive listing of franchisors by industry and business category.

The Franchise Option. DeBanks M. Henward, III, and William Ginalski. International Franchise Association, 1350 New York Ave., Suite 900, Washington, DC 20005. $26.00 hard cover, $18.00 soft bound.

A complete guide to franchising. How to franchise or expand your business through franchising including legal and regulatory issues.

Franchise Restaurants. The National Restaurant Association, 311 1st St., N.W., Washington, DC 20001 $30.

Statistical appendix highlighting franchise restaurant growth between 1973 and 1988. Includes sales and establishment data, employment, international franchising, and minority ownership.

Franchise Suitability Questionnaire. Dr. Alfred J. Modica. Published by ADA Publishing, 28 Sandrock Avenue, Dobbs Ferry, NY 10522. 1986, 15 pp. $6.95 including mailing.

Are you mentally and physically attuned to the world of franchising? Save yourself considerable financial loss, wasted effort, and loss of health. The questionnaire asks you soul-searching questions only you can answer. Know yourself. Self-scoring sheet provided.

Franchise World. Published by Franchise Publications, James House, 37 Nottingham Road, London SW 17 7EA, England. Quarterly subscription 25 English pounds annually.

A magazine with current franchise topics and featuring business opportunities in franchising in the United Kingdom.

Franchise Rights—A Self-Defense Manual for the Franchisee. Alex Hammond. Hammond & Morton, 54 Riverside Drive, New York, NY 10024. 1980. $29.95.

Contains some perceptive insight into the franchisor/franchisee relationship and, in advising franchisees, highlights some of the pitfalls which can ensnare the unwary franchisor.

Franchising. Gladys Glickman, Matthew Bender & Co., Inc., 1275 Broadway, Albany, NY 12201. 1979 Revision. 4 volumes, 15, 15A, 15B, and 15C of the Business Organization Series. $340.

A legal look at franchising—for both the franchisor and the franchisee, including franchise relationships, legal and business problems, and development of the franchise-distribution agreement with legal citations footnoted. Also covers the legal, tax, and estate-planning problems facing the franchisee. Full text of state laws.

Franchising. Dr. Alfred J. Modica. Published by Quick Fox, distributed by ADA Publishing, 28 Sandrock Ave., Dobbs Ferry, NY 10522. 1981, 159 pp. $14.95.

Provides the practical advice necessary to succeed in franchising. Geared to special situation service related franchise. How to get into your own franchise business for less than $5,000.

Franchising—The How-To Book. Lloyd Tarbutton. International Franchise Association, 1350 New York Ave., N.W., Suite 900, Washington, DC 20005. $18.00

A practical guide that deals with every aspect of starting out in franchising and building a successful franchising operation.

Franchising: How to Successfully Select a Money Making Business of Your Own. Bruce Scher. Bay Publishing Co., 316 Fifth Ave., New York, NY 10001, 143 pp. $1.95.

New consumer guide written for the individual considering a career in franchising. Lists the eight major mistakes overlooked in the selection process. Shows how to investigate and evaluate all franchise opportunities.

Franchising in the Economy—1988-90. International Franchise Association, 1350 New York Ave., Suite 900, Washington, DC 20005. $25.00.

Summarizes the results of a special survey of franchisors.

Franchising: A Planning and Sales Compliance Guide. Commerce Clearing House, 4025 W. Peterson Ave., Chicago, IL 60646. 260 pp. $35.00

Provides a realistic discussion of the business planning and legal considerations as well as procedural tasks to be reviewed before setting up, selling, and running a franchise program.

Franchising Realities & Remedies. Harold Brown. Law Journal Seminal Press, 111 Eighth Ave., New York, NY, 10011. Summer 1986. $70.

Outlines sound courses of action that franchisees may consider and sound principles against which franchisors must examine their operations if their enterprises are to avoid destruction through legal attacks.

Franchising: Regulation of Buying and Selling a Franchise.
Philip F. Zeidman, Perry C. Ausbrook and H. Bret Lowell. Bureau of Nat'l Affairs, 9435 Key West Ave., Rockville, MD 20850 (CPS Portfolio #34. $50.)

Provides a how-to guide to franchise registration and disclosure and an in-depth analysis of the legal requirements for determining when a franchise exists.

Franchising: The Inside Story.
John Kinch, International Franchise Association, 1350 New York Ave., Suite 900, Washington, DC 20005. $18.00.

How to start your own franchise business and succeed including some basic and essential steps.

Franchising Opportunities.
International Franchise Association, 1350 New York Ave., N.W., Suite 900, Washington, DC 20005. $22 per year.

IFA's bi-monthly magazine that gives you all the news on what's happening in franchising—operational, legal, legislative coverage plus in-depth interviews with franchisors, profiles on new members, meeting announcements, and tidbits on individual franchise company events.

FTC Franchising Rule: The IFA Compliance Kit.
International Franchise Association, 1350 New York Ave., N.W., Suite 900, Washington, DC 20005. $120.

A comprehensive overview of the FTC rule and the various state of disclosure requirements rounded out with explanatory analyses, comparisons, and checklists prepared by IFA legal staff. Packaged in a handy 3-ring binder, the kit includes an update service of all advisory opinions issued.

Government Regulation of Real Estate Franchising.
Peter D. Baird, John L. Hay, and Judith M. Baily. Appears in American Bar Association publication, *Real Property, Probate and Trust Journal*, Pates 580-619. Vol. 12, Fall 1977. Can be found in any law library.

An excellent summary and guide to regulatory issues and actions facing real estate franchisors.

The Guide to Franchising.
M. Mendelsohn. Pergamon Press, Inc., Fairview Park, Elmsfork, NY 10523. 4th Edition. 1985, 275 pp. $48.

A referenced guide to the basic principles of U.K. franchising the meaning, advantages and disadvantages are detailed. Types of products and services, selection, fees, leasing, contracts, services, training and the future of franchising are discussed. Examined are the operations of eight established U.K. franchisors. Information on entering the U.K. market from abroad also is provided.

How To Be a Franchisor.
Robert E. Kushell and Carl E. Zwisler III, International Franchise Association, 1350 New York Ave., N.W., Suite 900, Washington, DC $7.00.

This booklet provides step-by-step details about how to launch a franchise program. Written from both the operational and legal perspectives, it provides necessary reading for all potential franchisors.

How To Evaluate a Franchise.
Martin Mendelsohn. Franchise World, James House, 37 Nottingham Road, London SW 17 7EA, England. Check for price.

A guide for those who are planning to set up on their own in a franchise business.

How To Franchise Your Business.
Mack A. Lewis. Pilot Industries, Inc., 103 Cooper St., Babylon, NY 11702. 1990. 48 pp. $3.50.

This book shows step-by-step procedures to follow to franchise a business. The information given is not theoretical. Actual franchise operations were started and successfully marketed using these methods.

How To Organize a Franchise Advisory Council.
International Franchise Association, 1350 New York Ave., N.W., Suite 900, Washington, DC 20005. $10.

A major contribution to smoother franchisee relations, this publication explains the benefits of councils and tells in detail how to set them up.

How To Organize and Operate a Small Business, 7th Ed.
Baumback et al. Prentice-Hall, 200 Old Tappan Rd., Old Tappan, NJ 07675. 1985. 612 pp. (013-425736-7).

Role of small business in the economy. Buying a going concern. Justifying a new business. Acquiring a franchise. Financing and organizing the business, etc.

How To Prepare Effective Business Program Blueprints.
David D. Seltz, Addison-Wesley, Gen. Books Div., Reading, MA 01867. 1981, 167 pp. $25.95.

The book shows how to develop a system for "blueprinting" any new venture or concept, tells how to sell others on the merits of a program, and, most importantly, helps to determine the feasibility of a program.

How To Select a Franchise.
Robert McIntosh, International Franchise Association, 1350 New York Ave., N.W., Washington, DC 20005. $15.00.

A workbook and cassette tape designed to help individuals decide whether and how to become a franchisee.

The Info Franchise Newsletter.
Info Press, 736 Center St., Lewiston, NY 14092. Monthly. $80 annual subscription, $147 for 1 year.

An 8-page newsletter concerning recent franchise legislation, franchise litigation, and other current news in the franchise world.

International Franchising: An Overview. Science Publishing Co., Inc., P.O. Box 1663, Grand Central Station, New York, NY 10163. $61.50.

A volume containing papers presented by the Int'l Franchising Law Committee on the Int'l Bar Association's section on business law. Includes a survey of more than 20 countries and an introduction to franchising and its legal implications in those territories.

Investigate Before Investing: Guidance for Prospective Franchisees. Jerome L. Fels and Lewis G. Rudnick. International Franchise Association, 1350 New York Ave., N.W., Suite 900, Washington, DC 20005. 1974. 32 pp. $5.00.

Explains how to investigate and evaluate franchise offerings before investing.

Is Franchising for You? Robert K. McIntosh, International Franchise Association, 1350 New York, Ave., N.W., Suite 900, Washington, DC 20005. $5.00.

Basic primer for prospective franchisees with emphasis on self-evaluation to determine whether the opportunities and challenges offered by a franchise system meet the ambitions and abilities of a propective franchisee.

Legal Aspects of Selling and Buying. Shepard's/McGraw-Hill, P.O. Box 1235, Colorado Springs, CO 80901. 596 pp. $85 plus $4 postage.

The first practical how-to guide for antitrust, franchising, and distribution law.

Negotiate Your Way to Success. David D. Seltz and Alfred J. Modica. Published by Farnsworth Publishing Company, Inc., distributed by ADA Publishing, 28 Sandrock Avenue, Dobbs Ferry, NY 10522. 1980. 190 pp. $12.95 including mailing.

A must reading for those interested in negotiation for a franchise. Advice on "reading fine print" to winning points by being negative. Ingenious strategies. The examples are endless.

Pilot's Question and Answer Guide to Successful Franchising. Pilot Industries, Inc., 103 Cooper St., Babylon, NY 11702. 32 pp. $2.00.

Discussion of the franchise system with question and answer guide and checklist.

Protecting Your Franchising Trademark and Trade Secrets. Donald A. Kaul. International Franchise Association, 1350 New York Ave., N.W., Suite 900, Washington, DC 20005. $10.

An overview of the techniques which a franchiser can use to protect the trademark under which he operates.

Starting a Business After 50. Samuel Small. Pilot Industries, Inc., 103 Cooper St., Babylon, NY 11702. 1990. 48 pp. $2.50.

Information on how to establish a small business, a franchise business, and a business at home. Includes a list of over 175 franchise opportunities.

Survey of Foreign Laws and Regulations Affecting International Franchising, compiled by the Franchising Committee of the Section of Antitrust Law of the American Bar Association. Publications Planning and Marketing, American Bar Association, 705 N. Lake Shore Dr., Chicago, IL 60611. $50.

Developed from survey work in 20 separate countries, the book provides current information on such topics as the business climate and legislation affecting foreign franchisors; tax aspects; customs; and import-export controls; forms of doing business; labor; trademarks; antitrust laws; insurance/liability; and investment incentives.

Twenty-One Questions. International Franchise Association, 1350 New York Ave., N.W. Suite 900, Washington, DC 20005. $2.25.

The most commonly asked questions about franchising are answered by IFA.

Understanding Franchise Contracts. David C. Hjelmselt. Pilot Books, Inc., 103 Cooper St., Babylon, NY 11702. $3.95.

Analyzes the various aspects of a franchise contract and the Federal Trade Commission full disclosure regulation.

The Franchise Advantage: Donald A. Borian and Patrick J. Borian. National BestSeller Corp., 955 American Lane, Schaumburg, IL 60173. 1987. 235 pp. $18.95.

Explains in detail what franchising is, comparing it point by point with other forms of business expansion.

Own Your Own Franchise: Everything you need to know about the best franchise opportunities in America. Ray Bard and Sheila Henderson, Addison-Wesley, Gen. Books Div., Reading, MA 01867. 1987. 455 pp. $14.95.

This guide provides detailed information on 160 top franchises. Each franchise profile includes statistics, the business, what it takes, getting started, making it work, and getting more information. Introduction provides 92 question checklist for 5 critical areas when choosing a franchise. Indexes for type of franchise, investment amounts, and geographical area facilitate reader's research.

FRANCHISE COMPANY DATA

*Denotes Member International Franchise Association

AUTOMOTIVE PRODUCTS/SERVICES

*AAMCO TRANSMISSIONS, INC.
One Presidential Boulevard
Bala Cynwyd, Pennsylvania 19004
Don Limbert, Director of Franchise Development

Description of Operation: AAMCO centers service transmissions for all vehicles. Services include unique "Lifetime Warranty" for as long as customer owns car (honored at AAMCO centers throughout U.S. and Canada).

Number of Franchisees: 700 in U.S. and Canada

In Business Since: 1963

Equity Capital Needed: Approximately $48,000

Financial Assistance Available: To qualified applicants.

Training Provided: A comprehensive 5 week training course is provided at the company headquarters.

Managerial Assistance Available: Consulting and operations departments continually work with each center to insure proper operation. Technical training seminars and video tapes are available.

Information Submitted: April 1990

ABT SERVICE CENTERS
Division of ABT SERVICE CORPORATION
2339 South 2700 West
Salt Lake City, Utah 84119

Description of Operation: Alignment—Brakes—Tune-up repair centers which specialize in the one-day, high profit automobile and truck service needs. Guaranteed, fast, economical service performed in a "new" 8-bay facility, with the "right" equipment and the "right" training, is the backbone of this franchise. A strong managerial background is essential—training will provide the rest.

Number of Franchisees: 5 in 2 States

In Business Since: 1977

Equity Capital Needed: $51,000 (includes $10,000 operating capital).

Financial Assistance Available: Franchise includes 8 bay facility, signs, equipment, training with no need for additional equipment. Should a franchisee want additional equipment, financing through leasing companies, banks and ABT is available to qualified applicants. Franchisee must be financially qualified to guarantee construction.

Training Provided: 2 weeks will be spent in an ABT Service Center and at the company headquarters in Salt Lake City, Utah. This schedule will be increased if necessary. ABT operational people will then shift to franchisee's center for the training of his manpower. A grand opening will be prepared and held during this period.

Managerial Assistance Available: On a regular basis ABT personnel visit the franchisee to provide consultation in day to day operations and to analyze monthly progress. ABT provides operation manuals, training manuals, bookkeeping systems, insurance programs, advertising assistance and other management tools.

Information Submitted: April 1990

ACC-U-TUNE & BRAKE
2510 Old Middle Field Way
Mountain View, California 94043
Stan Shore, Chief Executive Officer

Description of Operation: ACC-U-TUNE & BRAKE centers specialize in automotive tune-ups, brakes, oil changes, air conditioning, state inspections and other minor repair and auto maintenance services. Typical tune-up and complete lube, oil and filter change is less than $68, is done in about 1 hour while customer waits, and is guaranteed in writing for 12,000 miles. Prices include both parts and labor.

Number of Franchisees: 10 in California and 8 company-owned centers.

In Business Since: 1975

Equity Capital Needed: $50,000 and approved credit rating.

Financial Assistance Available: Total investment of $140,000; financial assistance available.

Training Provided: Extensive pre-opening training, classroom training (about 2 weeks) and 4 weeks on-the-job training. Training includes technical aspects of repair work, bookkeeping, marketing, customer relations, shop maintenance, sales.

Managerial Assistance Available: Complete technical manuals, advertising manuals, and operations manuals covering all day-to-day aspects of managing a profitable tune-up center.

Information Submitted: April 1990

*ACTION AUTO, INC.
2128 South Dort Highway
Flint, Michigan 48507
Richard A. Sabo, President

Description of Operation: Retail auto parts, service and gasoline store.

Number of Franchisees: 68 company stores in Michigan plus 2 franchises.

In Business Since: 1976

Equity Capital Needed: Minimum investment of $140,000, excluding real estate.

Financial Assistance Available: None

Training Provided: Retail sales and automotive repair—30 days (combination of classroom and store/service center).

Managerial Assistance Available: 7-week management program—time being spent in corporate office in the accounting, data processing, and personnel departments; distribution center; and store location.

Information Submitted: April 1990

AID AUTO STORES, INC.
475 Doughty Boulevard
P. O. Box 1100
Inwood, New York 11696
Philip L. Stephen, President

Description of Operation: Retail sales of automotive parts, tools and accessories.

Number of Franchisees: 88 in New York and New Jersey

In Business Since: 1954

Equity Capital Needed: $140,000

Financial Assistance Available: None

Training Provided: Continual assistance after initial training.

Managerial Assistance Available: All necessary to properly train franchisee to maintain a stable business.

Information Submitted: April 1990

AL & ED'S AUTOSOUND
516 Monterey Pass Road
Monterey Park, California 91754
Michel Odle, Sales Manager

Description of Operation: Al & Ed's Autosound sells, installs and services mobile electronics products such as cellular telephones, auto security devices and car stereos. Turnkey retail stores.

Number of Franchisees: 11 in California

In Business Since: 1954

Equity Capital Needed: $45,000, complete franchise $93,000 to $165,000.

Financial Assistance Available: Yes.

Training Provided: 4-week training program in sales, administration and technical procedures. 2 weeks at corporate location and 2 weeks in-store location.

Managerial Assistance Available: Training and installations manuals provided. Franchisor locates sites, offers continuing field consultation in problem solving and keeps franchisee abreast of innovations and changes in industry. Franchisor assists in marketing strategy and trends.

Information Submitted: April 1990

AMERICAN TRANSMISSIONS
38701 Seven Mile Road
Suite 105
Livonia, Michigan 48152
John F. Folino, President

Description of Operation: American Transmissions centers service all types of transmissions, foreign or domestic. Specially trained mechanics are on-site.

Number of Franchisees: 17 in Michigan and Ohio

In Business Since: 1979

Equity Capital Needed: Approximately $83,000 depending upon location.

Financial Assistance Available: Personnel from American Transmissions can arrange for financial assistance, or franchisee has the option to acquire for his own outside financing.

Training Provided: A 2-week training program is offered which directs the new franchisee in management, advertising techniques, warranty and adjustment procedures, etc. This program consists of classroom and on-site training. Additional training programs and refresher courses will be made available on a regular basis.

Managerial Assistance Available: The home office continually works with the franchisee and his operation. Complete manuals are provided which cover operation, marketing, inventory, etc.

Information Submitted: April 1990

AMMARK CORPORATION
10 West Main Street
Carmel, Indiana 46032
Curtis J. Butcher, President

Description of Operation: Service, installation and repair of automobile transmissions. Only area franchises available with the right to sub-franchise in your area.

Number of Franchisees: 29 franchise locations in operation in Indiana, Ohio, Kentucky, and Florida.

In Business Since: 1974

Equity Capital Needed: Operating capital of $2,000 per bay and the ability to obtain loan to pay for franchise, parts, equipment and inventory.

Financial Assistance Available: AmMark Corporation works closely with franchisee in attempting to locate outside financing sources.

Training Provided: Initial training of from 2 to 4 weeks is provided for each new franchisee.

Managerial Assistance Available: The company will provide up to 12 hours of consultation and technical services per year without charge to the franchisee; additional consulting services will be provided when a suitable fee has been agreed upon. The company will sponsor at least one seminar each year for franchise managers.

Information Submitted: May 1990

APPEARANCE RECONDITIONING CO., INC.
12833 Industrial Park Boulevard
Plymouth, Minnesota 55441
Daniel Almen, President

Description of Operation: Appearance Reconditioning Co., Inc., offers a complete service to the ever expanding used car market that reconditions the auto interior or wherever vinyls, plastics, cloth and leather are found. The priority of the Appearance Reconditioning Co., Inc., is to provide its franchisees with continued support.

Number of Franchisees: 6 in 6 states.

In Business Since: 1977

Equity Capital Needed: $13,500 minimum

Financial Assistance Available: A total investment of $25,000 is necessary for an Appearance Reconditioning Co., Inc., franchise. The minimum of $7,500 is needed with financing available to qualified franchisees. (An approved vehicle must be obtained which is not included in the franchise package.) The balance, if financed, is payable over 3 years. Franchise has option to arrange own outside financing.

Training Provided: A 1-week training course must be completed before each franchise is in operation. Within 30 days of completion, a representative from the home office provides the franchisee with continued training. The home office provides constant support with each of its franchisees.

Managerial Assistance Available: Appearance Reconditioning Co., Inc., provides continual management support in areas of market awareness, inventory control, bookkeeping, advertising and technical guidelines. A manual of operations and training is provided and each franchisee is expected to know it thoroughly. Problem solving is offered at any time for each franchisee.

Information Submitted: May 1990

APPLE POLISHING SYSTEMS, INC.
6103 Johns Road, Suite 102
Tampa, Florida 33634
Jimmy Morrison, National Sales Manager

Description of Operation: Apple Systems, Inc., is a unique paint sealant for use on automotive, marine and aviation vehicles. We have a full line of products to be applied on both commercial and individual vehicles, with up to a 5-year warranty.

Number of Franchisees: 3,000 in the United States.

In Business Since: 1979

Equity Capital Needed: $5,000.

Financial Assistance Available: Call the company.

Training Provided: Intensive 3-day mandatory training class is scheduled for all new franchisees and personnel.

Managerial Assistance Available: Apple Systems provides continual management assistance and training sessions to review and update sales and marketing techniques and to disseminate other information and training to assist franchisees.

Information Submitted: May 1990

ATLAS AUTOMATIC TRANSMISSION, INC.
10303 Northwest Freeway
Suite 201
Houston, Texas 77092
Doug Fletcher, Vice President of Marketing

Description of Operation: Service and repair of automobile transmissions, automatic and standard.

Number of Franchisees: 26 in Texas.

In Business Since: 1964

Equity Capital Needed: $30,000 to $50,000.

Financial Assistance Available: Atlas Transmission can work with franchisee to locate outside financing sources if needed.

Training Provided: 2 to 4 weeks of initial training provided for new franchisee.

Managerial Assistance Available: The home office provides field consultation and managerial assistance on as needed basis.

Information Submitted: May 1990.

AUTO ONE ACCESSORIES AND GLASS, INC.
580 Ajax Drive
Madison Heights, Michigan 48071
Michael Daniels, President

Description of Operation: Auto One Appearance and Protection Centers specialize in the service and installation of auto and truck replacement glass, burglar alarms, running boards, sunroof tops, rustproofing, paint sealant, fabric protection and a complete line of automotive accessories. Glass suppliers, tooling, sealant compounds, technical data, marketing are provided by Auto One.

Number of Franchisees: 28 in 2 states, Michigan and Florida.

In Business Since: 1963

Equity Capital Needed: $40,000 to $70,000.

Financial Assistance Available: None.

Training Provided: 1 week at corporation, 1 week at operational shop, 1 week on their site with follow-up assistance as needed.

Managerial Assistance Available: Auto One provides continuing management assistance in sales, marketing and technical operations. Field service managers are on staff to support franchisees. Technical manuals and operations manuals are continually updated. Advertising assistance is always available.

Information Submitted: May 1990

AUTOSPA CORP.
343 Great Neck Road
Great Neck, New York 11021
Joel Tenzer, Vice President, Franchising

Description of Operation: Autospa facilities provide a 10 minute oil change and lubrication service. Special bays eliminate the need for lifts and new technology dispenses oil without cans. Building is approximately 2,000 square feet. The operation is similar to a car wash since it is an assemblyline operation and a drive-thru.

Number of Franchisees: 110 in 12 states

In Business Since: 1981

Equity Capital Needed: $50,000 minimum

Financial Assistance Available: If franchisee has a good credit rating, company will arrange to have the equipment package consisting of tools, tanks, computerized cash register, T.V. cameras and monitors, equipment, and signs put on a monthly lease. This comes to $35,000 for the total equipment package. Franchisee will own equipment after 5 years.

Training Provided: 1 week training program at franchisor's headquarters for franchisee and his personnel.

Managerial Assistance Available: Autospa provides a continual management service during the term of the franchise agreement in such areas as bookkeeping, inventory control and advertising. Operations manuals are provided. Field representatives are provided to assist franchisees and visit locations. Autospa continually conducts marketing and research to maintain high consumer acceptance.

Information Submitted: May 1990

AUTO VALET, INC.
7110 Blondo Street
Omaha, Nebraska 68104
Marge Johnson, President

Description of Operation: Auto Valet offers full-time or part-time opportunities for an individual. We offer to the public a guaranteed paint protection for the vehicle, guaranteed interior protection, dry cleaning for the interior, under-coating, rust proofing, and other detail services. The dealer can be mobile or have a store location. Also offering window tinting and sun roofs.

Number of Franchisees: 11 in 5 states

In Business Since: 1978, starting franchising in 1982

Equity Capital Needed: From $3,000 to $25,000

Financial Assistance Available: None

Training Provided: On-the-job training, in house as well as on location.

Managerial Assistance Available: Management, advertisement and marketing assistance.

Information Submitted: April 1990

*AVIS SERVICE, INC.
900 Old Country Road
Garden City, NY 11530
Jay G. Sanderson, Director, Business Development

Description of Operation: Avis Service Inc., D/B/A Avis Lube Fast Oil Change Centers will provide basic preventive maintenance for automobiles and light trucks. Service will include oil change, oil filter change, lubrication of chassis, checking brake, differential, battery and windshield washer fluid.

Number of Franchisees: 75 in 25 States.

In Business Since: 1986

Equity Capital Needed: A net worth of $250,000 ($100,000 in liquid assets) is required.

Financial Assistance Available: Real estate and equipment financing is available to qualified franchisees.

Training Provided: Avis Service, Inc., shall provide a 2-week training course for franchise owners and managers, and on-the-job training of franchisees/initial technicians. Training will include instruction and product knowledge, identity, hiring/interviewing techniques, scheduling, benefits, incentive programs, how to train technicians, hands-on experience, computer operation, customer contact and selling skills, operating procedures, advertising/marketing programs.

Managerial Assistance Available: Avis Service, Inc. will furnish management assistance to franchisees on a continuing basis during the term of the franchise agreement. Assistance will include manuals on the operation of the business, system identity, real estate, advertising and accounting. Area managers will be available to work closely with the franchisee. He/she will periodically visit the lube center to discuss operations, advertising, new producers and merchandising, and quality standards, and to assist in hiring and training new employees.

Information Submitted: April 1990.

BARGAIN BRAKES & MUFFLERS
Cherry Hill Plaza
1415 Route 70 East, Suite 612
Cherry Hill, New Jersey 08034

Description of Operation: Bargain Brakes & Mufflers Centers have in-house staffs of finance, real estate, training, back-up support and marketing personnel. Bargain Brakes & Mufflers Centers offers complete discount Brake and Muffler Centers.

3

Number of Franchisees: 25 in New Jersey, Pennsylvania and Delaware.

In Business Since: 1985

Equity Capital Needed: Approximately $20,000.

Financial Assistance Available: Franchisor has financial personnel to arrange and/or assist in financing. Franchisee has option of arranging own financing.

Training Provided: Franchisee receives 2 weeks of formal classroom training, then 3 weeks of "hands-on" training in their centers.

Managerial Assistance Available: Full help and back-up support plus training "up-date" for the duration of the agreement.

Information Submitted: May 1990

*BIG O TIRE, INC.
11755 East Peakview Avenue
Englewood, Colorado 80111
Dennis Brooks, Vice President, Franchise Development

Description of Operation: Retail tire store selling tires, wheels, shocks and other automotive products and services.

Number of Franchisees: 330 in 15 States

In Business Since: 1962

Equity Capital Needed: $100,000 plus

Financial Assistance Available: Equipment leasing program.

Training Provided: Up to 90 days classroom and in-store training. Emphasis on sales, management, personnel and all phases of retail management.

Managerial Assistance Available: See offering circular.

Information Submitted: May 1990

BRAKE WORLD AUTO CENTERS
2640 Hollywood Boulevard
Hollywood, Florida 33020
Gerald D. Hopkins, President

Description of Operation: Brakes, alignment, front end repairs, mufflers, and other light repairs.

Number of Franchisees: 15 in Florida

In Business Since: 1970

Equity Capital Needed: $25,000

Financial Assistance Available: Will hold mortgage on balance.

Training Provided: On-the-job training in all phases of operation.

Managerial Assistance Available: Managerial assistance provided in any way possible.

Information Submitted: April 1990

CAP-A RADIATOR SHOPS OF AMERICA, INC.
dba CAP-A RADIATOR SHOPS
2879 Long Beach Road
Oceanside, New York
Joseph Fels, President

Description of Operation: Cap-A Radiator Shops are clean, attractive shops located in high trafficked areas designed to appeal to the retail customers for service of auto radiators, heaters and air conditioners.

Number of Franchisees: 7 in New York

In Business Since: 1971, franchise business established 1980.

Equity Capital Needed: $24,000

Financial Assistance Available: Franchisor is willing to render assistance to franchisee in locating outside financing.

Training Provided: Franchisor offers a complete 2 week training program at company headquarters, which includes training in technical and managerial aspects of operating a Cap-A Radiator Shop. Franchisee will also receive 1 week of training and assistance at his location.

Managerial Assistance Available: Franchisor offers many managerial and technical aids including complete operating manual (describing proper operation of a Cap-A Radiator Shop), text books on technical aspects of the business, advertising and merchandising programs, and a sustained program of cooperation for the duration of the franchise.

Information Submitted: May 1990

CAR-MATIC SYSTEMS, INC.
P. O. Box 12466
Norfolk, Virginia 23502
W. W. Vail, President

Description of Operation: Car-Matic System operates a 2 level merchandising program. A distributor covers an entire marketing area. Retail profit centers handle the direct-to-consumer sales. A Car-Matic distributor supplies the retail profit centers in his marketing area with rebuilt transmissions, engines, and other parts. He also operates a retail transmission and engine exchange center at the same location.

Number of Franchisees: 12 in 4 States

In Business Since: 1919

Equity Capital Needed: Approximately—Distributor $150,000, Retail Outlets $26,000

Financial Assistance Available: $37,500 assistance is available to qualified people for distributor franchise.

Training Provided: Complete overall training available.

Managerial Assistance Available: Initial training of 4 weeks, and continual consultation services available when needed.

Information Submitted: May 1990

CAR-X MUFFLER SHOPS
8430 West Bryn Mawr, Suite 400
Chicago, Illinois 60631
Ray Slonieski, Director, Franchise Development

Description of Operation: Retail automotive repair chain that specializes in exhaust, suspension, front end and brake repairs. Franchising since 1973, Car-X Muffler & Brakes is a component of Speedy Car-X Inc. which also includes the Speedy Muffler King and Pit Stop chains.

Number of Franchisees: Presently operating over 135 Car-X Muffler & Brake locations in the mid-west United States. Speedy Car-X has currently over 700 locations worldwide, both company-owned and franchised.

In Business Since: 1971

Equity Capital Needed: $180,000-$200,000. Franchise fee $18,500.

Financial Assistance Available: Provide assistance to franchisee to help secure financing. Equipment financing packages from outside sources are also available.

Training Provided: Franchisor provides complete training program which is 6 weeks long: 3 weeks in Ann Arbor, MI, 1 week on-the-job training, 1 week at headquarters, 1 week shop opening.

Managerial Assistance Available: Franchisor assists new franchisees in site selection, financing, shop operations, local marketing, sales and financial statement analysis. Field supervisors are also available for inventory, sales updates and training.

Information Submitted: April 1990

CHAMPION AUTO STORES, INC.
5520 North Highway 169
New Hope, Minnesota 55428
Earl Farr, Director of Franchising

Description of Operation: Retail sale of automotive parts, accessories and tires.

Number of Franchisees: 119 in 9 States

In Business Since: 1956

Equity Capital Needed: $75,000 to $100,000

Financial Assistance Available: None

Training Provided: Sales and management training with minimum required by franchisor of 20 days.

Managerial Assistance Available: Franchisor gives assistance in advertising, inventory control, purchasing, sales, merchandising, expense control and employee management throughout the affiliation.

Information Submitted: April 1990

CLASSIC SHINE AUTO FITNESS CENTERS
428 West Putnam Avenue
Greenwich, Connecticut 06830

Description of Operation: The Classic Shine system offers the highest quality detailing service, featuring meticulous cleaning, polishing, waxing, compounding, of not only the exterior, but also the engine, wheels, trunk, upholstery, floormats, rugs, dashboard and door jambs. ALL CLEANING IS DONE BY HAND 1-800-72-SHINE.

Number of Franchisees: 9

In Business Since: 1984, started franchising in 1987.

Equity Capital Needed: $66,000-$120,000

Financial Assistance Available: None

Training Provided: 1 week at company headquarters and 3 days in the field.

Managerial Assistance Available: Ongoing managerial assistance provided.

Information Submitted: April 1990

CLEANCO INC.
8018 Sunnyside Road
Minneapolis, Minnesota 55432
James A. Trapp, President

Description of Operation: Truck washing—mobile units and drive-thru. A complete chemical wash.

Number of Franchisees: 16 in Minnesota, Wisconsin, Illinois, Georgia and Florida

In Business Since: 1963

Equity Capital Needed: $20,000

Financial Assistance Available: None

Training Provided: 1 week full training in Minneapolis, Minnesota.

Managerial Assistance Available: Ongoing in all areas of the franchise.

Information Submitted: May 1990

CONTINENTAL TRANSMISSION INTERNATIONAL
2328 Fort Street
Lincoln Park, Michigan 48146
Aaron Conley, Jr.

Description of Operation: Auto and truck transmission service.

Number of Franchisees: 1 plus 4 company-owned in Michigan.

In Business Since: 1978

Equity Capital Needed: Minimum $25,000

Financial Assistance Available: None

Training Provided: 2 weeks classroom, 2 weeks shop.

Managerial Assistance Available: Continental provides ongoing assistance such as bookkeeping, advertising, inventory control; will provide operating manual. Visit center on an ongoing basis.

Information Submitted: May 1990

*COTTMAN TRANSMISSION SYSTEM, INC.
240 New York Drive
Fort Washington, Pennsylvania 19034
Greg Mowry, National Sales Manager

Description of Operation: Cottman Transmission Centers repair, service and remanufacture automatic transmissions for wholesale and retail trade. Operator does not need previous automotive experience.

Number of Franchisees: 129 throughout the United States and Canada

In Business Since: 1962

Equity Capital Needed: $35,000 (total cost: $97,500)

Financial Assistance Available: A financial package designed to aid franchisee in loan negotiations with lending institutions.

Training Provided: 3 weeks training at the home office and 1 week training at operator's location. Continued assistance through operational support.

Managerial Assistance Available: The home office continually works with each operator on all phases of operation, advertising, sales, management, employee relations, remanufacturing techniques, etc.

Information Submitted: May 1990

DAN HANNA AUTO WASH
2000 S.E. Hanna Drive
Portland, Oregon 97222
Art Guariniello

Description of Operation: Automatic drive-thru, roll over and conveyorized car washes.

Number of Franchisees: 9 plus 31 company-owned

In Business Since: 1954 franchising since 1985

Equity Capital Needed: Total investment ranges depending on location from $350,000-$2,000,000.

Financial Assistance Available: Available to qualified applicant.

Training Provided: 4 weeks training at headquarters and 2 weeks at location.

Managerial Assistance Available: Continuous support with manuals, seminars, field representatives, hotlines and grand opening support.

Information Submitted: May 1990

DETAIL PLUS CAR APPEARANCE CENTERS
P. O. Box 14276
Portland, Oregon 97214
R. L. Abraham

Description of Operation: Complete automatic car wash business with options to do auto detailing, including waxing and polishing.

Number of Franchisees: 100 in 20 States and 6 countries.

In Business Since: 1982

Equity Capital Needed: Minimum cash $50,000. Total investment $100,000-$150,000.

Financial Assistance Available: Yes

Training Provided: On-site for time required. Training in factory locations as required by customer. Market study, site selection, financial engineering, layout, building design, services, equipment, installation, drawings, construction, supervision, training, operations management.

Managerial Assistance Available: Complete management training in all phases.

Information Submitted: April 1990

DR. NICK'S TRANSMISSIONS, INC.
150 Broad Hollow Road
Melville, New York 11747
Richard G. Brown, Franchise Director

Description of Operation: Transmission Service Centers provide quality repairs to all types of auto and light duty commercial vehicles in both the retail and wholesale trade.

Number of Franchisees: 32 Centers

In Business Since: 1972—Franchising since 1977

Equity Capital Needed: Up to $75,000. $21,500 franchise fee, $10,000 working capital required—remainder depending on inventory, lease equipment available, leasehold improvements necessary and personal credit rating.

Financial Assistance Available: Financial advice and counseling is available when necessary and upon request. The prospective franchisee is responsible for an investment to cover initial licensing fees and operating capital.

Training Provided: A comprehensive home office training program in all phases necessary to successfully operate your transmissions center. Also continuous field support and counseling.

Managerial Assistance Available: Prospective franchisee need not have any automotive technical experience. We provide ongoing training and assistance in all phases of center operations, including but not restricted to center management. Personnel selection and financial management. A professional co-op advertising program. Site selection assistance. Regular monthly meetings.

Information Submitted: May 1990

*DR. VINYL & ASSOCIATES, LTD.
13665 East 42nd Terrace South
Independence, Missouri 64055

Description of Operation: Dr. Vinyl franchisees provide a mobile wholesale service to the auto dealership community in their franchise territory. The service includes vinyl, leather and dashboard repair to car interiors and tops as well as complete recoloring of vinyl and leather, either to match or change colors; also installation of pin stripes, side moldings, and other cosmetic add-ons.

Number of Franchisees: 100 in 30 States.

In Business Since: 1972

Equity Capital Needed: Minimum franchise is $20,000, which includes all materials and training but does not include necessary vehicle.

Financial Assistance Available: Qualified applicants may receive financing assistance up to 40 percent of the required investment.

Training Provided: 2 weeks of training is required by the franchisor at the Kansas City headquarters. Franchisee is only responsible for room and board during training interval.

Managerial Assistance Available: All managerial and technical assistance is provided during the 2 week training period in Kansas City, Missouri. Technical, sales, accounting and business practices are included.

Information Submitted: April 1990

DURA-BUILT TRANSMISSION CENTERS, INC.
455 University Avenue, Suite 100
Sacramento, California 95825
Jay Beyers, Chairman

Description of Operation: Automotive transmission and driveline repair and service centers.

Number of Franchisees: 23 in Western region of United States

In Business Since: 1971, franchising since 1982

Equity Capital Needed: $55,000 minimum cash required includes initial franchise fee and working capital. Total investment $110,000-$125,000.

Financial Assistance Available: Dura-Built will assist in the preparation of all required documents for lender.

Training Provided: Dura-Built requires satisfactory completion of our comprehensive 4 week training program by all franchisees. One week post opening on-site training for franchisee and staff members. In addition: telephone consultation, quarterly on-site reviews, quarterly seminars, and one week management schools, plus operations manuals and video training tapes.

Managerial Assistance Available: Site selection, on-site pre-opening set-up; lease negotiation or purchase assistance; model inventory program; integrated computer software program; accounting and bookkeeping procedures; advertising and marketing programs; personnel manual; government agency regulation manual; operations manual complete with updates—all included in the franchise fee.

Information Submitted: April 1990

ECONO LUBE N'TUNE, INC.
4911 Birch Street
Newport Beach, California 92660

Description of Operation: "Turn-key" franchise offering full-service menu specializing in 10 minute lube, oil and filter change, 30 minute tune-up, smog inspection and certification, brakes, air conditioning service, transmission service, valve adjustments, belts, hoses and shock absorbers. Company builds 5 or 6 bay free-standing buildings.

Number of Franchisees: 141 in 11 States.

In Business Since: 1973

Equity Capital Needed: Approximately $160,000

Financial Assistance Available: $80,000 O.A.C.

Training Provided: Mandatory 3 weeks in all phases of operation.

Managerial Assistance Available: Day to day managerial and technical assistance is provided throughout the life of the franchise.

Information Submitted: May 1990

END-A-FLAT
172b Washington Road
Suite 205
Pittsburgh, Pennsylvania 15241
Gary B. Griser, Vice President

Description of Operation: A revolutionary product that eliminates flat tires. Distributorship available in all major cities. End-A-Flat offers each distributor a protected territory.

Number of Franchisees: 10 locations

In Business Since: 1982

Equity Capital Needed: $10,000 inventory plus working capital.

Financial Assistance Available: None

Training Provided: Company training in all phases of operations.

Managerial Assistance Available: Ongoing assistance.

Information Submitted: April 1990

ENDRUST INDUSTRIES
1725 Washington Road
Suite 205
Pittsburgh, Pennsylvania 15241

Description of Operation: Engaged in establishing dealerships for Endrust Auto Appearance & Detailing Centers. Services include wash, wax, interior cleaning, detailing, rustproofing, under-coating, sound deadening, exterior paint protection, fabric protection, car alarms, etc. Can be established as a separate center or a supplement to a present automotive business.

Number of Franchisees: 80 dealerships

In Business Since: 1969

Equity Capital Needed: $30,000

Financial Assistance Available: None

Training Provided: Company training in all phases of operation, on-going support.

Managerial Assistance Available: All that is required by dealer.

Information Submitted: April 1990

FANTASY COACHWORKS LTD
6034 S. Lindbergh
St. Louis, Missouri 63123
James Smoot, Jr., President

Description of Operation: A new concept in automotive retailing, the "Auto Boutique" features practical and functional motoring accessories for all cars, vans, imports and pickups, plus designer wearables for the driving enthusiast. Packaged in "high fashion" themes. Professional installation available.

Number of Franchisees: 25 in 4 States

In Business Since: 1975

Equity Capital Needed: $20,000 per single unit

Financial Assistance Available: Finance package preparation assistance.

Training Provided: 2 weeks intensive training at an existing boutique, operations manual, bi-monthly newsletter, site selection and grand opening planning and assistance.

Managerial Assistance Available: Managerial assistance provided in advertising, public relations, promotions, accounting/bookkeeping, co-op buying, product testing, sales, personnel, periodic visits from company field consultants.

Information Submitted: April 1990

THE FIRESTONE TIRE & RUBBER COMPANY
1200 Firestone Parkway
Akron, Ohio 44317
W. F. Tierney, Dealer Sales Manager

Description of Operation: Complete business franchise includes all phases of selling tires, auto supplies, and automotive services, backed up with national and local television, radio and newspaper advertising, periodic retail sales plans, display materials, and many other sales and merchandising plans for increased sales and profits. Master-care service program available to qualified operators. Complete identification program includes illumination signs available where practicable.

Number of Franchisees: Over 7,000 direct, including many associate dealers operating throughout the USA and Canada.

In Business Since: 1900

Equity Capital Needed: $85,000 or more; varies as to locations, business, equipment and inventory.

Financial Assistance Available: Sales and credit personnel counsel and assist franchisee to obtain necessary assistance through local source or through company's assistance programs.

Training Provided: Home office and field personnel are available at all times to train the dealer and his employees in all phases of sales and business management. This continuous program helps to insure an efficient and successful operation. Forms, self-training programs, on-the-job training programs, etc., are constantly being revised and up-dated to keep dealer informed on all aspects of his business.

Managerial Assistance Available: Home office and local sales personnel are available to give assistance on any matter requested, including all phases of retail selling.

Information Submitted: April 1990

FLY-N-HI, INC.
1661 East Camelback Road
Suite 118
Phoenix, Arizona 85016
Paul Harris, Marketing Director

Description of Operation: Retail business providing specialty parts, accessories and services for the offroad vehicle and sport truck market. Typical equipment includes shock absorbers, suspension kits, tires and wheels, seats and safety equipment, bed bars and grill guards, lights, winches and ground effects kits.

Number of Franchisees: 6

In Business Since: 1979

Equity Capital Needed: $150,000-$200,000

Financial Assistance Available: None

Training Provided: 2 weeks at home office in business and sales techniques, inventory control and FLY-N-HI methods and products. One week on-site training and assistance after opening.

Managerial Assistance Available: On-going technical support available during development and operational phases. Assistance in grand opening of FLY-N-HI Offroad Center. Annual workshops and seminars also provided for all franchisees. Full manuals provided by franchisor.

Information Submitted: April 1990

*GIBRALTAR TRANSMISSIONS
5 Delaware Drive
P. O. Box 5459
Lake Success, New York 11042
Dennis Ballen, President

Description of Operation: Gibraltar Transmissions Centers specialize in quality repair, rebuilding and servicing of automotive transmissions and replacement of radiators.

Number of Franchisees: 71 in 11 States

In Business Since: 1974—franchising since 1977

Equity Capital Needed: Approximately $120,000

Financial Assistance Available: Sales and administrative personnel assist franchisee to obtain necessary assistance through financial institutions.

Training Provided: We have a 5 week training program: 2 weeks on site training.

Managerial Assistance Available: Continuous management and technical assistance.

Information Submitted: April 1990

B. F. GOODRICH COMPANY
Tire Group
500 South Main Street
Akron, Ohio 44318 D/0636
Dealer Sales Marketing Operations

Description of Operation: Establishes a total franchise to sell and service B. F. Goodrich tires and related automotive service merchandise. Franchise is supported by effective national advertising coupled with all necessary marketing support.

Number of Franchisees: Thousands of direct dealers and associate dealers throughout the United States.

In Business Since: 1870

Equity Capital Needed: Varies as to market, style of business, projected volume, etc.

Financial Assistance Available: Assistance is provided to help franchisee obtain required financing through local sources and/or franchisor's assistance programs. Required financing is dependent upon market potential, requirements and projected profitability.

Training Provided: Training on a continuous basis is provided by the company on salesmanship, product knowledge, servicing techniques and business management.

Managerial Assistance Available: Sale as "Training" above.

Information Submitted: April 1990

THE GOODYEAR TIRE & RUBBER COMPANY
1144 East Market Street
Akron, Ohio 44316
H. M. Harding, Manager, Tire Centers Division

Description of Operation: Retail and wholesale sale of tires, tire and automotive service and other car and home related merchandise. These are marketed through a long-established independent dealer organization and a more recently developed chain of franchised tire centers.

Number of Franchisees: Approximately 4,500 independent Goodyear dealers, including 650 tire center franchisees in most States.

In Business Since: 1898. Tire center franchise program has operated since 1968.

Equity Capital Needed: Varies for regular Goodyear dealership. $50,000 minimum required for tire center.

Financial Assistance Available: Lease real estate; equipment and fixtures, long-term note line as needed and justified; and open account credit as needed and justified.

Training Provided: Formal 10 weeks training plus continued on-the-job training.

Managerial Assistance Available: Business counsel and data processing available on a continuing and permanent basis. Program also includes local, cooperative advertising to tie-in with national advertising, display and point-of-sale advertising, identification and fixture assistance, monthly and quarterly marketing and merchandising program; complete sales training program.

Information Submitted: April 1990

*GREASE 'N GO, INC.
526 East Juanita, #6
Mesa, Arizona 85204

Description of Operation: Grease 'n Go 3-bay quick-lube centers provide 10-minute lube and oil service and other fluid-maintenance services for all vehicles, using nationally advertised brand-name products.

Number of Franchisees: 18 open and 45 sold in 9 States.

In Business Since: 1984

Equity Capital Needed: $98,900 including franchise fee and operating capital.

Financial Assistance Available: Grease 'n Go assists as needed in preparing bank packets and in arranging financing, but does not offer financial assistance directly.

Training Provided: Grease 'n Go provides classroom and hands-on training to franchisee or designated manager and initial staff as well as ongoing training to new employees.

Managerial Assistance Available: On-call franchise supervisor provides support in all operational areas at no additional charge.

Information Submitted: April 1990

*GREASE MONKEY INTERNATIONAL, INC.
Subsidiary of: GREASE MONKEY HOLDING CORP.
1660 Wynkoop Street, Suite 1160
Denver, Colorado 80202
Arthur P. Sensenig, President

Description of Operation: Franchisor is in the business of providing convenient quick-service lubrication and oil changes for automobiles and trucks and of licensing franchisees to use the mark Grease Monkey, The 10 Minute Lube and Oil Pros, and other trademarks, service marks, copyrights and concepts regarding the establishment of operation of automotive lubrication centers.

Number of Franchisees: 358 open or under development contracts in 33 States.

In Business Since: 1978

Equity Capital Needed: $125,000 liquid. $100,000 net worth.

Financial Assistance Available: Equipment leasing programs are normally available for certain items and construction funds for building available from company.

Training Provided: The franchisor will provide training and instruction to franchisee and its employees in the operation and management of each center.

Managerial Assistance Available: Franchisor provides a recommended system of accounting and internal accounting control, grand opening and promotional advertising package, technical advice and assistance re: installation of equipment, construction of building, technical service. Manuals are provided for marketing, operations and accounting. The company maintains national and regional advertising programs, and has a system of quality control over all franchisees to maintain uniform quality of the products, services and inventory control. Franchisor also protects its trade and service marks.

Information Submitted: May 1990

GREAT BEAR AUTO CENTERS, INC.
100 Merrick Road, Suite 206
Rockville Centre, New York 11570
Ken Loderhose, Vice President

Description of Operation: Great Bear Auto Centers specialize in automotive aftermarket sales and installation of parts for front end, brakes, shocks, alignment, mufflers, springs and tune-ups. All work performed by specially trained mechanics. Franchisees do not require an automotive background but should have some managerial experience.

Number of Franchisees: 55 in New York, New Jersey and Florida

In Business Since: 1934

Equity Capital Needed: $75,000

Financial Assistance Available: A minimum investment of $150,000 is necessary to open a Great Bear Auto Center in a major marketing area. Company will assist in obtaining financing for franchisees with good credit references.

Training Provided: Basic training at company headquarters followed by field training at the franchisee's own location to guarantee a well-planned operation and an organized opening.

Managerial Assistance Available: Continued managerial, technical and advertising assistance at all times during the time of the franchise.

Information Submitted: April 1990

GUARANTEED TUNE UP
101 Eisenhower Parkway
Roseland, New Jersey 07068
William Okita, President

Description of Operation: Automotive tune-up and automobile repair service business.

Number of Franchisees: 7 in New Jersey, New York, North Carolina and Pennsylvania.

In Business Since: 1984

Equity Capital Needed: Turnkey operation approximately $96,000; $25,000 cash, and balance financed, to qualified investors.

Financial Assistance Available: Will assist in securing outside financing.

Training Provided: An intensive 1 week training program is provided for shop managers, mechanics or owners.

Managerial Assistance Available: Continuous managerial assistance is provided in all phases of operation to insure proper operation of the business.

Information Submitted: May 1990

J. D. BYRIDER SYSTEMS, INC.
1800 North Wabash Road
Suite 202

Marion, Indiana 46952
James F. DeVoe, President
Randy K. Buzzard, Vice President, Field Operations

Description of Operation: J. D. Byrider System, Inc., is a system for the establishment, development, and operation of a primarily used automobile sales location(s) and a related business providing financial arrangements for primarily used automobiles to consumers with marginal credit. These consumers make up to 50 percent of the automobile buying market. A complete system of management procedures and sophisticated analysis software is the key to the franchise system.

Number of Franchisees: 10 in 6 States including 1 company-owned operation.

In Business Since: 1979, franchising since 1989

Equity Capital Needed: Average $50,000 start-up with average total investment of $150,000-$250,000.

Financial Assistance Available: Total assistance and guidance in preparation of supplied documents for business presentations to recommended and all other banks, lending institutions, etc.

Training Provided: Franchisee(s) shall attend, prior to opening, a management and operations course of 4 business days at franchisor's headquarters with involvement in company-owned operation during training. An initial on-site assistance program of 5 business days is also provided during the first month of operation of franchisee's business. Training includes an understanding of financial controls; promotion and merchandising methods, techniques and procedures; procedures for operation; marketing and advertising techniques; deployment of labor; and maintenance of quality standards.

Managerial Assistance Available: In addition to the above, franchisor visits operations frequently to provide assistance, especially in the area of proper management of forecast and results through franchisor's staff.

Information Submitted: April 1990

JIFFIWASH, INC.
P. O. Box 2489
San Francisco, California 94126
Merle Akers, President

Description of Operation: Service institutional clients at their locations, washing, brushing and cleaning their fleet of vehicles from a Jiffiwash mobile unit equipped with patented pressure washing equipment. Work is done mostly in the evenings and on weekends when rolling stock is parked in their respective yards.

Number of Franchisees: 31 now—exclusive franchises in 10 States

In Business Since: 1959

Equity Capital Needed: $5,000-$25,000

Financial Assistance Available: Franchisee is to arrange own financing for the purchase price. $5,000-$20,000 is needed to purchase a Jiffiwash franchise. The additional $5,000 is necessary to defray initial operating expenses for the first 6 months the franchisee is in business, or until such time sufficient revenue is generated for the franchisee to be self-sufficient with positive cash flow.

Training Provided: 1 week of on-site training with established Jiffiwash Dealer washing vehicles and making sales calls. Optional: a visit to the home office in San Francisco for additional sales training and a training period at the Jiffiwash machine shop to acquaint franchisee with Jiffiwash patented equipment. Franchisee to pay all expenses incurred during training period.

Managerial Assistance Available: Jiffiwash will do all accounting functions on behalf of franchisee until the franchise is terminated. Jiffiwash will conduct periodic sales campaign in and around the area serviced by franchisee. Franchisee is to follow up leads thus generated, calling on interested parties selling the Jiffiwash Mobile Washing Service in and around his service area. Jiffiwash machine shop is available for technical assistance during normal shop hours. All equipment received by the franchisee is

covered by a 90-day warranty. After the warranty period, replacements will be shipped, at cost, to franchisee to keep the equipment working on-the-job.

Information Submitted: May 1990

*JIFFY LUBE INTERNATIONAL, INC.
P.O. Box 2967
Houston, Texas 77252-2967
Franchise Development Department

Description of Operation: Largest quick lube system in the industry.

Number of Franchisees: 1,015

In Business Since: 1979

Equity Capital Needed: Approximate total investment $200,000, initial cash needed $60,000.

Financial Assistance Available: Jiffy Lube International, Inc., may assist franchisees in locating sources of financing.

Training Provided: Jiffy Lube International, Inc., provides a mandatory course to franchisee or approved manager which consists of working at a Jiffy Lube Service Center for 2 weeks. You must also attend a standard operations training course for an additional 2 weeks at Jiffy Lube headquarters.

Managerial Assistance Available: Jiffy Lube International, Inc., provides continual management service for the life of the franchise in such areas as accounting, advertising, policies and procedures and operations. Complete manuals are provided. Regional managers are available to work closely with franchisees and visit service centers regularly to assist in solving problems.

Information Submitted: April 1990

JOHNNY RUTHERFORD TUNE/LUBE CORP.
2525 N.W. Loop 410
San Antonio, TX 78265

Description of Operation: Simultaneous automotive tune-up and oil change service, including diagnostics, carburetor service, fuel injection service, a/c recharge service and transmission fluid and filter service.

Number of Franchisees: 3

In Business Since: Incorporated in 1984, franchising since 1986

Equity Capital Needed: $30,000 initial investment; total $90,000-$110,000.

Financial Assistance Available: None

Training Provided: 2 week training course includes everything from everyday paperwork to operating sophisticated diagnostic systems. Forty hours on daily operations and 40 hours on computer diagnostic system include P.C. operations, cash procedures, opening and closing the center, customer relations, employee evaluations, scheduling and more.

Managerial Assistance Available: Site selection, advertising/marketing, accounting and field support.

Information Submitted: May 1990.

KENNEDY TRANSMISSION
5740 Humboldt Avenue South
Bloomington, Minnesota 55431
Dennis A. Bain, Vice President

Description of Operation: Kennedy Transmission offers a unique, single purpose service. Each store is approximately 4,000 square feet with ample parking and is open 5 days per week.

Number of Franchisees: 14 in Minnesota

In Business Since: 1962

Equity Capital Needed: Approximately $35,000; total investment is approximately $100,000.

Financial Assistance Available: Franchisee to arrange own financing.

Training Provided: Franchisor will assist franchisee in setting up the operation, and ordering equipment and supplies, and will assist on-site during first 10 days of operation.

Managerial Assistance Available: Field managers are available on an "as-needed" basis to assist franchisees. In addition, periodic visits and training sessions are conducted by franchisor.

Information Submitted: April 1990

*KING BEAR ENTERPRISES, INC.
1390 Jerusalem Avenue
North Merrick, New York 11566

Description of Operation: Automotive repairs, brake, front-end, shock, mufflers, and under-car repairs. All parts are sold to franchisees at jobber prices, or less.

Number of Franchisees: 61 in New York, New Jersey and California.

In Business Since: 1973

Equity Capital Needed: $60,000

Financial Assistance Available: Limited financing available, to qualified individuals.

Training Provided: In-shop training for 2 weeks, plus full management training in our home office. Additional training provided in franchisee's shop on a continuing basis and assistance at all times thereafter.

Managerial Assistance Available: A divisional field consultant works with each franchise dealer to promote success with updated marketing formulas, technical information, and sales training.

Information Submitted: April 1990

*LEE MYLES ASSOCIATES CORP.
25 East Spring Valley Avenue
Maywood, New Jersey 07607
Bob Zia, Chief Executive Officer

Description of Operation: Lee Myles Franchised Transmission Centers offer complete one-stop transmission service. These centers perform complete quality automatic transmission service, from minor adjustments through and including major repairs and reconditioning. It is not necessary for franchisees to have a technical background: Lee Myles provides a comprehensive training course and shop set-up assistance by a training staff equipped with experience and knowledge of developments of 35 years in the automotive field.

Number of Franchisees: 100 in 8 States and Puerto Rico

In Business Since: 1040

Equity Capital Needed: $100,000

Financial Assistance Available: Assistance in obtaining partial financing to qualified individuals.

Training Provided: 2 week training course, parent company classroom. Staff of experienced field consultants provides continuing guidance and assistance at all times thereafter.

Managerial Assistance Available: A unit manager works with each franchise dealer to promote success with updated marketing formulas, technical information, and sales training.

Information Submitted: April 1990

LENTZ U.S.A. SERVICE CENTERS
1001 Riverview Drive
Kalamazoo, Michigan 49001
Gordon Lentz

Description of Operation: Auto under-car repair—mufflers, brakes, shocks and alignment.

Number of Franchisees: 3

In Business Since: 1983

Equity Capital Needed: $80,000-$100,000

Financial Assistance Available: 2 to 4 weeks in all phases of operation.

Managerial Assistance Available: Continuous.

Information Submitted: April 1990

LUBEPRO'S INTERNATIONAL, INC.
1900 N. Roselle Rd.
Suite #403
Schaumburg, Illinois 60195
David Beebe, Franchise Director

Description of Operation: Automotive—quick lubrication and oil change franchise.

Number of Franchisees: 29 in 7 states.

In Business Since: 1978

Equity Capital Needed: $100,000 liquid, $300,000 net worth.

Financial Assistance Available: Direction to 3rd party lenders and build to suit developers.

Training Provided: 17 days of training including on location.

Managerial Assistance Available: Field service provided periodically and on-site evaluation.

Information Submitted: April 1990

*MAACO ENTERPRISES, INC.
381 Brooks Road
King of Prussia, Pennsylvania 19406
Linda Kemp, Franchising Sales Administrator

Description of Operation: MAACO Auto Painting and Body Centers are complete auto painting and collision repair centers. Knowledge of the auto paint business is not necessary as MAACO provides a thorough training course and shop opening assistance by a staff fully experienced in the field.

Number of Franchisees: 409 open.

In Business Since: 1972

Equity Capital Needed: $65,000—cost of complete franchise $188,990.

Financial Assistance Available: MAACO will consider applicants with $65,000 investment capital and will assist franchisee in applying for balance required. MAACO, however, does not in any way guarantee financing.

Training Provided: Complete 3 week training program in company's home office as well as initial training in franchisee's own shop.

Managerial Assistance Available: Continuous as long as the franchise is in operation.

Information Submitted: April 1990

*MAD HATTER MUFFLER INTERNATIONAL, INC.
11290 Park Boulevard #200
Seminole, Florida 34642
Joseph Kotow, President

Description of Operation: Complete undercar specialists offering fast, professional automotive services such as exhaust repair, brakes, struts and shock absorbers, front end alignment, and lubrication. Computerized inventory control and billing procedures, in an updated, clean, sales inducing atmosphere.

Number of Franchisees: 97 in 17 States

In Business Since: 1986

Equity Capital Needed: $98,500 to $113,500 is total investment for inventory, equipment, signs, lease deposits, utility deposits, start-up expenses and working capital.

Financial Assistance Available: Minimum of $25,000 cash required. Franchisee will receive assistance in obtaining necessary financing through various financial institutions including banks, business finance companies and SBA.

Training Provided: Training for franchisee and one employee. 4 week training classes conducted by industry professional in Chicago and Florida National Training Center. Training will cover all aspects for successful shop operation. Weekly shop analysis, monthly territorial meetings, continuous and follow-up training provided by franchisor.

Managerial Assistance Available: A complete operations manual is provided along with computer training and accounting procedures. Technical bulletins issued on periodic basis. Toll free incoming WATS line for immediate access.

Information Submitted: May 1990

MALCO PRODUCTS, INC.
361 Fairview Avenue
P. O. Box 892
Barberton, Ohio 44203
J. Ginley

Description of Operation: Distributorship to sell complete line of automotive chemical specialties including cleaners, oil additives, brake fluid, etc., to service stations, garages, new and used car dealers, and industrial outlets. He is assigned a territory that can support him. The distributor and his men travel the area using step vans, selling to the above accounts.

Number of Franchisees: 430 throughout the United States

In Business Since: 1953

Equity Capital Needed: $6,000 for inventory investment only.

Financial Assistance Available: None

Training Provided: Thorough field and product training in the distributor's area by regional sales manager. Periodically during the year the regional sales manager spends time with the distributor and salesmen for training both in product knowledge and field training.

Managerial Assistance Available: Distributor sales meetings are held twice a year for further training. Complete managerial assistance provided through company personnel and field representatives.

Information Submitted: May 1990

MARK I AUTO SERVICE CENTERS, INC.
10825 Old Halls Ferry
St. Louis, Missouri 63136

Description of Operation: Mark I Auto Service Centers, Inc., offers computerized automotive diagnostic and repair services on all vehicles. The company employs nationally certified mechanics and offers appointments and service while-you-wait and extensive guarantees, all at reasonable prices. Center is a complete "turn-key" operation, including all equipment, tools, furniture, fixtures, signs, inventory, forms, and procedures. No prior automotive experience is required.

Number of Franchisees: 2 plus 5 company-owned in Missouri

In Business Since: 1971

Equity Capital Needed: Total investment is approximately $85,000, with about $45,000 required in cash.

Financial Assistance Available: Mark I will indirectly assist franchisee in possibly acquiring financing through equipment manufacturers and other suppliers. Mark I will offer substantial savings on equipment, tools and auto parts through its own automotive warehouse.

Training Provided: Franchisee is required to attend an extensive 2 week classroom and on-the-job training session at an operational center. In addition, a company representative will spend the first week at the franchisee's center for the grand opening. Continual training and advice is provided as needed.

Managerial Assistance Available: Mark I Auto Service Centers, Inc., provides a complete operations manual. Mark I also provides regular on-site visits from company representatives to assist franchisee. Updated technical and business bulletins are sent regularly. Regular meetings are held with franchisees and company personnel. Mark I offers, as an option, computerized accounting and statistical analysis to its franchisees.

Information Submitted: May 1990

*MEINEKE DISCOUNT MUFFLER SHOPS, INC.
First Citizens Bank Plaza
128 South Tryon Street, Suite 900
Charlotte, North Carolina 28284
Ron Smythe, President

Description of Operation: Meineke Discount Muffler Shops, Inc., offer fast, courteous service in the merchandising of automotive exhaust systems, shock absorbers, struts and brakes. Unique inventory control and group purchasing power enable Meineke dealers to adhere to a "discount concept" for delivering quality service. No mechanical skills required.

Number of Franchisees: 953 in 46 States and Canada.

In Business Since: 1972

Equity Capital Needed: $69,800. Total of $107,200 investment for inventory, equipment, signs, furniture, fixtures, estimated lease, utility deposits, start-up costs and working capital.

Financial Assistance Available: Third party financing available to qualified applicants.

Training Provided: 4 weeks schooling and on-the-job training at Charlotte headquarters. In addition, Meineke provides continuous field supervision and group opertional meetings.

Managerial Assistance Available: Meineke Discount Muffler operations manual provides clear and concise reference for every phase of the business. Home office staff analysis of weekly reports is provided on a continuous basis.

Information Submitted: April 1990

MERLIN MUFFLER AND BRAKE
33 West Higgins Road
Suite 2050
South Barrington, Illinois 60010
Mark M. Hameister, Manager of Franchise Development

Description of Operation: Merlin is an upscale automotive specialty shop providing full underbody automotive services including exhaust, brake, ride control and oil/lubrication services.

Number of Franchisees: 33 in Illinois, Georgia, Texas and Michigan. 8 company-owned in Illinois, Wisconsin and Georgia.

In Business Since: 1975

Equity Capital Needed: $160,000 is necessary to open a Merlin's Muffler and Brake franchise. This includes equipment, inventory, working capital and start-up expenses.

Financial Assistance Available: Minimum $45,000 cash required. Subject to individual qualification, franchise is readily financable through third parties such as banks, business finance/leasing companies, etc.

Training Provided: Franchisees and their designated managers must attend and successfully complete a 5 week training program conducted at Merlin's headquarters in Illinois. Training will cover sales techniques, shop management, product installation, communication and personnel policies and procedures.

Managerial Assistance Available: Technical and managerial support provided on a continuing basis.

Information Submitted: April 1990

MERMAID MARKETING INC.
526 Grand Canyon Drive
Madison, Wisconsin 53711
Peter H. Aspinwall, President
John M. Aspinwall, Vice President

Description of Operation: Mermaid Car Wash is a service business franchise devoted to the total service washing, cleaning, waxing and detailing of cars, vans and pick-up trucks.

Number of Franchisees: 5 in Wisconsin, Minnesota and Illinois.

In Business Since: 1984

Equity Capital Needed: $200,000 to $400,000

Financial Assistance Available: Mermaid Marketing, Inc., indirectly offers financing to the franchise on the initial franchise fee. The franchisor will not guarantee any note, lease or other payments and has no agreement with any lender to offer financing.

Training Provided: Provide training for franchisee, managers, assistant managers, salespersons, off-line persons, and cashiers at Madison, Wisconsin for a period up to 60 days after opening at no additional charge.

Managerial Assistance Available: Mermaid Marketing, Inc., provides complete training, assistance and consultation for the life of the franchise. This service provides the franchisee with technical and operational help at all times for the duration of the franchise.

Information Submitted: April 1990

*MIDAS INTERNATIONAL CORPORATION
225 North Michigan Avenue
Chicago, Illinois 60601

Description of Operation: Automotive exhaust system, brake, shock absorbers, alignment and suspension. Shops offer fast service "while you wait" in clean, pleasant, modern surroundings.

Number of Franchisees: 1,608 in 50 States plus 119 company-owned shops with another 630 units internationally.

In Business Since: 1956

Equity Capital Needed: $200,000 to $230,000 investment for inventory, equipment, sign, furniture, fixtures, fees and working capital for a standard 6 bay shop.

Financial Assistance Available: Franchisee will receive assistance in obtaining necessary financing from appropriate lending agencies with which Midas has working arrangements.

Training Provided: Both a dealer orientation program and on-the-job training programs are initially provided, followed by continuous in-the-shop field counseling and periodic dealer seminar-type meetings on all aspects of shop operations. All new dealers must attend a formal 4 week training program at National Training Center, Palatine, Illinois.

Managerial Assistance Available: A shop operator's manual is provided along with recordkeeping and accounting manual. Training received from regional directors covers all aspects of management, marketing, and sales.

Information Submitted: April 1990

*MIGHTY DISTRIBUTION SYSTEM OF AMERICA, INC.
50 Technology Park/Atlanta
Norcross, Georgia 30092
Timothy Galfas II

Description of Operation: The Mighty franchise sells a complete automotive parts and services system to independent repair shops, service stations, fleet operators, and new car and truck dealers. Inventory control for the customer, a unique double guarantee and diagnostic assistance capabilities are important parts of the system.

Number of Franchisees: 193 in 45 States

In Business Since: 1963; franchising since 1970

Equity Capital Needed: $75,000 to $250,000

Financial Assistance Available: Franchisor will assist in preparation of loan application and in locating sources of financing.

Training Provided: Franchisees are provided with a 2 week business management and sales technique course at the home office in Norcross, Georgia and on location in franchisee's territory. Periodic visits are scheduled to assist franchisees in the overall conduct of their businesses. 9-1/2 days of seminars a year are scheduled for franchisees for product, marketing, sales, business and productivity management training.

Managerial Assistance Available: Business management seminars located throughout the country as well as on-site assistance; product and technical assistance hotlines; computer services and monthly individual profit and loss statements for participating franchisees.

Information Submitted: April 1990

MILEX OF AMERICA, INC.
4914 North Lincoln Avenue
Chicago, Illinois 60625

Description of Operation: Milex service centers provide written warranties on all work performed. Although tune-ups and brake services are the mainstay of the operation, other car care services may be offered subject to Milex approval. Milex shops are equipped with the latest computerized diagnostic equipment to give an exclusive Milex diagnosis. Milex franchisees come from many different walks of life; some have a mechanical background—others do not.

Number of Franchisees: 32 in Illinois

In Business Since: 1972

Equity Capital Needed: $35,000 minimum

Financial Assistance Available: The total investment range is $119,500, depending on the equipment needed in the location. Milex Finance Department will assist the franchisees by recommending procedures by which such loans previously have been obtained and will counsel in preparing any applications or presentations necessary to submit to the lending institutions or government agencies.

Training Provided: Prior to the opening of a center for business, a new franchisee must attend Milex's comprehensive training program, which takes place in a classroom and/or service center for a period of 24 working days.

Managerial Assistance Available: Since 1972, most principals of Milex have been successfully owning and operating auto care service centers specializing in tune-ups and brakes. Continuous managerial and sales counseling is provided throughout the life of the franchise. The Operations Division will put special emphasis on counseling the franchisees during their first year in business. Ongoing counseling in such areas as advertising, accounting, complete operating procedure manuals, and forms and directions is provided.

Information Submitted: May 1990

MING OF AMERICA, INC.
7526 Metcalf
Overland Park, Kansas 66204

Description of Operation: Automotive beautification and protection services, including Ming Mirror Finish, complete appearance reconditioning, Ming custom rust protection.

Number of Franchisees: 43 in the United States and 2 countries.

In Business Since: 1968

Equity Capital Needed: $49,600-$68,800

Financial Assistance Available: Ming of America, Inc., will assist in preparation of loan application and in locating sources of financing.

Training Provided: 3 week mandatory training program for manager and 1 employee at the corporate training center. 1 week training provided on-site at time of store opening.

Managerial Assistance Available: Technical and managerial support is provided on a continuing basis, including operations manuals, on-site inspections and updated technical information.

Information Submitted: May 1990

MIRACLE AUTO PAINTING
Division of MULTIPLE ALLIED SERVICES, INC.
Century Plaza One Building
1065 East Hillsdale Boulevard
Suite 110
Foster City, California 94404

Description of Operation: Miracle Auto Painting offers quality body repair work and baked enamel auto painting with a written guarantee at a volume-producing low price. Miracle provides high quality, rapid service and lowest cost through the production line process. Assistance is provided to the franchisee in site selection, equipment installation, and sales promotion. Supplies and materials are available through Miracle's volume purchasing.

Number of Franchisees: 46 in California, Oregon, Arizona, Nevada and Texas

In Business Since: 1953

Equity Capital Needed: $35,000 minimum

Financial Assistance Available: The franchisee usually needs a minimum of $79,000 cash to establish the business on a profitable basis.

Training Provided: A 4 week training course is scheduled for new franchisees. Two weeks of the training is at a Miracle location and 2 weeks at the franchisee's location. Training covers systems and procedures for production painting and bodywork as well as sales and business procedures. Miracle operates training centers in San Mateo and Foster City, California.

Managerial Assistance Available: Miracle provides continuing consultation not only for production techniques and procedures but also for sales and business management, accounting and record keeping and employee recruiting and training.

Information Submitted: April 1990

MOBILE AUTO TRIM, INC.
10500 Metric Drive
Dallas, Texas 75243
C. F. "Butch" Davis, Jr., President

Description of Operation: Mobile Auto Trim, Inc., provides the franchisee the opportunity to offer their prospective market area with one of the most complete mobile reconditioning and trim concepts in the country. Services include body side molding, pin striping, custom dye for carpet, vinyl, and leather surfaces, vinyl repair, trunk reconditioning, auto paint chip repair, windshield repair, etc. No prior experience required; methods and techniques highly effective towards success.

Number of Franchisees: 15 in Texas, Oklahoma, Louisiana, Arkansas, Indiana, and Michigan plus 10 company-owned.

In Business Since: 1981

Equity Capital Needed: $10,000 minimun

Financial Assistance Available: Total investment for a Mobile Auto Trim franchise operation is approximately $25,000. Investment includes $15,000 franchise fee and $10,000 equipment and supplies.

Training Provided: Complete 3 day administrative orientation required at home office in Dallas, Texas followed by a 4 week field training program. Training program includes establishment of customer base, familiarization with product line, and how to professionally and proficiently perform the range of services offered through Mobile Auto Trim.

Managerial Assistance Available: In addition to initial training program outlined above, Mobile Auto Trim provides continual management services for the life of the franchise (i.e., bookkeeping, advertising, inventory control). Complete manuals of operations, solving any problems of the franchise operation. Dissemination of new methods and products as they are tested and become available.

Information Submitted: May 1990

MOBILE TRIM TEAM
1239 Braselton Highway
Lawrenceville, Georgia 30243
Ken Clark

Description of Operation: Company has a wide variety of repair services and complete upholstery to new and used car dealers, restaurants, motels, hotels, hospitals or wherever there is work to be done.

Number of Franchisees: 18 in 8 States.

In Business Since: 1972

Equity Capital Needed: $28,000-$29,500

Financial Assistance Available: None

Training Provided: 3 weeks minimum in shop and field training.

Managerial Assistance Available: Ongoing seminars in all phases of operations.

Information Submitted: May 1990

MORALL BRAKE CENTERS
160 Larrabee Road
Westbrook, Maine 04092
Gary T. Tryon, Vice President

Description of Operation: Morall Brake Centers provide fast, efficient, low cost automotive brake service. Morall Brake Centers carry complete brake part inventories as well as all equipment to perform required services. All work is backed by Morall's unique Lifetime Guarantee. Using Morall techniques, most vehicles can be serviced in one hour or less. All makes and models of vehicles are serviced up to one ton trucks.

Number of Franchisees: 24 in Maine and Massachusetts, New Hampshire, Connecticut, New Jersey, and Maryland, plus 23 corporate owned stores.

In Business Since: 1978, franchising since 1984

Equity Capital Needed: Total investment required is $118,000, which includes $24,000 franchise fee and $20,000 working capital. Approximately 80 percent of tools and inventory can be financed.

Financial Assistance Available: None currently

Training Provided: 2 weeks mandatory training at franchisor's training facility. Includes technical development, management seminar, inventory control, sales, employee relations and on-the-job training at a company-owned center. Follow-up training at franchisee's location conducted by a Morall representative for an additional 3 weeks.

Managerial Assistance Available: Morall provides continuous managerial development through periodic training meetings of franchisees. Besides a comprehensive operations manual, Morall also provides a complete system of forms, work orders, and guarantees, as well as a brake service technical bulletin file. A regional manager is available to assist in training, management, sales and inventory control.

Information Submitted: April 1990

MOTORWORK, INC.
4210 Salem Street
Philadelphia, Pennsylvania 19124

Description of Operation: Automotive franchise specializing in motor replacement, one of the most expensive repairs performed on today's cars and by far one of the most profitable. Our unique business offers the customers an alternative to the rising cost of new car prices. Major engine failure is the big reason for new car purchases. With Motorwork centers providing this specialized repair, customers can actually save thousands of dollars.

Number of Franchisees: 22 in 7 States.

In Business Since: 1987

Equity Capital Needed: $65,000-$90,000

Financial Assistance Available: Partial financing available to qualified applicants.

Training Provided: 2 week training in home office and franchisee's location. Training is provided to management and staff.

Managerial Assistance Available: Continuous field support and newsletters and day-to-day operations.

Information Submitted: May 1990

*MOTRA CORP.
4912 North Lincoln
Chicago, Illinois 60625
Werner E. Ament, Chairman of the Board

Description of Operation: MOTRA Transmission Service Centers provide transmission rebuilding and repair services with warranties from 6 months to lifetime. MOTRA Centers provide free 23-point diagnostic Motra checks. MOTRA will make recommendations as to the equipment requirements for each center. Franchisee does not need a mechanical background.

Number of Franchisees: 42 in Illinois, Arizona and Florida

In Business Since: 1980

Equity Capital Needed: $17,500

Financial Assistance Available: The total investment is $89,500 depending upon the equipment needed in the location. MOTRA will assist the franchisee by recommending procedures by which such loans previously have been obtained and will counsel in preparing any applications or presentations necessary to submit to the lending institutions or government agencies.

Training Provided: Prior to opening center for business, franchisee must attend MOTRA's comprehensive training program.

Managerial Assistance Available: The principals of MOTRA have over 30 years of successful experience in owning and operating transmission shops, and continue to own and operate MOTRA Centers. Continuous managerial, technical, and sales counseling is provided throughout the life of the franchise. The Operations Division will put special emphasis on operators during the first year in business. Ongoing counseling in such areas as advertising and accounting is provided. Complete operating procedure manuals and forms and directions are provided. Operations director and other representatives are available to counsel franchisees through MOTRA's Operations Division.

Information Submitted: May 1990

*MR. TRANSMISSION INC.
P. O. Box 111060
Nashville, Tennessee 37222-1060
Jack Yost

Description of Operation: Transmission repair centers.

Number of Franchisees: 80 in 16 States

In Business Since: Incorporated in 1962

Equity Capital Needed: Approximately $105,000 ($82,500 franchise fee, $2,500 inventory, capital and start-up cost).

Financial Assistance Available: Will assist the franchisee in obtaining financing.

Training Provided: A 4 to 6 weeks in-office/on the job training school is required of franchisee.

Managerial Assistance Available: A review of the franchisee's business is made monthly by the home office; a seminar of the office staff periodically visits the franchisee to offer assistance; the franchise shop is periodically audited; and if the franchisee needs assistance, the Nashville office can provide it.

Information Submitted: April 1990

MUFFLER CRAFTERS, INC.
4911 Birch Street
Newport Beach, California 92660

Description of Operation: A complete 'turnkey' muffler, brakes and front end alignment operation.

Number of Franchisees: 7 in California

In Business Since: Parent company 1973

Equity Capital Needed: Approximately $80,000

Financial Assistance Available: None

Training Provided: 6 weeks training in all phases of operation. We hire and train all employees.

Managerial Assistance Available: Day-to-day managerial and technical assistance is provided.

Information Submitted: May 1990

MULTISTATE TRANSMISSION CO., INC.
29200 Vassar Avenue
Suite 501
Livonia, Michigan 48152
Aaron A. Reavis, Vice President

Description of Operation: Multistate Transmission Centers service, repair and replace all types of standard and automatic transmissions for automobiles, small truck and RVs. They are usually in a building large enough to service 5 or 6 vehicles with outside parking for up to 20 cars. Each center is completely equipped with new and unique labor saving and parts reconditioning equipment.

Number of Franchisees: 43 in 9 States

In Business Since: 1973

Equity Capital Needed: Subject to franchisees' financial status.

Financial Assistance Available: A total investment of $85,500, excluding working capital, is required. Because of the amount of equipment involved in a Multistate Transmission Center, and depending upon the individual licensee's credit standing, financing can usually be arranged.

Training Provided: 2 weeks of intensive management training is provided at the home office and then additional on-site training is given during the opening period.

Managerial Assistance Available: Multistate Transmissions provides operational support in both management and technical services. Field operation managers visit each center on a periodic basis.

Information Submitted: April 1990

*NATIONAL CAR CARE CENTERS, INC.
2470 Windy Hill Road
Marietta, Georgia 30067
D. J. Zachman, President

Description of Operation: National provides specialty automotive services with emphasis on brake and exhaust systems, shock absorbers and MacPherson struts, trailer hitches and towing systems, quik lube, and filter and ACD service quick oil/filter change. Each center offers fast service and popular prices in well equipped, clean facilities. Franchisee does not need a mechanical background.

Number of Franchisees: 12 in Georgia, Florida and Louisiana.

In Business Since: 1977

Equity Capital Needed: Total investment between $90,000 and $110,000.

Financial Assistance Available: Financial packages and leasing are available to qualified franchisee's through various approved sources. Assistance is available in preparing and presenting financial packages to lending institutions or government agencies. Joint ventures can be coordinated and other financial assistance extended based on the personal financial statement of the applicant.

Training Provided: National provides a unique 3 phase technical and management training program for franchisee and manager. Hands-on training is provided at National headquarters. Assistance is also provided prior to and during grand opening. Ongoing support, assistance and training is rigidly structured and includes field counseling, periodic meetings on all aspects of center management and technical updates.

Managerial Assistance Available: An extensive operations manual is provided and complete managerial assistance is provided on a continuing basis through company personnel and field supervisors.

Information Submitted: May 1990

NOVUS WINDSHIELD REPAIR AND SCRATCH REMOVAL
10425 Hampshire Avenue South
Minneapolis, Minnesota 55438
Gerald E. Keinath, President

Description of Operation: Using the exclusive NOVUS patented process, professionally trained franchisees repair, rather than replace, stone-damaged windshields. NOVUS franchisees are the experts in windshield repair and offer a money-saving service to fleets, insurance companies, government agencies, and consumers. Franchisees work out of their home or from a fixed location. NOVUS has also developed a process for removing scratches from windshields and other laminated glass.

Number of Franchisees: 600

In Business Since: 1972

Equity Capital Needed: Approximately $10,000

Financial Assistance Available: None

Training Provided: 5 day factory training at the NOVUS international headquarters includes technical training, sales and marketing classes and seminars on general business operations.

Managerial Assistance Available: Ongoing technical sales assistance provided by professional staff. Newsletters, conventions, regional meetings, and ongoing research and development are included.

Information Submitted: May 1990

*OIL CAN HENRY'S
1650 N.W. Front Avenue
Suite 120
Portland, Oregon 97209
Chris Shepanek, Director of Franchise Development

Description of Operation: Oil Can Henry's are quick lube/fast oil change professionals, offering a 20 point courtesy check as well as additional preventive maintenance services on auto filters and fluids.

Number of Franchisees: 16 in Oregon, Florida, Washington and Arizona.

In Business Since: Franchising since 1987, in business since 1978.

Equity Capital Needed: $75,000 liquidity with net worth of $150,000.

Financial Assistance Available: Franchisor estimates a total investment of $60,000 to $75,000, which includes franchise fee of $25,000, pre-paid expenses such as security deposits, and first and last month's rent, opening inventory, and working capital. Leasebacks for land and building are possible; equipment financing is available through suppliers. Franchisee has option to arrange own outside financing.

Training Provided: No tuition charged. 5 weeks intensive training required for operator and available for managerial personnel; conducted in classroom facility and company service center. Additional training assistance at franchisee's service center prior to opening. Opening team of four supervises and assists in training of franchisee's crew. Ongoing training provided for new procedures, new equipment, managerial techniques, etc., during life of the franchise.

Managerial Assistance Available: Oil Can Henry's provides coaching and counseling for the full term of the franchise through the franchise consultant. The consultant is a technical expert as well as a business generalist able to offer assistance in administrative controls, marketing and advertising; he visits each center on a regular basis. Complete manuals on operations are provided along with in-center crew training. Oil Can Henry's conducts ongoing marketing and product research to maintain high customer acceptance.

Information Submitted: April 1990

OIL EXPRESS NATIONAL, INC.
22 Orchard Place
Hinsdale, Illinois 60521
Daniel R. Barnas, Executive Vice President

Description of Operation: 10 minute oil, filter and lubrication service for cars and trucks.

Number of Franchisees: 30 in Illinois, Indiana and Tennessee

In Business Since: 1979

Equity Capital Needed: $75,000 minimum

Financial Assistance Available: Independent oil company loans.

Training Provided: Complete operations for at least 10 days plus management school.

Managerial Assistance Available: Above training, plus store development and advertising and site location assistance.

Information Submitted: April 1990

PARTS PLUS
Sponsored by ASSOCIATION OF AUTOMOTIVE AFTERMARKET DISTRIBUTORS
5050 Poplar Avenue, Suite 2020
Memphis, Tennessee 38157
Alan Hunsaker, Director of Marketing

Description of Operation: Affiliation is a jobber (auto parts store) operation wholesaling and/or retailing automotive parts, supplies, equipment and accessories. Inventory selection is from over 200 brand names and nationally advertised product lines.

Number of Franchisees: 2,400 in 48 States

In Business Since: Affiliating since 1957

Equity Capital Needed: Varies on basis of inventory investment.

Financial Assistance Available: Arranged if franchisee has outside collateral.

Training Provided: General management, to include bookkeeping and accounting system, operations manual, advertising and merchandising programs, market surveys, product and technical clinics; companies retain field representatives as well as specialty sales representatives.

Managerial Assistance Available: Maintain daily contact through field representatives and/or through WATS telephone calls to assist jobber in any phase of his business and to supplement written operating manuals, bookkeeping and accounting system manuals, cost books, catalog services. Financial ratios, expense control and inventory control are designed to improve the jobber's sales, profits and return on investment. Owners have the option of utilizing in-store computer terminal that accomplishes the following: inventory management, accounts receivable, sales analysis, profit analysis and general ledger.

Information Submitted: April 1990

PLUG BUGGY, INC.
7501 Gynor Avenue
Van Nuys, California 91406
Edward R. Hier, President

Description of Operation: Mobile auto parts distribution (auto parts store on wheels). Selling auto parts wholesale to repair garages, service stations, and dealers both foreign and American from an attractive, well organized van in a protected area.

Number of Franchisees: 10 in California and Hawaii

In Business Since: 1970, franchised since 1979

Equity Capital Needed: $27,500

Financial Assistance Available: Franchisor will assist in obtaining franchisee his own financing.

Training Provided: Product knowledge, product identification, sales, accounting, buying and selling.

Managerial Assistance Available: Ongoing field assistance, technical assistance from franchisor and manufacturers' representatives.

Information Submitted: May 1990

PRECISION TRANSMISSION
1180 Medical Court
Suite A
Carmel, Indiana 46032
L. D. Hinshaw

Description of Operation: The centers provide vehicle transmission repair, replacement and maintenance services, in accordance with guidelines and regulations prescribed by the franchisor. For inquiries from Florida call 813/793-1211 and from Kentucky and Tennessee call 502/444-0151.

Number of Franchisees: 5 in Florida, 1 in Kentucky and 1 in Tennessee.

In Business Since: 1989

Equity Capital Needed: Approximately $108,500, plus building renovation and lifts if required of franchisee ($27,000 franchise fee and $81,500 inventory, capital and start-up costs).

Financial Assistance Available: Work closely with franchisee in attempting to locate outside financing sources.

Training Provided: Initial training of from 2 to 4 weeks is provided for each new franchisee.

Managerial Assistance Available: The company will provide up to 12 hours of consultation and technical services per year without charge to the franchisee, and additional consulting services will be provided when a suitable fee has been agreed upon. The company will sponsor at least one seminar each year for franchise managers.

Information Submitted: June 1990

*PRECISION TUNE INC.
1319 Shepard Drive
P.O. Box 379
Sterling, Virginia 22170
Donald E. Ervin, Chairman and Chief Executive Officer

Description of Operation: Precision Tune, Inc., is America's largest automotive tune-up specialty franchise. No automotive or mechanical experience is needed. Precision Tune centers are usually 4-6 bays and are open 6 days a week. Franchisees may offer oil change and lubrication services. Franchisees may either convert an existing building into a Precision Tune center or construct the center. Precision Tune centers specialize in both tune-ups and engine performance repair and maintenance for newer computer-assisted vehicles. Precision Tune centers provide a cost effective alternative to higher priced repair facilities with no sacrifice in quality.

Number of Franchisees: 525 centers in operation in 40 States—80 additional centers sold and not yet open.

In Business Since: 1975

Equity Capital Needed: Approximately $135,000-$150,000 total capital required—this includes franchise fee, advertising, working capital, equipment, inventory, etc. ($30,000 cash plus the ability to finance balance.)

Financial Assistance Available: Sources provided.

Training Provided: 5 weeks, 2 weeks management and technical training at corporate headquarters. No mechanical or technical experience necessary.

Managerial Assistance Available: Management assistance is provided through Precision Tune Corporate Headquarters' Operations Department, video training tapes, in-field seminars, correspondence courses, and corporate produced training manuals.

Information Submitted: April 1990

PROLUBE
625 East Merritt Avenue
Merritt Island, Florida 32953
Joe Haggard, President

Description of Operation: Prolube is a professional drive-thru lubrication center. 34 service and inspection items, including oil and filter change, chassis lube, top off of all fluids and courtesy service items, are completed in 12 minutes with a highly trained, uniformed crew working in a very precise, methodical sequence.

Number of Franchisees: 4 company-owned and 3 franchisees in Florida.

In Business Since: 1979

Equity Capital Needed: Total cost of complete unit is $250,000 to $350,000 depending on location selected.

Financial Assistance Available: May be financed with routine mortgage or built-to-suit by others and rented.

Training Provided: 2 weeks at Prolube training center, Cocoa Beach, Florida.

Managerial Assistance Available: All operating manuals, building plans, training and continuous consulting services are provided.

Information Submitted: April 1990

QUAKER STATE MINIT-LUBE, INC.
1385 West 2200 South
Salt Lake City, Utah 84119
Bradley J. Carter, Franchise Director

Description of Operation: Quaker State Minit-Lube centers provide a full range of lubrication services performed expertly in about 10 minutes in clean, attractive surroundings, and with no appointment necessary. Our service includes: drain oil and replace with up to five quarts of Quaker State premium quality oil, install new oil filter, lubricate chassis, check and fill battery fluid, check and fill transmission/transaxle fluid, check wiper blades, check and fill differential, check and clean air filter, check and fill windshield washer fluid, check pressure in all tires, wash outside of windows, and vacuum interior of vehicle. We also supply new air filters and wiper blades when requested.

Number of Franchisees: 101 franchise locations and 276 company operated facilities located in 21 States and Canada.

In Business Since: 1977

Equity Capital Needed: Financial requirements include a net worth of $275,000 per center of which $125,000 needs to be liquid. The $125,000 liquidity is necessary for start up costs.

Financial Assistance Provided: None

Training Provided: Franchisor provides a complete training program covering all aspects of the business prior to store opening with ongoing technical support and training after store opening.

Managerial Assistance Available: Ongoing technical support and training available for franchisees through Quaker State Minit-Lube's operations personnel. Franchisees are also updated on operating procedures through technical service bulletins and quarterly consultations.

Information Submitted: April 1990

SAF-T AUTO CENTERS
R & R ENTERPRISES, INC.
209 Forbes Avenue
New Haven, Connecticut 06512
Richard G. Bilodeas, President

Description of Operation: SAF-T Auto Centers is an owner-operated auto repair shop offering steering, suspension, brakes, mufflers, lubrication and minor repair. Our main effort is to give good mechanics a business opportunity to capitalize on their trade. Ability, skill and talent to do auto repair are a Prerequisite.

Number of Franchisees: 9 in 2 States plus 1 company-owned.

In Business Since: 1978

Equity Capital Needed: Minimum $32,500—maximum $65,000.

Financial Assistance Available: Assistance in third-party financing to qualified applicants.

Training Provided: 1 week in your franchise on site geared toward managerial aspects and administrtive operations. Ability, skill and talent to do auto repair are a prerequisite.

Managerial Assistance Available: Ongoing.

Information Submitted: April 1990

SPARKS TUNE-UP, INC.
1400 Opus Place, Suite 800
Downers Grove, Illinois 60515

Description of Operation: Tune-ups are an $8.7 billion market in the United States; under-the-hood is a $23.6 billion market. Sparks intends to be a major player in this market while providing engine diagnostics, fuel injector cleaning, air conditioning servicing, radiator flush and fill, and lube and oil changes to the motoring public. GKN purchased Meineke in 1963 and has been the driving force behind their growth since that time. Sparks was acquired by GKN Automotive in 1987.

Number of Franchisees: 132 in 29 States.

In Business Since: 1981

Equity Capital Needed: $50,000

Financial Assistance Available: The franchisee is responsible for the total investment of $127,834. Sparks' finance department will assist the franchisee by recommending procedures by which such loans have been previously obtained, and will assist in preparing any applications or presentations necessary to be submitted to lending institutions or government agencies.

Training Provided: An intensive 3 week training program is scheduled at the Corporate Headquarters, and another 3 weeks of training at the franchisee's Sparks center by a full-time Sparks Tune-Up, Inc. employee when the center opens.

Managerial Assistance Available: Sparks Tune-Up, Inc., provides continual management services for the life of the franchise in such areas as advertising, inventory control and accounting. Complete operating procedures manuals, technical manuals, forms and directions are provided. An operations director and field representative are available to work closely with the franchisee both by phone and by visiting the centers regularly to assist whenever needed. Sparks' operations department will hold regional meetings and conventions for the franchisees, and conduct marketing and product research to assure the best service available to our customers.

Information Submitted: April 1990

SPEEDEE OIL CHANGE & TUNE-UP
6660 Riverside Drive
Suite 101
Metairie, Louisiana 70003
Kevin Bennett, Vice President/Director of Franchising

Description of Operation: Specializing in 9 minute oil changes and 30 minute tune-ups. Also perform transmission services, radiator flushes, and related fluid maintenance.

Number of Franchisees: 275 in 18 States.

In Business Since: 1980

Equity Capital Needed: $75,000-$150,000

Financial Assistance Available: Supplier financing on equipment.

Training Provided: 2 week training class, covering the operation of the shop.

Managerial Assistance Available: Site selection, construction, advertising, accounting, public relations and ongoing support and training.

Information Submitted: May 1990

SPEEDY MUFFLER KING
8430 West Bryn Mawr
Suite 400
Chicago, Illinois 60631
Ray Slonieski, Director, Franchise Development

Description of Operation: Retail automotive repair chain that specializes in exhaust, front end suspension and brake repairs. Franchising since 1986, Speedy Muffler King is a component of Speedy Car-X Inc. which also includes the Car-X Muffler & Brake and the Pit Stop chains. Speedy is granting franchises in the Eastern U.S.

Number of Franchisees: Presently operating 581 company-owned units in the United States, Canada and Europe, and 15 franchised shops in the Eastern U.S.

In Business Since: 1956

Equity Capital Needed: $180,000-$200,000. Franchise fee $18,500.

Financial Assistance Available: Provide assistance to franchisee to help secure their own financing. Equipment financing packages from outside sources are also available.

Training Provided: Franchisor provides complete training program, which is 6 weeks long: 3 weeks in Ann Arbor, Michigan, 1 week on-the-job training, 1 week at headquarters, 1 week shop opening.

Managerial Assistance Available: Franchisor assists new franchisees in site selection, financing, shop operations, local marketing and sales, financial statement analysis. Field supervisors are available for inventory and sales updates and training.

Information Submitted: April 1990

SPEEDY TRANSMISSION CENTERS
1239 E. Newport Center Drive, #115
Deerfield Beach, Florida 33442
D'Arcy J. Williams, President

Description of Operation: Speedy Transmission Centers repair, rebuild, and recondition automatic and standard transmissions for automobiles and trucks. Franchisees do not require a mechanical background. Trained mechanics are used for the technical aspect of the operation.

Number of Franchisees: 19 in Florida, Georgia, North Carolina, New York and California.

In Business Since: 1983

Equity Capital Needed: Total investment $60,000

Financial Assistance Available: Financial packages are available to qualified franchisees through various suppliers of the franchisor. Both financing and leasing is available in most areas. Franchisor will assist applicant in preparing and the presenting of a financial plan to secure financing.

Training Provided: Prior to opening the franchisor provides a 3 week course covering sales, management systems, advertising, accounting and operations management and on-the-job training.

Managerial Assistance Available: The franchisor assists in securing a location, building design and layout, initial equipment and stock ordering, pre-opening and post opening operations and management supervision by the operations department. Continued periodic operations support, advertising and technical support are supplied on an "ongoing basis."

Information Submitted: April 1990

SPOT-NOT CAR WASHES
(A Division of RACO CAR WASH SYSTEMS, INC.)
2011 West Fourth Street
Joplin, Missouri 64801

Description of Operation: The Spot-Not Car Wash franchise system is a division of RACO Car Wash Systems, Inc., an acknowledged leader in the car wash industry for nearly 20 years. Spot-Not's technological superiority is recognized in the industry and the company continues to be a pioneer in the development of brushless, frictionless car washing and exclusive No-Spot Rinse systems.

Number of Franchisees: 32 in 6 states.

In Business Since: 1968 as RACO Car Wash Systems, Inc.; franchising since 1985.

Equity Capital Needed: 15-25 percent of total investment.

Financial Assistance Available: Assistance in preparation of presentation to lending institutions.

Training Provided: 6 days of comprehensive factory-based, technical and management training; additional 5 to 7 days training at franchisee site, following startup. Full complement of operations manuals. Franchisees do not need a technical background, but should be strongly motivated to achieve success through owning their own business.

Managerial Assistance Available: The Spot-Not management team assists franchisees in site selection, start-up and ongoing training, marketing and advertising planning and implementation, and operational management.

Information Submitted: May 1990

STAR TECHNOLOGY WINDSHIELD REPAIR, INC.
P. O. Box 724706
Atlanta, Georgia 30339
David A. Casey, General Manager

Description of Operation: The franchisor develops, owns and operates, and authorizes franchisees to operate and own mobile and fixed windshield repair business using franchisors' registered trademarks and exclusive ADP windshield repair system. Many franchises are operated as mobile service units in conjunction with an answering service and post office box for mailing and collection of receipts. The primary business of the franchise is the mobile repair of rock damaged windshields, guaranteeing the windshield against further breakage for the life of the windshield. Complete customer satisfaction is guaranteed. The income base is primarily provided by service to commercial fleets, car sales lots, auto rental, insurance independent motorists.

Number of Franchisees: 140 in 38 States.

In Business Since: 1983

Equity Capital Needed: $14,000 to $35,000, includes franchise fee, all equipment and materials, training and city set-up and 3 months personal expenses.

Financial Assistance Available: 70 percent down payment required. Franchisor will finance remainder to persons with approved credit.

Training Provided: An intensive 2 week training course is mandatory: 1 week at the national training center in Boulder, Colorado, and 1 week in the franchisee's territory setting up working accounts with a certified corporate senior technician. Training manuals, operation manuals, account cross reference catalogues, a complete bookkeeping system, all equipment and accessories, complete uniform package, all printed materials, continuous newsletters and follow-up marketing support are included in the franchise package.

Managerial Assistance Available: A full-time corporate staff is available to provide technical assistance, counsel and marketing guidance as needed. A full-time national account marketing department is in effect. Seminars and advanced training are available full-time. An annual convention is held.

Information Submitted: May 1990

SUN COUNTRY AUTO CENTERS INC.
2005 East Michigan Avenue
Jackson, Michigan 49202
Hank Weber, President
John D. Laird, Chairman

Description of Operation: Auto appearance and protection services specialists featuring restyling, detailing, electronics and accessories. Products include: sun roofs, running boards, window tinting, auto alarms, convertible conversions, graphics, glass, and protective coatings.

Number of Franchisees: 14 outlets

In Business Since: 1988

Equity Capital Needed: Cash investment $45,000 to $90,000

Financial Assistance Available: Financing available for equipment, fixtures and signs.

Training Provided: 2 weeks plus continual training on inspection basis.

Managerial Assistance Available: Complete manuals of operation, training school, forms, technical assistance, marketing, and advertising.

Information Submitted: April 1990

SUPERFORMANCE FRANCHISING, INC.
2950 Airway Avenue A5
Costa Mesa, California 92626
Geoff Hirson, President

Description of Operation: Independent repairs and service to Mercedes Benz, BMW and Porsche. Fully computerized, unique customer service, and full support from franchisor, including training, hiring, and inventory purchasing.

Number of Franchisees: 4 plus 3 company-owned in California.

In Business Since: 1980

Equity Capital Needed: Capital requirements $125,000-$207,000.

Financial Assistance Available: Introduction to financial institutions.

Training Provided: Minimum 20 days—up to 90 days.

Managerial Assistance Available: Complete managerial assistance, including bookkeeping, estimating, invoicing, technical updates, price increases. District manager to work closely with franchisee in all areas of the business, including customer relations, advertising, and technical problems.

Information Submitted: May 1990

*TIDY CAR INTERNATIONAL, INC.
P. O. Box 7024
Troy, Michigan 48007-7024

Description of Operation: The Tidy Car format is specifically designed to meet the needs of today's on-the-go, quality conscious consumer by offering a spectrum of automotive detailing services and accessories that range from those performed on a low cost, while-you-wait basis to full service long-term appearance with protective warranties.

Number of Franchisees: 121

In Business Since: 1976

Equity Capital Needed: $41,700-$59,000

Financial Assistance Available: None

Training Provided: The 4 week training period is comprised of extensive schooling in all services offered in addition to management techniques. Ongoing training is also available via schools, seminars, and national meetings.

Managerial Assistance Available: With site selection, lease negotiations, display set up, and inventory requirements. Product orders can be placed with home office personnel who also arrange shipment; marketing staff assists with advertising selection and placement while field staff visit and work with the franchisee on an ongoing basis.

Information Submitted: April 1990

*TKD NORTH AMERICA LTD.
1290 East Maple
Troy, Michigan 48084
Deane Presar, Vice President

Description of Operation: Retail automotive appearance centers provide rust protection, paint glaze, fabric protection, sunroofs, window tinting, security systems, body trim, luggage racks, running boards, bedliners and interior-engine reconditioning. Wholesale programs available at franchise option.

Number of Franchisees: 80 outlets in U.S. and Canada

In Business Since: 1967

Equity Capital Needed: Franchise fee is $15,000 with up to $7,500 returnable for signage and opening advertising. Equipment and start-up inventory approximately $15,000 additional.

Financial Assistance Available: Yes

Training Provided: Complete technical training, both theory and hands-on, plus comprehensive business management, advertising, and sales training is provided at company expense. Franchisee is responsible for transportation, food, lodging for 2 week training course.

Managerial Assistance Available: Beyond classroom training, technical and management manuals are issued at graduation which are continually updated. Supported by field service and quality control personnel regularly helping franchisee in his own territory. Advertising representatives also aid dealers.

Information Submitted: April 1990

TRUCKALINE SUSPENSION CENTERS, INC.
1420-B Highway 12 East
Altoona, Wisconsin 54720
Mike Sheikh, Executive Vice President

Description of Operation: Truckaline Suspension Centers are unique truck repair facilities specializing in the repair and maintenance of heavy duty truck suspension systems and truck wheel alignment serving the needs of truck fleet operators of all sizes. Each center is equipped with modern state of the art equipment and is designed to provide efficient and timely service in a professional manner. Prior industry knowledge is not required as Truckaline provides thorough training and store opening assistance.

Number of Franchisees: 1 operating, 2 under development

In Business Since: 1978, franchising since 1990

Equity Capital Needed: $50,000 minimum cash. Total investment: $550,000 plus.

Financial Assistance Available: Minimum $50,000 cash is required. Truckaline offers financial assistance by soliciting investor/lender funds for the remaining balance and providing loan guarantees on behalf of franchisee.

Training Provided: Truckaline provides a comprehensive training program to franchisee and his initial supervisory staff at Truckaline headquarters. Training is also provided at franchisee's location for all other initial employees by Truckaline corporate staff.

Managerial Assistance Available: Truckaline offers comprehensive store opening assistance and thereafter continued management support in such areas as accounting, advertising, store operations and more.

Information Submitted: April 1990

*TUFFY ASSOCIATES CORP.
dba TUFFY SERVICE CENTERS, INC.
1414 Baronial Plaza
Toledo, Ohio 43619
Eric Schmitt, Director of Franchise Sales

Description of Operation: Retail sales and installation of exhaust, brakes, suspension including front end, alignment, oil and lube

Number of Franchisees: 120 in 7 States

In Business Since: 1970

Equity Capital Needed: $60,000-$70,000 capital injection required. Total investment (exclusive of land and building) is $135,000-$150,000. This includes equipment, inventory, start-up expenses, working capital and initial franchisee fee of $18,500.

Financial Assistance Available: Financing/Leasing is available to qualified applicants. Tuffy will also assist franchisees in obtaining bank financing.

Training Provided: Initial and ongoing training is available at Tuffy Technical Center for franchisees, managers and technicians. In addition, in-market training is available. Shop opening assistance and training are also provided.

Managerial Assistance Available: Tuffy provides ongoing operational management and advertising assistance through district managers and our advertising department.

Information Submitted: April 1990

*TUNEX INTERNATIONAL, INC.
556 East 2100 South
Salt Lake City, Utah 84106
Boyd Enniss, Director of Franchise Operations

Description of Operation: Attractive 6-8-bay Tunex Automotive Centers offer complete engine performance services. Tunex is the innovator of high tech tune-up technologies, specializing in analysis and repair of ignition, fuel, and computerized engine control systems, full service of the engine cooling and the automotive air conditioning system, and the (newly added) Tunex Lube and Oil Service, using the latest equipment and skilled technicians. Franchisee does not need automotive experience. Sales skills and a good business background are desirable.

Number of Franchisees: 12 operating in 3 Western States plus 8 company-owned.

In Business Since: 1972

Equity Capital Needed: $65,000 plus adequate credit to lease $40,000 worth of equipment. Capital includes $15,000 working capital and $19,000 franchise fee.

Financial Assistance Available: Direct financial assistance is not available; however, guidance in preparing application for SBA guaranteed or commercial loans can be provided.

Training Provided: 2 weeks training is provided for franchisee/manager at company headquarters and the service centers, which includes opening week training in the franchisee's center.

Managerial Assistance Available: Technical and managerial support provided on a continuing basis.

Information Submitted: April 1990

ULTRA WASH, INC.
2335 Naomi Street
Houston, Texas 77054
Brian Peskin, President

Description of Operation: A state-of-the-art mobile pressure washing franchise specializing in truck fleet washing at the customer's location. All equipment, training, and initial supplies are included. An on-site salesman will come to franchisee's area to secure sales of $75,000.

Number of Franchisees: 32 in 6 States.

In Business Since: 1981, franchising since 1984.

Equity Capital Needed: $25,000 cash. Total franchise is approximately $54,000.

Financial Assistance Available: Sources provided.

Training Provided: 2 week training at corporate headquarters in Houston, Texas, plus 1 week on location. Sales specialist goes to franchisee's area to assist in securing sales. Ongoing support is continual in the form of monthly newsletters, videotapes, etc.

Managerial Assistance Available: Over 15 years fleet washing experience. Mr. Peskin has been a manager with a Fortune 500 company. Our sale's expertise numbers over 12 in selling this service to truck fleet managers. We have over 5 man-years in equipment design and the washing equipment can bring in more sales per system than any other competitor due to its vastly reliable design.

Information Submitted: April 1990

VALVOLINE INSTANT OIL CHANGE FRANCHISING, INC.
P. O. Box 14046
Lexington, Kentucky 40512
Michael P. Booth, Director of Franchising

Description of Operation: Quick lube service center offering oil change, filter and lubrication plus maintenance check—all in about 10 minutes with no appointment necessary. Franchisee leases or purchases own building with site selection assistance from franchisor. Financing is available for qualified applicants. Franchisee benefits from oldest trademark in the petroleum industry and connection to nation's third largest marketer of motor oil. Subsidiary of Ashland Oil, Inc.

Number of Franchisees: 10 in 8 States.

In Business Since: 1989

Equity Capital Needed: $84,000-$132,000 depending on location and site development.

Training Provided: 6 weeks for owners, operations managers at corporate headquarters, company-owned service centers.

Management Assistance Available: Operations (including system set-up, inventory control, accounting and employee training) and marketing assistance provided.

Information Submitted: April 1990

VICTORY LANE QUICK OIL CHANGE
2610 West Liberty
Ann Arbor, Michigan 48103
John Stegeman, Director of Franchising

Description of Operation: Quick oil change centers in which vehicles are given oil and filter change, chassis lubed and all fluids filled in addition to windows cleaned, tires checked and inflated to correct pressure and a general vehicle inspection, all done in 10 minutes on a drive-thru basis.

Number of Franchisees: 38 in 11 States.

In Business Since: 1980

Equity Capital Needed: $65,000

Financial Assistance Available: Franchisee to arrange own financing.

Training Provided: 1 week training course in Ann Arbor, Michigan covering site and personnel selection, pre-opening requirements, marketing, advertising, P&L statements, accounting and control procedures. In addition, 25 hours are designated for on-site training.

Managerial Assistance Available: Victory Lane will provide continual assistance in "overseeing" the complete operation of the franchise. Manuals, technical bulletins, slide presentations and continual training are provided. In addition, an area supervisor will assist in franchisee's initial opening in an on-site capacity and continue to oversee the operation on an ongoing basis.

Information Submitted: May 1990

WASH-O-TEL, INC.
1500 Louisville Avenue
Monroe, Louisiana 71201
Wayne Williamson, President

Description of Operation: We are in the vehicle maintenance service and we provide top quality cleaning and waxing service with our own hand applied technique while consuming no more than 1 gallon of water. A patented detergent combined with hand work makes the system successful.

Number of Franchisees: 15 plus 11 company-owned in Louisiana, Oklahoma, Texas, Tennessee, Arkansas and Florida

In Business Since: 1982

Equity Capital Needed: $15,000 franchise fee.

Financial Assistance Available: Possible source of financing provided.

Training Provided: 3 days corporate training and 3 days in field training.

Managerial Assistance Available: Ongoing assistance of both types, as needed by franchisee.

Information Submitted: May 1990

*WESTERN AUTO
2107 Grand Avenue
Kansas City, Missouri 64108

Description of Operation: Retailing of hard lines and other home items—principal lines are automotive, lawn and garden and wheel goods, appliances, and electronics.

Number of Franchisees: Over 1,700 stores in all States except North Dakota. Dealer stores in 3 countries.

In Business Since: 1909: Began dealership in 1935

Equity Capital Needed: $75,000 minimum

Financial Assistance Available: Financing available on store fixtures. Floor planning of major items and deferred terms on some seasonal merchandise offered. Other financial assistance extended depending on personal financial statements of prospects.

Training Provided: 4 week training course, 4 weeks hands-on training in a company operated store. Company personnel continue to offer training, counseling and sales assistance after formalized training school is completed.

Managerial Assistance Available: Dealer contacted regularly in store by company personnel, offering counseling on sales, credit and store operation.

Information Submitted: May 1990

*ZIEBART CORPORATION
1290 East Maple Road
Troy, Michigan 48084
Carl W. Bennett, Director of Franchise Development

Description of Operation: While once known only for rustproofing, today's Ziebart center is devoted to the complete protection and appearance of automobiles. The expanded line now includes detailing services, window tinting, graphics, alarms, sunroofs, and running boards.

Number of Franchisees: 565 in 31 States and 35 countries.

In Business Since: 1962

Equity Capital Available: $68,000-$97,400 which includes the franchise fee.

Financial Assistance Available: None

Training Provided: The 5 week training period is comprised of an extensive schooling in all services offered in addition to management techniques. Ongoing training is also available via schools, seminars, and national meetings.

Managerial Assistance Available: With site selection, lease negotiations, display set up, and inventory requirements. Product orders can be placed with home office personnel who also arrange shipment; marketing staff assist with advertising selection and placement while field staff visit and work with the franchise on an ongoing basis.

Information Submitted: April 1990

AUTO/TRAILER RENTALS

AFFORDABLE USED CAR RENTAL SYSTEM, INC.
51 Gerard Avenue
Matawan, New Jersey 07747
Charles Vitale

Description of Operation: Affordable license is available to new car **dealers only.** It provides training, forms, follow-up and insurance for new car dealers desiring to enter the used car rental business. Price of license includes all forms necessary. District representatives call on dealer members regularly in person.

Number of Franchisees: 297 in 41 States

In Business Since: 1981

Equity Capital Needed: $30,000-$50,000.

Financial Assistance Available: None

Training Provided: 3 days at training. Training program mandatory.

Managerial Assistance Available: Affordable has trained executives to personally counsel dealers on regular basis. Forms are provided at no cost. Advertising techniques are exchanged. Low cost insurance is available but not compulsory. All former new car dealers, auto manufacturers' former employees and rental professionals eligible.

Information Submitted: May 1990

A.I.N. LEASING SYSTEMS
501 Burnside Avenue
Inwood, New York 11696
Garry Rothbaum

Description of Operation: An automobile and equipment leasing franchise. A.I.N. provides training, marketing plan, and all necessary lease financing.

Number of Franchisees: 265 nationwide

In Business Since: 1980

Equity Capital Needed: $25,000

Financial Assistance Available: None

Training Provided: 4 days of training covers, marketing and merchandising.

Managerial Assistance Available: Ongoing support and assistance.

Information Submitted: May 1990

AIRWAYS RENT A CAR CO.
4025 North Mannheim
Schiller Park, Illinois 60176
Michael H. Zaransky, President
Howard Maybloom, Director of Franchising

Description of Operation: Car rental firm in business 23 years. Offers national reservations system including 800 number and airline automated system listing operated by American Airlines Direct Marketing Corp. Cooperative advertising and promotional agreement with General Motors. Ranked 11th largest car rental firm.

Number of Franchisees: 64

In Business Since: 1967

Equity Capital Needed: $150,000

Financial Assistance Available: Arrange for auto purchase financing.

Training Provided: Comprehensive at franchisor's premises for up to 2 weeks.

Managerial Assistance Available: Throughout franchise term.

Information Submitted: April 1990

AMERICAN INTERNATIONAL RENT A CAR
One Harborside Drive
Boston, Massachusetts 02128

Description of Operation: American International is a worldwide network of car rental operations servicing customers at airport, suburban, and downtown locations. All outlets are franchised-owned; there are no corporate locations.

Number of Franchisees: The American International network consists of over 1,300 locations in more than 25 countries throughout North America, Europe, the Middle East, South America, and the Caribbean.

In Business Since: 1968

Equity Capital Needed: Varies with size and location of the territory. Average initial franchise investment: $50,000.

Financial Assistance Available: Arrangements are discussed on an individual basis.

Training Provided: Initial training available at the corporate headquarters location. Complete operations manuals are provided and updated by the Systems Office. Ongoing consultation and assistance will be provided as needed.

Managerial Assistance Available: The management team at American International assists new franchisees in selecting sites, financing and managing their fleets, analyzing financial statements, obtaining corporate accounts, and government contracts, and local marketing and advertising. American International has standardized everything their franchisees need, including signs, rental agreements, uniforms and promotional materials.

Information Submitted: May 1990

AVIS RENT A CAR SYSTEM, INC.
Licensee Relations Department
900 Old Country Road
Garden City, New York 11530

Description of Operation: Avis is in the business of renting passenger cars to members of the general public directly and through franchisees who purchase Avis car rental franchises from Avis. Avis offers franchises within the United States for car rental (including the sale of used cars) and truck rental and leasing.

Number of Franchisees: Over 700 locations throughout the United States.

In Business Since: 1946

Equity Capital Needed: Varies according to the size of franchised area.

Financial Assistance Available: None

Training Provided: An Avis field director will spend approximately 1 week prior to or during the opening of the franchised business to assist the franchisee, to acquaint the franchisee with the Avis car rental system and to assist in training rental sales agents.

Managerial Assistance Available: Avis personnel are available for consultation on advertising, promoting, operating and developing the franchisee's car rental business. Periodic business conventions will be held.

Information Submitted: May 1990

*BUDGET RENT A CAR CORPORATION
200 North Michigan Avenue
Chicago, Illinois 60601
Rick J. Santella, Assistant Vice President
Franchise Acquisitions and Development

Description of Operation: Automobile and truck rental.

Number of Franchisees: 3,049 locations worldwide.

In Business Since: 1958, franchising since 1960.

Equity Capital Needed: Varies with size of operation.

Financial Assistance Available: None

Training Provided: Full training, advertising and marketing, and financial analysis services are provided to licensees.

Managerial Assistance Available: During the term of the franchise, Budget has a complete management team available to assist licencees in areas of franchising, operations, promotions, local marketing, advertising, trucks, training and insurance. Site selection assistance is provided prior to the opening of each location.

Information Submitted: April 1990

DOLLAR RENT A CAR SYSTEMS, INC.
6141 West Century Boulevard
Los Angeles, California 90045
E. Woody Francis

Description of Operation: Automobile and truck rental. Heavy concentration in airport operations.

Number of Franchisees: Over 1,800 worldwide. Locations throughout Europe, Middle East and Africa will be under Inter-Rent-Dollar.

In Business Since: 1966

Equity Capital Needed: Approximately $100,000

Financial Assistance Available: Occasionally assist in financing.

Training Provided: Standardized accounting system set up. Operational training by franchisor's representative at site.

Managerial Assistance Available: Assistance in site selection. Standardized free-standing building. Consultant on-site during construction. Guidance in selection and balance of fleet. Continuing guidance in accounting and operations. Nationwide advertising campaign, co-op program available, and nationwide reservations service.

Information Submitted: May 1990

EQUITY AUTO & EQUIPMENT LEASING CORP.
24700 Northwestern Highway
Suite 134
Southfield, Michigan 48034
Dennis M. Lynch

Description of Operation: Equity is an independent lessor of autos and equipment of all types. To our knowledge, our franchise opportunity is unique.

Number of Franchisees: 54 in Michigan; 5 in Florida

In Business Since: 1986

Equity Capital Needed: Total investment—$10,000.

Financial Assistance Available: 50 percent financing available to qualified applicants.

Training Provided: 12 hours of training are provided.

Managerial Assistance Available: Franchisees receive an operations manual and ongoing home office support.

Information Submitted: April 1990

FAMILY RENT-A-CAR, INC.
1827 West Capital Avenue
Grant Island, Nebraska 68801
Robert Noden

Description of Operation: This business is designed to rent used cars for a more competitive price than from local competition; dealers may adjust prices to their own area cost factor, depending on what fits well with competition in their town.

Number of Franchisees: We have 56 dealers across the United States.

In Business Since: 1982

Equity Capital Needed: Equity needed can vary according to individual needs from $150,000 to $50,000. The dealer may start with as small a fleet as he wishes, and we also have the correct insurance available.

Financial Assistance Available: None

Training Provided: Every franchisee is trained on all details at his own town by one of our company representatives.

Managerial Assistance Available: The management is available by phone during all hours of every work day for any help or guidance.

Information Submitted: April 1990

FREEDOM RENT-A-CAR SYSTEM
P. O. Box 2345
Bartlesville, Oklahoma 74005
Neil Wilderom, President

Description of Operation: Freedom Rent-A-Car offers daily car and truck rentals throughout the United States. Operators offer new and used rental cars to both airport and local markets at inexpensive rates.

Number of Franchisees: 165 locations in 35 States

In Business Since: 1982

Equity Capital Needed: Varies in size of franchise territory.

Financial Assistance Available: Franchisor will assist licensee in obtaining vehicle financing from lending institutions. Franchisor will extend financing for a portion of franchise purchase to select licensees.

Training Provided: Each licensee receives a comprehensive 3-day classroom training course in Bartlesville, Oklahoma, and on-site training within first 2 weeks of operation. The training program is open to any new staff members on continuing basis.

Managerial Assistance Available: Periodic reviews conducted by regional managers qualified in all aspects of the car rental industry. Operating manuals and a toll-free number maintained for licensee assistance.

Information Submitted: May 1990

HERTZ CORPORATION
225 Brae Boulevard
Park Ridge, New Jersey 07656-0713

Description of Operation: Hertz System, Inc., offers franchises for the conduct of car and truck rental and leasing businesses in the United States under the "Hertz" name.

Number of Franchisees: Over 1,100 car and truck rental locations in all states except Florida and Hawaii.

In Business Since: 1918

Equity Capital Needed: Varies according to franchise-operating capital as required by location.

Financial Assistance Available: None

Training Provided: Zone System Manager trains new franchisee before operation opens with Hertz Starter Kit (kit includes all forms needed to run a location). Visits by System Manager on a periodic basis. Manager rental representative training classes. Manuals and guides for running a location issued. Corporate training class available to franchisees. Annual business meeting.

Managerial Assistance Available: Accounting and operational guides are provided to run the location. Visits by Corporate Zone System Manager to act as a liaison between the corporate and licensee locations. All forms and training classes provided business (e.g., insurance, advertising, accounting, etc.).

Information Submitted: May 1990

PAYLESS CAR RENTAL
2350/N 34th Street
St. Petersburg, Florida 33713
Jay Vahl, President

Description of Operation: Automobile renting of current model cars.

Number of Franchisees: 130 in 50 States and 5 in foreign countries.

In Business Since: 1971

Equity Capital Needed: Varies—franchise fee plus $25,000 to $150,000.

Financial Assistance Available: Assistance in establishing necessary lines of credit with which to acquire vehicles. Assistance in procuring fleet insurance.

Training Provided: Theory complete with policies, procedures and automated reservation systems. On-the-job training, 1-3 days. Opening assistance and review, 1-3 days. Follow-up visit and review, quarterly.

Managerial Assistance Available: Training as necessary in vehicle procurement, insurance procurement, office and counter procedures, customer qualifications, hiring and training personnel, business development, advertising, accounting, vehicle disposal and fleet maintenance procedures. Periodic visits, regional and international meetings.

Information Submitted: May 1990

PRACTICAL RENT-A-CAR
705-B Yucca
Boulder City, Nevada 89005
Bert Frost, General Manager

Description of Operation: Practical Rent-A-Car is America's alternative car rental agency. We offer affordable car rental franchises to people committed to service. New car prices make new car rentals prohibitive for the majority of people, renting used cars is right for the 1990s.

Number of Franchisees: 13 in 6 States

In Business Since: Practical Rent-A-Car was trademarked in Canada in 1984. Micro Instrument Corp of Rochester, New York purchased the United States rights to the trademark in March 1989.

Equity Capital Needed: $12,500 to $275,000

Financial Assistance Available: None

Training Provided: Mandatory training program conducted at the franchisee's location or at corporate headquarters. The training program covers general policies, fleet purchasing and management, rental counter management, financial information, record keeping, personnel, customer relations, and advertising and promotion.

Managerial Assistance Available: On-site opening assistance, continuing management, marketing, operation and technical assistance to franchisee and employees.

Information Submitted: April 1990

RENT-A-WRECK OF AMERICA, INC.
6053 West Century Boulevard
Suite 550
Los Angeles, California 90045
Henry Gross, Vice President

Description of Operation: Automobile rental and leasing.

Number of Franchisees: 347 in 46 States, Australia and New Zealand.

In Business Since: 1977

Equity Capital Needed: Capitalization $26,000 to $139,000. Each new franchise pays an initial license fee which ranges from $4,000 to $30,000 depending on the size and location of his market.

Financial Assistance Available: See automobile financing available.

Training Provided: Each new licensee attends mandatory 4-day intensive training course in Los Angeles which covers all aspects of the operation of a Rent-A-Wreck facility in compliance with the standards set by the company. Ongoing training is provided through regional meetings, regional representatives, national conventions and refresher courses as well as personal visits to the franchisee by the company's experienced operations staff.

Managerial Assistance Available: During the 4-day training period management and technical training are the foremost areas addressed to prepare new licensees in running a Rent-A-Wreck operation; licensees are free to send new management personnel to Rent-A-Wreck school as needed. A complete operations manual, as well as rental business forms with directions for their use, and a marketing planner, containing advertising and promotional materials, are provided. Experienced Rent-A-Wreck personnel are available by telephone for ongoing consultation and assistance.

Information Submitted: April 1990

THRIFTY RENT-A-CAR SYSTEM, INC.
P. O. Box 35250
5330 East 31st Street
Tulsa, Oklahoma 74153-0250

Description of Operation: Franchisor of automobile renting and leasing business throughout the world.

Number of Franchisees: 770 locations worldwide.

In Business Since: 1950, franchising since 1962.

Equity Capital Needed: Varies in proportion to the size and potential of the franchise area.

Financial Assistance Available: Franchisor will assist licensee in obtaining vehicle financing from lending institutions.

Training Provided: Company maintains and operates an ongoing car rental operation which is used exclusively for the training of licensees, testing of marketing theories and programs. In addition, field assistance is provided by trained personnel at the time of opening, and periodically thereafter.

Managerial Assistance Available: Thrifty furnishes continuing management assistance to its licensees by way of a headquarters staff trained in all areas of the car rental operation, including financial, legal, operational, sales and marketing, insurance, and vehicle purchases and disposal. Trained regional directors call on the licensee on a regular basis offering assistance designed to insure the success of the licensee.

Information Submitted: April 1990

UGLY DUCKLING RENT-A-CAR
1240 East Missouri
Phoenix, Arizona 85014

Description of Operation: Each franchise is individually owned and operated. Rental of preowned vehicles aimed at local market with few customers at or from airports. Licensee provides capital and vehicles except as noted below. Current licensees include new and used car dealerships and related automotive businesses such as body shops, tune-up centers, transmission repair shops, etc.

Number of Franchisees: 300 in United States.

In Business Since: 1977

Equity Capital Needed: $30,000 to $50,000

Financial Assistance Available: None

Training Provided: Fully comprehensive 4 day training program.

Managerial Assistance Available: 800 number available for all problems relative to the business. Zone managers and service representatives available for technical assistance. Monthly information and bulletins keep franchisees abreast of market development.

Information Submitted: April 1990

U-SAVE AUTO RENTAL OF AMERICA, INC.
7525 Connelley Drive
Suite A
Hanover, Maryland 21076
William Edwards, National Sales & Marketing Manager

Description of Operation: U-Save has been named to *Inc's* list of 500 fastest growing private companies and *Entrepreneur's* list of 500 top franchises for four consecutive years. U-Save franchisees focus on the hometown market and insurance replacement.

Number of Franchisees: 495 in 45 States

In Business Since: 1979

Equity Capital Needed: $15,000-$150,000

Financial Assistance Available: None

Training Provided: Training by State or Regional Manager is provided, as is a comprehensive training and policy manual and guides for operation. State Managers visit franchises regularly.

Managerial Assistance Available: Regular visits by State and Regional Managers, toll free number to home office. National annual convention held each year. Assistance available in all phases of rental and reservation system (i.e. accounting, legal, insurance, etc.) Operating forms, brochures, specialty advertising products, uniforms are available. TV, radio and newspaper advertisements are also available.

Information Submitted: May 1990

BEAUTY SALONS/SUPPLIES

ACCENT HAIR SALONS, INC.
211 South Main Street
Suite 1130
Dayton, Ohio 45402
Claude Patmon, President

Description of Operation: Retail chain hair salons directed at the black segment of the hair care market, providing a full range of hair care services, emphasizing exceptionally high quality, convenient walk-in service, and competitive prices; located in high traffic malls or major shopping centers. These salons are distinctively decorated reflecting quality and efficiency, occupy 2,000 to 2,800 square feet and are able to service 16 to 18 customers at one time.

Number of Franchisees: 9 in 6 States

In Business Since: 1981

Equity Capital Needed: Minimum cash required, $35,000; total capital required, $125,000.

Financial Assistance Available: Direct financing provided for construction of leasehold improvements by the franchisor to qualified applicants.

Training Provided: A comprehensive 3 week training program in all facets of salon operations. Continuous training at the unit level.

Managerial Assistance Available: Complete support system including site selection, unit design, pre-opening hiring and training of operating personnel, opening advertising, and continuous field support in all aspects of salon operations.

Information Submitted: April 1990

AMERICUTS
501 West Glenoaks Boulevard
Suite 201
Glendale, California 91202
Victor Seprakian

Description of Operation: Americuts offers a full service franchise concept providing both men and women a complete hair care package—dedicating its energies and resources to cutting hair better and in a better environment. The marketing emphasis of the franchise salons is on the precision hair stylists employ and on building exceptional stores with a bustling trade based on repeat and new customers. In addition to new franchise outlets, franchises may be available for fully improved, operational, company-owned shops.

Number of Franchisees: 3 plus 4 company-owned in California

In Business Since: 1982

Equity Capital Needed: Total investment, including initial franchise fee, ranges from $65,000 to $92,000 depending on the size and leasehold improvements of franchise outlets.

Financial Assistance Available: None

Training Provided: The franchise requires 1 person employed in a managerial capacity and 3 licensed operators to be trained prior to the opening of the franchise. Training is generally 1 week and includes shop management and business operations and procedures. The training program includes both classroom and practical instruction.

Managerial Assistance Available: The franchisor provides members of its operations staff and shop personnel to assist franchisee in the operation of the shop, in establishing shop procedures and training shop personnel. The franchisor also provides a staff and shop personnel at its expense for up to 4 weeks following the opening of the franchise outlet. Periodically, franchisor may make available advertising plans and advice and in-shop promotional materials for franchisees' use and may assist in designing special advertising and promotional programs. Additional training courses or programs may become available to franchisee at the discretion of the franchisor to include sales techniques, training of personnel, performance standards and advertising programs.

Information Submitted: May 1990

*THE BARBERS, HAIRSTYLING FOR MEN AND
WOMEN, INC.
300 Industrial Boulevard
Minneapolis, Minnesota 55413
Vaughn Berg, Executive Vice President of Franchise
Sales and Development

Description of Operation: A completely systemized men's and women's hairstyling shop with inventory controls, accounting systems, advertising, public relations, and business management programs.

Number of Franchisees: 82 in 9 States plus 8 company-owned.

In Business Since: 1963

Equity Capital Needed: $90,000

Financial Assistance Available: Investor partners welcomed.

Training Provided: Management and technical, 2 week, then quarterly seminars.

Managerial Assistance Available: Business management, including advertising, public relations, accounting and recordkeeping, training in hairstyling and all related services.

Information Submitted: April 1990

*COMMAND PERFORMANCE
Baldwin Park
7 Alfred Street
Woburn, Massachusetts 01801
Dennis Brown, C.O.O.

Description of Operation: Precision haircutting and styling salons for men and women. Company encourages owner-operators.

Number of Franchisees: 90 in 30 States plus 130 company-owned.

In Business Since: 1976

Equity Capital Needed: Total cost to purchase, construct and open salon: $41,500 to $124,500.

Financial Assistance Available: Various combinations of approved leasing and financing alternatives.

Training Provided: In addition to recruiting and training the salon's manager and staff, the franchisor conducts a comprehensive 30 hour initial training course for its franchisees in all phases of operations, advertising, promotion, legal and financial considerations.

Managerial Assistance Available: In addition to initial site selection, lease negotiations, hiring and training of staff, and construction advice, the franchisor furnishes continuing management, marketing, operational and technical assistance to franchisee and his/her employees.

Information Submitted: May 1990

*COST CUTTERS FAMILY HAIR CARE SHOPS
A Division of THE BARBERS, HAIRSTYLING FOR MEN
& WOMEN, INC.
300 Industrial Boulevard NE
Minneapolis, Minnesota 55413
Vaughn Berg, Executive Vice President of Franchise
Sales and Development

Description of Operation: No-frills hair care services and related retail products for men, women and children.

Number of Franchisees: 370 in 28 States and 4 in Canada plus 3 company-owned.

In Business Since: 1982

Equity Capital Needed: $80,000

Financial Assistance Available: Leasing

Training Provided: Mandatory 2 week program for the franchisee and manager to include operating and management skills, customer relations, handling of personnel, inventory control, advertising and promotional techniques.

Managerial Assistance Available: Additional training for stylists available upon request at charges based on the type, location and duration of training provided. Such training may be custom designed to fit the franchisees' needs.

Information Submitted: April 1990

CUSTOM CUTS, INC.
13850 Manchester Road
St. Louis, Missouri 63011
Robert Hanson, President

Description of Operation: Family hair care centers.

Number of Franchisees: 6 plus 7 company-owned units.

In Business Since: 1985

Equity Capital Needed: Approximately $95,000, which includes franchise fee.

Financial Assistance Available: None

Training Provided: Complete training provided in operating a family hair care center.

Managerial Assistance Available: Continuous in all operations of the franchise.

Information Submitted: May 1990

DAVID ALAN'S CUTS FOR KIDS
15 Engle Street
Englewood, New Jersey 07631
Ronald Sommers

Description of Operation: Children's hair salon.

Number of Franchisees: 2 plus 1 company-owned in New Jersey.

In Business Since: 1986

Equity Capital Needed: Approximately $80,000.

Financial Assistance Available: WIll assist in obtaining financing.

Training Provided: Complete training in operating a children's hair salon.

Managerial Assistance Available: Ongoing in all operations of the salon.

Information Submitted: May 1990

EASY HAIR FRANCHISE, INC.
1257-H Kennestone Circle
Marietta, Georgia 30066
Don Westbrook, President

Description of Operation: Value priced hair care salon. Computerized operations with full-time manager. Stores approximately 1,500 square feet.

Number of Franchisees: 11 in Georgia

In Business Since: 1986

Equity Capital Needed: $30-40,000 cash plus $50-$60,000 equity.

Financial Assistance Available: We will assist in obtaining satisfactory financing.

Training Provided: 2 weeks prior to opening, 1 week on operations and 1 week on actual daily business.

Managerial Assistance Available: Pre-opening training for all parties involved. Regular owner and manager meetings, plus shop visits and constant management availability.

Information Submitted: May 1990

FAMILY HAIRCUT STORE
398 Hebron Avenue
Glastonbury, Connecticut 06033
Randall Gibbons, President

Description of Operation: The Family Haircut Store is a modern, convenient store designed to meet the needs of the busy American family by providing full service haircare at affordable prices. Our policies—appointments never necessary and customer satisfaction guaranteed—give us a high customer base and exceptionally high repeat business.

Number of Franchisees: 23

In Business Since: 1985

Equity Capital Needed: $53,400-$98,600

Financial Assistance Available: None

Training Provided: A full week of training is provided focusing on marketing strategies and programs, managerial techniques, staffing, financial controls, operating procedures, in-store training.

Managerial Assistance Available: Corporate office provides ongoing support in advertising and promotions, daily operations, and new haircare techniques and products, as well as any information that pertains to the business.

Information Submitted: May 1990

FANTASTIC SAM'S, THE ORIGINAL FAMILY HAIRCUTTERS
3180 Old Getwell Road
P. O. Box 18845
Memphis, Tennessee 38181-0845
Sam M. Ross, Chairman of the Board
George H. Carnall II, President

Description of Operation: The company sells licenses for Fantastic Sam's, the Original Family Haircutters, a unique retail haircare establishment oriented to the demands, pocketbooks and convenience of all American families.

Number of Franchisees: Over 2,200 stores in 45 States and 4 countries.

In Business Since: 1974

Equity Capital Needed: (1) One Fantastic Sam's store—$58,700-$120,500, which includes the license fee and all amounts to open that store. (2) Regional license to sell and provide service to Fantastic Sam's licensees within that region—$25,000-$300,000.

Financial Assistance Available: The company provides payment terms on initial product inventory and will finance shop equipment to qualified licensees.

Training Provided: The company provides training classes for all licensees, their shop managers, hairstylists and staff members in the company's training facilities. Further, experienced trainers assist all of the licensees in their store openings, provide seminars around the country and Canada, conduct in-store consultation and training, and provide a complete technical training program.

Managerial Assistance Available: In-store seminars and regional seminars are provided to all licensees and their store managers. Additionally, week long management classes and daily training classes for all licensees and their store managers are scheduled regularly at the training facilities of the company.

Information Submitted: May 1990

*FIRST CHOICE HAIRCUTTERS, LTD.
6465 Millcreek Drive
Suite 205
Mississauga, Ontario L5N 5R3
George Kostopoulos, Director of Franchise Development

Description of Operation: First Choice Haircutters is in the business of providing high volume, low cost retail haircutting and hair care services for the entire family. Our a la carte price structure allows customers to purchase only services required: cut, shampoo, style dry, perms, etc. Convenience emphasized—no appointments, one-stop shopping for entire family.

Number of Franchisees: 170 franchised units plus a strong corporate base of 75 stores; strategically located in the United States and Canada.

In Business Since: 1980

Equity Capital Needed: The range of unencumbered funds required is $35,000 to $40,000. The range of total investment required for a single store franchise including franchise fees, furniture and equipment, estimated leaseholds, grand opening, advertising and working capital would be $75,000 to $80,000. An area franchise including 2 shops, complete as indicated would require approximately $80,000 in unencumbered funds, and about $80,000 available through financing plus living expenses for a period of 3-6 months. The amounts include all applicable franchise fees.

Financial Assistance Available: Preparation of proformas and assistance in obtaining bank financing.

Training Provided: 2 week complete franchisee training program includes operations, site selection and lease negotiations, advertising, staff hiring and motivation. Plus 10-13 days on-site store opening assistance and continued support. Plus 2 store visits per year by a training officer/operations manager for updates, reviews and progress reports. Plus operations and training manuals, video training tapes, television commercials and radio ads. All included in the franchise fee.

Managerial Assistance Available: All haircutters are trained in the First Choice Haircutters method of cutting and customer service techniques. On-site opening assistance, frequent shop visits, ongoing support and consultation, franchisee seminars, advertising advisory council and refresher course.

Information Submitted: April 1990

FIRST PLACE, INC.
2100 River Chase Center
Suite 406
Birmingham, Alabama 35244
Michael Darnell, President

Description of Operation: Family hair care center servicing the entire family. The stores are characterized by a distinctive interior design, color scheme, layout and specially designed decor.

Number of Franchisees: 13 stores including company-owned.

In Business Since: 1977

Equity Capital Needed: $64,225 to $92,200

Financial Assistance Available: None

Training Provided: Training consists of an initial 2 week session on procedures and techniques for hair care, methods of implementing operating cash and financial controls, and manuals including advertising and marketing programs.

Managerial Assistance Available: During the first week of franchisee's opening, franchisor provides an employee at franchisee's location for opening assistance. Franchisor offers continuing services relating to the conduct of franchisee's business.

Information Submitted: May 1990

GREAT CLIPS, INC.
3601 Minnesota Drive
Minneapolis, Minnesota 55435
Raymond L. Barton, President

Description of Operation: A Great Clips shop is a high quality, high volume haircutting shop for the entire family.

Number of Franchisees: 201 in 12 States

In Business Since: 1982

Equity Capital Needed: $62,500 to $87,000

Financial Assistance Available: Assistance in preparing bank presentations.

Training Provided: Complete franchisee and staff training and assistance including site selection, lease negotiations, manager selection, equipping and supply a Great Clips shop, and professional advertising and promotion programs.

Managerial Assistance Available: Professional technical training and assistance for all shop managers and stylists. Regularly scheduled visits from Great Clips field consultants. Continuing advertising and promotion support and assistance.

Information Submitted: April 1990

*GREAT EXPECTATIONS PRECISION HAIRCUTTERS
125 South Service Road
P. O. Box 265
Jericho, New York 11753
Don vonLiebermann, President

Description of Operation: Great Expectations is a distinctive haircutting establishment primarily servicing men and women aged 18-49, appealing to the contemporary hair care customer. The franchise package offers a thoroughly modern, attractively designed shop, streamlined equipment, operational support, training, site selection and personnel recruitment.

Number of Franchisees: 185 in 40 States

In Business Since: 1955

Equity Capital Needed: Total initial investment $83,100 to $176,500.

Financial Assistance Available: Financial assistance available to qualified applicants.

Training Provided: In-salon training about 10 days. Pre-opening training in franchisee's salon and complete supply of manuals.

Managerial Assistance Available: Technical training and seminars, new styling techniques, and management training. Advertising materials and promotions.

Information Submitted: April 1990

HAIR BEARS
P. O. Box 1415
Mt. Pleasant, South Carolina 29465
Dolph Rodenberg

Description of Operation: Upscale hair salon catering to children ages birth to 19.

Number of Franchisees: 2

In Business Since: Franchising since 1989

Equity Capital Needed: $53,700-$69,000. Includes franchise fee and initial operating capital.

Financial Assistance Available: No financial assistance available.

Training Provided: Extensive. No need for experience or knowledge in cosmetology field. Ideal second business.

Managerial Assistance Available: Ongoing

Information Submitted: April 1990

*HAIRCRAFTERS
125 South Service Road
P. O. Box 265
Jericho, New York 11753
Don vonLiebermann, President

Description of Operation: Full service hair care salons servicing men and women, combines popular unisex styling services with the traditional selection to meet the needs of all ages. The franchise package offers a thoroughly modern, attractively designed shop, streamlined equipment, operational support, training, site selection and personnel recruitment.

Number of Franchisees: 387 in the United States and Canada.

In Business Since: 1955

Equity Capital Needed: $73,000 to $131,500

Financial Assistance Available: Financial assistance available to qualified applicants.

Training Provided: In-salon training about 10 days. Pre-opening training in franchisee's salon and complete supply of manuals.

Managerial Assistance Available: Technical training and seminars, new styling techniques, and management training. Advertising material and promotions.

Information Submitted: April 1990

HAIRCUTS COMPANY
20900 Swenson Drive
Suite 100
Waukesha, Wisconsin 53186
Ken Smith/Bernard J. Conway

Description of Operation: Haircuts operates a chain of family affordable hair care shops. Locations are in strip mall centers and are approximately 1,500 square feet. Haircuts provides site location, remodeling plans and a complete operations manual to each franchisee. Television commercials and print promotions are a part of the extensive marketing plan available to franchisees.

Number of Franchisees: 5 plus 22 company-owned in Ohio, and Wisconsin.

In Business Since: 1983, franchising since 1985.

Equity Capital Needed: $85,000-$95,000 total investment.

Financial Assistance Available: While Haircuts does not provide any direct financing to franchisees, assistance is provided in obtaining outside financing.

Training Provided: Separate training programs are conducted for franchisees and their personnel. Haircuts provides franchisees with on-site assistance during shop opening process.

Managerial Assistance Available: Haircuts provides ongoing quality control assurance through field operations management. Marketing and advertising programs are implemented in conjunction with the franchisees.

Information Submitted: May 1990

HAIR N' THINGS
21655 Coolidge
Oak Park, Michigan 48221
Shirley Banks, President

Description of Operation: Hair N' Things is a multifaceted hair salon designed to promote and market services within the beauty hair care industry. In keeping with the current trends, all Hair N' Things salons offer facial treatments, manicures, pedicures and cosmetics, in addition to hair care treatments.

Number of Franchisees: 3

In Business Since: 1978

Equity Capital Needed: $57,000: $20,000 is the franchise fee, $37,000 is for fixtures, equipment, inventory and supplies.

Financial Assistance Available: Financial assistance is provided by the franchisor.

Training Provided: Franchisee is enrolled in training classes.

Managerial Assistance Available: Managerial assistance is provided in all operation phases of the business.

Information Submitted: June 1990

*HAIR PERFORMERS
c/o JOHN F. AMICO & CO., INC.
7327 West 90th Street
Bridgeview, Illinois 60455
Gary R. Dobson, Vice President of Franchise Development

Description of Operation: Family hair care center which provides styling and hair cutting for the entire family. Most franchisees operate store on limited hours (8 to 10). All business and management aids provided. Regional offices and training facilities throughout the U.S. Two basic schools in Chicago.

Number of Franchisees: 217 franchised units in 17 States, plus 9 company-owned.

In Business Since: 1962

Equity Capital Needed: $40,000 to $80,000

Financial Assistance Available: None

Training Provided: Staffing, recruiting, management selection and training provided for franchisees. Training conducted at home office, regional offices, company-owned college and in-store programs.

Managerial Assistance Available: Complete site selection, lease negotiations, salon design, full staffing and continual management assistance and full training at Hair Performers college.

Information Submitted: April 1990

JOAN M. CABLE'S LA FEMMINA BEAUTY SALONS, INC.
3301 Hempstead Turnpike
Levittown, New York 11756
John L. Wagner, Vice President

Description of Operation: Joan M. Cable's La Femmina Beauty Salons, Inc., offers qualified applicants franchises to operate retail ladies' beauty parlors under its name. La Femmina offers total service to women with complete haircare and grooming services including manicures, pedicures, and facials, using only the highest quality name brand products—all at affordable prices and convenient hours for today's active women.

Number of Franchisees: 7 in New York/Long Island areas.

In Business Since: 1974

Equity Capital Needed: Total investment ranges from $27,265 to 33,265.

Financial Assistance Available: Franchisor will possibly assist franchisee in obtaining appropriate financing or franchisor may offer a portion of such financing for the purchase of all necessary machinery and equipment.

Training Provided: The training program shall last no less than 5 days and provides the franchisee with the certain knowledge to assist the franchisee in the operation of the La Femmina Beauty Parlor. Throughout the training program, which will be held on a one-to-one basis, such topics as payroll, advertising, insurance, products, and scheduling will be discussed in conjunction with the direct use of the operations manual.

Managerial Assistance Available: Joan M. Cable's La Femmina Beauty Salons, Inc., provides continual and ongoing training and management service for the term of the franchise in areas of bookkeeping, advertising, workshops, seminars and promotional programs, all on an as needed basis.

Information Submitted: April 1990

JOAN M. CABLE'S LA FEMMINA BEAUTY SALONS, INC.
dba THE LEMON TREE
3301 Hempstead Turnpike
Levittown, New York 11756
John L. Wagner, Vice President

Description of Operation: Joan M. Cable's La Femmina Beauty Salons, Inc., offers franchises to qualified applicants. Franchises to operate unisex haircutting establishments under the name of The Lemon Tree, a Unisex Haircutting Establishment. Lemon Tree offers complete haircare and grooming service to men, women and children using only the highest quality name brand products, all at affordable prices and convenient hours for today's active people.

Number of Franchisees: 58 in Long Island/Staten Island/Brooklyn, Westchester, New Jersey, Connecticut and Maryland.

In Business Since: 1976

Equity Capital Needed: Total investment ranges from $26,600 to $33,100.

Financial Assistance: Franchisor will possibly assist franchisee in obtaining appropriate financing or franchisor may offer a portion of such financing for the purchase of all necessary machinery and equipment.

Training Provided: The training program shall last no less than 5 days and provides the franchisee with the certain knowledge to assist the franchisee in the operation of the Lemon Tree, a Unisex Haircutting Establishment. Throughout the training program, which will be held on a one-to-one basis, such topics as payroll, advertising, insurance, products, and scheduling will be discussed in conjunction with the direct use of the operations manual.

Managerial Assistance Available: Joan M. Cable's La Femmina Beauty Salons, Inc., provides continual and ongoing training and management service for the term of the franchise in areas of bookkeeping, advertising, workshops, seminars and promotional programs, all on an as needed basis.

Information Submitted: April 1990

LORD'S & LADY'S HAIR SALONS
450 Belgrade Avenue
Boston, Massachusetts 02132
Michael M. Barsamian, President
Harry G. Mitchell, Executive Vice President and Treasurer

Description of Operation: Professional haircutting for men and women is the main service of a full service operation requiring a minimum of 15 hours per week from the franchisee. The salons have a wide range of professional hair care products including a private label Lord's & Lady's line.

Number of Franchisees: 12 franchises plus 12 company-owned units in 7 States.

In Business Since: Lord's & Lady's began operations in 1971 and has been franchising since 1978.

Equity Capital Needed: "Turnkey" operation ranges from $80,000 to $140,000. This includes a $25,000 franchise fee.

Financial Assistance Available: Reduced royalties during initial year of operations; reduced franchise fee for multi-salon commitments and exclusive territory agreements.

Training Provided: Comprehensive management and business training programs for franchisee and manager. The director of education and members of the Lord's & Lady's styling team provide in-salon technical and motivation training workshops on a periodic basis.

Managerial Assistance Available: Four operations supervisors provide regular salon managerial assistance. The corporate office has several certified public accounts to assist franchisees with such matters as corporate structure, accounting, bookkeeping systems, cash budgeting, tax planning and inventory purchasing and control. The company also provides support and guidance in advertising, marketing and merchandising programs.

Information Submitted: May 1990

MAGICUTS, INC.
2105 Midland Avenue
Scarborough, Ontario
Canada M1P 3E3
Brian Luborsky, President

Description of Operation: Magicuts Great Haircut for Everyone offers what people demand today—style, value and convenience. Magicuts salons specialize in perming and coloring in addition to cutting and styling. With nearly 200 stores operating in prime shopping centers in the United States and across Canada, the Magicuts system is a complete and comprehensive franchise opportunity. The system is proven, successful and growing.

Number of Franchisees: 6 in California, 36 in Canada.

In Business Since: 1981

Equity Capital Needed: Investment of $60,000 to $80,000 per store (includes franchise fee).

Financial Assistance Available: Financial assistance is not available for Magicuts.

Training Provided: The training will be conducted by either another existing successful multiple-store franchisee or staff from Magicuts head office—your choice.

Managerial Assistance Available: Ongoing. You will be assigned a "mentor" franchisee to assist you until you know the business. Magicuts head office staff are always a phone call or visit away.

Information Submitted: April 1990

THE MANE EVENT FRANCHISING CO., INC.
dba AUTUMN ROSE HAIR DESIGNERS
225-A Main Street
Farmingdale, New York 11735
Lee Meyer, President

Description of Operation: The franchise offered is for the establishment and operation of a hair care salon featuring traditional "beauty parlor" services, such as full sets, in addition to basic haircutting, styling and hair care services, at a designated location under the name Autumn Rose Hair Designers. The marketing emphasis of the franchise salons is haircutting and styling for women as the primary market target, although services are available to men. Personalized attention in a relaxing atmosphere

is stressed. Private brand hair care products packaged under the name Autumn Rose are also featured at franchise salons for retail sales to customers.

Number of Franchisees: 4 in New York

In Business Since: 1979

Equity Capital Needed: Initial estimated total cost, including initial franchise fee, ranges between $24,945 to $56,250.

Financial Assistance Available: Initial franchise fee of $9,500 may be paid in installments. Most installment payment plans require the franchisee to pay at least $3,500 upon signing the franchise agreement, at least $1,500 upon signing the sublease for the franchise premises, and the balance of the initial franchise fee by no later than 3 months after the franchise salon opens for business. However, in individual cases different payment plans may be available.

Training Provided: Initial training is in 2 parts: hands-on training at a company-owned location and on-site assistance at the franchise location following the opening of the franchise business to the public. The length of the initial training program varies in individual cases depending on the franchisee's prior business and trade experience. Training covers all aspects of the Autumn Rose franchise system. There is no training fee (fee is included in initial franchise fee), except the franchisee is responsible for all personal expenses incurred in attending the training program. An unlimited number of employees and managers of the franchisee may attend the initial training program.

Managerial Assistance Available: The franchisor will periodically inspect the franchise premises to provide on-site operations assistance. Franchisees will be provided with the names of recommended suppliers for equipment, signs, fixtures, nonproprietary supplies and materials. The franchisor may periodically make available advertising plans and advice and in-shop merchandising materials for franchisees' local use and may assist in designing special advertising and promotional programs for individual market regions. The franchisor will periodically offer free optional and mandatory workshops for franchisees and their employees in haircutting and hair styling and may hold franchisee conferences to discuss sales techniques, training of personnel, performance standards, advertising programs and merchandising procedures.

Information Submitted: May 1990

THE MANE EVENT FRANCHISING CO., INC.
dba THE MANE EVENT UNISEX HAIR DESIGNERS
225-A Main Street
Farmingdale, New York 11735
Lee Meyers, President

Description of Operation: The franchise offered is for the establishment and operation of a precision unisex haircutting, styling and hair care salon at a designated location under the name The Mane Event Unisex Hair Designers. The marketing emphasis of the franchise salons is on servicing all members of the family as well as the working population. Franchise salons are required to be open for extended hours, 7 days a week, with limited holiday closings to accommodate this diverse potential market. Private brand hair care products packaged under the name The Mane Event are also featured at franchise salons for retail sale to customers.

Number of Franchisees: 12 plus 3 company-owned in New York

In Business Since: 1979

Equity Capital Needed: Initial estimated total cost, including initial franchise fee, ranges from $24,945 to $56,250.

Financial Assistance Available: Initial franchise fee of $9,500 may be paid in installments. Most installment payment plans require the franchisee to pay at least $3,500 upon signing the franchise agreement, at least $1,500 upon signing the sublease for the franchise premises, and the balance of the initial franchise fee by no later than 3 months after the franchise salon opens for business. However, in individual cases different payment plans may be available.

Training Provided: Initial training is in 2 parts: hands-on training at a company-owned location and on-site assistance at the franchise location following the opening of the franchise business to the public. The length of the initial training program varies in individual cases depending on the franchisee's prior business and trade experience. Training covers all aspects of The Mane Event franchise system. There is no training fee (fee is included in initial franchise fee), except the franchisee is responsible for all personal expenses incurred in attending the training program. An unlimited number of employees and managers of the franchisee may attend the initial training program.

Managerial Assistance Available: The franchisor will periodically inspect the franchise premises to provide on-site operations assistance. Franchisees will be provided with the names of recommended suppliers for equipment, signs, fixtures, non-proprietary supplies and materials. The franchisor may periodically make available advertising plans and advice and in-shop merchandising materials for franchisees' local use and may assist in designing special advertising and promotional programs for individual market regions. The franchisor will periodically offer free optional and mandatory workshops for franchisees and their employees in haircutting and hair styling and may hold franchisee conferences to discuss sales techniques, training of personnel, performance standards, advertising programs and merchandising procedures.

Information Submitted: May 1990

PRO-CUTS, INC.
3716 Rufe Snow Drive
Fort Worth, Texas 76180-8088
Don Stone, Executive Director

Description of Operation: Pro-Cuts offers professional haircuts at affordable prices for the whole family. In addition to quality haircuts, Pro-Cuts offers shampoos, blowdrys and a line of haircare products. Stores normally employ 6-8 stylists and are open Monday through Saturday.

Number of Franchisees: 95 in Texas, Oklahoma, New Mexico, and Louisiana

In Business Since: 1982

Equity Capital Needed: $60,000 to $85,000

Financial Assistance Available: Existing franchisees.

Training Provided: Extensive training for the franchisee is available with ongoing support for a long term relationship. All stylists are trained by the Pro-Cuts executive training staff.

Managerial Assistance Available: Ongoing, extensive training for managers. Special management development classes available. Shops are overseen by our field staff who provide quality control and operations assistance.

Information Submitted: April 1990

SNIP N' CLIP
6804 West 75th Street
Overland Park, Kansas 66212
Ronald M. Mitchell

Description of Operation: Family haircut shops.

Number of Franchisees: 26 franchised plus 30 company-owned.

In Business Since: 1982

Equity Capital Needed: $35,000. The Snip N'Clip investment package includes all equipment and leasehold improvements for a finished, turnkey operation.

Financial Assistance Available: None

Training Provided: Offering up-to-date workshops in hairstyling, retraining and communications. Periodic visits by Snip N' Clip supervisory personnel to all shops will keep shops and staffs up to date on the latest trends, hairstyles, products and specific promotions.

Managerial Assistance Available: Use of operations manual to ensure consistency of operations.

Information Submitted: April 1990

SUPERCUTS
555 Northgate Drive
San Rafael, California 94903
Teresa A. Guerin, Director of Franchise Sales

Description of Operation: Supercuts shops provide affordable, stylish, custom hair care for men, women and children. Supercuts success is founded on the simple concept of precision, mistake proof, guaranteed haircuts—made possible by technical advances pioneered by Supercuts, and supported by a training program unrivaled in the industry. Single and multiple unit franchises available. Industry experience not required.

Number of Franchisees: 150 with 523 open shops in 36 States. We have an additional 60 corporate-owned shops.

In Business Since: 1975

Equity Capital Needed: $54,300-$132,900 is the estimated cost to open a shop and includes the franchise fee.

Financial Assistance Available: None

Training Provided: Training begins with a course on site selection and lease negotiations. Franchisee training course is an intensive 1 week training course which includes shop build-out, operations, accounting, personnel and marketing. A 1 week advanced operations training is also available on an ongoing basis without additional charge. All haircutters are trained in the Supercuts technique and shop managers also attend specialized training.

Managerial Assistance Available: Extensive field staff provide quality control and operations assistance as well as refresher courses for haircutters. Regional offices along with corporate headquarters provide ongoing assistance in all phases of the business.

Information Submitted: April 1990

*THIRD DIMENSION CUTS, INC.
8015 Broadway
Everett, Washington 98203
Rob Jurries, New Development Director

Description of Operation: Third Dimension Cuts offers a unique design and no appointment style hair salon for men and women with a concept that appeals to the largest segment of the population. You need not be a hair stylist to own or operate.

Number of Franchisees: 13 plus 31 company-owned in Alaska, Idaho, Washington, Oregon and Utah.

In Business Since: 1979

Equity Capital Needed: Approximately $25,000

Financial Assistance Available: Investment is between $65,000 to $120,000 of which approximately $25,000 is start up capital for franchise fee, down payments, grand opening advertising, and start up capital depending on financial arrangements.

Training Provided: Training is done at the nearest location or 3D headquarters and consists of 25 to 120 hours training in all aspects of the operation; all manuals and operation formulas are provided.

Managerial Assistance Available: Third Dimension Cuts offers handbooks, manager manuals, and continued hair styling training from company representatives, plus national company training from products companies throughout the life of the franchise.

Information Submitted: May 1990

WE CARE HAIR
c/o JOHN AMICO & CO.
7327 West 90th Street
Bridgeview, Illinois 60455

Description of Operation: Family style budget hair care centers which provide styling and hair cutting for the entire family.

Number of Franchisees: 24 plus 3 company-owned.

In Business Since: 1988

Equity Capital Needed: Total investment $59,000-$118,000

Financial Assistance Available: Assist in obtaining financing.

Training Provided: Staffing, recruiting, management selection and training provided for franchisees. Training conducted at home office, regional offices, company-owned college and in-store programs.

Managerial Assistance Available: Complete unit selection, lease negotiations, salon design, full stafing and continual management assistance.

Information Submitted: May 1990

BUSINESS AIDS AND SERVICES

A CHOICE NANNY
ACN Franchise Systems, Inc.
8950 Route 108, Gorman Plaza #217
Columbia, Maryland 21045
Department of Franchise Development

Description of Operation: Own your own child care referral business! Recruit, screen, and train private nannies for working parents seeking quality in-home child care. Franchise fee includes computer hardware and software, classroom and on-the-job training, ongoing support, and advertising/public relations package. Each office requires 350-500 square feet and is located within professional building.

Number of Franchisees: 24 franchised units.

In Business Since: Parent company—7 years. Franchise company—3 years.

Equity Capital Needed: Minimum requirements: $40,000 liquidity, $100,000 net worth, and the ability to sustain self without a salary for 6 to 12 months.

Financial Assistance Available: None

Training Provided: Comprehensive classroom instruction and procedures practice (8 days at corporate headquarters). Training updates available as applicable. Multiple manuals assist in training staff and support daily activities.

Managerial Assistance Available: Ongoing support via telecommunications and personal visitations. Purchasing assistance provided.

Information Submitted: April 1990

ADTEL FRANCHISE SYSTEMS, INC.
1661 East Camelback Road
Suite 118
Phoenix, Arizona 85016
Paul Harris, Marketing Director

Description of Operation: Sales and distribution of customized audio tapes to businesses for telephone systems with "hold" capabilities. Product provides corporate image enhancement and makes productive use of time clients are put on hold.

Number of Franchisees: 6

In Business Since: 1989

Equity Capital Needed: $20,000

Financial Assistance Available: None

Training Provided: 1 week intensive training in business procedures and sales and marketing techniques. After opening, additional on-site training provided. Annual training workshops and seminars on latest techniques also provided.

Managerial Assistance Available: Ongoing technical support regarding marketing and sales techniques, and technical support with the production of tapes for clients. Full manuals provided by franchisor.

Information Submitted: April 1990

ADVANTAGE PAYROLL SERVICES
800 Center Street
P. O. Box 1330
Auburn, Maine 04211

Description of Operation: Franchisees provide a complete payroll and payroll tax filing service to small businesses. Small computers in the franchised offices are linked to the company's computer center in a unique shared distribution of responsibilities.

Number of Franchisees: 22 in 13 states, 1 company-owned.

In Business Since: 1967

Equity Capital Needed: $13,000-$20,000 including equipment, franchise fee, and training. Additional working capital for personal living expenses required.

Financial Assistance Available: $5,000 at 10 percent over 4 years. No payments required during the first year.

Training Provided: Up to 2 weeks at company headquarters with a minimum of 10 days in field. Ongoing service and support.

Managerial Assistance Available: Ongoing

Information Submitted: April 1990

AFTE ENTERPRISES, INC.
13831 Northwest Freeway
Suite 335
Houston, Texas 77040
Ken Jaeger

Description of Operation: Computerized bookkeeping, tax and business consulting service. Proven method of acquiring clients.

Number of Franchisees: 13 in 7 States

In Business Since: 1986

Equity Capital Needed: $5,000

Financial Assistance Available: None

Training Provided: 2 weeks training.

Managerial Assistance Available: Continuous guidance and support by all company personnel when and as needed. Regular contact by phone and through the mail during the life of the agreement.

Information Submitted: April 1990

AIT FREIGHT SYSTEMS, INC.
1350 North Michael Drive, Suite D
Wood Dale, Illinois 60191
Herbert L. Cohan, Director of Corporate Development

Description of Operation: Air freight forwarder offering expedited air and surface transportation services.

Number of Franchisees: 5 in 5 States plus 1 company-owned in Illinois.

In Business Since: 1979

Equity Capital Needed: Costs vary from $10,000 to $30,000 depending on locale. Contact company for full particulars.

Financial Assistance Available: None

Training Provided: At corporate headquarters and at franchisee's location as needed.

Managerial Assistance Available: Continuous management guidance during the life of the franchise agreement in such areas as accounting, policies, procedures, operations and sales.

Information Submitted: April 1990.

AIR BROOK LIMOUSINE
115 West Passaic Street
Rochelle Park, New Jersey 07662
Conrad Rehill, Director of Franchising

Description of Operation: Provide transportation service to the general public, including corporations, travel agencies, group and individuals with a fleet of late model sedans, station wagons, vans and stretch limousines. Areas of operation include the metropolitan New York area as well as Rockland, Orange County, New York and New Jersey, including the Atlantic City area. Complete service is also provided to and from the major metropolitan airports.

Number of Franchisees: 125 in New Jersey

In Business Since: 1969

Equity Capital Needed: $9,500—new sedan, $14,500—new van or stretch limousine.

Financial Assistance Available: Air Brook will finance up to $5,000 on a $9,500 investment and up to $6,000 on a $14,500 investment at no interest charge.

Training Provided: 5 day program consisting of 3 days classroom training and 2 days on-the-road training. This program is available for owners and their employed drivers.

Managerial Assistance Available: Air Brook actively markets its services through a team of sales professionals and maintains a fully-staffed reservations and dispatch departments 7 days to coordinate work. Air Brook also provides all accounting and bookkeeping services at no cost; in addition, Air Brook provides all necessary vehicle liability insurance.

Information Submitted: April 1990

ALL AMERICAN SIGN SHOPS, INC.
1460-A Diggs Drive
Raleigh, North Carolina 27603
Doug Lipscomb, Director of Marketing

Description of Operation: Retail sign shop specializing in small signs. Concept puts you in business with minimum capital and reduces overhead expenses. 24 hour service for the consumer.

Number of Franchisees: 14 in 6 States

In Business Since: 1984, franchising since 1987

Equity Capital Needed: $30,000-$50,000, franchise fee $10,000.

Financial Assistance Available: Equipment leasing assistance available.

Training Provided: Yes

Managerial Assistance Available: Ongoing

Information Submitted: April 1990

ALLAN & PARTNERS
603 Lawyers Building
428 Forbes Avenue
Pittsburgh, Pennsylvania 15219
Allan L. Hyman, General Partner

Description of Operation: Executive marketing, outplacement, resume services to corporate and private sector clients.

Number of Franchisees: 2 in 2 States

In Business Since: 1972—franchise operations since 1984

Equity Capital Needed: $30,000

Financial Assistance Available: None

Training Provided: Initial year's start up training approximately 30 days and approximately 10 days training each succeeding year. All selected franchises are appointed senior consultants and receive, with no additional cost, a complete set of training, operations, and client information manuals which outline company policy and operations methods; computerized resume reference files; 2 weeks of initial training plus 1 week of advanced training in Pittsburgh, Pennsylvania; periodic field training in the franchisee's office as needed. Training and individual assistance continue through experienced home office personnel and senior partners to be assigned in the future.

Managerial Assistance Available: Each franchisee is trained in the use of PAAR Plan-A job search program for professional, executive, technical and other white collar workers that is based on effective and proven marketing and communications procedures. Full assistance is provided continuously to franchisees and their clients by home office personnel. In addition, the company provides professional writing, research and computer support services to franchisees and their clients.

Information Submitted: May 1990

*AMERICAN ADVERTISING DISTRIBUTORS, INC.
234 South Extension Road
Mesa, Arizona 85202
Al Shindelman, Managing Director, Franchise Operations

Description of Operation: American Advertising Distributors, Inc., has trademarked techniques, methods, experience and know how in establishing a professional direct mail business. Franchisee shall have the exclusive marketing license for a particular territory. The company has complete 80,000 square feet facilities for the printing and production of coupons and other mailing pieces, for nationwide delivery.

Number of Franchisees: 111 in most States.

In Business Since: 1976

Equity Capital Needed: $25,000 to $50,000.

Financial Assistance Available: None

Training Provided: 4 weeks comprehensive training: 2 weeks at company's home office, 1 week at a similar operation and 1 week in the licensee's territory by an authorized trainer.

Managerial Assistance Available: Provided in training school. Further training at regional sessions 2-3 times per year. Also, national convention once a year. Support network to guide franchisee through various stages of growth.

Information Submitted: March 1990

AMERICAN BUSINESS ASSOCIATES FRANCHISE CORP.
475 Park Avenue
New York, New York 10016
Jerome P. Feltenstein, President

Description of Operation: ABA offers a unique system for executive networking councils. Each franchise operates 5 councils in a specific geographic area. A business category can be represented by only one company so there is no competition.

Number of Franchisees: 11 in 3 States.

In Business Since: 1983

Equity Capital Needed: $25,000-$80,000

Financial Assistance Available: 60 percent financeable

Training Provided: 1 week intensive training, working with existing ABA councils and ABA representatives.

Managerial Assistance Available: ABA offers continual advisory services, as well as financial administration, and national and public relations.

Information Submitted: May 1990

AMERICAN COLLEGE PLANNING SERVICE, INC.
94B Jefryn Boulevard East
Deer Park, New York 11729
Richard A. Simeone, President
Randy G. Romano, Vice President

Description of Operation: ACPS Planning Centers help families afford the high cost of a college education. Services help parents of college bound students, regardless of income, to qualify and apply for maximum college funding.

Number of Franchisees: 9 in 5 States.

In Business Since: 1984

Equity Capital Needed: Total investment $20,000.

Financial Assistance Available: None. The company will assist franchisees with financing arrangements.

Training Provided: 1 week training at company's training center. Ongoing training and assistance at the company's training center and at franchise center location.

Managerial Assistance Available: ACPS provides complete managerial assistance in all phases of operation including franchisee's pre-opening and start up, marketing, training, accounting and day-to-day operations. Complete manuals are provided.

Information Submitted: April 1990

AMERICAN HERITAGE AGENCY, INC.
Heritage Building
104 Park Road
West Hartford, Connecticut 06119

Description of Operation: 1 wedding consulting business furnishes services tailored to the needs of the brides-to-be.

Number of Franchisees: 6 in Connecticut, Massachusetts and New York

In Business Since: 1925

Equity Capital Needed: $500-$10,000

Financial Assistance Available: Financing of up to 50 percent of the franchise fee provided credit standards can be met.

Training Provided: 12 days of formal classroom training and on-the-job training at established office; up to 30 days training at franchisee's own office; periodic briefings and meetings.

Managerial Assistance Available: Liaison officer available to help in solving problems, expanding operations and suggesting improvements.

Information Submitted: May 1990

AMERICAN INSTITUTE OF SMALL BUSINESS
7515 Wayzata Boulevard, Suite 201
Minneapolis, Minnesota 55426

Description of Operation: The American Institute of Small Business is a publisher of books and educational materials on Small Business and Entrepreneurship and provides seminars on How to Start and Operate a Small Business. Publications including books and software are sold to individuals, libraries, companies, secondary and postsecondary high schools, colleges and universities. Seminars are offered to individuals wishing to set up their own small business.

Number of Franchisees: 5

In Business Since: 1985, in franchising since 1988.

Equity Capital Needed: $5,000

Financial Assistance Available: None

Training Provided: The American Institute of Small Business provides 1 day of training at their home offices and conducts the first seminar on How To Set Up and Operate Your Own Small Business in the city of the franchisee. A prompter book and materials are provided. Literature on all books and educational materials are supplied.

Managerial Assistance Available: The Institute provides all necessary management assistance relative to the company's manner of doing business.

Information Submitted: April 1990

AMERICAN POST 'N PARCEL, INC.
315 West Pondera Street, Suite F
Lancaster, California 93534-3681
Harry Klemm, President

Description of Operation: Emphasis is placed on packaging and shipping parcels and freight up to 1,000 lbs. using state-of-the-art equipment and techniques. Other related services include mail box rentals, FAX, photocopying and retail supplies.

Number of Franchisees: 5 in 2 States plus 1 company-owned.

In Business Since: 1986

Equity Capital Needed: Cash requirement—$42,000-$68,000.

Financial Assistance Available: None

Training Provided: 1 week comprehensive training at corporate training center plus on-site assistance as needed.

Managerial Assistance Available: Continuous service from our operations department. Site selection assistance. Equipment leasing assistance. Performance evaluation continuous. Promotional assistance throughout franchise term.

Information Submitted: April 1990

AMERISPEC HOME INSPECTION SERVICE
1507 West Yale Avenue
Orange, California 92667
Sheilah Hyman, Vice President, Sales

Description of Operation: Residential inspection services offered to home buyers, sellers and referral services (i.e., real estate brokers).

Number of Franchisees: 85

In Business Since: 1987

Equity Capital Needed: Capital requirement $5,300-$12,250 plus working capital. Franchise fee ranges from $12,900-$18,900.

Financial Assistance Available: None

Training Provided: Required to complete 2 week intensive management institute at corporate headquarters.

Managerial Assistance Available: Complete operations. Technical and business development manuals. Ongoing marketing assistance.

Information Submitted: May 1990

AN INTERNATIONAL WORLD OF WEDDINGS, INC.
12012 S.E. 122nd Avenue
Portland, Oregon 97236
Francine M. Hansen, President

Description of Operation: The company's principal business is as a franchisor of business opportunities to own and operate bridal consulting and wedding design firms, not only planning and creating traditional Christian ceremonies, but also creating custom ethnic and religious ceremonies for Hindu, Buddhist, Jewish and Moslem brides and co-ordinating a variety of formal occasions, such as proms, balls, cotillions and anniversary parties. The rental of bridesmaid gowns, wedding gowns, and other formal women's attire also included in the franchise.

Number of Franchisees: 4 in Oregon and 3 in Washington

In Business Since: 1973

Equity Capital Needed: $17,500-$31,500

Financial Assistance Available: None at present.

Training Provided: A 1 week training program includes comprehensive training for 2, covering all aspects of wedding, consultation, planning, and design. The training is conducted by 7 qualified instructors in Portland, Oregon, teaching not only traditional American wedding planning, but also the planning of many authentic ethnic or religious rituals, including but not limited to the Hindu, Buddhist, Jewish and Moslem weddings.

Managerial Assistance Available: Complete support system including confidential operations manuals, training manuals, full color photo presentation manual, initial supply of brochures, flyers, coupons, newspaper slick ads, business cards and VHS tape to assist franchisee in selling the service. Regional representatives to assist in ongoing advice and counseling, and a newsletter with the most up-to-date information in the wedding industry. Regional and/or national advertising through a co-operative effort in combining our advertising dollars.

Information Submitted: May 1990

ANSWERING SPECIALISTS
119 West Doty Avenue
Summerville, South Carolina 29483
Arthur F. (Bud) Doty, III, President

Description of Operation: A live telephone answering service with emphasis on quality. Answering Specialists brings 18 years of experience to the market. Answering Specialists seeks locations only in the Southeast at this time.

Number of Franchisees: 1 company-owned unit.

In Business Since: 1989

Equity Capital Needed: $35,000 to $45,000 total investment.

Financial Assistance Available: None

Training Provided: We provide ongoing training at our location.

Managerial Assistance Available: Ongoing

Information Submitted: April 1990

ASI SIGN SYSTEMS
548 West 28th Street
New York, New York 10001
Tim Jones, National Sales Director

Description of Operation: ASI Sign Systems, Inc., offers franchises that give the license and right to operate a sign business using the ASI Sign System. The ASI Sign System consists of various components including patented manufacturing techniques, equipment, materials and supplies, proprietary business and marketing formats, general know-how and information that enables the franchisee to manufacture subsurface imaged signs, obtain from qualified sources other kinds of finished signs as well as materials and consumable supplies, provide sign planning services and conduct a complete professional architectural sign business.

Number of Franchisees: 31 in 25 States plus 3 in Canada

In Business Since: 1977

Equity Capital Needed: $50,000 initial license fee (which includes certain computer software, equipment and start-up inventory) plus $75,000 to $125,000 to cover additional equipment, supplies, rental space, salaries, insurance and operating capital.

Financial Assistance Available: The franchisor offers, at its option, financial assistance on a portion of the initial fee.

Training Provided: An intensive 5 day training course is held for all new franchisees at the home office. An additional 3 days of training and start-up assistance is held at the franchisee's location.

Managerial Assistance Available: ASI Sign Systems provides ongoing assistance in sales, marketing, manufacturing and administration. Comprehensive operations manuals are provided. ASI has field personnel who regularly visit and work with the franchisees in all phases of the business.

Information Submitted: April 1990

ASSET ONE
230 East Wheeling Street, Suite 101
Lancaster, Ohio 43130
Raymond A. Strohl, President

Description of Operation: Financial and investment planning service for the public. Advice given on budgeting, plans to reduce taxes on the Federal, State, and local levels, and advice given on various investments. Advice given on sources of real estate and business loans and financing.

Number of Franchisees: 5 in Ohio, Florida, and California.

In Business Since: 1989

Equity Capital Needed: Varies

Financial Assistance Available: Yes

Training Provided: Yes

Managerial Assistance Available: Perpetual assistance as needed.

Information Submitted: April 1990

*ASSOCIATED AIR FREIGHT, INC.
3333 New Hyde Park Road
New Hyde Park, New York 11042
Walter G. Mahland, Vice President, Development

Description of Operation: Associated Air Freight currently ranks in the top 15 air freight forwarders. Franchisees must have either transportation sales experience or an extensive background in business-to-business sales. Each location is staffed with customer service and operations personnel in addition to sales personnel. Associated offers an extensive product line including domestic same day, overnight, second day and international prior-

ity service, 3-5 day deferred, and courier express service. Inventory requirements are minimal, and inventory items are provided free of charge during the first year of operation.

Number of Franchisees: Associated has 11 company-owned locations, 2 franchises, 36 joint-venture operations in the U.S., and 10 international joint-venture operations as well as 300 U.S. and 100 international agents.

In Business Since: 1958

Equity Capital Needed: $20,000-$50,000, depending on market area (this includes franchise fees of $5,000-$15,000).

Financial Assistance Available: Associated offers indirect financing. Also, franchisees have immediate credit with all suppliers, and Associated assists in marketing for first year of operation at no cost to franchisee. Franchisees are not required to purchase trucks or aircraft. Approximately 40 percent of working capital is spent on facility and the remaining on staffing.

Training Provided: Training consists of 5 days training at world headquarters to include sales, marketing and advertising presentations and demonstrations of accounting and billing procedures, routing guidelines, reporting and claims. An additional 5 days training is held at an Associated field location to include joint sales calls and hands-on operational training.

Managerial Assistance Available: Associated provides ongoing assistance in the management of the franchise operation. Associated handles the majority of accounting functions, including accounts receivable and accounts payable to suppliers. On a monthly basis, Associated does an analysis of each franchise location and provides directional support. Franchisees benefit from national account purchasing arrangements with major airlines. Special attention is paid to the support of each newly opened office.

Information Submitted: April 1990

BARTER EXCHANGE, INC.
Twin Towers
1106 Clayton Lane
Suite 480 West
Austin, Texas 78723
Jerome Antil, Chief Operating Officer

Description of Operation: Barter Exchange, Inc., operates as a third party record keeper for businesses (clients) throughout the U.S. and abroad. Clients are able to buy and sell goods and services for trade dollars instead of cash. The national headquarters in Austin is responsible for billing, receiving, monthly statements, credit lines, and long-term loans. Each franchise office registers new clients and brokers each client's product/service. Client's financial position is enhanced by the new sales generated and the ability to offset cash expenses with the trade dollars received for their goods and services. BEI provides each client with a client directory, client cards (similar to credit cards), and a subscription to BEI's bi-monthly newspaper, *Tradewinds*. BEI provides each franchisee with a computer hardware and software package which includes BarterLine, a central computer access system.

Number of Franchisees: 15 in 11 States

In Business Since: 1983

Equity Capital Needed: $60,000

Financial Assistance Available: Financing of part of the franchise fee available to qualified individuals in select situations.

Training Provided: BEI provides up to 6 weeks of training including 1-2 weeks at the corporate office, 1 week with an existing franchise and 3 weeks in the franchisee's market. Also included is ongoing Tradebroker training, and quarterly, regional and annual meetings.

Managerial Assistance Available: BEI processes all new clients, generates client cards, sets up client accounts in the data base, and provides ongoing accounting services with monthly statements. BEI also provides toll-free WATS lines for authorizations on transactions. Along with this administrative support, BEI provides all printed brochures, directories, newspapers, and logos for creation of letterhead, envelopes, etc. BEI provides operations and sales manuals that direct and instructs the franchisee in virtually every aspect of the business along with weekly management reports.

Information Submitted: April 1990

BINEX-AUTOMATED BUSINESS SYSTEMS, INC.
4441 Auburn Blvd., Suite E
Sacramento, California 95841
Walter G. Heidig, President

Description of Operation: Binex licenses offer a broad range of computerized services to small and medium sized businesses. Services include financial reports, general ledgers, accounts receivable, accounts payable, job cost, and payroll. Specialized computer services are also available, and you can develop your own. You may operate your business in various ways from a bookkeeping office to a full computer service. The computer programs are licensed to you for use on your computer or a central Binex computer. Complete small business computer systems may be installed in your client's office.

Number of Franchisees: 60 in 21 States, Canada, and New Zealand.

In Business Since: 1965

Equity Capital Needed: $8,500. The fee covers training, manuals, and startup supplies. No expensive equipment is required.

Financial Assistance Available: A computer can be purchased for $2,000. Lease arrangements available if a computer is purchased.

Training Provided: Home study course and 1 week home office. Individuals may return for further training as needed.

Managerial Assistance Available: Support is provided on a continuous basis. Frequent newsletters are sent out covering a variety of subjects including business operation, marketing, technical, taxes, etc. New programs and services are developed, documented, and made available regularly to all licensees. Periodic regional meetings provide upgrading and review.

Information Submitted: April 1990

THE BREAD BOX
1010 South Taylor
Little Rock, Arkansas 72204
John Reynolds, President

Description of Operation: The Bread Box is a co-op direct mail advertising company. Our licensees provide the local business owners in their territories with media that target his advertising in a specific geographical area. All printing and production is handled by The Bread Box from their corporate headquarters in Little Rock, Arkansas. No inventory required and low overhead operation for our licensees.

Number of Franchisees: 3 in Arkansas, Texas and Tennessee.

In Business Since: 1976

Equity Capital Needed: $8,000-$15,000

Training Provided: 1 week classroom training program is mandatory for all new franchisees. Field training is available. Complete operations manual, sales presentation manual and coupon library are provided.

Managerial Assistance Available: Regional and annual meetings, work shops, home office support on a continuous basis, periodic newsletters, awards and incentive programs.

Information Submitted: April 1990

BROKER ONE
230 East Wheeling Street, Suite 101
Lancaster, Ohio 43130
Raymond A. Strohl, President

Description of Operation: Stockbroker offering stocks, bonds, options, mutual funds, penny stocks, tax shelters, retirement plans, diamonds, precious metals, commodities, managed commodity accounts, rare coins and loan brokering.

Number of Franchisees: 7 in Ohio, Florida, California, Pennsylvania, Louisiana and Arizona.

In Business Since: 1983

Equity Capital Needed: Varies

Financial Assistance Available: Yes

Training Provided: Varies, depending on the background and experience of the franchisee.

Managerial Assistance Available: Perpetual assistance as needed.

Information Submitted: April 1990

BUDGET SIGNS
4109 Brown Trail
Suite 100
Colleyville, Texas 76034
Robert S. Phillips, Jr., President

Description of Operation: Computer generated quick sign stores.

Number of Franchisees: 20

In Business Since: 1989

Equity Capital Needed: $80,000 to $100,000

Financial Assistance Available: None

Training Provided: 2 week training school, 1 week on-site. Additional training as needed.

Managerial Assistance Available: Continuous

Information Submitted: April 1990

*THE BUILDING INSPECTOR OF AMERICA
684 Main Street
Wakefield, Massachusetts 01880
Larry Finklestone, Director of Marketing

Description of Operation: The Building Inspector of America is a national organization of home and building inspection consultants. The service is used primarily by buyers of homes, condominiums and property investors. It is designed to alert buyers to potential problem areas as well as show buyers how to maintain their property and possibly save money by conserving on energy.

Number of Franchisees: 73 in 27 States

In Business Since: 1985

Equity Capital Needed: $15,000 and up depending on size of territory.

Financial Assistance Available: None

Training Provided: Intense 2 week in-field and in-franchisee. Audio and video tapes provided. Workbook on sales promotion and advertising is included.

Managerial Assistance Available: Extensive ongoing market research for franchisee benefit. Report writing clinics and sales training and promotion workshops run several times a year at corporate headquarters. Regular newsletters, slide show programs, national referral system in place.

Information Submitted: April 1990

BUSINESS AMERICA ASSOCIATES, INC.
300 Cedar Boulevard
Pittsburgh, Pennsylvania 15228
Thomas D. Atkins, President

Description of Operation: Listing and sales of businesses. Listings of businesses for sale are shared by all offices on a confidential basis. Buyers are prequalified by interview in franchise office locations. Franchises are offered for sale as well as established businesses.

Number of Franchisees: 4 in Pennsylvania

In Business Since: 1984

Equity Capital Needed: $45,000

Financial Assistance Available: Terms may be considered.

Training Provided: 1 week at corporate offices and 1 week at franchisee's location. Training by video with training manual. All forms and systems provided.

Managerial Assistance Available: Ongoing support with regular meetings for franchise owners.

Information Submitted: April 1990

BUSINESS CONSULTANTS OF AMERICA
Affiliate of: HORIZONS OF AMERICA
P. O. BOX 4098
Waterbury, Connecticut 06714
Gregg Nolan, Franchise Director

Description of Operation: Franchisor offers time tested practice, dealing with advisory services for small and medium sized business operations. Training in services to include: management, market, tax advisory and financial advisory services. Additional training to include programs for mergers/acquisition, business brokerage and franchise coverage. Franchisor provides a client lead service through a computer hookup to franchisee's office.

Number of Franchisees: 26 in 11 States.

In Business Since: 1973

Equity Capital Needed: $20,000 plus $5,000-$10,000 working capital. Computer equipment optional.

Financial Assistance Available: Assistance with bank/government financing/franchisor financing.

Training Provided: 3 weeks intensive training at franchise headquarters, 1 week at franchisee's office, followed by 2 months cassette courses packaged by franchisor and other professional organizations. Continuing franchisor advisory newsletters and tapes. Fully computerized national listing and consulting service.

Managerial Assistance Available: Technical and advisory services at discretion of franchisee. Continued services on an as needed basis from franchisor. Additional memberships arranged in professional associations.

Information Submitted: May 1990

BUSINESS DIGEST, INC./BUSINESS PEOPLE
650 Main Street
South Portland, Maine 04106
Leo Girr or Patti Crabtree

Description of Operation: *Business Digest* is the first franchised monthly business publication that pays special attention to local small- and medium-size businesses of all sizes.

Number of Franchisees: 17 in 9 States

In Business Since: 1976

Equity Capital Needed: $175,000 (approximately) depending on the market and size of trade area. (Includes $40,000 franchise fee.)

Financial Assistance Available: Franchisor will assist in obtaining working capital and equipment loans.

Training Provided: Minimum 3 day initial training at franchisor's headquarters.

Managerial Assistance Available: Because of the nature of the publishing business the franchisor will assist the franchisee in selecting copywriters, layout and design staff, coordinate the relationship with printers and train the franchisee's sales staff on the techniques of selling advertising. Further, as the franchisee gains experience, the franchisor will assist in incorporating other income sources at the franchisee's level, such as business opportunity shows and ways to derive income from the equipment involved in running a magazine.

Information Submitted: April 1990

BUSINESS STARTERS INC.
4113 Yancey Street
Charlotte, North Carolina 28217

Description of Operation: Small and medium sized business consulting for wholesalers, retailers and service businesses in the area of finance, management, operations and marketing.

Number of Franchisees: 5

In Business Since: 1988 and began offering franchising in 1990.

Equity Capital Needed: $8,995 for franchise fee, range of $1,500-$7,000 for start-up and initial living expenses.

Financial Assistance Available: None at this time.

Training Provided: Complete training program over a 90 day period. 2 days at corporate followed by field support assistance and training, followed by an optional return to corporate for a 2 day advanced training course.

Managerial Assistance Available: Complete support system provided for a monthly fee of $200, including consultant support and marketing support. Business Starters Inc. provides a public relations vehicle which allows the consultant to become the recognized expert in the field of small business in their area through the use of a public relations campaign, brochure mailings, newspaper articles, advertising and promotional press releases. All products, materials and supplies are provided, as well as actual analysis of client situations, including recommendations, solutions and consulting guides. Lines are provided for consultant.

Information Submitted: July 1990

BUYING AND DINING GUIDE
80 Eighth Avenue
Suite 315
New York, New York 10011
Allan Horwitz, President

Description of Operation: *Buying and Dining Guide* is a unique money-maker for the publishers and the advertisers. A free publication offering total market coverage of the active "buyers" and "diners" throughout the area, it's a direct route to prime spenders—those who enjoy spending money even more than they like saving it. Publishing and distribution costs are minimal, and the advertiser receives 14 days of effective advertising—and at the price of just a single ad.

Number of Franchisees: 5

In Business Since: 1980, franchising since 1989

Equity Capital Needed: $19,900 with a money-back guarantee.

Financial Assistance Available: 80 percent financing to qualified applicants.

Training Provided: 8 days of classroom, infield and on-site training for franchisees and their employees. Covers how to sell advertising, acquire co-op from manufacturers, profit from barter, service accounts, ad design, layout, distribution, and bookkeeping. Includes confidential operations manual, audio and video cassettes, training films and video-taped role playing sessions.

Managerial Assistance Available: Continuous assistance provided by the home office. Includes our unique "head start" program to get you off to a flying start, with $1,000 free printing, a direct mailing to your prospects by the company, and our special charter advertiser program to produce immediate income for both the franchisee and his advertisers. In addition, the company contributes $1,000 for each new franchise plus 12 percent of all royalty fees for direct mailing, sweepstakes, and other promotions funded entirely by the company to make the franchisees more successful.

Information Submitted: April 1990

BUY LOW ENTERPRISES, INC.
801 North Cass Avenue
Suite 104
Westmont, Illinois 60559
Irv Silver, President
Russell B. Chevalier, Vice President

Description of Operation: To provide merchandising displays, sales promotions and advertising under the trade name of "Buy Low" to franchisees engaged in the sale of alcoholic beverages at retail for consumption off premises.

Number of Franchisees: 83 in Illinois

In Business Since: Incorporated by Low Enterprises, Inc., under the law of Illinois on October 1960.

Equity Capital Needed: Franchisee and initial investment is estimated at a low-high range of $500-$1,000.

Financial Assistance Available: Neither the franchisor nor any agents directly or indirectly offers any financial management to franchisees.

Training Provided: There are training programs supplied by the franchisor.

Managerial Assistance Available: The licensor is obligated to (1) permit the licensee to represent himself as a "Buy Low" store, (2) permit licensee to use its service marks, trademarks, trade names and logotypes, in accordance with licensor's policy, (3) provide assistance to the licensee in establishing a retail promotional plan for the location, including merchandise displays and general sales promotion and advertising, and (4) place advertisements in newspapers and other media chosen solely by licensor and published and circulated in the greater metropolitan Chicago land area at least once each week. Other various assistance may be provided by the franchisor on a voluntary basis to franchisees in addition to the above.

Information Submitted: May 1990

CARING LIVE-IN'S, INC.
214 East 72nd Terrace
Kansas City, Missouri 04114
George Fetekamp, President

Description of Operation: Consultation and referral service for elderly.

Number of Franchisees: 10 in Missouri, Texas, Kansas, Ohio and Florida

In Business Since: 1982

Equity Capital Needed: $10,000 to $15,000

Financial Assistance Available: None

Training Provided: 4 days of training in all phases of operation.

Managerial Assistance Available: Ongoing consultation.

Information Submitted: May 1990

CA$H PLUS
4020 Chicago Avenue
Riverside, California 92507
Jerry E. Todd

Description of Operation: Check cashing service and related services.

Number of Franchisees: 11

In Business Since: 1989

Equity Capital Needed: $40,000

Financial Assistance Available: None

Training Provided: As much time as necessary at company-owned store and follow-up at location.

Managerial Assistance Available: From beginning to end. We assist, coach, train, help, do whatever is necessary to put you into business. Protected areas, follow-up, country managers, a complete system to assure your success.

Information Submitted: April 1990

*CHECK CHANGERS
2 West Madison
Suite 200
Oak Park, Illinois 60302
Ted Malone, Operation Development Manager

Description of Operation: Check cashing centers.

Number of Franchisees: 12 plus 47 company-owned.

In Business Since: 1964, franchising 1989

Equity Capital Needed: $21,500 start-up cash. $50,000-$70,000 total investment.

Financial Assistance Available: None

Training Provided: Complete training in operating a check cashing center.

Managerial Assistance Available: Continuous

Information Submitted: June 1990

CHECKCARE ENTERPRISES, INC.
3907 Macon Road
Columbus, Georgia 31907
Michael Stalnaker, Vice President, Franchise Development

Description of Operation: Checkcare Systems' franchisees provide a check guarantee and verification service for its members. The system utilizes proprietary sales, collection and administrative software with data line to franchisor.

Number of Franchisees: 30 in 8 States

In Business Since: 1983

Equity Capital Needed: $30,000

Financial Assistance Available: Limited financing available to qualified individuals.

Training Provided: Complete 1 week training program at home office.

Managerial Assistance Available: On-site support and evaluation as necessary.

Information Submitted: April 1990

CHECK-X-CHANGE CORPORATION
111 S.W. Columbia
Suite 1080
Portland, Oregon 97201
Jean Gaines, National Development Coordinator

Description of Operation: Check cashing for a fee, money order sales, and photo I.D.'s.

Number of Franchisees: 102 in 21 States

In Business Since: 1982

Equity Capital Needed: $90,000-$100,000

Financial Assistance Available: None

Training Provided: 2 weeks at corporate headquarters

Managerial Assistance Available: On-site training after opening, continuing on-site consulting on as needed basis.

Information Submitted: April 1990

*CHROMA COPY FRANCHISING OF AMERICA, INC.
423 West 55th Street
New York, New York 10019
Amnor Bartur

Description of Operation: Photographic service for business.

Number of Franchisees: 15 in 10 States

In Business Since: 1982

Equity Capital Needed: $300,000

Financial Assistance Available: None

Training Provided: Management, printmaking, sales 2 weeks.

Managerial Assistance Available: Organizing assistance relating to all areas of the operation is provided as needed by each franchise.

Information Submitted: May 1990

CLOSET-TIER, INC.
5822 Forward Avenue
Pittsburgh, Pennsylvania 15217
Arlene Mogerman, Franchise Coordinator

Description of Operation: Closet and storage area organization system made up of component parts for versatile use.

Number of Franchisees: 2 in Pennsylvania

In Business Since: 1976

Equity Capital Needed: $50,000

Financial Assistance Available: None

Training Provided: 8 days of intensive training in the corporate office and shop, 1 week in franchisee operation before opening and 1 week after opening. Ongoing support by phone and field representatives.

Managerial Assistance Available: The franchisor is available for assistance by phone or field representatives any time for franchisee assistance.

Information Submitted: May 1990

*COMMUNICATIONS WORLD INTERNATIONAL, INC.
14828 West 6th Avenue
Suite 13B
Golden, Colorado 80401
Aletha Zens, Franchise Director

Description of Operation: Sale and service of business telephone systems to companies with 2 to 250 employees.

Number of Franchisees: 61 in 16 States

In Business Since: 1979

Equity Capital Needed: $40,000, $10,000 cash and $30,000 line of credit, for sales franchise. $100,000, $40,000 cash and $60,000 line of credit for master franchise.

Financial Assistance Available: Yes

Training Provided: Initial 5 days at company headquarters, involving administrative and product knowledge. On-site quarterly, yearly national conference/convention.

Managerial Assistance Available: Continuous technical help via 800 number. Managerial support, researching acceptable product lines; providing sales advice. Business telephone centers are established in each city to provide administrative, service and demonstration back-up.

Information Submitted: April 1990

*COMPREHENSIVE ACCOUNTING CORPORATION
2111 Comprehensive Drive
Aurora, Illinois 60505
John F. Kean

Description of Operation: Comprehensive franchises, independent accountants to provide a monthly computerized accounting, bookkeeping, tax and business consultation service to small- and medium-sized businesses of all types. Services include complete computerized preparation of monthly balance sheets, operating statements, general ledger and payroll ledgers, accounts receivable, and job cost statements. Comprehensive trains its franchisees to use the Comprehensive Client Acquisition System. The franchisee can build his practice as fast as he is able to grow and maintain quality service.

Number of Franchisees: Approximately 240 in 40 States and Puerto Rico

In Business Since: 1949; licensing since 1965

Equity Capital Needed: $25,000 initial franchise fee; $20,000 deferred franchise fee.

Financial Assistance Available: The initial franchise fee is paid in cash. The $20,000 deferred franchise fee and $10,000 computer equipment may be financed.

Training Provided: The franchisee is required to complete a 4-week course at the corporate headquarters after sufficient home study preparation in Comprehensive's production methods. Training at corporate headquarters is divided equally between production and marketing. In addition, a post-graduate course lasting 1 week is given in the corporate headquarters.

Managerial Assistance Available: Comprehensive provides, on an ongoing basis, a consultant for production, marketing and practice management and a data processing consultant. Each consultant is available by phone or in person for each franchisee. Also provided are detailed production procedures and methods, client reporting forms, plus sales aids for use in obtaining accounts, one professional film portraying Comprehensive's service to prospective clients, desk top visual for client presentation, sample computer financial statements and various sales brochures. Comprehensive gives the franchisee the benefit of Comprehensive's experience gained through current licensees who are providing services for 20,000 monthly accounting, bookkeeping, tax and business consultation service clients. A management information system provides statistics monthly and annually of continuing education and interchange of ideas. Other seminars are conducted for franchisee's staff and clients.

Information Submitted: May 1990

COMPUTER CAR
131-61 40 Road
Flushing, New York 11354
Rod Barfield, President

Description of Operation: Quality transportation service provided with sedans and limousines to corporate clients within New York City and the surrounding metropolitan area.

Number of Franchisees: 190

In Business Since: 1987

Equity Capital Needed: $12,000

Financial Assistance Available: None

Training Provided: 80 hours of training both in the classroom and on the road. This includes company procedure, map skills, etc.

Managerial Assistance Available: Management personnel is available to help the franchisees with their recordkeeping and having their franchise expenses paid directly from their earnings.

Information Submitted: May 1990

CONVENIENCE MONEY CENTERS, INC.
1155 S. Havana
Unit 43
Aurora, Colorado 80012
James Brown, Franchising

Description of Operation: Variety of financial services: cash checks, sell money orders, postage, postal services. Also offer notary service, Western Union, utility payments, and other related services.

Number of Franchisees: 5 in Colorado, Oregon, Louisiana and Arizona.

In Business Since: 1982

Equity Capital Needed: $75,000

Financial Assistance Available: Finance plan available.

Training Provided: All facets of check cashing operations (5 years duration).

Managerial Assistance Available: We offer complete training in all phases of check cashing business (5 years duration).

Information Submitted: May 1990

CORPORATE FINANCE ASSOCIATES
1801 Broadway
Suite 1200
Denver, Colorado 80202
Robert Prangley

Description of Operation: Financial consultants on loans, mergers—acquisition brokers. For executives only.

Number of Franchisees: 48 in 18 States plus 2 international offices.

In Business Since: 1956

Equity Capital Needed: $35,000 for operating capital

Financial Assistance Available: No financial assistance except for sources for loan and venture funds.

Training Provided: For executives—one on one. Operating manuals are provided. Semi-annual seminars and periodic regional meetings. Total of 8 training days annually.

Managerial Assistance Available: Ongoing—case by case training.

Information Submitted: April 1990

CORRECT CREDIT CO. OF HOWELL, INC.
P. O. Box 537
Howell, New Jersey 07731
Pat Fasano, President

Description of Operation: Credit restoration service. Each office is approximately 500 square feet with 2-1/2 salespeople, who see clients in their homes 6 days a week.

Number of Franchisees: 8 in Pennsylvania, Massachusetts, Florida and Georgia.

In Business Since: 1983

Equity Capital Needed: $6,500, total fee $19,500

Financial Assistance Available: Approximately $3,000-$5,000 operating capital needed for office and advertising for first 6 weeks. A portion of the investment finances to qualified applicants—$11,000.

Training Provided: In-out office training for 1 week and follow up at franchisee's office whenever needed.

Managerial Assistance Available: Always available to assist franchisees whenever needed.

Information Submitted: April 1990

CREATIVE CARD INTERNATIONAL, INC.
2120 South Green Road
South Euclid, Ohio 44121
Larry Sommers, Franchise Director

Description of Operation: "Creative"—dynamic photo advertising. One of the fastest growing industries of the 90's is photographic advertising. If you qualify you can get a head start with a franchise(s) of your own. We offer extensive training and support along with state of the art equipment and concepts. We offer over 48 products including photo business cards, post cards, business reply, magnet cards, presentation folders, fun photos with graphics, etc. We are the "Franchise for the 90's."

Number of Franchisees: 3

In Business Since: 1988

Equity Capital Needed: $18,000/$31,000

Financial Assistance Available: None

Training Provided: 1 week in Cleveland, 2 days on-site.

Managerial Assistance Available: Ongoing assistance.

Information Submitted: April 1990

DATA DESTRUCTION SERVICES, INC.
dba DDS FRANCHISE CORPORATION
8-G Gill Street
Woburn, Massachusetts 01801
Richard Hannon, President

Description of Operation: DDS Franchise Corporation offers a unique new business—a mobile shredding service providing on-site shredding of confidential documents or materials. Franchisor provides a completely equipped vehicle. Customers are high tech, governmental, banks, insurance companies and medical facilities.

Number of Franchisees: 1 company-owned unit in New England

In Business Since: 1982, franchising since 1989

Equity Capital Needed: $106,000-$131,000

Financial Assistance Available: None

Training Provided: A 2 week training program is provided by the franchisor.

Managerial Assistance Available: Continual operating support is provided in all aspects of business operation.

Information Submitted: April 1990

DEBIT ONE, INC.
9387 Dielman Industrial Drive
St. Louis, Missouri 63132
Arthur Cohen

Description of Operation: Debit One offers a unique concept in bookkeeping services. Our mobile vans are a custom designed office with computer and software used to travel to the client's place of business where their bookkeeping is done "at the door of their store."

Number of Franchisees: 65 in 26 States

In Business Since: 1983

Equity Capital Needed: $44,025 minimum plus $5,000 operating capital.

Financial Assistance Available: Franchisee provides no financial assistance but the $26,025 for the vehicle and equipment can be financed through local banks or leasing company.

Training Provided: Intensive 80 hours mandatory training course is scheduled for all new franchisees and/or their personnel. 56 hours of training are conducted at the home office and 24 hours are held in franchisee's territory.

Managerial Assistance Available: Debit One provides continued management service. Complete manuals of operations (computer and sales) and directions are provided. A director of franchisees is available to work closely with franchisee and to assist in solving problems. Debit One provides a bi-monthly newsletter in order to keep the franchisees up to date on any software changes, changes in tax laws, etc.

Information Submitted: May 1990

DELIVEREX SERVICE CENTERS
3401 Nevada Avenue North
Minneapolis, Minnesota 55427
John D. Jerome, President

Description of Operation: Off-site storage, management and delivery of medical industry records, business records and computer tapes.

Number of Franchisees: 20 nationwide

In Business Since: 1973

Equity Capital Needed: Approximately $150,000

Financial Assistance Available: None

Training Provided: 2 weeks home office training and assistance as needed at franchise location.

Managerial Assistance Available: Ongoing as needed.

Information Submitted: May 1990

*DIAL ONE INTERNATIONAL, INC.
175 South Third Street, Suite 320
Columbus, Ohio 43215
Bill Ledbetter, President

Description of Operation: Must be a qualified property service or selected retail company operator, with good recommendations from customers, suppliers and financial institutions. Franchisees may be in one or more of over 45 trades and services.

Number of Franchisees: 865 nationally and 125 internationally.

In Business Since: 1982

Equity Capital Needed: Master district approximately $100,000-$175,000 and working capital.

Financial Assistance Available: Local financing where applicable.

Training Provided: Monthly management training for owners and managers, periodic (quarterly) for employees.

Managerial Assistance Available: Management workshops, support groups and technical counsel where applicable.

Information Submitted: May 1990

DIXON COMMERCIAL INVESTIGATORS, INC.
728 Center Street
Lewiston, New York 14092
E. L. Dixon, President

Description of Operation: Complete range of credit and collection services. Territories available by city or state/province (U.S. and Canada locations available).

Number of Franchisees: 6 in New York, Pennsylvania, Ohio, California and Canada.

In Business Since: 1956

Equity Capital Needed: $5,000

Financial Assistance Available: None

Training Provided: 1 or 2 weeks head office training. Continuous supervision and aid afterwards.

Managerial Assistance Available: Franchisee is trained in all areas of credit collection. Franchisee is in continuous contact with head office.

Information Submitted: April 1990

DYNAMIC AIR FREIGHT, INC.
1732 Old Minters Chapel Road
Suite 100
Grapevine, Texas 76051
E. G. McGuire

Description of Operation: Dynamic Air Freight is an air freight forwarder, transporting a customer's cargo from pick-up at the point or origin to delivery at destination. The company's purpose is to provide effective and efficient air freight forwarding services to businesses, industry, institutions and governmental entities.

Number of Franchisees: 20 in 10 States and 3 countries.

In Business Since: 1978

Equity Capital Needed: $30,000

Financial Assistance Available: $307,500 for qualified individuals. The company offers to finance up to three quarters of the franchisees initial license fee. The company does not offer financing for any other purpose relating to either the establishment or operation of the franchise business.

Training Provided: 2 week mandatory training program is provided all new franchisees and their management personnel. Training program is conducted at both the company's headquarters and the franchisee's outlet.

Managerial Assistance Available: Dynamic provides continual administrative and managerial assistance for the life of the franchise business. Complete manuals of operations are provided each franchisee.

Information Submitted: April 1990

EBC FRANCHISE GROUP, INC.
1080 Holcomb Bridge Road
Building 100, Suite 310
Roswell, Georgia 30076
Tom N. Dye

Description of Operation: EBC provides offices and shared secretarial services to companies and executives that are efficient, cost effective and enhance their business image and performance.

Number of Franchisees: 4 in 2 States.

In Business Since: 1982

Equity Capital Needed: $90,000-$150,000 excluding a franchise fee of $25,000.

Financial Assistance Available: None

Training Provided: Training at the Atlanta office and ongoing on franchisee location.

Managerial Assistance Available: Managers are available for training; quarterly sales meetings.

Information Submitted: April 1990

ECONOTAX
a/k/a Taxpro, Inc.
5846 Ridgewood Road, Suite B-101
Jackson, Mississippi 39211
James T. Marsh, E.A. or Chip Johnson, E.A.

Description of Operation: ECONOTAX provides the public with a full range of professional tax services, including tax preparation, audit assistance, electronic filing, and refund anticipation loans. ECONOTAX franchisees find their practices compatible with a wide range of financial service, bookkeeping, small business service, and other endeavors.

Number of Franchisees: 56 offices in current operation.

In Business Since: 1965, franchising since 1968

Equity Capital Needed: Initial franchise fee is $2,500. Computer adequate to run tax software recommended. Estimated other start-up costs are $500 to $1,500.

Financial Assistance Available: Partial financing of computer hardware, software, and initial franchisee fee available.

Training Provided: ECONOTAX provides a self-guided study course for franchisees and employees in tax preparation and tax law. Franchisees are provided an initial practice management seminar at the company's offices. ECONOTAX sponsors accredited continuing professional education seminars and courses, regular updates and bulletins, and maintains a toll-free "hot line."

Managerial Assistance Available: Assistance is provided in the provision of advertising and marketing materials; recruiting, hiring, and training programs; work scheduling and internal controls and procedures; resolution of tax questions; electronic filing, RAL, and computer support; and general management assistance.

Information Submitted: April 1990

EGAL, Inc.
12345 West 95th Street, Suite 203
Lenexa, Kansas 66215
Timothy J. Warkins

Description of Operation: EGAL, Inc. is a home inspection and radon screening franchisor, offering home inspection and radon screening for residential real estate. No office is required; it can be operated out of your house and EGAL supplies you with most materials and equipment needed to start the business.

Number of Franchisees: 16

In Business Since: 1987

Equity Capital Needed: $12,800

Financial Assistance Available: None

Training Provided: 1 week to 10 days training is required at EGAL's home office.

Managerial Assistance Available: We will assist you in areas of management of the business.

Information Submitted: April 1990

E. K. WILLIAMS & CO.
8774 Yates Drive, Suite 210
Westminister, Colorado 80030
David H. Hinze, Franchise Director

Description of Operation: EKW is a business management service specializing in the "how-to" of maximizing small business profits through a network of franchised offices. This network of local offices provides the most up-to-date accounting, tax and business counseling services plus a wide range of computer services to independently owned businesses. EKW has developed and marketed recordkeeping systems for small businesses, and these systems and the business management services EKW offers have received the endorsement of numerous organizations which represent potential management service clients.

Number of Franchisees: 301 franchised offices in 50 States.

In Business Since: 1935 and franchising since 1947

Equity Capital Needed: Will vary by market. Minimum $40,000.

Financial Assistance Available: None

Training Provided: A 3 week initial training course is conducted at EKW national training center to instruct in the day-to-day business operations and techniques. Field training sessions are conducted throughout the year.

Managerial Assistance Available: After the initial training course EKW field staff provides on-site follow-up counseling, assistance and guidance in all phases of business operations manuals, and EKW conducts field training sessions throughout the year. National marketing department works to secure endorsements of national companies which represent potential clients to the franchisee. Computer system software for processing client work is supported from the corporate office by an in-house staff of data processing professionals.

Information Submitted: April 1990

ENTREES ON-TRAYS, INC.
3 Lombardy Terrace
Fort Worth, Texas 76132
Don Shipe, President-Owner

Description of Operation: Entrees On-Trays, Inc., is a dinner delivery service serving the finer restaurants of the metropolitan areas. Deliveries are made to residences, hospitals and businesses. Franchisee can operate from home with extremely low overhead.

Number of Franchisees: 5 in Ft. Worth/Dallas metroplex.

In Business Since: 1986

Equity Capital Needed: $12,500 initially to $17,500 ultimately.

Financial Assistance Available: None

Training Provided: On-site in Ft. Worth; however, the simplicity of the operation requires very little training.

Managerial Assistance Available: Since the owner operates a franchise in Ft. Worth and will continue to do so, he can provide timely and "on-the-job experience" assistance on a continuing basis.

Information Submitted: April 1990

EZ DMV, INC.
100 North Harbor Boulevard #5
Santa Ana, California 92703
Harprit Leavell, President

Description of Operation: EZ License Centers provide all of the services of a Department of Motor Vehicles in the State of California, with the exception of driver's licenses. They offer every service from registrations, transfers, license plates, personalized license plates, out-of-state transfers, and all of the other complex transactions. They charge fees from $5 to $25. The documentation and acquisition of all the required documents and forms are taken care of at these centers without the long lines and bureaucratic hassles. The centers also offer related services such as passport photos, fingerprinting, notary public and other profit oriented services.

Number of Franchisees: 2 company centers and 1 franchised center in California.

In Business Since: 1982, franchising since 1989.

Equity Capital Needed: Approximately $55,000 to $67,000 depending on size and location of shop.

Financial Assistance Available: The company will assist the franchisee in applying for financing. The company will not make direct loans to the franchisee.

Training Provided: 4 weeks of comprehensive training in all aspects of store operations, DMV procedures, and marketing, 1 week of which is in the franchisee's center.

Managerial Assistance Available: Site selection, equipment lists, shop layouts, procedure seminars and ongoing support.

Information Submitted: May 1990

FASTSIGNS
4951 Airport Parkway, Suite 530
Dallas, Texas 75248
Carmen Cohn

Description of Operation: High-tech, computerized, retail sign stores with 1-day service.

Number of Franchisees: 75

In Business Since: 1985

Equity Capital Needed: $80,000-$90,000 plus working capital.

Financial Assistance Available: None

Training Provided: 3 weeks in Dallas, Texas.

Managerial Assistance Available: Opening assistance for 1 week.

Information Submitted: April 1990

FAX-9
1609 South Murray Boulevard
Colorado Springs, Colorado 80916

Description of Operation: National public fax service-franchises are piggyback operations to be run from existing businesses, known as host locations.

Number of Franchisees: Currently over 350 franchises sold with 250 opened sites in 47 States and Canada.

In Business Since: 1988

Equity Capital Needed: $3,500 with a minimum cash requirement of $1,500-$1,800.

Financial Assistance Available: None

Training Provided: A franchise representative installs the fax machine and provides training on the equipment and bookkeeping.

Managerial Assistance Available: Ongoing marketing support in promoting the business.

Information Submitted: April 1990

FINANCIAL EXPRESS
dba FINANCIAL EXPRESS SYSTEMS, INC.
14679 Midway Road, Suite 102
Dallas, Texas 75244
David A. Vernon, Director of Franchise Development

Description of Operation: Financial Express provides efficient, on-site bookkeeping, payroll processing, tax preparation and general business consulting to the fastest growing market in the United States—small business. The exciting aspect of our business is our unique marketing program that attracts and retains clients. Our mobile offices add to our dynamic marketing plan.

Number of Franchisees: 3 in Texas and 3 corporate.

In Business Since: 1985

Equity Capital Needed: $50,000, plus a minimum of 6 months living expenses.

Financial Assistance Available: None

Training Provided: Intensive 2 week program with supporting manuals for computer/software, management, systems business development and consulting. Additional 1 week sales and marketing program conducted at franchisee's location. Continuous technical support and training classes.

Managerial Assistance Available: Monthly seminars and ongoing marketing and operational assistance are provided.

Information Submitted: April 1990

FINANCIAL TRANSACTION CORPORATION
7 Mt. Lassen Drive, Suite D-114
San Rafael, California 94903
Douglas R. Brim, Executive Vice President

Description of Operation: Real estate loan brokerage. Franchisee should be a licensed real estate person with experience in real estate finance.

Number of Franchisees: 16 in California

In Business Since: 1981

Equity Capital Needed: Approximately $10,000-$20,000

Financial Assistance Available: Per agreement.

Training Provided: Training manual, ongoing updates, seminars on underwriting and other important functions of real estate finance.

Managerial Assistance Available: Operations manuals and setting up assistance. Management seminars, advertising and recruiting assistance.

Information Submitted: April 1990

FINDERBINDER/SOURCE BOOK DIRECTORIES
4679 Vista Street
San Diego, California 92116
Gary Beals, CEO

Description of Operation: Add-on profit centers for existing small businesses.

Number of Franchisees: 25

In Business Since: 1974

Equity Capital Needed: $10,000-$12,000

Financial Assistance Available: None

Training Provided: Full day plus detailed manuals.

Managerial Assistance Available: Ongoing support.

Information Submitted: April 1990

FOCUS ON BINGO MAGAZINE
GUIDES PUBLISHING, INC.
One Anderson Avenue, Dept. FOB
P. O. Box 133
Fairview, New Jersey 07022
Louis C. Fernandez, President

Description of Operation: *Focus On Bingo* is a free bingo guide magazine whose main advertisers are bingo sponsors who otherwise are unable to advertise in most newspapers because of postal regulations. No experience necessary. We produce the complete magazine for you. Complete training and protected territory.

Number of Franchisees: 5 in 4 States

In Business Since: 1980

Equity Capital Needed: $1,800 license fee.

Financial Assistance Available: None

Training Provided: Complete training and continuous support.

Managerial Assistance Available: Continuous assistance via telephone "hot line" and periodic bulletins.

Information Submitted: May 1990

FOCUS ON HOMES MAGAZINE
GUIDES PUBLISHING, INC.
One Anderson Avenue, Dept. FOH
P. O. Box 133
Fairview, New Jersey 07022
Louis C. Fernandez, President

Description of Operation: *Focus On Homes* is a free pictorial "houses-for-sale" magazine whose main advertisers are the real estate agencies in your territory. No previous experience necessary. We produce the complete magazine for you. Complete training and protected territory.

Number of Franchisees: 10 in 5 States

In Business Since: 1980

Equity Capital Needed: $1,800 license fee.

Financial Assistance Available: None

Training Provided: Complete training and continuous support.

Managerial Assistance Available: Continuous assistance via telephone "hot line" and periodic bulletins.

Information Submitted: May 1990

THE FRANCHISE STORE
5100 Poplar, Suite 2116
Memphis, Tennessee 38137

Description of Operation: The franchise is a business utilizing certain methods of service and sales to the public for the marketing and sales of franchises from a central location throughout the United States through promotional efforts.

Number of Franchisees: Regions with sublicensees, in 43 States, Canada, United Kingdom, Australia, South America, Asia and Mexico.

In Business Since: 1976

Equity Capital Needed: $1,000 plus. Dependent on population of area served.

Financial Assistance Available: None

Training Provided: The training is available in Memphis, Tennessee, and extensiveness is dependent upon experience.

Managerial Assistance Available: See above

Information Submitted: April 1990

FRANKLIN TRAFFIC SERVICE, INC.
5251 Shawnee Road, P. O. Box 100
Ransomville, New York 14131
Richard D. Dearborn, Manager Sales/Franchising

Description of Operation: Franklin Traffic Service, Inc., is a prominent company providing its nationwide clientele with audit and payment of freight bills, management reporting, management services, and complete industrial traffic services.

Number of Franchisees: 6 in New York, Pennsylvania and Georgia.

In Business Since: 1969

Equity Capital Needed: $19,000-$25,000

Financial Assistance Available: $11,000-$14,000 required in advance. Financing on balance to qualified applicants.

Training Provided: Intensive 3 week, mandatory training program for all new franchisees. Training consists of in-house programs and time in the field with an existing franchisee.

Managerial Assistance Available: Franklin Traffic Service maintains a bonafide interest in all franchises. Manuals of operations, forms, and directions are provided. In-the-field assistance is provided on a regular basis. Franchisees benefit from all new marketing concepts which are developed. Franklin sponsors regular franchise meetings, and continually upgrades and maintains the highest level of quality possible.

Information Submitted: April 1990

GASCARD CLUB, INC.
2720 Loker Avenue, Suite G
Carlsbad, California 92008
J. R. Wheeler

Description of Operation: Computerized automated fuel management system.

Number of Franchisees: Over 700 open and operating in 38 States.

In Business Since: 1981

Equity Capital Needed: $50,000

Financial Assistance Available: Gascard Club will supply a list of contacts for franchisees who wish to lease equipment in place of purchasing equipment needed.

Training Provided: Minimum 5 days training at national headquarters in La Jolla, California, is required of new franchisees. Gascard's total program and C.R.T. hands-on are only 2 of the many subjects covered. Detailed training manuals are issued and updated for a continuing reference tool. Gascard advertising guidelines and new sales development ideas are passed on to franchisees. Sales training seminars are available to franchisees.

Managerial Assistance Available: Gascard Club provides member services, which is a franchisee's direct contact to any department in the event of questions or problems. A toll free customer service line is also available 24 hours a day, 7 days a week to meet franchisees' needs. Technicians are based at Gascard region offices across the nation for service as needed. Management and sales seminars and program enhancements are offered on a regular continuing basis.

Information Submitted: May 1990

*GENERAL BUSINESS SERVICES, INC.
20271 Goldenrod Lane
Germantown, Maryland 20874-4090
Robert Pirtle, President

Description of Operation: General Business Services franchised business counselors provide financial management, business counseling, tax planning, and computer services to small businesses and professionals. Supported by the GBS national office, franchisees provide clients the proper recordkeeping system, guaranteed correct tax return preparation, computer services, and financial planning services. GBS provides its business counselors and their clients with continuous training and support. The franchisee can be operated as either a sole proprietorship or corporation.

Number of Franchisees: Hundreds nationwide

In Business Since: 1962

Equity Capital Needed: Franchise fee is $25,000 (Plan I) or $15,000 (Plan II). Should also have sufficient operating capital for living expenses and for business "start-up" period—will vary by individual.

Financial Assistance Available: None

Training Provided: Initial and continuous training is provided. Approximately 32 days training provided during the first year and approximately 17 days training each year thereafter. GBS business counselors are trained in all aspects of counseling, client acquisition and operating an independent business based on GBS' 25-plus years experience. All new franchisees received without additional expense: (1) a 4-volume operations manual containing all operating instructions, company policies, and procedures; (2) 2 week basic training institute and 1 week advanced training institute at GBS' national training center; (3) 1 week individual training in the franchisee's own marketing area by an experienced business counselor; (4) necessary sales aids, client servicing and practice management forms; and (5) 12 days ongoing training and individual guidance through assigned field support manager.

Managerial Assistance Available: In addition to local assistance provided by an experienced field support manager, a staff of over 100 in the national office is available for managerial assistance and technical support as required; 20 continuing support services are provided franchisees: e.g., annual series of seminars for professional development and continuing education; business management self-study services; lending library of books, tapes and pamphlets; sales brochures, client advertising and ongoing public relations program; toll-free numbers for order placement, computer assistance and tax advisory services; ongoing communications through bi-weekly and monthly newsletters and field-represented President's Advisory Council.

Information Submitted: April 1990

GREETINGS INC.
P. O. Box 25623
Lexington, Kentucky 40524-5624
Carol L. Kargel, Vice President

Description of Operation: Greetings is a target market advertising company. Greetings addresses people with a need for information about the businesses in a given market, such as Home Owner Greeting, Campus Greetings, Apartment Greeting.

Number of Franchisees: 5 company-owned units in 3 States

In Business Since: 1984

Equity Capital Needed: $15,000 franchise fee, $12-$15,000 equipment and operating capital.

Financial Assistance Available: Franchisee to arrange own financing. Some assistance on franchise fee.

Training Provided: 1 week training in parent company, 1 week provided at franchisee location. Staff to provide continuing guidance and assistance at all times thereafter.

Managerial Assistance Available: Continuous as long as the franchisee is in operation.

Information Submitted: April 1990

*H & R BLOCK INC.
4410 Main Street
Kansas City, Missouri 64111
Franchise Information

Description of Operation: Preparation of income taxes and electronic filing.

Number of Franchisees: Over 8,800 offices worldwide of which approximately 4,800 are operated by franchisees.

In Business Since: 1955

Equity Capital Needed: $5,000-$8,000. Because very few new territories are available, in most cases, additional equity capital for purchase of an existing franchise is needed.

Financial Assistance Available: None

Training Provided: Individual and/or group training is held for all new franchisees. Each fall, a regional convention is held for all franchisees to discuss all phases of operation and new developments and ideas.

Managerial Assistance Available: A network of satellite franchise directors provides any and all assistance required or needed.

Information Submitted: April 1990

THE HEADQUARTERS COMPANIES
120 Montgomery Street
Suite 1040
San Francisco, California 94104
William R. Hughes

Description of Operation: Lease executive offices with complete support services. Offices and support services available to both full-time users and occasional users. Each client receives, in addition to use of office, a receptionist, telephone answering, secretarial, word processing, office supplies and an array of other support services such as radio paging, facsimile transmission, electronic document distribution, telex, conference rooms, furniture rental, printing, direct mail and more. The various services are made available to the business community in general, not only those using the office space. The office center functions as a business support service bureau for the entire city in which it is located. Company officials stress that the array of support services will continue to change as the new office technology unfolds in the future. The overall concept envisions licensed locations in both major and minor business cities across the country linked together in a communications network of office centers providing support services to the business community.

Number of Franchisees: 33 with 94 locations in 30 States and Europe.

In Business Since: 1967, franchising since October 1978

Equity Capital Needed: An initial investment of approximately $350,000.

Financial Assistance Available: None

Training Provided: License trademark only, no training.

Managerial Assistance Available: Marketing, advertising, sales and administration assistance.

Information Submitted: April 1990

HEIMER INSPECTIONS
1923 New York Avenue
Huntington, New York 11746
Irwin Heimer, Vice President, Marketing

Description of Operation: The Heimer Home Inspection Report gives the prospective home buyer a 40-50 page narrative report that informs the client of the total condition of the house; the good points, deficiencies and potential problem areas. The report is bound in a booklet and promptly submitted to the client.

Number of Franchisees: 3 in New York, Massachusetts, and New Jersey

In Business Since: 1985

Equity Capital Needed: Approximately $60,000

Financial Assistance Available: Co-signature on equipment available.

Training Provided: 2 weeks, 60 hour course given in the home office.

Managerial Assistance Available: Continuous

Information Submitted: May 1990

HOMES & LAND PUBLISHING CORPORATION
dba HOMES & LAND MAGAZINE
1600 Capitol Circle SW
Tallahassee, Florida 32310
Ken Ledford, Vice President, Sales

Description of Operation: Nation's largest publisher of community real estate magazines. Magazines are black/white or color and contain property listings of real estate companies. Franchisees sell advertising space to real estate brokers and distribute the magazines in the community. Separate franchises offered for quality magazines and for economy magazines.

Number of Franchisees: 300 under contract in 35 States

In Business Since: 1973

Equity Capital Needed: $6,000 for quality magazine; $1,500 for economy magazine.

Financial Assistance Available: None

Training Provided: 1 week orientation at company offices, including instruction in production, sales and financial management; field assistance provided for initial sales.

Managerial Assistance Available: Operating manuals and sales aids provided. Regional meetings and annual sales convention provide opportunities for further training and interaction. Home office technical assistance is provided by telephone; sales assistance is available from district sales managers.

Information Submitted: May 1990

HOMEWATCH CORPORATION
2865 South Colorado Boulevard
Denver, Colorado 80222
Paul A. Sauer, President

Description of Operation: A checking and sitting service which provides attentive care for people's homes, pets and elderly people. Homesitting 24 hours or overnight, companion sitting, and in-home personal services (errands), odd jobs and handyman services.

Number of Franchisees: 26 in 11 states

In Business Since: 1973

Equity Capital Needed: Initial fee is $6,000. The total investment not to exceed $10,000. Area development available.

Financial Assistance Available: Financial assistance available for multiple sales or large franchises.

Training Provided: 4-day (mandatory) training program at corporate office or on-site. Manuals, bookkeeping and advertising/marketing manuals. Continuous support and consultation, bi-monthly newsletters, and voice and video cassette telephone helpline.

Managerial Assistance Available: Continuous assistance available whenever needed. Newsletters, regional seminars, and national convention.

Information Submitted: April 1990

HOSTESS HELPER FRANCHISING, INC.
20 Whittlesey Road
Newton Centre, Massachusetts 02159
Ellen F. Hochberger, President

Description of Operation: Personalized party planning service.

Number of Franchisees: 1 company-owned.

In Business Since: 1973, franchising commenced in 1989.

Equity Capital Needed: $17,600-$25,000, which includes franchise fee.

Financial Assistance Available: None

Training Provided: Yes

Managerial Assistance Available: Yes

Information Submitted: April 1990

*HOUSEMASTER OF AMERICA, INC.
421 West Union Avenue
Bound Brook, New Jersey 08805
Robert J. Hardy, President

Description of Operation: HouseMaster of America is an organization of home inspection professionals. Qualified technical people conduct the inspections, while marketing-oriented people run the business end. Home buyers who want to know the condition of perhaps the largest investment of their lifetime are the primary users. There are no inventory requirements and no need for fancy office space. Suitable for ownership by men and women alike.

Number of Franchisees: 115 in 35 States

In Business Since: 1979

Equity Capital Needed: $17,000-$35,000, depending on the number of owner-occupied homes in area.

Financial Assistance Available: It is advised that an additional $10,000 to $15,000 is needed to get started. Sources of financial assistance are provided by the franchisor.

Training Provided: 3-day orientation training for the person who will run the business, 5-day technical training course for the designated technical director. Also provided are (1) sales and promotion manual, (2) operations manual, (3) technical training manual.

Managerial Assistance Available: Ongoing counseling in all aspects of the business. Administration of referral system (WATS Line), advertising, publicity and promotion programs, regular newsletters, both technical and sales, as well as bulletins, trade digests. Periodic seminars. Both technical and marketing research and development. A warranty program.

Information Submitted: April 1990

IDENT-A-KID SERVICES OF AMERICA, INC.
8430 Sixth Street North
St. Petersburg, Florida 33702
Robert King, National Director

Description of Operation: The IDENT-A-KID program provides parents with a laminated child I.D. card containing a child's photograph, physical description, and fingerprint. In case of an emergency, parents can provide the card to law enforcement or others to help in the quick, safe recovery of their child. Total turnkey package is $12,500 including computer, camera, assembly equipment, supplies, etc.

Number of Franchisees: 80 Total, 70 in the United States, 10 in Canada.

In Business Since: 1986

Equity Capital Needed: $12,000 total turnkey operation.

Financial Assistance Available: None

Training Provided: 3 days at the franchisee's home.

Managerial Assistance Available: Telephone assistance, information releases, and newsletter.

Information Submitted: April 1990

INCOTAX SYSTEMS, INC.
P. O. Box 1380
Lake Worth, Florida 33460
Richard B. Vondrak, President

Description of Operation: Incotax Systems is a volume, multi unit tax service system. It has developed an outstanding method of providing high quality, accurate tax returns to the public at a minimum cost.

Number of Franchisees: 15 in Florida and 3 in Arizona

In Business Since: 1967

Equity Capital Needed: $15,000

Financial Assistance Available: $10,000 of equity capital is prorated thru first year of operation.

Training Provided: Complete management and tax preparation training for 2 persons is conducted by the home office. Complete cost of training, including air fare, hotel, etc., is included in equity capital.

Managerial Assistance Available: Continuous home office inspection and management training is conducted. Home office consultation and management suggestions are made to all franchisees, complete procedural manuals and forms are furnished franchisees as well as monthly news bulletins.

Information Submitted: May 1990

INNOVATIONS IN CORPORATIONS, INC.
3333 Veterans Highway, Suite C-527
Ronkonkoma, New York 11779
David E. Gorman, President

Description of Operation: Singles matchmaking business. Calculated couples matchmaking parties use a new, innovative process to compatibly match hundreds of singles within minutes. Our parties virtually replace dating services.

Number of Franchisees: None. Previously sold licenses.

In Business Since: 1983

Equity Capital Needed: $10,000-$25,000

Financial Assistance Available: None

Training Provided: Training begins at franchisor's New York offices and continues at area parties. Further training is then provided at franchisee's location during grand opening period.

Managerial Assistance Available: Complete operations manuals are provided. Innovations in Corporations also provides management assistance in such areas as advertising, location referrals, system updates, policies and procedures.

Information Submitted: March 1990

INTERNATIONAL CONSULTING CENTERS
4695 MacArthur Court, Suite 1420
Newport Beach, California 92660
William James Long

Description of Operation: Business and franchise expansion and sales. Specialize in career planning and business expansion.

Number of Franchisees: 8

In Business Since: 1989

Equity Capital Needed: $20,000

Financial Assistance Available: Special financing for specific cultural groups.

Training Provided: 1 week home office and ongoing field training.

Managerial Assistance Available: This program is highly structured with technical and marketing support on a regional basis.

Information Submitted: April 1990

INTERNATIONAL MERGERS AND ACQUISITIONS
4300 North Miller Road
Suite 220
Scottsdale, Arizona 85251
Neil D. Lewis, President

Description of Operation: International Mergers and Acquisitions is a national affiliation of members engaged in the profession of servicing merger and acquisition minded companies on a confidential basis. Our program embraces all aspects essential to a successful merger or acquisition.

Number of Franchisees: 38 in 15 States

In Business Since: 1970

Equity Capital Needed: $10,000 minimum

Financial Assistance Available: A total investment of $10,000 is necessary.

Training Provided: Quarterly regional creative work sessions, plus orientation sessions for each new member as needed.

Managerial Assistance Available: International Mergers and Acquisitions provides complete procedures and operations manual, forms and product research to all members.

Information Submitted: May 1990

INTROMARKETING OF AMERICA
30161 Southfield
Suite 315
Southfield, Michigan 48076
James A. Mirro, President

Description of Operation: IntroMarketing of America provides product demonstration and other point-of-purchase or marketing services. Call (313) 540-5000.

Number of Franchisees: 2

In Business Since: 1987

Equity Capital Needed: $25,000 minimum (includes $9,500 franchise fee).

Financial Assistance Available: None

Training Provided: 2 week training program at corporate headquarters, plus 3 day on-site assistance.

Managerial Assistance Available: Aid in setting up payroll/billing system, advertising program, accounting system, demonstrator training, operations manual/forms, computer software system, promotional merchandise, product information, insurance needs and ongoing advice/consultation.

Information Submitted: May 1990

*JACKSON HEWITT TAX SERVICE
224 Groveland Road
Virginia Beach, Virginia 23452
Walter Ewell, Vice President, Franchise Development

Description of Operation: A Jackson Hewitt Income Tax franchise will offer computerized income tax preparation, bookkeeping, and other related services. Franchisees are licensed to use the Jackson Hewitt System, which includes proprietary software, accounting methods, merchandising, equipment selection, advertising, sales and promotional techniques, personnel training, and other related matters.

Number of Franchisees: 224 nationally

In Business Since: 1960

Equity Capital Needed: $16,000-$30,000 (estimated) including initial franchise fee.

Financial Assistance Available: Jackson Hewitt Inc., will not offer financing to any franchisee, either directly or indirectly.

Training Provided: Prior to franchisee's commencement of business Jackson Hewitt Inc., will provide a minimum of 5 days of training in all aspects of the operation and management of a Jackson Hewitt Income Tax Franchise, including the use of the computerized tax programs. In addition, annual refresher training is provided.

Managerial Assistance Available: Jackson Hewitt Inc., will provide assistance in advertising and marketing, recommendations and advice concerning site selection, ongoing advice and guidance as requested by franchisees concerning operations and tax problems as well as new and improved techniques and operating methods, business procedures, management and promotional materials, and updated software programs.

Information Submitted: April 1990

JAY ROBERTS AND ASSOCIATES INC.
82 North Chicago Street
Suite 105
Joliet, Illinois 60131-1362
John S. Meers

Description of Operation: Financial consultants specializing in government loan packaging, conventional business loans, private placements, real estate loans and general turn around and liquidity consulting.

Number of Franchisees: 29 in 19 States plus 1 company-owned.

In Business Since: 1963

Equity Capital Needed: $25,000 plus $5,000 franchise fee

Financial Assistance Available: None

Training Provided: 400 page training manual and optional 1 day training at our office.

Managerial Assistance Available: Ongoing

Information Submitted: April 1990

K & O PUBLISHING
P. O. Box 51189
Seattle, Washington 98115-1189
Warren E. Kraft, Jr., President

Description of Operation: K & O Publishing franchises a special interest newspaper called the *Bingo Bugle*. The franchisee has the opportunity to become the editor and publisher of his/her own newspaper even with no previous publishing experience. This publication is extremely popular with bingo players. The *Bingo Bugle* is America's largest group of bingo newspapers.

Number of Franchisees: 52 in 20 States and District of Columbia

In Business Since: 1982

Equity Capital Needed: $2,000-$10,000

Financial Assistance Available: None

Training Provided: Franchisor provides a 2 day seminar.

Managerial Assistance Available: An operation manual and ongoing assistance are provided by franchisor.

Information Submitted: April 1990

KELLY'S LIQUIDATORS, INC.
1310 N.W. 21st Street
Fort Lauderdale, Florida 33311
Edward Kelly, President

Description of Operation: Kelly's Liquidators is a unique clearing house service agency for bringing buyers and sellers of used, second-hand (or "pre-owned") personal property together (i.e., household goods, antiques, etc.). We sell piece-meal (by appointment), package-deal, or at one-day public sale (especially estates), NOT auctions! We charge 25 percent commission of gross sales on a contractual basis. We sell other people's goods on their premises.

Number of Franchisees: 4 in Florida (franchises available in Florida only)

In Business Since: 1954

Equity Capital Needed: $2,500 minimum

Financial Assistance Available: $2,000 is the cost of a franchise that must be paid before training begins. An additional $500 is needed for start-up and 3 months operations. Franchisee must arrange his own financing if necessary.

Training Provided: Intensive 5-day mandatory training course is given only to franchisee at Ft. Lauderdale. Training based on confidential manual of operations and supplemented wherever possible by on-the-job supervision by a Kelly's officer or experienced franchisee.

Managerial Assistance Available: KLI provides continuing managerial, technical and operational assistance for 6 months in such areas as obtaining contracts, listing, advertising, and selling, as they relate to the various methods of selling (i.e., appointment, package deal, or public sales—especially estates) and record control. A complete manual of operations is provided.

Information Submitted: April 1990

LASERQUIPT INTERNATIONAL, INC.
7615 Washington Avenue, South
Edina, Minnesota 55435
Jeffrey T. Gilmer, Vice President, Franchise Operations

Description of Operation: Laserquipt provides a service for regional, national and larger professional organizations utilizing laser printers and fax machines. This service involves the maintenance of the machines and the consumable components used in these machines. The franchisee promotes this service through a direct sales force and a follow-up technical staff.

Number of Franchisees: 8 locations in major urban areas.

In Business Since: 1986

Equity Capital Needed: Total cost to purchase and open.

Financial Assistance Available: None

Training Provided: Complete franchise training including recruiting, hiring, training of sales staff, lease consultation, inventory consultation, technical training, Laserquipt operational computer software training, personnel consultation, marketing to your customer list and advertising materials.

Managerial Assistance Available: Monthly ongoing sales training for sales staff at the training facilities of the company, sales and marketing manuals, advertising and promotional materials, qualified customer lead list, national advertising, national account referral program, personnel manual, technical manual and updates in the operational software program.

Information Submitted: April 1990

LEGALEZE, INC.
1661 East Camelback Road
Suite 118
Phoenix, Arizona 85016
Paul Harris, Marketing Director

Description of Operation: Preparation and sale of uncontested legal documents. A LEGALEZE Service Center services the general public not desiring the services of an attorney for preparation of documents such as bankruptcy, divorce, legal separation, living trust, living will, name change, power of attorney, quit claim deed, etc.

Number of Franchisees: 1

In Business Since: 1988, franchising since 1990.

Equity Capital Needed: $15,000-$20,000

Financial Assistance Available: None

Training Provided: 5-day at home office training and sales techniques, advertising standards, client counseling procedures, and operations procedures. 2-day on-site training and assistance after opening of LEGALEZE Service Center.

Managerial Assistance Available: Ongoing technical assistance support available during development and operational phases. Assist in grand opening of LEGALEZE Service Center. Annual workshops and seminars also provided for all franchisees. Full manuals provided by franchisor.

Information Submitted: April 1990

THE LETTER WRITER, INC.
9357 Haggerty Road
Plymouth, Michigan 48170
Ginny Eades, President

Description of Operation: Franchisor is offering for sale the right to use the trademarks and logos of The Letter Writer in connection with the operation of a resume writing, creative writing, letter writing, full secretarial services, answering service and technical writing/advertising service. Franchisor has developed training, policies and procedures, marketing and advertising procedures, accounting systems, printing and reproducing systems, supplier contacts, equipment contracts, methods of client development, methods of preparing client services and working with clients in operating a Letter Writer franchise.

Number of Franchisees: 1 including company-owned in Michigan.

In Business Since: 1981, franchising since 1985.

Equity Capital Needed: Franchise fee: $10,000. Equipment costs: $4,850.

Financial Assistance Available: Franchisor will advise and assist franchisee in obtaining necessary financing, including methods of purchasing or leasing equipment. Franchisor will require $5,000 as a down-payment and allow franchisee to pay the $5,000 balance in monthly payments of $833 for 6 months.

Training Provided: Franchisee or franchisee's designated manager will receive a combination of lecture, self-study and on-the-job training. Policies, procedures and methods of operation will be reviewed. Training will be given in both management and delivery of services to the public, including training in typing skills, resume writing, bookkeeping, advertising, hiring practices, use of equipment, purchasing and telephone methods—a minimum of 80 hours.

Financial Assistance Available: None

Training Provided: 2 weeks with ongoing support.

Managerial Assistance Available: Continuous in all phases of operation.

Information Submitted: May 1990

*MAIL BOXES ETC. USA
5555 Oberlin Drive
San Diego, California 92121
Anthony W. (Tony) DeSio, President & CEO

Description of Operation: Postal, business and communication centers. Provides more than 30 services to consumer, small and home-based businesses in the following areas: Mailbox service with 24-hour access, mail receipt and forwarding, rapid air shipping/receiving, parcel packaging and shipping, telephone messaging, copy and printing service, secretarial service, electronic mail, wire services and fax network, office supplies, notary, passport photos.

Number of Franchisees: 1,200 in 44 States, Puerto Rico, Canada, Mexico, and Japan.

In Business Since: 1980. Public company since 1986 traded on NASDAQ as (Mail).

Equity Capital Needed: Individual franchise—$43,000-$73,000 (includes $13,000-$31,000 leasehold improvements and $10,000-$15,000 working capital).

Financial Assistance Available: Yes.

Training Provided: Combination of classroom at MBE University and in-store training. Individual franchise—2 weeks at corporate and 1 week at franchise location. Area franchise—2 weeks at corporate and 2 weeks at franchise location.

Managerial Assistance Available: Initial assistance provided in setting up turnkey operation including site selection, lease negotiation, facility design, construction management (optional), set-up of facility, grand opening promotional assistance. Continuing assistance in local store marketing, advertising and public relations, promotions and new profit center development. Monthly newsletter and quarterly video newsletter.

Information Submitted: May 1990

MEDICAL INSURAFORM SERVICE
909 South St. Mary's
P. O. Box 3341
Sioux City, Iowa 51102

Description of Operation: A business that coordinates and processes all medicare and medical insurance claims. Medical reimbursement consultants, particularly of interest to people with medical background.

Number of Franchisees: 2 in Iowa

In Business Since: 1980

Equity Capital Needed: $35,000 to $40,000

Financial Assistance Available: None

Training Provided: 10 days to 3 weeks training in home office in all operations of the business.

Managerial Assistance Available: Monthly visits for the first 6 months of operations in addition to training.

Information Submitted: May 1990

*MIFAX SERVICE AND SYSTEMS, INC.
3022 Airport Boulevard
Box 5800
Waterloo, Iowa 50704
Sandy Halvorson, Franchise Director

Description of Operation: Mifax Service & Systems, Inc. sells Control-o-fax brand products nationwide. These products consist of computerized accounting systems sold to the healing arts community. Control-o-fax products have been advertised and sold to doctors since 1948. Exciting sales aids, training materials and marketing support have been developed over the years to help local franchised dealers get started immediately and stay on track. High residual income opportunity from the forms and supplies sold with the computers.

Number of Franchisees: 68 in all but 28 States

In Business Since: 1969

Equity Capital Needed: $10,000 franchise fee plus $50,000 in working capital recomended for the first year.

Financial Assistance Available: All but $7,500 financed on a 4 year note.

Training Provided: The initial investment of $10,000 provides for 3 weeks of formal classroom training for the franchisee and for 1 employee. Classroom training at the home office includes product knowledge, sales skills and time and territory management. Continuous field training provided to maintain selling skills and to help introduce new products in your market. Several regional meetings conducted throughout the year.

Managerial Assistance Available: Business and financial planning, assistance in recruiting of salespeople and service people. An operations manual covering all facets of the business is made available.

Information Submitted: May 1990

MILLION AIR INTERLINK
4300 Westgrove
Dallas, Texas 75248
Lou Pepper, President

Description of Operation: Aviation franchise or general aviation operators. Fixed Base Operations (FBO) provide fuel, maintenance charters, aircraft sales, etc., to the general aviation community.

Number of Franchisees: 26 in 11 States

In Business Since: 1985

Equity Capital Needed:

Financial Assistance Available: Finances franchise fee and leases refueling equipment.

Training Provided: Initial 2 day session in Dallas. Training done periodically at franchise location.

Managerial Assistance Available: Operational training on-site, manuals, monthly operational and marketing ideas, annual sessions, and semi-annual owners' meetings.

Information Submitted: May 1990

MONEY BROKER ONE
230 East Wheeling Street
Suite 101
Lancaster, Ohio 43130
Raymond A. Strohl, President

Description of Operation: Money broker offering loans and financing to individuals, businesses, and churches for financing almost any worthwhile project. We offer real estate loans and business loans, and there is no upper limit on the size of the loans. We also act as a business broker helping people and companies purchase and sell businesses.

Number of Franchisees: 10 in Ohio, Florida, California, Pennsylvania, Louisiana, Missouri, and New York.

In Business Since: 1983

Equity Capital Needed: None

Financial Assistance Available: Yes

Training Provided: Varies, depending on the background and experience of the franchisee.

Managerial Assistance Available: Perpetual assistance as needed.

Information Submitted: March 1990

*MONEY CONCEPTS INTERNATIONAL, INC.
Golden Bear Plaza
11760 U.S. Highway One
North Palm Beach, Florida 33408
John P. Walsh, President/Chairman

Description of Operation: Money Concepts International, Inc., is a financial services franchisor. Money Concepts provides its franchisees with a complete "turnkey" marketing system for a financial planning center.

Number of Franchisees: Over 350 in the United States, the Caribbean, United Kingdom, Australia, Canada and Northern Ireland.

In Business Since: 1979, franchising since 1982.

Equity Capital Needed: Capital requirements up to $100,000.

Financial Assistance Available: Money Concepts may accept a note for 50 percent or less of the franchise fee as a cash substitute for the full payment of the franchise fee upon execution of the agreement. There is no interest on the note, which shall be paid in no more than 10 installments, and within one year.

Training Provided: Franchise includes basic and advanced management seminars. Other training is available, such as product and marketing seminar, financial planning school, office administration seminar, equity products seminar, hard assets seminar. These schools and seminars each last 2 to 5 days.

Managerial Assistance Available: Council of Presidents meeting for all franchise presidents held each quarter (2 or 3 days). Back up support in all areas of franchise operations (both sales and administration) on an ongoing basis.

Information Submitted: May 1990

*MONEY MAILER, INC.
15472 Chemical Lane
Huntington Beach, California 92649
Kris O. Friedrich, President

Description of Operation: Money Mailer sells regional subfranchises through which its independent regions individually sell and service local franchises. Each of these independent local franchises provides an inexpensive but highly effective form of advertising to merchants, service businesses, and professionals in their local areas. Each region provides a wealth of sales aids and continuing marketing support to their local franchisees as well as complete production support from Money Mailer, including artwork, printing and mailing through the U.S. Post Office.

Number of Franchisees: 260 in 28 States.

In Business Since: 1979

Equity Capital Needed: Regional owner: $80,000-$125,000 (includes fee), local franchisee: $25,000-$140,000 (includes fee).

Financial Assistance Available: Yes

Training Provided: An intensive 5 week classroom/infield training is provided for regional owners. Local franchisees receive a mandatory 3 week training course that includes 1 week classroom training and 2 week field training in their local area.

Managerial Assistance Available: Money Mailer produces complete training manuals, forms and sales aids. The region owner is obligated to provide these materials as well as continuous consultation to the local franchisees for all aspects of the business. The region and local franchisee receive constant updates on the results of our product and market research. In addition, Money Mailer sponsors an annual convention and aids communication between regions, local franchisees and the corporate office with regional conferences and a bi-monthly newsletter.

Information Submitted: April 1990

MORTGAGE ASSISTANCE CENTERS, INC.
450 Seminole Boulevard
Casselberry, Florida 32707
Edward J. McTaggart

Description of Operation: Offering assistance to families who are behind with their house payments. We have several options available to solve 80 percent of the cases.

Number of Franchisees: 1 in Florida

In Business Since: 1983

Equity Capital Needed: $35,000 down payment

Financial Assistance Available: Yes

Training Provided: An extensive 2 week training period at the home office in Orlando, Florida, will show new office owners a working office atmosphere where they can have "hands-on training," followed by 1 week training in their office location.

Managerial Assistance Available: Each new office will receive assistance regarding office location, necessary forms and office management. In addition, each office will receive training in Orlando, Florida, prior to opening date. A manual of instructions is available covering all aspects of operation. Special group benefits are offered and available.

Information Submitted: May 1990

*MORTGAGE SERVICE ASSOCIATES
21 Brock Street, P. O. Box 690
North Haven, Connecticut 06473-0690
J. D. Raffone, President

Description of Operation: Property inspection, securing, maintenance and repair of foreclosed and distressed property as well as numerous other types of commercial and residential inspection services to banks, lenders, insurers and others. A custom computer software program and a well coordinated marketing effort make this an ideal opportunity. Over 700 agents nationwide. Ongoing contracts are transferred to franchisees.

Number of Franchisees: 2 in 10 States

In Business Since: 1975, franchising since 1986

Equity Capital Needed: Minimum equity capital $5,000-$7,500 per unit—minimum purchase 2 units.

Financial Assistance Available: To qualified individuals.

Training Provided: One 40-50 hour week comprehensive training at franchisors location in all aspects of operation including property inspection and maintenance procedures, general business practices, customer service, marketing, and computer operations.

Managerial Assistance Available: Staff support, on-site help with start-up, procedural updates and guides.

Information Submitted: April 1990

MR. SHIP N'CHEK
1661 East Camelback Road
Suite 118
Phoenix, Arizona 85016
Paul Harris, Marketing Director

Description of Operation: Multi-facet business involving mail services, packaging, shipping, check cashing and a variety of business support services operated as MR. SHIP N'CHEK Center. Clientele includes general public and businesses.

Number of Franchisees: 29

In Business Since: 1989

Equity Capital Needed: $55,000

Financial Assistance Available: None

Training Provided: 1 week at home office regarding sales techniques, advertising, business methods for packaging and shipping, check cashing procedures, and general business methods. On-site 3 day training and technical assistance after opening.

Managerial Assistance Available: Ongoing technical support available during development and operational phases. Assist in grand opening of MR. SHIP N'CHECK Center. Annual workshops and seminars also provided for all franchisees. Full manuals provided by franchisor.

Information Submitted: April 1990

MR. SIGN FRANCHISING CORP.
159 Keyland Court
Bohemia, New York 11716
Herb Miller, Vice President of Franchising Administration

Description of Operation: Sign business. Mr. Sign offers a unique concept in custom sign making—computerized vinyl/sign making services for both business and residential communities. Franchisees can offer a selection of over 100,000 different types of signs and they can duplicate supplied art work, such as a business customer's logo. The high quality, reasonable price and relatively quick turnaround of a Mr. Signs' sign is particularly appealing to the business and residential community.

Number of Franchisees: 103 in 26 States

In Business Since: 1985

Equity Capital Needed: $50,000

Financial Assistance Available: Franchisor assistance in financing.

Training Provided: Mr. Sign provides the franchisee with the entire computer equipment package, including proprietary copyrighted software, start-up inventory of supplies, a comprehensive 3-week training program and substantial ongoing technical and marketing support.

Managerial Assistance Available: Turnkey operation, including design and layout specification, site review, review of lease, grand opening package, sales and marketing manual and portfolio, total administration kit.

Information Submitted: April 1990

MUZAK
400 North 34th Street, Suite 200
Seattle, Washington 98103
Leslie Ritter

Description of Operation: Lease of special work and public area music programs to businesses of all kinds. Sound systems and related communication systems included as lease or sale to customers. Available franchises limited to U.S.; wide opportunities overseas.

Number of Franchisees: Approximately 183 in all 16 States plus 10 owned operations, 26 franchisees in 14 countries.

In Business Since: 1934

Equity Capital Needed: Varies—information from Muzak

Financial Assistance Available: None

Training Provided: Continuing sales and technical training sessions help at various sites.

Managerial Assistance Available: Field visits by Muzak corporate staff providing evaluations, assistance, progress reports on continuous basis. National advertising, sales brochures, equipment specification sheets, etc., provided at all times.

Information Submitted: May 1990

NAMCO SYSTEMS, INC.
7 Strathmore Road
Natick, Massachusetts 01760
Julie Stansky

Description of Operation: Professional advertising program for businesses sold by appointment.

Number of Franchisees: 37 in 17 States

In Business Since: 1952

Equity Capital Needed: $21,000-$35,000, depending on size of territories.

Financial Assistance Available: None

Training Provided: Classroom training consists of 4 days at franchisor's headquarters in Natick, Massachusetts, 2 weeks of field training in the franchisees' territory, subsequent regional meetings and advance training seminars, on-going support and advice.

Managerial Assistance Available: All administrative functions such as contract processing, artwork and initial client billing are done by franchisor. Franchisor produces and delivers the product. Franchisor provides a weekly newsletter and contests to motivate its franchisees.

Information Submitted: April 1990

NATIONAL HOUSING INSPECTIONS
1817 North Hills Boulevard NE
Knoxville, Tennessee 37917
Brad Raney, Rentals Supervisor

Description of Operation: National Housing Inspections is a service-oriented business performing individual inspections of residential and commercial properties for purchasers and/or sellers. Generally, inspections are 90 percent for "used" or existing housing and 10 percent for new homes. NHI makes NO appraisals, merely acts as "house detectives" enabling would-be purchasers to make better decisions, while oftentimes helping them receive better prices, terms.

Number of Franchisees: 301 in 47 States; 1 in Canada.

In Business Since: 1970

Equity Capital Needed: National Housing Inspections is rented for 60 day trial—"Try it before you buy it"—"Test before you invest." Rental fee applies to down payment. Rent is $29 for 60 days.

Financial Assistance Available: Full purchase price after down payment of $1,250 financed by parent company for up to 48 months, with 2 percent simple interest.

Training Provided: NHI's initial training is augmented by "trial-run" grading sessions and personal follow-up, if needed. Parent firm maintains computerized service of 125,000 housing items problems, causes, el al. available to dealer throughout life time of franchise.

Managerial Assistance Available: Continuing without cost during life of franchise and/or financing term, whichever is greater, including proven ad information, telephone dialogues, copyrighted inspection sheets and specialized inspection forms.

Information Submitted: May 1990

NATIONAL TENANT NETWORK, INC.
P. O. Box 1664
Lake Grove, Oregon 97035
Edward F. Byczynski, President

Description of Operation: Unique computerized tenant performance reporting system for residential and commercial tenants. Extremely high cash flow potential.

Number of Franchisees: 5 in Florida, Pennsylvania, Washington, California and North Carolina.

In Business Since: 1981

Equity Capital Needed: $15,000 to $25,000

Financial Assistance Available: Start-up financing

Training Provided: Computer and marketing for 3 month on-site period, when needed.

Managerial Assistance Available: Marketing assistance, bookkeeping, advertising and data control. Hardware and software supplies.

Information Submitted: May 1990

NATIONWIDE INCOME TAX SERVICE COMPANY
14507 West Warren
Dearborn, Michigan 48126
Carl Gilbert, President

Description of Operation: Preparation of State and Federal income tax returns for individuals.

Number of Franchisees: 32 franchised plus 8 company offices

In Business Since: 1965

Equity Capital Needed: Dependent on number of offices to be opened.

Financial Assistance Available: None

Training Provided: 2 day training period in home office in various phases of income tax preparation and in the systems and procedures developed by Nationwide Tax Service.

Managerial Assistance Available: The company (franchisor) will: assist franchisee in selecting sites most suitable for business; provide guidance for personnel recruitment, selection and training of employees; office layout and design counselling; franchisor designs advertising and promotional materials, recommends media and ad schedules; will maintain continuous liaison with franchisees through mail, telephone.

Information Submitted: April 1990

NEEDLE IN A HAYSTACK AUDIO VIDEO SERVICE CENTER
Gateway Building
Suite 216
Dulles International Airport
Washington, D.C. 20041
James Bowser, Director of Franchise Sales

Description of Operation: Needle in a Haystack Audio Video Service Center delivers what consumers want and need: fast, expert repair of their audio and video components and performance accessories and maintenance products to enhance their audio and video systems. Through service express and our national service center, franchisees can provide this service without the substantial investment a service operation normally demands.

Number of Franchisees: 9 in Ohio, Massachusetts and Virginia

In Business Since: 1974

Equity Capital Needed: A total investment of $87,000-$115,000 is needed (which includes the franchise fee).

Financial Assistance Available: Franchisor does not offer a financing program, but can recommend sources of financing to the franchisee.

Training Provided: An intensive 1 week store manager's training is held at the corporate office and flagship store on all facets of the day-to-day business. A 2 day training is held for the store owner on-site selection, store construction, pre-opening and store operations. On-site training as well as continuous communication with the franchisee is provided.

Managerial Assistance Available: Advertising materials, training seminars, newsletters and on-site support are provided, along with continuous communication regarding sales and service techniques.

Information Submitted: April 1990

*NETWORK BUSINESS SERVICES, INC.
3003 G Greentree Executive Campus
Marlton, New Jersey 08053
Bennett Sady, President

Description of Operation: A sophisticated professional retail office and shipping center.

Number of Franchisees: 8

In Business Since: 1988, franchising since 1989

Equity Capital Needed: Start-up cash of $41,000.

Financial Assistance Available: Will assist in franchising package.

Training Provided: 3 weeks of training provided.

Managerial Assistance Available: Ongoing

Information Submitted: June 1990

O'BRIEN BUDD, INC.
P. O. Box 1307
3620 Swenson
St. Charles, Illinois 60174

Description of Operation: O'Brien Budd, Inc. is a business forms distributor and product distribution center offering franchise opportunities. These franchises were designed with the needs of salespeople in mind, allowing them to concentrate on selling business forms, promotional materials and custom printing services.

Number of Franchisees: None to date—starting to offer spring of 1990.

In Business Since: 1911

Equity Capital Needed: An initial investment ranging from $13,500 to $49,750 includes a franchise fee ranging from $7,500 to $17,500. This initial investment further includes expenditures for rent, utility security deposits, printed materials, insurance, training, grand opening advertising, office equipment and supplies, working capital, vehicles and miscellaneous office expenses.

Financial Assistance Available: None

Training Provided: Franchisor will provide franchisee with an initial training and familiarization course of a minimum of 7 days in duration to be conducted at franchisor's headquarters.

Managerial Assistance Available: O'Brien Budd franchisees are given a confidential manual which gives in detail the complete operations of a franchise. Full assistance is provided in all areas of the O'Brien Budd program, including franchise sales services specialist who will work closely with the franchisee.

Information Submitted: April 1990

THE OFFICE ANSWER
One SeaGate
Suite 1001
Toledo, Ohio 43604
Steven B. Hanson

Description of Operation: By joining The Office Answer team, you'll offer telephone answering, typing, facsimile, copies, shipping and more! Because of Office Answer's exclusive telephone answering equipment, you'll be able to offer telephone answering by company name at a cost to you of only $3 per line per month! Your clients will also be able to receive their mail and have the use of a desk and an office to return calls, open mail, etc. A real Office Answer.

This business is ideal for adding to an existing business or can be opened in almost any location in just a matter of weeks! Because you'll cater to business clients, your business can be operated successfully during normal business hours. For more information about owning your own Office Answer franchise or territory, please write to the address above.

Number of Franchisees: 5 in 5 States

In Business Since: 1988

Equity Capital Needed: $12,000 total package.

Financial Assistance Available: Telephone system, computer, furniture, etc.

Training Provided: Training to be conducted at corporate headquarters in Toledo with all expenses including travel and lodging paid for. Franchisee get "hands-on" training, all necessary manuals and extensive marketing and advertising assistance.

Managerial Assistance Available: Continuous in all phases of operation.

Information Submitted: May 1990

THE OFFICE, LTD.
1111 South Alpine Road
Suite 201
P. O. Box 6391
Rockford, Illinois 61125
Basant Patel

Description of Operation: Custom secretarial service/word processing service.

Number of Franchisees: 1 in Illinois

In Business Since: 1974

Equity Capital Needed: $25,000

Financial Assistance Available: None

Training Provided: 2 weeks in home office, 1 week sales in the franchisee location, and continuing support through the years of the agreement.

Managerial Assistance Available: A book of operations is provided plus monthly newsletter. Personnel available to visit franchise location. A minimum of 2 yearly visits available on call for any problems. Hot line is open for calls from 8:00 a.m. to 5:00 p.m., Monday through Friday. An accounting, marketing and advertising package is provided.

Information Submitted: May 1990

OFFICE ONE
230 East Wheeling Street
Suite 101
Lancaster, Ohio 43130
Raymond A. Strohl, President

Description of Operation: Shared office facility offering office space, telephone answering service, photocopying, fax service, secretarial services, and other services to sales reps, various very small businesses, and professional people.

Number of Franchisees: 2 in Ohio

In Business Since: 1989

Equity Capital Needed: Varies

Financial Assistance Available: Yes

Training Provided: Yes

Managerial Assistance Available: Perpetual assistance as needed.

Information Submitted: April 1990

OUTDOOR FUN SIGNS
138 River Corner Road
Conestoga, Pennsylvania 14516
Dianne Shiffer

Description of Operation: Rental of all occasion lawn signs.

Number of Franchisees: 1

In Business Since: 1986

Equity Capital Needed: $15,000, total start up costs.

Financial Assistance Available: None

Training Provided: Manual and telephone support.

Managerial Assistance Available: See above.

Information Submitted: April 1990

PACKAGING PLUS SERVICES, INC.
20 South Terminal Drive
Plainview, New York 11803 USA
Bill Reichert

Description of Operation: Packaging Plus Services, Inc., is engaged in franchising service centers that offer convenient packaging, shipping, mailing and communication services to businesses, retailers, professionals, and residential customers. Packaging Plus Services offers all the convenient services that a full-time shipping department would provide to a large corporation, but on an "as needed" basis, and at a fraction of the cost.

Number of Franchisees: 125 in 15 States

In Business Since: 1985, franchising since 1986

Equity Capital Needed: $55,000-$85,000 including working capital.

Financial Assistance Available: Bank/sale lease back.

Training Provided: 2 week training at home office. 3 day in-store during grand opening. Training manuals, cassette training quarter update seminars.

Managerial Assistance Available: Ongoing, newsletters and 800 number for field assistance representatives.

Information Submitted: April 1990

*THE PACKAGING STORE, INC.
8480 East Orchard Road
Englewood, Colorado 80111
Richard T. Godwin, President

Description of Operation: Custom packaging and shipping service. Wholesale and retail sales of packaging supplies.

Number of Franchisees: 335 in 40 States

In Business Since: 1980

Equity Capital Needed: $30,000 to $40,000

Financial Assistance Available: None

Training Provided: Intensive, 1 week mandatory training session for all new franchisees and their employees in an authorized training store and opening assistance at franchise store.

Managerial Assistance Available: The Packaging Store provides continual management service for the life of the franchise in the areas of advertising and marketing, operations and management reviews. Complete manuals of operations, forms and directions are provided. Field managers are available in all regions to work closely with franchisees and visit stores regularly to assist in solving problems. The Packaging Store sponsors meetings of franchisees and conducts marketing and product research to maintain high Packaging Store consumer acceptance.

Information Submitted: April 1990

PADGETT BUSINESS SERVICES USA, INC.
160 Hawthorne Park
Athens, Georgia 30606
Hub Brightwell, Jr., Franchise Division

Description of Operation: PBS grants licenses to individuals who desire to operate their own accounting, income tax and business counseling practice, utilizing the unique forms and successful systems of operations developed by the franchisor. The PBS franchisee remains, at all times, in control of his practice subject only to quality control and performance prescribed by the franchisor. The franchisee markets small to medium-size businesses located in an area which franchisee is able to service from his assigned territory.

Number of Franchisees: 93 in 23 States and 11 in Canada

In Business Since: 1965, franchising since 1975

Equity Capital Needed: The PBS franchise fee is $14,500 with an additional training fee. First year operating capital is also necessary.

Financial Assistance Available: Yes—through a local financial institution.

Training Provided: The franchisor offers an initial 3 week training program. The first week of this program consists of training in the PBS systems and client services with emphasis on establishing and working with a large number of monthly clients. The second week consists of training in the PBS marketing techniques and the third week is held in an established franchise working with the office owner, employees, clients and prospective clients. A fourth week will be in field training conducted by a home office representative.

Managerial Assistance Available: PBS offers 2 seminars annually. One is a thorough 3 day income tax seminar, the other is a 2 day update on PBS procedures and new marketing techniques. There are no charges for these seminars. A year round income tax answering service is also included. Special visits to each franchise office are made to examine additional needs of franchisee and to update PBS forms, tax procedures and marketing advice. Re-training and new employee training are also available at no cost to the franchisee.

Information Submitted: April 1990

PAK MAIL CENTERS OF AMERICA, INC.
3033 South Parker Road, Suite 1200
Aurora, Colorado 80014
John E. Kelly, President

Description of Operation: Franchisor of retail convenience centers offering residential and business consumers a wide variety of packaging, shipping, mail, communications and related services as well as small business support.

Number of Franchisees: 210 in 37 States

In Business Since: 1984

Equity Capital Needed: $62,750—$82,300

Financial Assistance Available: None

Training Provided: Complete training program (11 days total) including technical, managerial, advertising and promotion and accounting and bookkeeping. This includes classroom, on-location (on-the-job) training and store opening assistance.

Managerial Assistance Available: Market survey, site selection assistance, lease negotiation assistance, building construction guidance, graphics package, start-up equipment, training, grand opening program and toll free "owners" hotline. Advertising and promotional materials, technical support, management visits and consultation. Purchasing discounts, research and development, monthly newsletter, annual convention and seminars.

Information Submitted: May 1990

*PARCEL PLUS, INC.
170 Jennifer Road
Suite 260
Annapolis, Maryland 21401
David G. Campbell, President

Description of Operation: Complete mail and business support services for all consumers with special emphasis toward the small business person. Services include packaging, shipping, mailbox

rentals, voice mail, secretarial, copying, fax, laser printing, and graphics. Expanding mail room management program for new and growing companies.

Number of Franchisees: 30 in 8 States

In Business Since: 1986

Equity Capital Needed: $50,000 plus

Financial Assistance Available: Leasing program for equipment.

Training Provided: 2 weeks with 1 week in store.

Managerial Assistance Available: Continuous sales support with sales manual plus comprehensive operations manual.

Information Submitted: April 1990

PARSON-BISHOP SERVICES, INC.
7870 Camargo Road
Cincinnati, Ohio 45243
Lou Bishop, President

Description of Operation: P-B's executive franchisees market P-B's guaranteed effective, low-cost accounts receivable management, collection and cash flow improvement plans. These exclusive plans provide solutions to an ongoing, basic business need. More than 90 percent of businesses are prospects. Build equity from long-term, repeat customers. You must have a sales, marketing or management background and be qualified to call on upper level management in corporations of all sizes.

Number of Franchisees: 43 franchisees with 58 territories in 23 States.

In Business Since: 1973

Equity Capital Needed: $23,000—$29,500

Financial Assistance Available: None

Training Provided: 1 week classroom training at home office. Two training visits to franchisee's area in first 6 months. National and regional seminars quarterly. Continuous one on one support.

Managerial Assistance Available: Constant advertising, marketing and public relations support plus videos and manuals. Computerized franchise management system.

Information Submitted: April 1990

PDP, INC. (Professional Dynametric Programs)
400 West Highway, Suite 201
Box 5289
Woodland Park, Colorado 80866
Bruce M, Hubby, President

Description of Operation: PDP provides a statistically based system that promotes effective in-house management and employee development. Franchisees train and implement the PDP System into small, medium and large client organizations. Applications of the PDP System include identifying motivators and stressors, reducing stress, opening lines of communication, job matching and selection, conflict resolution, team building and job performance improvement.

Number of Franchisees: Total of 26. There are 21 in 12 States, 4 in Canada and 1 in Australia.

In Business Since: 1978

Equity Capital Needed: Franchise fee of $29,500 plus $5,000—$10,000 working capital.

Financial Assistance Available: None

Training Provided: 1 week at home office, with overflow handled on weekend if necessary. Includes overview, philosophy of PDP training, hands-on implementation, marketing, pricing and operation.

Managerial Assistance Available: Home office staff is readily available to offer support in areas of program operation, data interpretation and client implementation. PDP's in-house research department provides field representatives and clients with up to date research information. Annual conferences/and regional meetings promote effective sales presentations and system applications.

Information Submitted: April 1990

PENNYSAVER
80 Eighth Avenue
Suite 315
New York, New York 10011
Allan Horwitz, President

Description of Operation: A free publication offering advertisers total market coverage of the households and businesses throughout the community. Usually delivered by mail, the Pennysaver is recognized as the number 1 local shopping guide throughout the U.S. Because the Pennysaver has no wasted or duplicated circulation and little editorial, the advertiser receives more circulation, and at a lower cost than with any daily or weekly newspaper. Many Pennysavers have started out in garages and basements, and have grown into multi-million dollar publishing empires.

Number of Franchisees: Over 300 throughout the United States.

In Business Since: 1973

Equity Capital Needed: $19,900 with a money back guarantee

Financial Assistance Available: Yes. 80 percent financing to qualified applicants.

Training Provided: 8 days of classroom, in-field and on-site training for franchisees and their employees. Teaches how to sell Pennysaver advertising, acquire co-op ads from manufacturers, profit from barter, service accounts, design ads, layout the publication, distribution, and bookkeeping. Includes confidential operations manual, audio and video tapes, training films and video-taped role playing sessions.

Managerial Assistance Available: Continuous assistance provided by the home office. Includes our unique "head start" program to get you off to a flying start with $1,000 free printing, a direct mailing to your prospects by the company, and our special charter advertising program to produce immediate income for the franchisee and his advertisers. In addition, the company contributes $1,000 per each new franchise plus 12 percent of all royalty fees for direct mailings, sweepstakes, and other promotions, funded 100 percent by the company to produce greater profits for all franchisees.

Information Submitted: April 1990

PETRO BROKERAGE & SERVICE, LTD.
1445 Falmouth Road
Centerville, Massachusetts 02632
Attn: John Wargin

Description of Operation: National group exclusively servicing petroleum marketers in the following essential areas: company and site appraisals, sales and divestiture service, merger and acquisition specialists, and consultant and valuation opinions.

Number of Franchisees: 11 covering 22 States

In Business Since: 1982

Equity Capital Needed: $9,500-$25,000 plus working capital.

Financial Assistance Available: Notes can be extended for 10 months at 10.5 percent.

Training Provided: 4 days in-house, and approximately 4 days in territory. Additional on-site and call-in reinforcement.

Managerial Assistance Available: Sales, financial, and operational furnished, with constant support and update monthly.

Information Submitted: May 1990

PEYRON ASSOCIATES, INC.
P. O. Box 175
Sellersburg, Indiana 47172
Dan Peyron, President and CEO

Description of Operation: Company licenses others to prepare tax returns in leading department and discount stores nationally. Prefer people already in tax return prep business but will train others. Minimum investment $2,000, which includes location, furniture, equipment, signs, advertising, training, and complete warranty package; $1,000 for each additional location. No restrictions on area or number of locations. Company also offers electronic filing and refund loans nationally. Sub franchising permitted but not required.

Number of Franchisees: 400 units in about 30 States

In Business Since: 1960

Equity Capital Needed: Minimum $500

Financial Assistance Available: None

Training Provided: Locally by any tax return prep school, college, course, etc.

Managerial Assistance Available: Monthly newsletters for tax return prepared the year round plus separate tax newsletter for clients, warranty back up for mistakes, audits, technical assistance on tax matters, etc. Also pay operators for audit work covered under warranty.

Information Submitted: May 1990

PILOT AIR FREIGHT CORPORATION
Route 352
P. O. Box 97
Lima, Pennsylvania 19037
John J. Edwards, President

Description of Operation: Pilot provides the service of handling air freight shipping requirements of their customers both domestically and internationally.

Number of Franchisees: 70 in 29 States, Canada and Puerto Rico.

In Business Since: 1970

Equity Capital Needed: $10,000-$30,000 determined by market.

Financial Assistance Available: None

Training Provided: 2 weeks classroom, Pilot headquarters, with emphasis on operation, customer service, sales and accounting procedures.

Managerial Assistance Available: Ongoing communications with corporate headquarters and visits by Pilot regional managers.

Information Submitted: May 1990

P.K.G.'S, INC.
4394 Glendale-Milford Road
Cincinnati, Ohio 45242
Thomas R. Sizer, President

Description of Operation: P.K.G.'s is an established and nationally recognized industry leader in a unique service business. P.K.G.'s provides both retail and commercial packaging and shipping services for customers wanting to pack and ship anything anywhere in the world. This proven concept provides a "hassle-free" retail store environment for sending an overnight letter or a baby grand piano. Our pick-up services for both retail and commercial/industrial customers provides for a total full service packaging and shipping program.

Number of Franchisees: 75 in 20 States.

In Business Since: 1983

Equity Capital Needed: Approximately $47,765

Financial Assistance Available: Yes—Financing available to qualified individuals through equipment and cabinetry leasing program.

Training Provided: P.K.G.'s provides each franchisee with a three phase training program. Initial training phase is a franchise orientation and development program. Second phase is a comprehensive multi-media hands-on training program for retail store owners, managers, and employees consisting of business operational instructions, franchisors' objectives, policies and procedures, utilization of all equipment and packaging technology involved in the operation of the franchise business. Extensive training in packaging, shipping, and customer service, marketing and advertising. Phase three involves in-store training and commercial sales and marketing on site in franchise owners retail location.

Managerial Assistance Available: P.K.G.'s provides each franchisee with field operations consultation and assistance on a continuing basis including demo site analysis, site selection, lease negotiations, turnkey store set-up and development, marketing and advertising programming and planning, operations planning, and routine field visits.

Information Submitted: April 1990

PNS, INC.
P. O. Box 428
Racine, Wisconsin 53401
Rexford M. Rossi, President

Description of Operation: PNS, Inc., (Pack'N Ship and Packy the Shipper) is a franchisor of local packing and shipping locations specializing in parcel post packages for the general public and small business. Generally this is an addendum to a retail or wholesale operation that adds this service to build additional in-store traffic and create extra cash sales.

Number of Franchisees: Over 1,200 in 48 States

In Business Since: 1981

Equity Capital Needed: $995-$1,295

Financial Assistance Available: Investment includes materials, equipment and introducing the program; no other funds are necessary except to replace supplies as needed.

Training Provided: Training on franchisee's premises by trained representative including audio-visual cassettes and operations manual.

Managerial Assistance Available: Periodic calls by representative—WATS line available for information on operations—strong support from home office for record maintenance and claim activity. A continuous co-op program instituted.

Information Submitted: May 1990

PONY MAILBOX AND BUSINESS CENTER, INC.
13110 Northeast 177th Place
Woodinville, Washington 98072
Robert E. Howell, President

Description of Operation: A commercial mail and shipping center combined with business services. A franchise offers rental of mailboxes, UPS, airborne, voice mail, copying, word processing (optional) and other services for the convenience of customers. Integration of local services is allowed by the franchisor.

Number of Franchisees: 16 franchises coast to coast including Florida, Tennessee, New Jersey, Washington and Illinois.

In Business Since: 1986

Equity Capital Needed: $46,000-$56,000 is necessary.

Financial Assistance Available: Franchisor does not provide financing. The equity capital purchases all the necessary equipment and supplies to begin operations. Estimated costs for leasehold improvements are included in the equity capital needed by the franchisee. Franchisee must arrange his or her own financing, if needed.

Training Provided: Intensive but personalized 3-4 day mandatory training course for all new franchisees. Course provided at home office and conducted by corporate officers who operate their own Pony Mailbox and Business Center. Refresher course given at no cost upon request of franchisee.

Managerial Assistance Available: Pony Mailbox and Business Center provides continual advisory assistance for the life of the franchise on the services offered by a franchisee and the marketing of the services. Franchisor furnishes manuals on operations; forms and directions are provided. Franchisor offers advisory assistance for new services introduced by franchisor and approved

services desired by the franchisee to meet local market conditions. Franchisor assists with location advice, layout and design of the franchise business.

Information Submitted: April 1990

POSTALANNEX+ SERVICE CENTERS
9050 Friars Road
Suite 400
San Diego, California 92108
Ralph Boden, Director of Franchise Development

Description of Operation: Postal, parcel, business and communications services. Complete postal, packaging, and parcel shipping services, facsimile, electronic funds transfer, copy and high speed duplicating, office and packaging supplies.

Number of Franchisees: 80 franchised outlets in California, Florida, Nevada, Oregon and Pennsylvania.

In Business Since: 1985, franchising since 1986

Equity Capital Needed: $55,000-$65,000 approximate turnkey cost including $19,500 franchise fee, site selection, lease negotiations, plans and training. Equipment leases available.

Financial Assistance Available: None

Training Provided: 1 week of classroom training and 1 week in-store training.

Managerial Assistance Available: Complete support staff to assist with operations, marketing, merchandising and accounting.

Information Submitted: April 1990

POWER DYNAMICS INTERNATIONAL
Box 498
Ranson, West Virginia 25438
F. J. Franke

Description of Operation: PDI operates as energy consultants to industry.

Number of Franchisees: 7 in 3 States.

In Business Since: 1989

Equity Capital Needed: $2,500

Financial Assistance Available: None

Training Provided: Field training and manual for home study.

Managerial Assistance Available: Continuous guidance by company when needed, calls via telephone and special visits when and as conditions require.

Information Submitted: April 1990

PRINCETON ENERGY PARTNERS, INC.
2221 Stackhouse Drive
Yardley, Pennsylvania 19067
David M. Brown, President

Description of Operation: Market comfort improvement and energy savings to the home owner and new construction markets and deliver an instrumented energy analysis and retrofitting service based on technology originally developed at Princeton University under a U.S. Department of Energy grant.

Number of Franchisees: 8 in Pennsylvania, New York and Minnesota.

In Business Since: 1981

Equity Capital Needed: $45,000 to $77,000

Financial Assistance Available: None

Training Provided: 1 week intensive training in Princeton, New Jersey, followed by a week of on-the-job training with other franchisees and a 3 day training at franchisee's location, followed a month later by a 2 day training at franchisee's location. Training covers all technical and marketing aspects of delivering instrumented energy analysis and retrofitting services in residential building markets.

Managerial Assistance Available: P.E.P. provides ongoing technical, marketing, and managerial assistance for the life of the franchise through its home office and field representatives. P.E.P. sponsors franchisee meetings and sponsors market development on behalf of franchisees. P.E.P. technical staff is closely connected to the residential energy research community.

Information Submitted: May 1990

PRIORITY MANAGEMENT SYSTEMS, INC.
500 108th Avenue, NE
Suite 1740
Bellevue, Washington 98053
Tee Houston-Aldridge, Manager, Franchise Marketing

Description of Operation: Priority Management is the one management training franchise in North America. Franchisees work with busy professionals and instruct them in the development of personal effectiveness skills.

Number of Franchisees: 125 in 38 States, 48 in Canada, 44 international in 7 countries.

In Business Since: 1984

Equity Capital Needed: $35,000 including franchise fee.

Financial Assistance Available: None

Training Provided: 2 weeks intensive training in the "Priority Management" program, 6 days in-house plus 1 week in field. Minimum 3 follow-up training sessions each year.

Managerial Assistance Available: Teach franchisee the "Priority Management" program. Sales techniques, presentation skills, marketing methods, bookkeeping, general business management skills. Work with franchisee on sales calls, conduct (at franchisee's request) first 2 workshops.

Information Submitted: April 1990

*PROFORMA, INC.
4705 Van Epps Road
Cleveland, Ohio 44131
John Campbell, Director of Franchise Development

Description of Operation: Business products. Distributors of business forms, commercial printing, office supplies, computer supplies. This is not a quick print shop or retail operation.

Number of Franchisees: 105 in 27 States

In Business Since: 1978, franchising started 1985

Equity Capital Needed: $75,000-$100,000

Financial Assistance Available: None

Training Provided: 1 week intensive training program covering industry/product knowledge and selling skills, ongoing field support.

Managerial Assistance Available: Franchise owner does not need to hire any administrative employees because most administrative functions are performed by franchisor. Franchisor answers franchisee's telephone (toll free number), generates billings, does computer input, logs cash receipts, and generates monthly business reports. Continuous managerial advice is available from an experienced team of professionals in selling, product knowledge, manufacturer sourcing, and administration.

Information Submitted: May 1990

PROPERTY DAMAGE APPRAISERS, INC.
P. O. Box 9230
Fort Worth, Texas 76107
John Tate, Vice President-Franchise Operations

Description of Operation: Property Damage Appraisers, Inc., grants franchises to highly qualified automobile damage appraisers in cities with sufficient business potential to provide a good income for the franchisee.

Number of Franchisees: 185 in all States except Montana, South Dakota, and Wyoming.

In Business Since: 1963

Equity Capital Needed: $5,000-$15,000

Financial Assistance Available: None. Property Damage Appraisers does not sell franchises. We provide all forms, procedure manual, advertising materials and marketing service. Equity capital required is needed to purchase office equipment, automobile, insurance, etc., necessary to start a business.

Training Provided: No formal training program is provided as only experienced appraisers are considered.

Managerial Assistance Available: Through a staff of regional managers we provide at least 2 weeks of intensive marketing support when an office opens. A bookkeeping system is provided at no cost to franchisee and is installed by a company accounting representative. Periodic visits are made by regional managers to market services of all franchisees.

Information Submitted: April 1990

PROPERTY INSPECTION SERVICE
1741 Saratoga Avenue
Suite 106
San Jose, California 95129
Ben Vitcov, President

Description of Operation: Property Inspection Service provides residential building inspections for the purpose of giving the prospective buyer a full disclosure of the structural and mechanical condition of the property. The inspection includes a roof to foundation inspection and the electrical, plumbing and heating systems.

Number of Franchisees: 11 in California

In Business Since: 1980

Equity Capital Needed: $50,000

Financial Assistance Available: None

Training Provided: Full training for field inspector and one office person. Training is performed at our San Jose location and includes 30 days of actual operational experience.

Managerial Assistance Available: Property Inspection Service provides all computer software including updates, all operational manuals and forms. A dynamic statewide marketing program and continuing education program is also provided to all franchises.

Information Submitted: April 1990

PROVE CONSUMER REPORTING SERVICES
A Division of the Taylor Group
4806 Shelly Drive
Wilmington, North Carolina 28405
Lorraine Taylor, President

Description of Operation: Since 1974, Prove Mystery Shoppers have been monitoring the quality of service employees provide patrons and provide an operations review for management along with suggestions and ideas on how to improve customer service. Training seminars provided on site for clients in all customer related areas.

Number of Franchisees: 35 franchisees

In Business Since: 1974

Equity Capital Needed: Franchise fees from $14,500 to $39,500.

Financial Assistance Available: To qualified buyers.

Training Provided: 10 day intensive training program, consists of classroom and field training. Includes operational and training manuals, video and audio aids.

Managerial Assistance Available: Additional and ongoing training and updates provided periodically or upon request.

Information Submitted: April 1990

PROVENTURE, INC.
79 Parkingway, Box 7169
Quincy, Massachusetts 02169
Leo F. Meady, Chairman

Description of Operation: Professional business brokers—specializing in the listing and sale of medium priced going businesses. Also represent franchise companies in the sale and location of their franchised units.

Number of Franchisees: 6 plus 1 company-owned in Massachusetts and New Jersey. Seeking franchisees for all areas of the U.S.

In Business Since: 1979

Equity Capital Needed: $15,000 franchise fee plus about $30,000 for working capital.

Financial Assistance Available: None

Training Provided: Intensive classroom training program for 1 week in Quincy, followed by on-the-job training in franchisee's own office. Assistance offered in recruiting and training commissioned sales staff. ProVENTURE prefers that franchisees (or their associates) have real estate licenses, or they obtain one as soon as possible.

Managerial Assistance Available: Continued training and management assistance for all franchised units. Parent company coordinates the distribution of "VENTURElist" to all offices. "VENTURElist" contains all the listings of all local offices. Participating franchisees share proportionally in the sale of business listed by one office and sold by another.

Information Submitted: May 1990

REALTY COUNSEL
2235 Crosby Herald Road
Lincoln, California 95648
D. LeMoine Bond, President

Description of Operation: Realty Counsel franchisees are independently practicing general real estate brokers who are interfacing single agency, flat fee consultive brokerage techniques as an alternative to the consumer over the traditional commission methods. Regional "broker consultant" licensing is selectively available to experienced brokers. Both non-contingent fee and contingent fee methods are used within the realty counsel sales methods.

Number of Franchisees: 8 in California

In Business Since: 1979

Equity Capital Needed: $8,500 minimum broker consultant license, $1,000 minimum initial fee for franchisee. No other projections are made. 5 percent royalty—$5,000 maximum per year.

Financial Assistance Available: Franchise financing available.

Training Provided: Broker reorientation, plus unlimited management consultation and support. No rookie recruiting or freshman training for salesmen. Only broker and franchisee training for the client related consultive broker. Periodic technical sessions and support media and personal telephone consultation. Video franchise and client sales presentation. Operations manuals and contracts.

Managerial Assistance Available: Continuous brokerage management assistance for the duration of the franchise. Advertising media packages, referrals. Because of the nature and degree of sophistication required of a Realty Counsel, the firm recommends university and college post graduate training plus certain approved certification and continuing education of the bar and realty professions.

Information Submitted: May 1990

*RECOGNITION EXPRESS INTERNATIONAL, LTD.
31726 Rancho Viejo Road
Suite 115
San Juan Capistrano, California 92675
Dennis Hunt, President

Description of Operation: Recognition Express franchise owners manufacture and sell corporate recognition and specialty advertising products—personalized badges, nameplates, plaques, awards, office signage, buttons, lapel pins, to name a few. Recognition Express is the oldest and largest chain of full service recognition shops. Our owners have been providing service to medium and large corporations. Our customers include Hilton Hotels, Century 21 Real Estate, Baskin Robbins, Rotary, Mary Kay Cosmetics, etc. Recognition Express dealers operate from a commercial location. Our shops feature state-of-the-art showrooms and do light manufacturing with the latest technology including computer engraving, automatic hot stamping, and automatic pinning machines. In addition, other items are offered that are purchased from approved trade suppliers.

Number of Franchisees: 70 throughout the U.S. and in 9 countries.

In Business Since: Founder began manufacturing name badges in 1972. BadgeMan franchises were first awarded in 1974 to part time, homebased owners who manufactured name badges only. Recognition express units tested since 1981, franchised since 1983.

Equity Capital Needed: $30,000

Financial Assistance Available: A total investment of $75,000 to $100,000 is needed to cover opening inventory, equipment, franchise fee, training costs, start-up promotion and advertising, as well as working capital. Financing can be arranged.

Training Provided: An intensive training course is conducted for the new owner at the home office. A field development person will help you in your new shop during opening. He will insure that you are capable of developing your business properly.

Managerial Assistance Available: Complete ongoing support and managerial assistance in all phases of the business.

Information Submitted: May 1990

RELIABLE BUSINESS SYSTEMS, INC.
19 Ransom Road
Newton, Massachusetts 02159
M. Michael Licker, President

Description of Operation: Firm publishes the Reliable Business and Tax Service System, a service designed to meet the needs of all businesses, offering them a bookkeeping system that complies with all Federal and State tax laws, together with an advisory service.

Number of Franchisees: 3 in Vermont and Massachusetts

In Business Since: 1955

Equity Capital Needed: $1,950

Financial Assistance Available: None

Training Provided: 1 week in-the-field training by another experienced distributor and further training at the home office if needed; continuous upgrading of distributor's knowledge.

Managerial Assistance Available: Continuous flow of new material; home office consultation available on an unlimited and continuous basis. Close contact with distributor maintained. Additional help regarding tax matters for client when called upon through home office accounting tax staff.

Information Submitted: May 1990

ROOM-MATE REFERRAL SERVICE CENTERS, INC.
P. O. Box 760328
Oklahoma City, Oklahoma 73176-0328
Florence S. Cook, President

Description of Operation: Room-Mate Referral Service Center is a service company that handles the placement of persons as roommates, for economic and a variety of other needs.

Number of Franchisees: 37 in Texas, Oklahoma, Pennsylvania, California and Georgia.

In Business Since: 1979

Equity Capital Needed: $3,500 to $30,000

Financial Assistance Available: Our franchise fee is determined by the population of the franchise area. The franchise can be from $7,500 to $45,000. We would carry one-third of the franchise fee on a promissory note.

Training Provided: We have a 3-1/2 day training session at the home office. We also help the franchisee find the right location, help with grand opening, and give ongoing assistance.

Managerial Assistance Available: We give continuous assistance for the life of the franchise. We assist with new advertising ideas and training on new services that we are adding. We are always available to solve any problems that may come up.

Information Submitted: April 1990

*SARA CARE FRANCHISE CORPORATION
1612 Lee Trevino
Suite 8
El Paso, Texas 79936

Description of Operation: Sales of Sara Care Service franchise—specializing in temporary companion aand home support personnel. Provides companion care, sleepovers, baby/child sitters, house sitters, hospital sitters, pet sitters, plant/garden sitters, drop-ins (companion, teens, pets, house) and sub-contracting services to all home health agencies and hospitals. We pride ourselves in being the largest franchisor of specialized services in the United States and the first company specifically organized to concentrate in the field of home support personnel.

Number of Franchisees: 46 in 18 States

In Business Since: 1978, franchising since 1983.

Equity Capital Needed: Capital requirement about $48,000.

Financial Assistance Available: None

Training Provided: A 5-business day intensive management training program at corporate headquarters. Training will continue even after the opening of your office to sharpen your skills and to make certain that your new business is operating as efficiently as possible. You even have the option of 1 week of on-site training at your location.

Managerial Assistance Available: You will have an effective support system behind you at corporate headquarters every step of the way. You will receive instructions and constant updates in the use of all Sara Care manuals and forms in addition to training in recruiting, interviewing, and applicant processing techniques as well as detailed training and handling customer requirements.

Information Submitted: May 1990

SELECTRA-DATE CORPORATION
2175 Lemoine Avenue
Ft. Lee, New Jersey 07024
Robert Friedman, President

Description of Operation: Computer-dating has been around since Art Linkletter started playing matching games with a Univac Computer in the late fifties. But that was just for laughs. Today it's for love and money, with a score of computer-dating firms throughout the country reporting brisk business. Selectra-Date, one of the pioneers, now offers a complete turnkey package that makes it possible for any reputable individual with a sound business or professional background to enter this fascinating work. Since all computer processing is handled entirely by the company, no technical knowledge is required.

Number of Franchisees: 9 in 10 States

In Business Since: 1967, oldest existing franchise operational since 1969

Equity Capital Needed: $7,000 to $10,000

Financial Assistance Available: The total required investment for promotional material, initial advertising, franchise fee, and forms and stationery is $9,000, of which Selectra-Date will finance $3,500 for qualified franchisees. In addition the franchisee should have sufficient capital to adequately equip his office and to see him through the first 30 days of operation.

Training Provided: A full-time Selectra-Date executive thoroughly trains each franchisee in all phases of the business during the first week he is in operation.

Managerial Assistance Available: Selectra-Date furnishes continuing individual guidance and support in all phases of the franchisee's operation.

Information Submitted: April 1990

SHIPPING CONNECTION, INC.
7220 West Jefferson Avenue, Suite 305
Denver, Colorado 80235
Betty Russotti, Vice President

Description of Operation: Shipping Connection is a retail convenience center that provides complete packaging and shipping services to the general public. Dealing with both business and individuals you can literally ship any item, any size, any place in the world. This business was founded by ex-United Parcel Service management personnel who will provide you with the packaging and shipping techniques recommended by the NSTC. The franchise locations also offer fax service, copies, giftwrapping and the sale of all types of packaging materials.

Number of Franchisees: 18 in Colorado, Kansas, Ohio, Minnesota, New Jersey, North Carolina plus 1 company-owned.

In Business Since: 1982; franchising since January 1987

Equity Capital Needed: $32,000-$46,000 (includes $14,500 franchise fee plus working capital).

Financial Assistance Available: Lease options on $7,000 in equipment, WAC.

Training Provided: An extensive 2 week training program provided at National Headquarters in Littleton, Colorado, one week on site.

Managerial Assistance Available: Site selection and lease negotiation assistance. Decor and equipment package. Franchisee is set up with negotiated discounts from suppliers and freight carriers. Co-op advertising program, continual follow-up and ongoing support, detailed operations manual.

Information Submitted: May 1990

SIGNS BY TOMORROW-USA, INC.
10730 Baltimore Avenue
Beltsville, Maryland 20705
Joseph E. McGuinness

Description of Operation: One day custom retail sign shops utilizing computer technology.

Number of Franchisees: 21 (includes 2 company-owned)

In Business Since: 1986

Equity Capital Needed: $85,000-$95,000

Financial Assistance Available: Equipment leasing plan is available.

Training Provided: 4 weeks, 2 in training center and 2 on location.

Managerial Assistance Available: Signs By Tomorrow offers a complete initial and ongoing training and support program.

Information Submitted: June 1990

THE SHIPPING DEPARTMENT, INC.
5880 Siegen Lane, Suite G
Baton Rouge, Louisiana 70809
Robert X. Hafele, President

Description of Operation: THE SHIPPING DEPT., INC. is structured to service a virtually untapped market in the moving business. Major movers do not like to handle moves under 2,100 lbs. The U.S. mail and UPS will not ship packages over 70 lbs. Until now, apartment dwellers, students, parents sending furniture to children, etc., had no economical way to move their things. THE SHIPPING DEPT., INC. fills the gap by expertly packing and shipping these goods via commercial carrier nationwide or worldwide. THE SHIPPING DEPT., INC. is the Small Load Specialist.

Number of Franchisees: 2 in 2 States

In Business Since: 1985

Equity Capital Needed: $26,000

Financial Assistance Available: None

Training Provided: THE SHIPPING DEPT., INC. provides an intensive mandatory course to franchisee or approved manager for a minimum of 2 weeks at our Baton Rouge facility. Follow-up help is also furnished.

Managerial Assistance Available: Help is provided to set up trucking and supply contracts. Special equipment, which we have developed, is available. Complete operating manuals are provided. Accounting and advertising material will be provided.

Information Submitted: April 1990

THE SIGNERY CORPORATION
614 West 5th Avenue
Naperville, Illinois 60563
Richard Gretz, President

Description of Operation: The Signery prompt service sign centers offer computer-generated signs and lettering from an attractive retail setting with reasonable store hours. No artistic/graphic design experience required. Ideal for husband and wife teams or multiple unit development.

Number of Franchisees: 30 in 6 States

In Business Since: 1986

Equity Capital Needed: $45,000-$85,000

Financial Assistance Available: The Signery offers a national equipment and supplies leasing program, and will provide assistance in the development of business plans.

Training Provided: Complete and extensive classroom and in-store training at corporate headquarters in Naperville, Illinois, lasting 3 weeks. Ongoing support and continued training from field personnel for life of agreement.

Managerial Assistance Available: Through a host of services including seminars, newsletters, in-store visits, and business planning meetings. The Signery provides ongoing support in creative design, profitable and effective business management, and advertising/marketing.

Information Submitted: April 1990

*SIGN EXPRESS
Clark Corporate Park
6 Clarke Circle
P. O. Box 309
Bethel, Connecticut 06801
Laurie Wright, Vice President

Description of Operation: Company offers complete sign center that offers 24-hour service. Signs are made by a signmaking computer and scanner, using 3M graphic materials, with complete design functions. Signs include indoor and outdoor signs, vehicle lettering, magnetic signs, banners, business signs, trade show exhibits, illuminated signs, etc. No prior experience is required.

Number of Franchisees: 22 in 10 States; 1 in Mexico

In Business Since: 1985, franchising since 1988

Equity Capital Needed: $50,000

Financial Assistance Available: Company provides full equipment financing.

Training Provided: 3 weeks comprehensive training in sign center operations, full business and marketing training; 2 weeks at company headquarters; up to 1 additional week on location with owner.

Managerial Assistance Available: Regular on-site visits to sign center owners; toll-free assistance, newsletters, conferences and workshops.

Information Submitted: May 1990

*SIGN STOP, INC.
256 Post Road West
Westport, Connecticut 06880
John Oudheusden, President

Description of Operation: Strong customer demand and new technology creates the opportunity to market high quality custom signs to small businesses. Operating from a store location and using computer-generated vinyl lettering, Sign Stop fabricates custom signs, trade exhibits, banners, graphs and charts, backlit awnings, and lettering for vans, trucks, and boats.

Number of Franchisees: 17 in the Northeast

In Business Since: 1985

Equity Capital Needed: $66,800

Financial Assistance Available: Independent company offers equipment lease.

Training Provided: No experience is necessary. We will train you, get you located and started, continue with on-site visits, and provide ongoing marketing and advertising assistance.

Managerial Assistance Available: Sign Stop offers ongoing marketing and advertising assistance, on-site visits, operations manuals, seminars and newsletters.

Information Submitted: April 1990

SIGN-TIFIC
175 East Fifth Street, Suite 700
St. Paul, Minnesota 55101
Daniel F. Gilroy, Vice President

Description of Operation: Azimuth Corporation is in the business of organizing the instant sign distribution channel through company and franchise instant sign retail stores (SIGN-TIFIC). These stores provide quality signs, posters and banners quickly and inexpensively.

Number of Franchisees: First franchises to be offered in April of 1990. Currently running 5 company stores, plus 3 prototype stores being run by a director of the company.

In Business Since: 1986

Equity Capital Needed: $85,000 plus working capital.

Financial Assistance Available: None

Training Provided: Complete training provided in Corporate Training Center. 4 weeks for Graphic Artists; 2 weeks for franchisee, store manager and production technician.

Managerial Assistance Available: SIGN-TIFIC provides continuing management, advertising, marketing and field support.

Information Submitted: April 1990

*SMI INTERNATIONAL, INC.
(SUCCESS MOTIVATION INSTITUTE, INC.)
1600 Lake Air Drive
Waco, Texas 76710
James Sirbasku

Description of Operation: The company's international franchise organization markets specialized management, sales, and personal development programs to individuals, companies, governments, and other organizations. Materials are printed and recorded, using modern learning methods, personal goal setting, and management by objective techniques.

Number of Franchisees: Approximately 2,000 in 50 States and 26 foreign countries.

In Business Since: 1960

Equity Capital Needed: $20,000

Financial Assistance Available: Financial assistance available.

Training Provided: Complete training program in printed and recorded form furnished with initial investment; continuous home office sales training and sales management seminars available monthly. Field sales training also available in many areas.

Managerial Assistance Available: Continuous sales consultant assistance provided by home office to distributors through use of monthly mailings, telephone and prompt response to mail communications.

Information Submitted: April 1990

SNC TELECOM PROBLEM SOLVERS
101 West Waukau Avenue
Oshkosh, Wisconsin 54901
Wally Petersen

Description of Operation: Providing sales, installation and consultation services to businesses with telecommunication problems. Customers include telephone and electric power utilities, interconnects and businesses with their own computer, telephone and data equipment. Proven product line with 15 year sales history. Only source for many items. Exclusive territories. Individual and master franchises available.

Number of Franchisees: 2 in Texas

In Business Since: 1986

Equity Capital Needed: $18,500-$47,400

Financial Assistance Available: None

Training Provided: Training and support provided by franchisor: intensive 8 day managerial, sales and technical training at corporate headquarters plus 5 days in-market start-up assistance. Comprehensive operations manual.

Managerial Assistance Available: Continuing technical support and seminars.

Information Submitted: May 1990

SOUND TRACKS RECORDING STUDIO, INC.
424 Parkway
Sevierville, Tennessee 37862
Rick Pemberton, President

Description of Operation: Sound Tracks allows the general public to record their voices on over 300 pre-recorded tapes. They can do audio or video productions in many of our studios across the United States.

Number of Franchisees: 30 in 14 States

In Business Since: 1984

Equity Capital Needed: Approximately $60,000. $40,000 minimum.

Financial Assistance Available: Finance of hard cost, such as equipment.

Training Provided: At the franchisee's location—1 week.

Managerial Assistance Available: At the franchisee's location—1 week.

Information Submitted: May 1990

SOUTHWEST PROMOTIONAL CORPORATION
P. O. Box 81023
San Diego, California 92138
Jerry Nesler, President

Description of Operation: SouthWest Promotional Corporation offers a proofs-of-purchase, advertising and marketing plan for franchisees to sell to radio, television and cable TV stations or to operate themselves. A franchisee's territory may include an area, one state, or more. The franchisee, besides receiving cash income from each station's advertising sales through the marketing plan, in addition receives a number of broadcast commercial spot announcements, as additional payment, with each station signed. The "network" of spot announcements may be sold to advertisers, by the franchisee, for additional franchisee income or barter. Potential franchisees may be multi-station representatives, experienced men and women advertising sales representatives or other experienced media sales persons. Telephone: 619/588-0664.

Number of Franchisees: 15 in the West

In Business Since: 1970—franchising since 1975

Equity Capital Needed: $10,000 area. Equity capital required for a territory is separately negotiated according to size and potential.

Financial Assistance Available: Yes

Training Provided: 2 weeks training in franchisee's own area or territory. Training by an experienced existing franchisee or by the franchisor. Also, additional assistance with any franchisee advertising sales through franchisor's existing account list and from account lists of other existing franchisees.

Managerial Assistance Available: Continual assistance for the life of the franchise.

Information Submitted: April 1990

SPEEDI-SIGN, INC.
P. O. Box 2882, 9 N. Fahm Street
Savannah, Georgia 31402
Karen Melton, Marketing Director

Description of Operation: Computerized sign shop chain offering paper and vinyl signs to businesses, institutions, government agencies, and individuals. Also offers add-on packages for screen-printing and sandblasting.

Number of Franchisees: 12 (including 4 company locations).

In Business Since: 1987

Equity Capital Needed: $30,000-$80,000

Financial Assistance Available: None

Training Provided: 1 week intensive classroom training in shop management, layout and design, marketing, advertising and accounting. 1 week in-store (hands-on) training in company stores. On-site assistance during opening phase as needed. Manuals provided.

Managerial Assistance Available: Optional ongoing support program available through monthly dues.

Information Submitted: April 1990

STORK NEWS OF AMERICA
6537 Raeford Road
Fayetteville, North Carolina 28304
John Nelson, Franchise Director

Description of Operation: Newborn announcement service. Announce new arrivals by large stork in front yard, office or any location desired by parents, grandparents, friends, etc. Also retail other pre-birth products, stork wiring in F.T.D. fashion.

Number of Franchisees: 78 in 28 States and Canada

In Business Since: 1984

Equity Capital Needed: $5,000

Financial Assistance Available: None

Training Provided: Book, telephone and visit the headquarters, newsletter.

Managerial Assistance Available: Assistance ongoing to help develop business.

Information Submitted: May 1990

STUFFIT COMPANY, INC.
12450 Automobile Boulevard
Clearwater, Florida 33520
Regina Anderson

Description of Operation: Co-operative direct mail advertising program.

Number of Franchisees: 17 in Florida, Louisiana, Alabama and New Jersey

In Business Since: 1978

Equity Capital Needed: $25,000

Financial Assistance Available: None

Training Provided: 1 week of training in plant for systems, product knowledge, and sales techniques. One week of training in the field to set up office procedures and make sales calls.

Managerial Assistance Available: Ongoing assistance to franchisees to help them with training and development of their geographical area.

Information Submitted: May 1990

SUPER COUPS
180 Bodwell Street
Avon, Massachusetts 02322
Scott Berry, President

Description of Operation: Super Coups franchises service local retailers and contractors by mailing money saving coupons to local residents. Corporate headquarters handles all manufacturing. Franchises' responsibilities include sales and service of local and regional advertisers and management of accounts and collection of payments due. Each protected territory totals 60,000 homes.

Number of Franchisees: 71 in 13 States

In Business Since: 1982

Financial Assistance Available: In addition to training, start-up manuals, samples, etc., mailings to the first 20,000 homes are free of charge. This provides the new owner with positive cash flow from the beginning.

Training Provided: Intensive 1 week training at corporate headquarters and field training of 1 week precede our ongoing education, which addresses the specific details an owner needs to know on a day-to-day basis to be successful in the field of co-operative direct mail advertising.

Managerial Assistance Available: Super Coups provides a wide range of managerial and technical assistance via 800 phone lines, meetings, franchise conferences, newsletter and bulletins. Coverage includes sales, marketing, bookkeeping, accounting, operations, recruitment, training, finance, and advertising layouts and design, as well as specific problem identification and solution forums.

Information Submitted: April 1990

TAX MAN, INC.
674 Massachusetts Avenue
Cambridge, Massachusetts 02139
Robert G. Murray, President

Description of Operation: Preparation of individual income tax returns. Interested in franchisees in New England Only.

Number of Franchisees: 8 in Massachusetts plus 15 company-owned units.

In Business Since: 1967

Equity Capital Needed: $4,500 minimum plus means of support for first 2 years.

Financial Assistance Available: Advertising support. Bookkeeping income opportunity for rest of year.

Training Provided: Tax preparation training (8 weeks). Tax office management training (3 days).

Managerial Assistance Available: Complete tax advice, management assistance, site selection, advertising and marketing.

Information Submitted: May 1990

TAX OFFICES OF AMERICA
Box 4098
Waterville, Connecticut 06714
Gregg Nolan, Franchise Director

Description of Operation: Income tax preparation for individuals and small businesses. Thorough training program, exclusive territories. Estate planning and business consulting services.

Number of Franchisees: 15

In Business Since: 1966

Equity Capital Needed: Approximately $12,000 plus $7,500 working capital.

Financial Assistance Available: Financing arranged through Horizons of America, Inc., parent company.

Training Provided: About 2 weeks training provided at Waterbury headquarters, 2 weeks at franchisee's location, plus a mail order course. If available in franchisee's area the company pays all expenses to a special training course set up by a nationally known organization.

Managerial Assistance Available: Company always available for counseling, plus on-site office organization.

Information Submitted: May 1990

THE TAYLOR REVIEW
A Division of the TAYLOR GROUP
4806 Shelly Drive
Wilmington, North Carolina 28405
Franklin E. Taylor, President

Description of Operation: Non-electronic employment verification services, which include vertification of employment history, educational background, criminal and public records review, attitude surveys toward honesty, drugs, alcohol and supervision, and skills testing to determine level of competency. In addition, tenant vertification for real estate companies.

Number of Franchisees: 5 franchisees

In Business Since: 1976

Equity Capital Needed: Franchise fee $7,500.

Financial Assistance Available: To qualified buyers.

Training Provided: 1 week intensive training at franchisor's headquarters. Training includes marketing, test administration, interviewing techniques (from polygraph theories), scoring procedures, vertification procedures, semi-annual national franchise advisory council conferences, ongoing on-line support.

Managerial Assistance Available: Additional and ongoing training and updates provided periodically or upon request.

Information Submitted: April 1990

TOTE-A-SHOWER, INC.
Rt. 1, Box 172
Toledo, Illinois 62468
Kathy Black, President

Description of Operation: Tote-A-Shower offers a unique at-home franchise business. Our franchisees may work out of their homes to rent large, special occasion greeting cards, and provide baby and bridal showers and birthday party services. Each franchisee is guaranteed an exclusive territory.

Number of Franchisees: 9 in Illinois, 3 in Indiana

In Business Since: 1985

Equity Capital Needed: $2,000

Financial Assistance Available: None

Training Provided: 1 day program plus VCR tape and training manual.

Managerial Assistance Available: Each new franchisee is given written instructions as well as on-the-spot assistance from an experienced franchisee owner at the first showing and during the first party.

Information Submitted: May 1990

TRANSFORMATIONAL TECHNOLOGIES
300 Drakes Landing Road, Suite 190
Greenbrae, California 94904
Mike McMaster, President

Description of Operation: Management consulting, management training and related organizational services.

Number of Franchisees: 50 in the United States, Canada and Europe.

In Business Since: 1984

Equity Capital Needed: $20,000 initial fee plus 3 months operating capital (variable).

Financial Assistance Available: None

59

Training Provided: 2 day orientation, 5 day program/technology training, 3 day advanced training program, 2 day business skills workshop, 3 days sales training, 240 hours video tape training.

Managerial Assistance Available: On-call coaching, site review, and 1 meeting annually for purpose of technical development.

Information Submitted: May 1990

TRAVEL MAGAZINE, INC.
2482 Lorrie Drive
P. O. Box 669051
Marietta, Georgia 30066
W. Ken Acree, Vice President

Description of Operation: Dining/entertainment/shopping guide providing information of interest to travelers. Revenue derived from advertising sold. *TV-Travel* is furnished free to hotels, who place it in their guest rooms for use by their guests. Low overhead; can operate from home; top earnings potential.

Number of Franchisees: 1 company owned unit.

In Business Since: 1983, franchising since 1987

Equity Capital Needed: Franchise fee $15,000. Total investment $2,000-$5,000 plus working capital.

Financial Assistance Available: None

Training Provided: 4 days of classroom training.

Managerial Assistance Available: Operations manual plus follow-up support.

Information Submitted: May 1990

*TRIMARK
184 Quigley Boulevard
P.O. Box 10530
New Castle, Delaware 19720
Wilmington, Deleware 19720
Contact: Gilbert Kinch, V.P. Sales and Marketing

Description of Operation: Co-op direct mail marketing company. Franchisor is a printing and publishing company in the business of co-op direct mail advertising, which consists of mailing advertisements, usually in the form of redeemable coupons and special discount notices, to homes throughout the United States. TRIMARK has refined the co-op concept, which brings together non-competitive business into a single "coupon" package. TRIMARK can assist the businessman in targeting his market area in as few as 10,000 homes or in excess of 20 million homes on an annual basis.

Number of Franchisees: 63 in 29 States

In Business Since: 1969, franchising since 1977

Equity Capital Needed: $5,000-$33,900 (varies with size of exclusive territory granted).

Financial Assistance Available: None

Training Provided: 1 week of intensive in-house classroom training. Franchisor has developed and provides to franchisee a system of operation, uniform standards, quality and uniformity of products and services offered. The training consists of procedures for layout design, artwork, printing, labeling and inserting. Heavy emphasis on marketing, sales, administration, procedures for bookkeeping, accounting. In-field training provided. Operation and sales manual provided.

Managerial Assistance Available: Continual regional meetings, field support, marketing, and technical assistance.

Information Submitted: May 1990

*TRIPLE CHECK INCOME TAX SERVICE
727 South Main Street
Burbank, California 91506
David W. Lieberman, President

Description of Operation: Triple Check Income Tax Service offers a unique method of operating a tax preparation business utilizing a proprietary interview worksheet system integrated with an all-encompassing training program and year-round technical assistance. Group promotional programs and a sophisticated, low cost computer service are also an integral feature of a Triple Check Franchise. Through a sister company, Triple Check Financial Services, Inc., a fully registered (NASD-SIPC) broker/dealer, franchisees also have the opportunity to qualify to provide financial and investment services to clients.

Number of Franchisees: 300 offices in 41 States

In Business Since: 1968

Equity Capital Needed: Ownership of a pre-existing business offering tax preparation services or approximately $5,000

Financial Assistance Available: Triple Check offers indirect financing in that the company may act as a guarantor with respect to loans made by an outside commercial bank in payment of the company's annual fees and for those participating in certain advertising programs. These loans are short-term (less than 1 year), made by an outside commercial bank.

Training Provided: Triple Check offers a comprehensive 66 hour training in the first year designed to familiarize franchisees and their employees with the "Triple Check" system, to improve their existing expertise as tax return preparers and to expand their knowledge of the tax laws. In addition, the company offers an annual training program consisting of 13 hours designed to maintain the expertise of its franchisees in tax theory. This training is given live via seminars in selected areas and made available to others through cassettes and workbooks.

Managerial Assistance Available: Triple Check provides ongoing technical assistance by providing year round "hot line" research, technical memoranda as to changes in the applicable laws and administrative practices related to the typical client expected to be served by franchisee. In addition, Triple Check provides various supplies and other items common to the operation of a tax preparation business on a substantial cost saving basis. Advertising and promotional programs are also an integral part of the ongoing service provided by the franchisor.

Information Submitted: April 1990

TV FACTS
1638 New Highway
Farmingdale, New York 11735

Description of Operation: TV Facts offers readers a localized weekly television guide with 7 days of national and local TV programming, cable TV, local news and advertising. Individually owned publications are operated by local associate publishers.

Number of Franchisees: 155 in 14 States and 2 countries.

In Business Since: 1971

Equity Capital Needed: $26,500-$28,500

Financial Assistance Available: None

Training Provided: 1 week home office training in sales, advertising and circulation.

Managerial Assistance Available: Continuous assistance is provided by home office and area supervisors.

Information Submitted: May 1990

TV FOCUS
Guides Publishing, Inc.
One Anderson Avenue
Fairview, New Jersey 07022
Lou Fernandez, President

Description of Operation: TV Focus weekly magazine is a free and localized TV, cable and shopping guide. It contains crossword puzzles, horoscope, and TV, movie and sports articles. It is designed to help local advertisers focus their advertising efforts effectively and economically on their immediate trading areas. No previous experience is necessary. No equipment, no inventory and no writing are required. Individually owned publication by associate publisher.

Number of Franchisees: More than 200 in 35 States

In Business Since: 1980

Equity Capital Needed: Distributorship fee of $1,800; $4,000 working capital suggested.

Financial Assistance Available: None

Training Provided: TV Focus provides the associate publisher with a comprehensive franchise operations manual. Continuous assistance is provided via telephone hot line and periodic memoranda.

Managerial Assistance Available: Continuous assistance is provided via a telephone hot line.

Information Submitted: May 1990

TV NEWS
COMMUNITY PUBLICATIONS OF AMERICA, INC.
80 Eighth Avenue
New York, New York 10011
Allan Horwitz, President

Description of Operation: *TV News* is an award-winning free community publication combining the 7-day readership of a *TV Guide* with the community saturation of a shopper, and the efficiencies of scale of a major national publication. *TV News* is an exciting editorial product that attracts readers, while the low advertising rates and concentrated circulation attract the advertisers. The publisher of *TV News* was formerly the sales strategy planner for the *Wall Street Journal*. As a leader in the publishing field he has been interviewed by Barbara Walters on "20/20" and appeared as a panelist on the "Phil Donahue Show."

Number of Franchisees: 7 in New York, and in South Carolina with no solicitation and no advertising.

In Business Since: 1973—TV News is a successful, respected and highly profitable publication, company-owned in New York. We stopped franchising in 1981 and began this new program in 1990.

Equity Capital Needed: $19,900 with a money back guarantee.

Financial Assistance Available: Yes—80 percent financing to qualified applicants.

Training Provided: 8 days of classroom, in-field and on-site training for the franchisees and their employees. Covers how to sell *TV News*, how to get co-op advertising, financial leverage thru barter, servicing of accounts, distribution, ad design, layout, and accounting. Includes extensive training manual, audio and video cassettes, numerous films, and video taped role-playing sessions.

Financial Assistance Available: Continuous assistance provided by the home office. Includes our unique start-up program to get you off to a flying start, with $1,000 of free printing, a direct mailing to your prospects by the company, and our special charter advertising program to produce immediate income for the franchisee and his advertisers. Also the company contributes $1,000 for each new franchise purchased plus 12 percent of all royalty fees for direct mailings, sweepstakes and special promotions to make the franchisees more successful.

Information Submitted: April 1990

TV TEMPO, INC.
P. O. Box 420215
Atlanta, Georgia 30342-0215
M. Usman Mirza

Description of Operation: TV Tempo, Inc., offers a unique system of "free" weekly television and cable TV scheduling and home entertainment guides. Each associate publisher (franchisee) owns and operates his/her local edition of TV Tempo magazine, which is distributed "free" in high traffic retail areas. Individual associate publishers place advertising around Saturday through Friday television scheduling listings and readership features such as crossword puzzle, horoscope and movie descriptions. No need for expensive equipment, fixtures or offices. Excellent cash flow and low operational costs. Excellent localized guides.

Number of Franchisees: 199 in 25 States

In Business Since: 1975

Equity Capital Needed: Approximately $35,000 up depending on the population of associate publisher area.

Financial Assistance Available: None, interim financing only.

Training Provided: 5 days in intensive classroom learning fundamentals of business operation. Follow-up field training at the actual site assisting the associate publisher to put into operation the techniques of a successful operation. Classroom training available on repeated basis for associate publisher, if needed. Periodic seminars conducted by home office.

Managerial Assistance Available: TV Tempo, Inc., offers guidance and assistance to franchisee on a continuing basis to enhance franchisee's ability and skills. Basic managerial control is always within the control of the associate publisher's business operations. Advertising rates are in the control of the associate publisher.

Information Submitted: May 1990

TWP ENTERPRISES, INC.
11128 John Galt Boulevard
Suite 512
Omaha, Nebraska 68137
Sanford Friedman, President

Description of Operation: The Wedding Pages (TWP) is a wedding planner (250 page book) that contains a 168 page wedding planner and an advertising section for local area advertisers. The local advertisers receive a monthly listing of brides-to-be names, addresses, phone numbers and wedding dates, making this the most targeted direct marketing tool available in the wedding market today. Franchisee sells the local advertising.

Number of Franchisees: 90 in 15 States and Washington, D.C.

In Business Since: 1982

Equity Capital Needed: $15,000 minimum

Financial Assistance Available: None

Training Provided: 2 day in-house training at home office in Omaha, Nebraska. 1 week in market with franchisee or franchisee's sales force for field training.

Managerial Assistance Available: Franchisor provides support for all questions regarding sales and servicing of the markets. Updating and creation of products is constantly done to maintain a quality product. Franchisor publishes the advertising section and the books.

Information Submitted: May 1990

VIDEO DATA SERVICES
24 Grove Street
Pittsford, New York 14534
Stuart J. Dizak

Description of Operation: Video taping services, legal, real estate, social, inventories and film and tape transfers.

Number of Franchisees: 206 in 42 States.

In Business Since: 1980

Equity Capital Needed: $18,000

Financial Assistance Available: Assistance in local banking financing.

Training Provided: 3 day school and continuous correspondence training.

Managerial Assistance Available: Marketing, technical consulting and co-op advertising.

Information Submitted: April 1990

VIDEO 5000
211 East 43rd Street
New York, New York 10017
Chuck Delaney, Vice President

Description of Operation: Video 5000 is a nationwide video franchise providing low cost professional post-production editing, protected territories, national sales support, promotional materials, and free technical and marketing training for members. Video 5000 franchises offered to wedding, special events (parties, graduations, bar mitzvahs, birthdays, anniversaries, etc.), industrial, and commercial videographers as well as Entrepreneurs.

Number of Franchisees: 82

In Business Since: 1988

Equity Capital Needed: $5,000-$10,000

Financial Assistance Available: None

Training Provided: Yes, free seminars held quarterly, nationwide.

Managerial Assistance Available: Complete operations manual (250 pp); management supervision and technical support in all phases, from equipment and start-up to selling, shooting, and editing professional video!

Information Submitted: July 1990

VOICE ENTERPRISES, INC.
70 West Streetsboro Street
Hudson, Ohio 44236
Joseph McClellan, National Franchise Director

Description of Operation: Voice messaging service bureaus, providing the transmission, storage and retrieval of verbal messages through a combination of computer and telephone equipment. Opportunities for single or master franchises available.

Number of Franchisees: 39 in 18 States and Washington, D.C.

In Business Since: 1986

Equity Capital Needed: Total investment: single franchise—$45,000. Metro franchise (multiple areas)—$225,000. Investment includes franchise fees, leased equipment and working capital.

Financial Assistance Available: Third-party leasing available for equipment packages.

Training Provided: All franchisees must attend an initial 10 day intensive training program at corporate office.

Managerial Assistance Available: Voice Enterprises provides continual managerial and field support during the life of the franchise in such areas as sales and marketing techniques, public relations services, equipment operations, accounting and information systems, business controls and personnel management. Operational manuals and training guides are provided as reference tools. Frequent seminars, training meetings and conventions are bringing our people the newest ideas in voice messaging. Metro franchisees in each region will provide ongoing field support for equipment and sales marketing.

Information Submitted: April 1990

*VR BUSINESS BROKERS, INC.
230 Western Avenue
Boston, Massachusetts 02134
Geoffrey G. Wheatley, President and CEO

Description of Operation: The only national network of franchised business brokerage offices. VR's market ranges from privately held companies under $1 million up to and including companies in the $5 million range. Additionally, VR has recently expanded its market base into the care and hospitality industries, providing customized brokerage services to these highly specialized industries as well. Also, VR has developed proprietary software packages for business evaluations, business listings, buyer profiles, and internal stats-tracking system. The VR Network is linked nationally via computer to form an exclusive VR multiple listing system, which provides every new franchisee an instant inventory of available businesses and buyers. VR also assists its offices in marketing, recruiting, advertising, public relations, initial and ongoing training, industry education.

Number of Franchisees: 140

In Business Since: 1979

Equity Capital Needed: Approximately $860,000-$120,000, which includes $35,000 franchise fee.

Financial Assistance Available: Yes

Training Provided: 2-week classroom at regional centers, plus 1 week (specialized) franchise sales training and 1 week (specialized) preferred investment training. Supplemented by continuing assistance of regional operations supervisors, bi-weekly regional seminars, and in-office training of sales associates.

Managerial Assistance Available: Regional operations supervision from experienced business brokers who assist franchisees in all aspects of their business: recruiting, training, advertising, marketing, sales, closings, office management, etc. In addition, full management support available by telephone, newsletter, bulletins, and a regular program of office visits by regional operations staff.

Information Submitted: May 1990

WEDDING INFORMATION NETWORK, INC.
11128 John Galt Boulevard
Omaha, Nebraska 68137
Kenneth L. Nanfito

Description of Operation: The Wedding Pages is a complete marketing program reaching the $28 billion wedding market. It is based around The Wedding Pages, a 160 page wedding planner, and a directory of local area advertisers. The book is distributed free to brides-to-be. Through the distribution, a list of brides and grooms-to-be is compiled. Involves the sale of space advertising and the list.

Number of Franchisees: 76 in 37 States

In Business Since: 1982

Equity Capital Needed: $20,000—$75,000 depending on market and area.

Financial Assistance Available: None

Training Provided: 2 day seminar in Omaha and 1 full week in the franchise market. Ongoing support provided.

Managerial Assistance Available: Operations manual detailing operation is provided and updated on an ongoing basis. Consulting on sales techniques, record keeping provided at owners request.

Information Submitted: April 1990

WESTERN APPRAISERS
Division of WEST/APP, INC.
P. O. Box 215742
Sacramento, California 95821
Bert F. Baumbach, President

Description of Operation: Western Appraisers provides material damage appraisals, total loss evaluation and mechanical failure inspections to major insurance companies, lending institutions and fleet operators.

Number of Franchisees: 33 in 7 States

In Business Since: 1960

Equity Capital Needed: $7,500 to $15,000 depending on population count of area desired.

Financial Assistance Available: None; exceptions may be made under certain circumstances.

Training Provided: Intensive 4 week training period at one of our California training offices prior to franchisee opening business.

Managerial Assistance Available: West/App, Inc. provides continued management service for the life of the franchise in such areas as work product quality control, customer development and profit structure. Many services such as medical insurance, manuals and printing can be purchased from West/App, Inc. at a considerable discount. Semi-annual training seminars are also provided.

Information Submitted: April 1990

CAMPGROUNDS

KAMP DAKOTA, INC.
103 West 20th Street South
Brookings, South Dakota 57006
M. L. Thorne, President

Description of Operation: Franchising of campgrounds to be used by camping and trailering vacationers.

Number of Franchisees: 36 nationwide

In Business Since: 1964

Equity Capital Needed: $50,000 and up

Financial Assistance Available: Other than assistance in preparation and presentation of loan requests to potential financiers, Kamp Dakota, Inc., offers no financial assistance.

Training Provided: Training is provided at each campground as required and as may be necessary.

Managerial Assistance Available: Managerial assistance offered franchisees on a continuous basis. Kamp Dakota, Inc., also provides franchisee with complete engineering and construction planning for their particular campground.

Information Submitted: May 1990

*KAMPGROUNDS OF AMERICA, INC.
P. O. Box 30558
Billings, Montana 59114
David W. Johnson

Description of Operation: Kampgrounds of America, Inc., (KOA) is America's largest system of campgrounds for recreational vehicles. The average campground contains 100 sites equipped with water and electrical hookups; many sites have sewer hookups. Each campground features clean restrooms with hot showers, a convenience store, laundry equipment and playground equipment. Most have swimming pools.

Number of Franchisees: Over 640 in the United States and Canada

In Business Since: 1962

Equity Capital Needed: $85,000 minimum

Financial Assistance Available: KOA does not provide direct financing to franchisees for campground construction. However, it does provide assistance in obtaining financing such as assisting the franchisee in preparing his prospectus, developing operating projections, and meeting with potential lenders.

Training Provided: KOA provides formal classroom training in campground development and campground operations for franchisees and their personnel. Each school (development and operations) lasts 3 days and several sessions are conducted throughout the year.

Managerial Assistance Available: KOA provides formal classroom training and continual engagement services for the life of the franchise in such areas as development, general operations, advertising and merchandising. In addition, complete manuals of development, operations and supply catalogs are provided. Regional consultants are available in all regions to work closely with franchisees. Each campground is visited regularly to insure conformance with standards and to assist franchisees in solving problems. KOA publishes a Kampground Directory annually and sponsors an annual meeting of franchisees.

Information Submitted: April 1990

***YOGI BEAR'S JELLYSTONE PARK
CAMP-RESORTS
LEISURE SYSTEMS, INC.**
Rt. 209
Bushkill, PA 18324
J A. Lovejoy, Chief Operating Officer

Description of Operation: Has designed a standardized method of marketing and operation under a nationwide system known as Jellystone Park Camp-Resorts. Jellystone has granted and desires to grant franchises for exclusive territories in which to operate a Jellystone Park Camp-Resort. Jellystone will also accept certain existing unaffiliated campgrounds for conversion to their system.

Number of Franchisees: 80 in 22 States and Canada

In Business Since: 1969

Equity Capital Needed: $12,500 to $100,000 plus. Depends on location, size and other considerations.

Financial Assistance Available: Up to 60% of franchise fee.

Training Provided: 1 week manager training school, opening assistance, and a manual.

Managerial Assistance Available: Consultation regarding acceptable site criteria and selection. Construction assistance by way of campground layout and building plans. Consulting engineering also available. Ongoing consultation on all facets of campground operation and promotion. Inspection visits to insure chainwide adherence to quality standards. Field consulting. A national 800 toll free reservation service is provided by the national office as well as a national directory and national advertising.

Information Submitted: May 1990

CHILDRENS STORES/FURNITURE/PRODUCTS

BABY NEWS CHILDREN'S DEPARTMENT STORES
23521 Foley Street
Hayward, California 94545
Roger E. O'Callaghan, President

Description of Operation: Baby News Children's Department Stores are a complete children's store offering everything from furniture, clothing, pre-school toys, and safety equipment. Baby News provides a training course and assistance of an experienced staff. Baby News Stores have been in the children's retail business for over 40 years.

Number of Franchisees: 50

In Business Since: 1949

Equity Capital Needed: $150,000

Financial Assistance Available: None

Training Provided: Yes, in both home office as well as store location.

Managerial Assistance Available: Yes, through home office support.

Information Submitted: April 1990

BABY'S ROOM USA, INC.
752 North Larch Avenue
Elmhurst, Illinois 60126
Richard G. Levine

Description of Operation: Retail infants and juvenile furniture and accessories.

Number of Franchisees: 43 in 21 States including 9 company-owned.

In Business Since: 1985

Equity Capital Needed: $88,000 to $199,000

Financial Assistance Available: No direct financial assistance; however, our in-house CPA is available for advice and counsel. In most cases we are able to negotiate 60 to 90 day terms on initial stock orders.

Training Provided: Complete 2 week training program for franchisee and up to 2 additional employees at our headquarters in Elmhurst, Illinois.

Managerial Assistance Available: An operations specialist will spend 1 week during the first month of operation. Regular visits by our field representatives thereafter. A complete operations manual covering all facets of the business as well as periodic newsletters. Two meetings per year which all franchisees attend.

Information Submitted: April 1990

*BELLINI JUVENILE DESIGNER FURNITURE CORPORATION
15 Engle Street, Suite 304
Englewood, New Jersey 07631
John Sterns

Description of Operation: Bellini offers exclusive juvenile designer furniture.

Number of Franchisees: 51 in 21 States, plus 7 company-owned.

In Business Since: 1982

Equity Capital Needed: $110,000-$140,000

Financial Assistance Available: The franchisor will assist the franchisee in applying to local banks for financing.

Training Provided: Training provided in New York or California locations for 2 weeks includes extensive training in furniture sales and merchandising.

Managerial Assistance Available: Additional assistance and direction given by direct phone, correspondence and store visits. Complete operations manual provided covering all aspects of the retail operation.

Information Submitted: May 1990

CHILDREN'S ORCHARD
253 Low Street
Newburyport, Massachusetts 01950
Dick Merrick, Vice President, Franchise Development

Description of Operation: The company sells franchises for the operation of a unique retail boutique that specializes in "nearly new" children's clothing and equipment.

Number of Franchisees: 45 franchises are sold, 36 are open in 7 States.

In Business Since: 1980

Equity Capital Needed: (1) A single franchise will range from $45,000 to $60,000. (2) A master franchise will range from $125,000 to $150,000.

Financial Assistance Available: None

Training Provided: The company provides training classes for all franchisees and their manager. The training is 2 weeks long and covers all aspects of the franchise operation.

Managerial Assistance Available: The franchisor provides ongoing assistance in advertising, buying and pricing, store operations, and store display.

Information Submitted: April 1990

LEWIS OF LONDON INC.
25 Power Drive
Hauppauge, New York 11788
Joel Rallo, President of Franchise Operations

Description of Operation: Retail juvenile furniture and accessories imported exclusively for Lewis of London stores.

Number of Franchisees: 6 in 5 States including 4 company-owned.

In Business Since: 1950

Equity Capital Needed: Determined by the area.

Financial Assistance Available: None

Training Provided: As much as needed for the franchisee to feel comfortable with the opening of his/her store. Full training is provided in all aspects of the business such as complete knowledge of sales, inventory help to start up books, and in tracking inventory, and full understanding of all fees and the billing procedures.

Managerial Assistance Available: Same as above

Information Submitted: May 1990

PREGNANT INC. 4 BABYS ONLY
8930 East Valley Boulevard
Rosemead, California 91770
Bernard Zwick, President

Description of Operation: The "4 Babys Only" and "4 Kids Only" retail baby and teen furniture stores are approximately 8,000 square feet, with off-site warehousing of 2,000 square feet. These specialty stores display imported and American name brand merchandise in addition to exclusive merchandise to "4 Babys Only." The unique geometric display distinguishes our supermarket effect.

Number of Franchisees: 10 in California, Arizona and Nevada.

In Business Since: 1970

Equity Capital Needed: $160,000-$200,000

Financial Assistance Available: Total investment ranges from $160,000-$200,000, $10,000 of which is the franchise fee. $60,000 is for leasehold improvements, deposits, fixtures, delivery truck, cash registers, computer equipment, etc. $90,000-$140,000 is for inventory depending on product mix and size of store.

Training Provided: A 116 page store operation manual and 5 days of in-store training and 2 days in our training center.

Managerial Assistance Available: "4 Babys Only" provides management advice and consultation in inventory control, operations, advertising, accounting and personnel. We provide purchasing information on a continual basis and pass on additional cash and volume discounts negotiated by "4 Babys Only" management team.

Information Submitted: May 1990

CLOTHING/SHOES

*ACA JOE, INC.
148 Townsend Street
San Francisco, California 94107
Ester Muller, President

Description of Operation: Men's retail, casual clothes.

Number of Franchisees: 15 plus 44 company-owned.

In Business Since: 1981, franchising since 1990

Equity Capital Needed: Total investment $150,000-$200,000.

Financial Assistance Available: None

Training Provided: Complete training provided in operating a men's clothing store.

Managerial Assistance Available: Continuous management assistance available.

Information Submitted: June 1990

ALBERT ANDREWS LTD.
111 Speen Street
Suite 510
Framingham, Massachusetts 01701
Andrew L. Stern, President

Description of Operation: Albert Andrews Ltd. is the marketer of men's custom tailored clothing. Franchisees use the Albert Andrews patented portable Computer Fitting System to measure men for suits, shirts, sport coats, slacks and accessories. Service is always in the *customer's* office, therefore, the business may initially be run out of the franchisee's home. Franchisee's goal is to saturate his exclusive territory by hiring sales associates to call on customers, at which point he will require a sales office.

Number of Franchisees: 1

In Business Since: Incorporated in 1986; Boston, Massachusetts operation since 1987; franchising since 1989.

Equity Capital Needed: $34,000-$85,000

Financial Assistance Available: Albert Andrews Ltd. may assist in financing the equipment (up to $11,000).

Training Provided: Complete training in the use of measuring equipment, sales and marketing techniques and day-to-day operations. Self-study required prior to formal training.

Managerial Assistance Available: Continuous guidance by all company personnel when and as needed; calls via telephone and in person on continuous basis during life of license agreement in all aspects of the business. Special visits in person when and as conditions require.

Information Submitted: April 1990

*ATHLETE'S FOOT MARKETING ASSOCIATES, INC.
3735 Atlanta Industrial Parkway
Atlanta, Georgia 30331
Joe DeMarco, Director of Sales/Marketing

Description of Operation: Company franchises its name and services, on a national basis, to individually owned stores that specialize in athletic shoes offering top quality retail priced lines of shoes and related clothing. Company also offers a private label program that enhances the bottom line profitability of its franchised stores.

Number of Franchisees: 500 in the United States, Japan, Australia and France.

In Business Since: 1971

Equity Capital Needed: $19,500 for franchise fee plus approximately $100,000 to $150,000 investment including opening inventory.

Financial Assistance Available: No financing provided by headquarters company. They do provide a package to present to bankers, and will assist in helping to negotiate loan package.

Training Provided: 2 weeks intensive training program provided by headquarters prepares franchisee for complete operation of store. Written manuals also provided.

Managerial Assistance Available: Assistance in lease negotiations and site selection. Complete competitively priced package for store design and construction. Continuous ongoing help in the form of store visitations by franchise coordinators.

Information Submitted: April 1990

ATHLETIC ATTIC MARKETING, INC.
P. O. Box 14503
Gainesville, Florida 32604
C. J. Collins, Director of Franchise Sales

Description of Operation: A retail sporting goods operation specializing in the sale of active-wear apparel, athletic footwear and related sporting goods (racquetball, tennis, soccer, etc.).

Number of Franchisees: 145 in 40 States, District of Columbia, Puerto Rico, New Zealand and Japan.

In Business Since: 1974

Equity Capital Needed: $15,000 for franchise fee. $125,000 to $175,000 total investment. Minimum $45,000 cash required.

Financial Assistance Available: No financial assistance is provided by the franchisor; however, all necessary information for loan applications is available.

Training Provided: Training program includes 1 week of classroom instruction in all aspects of store operations and 1 week of in-store instruction at franchisor's training store.

Managerial Assistance Available: Assistance includes, but not limited to, the following: site selection, lease negotiations, store design, basic construction drawings, product mix assistance, opening suppliers accounts, accounting systems, inventory systems, on-site opening assistance, complete operations manual, advertising manual, local advertising materials, national advertising and publicity support, monthly management and newsletters, annual sales meetings.

Information Submitted: May 1990

ATHLETIC ATTIC MARKETING, INC.
dba ATHLETIC LADY
P. O. Box 14503
Gainesville, Florida 32604
C. J. Collins, Director of Franchise Sales

Description of Operation: A retail sporting goods operation specializing in the sale of women's fashion active wear and footwear (aerobic, tennis, running, swimming, etc.).

Number of Franchisees: 5 in Georgia, Florida, and North Carolina.

In Business Since: Athletic Attic—1974—started franchising Athletic Lady in 1983

Equity Capital Needed: $15,000 for initial fee. $125,000 to $175,000 total investment. Minimum $45,000 cash required.

Financial Assistance Available: No financial assistance is provided by franchisor. However, all necessary information for loan application is available.

Training Provided: Training program includes 1 week of classroom instruction in all aspects of store operation and 1 week of in-store instruction at franchisor's training store.

Managerial Assistance Available: Assistance includes, but is not limited to, the following: site selection, lease negotiations, store design, basic construction drawings, product mix assistance, opening suppliers accounts, accounting systems, inventory systems, on-site opening assistance, complete operations manual, advertising manual, local advertising materials, national advertising and publicity support, monthly management and newsletters, annual sales meetings.

Information Submitted: May 1990

BAGS & SHOES, INC.
P. O. Box 51273
Jacksonville Beach, Florida 32240
W. H. Bonneau, President

Description of Operation: Step into leather with over 100 designer and brand name bags and shoes. A warehouse outlet for $20,000 to $40,000. A designer and brand name Bag & Shoes store for $75,000 to $150,000. We tailor your business to meet your individual needs and resources, offering our turnkey operations, which are geared for high traffic strip centers and malls for a flat fee or on a plus basis with no hidden charges. All inventory is guaranteed to sell.

Number of Franchisees: 37

In Business Since: 1985

Equity Capital Needed: $50,000 to $150,000

Financial Assistance Available: None

Training Provided: We will hire and train sufficient personnel at your Bags & Shoes Boutique. Our program is ideal for absentee ownership.

Managerial Assistance Available: Bags & Shoes will continually provide you with the latest in fashion footwear and handbags. We will make available to you our expertise in buying, pricing, merchandising and advertising on a cost plus basis.

Information Submitted: April 1990

FASHION CROSSROADS
2130 North Hollywood Way
Burbank, California 91505
Bob Deutsch, Director of Franchise Development

Description of Operation: FASHION CROSSROADS (formerly Mode O'Day Company) presently operates and licenses women's apparel specialty shops. These stores specialize in popular and moderately priced merchandise in size ranges that may include junior, misses, and large sizes. Licensees do not purchase inventory from FASHION CROSSROADS; all FASHION CROSSROADS inventory is placed in licensee's store on consignment.

Number of Franchisees: Approximately 250 in 27 States.

In Business Since: 1933

Equity Capital Needed: Variable—estimated range: $15,000 to $30,000 to cover initial license fee, lease deposit, leasehold improvements, equipment and fixtures, working capital, insurance and security deposit.

Financial Assistance Available: No merchandise investment, all merchandise supplied on consignment. Licensee pays FASHION CROSSROADS for merchandise after it has been sold to the ultimate consumer. FASHION CROSSROADS requires a security deposit from all licensees.

Training Provided: Mandatory training is conducted at the National Training Center of FASHION CROSSROADS. FASHION CROSSROADS customarily provides a 2 week training period for each new licensee by company trainers. There is no charge to licensee for training. Additional licensee training is provided in the form of FASHION CROSSROADS continuous in-store training program, which is based upon periodic visits by the licensee's field consultant, a FASHION CROSSROADS employee, and various training materials prepared by FASHION CROSSROADS. The licensee's field consultant will visit the licensee's store at regular intervals in order to provide the licensee with guidance concerning operation and management of store.

Managerial Assistance Available: FASHION CROSSROADS agrees from time to time to provide and make available to licensee retail operations assistance and supplies. The assistance provided by FASHION CROSSROADS shall include, but not be limited to, training of licensee; supervision and assistance in store leasing, store operation, personnel management, inventory control, advertising, sales promotion, and window display; providing without additional charge store improvement plans, lay-out plans, advertising productions, seasonal window backgrounds, window signs, interior signs and merchandise bags; and making available insurance, store fixtures, gift boxes, sales checks, bookkeeping supplies and other miscellaneous items. Licensee is not required to make use of any or all of these services in order to obtain merchandise on consignment.

Information Submitted: April 1990

FASHION LTD.
P. O. Box 51273
Jacksonville Beach, Florida 32240
W. H. Bonneau, President

Description of Operation: We offer over 3,000 designer and brand name fashions, footwear and accessories at below wholesale pricing. You are able to offer your customers current season styles at 25 to 75 percent savings and all inventory is guaranteed to sell. We offer site selection, lease negotiation, design fixturing, and inventory control. We will tailor a theme store of your choice to fit your budget.

Number of Franchisees: 73 units

In Business Since: 1985

Equity Capital Needed: $25,000 to $100,000

Financial Assistance Available: We will assist in a business plan.

Training Provided: Complete training is provided at licensee's store location for 1 week in hiring, merchandising, pricing control and customer relations.

Managerial Assistance Available: Managerial assistance is continued as long as purchasing is through Fashion Ltd. since licensees have the option of purchasing from anyone.

Information Submitted: April 1990

FLEET FEET, INCORPORATED
1555 River Park Drive, Suite 102
Sacramento, California 95815
Sally Edwards, President/CEO

Description of Operation: Retail, active name brand shoes, apparel, and accessories with a strong emphasis on a health oriented fitness lifestyle. Owners must be actively involved in physical fitness.

Number of Franchisees: 35 locations in 11 States

In Business Since: Retail business 1975, franchise since 1978.

Equity Capital Needed: $25,000-$50,000

Financial Assistance Available: Financial advice and assistance in preparing papers and business plan for financial institution. The total capitalization costs range from $85,000-$125,000.

Training Provided: Strenuous 2 week training program in Sacramento, and 1 week on-site assistance before store opening. Ongoing support with manuals, computerized accounting package, workbooks, toll-free telephone consulting, national buying programs, and more.

Managerial Assistance Available: Ongoing weekly bulletin, "Fleet Feet Weekly Memo," to announce inventory and management news. Weekly phone calls to each franchise to offer assistance. Warehouse facilities which offer franchises inventory goods. Franchisee/franchisor meetings three times annually to improve managerial, technical, and other business skills. Discount buying programs.

Information Submitted: April 1990

FORMAL WEAR SERVICE
639 V.F.W. Parkway
Chestnut Hill, Massachusetts 03267
Jay Kuritsky

Description of Operation: Formal specialists in the sale and rental of men's formal clothes. Dealers receive stock plus photo album of every fashion and color we stock plus rental and sales catalog.

Number of Franchisees: 34 in Massachusetts, New Hampshire, New York and Connecticut.

In Business Since: 1940

Equity Capital Needed: $65,000 minimum for stock and fixtures.

Financial Assistance Available: Formal Wear Service will finance if franchisee has good credit rating.

Training Provided: 2 weeks at store. Complete training course in all aspects of formal rental business to all franchisees plus a 60 page book "Can A Nice Guy Succeed in Formals."

Managerial Assistance Available: The home office provides bookkeeping, inventory control and national and local cooperative advertising.

Information Submitted: April 1990

*GINGISS INTERNATIONAL, INC.
180 North LaSalle Street
Chicago, Illinois 60601
John Heiser, Vice President

Description of Operation: Specialists in the sale and rental of men's formal wear.

Number of Franchisees: 208 in 36 States

In Business Since: 1936 franchising since 1968

Equity Capital Needed: $40,000-$95,000

Financial Assistance Available: Through external sources franchisor arranges and guarantees $65,000 financing for opening inventory.

Training Provided: 2 week comprehensive training at Gingiss International Training Center in Chicago approximately 1 month before center's opening. One week on-site training during initial opening week. Regular visits by training directors and various department heads on a continuing basis.

Managerial Assistance Available: Franchisor provides regular visits by field training advisors, a comprehensive instructional manual, periodic bulletins, semi-annual meetings.

Information Submitted: April 1990

JILENE, INC.
4910 Cervato Way
Santa Barbara, California 93111

Description of Operation: Jilene offers two different opportunities to the retail clothing business. One store is called Kimo's Polynesian Shop, which specializes in colorful clothing for women and men. The other store is called Shandar, which specializes in quality women's fashions. Jilene provides expert site selection, complete retail training program, professional buying service, merchandise control system, and advertising and sales promotion assistance.

Number of Franchisees: 10 in California and Florida

In Business Since: 1969

Equity Capital Needed: $35,000 and up depending on size of store.

Financial Assistance Available: None

Training Provided: 2 weeks training provided in franchisee's store. Training covers all general aspects of a retail clothing store operation. A complete operations manual is provided to each store owner.

Managerial Assistance Available: After initial 2 week training period Jilene is always available for assistance for the duration of the franchise contract. Jilene also functions as a buying service for the franchisee.

Information Submitted: May 1990

JUST PANTS
M L C Stores Ltd.
1034 Bonaventure Drive
Elk Grove Village, Illinois 60007
Bernard Bloomenkranz

Description of Operation: Geared to factory outlet centers. Just Pants Warehouse and What A Deal Stores (ladies sportswear nothing over $12).

Number of Franchisees: 7 franchisees, 73 stores in 10 States

In Business Since: 1969

Equity Capital Needed: Regional mall $108,000 to $202,500. No initial franchise fee. Investment covers site selection and development, inventory, fixtures and working capital.

Financial Assistance Available: None

Training Provided: Just Pants will furnish a training program consisting of on-the-job-training plus much additional instruction to the manager with respect to other aspects of the business. The licensee will be responsible for the travel and living expenses and the compensation of the manager while enrolled in the training program.

Managerial Assistance Available: Operating assistance will include advice and guidance with respect to (1) buying pants, tops and other merchandise; (2) additional products authorized for sale by Just Pants stores; (3) hiring and training of employees; (4) formulating and implementing advertising and promotional programs; (5) pricing and special sales; (6) the establishment and maintenance of administrative, bookkeeping, accounting, inventory control and general operating procedures. Further, Just Pants will advise the licensee from time to time of operating problems of the store disclosed by financial statements submitted to or inspections made by Just Pants. Just Pants will make no separate charge to the licensee for such operating assistance.

Information Submitted: May 1990

THE KIDDIE KOBBLER LTD.
68 Robertson Road
Suite 106
Nepean, Ontario
K2H 8P5 Canada
Fred Norman, President

Description of Operation: Largest franchisor of children's full line shoe stores in North America. Stores carry complete lines of America's leading children's branded footwear for all seasons as well as athletic, orthopedic and dancewear needs.

Number of Franchisees: 70 in Massachusetts, Connecticut and Canada

In Business Since: 1951

Equity Capital Needed: 50 percent of investment. Total investment $170,000 to $180,000.

Financial Assistance Available: Assistance in preparation of loan application and possible SBA financing.

Training Provided: Minimum 2 months in-store training with an established franchisee, covering all phases of customer service and recordkeeping, marketing, ordering, store maintenance, on-site assistance before and after grand opening.

Managerial Assistance Available: Regular visits by field consultants, operations manual, buying assistance, regular information memos, head office personnel on-call for advice, franchise meetings semi-annually, advertising assistance, new products advisory, leasing and store design services.

Information Submitted: April 1990

LANZ FRANCHISING, INC.
8680 Hayden Place
Culver City, California 90232
Christofer Scharff

Description of Operation: Classic yet contemporary women's wear specialty stores. Featuring full line of Lanz quality merchandise in the upper-moderate pricelines and other well-known brands. Each fashion store is uniquely tailored to reflect the tastes of the women and the flavor of the community in which they do business.

Number of Franchisees: 29 stores including company-owned in California and Utah.

In Business Since: 1983

Equity Capital Needed: $125,320 to $308,030

Financial Assistance Available: 100 percent financing available for Lanz merchandise. Company provides assistance in developing proposals for obtaining financing.

Training Provided: 10 day extensive management training program, conducted at the corporate headquarters in Los Angeles, and in the California apparel mart with our staff of buyers. The program consists of seminars covering all areas essential to the operation of a Lanz Fashion Store.

Managerial Assistance Available: Prior to the grand opening, a Lanz area supervisor will help train local staff. The areas covered in these training sessions include product knowledge, multiple-sales technique, customer service, development of a personal trade file and more. As part of the ongoing training and support system, the area supervisor will visit the fashion store periodicallly to make recommendations and provide basic training for sales staff and ascertain that all stores are adhering to Lanz standards.

Information Submitted: May 1990

THE MARK-IT STORES, INC.
316 Yale
P. O. Box 187
St. Joseph, Missouri 64504
Tim Burtner, President

Description of Operation: The Mark-It Stores franchise system consists of retail stores in regional malls. We specialize in imprinted sportswear and accessory items. Average store size of 700 square feet. We operate a complete screenprinting plant.

Number of Franchisees: 28 in 17 States

In Business Since: 1975

Equity Capital Needed: $35,000 to $85,000

Financial Assistance Available: None

Training Provided: 2 days in store, 2 days in office. Available for assistance when needed.

Managerial Assistance Available: Monthly newsletters, product location service, advertising assistance, store display.

Information Submitted: April 1990

PARTY FASHIONS INTERNATIONAL, INC.
2551 Pacific Coast Highway
Rolling Hills Plaza
Torrance, California 90505
Satish Mehta, President

Description of Operation: Party Fashions offers high fashion, high quality formal wear and accessories for rental or sales, suitable for women ranging from age 15 and up. Designer gowns and accessories are most appropriate for proms, graduations, cocktail parties, black tie, mother of the bride/groom, or for any other special occasion. The stores are characterized by a distinctive interior design, color scheme, layout, and specially designed decor.

Number of Franchisees: 1 company-owned

In Business Since: 1989

Equity Capital Needed: $133,000-$159,000 for a single store franchise includes franchise fee, furniture and fixtures, computer and custom software, leaseholds, grand opening, advertising, inventory and working capital.

Financial Assistance Available: Assistance in preparing bank presentations to secure up to one third financing through various outside financial institutions.

Training Provided: 2 weeks prior to opening. Franchise training program includes day-to-day store operations, customer relations, inventory control, advertising and promotional techniques, record keeping.

Managerial Assistance Available: The franchisor furnishes continuing management, marketing, new sources of merchandise, payment terms and discount negotiations from vendors, operational and technical assistance to franchisee and his employees.

Information Submitted: April 1990

PRESIDENT TUXEDO, INC.
32185 Hollingsworth
Warren, Michigan 48092
Michael A. Sbrocca, Vice President

Description of Operation: President Tuxedo stores rent and sell the finest in men's formal wear and accessories. Each store is approximately 1,000-1,500 square feet and usually located in regional malls or high traffic, easily accessible street locations. President Tuxedo specializes in servicing proms, weddings, fraternal groups, and black tie occasions.

Number of Franchisees: 14 plus 31 company-owned stores in Michigan, Ohio, Colorado and California.

In Business Since: 1970; the concept of franchising began in 1985

Equity Capital Needed: Between $60,000-$100,000 plus good credit.

Financial Assistance Available: President Tuxedo will help in arranging credit with all suppliers and manufacturers. President Tuxedo will also locate, negotiate, and secure leases for stores.

Training Provided: A complete 2 week training course is given for every franchisee at President Tuxedo's training facilities in Warren, Michigan. After the in-house training, a President Tuxedo field supervisor will be on hand for the official opening plus the following 2 weeks, or longer.

Managerial Assistance Available: President Tuxedo will have a field supervisor available to the franchisee on an ongoing basis, including help with local promotions, buying, store operations, merchandising, and any accounting support needed. President Tuxedo is dedicated to continuing the high quality standards our customers have come to expect. Therefore, we feel obligated to give our franchisees any and all support necessary to have an efficient and profitable business.

Information Submitted: May 1990

SALLY WALLACE BRIDES SHOP, INC.
2210 Pine Terrace
Scotch Plains, New Jersey 07076
John Van Drill, President

Description of Operation: Sally Wallace Brides Shops offer a complete bride shop and bridal service. Wedding gowns, bridesmaids, mothers, party, cocktail, dance and formals plus all accessories. Inventory consists of all the leading designers and manufacturers. Advertised in Brides and Modern Bride Magazine.

Number of Franchisees: 12 in 5 States

In Business Since: 1955

Equity Capital Needed: $50,000

Financial Assistance Available: A total investment of approximately $50,000 is needed for a complete turnkey operation including inventory and $5,000 operating fund back-up. We will finance 30 percent if franchisee has good credit reference.

Training Provided: 3 week mandatory training course in one of our shops. Trainer spends 1 week with franchisee to open new shop. Six months follow-thru by trainer with close supervision via written reports and telephone.

Managerial Assistance Available: Continuous. Consultant buyer and merchandise manager supervision on a weekly basis, checking sales, money, inventory and cost controls. Field personnel available as needed, to visit shops and assist in solving problems. Buying service supplies as part of franchise agreement.

Information Submitted: May 1990

SECOND SOLE, INC.
300 Montgomery Street, 3rd Floor
San Francisco, California 94104
Anastasia Oung, President

Description of Operation: Athletic shoe retail stores combined with athletic shoe resoling operations.

Number of Franchisees: 54 in 6 States

In Business Since: 1976

Equity Capital Needed: $70,000 to $100,000 ($10,000 franchise fee plus inventory, leasehold improvements, machinery, etc.).

Financial Assistance Available: None

Training Provided: A comprehensive training program is conducted in San Diego and includes all aspects of athletic shoe sales and resoling as well as buying systems, inventory systems, advertising and promotional activities. Training course lasts a minimum of 7 days and a maximum of 14 days.

Managerial Assistance Available: Second Sole provides management assistance and consultation for the life of the franchise. Complete manual of operations, forms and systems are provided as well as complete seasonal advertising assistance on a quarterly basis. Second Sole management is continually available to assist in problem solving.

Information Submitted: May 1990

SOX APPEAL
Designers Guild Building
401 North Third Street
Suite 490
Minneapolis, Minnesota 55401
Bill Travis, Vice President, Franchise Sales

Description of Operation: Sox Appeal businesses are retail establishments that sell specialty and quality socks, hosiery and a limited number of approved items such as Sox Appeal t-shirts and sweatshirts, footsie roll mailing tubs, slipper socks, washing bags and washing soap. Sox Appeal imports from 5 different countries and is currently completing a private label program. Each store is approximately 500-900 square feet.

Number of Franchisees: 18 throughout the U.S.

In Business Since: Sox Appeal originally started in 1984 and the franchise program started in 1986.

Equity Capital Needed: Low $115,800—High $170,600. Sox Appeal currently does not provide financial assistance.

Training Provided: The training program will include classroom and on-the-job instruction on basic operations, product knowledge, merchandising, employee relations, customer relations and other topics selected by Sox Appeal. The training program will be for no less than 4 days.

Managerial Assistance Available: Sox Appeal provides continual management services for the life of the franchise in such areas as bookkeeping, advertising, inventory control and day-to-day operations. Complete and updated training manuals of the operations, forms and directions are provided. A franchise coordinator is available to work closely with the franchisees and visit the stores periodically. A Sock Market Report is mailed after each buying market to keep the franchisee informed on what is approved merchandise to buy.

Information Submitted: April 1990

SPORTS FANTASY MARKETING, INC.
P. O. Box 1380
Columbus, Georgia 31902-0980
Reese Davis, Vice President

Description of Operation: A Sports Fantasy Store specializes in "The Clothes of the Pros." The stores are typically 1,000 square feet and carry professional and collegiate licensed sporting apparel and novelty items.

Number of Franchisees: 5 including company-owned in Kentucky, Georgia, Florida, and South Carolina.

In Business Since: 1986

Equity Capital Needed: $60,000-$90,000

Financial Assistance Available: None available—Sports Fantasy assists franchisee in developing a business plan for third party financing.

Training Provided: Sports Fantasy marketing provides intensive 1 week training at the company headquarters and store in Columbus, Georgia, in all phases of operations, merchandising, inventory control, bookkeeping, and purchasing.

Managerial Assistance Available: Ongoing managerial and business operations assistance to maximize store performance via phone contact, company newsletter, promotional and point of sales programs.

Information Submitted: May 1990

STARLIT SOIREE
20 East Camelback Road
Phoenix, Arizona 85012
Michele R. Stone, President
Debbie L. Weller, Vice President
Gordon G. Giles, Director of Marketing

Description of Operation: STARLIT SOIREE is in the business of renting ladies' designer formal wear, similar to men's tuxedo shops. Designer dresses, evening gowns, jewelry, shoes, handbags and furs are offered. Clients receive personalized service from fashion experts who assist in selecting the perfect attire and matching accessories for the ladies' special event. Customers enjoy convenient, one stop shopping and are able to rent at a fraction of the retail purchase price. Rentals range from $55 to $225 on designer dresses typically retailing from $300 to $2,500.

Number of Franchisees: 3 in Arizona and California plus 1 company-owned store.

In Business Since: 1986

Equity Capital Needed: $75,000-$95,000 includes the franchise fee, leasehold improvements, inventory, furniture and fixtures, advertising and working capital.

Financial Assistance Available: None

Training Provided: 1 week of in-store training plus assistance and support in site selection, buying of inventory, advertising materials and all business system methods. In addition, a comprehensive training and operations manual is provided.

Managerial Assistance Available: Consistent, ongoing support is provided by corporate in the areas of showroom systems and sales, as well as administrative systems for personnel, inventory control, and record keeping.

Information Submitted: May 1990

T-SHIRTS PLUS
P. O. Box 20608
3630 I-35 South
Waco, Texas 76702-0608
Larry Meyer, President

Description of Operation: T-Shirts Plus is the world's largest franchise retail specialty chain offering the very best in imprinted sportswear and customized activewear. Each store is independently owned and positioned in major shopping malls throughout the United States, operating in 47 states with more than 175 franchise stores.

Number of Franchisees: 180 in 47 States

In Business Since: 1975

Equity Capital Needed: $135,000-$165,000

Financial Assistance Available: Loan placement assistance.

Training Provided: T-Shirts Plus provides a 2 day orientation training meeting for new franchisees to expose them to all of the essential elements in the store opening process. T-Shirts Plus provides 7 days of intensive retail training, both in classroom and on-site environments at its Waco, Texas, headquarters, prior to store opening. In addition, the company requires its franchisees to train in an existing T-Shirts Plus store for a minimum of 2 days prior to store opening.

Managerial Assistance Available: Each franchisee receives a comprehensive set of operating manuals, as well as company, regional, and on-site support and consultation. In addition, a store opening team is on hand to assist in stocking, merchandising, and first-day operations. The company's most talented franchisees are appointed as Franchisee Partners and are responsible for providing operational support and assistance, as well as store opening support, to all franchisees within their geographic region.

Information Submitted: April 1990

WILD TOPS
NATIONAL DEVELOPMENT GROUP, INC.
74 Main Street
Framingham, MA 01701
Richard Gold, President

Description of Operation: Wild Tops T-Shirt Stores are contemporary in design and are located in major regional malls. Average location size is 400 to 1,000 square feet. Wild Tops features an extensive selection of imprinted sportswear highlighted by T-shirts, sweatshirts, custom flock lettering, numbers, transfers, trendy fashion tops, sweaters, infantwear and related items.

Number of Franchisees: 37 franchised and 3 company-owned.

In Business Since: Predecessor: 1980; current company 1985

Equity Capital Needed: $40,000 and leasehold improvements.

Financial Assistance Available: The total investment of $40,000 and construction (if any) includes all equipment and fixtures such as heat press, cash register, press table, cash and wrap table counter, glass shelving, decal display book, promotional advertising, lease negotiation, home office training and inventory.

Training Provided: Intensive on-the-job training at Wild Tops training center will last 1 week and cover the following topics: store opening and closing, transfer application, purchasing, store set-up, advertising, hiring procedures, customer relations, etc.

Managerial Assistance Available: Wild Tops representatives will be present for all franchisees' grand openings and home office personnel are available on a daily basis to assist franchisees on a consultancy basis. A manual is also provided that outlines all policies, forms and procedures.

Information Submitted: May 1990

CONSTRUCTION/REMODELING
MATERIALS/SERVICES

ABC SEAMLESS, INC.
3001 Piechtner Drive, SW
Fargo, North Dakota 58103
Jerry Beyers, President

Description of Operation: ABC franchise sales for seamless steel siding, seamless gutters. All products manufactured on location. ABC seamless steel siding replaces the obsolescent method of applying siding in 12' lengths. Factory direct suppliers.

Number of Franchisees: 410 in 22 States and Canada

In Business Since: 1973

Equity Capital Needed: $30,000-$50,000

Financial Assistance Available: Leasing available for equipment to qualified buyers, through national lease companies.

Training Provided: Training in sales, product information and application.

Managerial Assistance Available: Accounting services—product service—equipment service.

Information Submitted: May 1990

*ACRYSYL INTERNATIONAL CORPORATION (AIC)
11 South 11th Street
P. O. Box 7858
Reading, Pennsylvania 19603
Dr. Donald G. Snyder, President

Description of Operation: AIC is engaged in franchising nationwide a unique patent-pending 3-stage elastomeric roofing and siding coating system called AcrySyl.

Number of Franchisees: 20 in Pennsylvania, New Jersey, North Carolina, and South Carolina

In Business Since: 1982

Equity Capital Needed: License fee minimum $15,000 plus $20,000 initial operating capital.

Financial Assistance Available: None

Training Provided: Technical aspects of the AcrySyl line of products; estimates; evaluations; application procedures; customer service and relations; marketing, management, and administrative procedures. Individual training in the field. Ongoing assistance on unusual roofing/siding service-related matters. Group meetings or training sessions to exchange marketing, administrative, and technical know-how among franchisees and for the transfer of specialized and advanced technical information and procedures from AIC to franchisee personnel.

Managerial Assistance Available: See above.

Information Submitted: May 1990

ADD-VENTURES OF AMERICA, INC.
38 Park Street Station
Medfield, Massachusetts 02052
Thomas D. Sullivan, President

Description of Operation: Add-Ventures of America, Inc., specializes in remodeling construction for both residential and commercial tradesman. Developed business system and documentation for assisting carpenters/general contractors in administrating their operations. Region franchise owners have exclusive rights to sell local franchises in defined territories.

Number of Franchisees: Regional franchise owners—2, local franchiseowners—12.

In Business Since: 1977

Equity Capital Needed: Regional franchise ($45,000), local franchise ($2,500).

Financial Assistance Available: Will assist in arranging financing.

Training Provided: Initial 10 day training, spread over 2-3 different sessions at regional franchise owner's location.

Managerial Assistance Available: Assistance in preparation of business plan and ongoing management training.

Information Submitted: May 1990

AMERICAN CONCRETE RAISING, INC. (ACRI)
918 Fairway Drive
Bensenville, Illinois 60106
John G. Meyers, President

Description of Operation: ACRI offers the exclusive service of raising concrete walks, drives, patios, warehouses, highways and any concrete slab that has settled or sunken due to improper sub-soil preparation by the method of pressure injection. The service offers the benefit of substantial savings over concrete replacement. The method, developed in the mid-30s, is approved by State and local governments.

Number of Franchisees: 1 in Illinois

In Business Since: 1983

Equity Capital Needed: $40,000-$60,000

Financial Assistance Available: None

Training Provided: 10 days initial training at franchisor's location, learning all aspects of the operations and installations; ongoing training as needed for the franchisee's successful operation.

Managerial Assistance Available: Franchisee is trained in all areas of management. ACRI provides help in advertising and public relations. ACRI also develops and researches new services and products to add to the franchisee's operation.

Information Submitted: April 1990

AMERICAN LEAK DETECTION
1750 East Arenas
Suite 7
Palm Springs, California 92262
Dick Rennick, Chief Executive Officer

Description of Operation: Electronically locates leaks in pools, spas, fountains, under concrete slabs of homes and commercial buildings. Locates hidden and concealed sewer lines, septic tanks, etc. Building energy loss, roof moisture analysis by the use of infrared thermography. Locate and repair drain, waste and sewer leaks.

Number of Franchisees: 110 in 10 States, and 2 in Australia

In Business Since: 1975, franchising since 1985

Equity Capital Needed: $20,000

Financial Assistance Available: Franchises start at $40,000—a portion can be financed in-house by franchisor with good credit rating.

Training Provided: 4 to 6 week training—50 hours plus per week—very intensive course. Ongoing quarterly training.

Managerial Assistance Available: Ongoing public relations and marketing support given periodically or upon special request. Yearly training conventions and sales meetings, continual equipment and technique updates.

Information Submitted: April 1990

ARCHADECK WOODEN PATIO DECKS
P. O. Box 5185
Richmond, Virginia 23220
Richard Provost, President

Description of Operation: Archadeck (R-KA-DEK) markets, sells, and builds custom-designed, stick-built wooden patio decks for residential, builder, and commercial clients.

Number of Franchisees: 32 in 15 States and Japan.

In Business Since: 1980, franchising since 1984

Equity Capital Needed: $40,000-$60,000

Financial Assistance Available: None

Training Provided: Minimum 10 days intensive training covering the areas of office management; marketing and advertising; sales; construction documentation and management; and design and estimating.

Managerial Assistance Available: Unlimited managerial support via telephone and mails. Regular on-site services include support in all facets of business with special emphasis on sales support and business management. We provide working drawings for each project with specs, details, and material takeoffs. We also have an architectural rendering service and an in-house advertising agency.

Information Submitted: May 1990

BASEMENT DE-WATERING SYSTEMS, INC.
162 East Chestnut Street
Canton, Illinois 61520
Robert Beckner, Marketing Director

Description of Operation: Basement De-Watering Systems, Inc. (BDW) is the nation's largest network of professionally trained and authorized professionals, servicing residential and commercial waterproofing and radon testing and mitigation markets in 36 states and Canada. BDW offers a 2-in-1 business opportunity through year-round installations of both water seepage control systems and the Safe-Aire Patented Radon Mitigation System. The patented Safe-Aire System employs an Environmental Protection Agency proven method that is capable of removing high concentrations of radon gas and structural water seepage in a single system application. Both the Basement De-Watering and Safe-Aire Systems utilize a unique method of interior perimeter baseboard channelization that is marketed and installed by our authorized dealers exclusively.

Number of Franchisees: 23 franchises, plus 1 company store, plus over 100 dealers.

In Business Since: 1978

Equity Capital Needed: $24,000 to $45,000 is the approximate cost of original start-up; includes extensive training, specialized tools, marketing materials, inventory, and supplies. Initial product inventory is structured to recoup all or a large portion of original investment.

Financial Assistance Available: Franchisor does not at present offer any specific kind or amount of financing.

Training Provided: The initial 1 week course is conducted at the home office in both water seepage control and radon testing and mitigation. Ongoing training is available for franchisee and future employees at the home office, at no additional cost for course studies.

Managerial Assistance Available: Advertising, marketing, and management materials are initially provided during training. Ongoing support materials are provided throughout the year. Additionally, dealers are supported through in-house products catalog, in-house advertising layout support, radio and TV program support, and ongoing marketing materials support. Franchisor serves as continual technical consultant for franchisee via toll-free service hot-line. Continual market awareness and research are provided bi-monthly to all authorized dealers through BDW/SA Newsletter.

Information Submitted: April 1990

BATHCREST INC.
2425 South Progress Drive
Salt Lake City, Utah 84119
Scott Peterson, President

Description of Operation: Specializing in porcelain resurfacing on bathtubs, sinks, ceramic wall tile, kitchen appliances, chip repair on new tubs, fiber glass and acrylic spa repair. Bathcrest Inc. services motels, hotels, apartment houses, home owners, contractors, and repairs for manufacturers of new porcelain bathroom fixtures.

Number of Franchisees: 153 in 35 States, 3 in Canada

In Business Since: 1979

Equity Capital Needed: $24,500

Financial Assistance Available: None

Training Provided: 5 days of on-the-job training by trained technicians. Complete equipment, printed materials, supplies, advertising, and enough Glazecote to return investment. Yearly dealers' meetings and newsletters. Protected territory.

Managerial Assistance Available: Continual support.

Information Submitted: April 1990

BATH GENIE, INC.
69 River Street
Marlborough, Massachusetts 01752
John J. Foley, President

Description of Operation: The franchisor, through a uniquely developed and refined process, offers the service of restoring and resurfacing bathroom fixtures. This service includes the restoration, recolor and recoating of standard bathroom fixtures which include bathtubs, sinks, wall tiles, fiberglass and acrylic and chip repair.

Number of Franchisees: 27 in 9 States and Canada

In Business Since: 1978

Equity Capital Needed: $24,500

Financial Assistance Available: The franchisor does not offer any specific kind or amount of financial assistance to prospective franchisees. Assistance is rendered to prospective franchisees with regard to mode and method of financing where needed.

Training Provided: Prior to the start of the franchise business, the franchisor has the obligation to provide full training for a period of approximately 4 to 5 days in all phases of the business to include on-the-job training, revelation of all technical aspects and procedures of the business, and instruction with regard to marketing, public relations and accounting procedures. Training is mandatory.

Managerial Assistance Available: Beyond the training period, the franchisor keeps a continual liaison with the franchisee with regard to all details pertaining to training of personnel, public relations, marketing, and with regard to advertising. In addition the franchisor provides the franchisee with periodical newsletters and newsworthy items pertaining to doings in the industry and also with regard to pertinent changes in the law and other factors that affect the conduct of the franchisee's problems of any kind or nature directly with the home office of the franchisor. All such communications are attended to by the franchisor's office immediately upon notification from the franchisee.

Information Submitted: April 1990

*B-DRY SYSTEM, INC.
1341 Copley Road
Akron, Ohio 44320
Joseph Garfinkel, Vice President

Description of Operation: Franchisor has developed and formulated unique procedures and techniques for the operation of a basement waterproofing business. Franchisor provides to franchisee a uniform system of procedures for the operation of a B-Dry franchise including the right to use the B-Dry patented process and the use of B-Dry logos and trademarks.

Number of Franchisees: 80 franchises in 25 States and Canada

In Business Since: 1958

Equity Capital Needed: $20,000-$45,000

Financial Assistance Available: Up to 50 percent of the initial franchisee fee may be extended up to 24 months at no interest.

Training Provided: Franchisor provides the complete initial training on all aspects of technical, marketing, and administrative phases of the operation. Initial training approximately 10 days. Regular follow-up training provided at no charge.

Managerial Assistance Available: During operation of franchise, regular managerial and technical assistance is provided on an ongoing basis.

Information Submitted: May 1990

BOMANITE CORPORATION
P. O. Box 599
Madera, California 93639-0599
Daryl Derus, Director of Licensing

Description of Operation: The company sells licenses to operate a concrete contracting business using the company's proprietary processes, materials and equipment, and use of trademarks. Bomanite is the originator and world leader in the field of coloring and imprinting patterns and textures on concrete slabs. Franchisees must already be, or have the qualifications to be, a skilled concrete contractor.

Number of Franchisees: 90 in the U.S. and Canada, plus 27 Master Licensees and 58 Sublicensees in 27 countries.

In Business Since: 1970

Equity Capital Needed: $20,000 to $30,000 initial investment.

Financial Assistance Available: Time payment on portion of initial investment available in smaller U.S. cities.

Training Provided: 1 week training program at home office, followed by 2 or 3 days additional training at franchisee's location. Training manual, training videos and marketing kit provided.

Managerial Assistance Available: The company sponsors periodic meetings and workshops and other types of continuing education, training and assistance, including newsletters and technical bulletins. Continuing national marketing and advertising services for the benefit of the franchisees are provided by the company.

Information Submitted: August 1990

BRITETECH ENVIRONMENTAL, INC.
6350 McDonough Drive
Norcross, Georgia 30093
A. Whitworth, Franchising Administrator

Description of Operation: BriteTech is one of the nation's leading Indoor Environmental Quality (IEQ) companies serving the commercial building marketplace. Our franchisees are trained in IEQ source identification, remediation and preventive services. Our franchisees come from all former occupational backgrounds, and receive ongoing professional support as well as local and national marketing.

Number of Franchisees: 20

In Business Since: 1988

Equity Capital Needed: $35,000-$50,000

Financial Assistance Available: None

Training Provided: 1 week training in Atlanta includes procedures for diagnostics, remediation, marketing, and complete operational manuals.

Management Assistance Available: Continuing advertising and promotional support and assistance. Ongoing professional and technical support available thru a toll-free 800 number.

Information Submitted: April 1990

*****CALIFORNIA CLOSET CO.**
21300 Victory Boulevard, Suite 1150
Woodland Hills, California 91367
Neil Balter

Description of Operation: Custom closet installation—complete interior renovation and designed individually. Space savers. Double hanging space. A place for all articles in a closet.

Number of Franchisees: 100 in 23 States, Canada/Australia

In Business Since: 1979

Equity Capital Needed: $200,000

Financial Assistance Available: None

Training Provided: Initial 2 weeks ongoing sales, installation and bookkeeping.

Managerial Assistance Available: Ongoing—advertising, sales and carpentry.

Information Submitted: May 1990

CHIMNEY RELINING INTERNATIONAL, INC.
105 West Merrimack Street
P. O. Box 4035
Manchester, New Hampshire 03108
Clifford R. Martel, President

Description of Operation: Using the PermaFlu Chimney Lining System, the PermaFlu franchisee can reline cracked, crooked or deteriorated chimney flues and restore them to safe, efficient use with any heating fuel, including wood, oil, gas and coal. Complete contractor package includes a mortar mixer mounted on a hopper which flows into a pump. Special PermaFlu Mix pumped into chimney around inflated rubber flue-former. When mix hardens, former is deflated and removed. New round flue. All cracks sealed.

Number of Franchisees: 35 in 21 States and Canada. Affiliate in United Kingdom.

In Business Since: 1981

Equity Capital Needed: $14,700, $11,700 or $6,900

Financial Assistance Available: Will provide model business plan.

Training Provided: 1 week intensive training in actual on-the-job chimney relining work; also classroom work reviewing operations guidelines, marketing, estimating, profit and cost analysis; warehouse instructions on maintenance of PermaFlu Chimney Lining System.

Managerial Assistance Available: Guidance in advertising and publicity, office operations, use of programmed estimating computer (provided by CRI); letters of introduction on franchisee's behalf sent with complete testing and descriptive package to franchisee's local (1) building inspectors, (2) insurance adjusters, (3) fire marshals, (4) real estate brokers and (5) local newspapers. Advertising and publicity sales lead program on monthly basis—Permaflu information sent to franchisee's customer, with copy to franchisee. Full package of franchisee identity materials provided—business cards, letterheads, invoices, envelopes and brochures, all custom printed with the franchisee name, address, etc.

Information Submitted: May 1990

CLASSIC STORAGE
12 Sterling Lane
Scotts Valley, California 95066
Bart L. Ross, CEO

Description of Operation: CLASSIC STORAGE, the premier builder of quality residential and commercial storage buildings, offers a unique opportunity in owning your own business. No previous experience required; we completely train you in manufacturing, marketing, sales and day-to-day operations. Exclusive territory, sales assistance, technical support, strong ongoing marketing support, low investment, low overhead. Take charge of your future.

Number of Franchisees: 7 in California

In Business Since: 1988

Equity Capital Needed: Investment ranges between $24,500-$50,000.

Financial Assistance Available: Financial assistance is available up to $9,000.

Training Provided: 1 week at home office and 1 week at franchisee's location.

Managerial Assistance Available: Continuous in all phases of management including lease negotiations, site selection and all business services.

Information Submitted: April 1990

THE CLOSET FACTORY
12800 South Broadway
Los Angeles, California 90061
Nancy Seyfert, Franchise Director

Description of Operation: The Closet Factory designs, builds and installs premium custom closet systems to customer specifications.

Number of Franchisees: 3 in California (plus 1 company-operated), 1 in New Jersey, 3 in New York.

In Business Since: 1983; franchising since 1986.

Equity Capital Needed: $89,000 to $119,500, with total investment ranging from approximately $104,000 to $144,500.

Financial Assistance Available: None

Training Provided: Extensive comprehensive training program at headquarters and on-site including sales, marketing, customer service, design, manufacturing, installation and operational management.

Managerial Assistance Available: Site selection, equipment purchasing, personnel selection, inventory control and general operational guidance. Ongoing counseling in all aspects of the business.

Information Submitted: May 1990

CLOSETS TO GO, INC.
9540 S.W. Tigard Street
Tigard, Oregon 97223
Jeffrey V. Turner, Franchise Director

Description of Operation: Closets To Go is a specialty product and service company offering a unique portable closet and storage system that appeals to everyone. The unique concept behind Closets To Go is providing quality, instant service and fair prices to its customers, while eliminating the expense of manufacturing for its franchisees.

Number of Franchisees: 2 in California and Washington

In Business Since: 1985

Equity Capital Needed: $32,300 Small Market Franchise to $118,900 Large Market Franchise. Includes franchise fee, training expenses, initial inventory, complete start up expenses and working capital.

Financial Assistance Available: Vehicle and computer equipment can be leased.

Training Provided: 2 week training corporate store with an additional 2 weeks at franchise location.

Managerial Assistance Available: Continuous and ongoing support.

Information Submitted: April 1990

CLOSETTEC FRANCHISE CORPORATION
123 East Street
Dedham, Massachusetts 02026
Eliot Cubell

Description of Operation: Custom designed closets and storage systems for both the consumer and commercial markets. Using furniture grade wood products and European steel hardware to create custom designed and installed fully adjustable storage systems.

Number of Franchisees: 56 in 28 States

In Business Since: 1985

Equity Capital Needed: $155,200

Financial Assistance Available: None

Training Provided: 2 weeks initial training for owners and managers at corporate office. Additional 1 week courses for other personnel. Ongoing regional seminars and on-site training and support.

Managerial Assistance Available: Ongoing in all phases of the business.

Information Submitted: April 1990

COLLEGE PRO PAINTERS (U.S.), LTD.
(student franchises)
College Pro's PAINTERS PLUS

(full-time franchise contractor)
400 Riverside Avenue
Medford, Massachusetts 02155
Kenneth J. Cleary, Vice President

Description of Operation: Students Division: Students are selected each fall to participate in the program. They are given territories in which they are to operate their own painting franchise; these territories are usually their own home town area. During the winter and spring they are taught all the aspects of operating a painting business through attending two three day classroom sessions and one three day practical on-site training session. These are weekend sessions. After school is complete they begin operations and paint between 40 to 50 homes before going back to school. Full-Time Franchise: Any person willing to operate a hands-on painting business year round will receive all the benefits of an association with the world's largest painting company. Training, financial assistance, marketing program, insurance, and expert support are all included.

Number of Franchisees: Students: 295 in 20 States full-time: 17 in 4 States

In Business Since: 1971

Equity Capital Needed: None

Financial Assistance Available: $2,500 is prepaid expenses and advertising.

Training Provided: 6 days of classroom, 8 days of in-the-field training.

Managerial Assistance Available: Ongoing advice and assistance are available from experienced people at any time to the franchisee.

Information Submitted: March 1990

EASI-SET INDUSTRIES
Rt. 28
Midland, Virginia 22728
Ashley Smith, President

Description of Operation: ESI provides a service to concrete products producers who are seeking diversification and to persons interested in establishing a precast concrete business. The approach is to supply them fulll developed standards products which have been proven successful and profitable and to provide them an ongoing comprehensive program of service.

Number of Franchisees: 40 in 14 States, Canada, Belgium and Spain.

In Business Since: 1978

Equity Capital Needed: Varies with product selected and franchisee's manufacturing capabilities. Range $35,000-$215,000

Financial Assistance Available: None

Training Provided: Production training—1-2 weeks, sales training—1-2 weeks.

Managerial Assistance Available: Marketing consultation, production consultation, provide co-op regional advertising, and quarterly field visits.

Information Submitted: May 1990

ELDORADO STONE CORPORATION
P. O. Box 27 Z
Carnation, Washington 98014
John E. Bennett, President

Description of Operation: Franchisee will manufacture and sell Eldorado Stone, simulated stone and brick building products. No technical background is necessary.

Number of Franchisees: 25 in 16 States and international

In Business Since: 1969

Equity Capital Needed: $46,000 minimum

Financial Assistance Available: None

Training Provided: Company provides 1 week of training in an established manufacturing plant, 1 week in franchisee's plant, and continuous supervision thereafter.

Managerial Assistance Available: Company provides continuous managerial assistance and sponsors annual meetings of franchisees.

Information Submitted: April 1990

EUREKA LOG HOMES INC.
Industrial Park, Commercial Avenue
Box 426
Berryville, Arkansas 72616
Bill Smith, President

Description of Operation: Wholesaling through an international network of distributors and dealers.

Number of Franchisees: 300 in 38 States, Japan and Switzerland

In Business Since: 1976

Equity Capital Needed: $19,700 for 2,000 square foot log home display model.

Financial Assistance Available: None

Training Provided: Excellent training manual and constant assistance from international marketing and production division.

Managerial Assistance Available: Same as above

Information Submitted: June 1990

EXOTIC DECKS, INC.
Four Seasons
5005 Veterans Memorial Highway
Holbrook, New York 11741
Tony Russo

Description of Operation: For experienced deck builders, an Exotic Deck franchise offers the following benefits: Exclusive Tuff-Talk Tropical Hardwood (much heavier than teakwood), not available anywhere else, price comparable to redwood, extraordinary stainless steel fastening equipment, very low investment, marketing and advertising program and much more. Exotic Decks is a new franchise concept from the renowed Four Seasons Design & Remodeling Center organization.

Number of Franchisees: 3 company-owned units.

In Business Since: 1989

Equity Capital Needed: Varies, but franchise fee is between $2,500-$5,000.

Financial Assistance Available: None

Training Provided: Training is provided in all phases of operation.

Managerial Assistance Available: Ongoing

Information Submitted: April 1990

FERSINA WINDOWS, INC.
14201 F & G South Lakes Drive
South Point Business Park
Charlotte, North Carolina 28217
Chuck McGill

Description of Operation: Sales/manufacture of solariums/windows.

Number of Franchisees: Over 2,500 in 21 countries.

In Business Since: 1980

Equity Capital Needed: Cash requirements $30,000-$35,000. Total investment up to $100,000.

Financial Assistance Available: Up to 70 percent financing available.

Training Provided: Training provided.

Managerial Assistance Available: Ongoing

Information Submitted: April 1990

FLEX-SHIELD INTERNATIONAL, INC.
P. O. Box 1790
636 West Commerce
Gilbert, Arizona 85234
Charles Carroll

Description of Operation: Total maintenance products for the floor to the roof. Cold applied elastomeric roof system—the toughest rubber nonbrake roof system manufactured—the quickest to install, the best warranty. Also features commercial floor care products and service.

Number of Franchisees: 12 including company-owned

In Business Since: 1976

Equity Capital Needed: $25,000 franchise fee. Initial investment of $50,000 to $150,000.

Financial Assistance Available: Yes, some on both franchise fee and equipment.

Training Provided: Complete 5 day training in Gilbert, Arizona, with classroom and on-the-job training. Continued training on-site for several installations and follow-up training on an ongoing basis.

Managerial Assistance Available: Complete corporate resource staff and new product development staff for ongoing assistance.

Information Submitted: May 1990

FOREST HILL ENTERPRISES, INC.
2320-B Hunters Way
Charlottesville, Virginia 22901
Walter L. Lumpp, President

Description of Operation: The company sells licenses for Forest Hill Associates Remodeling and Restoration specialists. Residential and light commercial remodeling companies specializing in restoring properties after an insurance claim.

Number of Franchisees: 36 offices in 14 States.

In Business Since: 1984, with 12 years prior experience in insurance restoration before starting franchising.

Equity Capital Needed: Licensing fees range from $25,000 to $35,000. Company suggests an additional $25,000 to $50,000 additional working capital available.

Financial Assistance Available: None

Training Provided: 1 week classroom schooling in corporate office. 3-6 weeks field training in existing offices.

Managerial Assistance Available: On-site assistance and regional seminars available. Regional managers provide regular site visits and assistance. Continuous phone support available through corporate office on business management, estimating, computer software and technical matters.

Information Submitted: April 1990

*FOUR SEASONS DESIGN AND REMODELING CENTERS
Four Seasons Marketing Corp.
5005 Veterans Memorial Highway
Holbrook, New York 11741
Marcus Peters

Description of Operation: We provide an expanded product line for total remodeling services. Our franchisees offer our exclusive product line, which includes solariums and greenhouse additions, clad/wood doors and windows, patio rooms, skylights and entry doors. Qualified candidates are given an opportunity to be a part of the $140 billion plus remodeling industry. The Four Seasons name presents a uniform image of quality, reliability and confidence to consumers.

Number of Franchisees: 271 in 48 States and 9 countries.

In Business Since: 1975

Equity Capital Needed: Varies

Financial Assistance Available: No financing available

Training Provided: We provide training in sales techniques, lead management, marketing and installation of our products at our national training center. Field support and ongoing training through our six regional offices.

Managerial Assistance Available: Four Seasons will provide ongoing administrative, sales, installation and service training and guidance during the life of the franchise. Complete manuals, forms and directions are provided. Regional sales and service representatives are available to work closely with the franchisees.

Information Submitted: April 1990

GARAGEMAN
2825 Tahquitz McCallum Way
Palm Springs, California 92262

Description of Operation: Garageman dealers specialize in the sale, assembly and installation of storage modules. The main marketing thrust is to garages, but the modules are also installed in business and professional offices.

Number of Franchisees: 7

In Business Since: 1987

Equity Capital Needed: $104,000-$163,000

Financial Assistance Available: None

Training Provided: Garageman provides consulting and advisory assistance on an ongoing basis and conducts a mandatory 1 to 2 week initial training program at its headquarters and in the field for franchisees and their employees, who are responsible for their own transportation, meals and lodging.

Managerial Assistance Available: Garageman provides, at a nominal cost to its franchisees, catalogues, newspaper ad mats, television commercials, direct mail pieces and other promotional material.

Information Submitted: April 1990

HERITAGE LOG HOMES, INC.
Box 610
Gatlinburg, Tennessee 37738

Description of Operation: Manufactures pre-cut log home(s) kits in various attractive design plans for year-round living. Meets all national building codes, HUD approval and material grades for quality. Sells through dealership and provides training and development of sales force.

Number of Franchisees: 54 in 22 States

In Business Since: 1974

Equity Capital Needed: $50,000 to $100,000 model home construction on commercial lot.

Financial Assistance Available: Co-op advertising after open house/grand opening. Construction and permanent mortgage financing.

Training Provided: 2 days sales, policies and technical training at national headquarters in Gatlinburg, Tennessee. Annual follow-up.

Managerial Assistance Available: Technical assistance construction training provided upon delivery of model home.

Information Submitted: May 1990

HYDROFLO SYSTEM BASEMENT WATERPROOFING
3729 Linden, Southeast
Wyoming, Michigan 49548
Wayne L. Nichols, Jr., President

Description of Operation: Franchisor has developed unique procedures for waterproofing an entire basement within one day without the use of any chemicals. All work carries a life-of-structure guarantee against leakage, regardless of ownership. Franchises are geared for high volume through refined marketing techniques.

Number of Franchisees: 3 in Michigan and Indiana

In Business Since: 1972

Equity Capital Needed: $50,000

Financial Assistance Available: Franchisor will assist in securing financial assistance through leasing companies.

Training Provided: 4 to 6 weeks intensive classroom and on-the-job training at the home office and at the franchisees location.

Managerial Assistance Available: Monthly personal assistance by both marketing representatives and installation supervisors.

Information Submitted: April 1990

KITCHEN SAVERS, INC.
715 Rose Street
La Crosse, Wisconsin 54603
Cliff LeCleir, President

Description of Operation: Kitchen Savers remodels kitchen cabinets by first removing the existing doors and drawer fronts. Then we reface the existing framework with 1/8", 3-ply oak paneling. The old doors and drawer fronts are then replaced with new, 3/4" solid oak doors and drawer fronts.

Number of Franchisees: 11 plus 1 company-owned

In Business Since: 1982

Equity Capital Needed: Total investment: $11,000-$40,000, franchise fee: $7,500-$12,500.

Financial Assistance Available: Assistance and advice.

Training Provided: 2 days of extensive training at home office and 3 days at franchisee's location.

Managerial Assistance Available: Ongoing training and consultation will be provided upon request.

Information Submitted: April 1990

KITCHEN TUNE-UP
131 North Roosevelt
Aberdeen, South Dakota 57401
David Haglund, President

Description of Operation: Kitchen Tune-Up offers wood care and maintenance for the home and office. Our nine step process revitalizes and rejuvenates "tired" looking cabinets. Our franchises also offer door replacement built to specifications and closet systems available in over 300 colors. Kitchen Tune-Up is a home-based business that requires no inventory.

Number of Franchisees: 62 in 24 States

In Business Since: 1988

Equity Capital Needed: $11,495-$11,995; this includes $9,995 franchise fee.

Financial Assistance Available: None

Training Provided: Complete 3 day training program at franchisor location and an additional 2 day follow up training at franchise location.

Managerial Assistance Available: Kitchen Tune-Up offers a complete management training program including use of our operations and marketing manual. Kitchen Tune-Up visits its franchisees on a regular basis and offers regional training schools to update them on industry trends and improvements.

Information Submitted: April 1990

LAVASTONE INTERNATIONAL, INC.
P. O. Box 26699
Dallas, Texas 75226
Jack G. Busby, President

Description of Operation: Manufacturing and sales of a complete system and product line: Lavastone, Lite Stone, Fireplace Surrounds, Lava Crete, Lavastone Grout, and Lavastone Sealer.

Number of Franchisees: 8

In Business Since: 1969

Equity Capital Needed: Determined by size of operation and franchise territory.

Financial Assistance Available: None

Training Provided: Company provides 2 weeks of comprehensive training in franchisee's plant, plus 2 weeks training in sales. Company personnel are available upon request at all times.

Managerial Assistance Available: Company provides continuous managerial assistance and sponsors semi-annual meetings for franchisees each year. A manual is provided for all policies and procedures.

Information Submitted: April 1990

THE LINC CORPORATION
4 North Shore Center
Pittsburgh, Pennsylvania 15212
Preston D. Bond, President

Description of Operation: Franchising leading existing independent heating and air conditioning contractors to offer commercial and industrial building owners and operators a full service heating, ventilating and air conditioning maintenance program (LINC Service). This program also includes energy management, system installation, replacement, repair and modernization and 24-hour emergency service. As part of the LINC System franchise arrangement, the contractor is provided with computerized programs for customer invoicing, accounting and management information reporting. The computerized programs are part of the LINC System, which links a computer terminal in each franchisee's office to a main computer at the Linc Corporation headquarters in Pittsburgh. This total franchise program, which is unique in the industry, offers independent contractors a comprehensive and cost-effective maintenance and service program for today's professional HVAC contractors.

Number of Franchisees: 90 in 37 States

In Business Since: 1974

Equity Capital Needed: Not applicable; only franchising existing businesses. (Approximately $35,000 initial cost.)

Financial Assistance Available: $25,000 of initial fee with interest.

Training Provided: Business format, management, marketing, sales and operations.

Managerial Assistance Available: Ongoing consultation is available without charge. Initial start-up training is a minimum of 15 instructor days.

Information Submitted: April 1990

LINDAL CEDAR HOMES, INC.
P. O. Box 24426
Seattle, Washington 98124
Sir Walter Lindal, Chairman

Description of Operation: Manufacture and sale of Cedar Homes including precut Cedar Homes and Cedar Log Homes.

Number of Franchisees: 346 in all 50 States

In Business Since: 1945

Equity Capital Needed: $5,000 minimum, none to Lindal (no franchise fee).

Financial Assistance Available: Long-term mortgage financing for homes sold.

Training Provided: 5 days training seminar initially. 1 day seminars 3 times a year.

Managerial Assistance Available: Area representative continually assists.

Information Submitted: May 1990

MAGNUM PIERING INC.
720 A. West Fourth Street
Eureka, Montana 63025
Tom Zagel, Vice President

Description of Operation: Raising, leveling and stabilizing settled buildings, foundations, using steel piers to bedrock.

Number of Franchisees: 8 in 7 States

In Business Since: 1985

Equity Capital Needed: $35,000 includes one half of franchise fee, supplies, equipment, materials, and training.

Financial Assistance Available: Partial financing of the franchise fee with no interest charged.

Training Provided: Complete training in office procedure, advertising, estimating presentation of contracts, closing and all facets of piering, including "hands-on" field work.

Managerial Assistance Available: Franchisor features thorough training in both managerial and technical aspects and offers ongoing support without reservation.

Information Submitted: April 1990

MASTER REMODELERS NATIONAL, INC.
11747 Firestone Boulevard
Norwalk, California 90650
Leslie D. Wilson, President

Description of Operation: Franchising of home remodeling contractors.

Number of Franchisees: 6 in California

In Business Since: 1981

Equity Capital Needed: $7,500 plus business office—$20,000 working capital.

Financial Assistance Available: $3,500 deposit on franchise purchase price with monthly payments of $200 until paid in full.

Training Provided: Sales and management training provided before start-up of operation. Ongoing sales training for sales personnel plus help as needed regarding management.

Managerial Assistance Available: Additional training in management or sales and marketing assistance as company deems necessary.

Information Submitted: May 1990

MIRACLE METHOD BATHROOM RESTORATION
3732 West Century Boulevard
Suite 6
Inglewood, California 90303
Brian Pearce, President

Description of Operation: Homes, apartments and hotels older than 20 years need improvements in bathrooms and kitchens. Replacement of fixtures or tile costs thousands, refinishing them cost only hundreds! Plus, 30 to 50 percent of all fixtures are damaged during construction! YOU can fulfill this existing demand in your home town. Our franchisees use a unique system, proven for its outstanding durability and ease of application.

Number of Franchisees: 116 in 14 States and 15 countries.

In Business Since: 1977

Equity Capital Needed: $30,000-$35,000 depending upon franchise type and business strategy.

Financial Assistance Available: Local franchises financed for staff with 1 year experience with Miracle. Master licenses financed for qualified franchise industry professionals.

Training Provided: Two phase program delivered at one of 4 training facilities and in new office location.

Managerial Assistance Available: Monthly individual production analysis, advertising recommendations, sales assistance, toll free hot line to headquarters, newsletters, etc.

Information Submitted: April 1990

MR. BUILD HANDI-MAN SERVICES, INC.
628 Hebron Avenue
Glastonbury, Connecticut 06033
Thomas Tyska, President/CEO

Description of Operation: Mr. Build Handi-Man Services offers residential and commercial property owners a central source for small repair maintenance and renovation work. Each franchisee has a protected territory and is tied into a regional central dispatch by computer.

Number of Franchisees: 20

In Business Since: 1989

Equity Capital Needed: $30,000-$40,000

Financial Assistance Available: None

Training Provided: 1 week initial and then ongoing 1-day workshop.

Managerial Assistance Available: Pre-opening and opening, central data processing, central purchasing, field operations evaluation, inventory control, regional or national meetings.

Information Submitted: May 1990

MR. BUILD INTERNATIONAL
628 Hebron Avenue
Glastonbury, Connecticut 06033
Thomas Tyska, President/CEO

Description of Operation: National franchisor of residential and commercial remodeling, maintenance, service and repair tradespeople.

Number of Franchisees: Over 500 throughout the United States, Canada and Japan.

In Business Since: 1981

Equity Capital Needed: $9,900 franchise fee, depending on classification, plus net worth requirements.

Financial Assistance Available: Various financing programs available through independent lending institutions if franchisee qualifies.

Training Provided: Management on a continuous basis.

Managerial Assistance Available: Various industry-related personnel, sales and management courses available on a continuous basis.

Information Submitted: May 1990

MR. BUILD PLUS, INC.
628 Hebron Avenue
Glastonbury, Connecticut 06033
Thomas Tyska, President/CEO

Description of Operation: Mr. Build Plus is a home improvement showroom where consumers choose materials, get project designs and cost estimates and arrange installation. The showrooms feature kitchen and bathroom layouts, as well as ideas and concepts for other remodeling, renovating and additions. They also provide interior decorating.

Number of Franchisees: 6

In Business Since: 1987

Equity Capital Needed: $90,000-$221,000

Financial Assistance Available: None

Training Provided: 1 week initial training at Connecticut headquarters.

Managerial Assistance Available: Central data processing, central purchasing, field operations evaluation, field training, initial store opening, inventory control, newsletter, regional or national meetings, telephone hotline.

Information Submitted: May 1990

NATURE LOG HOMES
Rt. 2, Box 164, South Kings Highway
Noel, Missouri 64854
Ernest Bramlett, President

Description of Operation: International log home manufacturer.

Number of Franchisees: 137 in 23 States

Equity Capital Needed: $40,000-$50,000 (log model home)

Financial Assistance Available: 50 percent is provided to qualified applicants.

Training Provided: Expense-free at our national office, excluding travel.

Managerial Assistance Available: Technical manual, blueprints and etc.

Information Submitted: April 1990

NEW ENGLAND LOG HOMES, INC.
2301 State Street
P. O. Box 5427
Hamden, Connecticut 06518

Description of Operation: New England Log Homes, Inc. (NELHI), manufactures precut, hand-peeled log homes from pine timber. Over 40 models are available encompassing a wide variety of home sizes and styles. NELHI can also design and manufacture custom homes. Franchise dealers are established from Maine to Florida and as far West as California. The dealer is required to erect a model home which serves as his office. This is provided at dealers cost.

Number of Franchisees: 70 nationwide.

In Business Since: 1969

Equity Capital Needed: $100,000-$150,000 (this includes the log home cost, land, furnishings, etc., which are then the franchisee's personal property).

Financial Assistance Available: Yes

Training Provided: 5 days classroom in Hamden, Connecticut, 5 days construction when model home erected. A yearly sales meetings is designed to upgrade the dealers in the latest changes in the log homes, sales methods, etc.

Managerial Assistance Available: Yes, depending on the individual's needs, assistance is provided by regional managers in franchisee's area as well as by corporate staff.

Information Submitted: May 1990

NORTHERN PRODUCTS LOG HOMES, INC.
P. O. Box 616, Bomarc Road
Bangor, Maine 04401-0616
Judi Perkins, Director of Marketing

Description of Operation: Northern Products Log Homes, Inc., manufactures pre-cut log home packages for both residential and commercial use. The company offers 58 standard models and a free custom design service. Franchised dealers are required to purchase and erect a display building that may also be used as the franchisee's residence.

Number of Franchisees: 27 in 19 States

In Business Since: 1968

Equity Capital Needed: $66,600-$199,980 (includes cost of log home, equipment, furnishings, signage and sales and promotional material).

Financial Assistance Available: Construction financing.

Training Provided: Mandatory initial training and orientation at main office in Bangor, Maine. Further training at the franchisee's location. Annual national sales training and business meeting held.

Managerial Assistance Available: Managerial and technical assistance provided as required or requested throughout the term of the franchise.

Information Submitted: April 1990

NOVUS PLATE GLASS REPAIR, INC.
10425 Hampshire Avenue, South
Minneapolis, Minnesota 55438
Gerald E. Keinath, President

Description of Operation: Using the exclusive NOVUS patented process, professionally-trained franchisees repair, rather than replace, BB and stone-damaged plate glass windows. NOVUS franchisees are the experts in plate glass repair, and offer a money-saving service to contractors, store owners, banks, and other businesses that use plate glass windows. Franchisees work out of their home or from a fixed location. This company is affiliated with NOVUS Windshield Repair, which has over 1,500 dealers worldwide.

Number of Franchisees: 6

In Business Since: 1972 (franchising since 1982).

Equity Capital Needed: Approximately $12,000 (depending on size of exclusive area).

Financial Assistance Available: None

Training Provided: 3 day factory training at the NOVUS international headquarters includes technical training, sales and marketing classes and seminars on general business operations.

Managerial Assistance Available: Ongoing technical and sales assistance provided by professional staff. Newsletters, conventions, regional meetings, and ongoing research and development are included.

Information Submitted: May 1990

O.P.E.N. AMERICA, INC.
2390 East Camelback Road
Suite 304
Phoenix, Arizona 85016

Description of Operation: O.P.E.N. America, Inc., is a national franchisor of building maintenance contracts, currently with regional offices in Phoenix, Los Angeles, and Seattle. The franchisee receives training in operations and sales, an equipment and supplies package, and a specific amount of initial business to get started. Franchisee will provide janitorial and related services to the building owners, managers and tenants on a contract basis. The franchisor will provide ongoing administrative and billing services to the franchisee.

Number of Franchisees: 265 in California, Washington, and Arizona.

In Business Since: 1983

Equity Capital Needed: As low as $5,000 and $90,000 for local franchise and master franchise, respectively. Total investment of $6,000 to $150,000.

Financial Assistance Available: Available

Training Provided: Franchisor trains franchisees in operation techniques as well as in marketing and sales at the franchisor's regional offices and in the field from 2 days to 6 weeks.

Managerial Assistance Available: Franchisees are provided with confidential operations manual and a marketing manual. Franchisees are kept abreast of all new products and techniques in the building maintenance field. The franchise director is available at all times to the franchisee to offer assistance in all areas.

Information Submitted: April 1990

PAUL W. DAVIS SYSTEMS, INC.
8933 Western Way
Suite 12
Jacksonville, Florida 32256
Paul W. Davis, President

Description of Operation: Paul W. Davis Systems, Inc., is a totally computerized insurance restoration contracting company with approximately 80 percent of its business obtained from insurance adjusters for the repair of fire, water and windstorm damage; the other 20 percent comes from home and commercial improvements. A unique system of computer estimates and cost controls enables our franchisees to experience early success with no previous experience in this field. A good personality and a willingness to work are required.

Number of Franchisees: 90 in 25 States

In Business Since: 1966

Equity Capital Needed: The franchise fee is $35,000. The franchise needs $25,000 operating capital. $42,500 minimum cash required to start.

Financial Assistance Available: Franchisor finances part of franchise fee with payment tied to sales income.

Training Provided: Franchisee trains in home office school for 3 weeks. Franchisor works with franchisee on location. Franchisor can assist in all recruiting, hiring and training.

Managerial Assistance Available: Managerial and technical assistance continues throughout the life of the franchise including computer software and other management programs.

Information Submitted: June 1990

PERMA CERAM ENTERPRISES, INC.
65 Smithtown Boulevard
Smithtown, New York 11787
Joseph Tumolo, President

Description of Operation: Resurfacing and repair of porcelain and fiberglass bathroom fixtures such as tubs, sinks and wall tile with Perma Ceram's Porcelaincote. Process used in private homes, apartments, hotels/motels, institutions, etc. Available in white and all colors. Established national accounts.

Number of Franchisees: Approximately 175 in 39 States, Bermuda, Bahamas, Canada and Puerto Rico

In Business Since: 1975

Equity Capital Needed: $19,500 total investment. Includes all equipment, materials, supplies and training.

Financial Assistance Available: 100 percent financing available through independent lending institutions.

Training Provided: 5 days training at established location. All expenses included in cost of dealership. Technical training, sales training, management, marketing, etc. Operation manual provided.

Managerial Assistance Available: Advertising, sales and promotional materials; ongoing managerial and technical assistance provided. Continual updating of information provided through bulletins, newsletters, personal contact. Return visits to training facility available if necessary.

Information Submitted: May 1990

PERMA-GLAZE, INC.
1200 North El Dorado Place
Suite A-110
Tucson, Arizona 85715
Dale R. Young, President

Description of Operation: Perma-Glaze specializes in the restoration and refinishing of bathroom and kitchen fixtures such as bathtubs, sinks and ceramic wall tiles. Materials to be refinished consist of porcelain, fiberglass, acrylic, cultured marble, formica, kitchen appliances, whirlpool tubs, shower enclosures and most building materials. Service includes chip repair, fiberglass and acrylic spa repairs, restoration and recoating of fixtures. Available in any color including white. All work under complete warranty. Perma-Glaze services home owners, apartments, hotels/motels, institutions, hospitals, contractors, property managers, plumbing contractors and many more.

Number of Franchisees: 97 in 28 States and 3 countries

In Business Since: 1978; sale of franchise began in 1983.

Equity Capital Needed: $16,500 to $19,500 includes all training, equipment and supplies with enough product to earn back your initial investment.

Financial Assistance Available: Franchisor does not offer any specific kind or amount of financial assistance to prospective franchises. Assistance is rendered to prospective franchises with regard to mode and method of financing and payment where a small amount of assistance is needed.

Training Provided: 5 day (hands-on) training session by trained technician at established location. Lodging and air fare included in cost of franchise. Technical training provided with operations manual, hotline service and newsletter.

Managerial Assistance Available: Info provided for support in advertising, sales, promotional sales, mailing lists, business contacts. Advertising format for yellow pages, newspapers and manazines plus availability of material for TV commercial. Continual exposure from national advertising in popular well known magazines as well as many trade publications. Continual updating of information provided through bulletins, newsletters and personal contact.

Information Submitted: April 1990

PERMA-JACK CO.
9066 Watson Road
St. Louis, Missouri 63126
Joan L. Robinson, President

Description of Operation: A fast inexpensive building foundation stabilizing system. Hydraulically driven steel pipe columns support the building foundation on rock or equal load bearing.

Number of Franchisees: 16 in 9 States

In Business Since: 1974, incorporated 1975

Equity Capital Needed: Inventory and working capital $60,000. Franchise fee, according to population, $7,500 to $20,000.

Financial Assistance Available: None

Training Provided: Field training and complete instructions are given at the St. Louis, Missouri, home office. Further training at the franchisee's location and job sites. Continuing informational assistance and training are given. Art work, layouts, and outlines for advertising and suggested business forms and brochures are included.

Managerial Assistance Available: Managerial and technical assistance provided throughout length of franchise. Top management makes field visits as deemed necessary.

Information Submitted: April 1990

PORCELAIN PATCH & GLAZE COMPANY OF AMERICA
140 Watertown Street
Watertown, Massachusetts 02172
Philip J. Gleason

Description of Operation: Refinishing, spraying, glazing, spot-blending and patching of porcelain and enamel finishes of all kinds, spray painting of lacquer and lacquer blending work of all kinds. Performed for appliance stores, home owners, movers, apratment house owners, plumbers, distributors of major appliances, dentists. A shop is not necessary.

Number of Franchisees: 15 in 15 States

In Business Since: 1938

Equity Capital Needed: $3,500

Financial Assistance Available: 50 percent down to good credit risks.

Training Provided: 10 days at main office

Managerial Assistance Available: Periodic visits, direct mail advertising.

Information Submitted: June 1990

PORCELITE INTERNATIONAL, INC.
15745 Crabbs Branchway
Rockville, Maryland 28855
M. D. Berardi, President

Description of Operation: The Porcelite franchise offers a process for the repair and refinishing of porcelain plumbing fixtures such as bathtubs and sinks for both commercial and residential use. Chips are repaired and complete fixtures refinished and restored. Used in homes, motels, apartment houses, etc. In white or choice of any color.

Number of Franchisees: 72 in 26 States

In Business Since: 1963

Equity Capital Needed: $17,500 minimum

Financial Assistance Available: None

Training Provided: 5 day training session from 9 am to 5 pm covering all aspects of procelain repair, refinishing, and restoration.

Managerial Assistance Available: Advertising and sales promotional materials, continuing guidance and assistance are required. Operations manual provided.

Information Submitted: June 1990

REDI-STRIP CO., INC.
9910 Jordon Circle
Santa Fe Springs, California 90670
J. Paul Derlinger, President

Description of Operation: The Redi-Strip system offers a unique nondestructive paint and coating removal by a simple immersion system. The electrolytic deruster immersion "floats" the rust off of steel parts with no metal loss. Redi-Strip provides the tanks, chemicals and some other equipment to start your business.

Number of Franchisees: 23 in 16 States and Canada

In Business Since: 1951

Equity Capital Needed: $40,000 to $89,000. No franchise fee or royalties are involved.

Financial Assistance Available: This would be answered by J. Paul Deringer.

Training Provided: Intensive 1 week mandatory work and training program at one of our plants. One week at the franchise location.

Managerial Assistance Available: Redi-Strip is available at all times to answer any and all questions.

Information Submitted: May 1990

RYAN HOMES, INC.
100 Ryan Court
Pittsburgh, Pennsylvania 15205
Edward L. Smith

Description of Operation: Ryan Homes, Inc., is a residential single family homebuilder. Ryan is presently one of the largest builders in the country. They offer individuals complete systems and products to allow them to build and sell houses in preselected markets.

Number of Franchisees: 7 in 7 States

In Business Since: 1948

Equity Capital Needed: $150,000-$250,000

Financial Assistance Available: Franchisor will provide no assistance in financing operation. Franchisor provides construction financing for model homes and sold houses and assistance in securing permanent mortgages for customers.

Training Provided: Initial training includes Ryan manager spending approximately 4 months on-site with franchisee to set up systems and start up operation. Ryan has ongoing field training and franchisee can attend Ryan training center for any of 16 courses.

Managerial Assistance Available: Field support is administered by a staff and is involved in marketing, merchandising, sales, construction, administration and management. Field staff works closely with franchisee in all phases of operation.

Information Submitted: June 1990

THE SCREEN MACHINE
P. O. Box 1207
Sonoma, California 95476
Wayne T. Wirick, President

Description of Operation: The Screen Machine is a mobile repair service franchise, engaged in the business of providing rescreening for doors and windows, installation of new door screens and window screens, and related services including security hardware installation. The screening and related services are provided at the customer's home or place of business.

Number of Franchisees: 4 in California, plus 1 company owned in Sonoma.

In Business Since: 1986

Equity Capital Needed: Minimum cash requirement of $25,000. Includes $13,500 franchise fee, $9,030 equipment, $2,320 inventory.

Financial Assistance Available: None

Training Provided: Comprehensive 1 week program at company training facility in Sonoma. The training will cover all areas of operations including product manufacturing, accounting, inventory control, customer service and relations, financial management and control, advertising and promotion.

Managerial Assistance Available: The Screen Machine support staff including all officers of the company are readily available to give continuous assistance in all areas of operations and development.

Information Submitted: April 1990

THE SCREENMOBILE CORP.
457 West Allen #107
San Dimas, California 91773
Monty M. Walker, President

Description of Operation: Mobile window and door screening and rescreening service.

Number of Franchisees: 40 in California, Arizona, Idaho and Texas.

In Business Since: 1982

Equity Capital Needed: $33,000

Financial Assistance Available: None

Training Provided: Field training, shop training, classroom training, approximately 2 weeks.

Managerial Assistance Available: Ongoing 24 hour telephone and field assistance.

Information Submitted: April 1990

SERVICE AMERICA
6840 Roswell Road
Suite 2A
Atlanta, Georgia 30328
Ron Smith, President

Description of Operation: Service America offers a unique service/replacement marketing program for existing heating and air conditioning dealers.

Number of Franchisees: 75 in 21 States

In Business Since: 1984

Equity Capital Needed: $75,000

Financial Assistance Available: None

Training Provided: 10 days of initial training is provided at the home office school.

Managerial Assistance Available: Service America provides continual ongoing management service for the life of the franchise.

Information Submitted: May 1990

SMOKEY MOUNTAIN LOG HOMES
P. O. Box 549
Maggie Valley, North Carolina 28751

Description of Operation: Manufacturer of pre-fabricated log homes.

Number of Franchisees: 16 in Virginia, North Carolina, South Carolina, Georgia and Florida.

In Business Since: 1974

Equity Capital Needed: No franchise fee or liability. However, dealer must be capable of erecting a model home.

Financial Assistance Available: Financing must be obtained through various established loan institutions.

Training Provided: Franchisee is required to familiarize himself/herself with Smokey Mountain Log Home production methods by visiting the production facility in Maggie Valley, North Carolina. Knowledge of construction related procedures is a prerequisit. A paid 2 day training seminar is offered.

Managerial Assistance Available: Technical assistance in the field on a personal basis is provided along with a dealer support kit that has been compiled to aid advertising and marketing of Smokey Mountain Log Home kits.

Information Submitted: June 1990

SPEED FAB-CRETE CORPORATION INTERNATIONAL
1150 East Mansfield Highway
P. O. Box 15580
Fort Worth, Texas 76119
David Bloxom, Jr., President

Description of Operation: Speed Fab-Crete is a patented precast concrete building system using lightweight loadbearing concrete wall panels as its core component. Each franchise acts as a manufacturer, general contractor, and sub-contractor. The franchisor provides complete training program and technical back-up support services.

Number of Franchisees: 2 in 2 States

In Business Since: 1968

Equity Capital Needed: $30,000-$50,000

Financial Assistance Available: None

Training Provided: Minimum 1 week training provided by franchisor at national headquarters for franchisee and key personnel. Periodic 1 and 2 day training seminars held at national headquarters

Managerial Assistance Available: On-site managerial assistance periodically provided at expense of franchisor. On-site technical assistance on request of franchisee. Complete manuals of operations, forms, and directions as provided.

Information Submitted: April 1990

SPR INTERNATIONAL BATHTUB REFINISHING, INC.
3398 Sandford Drive
Marietta, Georgia 30066
Larry Stevens, Franchise Director

Description of Operation: SPR franchise system offers confidential technical knowhow and an exclusive chemical system to repair, refinish or change color on porcelain, fiberglass, cultured marble bathtubs, sinks, appliance surfaces, counter tops, etc. SPR also offers a system for ceramic tile restoration that includes leakproofing ceramic walls and floors, stain and mildew removal, regrouting sealing or complete color change without removal. SPR franchise system includes use of all trademark and service marks including the service trucks, etc., for the use of all dealers.

Number of Franchisees: 16 in 9 States and 1 in Canada

In Business Since: 1971

Equity Capital Needed: $500-$10,000

Financial Assistance Available: Yes

Training Provided: 2 weeks training for franchisee and personnel at home office and on-the-job training. SPR also provides periodic training year round to assist franchisee and employees in any aspect of their business at no charge on VHS video training tapes.

Managerial Assistance Available: SPR provides continual management aid for the life of the franchise, including advertisement formats for newspapers, magazines, TV commercials, etc. Co-op advertisement is also available. Complete manual of operations and directions is provided. SPR personnel offers telephone consultation daily on problem solving.

Information Submitted: April 1990

STUDIO BECKER KITCHENS
2000 Powell Street, Suite 1650
Emeryville, California 94608
Jostein Stokkan, President

Description of Operation: Studio Becker Kitchens is a high end kitchen showroom selling the high quality German Beckermann cabinets. The franchise is set up as a complete one-stop design and planning service for retail customers, architects, contractors and builders in need of residential kitchens.

Number of Franchisees: 8

In Business Since: Abroad in 1946, in U.S.A. 1987

Equity Capital Needed: Minimum of $85,000

Financial Assistance Available: None

Training Provided: 1 week in franchisor's office and 1 week at the showroom and as needed.

Managerial Assistance Available: Yes, as needed with management, pricing, advertising, ocean transport, customs clearance, local delivery, bookkeeping, site selection and lease negotiating and product information, among others.

Information Submitted: April 1990

SURFACE SPECIALISTS, INC.
Route 3, Box 272
Isanti, Minnesota 55040
Wayne McClosky, President

Description of Operation: Repair, refinishing, recoloring of acrylic spas, formica countertops, cultured marble vanities and whirlpool tubs, fiberglass tubs and showers, porcelain tubs and sinks. PVC tubs and showers and kitchen appliances. Factory authorized warranty service for 33 plumbingware manufacturers. Service work for apartments, hospitals and major hotel/motel chains. Supplier of repair materials to acrylic spa and PVC tub manufacturers.

Number of Franchisees: 14 in 11 States and New Brunswick, Canada.

In Business Since: 1980

Equity Capital Needed: $20,500 includes franchise fee.

Financial Assistance Available: Finance $3,500 of the $14,500 franchise fee, payable over 3 years at 10 percent interest. Fee includes equipment and material to complete $10,000 to $15,000 in service work.

Training Provided: 2 weeks at the Minnesota location. After training we contact all manufacturers, distributors, etc.

Managerial Assistance Available: Continual management service for the duration of the franchise in all phases including bidding, technical problems, new services and materials, and problem solving.

Information Submitted: April 1990

TIMBERMILL STORAGE BARNS, INC.
P. O. Box 218
Sonoma, California 95476
Thomas N. Hoover, President

Description of Operation: Timbermill Storage Barns, Inc., prefabricates, sells and constructs on-site storage barns. These barns are constructed of top quality materials purchased locally by the franchisee. Some prefabriction is required before construction takes place at the job site.

Number of Franchisees: 26 nationwide

In Business Since: 1985

Equity Capital Needed: $18,000

Financial Assistance Available: None

Training Provided: Extensive 5 day training program at franchisee's location designed to educate him in all aspects of the Timbermill business plan. The loan of the Timbermill operations

manual that includes such topics as material inventory, purchasing and construction procedures, marketing, bookkeeping, and much more.

Managerial Assistance Available: Total training and ongoing assistance with advertising, technical bulletins and managerial support. Conducts market research to aid franchisees in promoting their products. Timbermill Storage Barns, Inc., provides all assistance necessary to achieve and maintain the high quality that is becoming a trademark with our barns.

Information Submitted: April 1990

*UNION CARBIDE MARBLE CARE, INC./MARBLE LIFE
39 Old Ridgebury Road
Location K
Danbury, Connecticut 06817
Richard M. Brockmann, President

Description of Operation: Marble restoration and preservation service for commercial facilities and residences.

Number of Franchisees: 3 plus 1 company-owned.

In Business Since: 1989, franchising since 1990

Equity Capital Needed: Total investment $57,000-$80,000.

Financial Assistance Available: None, assistance program for bank financing and SBA.

Training Provided: Full training program is provided.

Managerial Assistance Available: Complete managerial assistance program is available.

Information Submitted: June 1990

WALL FILL WORLDWIDE, INC.
649 Childs Street
Wheaton, Illinois 60187
Edmund G. Lowrie, President

Description of Operation: Business format franchise. Trains the franchisee in the areas of sales, management, and basic installation procedures. The business operation consists of the sale and installation of siding, gutters, windows and doors.

Number of Franchisees: 2 in Illinois including company-owned.

In Business Since: 1986—Parent in business since 1928.

Equity Capital Needed: $31,250

Financial Assistance Available: None

Training Provided: 10 days in sales, basic installation, crew management, and office management.

Managerial Assistance Available: Ongoing—intensive in first 5 days of operation.

Information Submitted: June 1990

THE WINDOWS OF OPPORTUNITIES, INC.
711 Rigsbee Avenue
Durham, North Carolina 27701
Conrad Harris

Description of Operation: The Windows of Opportunities offers franchises in "The Window Man," for exclusive solid vinyl replacement windows and new construction vinyl windows, sun and garden room enclosures and state of the art wireless security systems.

Number of Franchisees: 24 in North Carolina, South Carolina, Georgia, and Virginia

In Business Since: 1983

Equity Capital Needed: Varies from $15,000 to $35,000.

Financial Assistance Available: Financing assistance to qualified applicants.

Training Provided: Extensive 1 week training at corporate training center in Durham, North Carolina. On-site start-up support and continual ongoing training and operational support.

Managerial Assistance Available: Assistance in management, sales and marketing, business operations, advertising, lead operations, etc.

Information Submitted: April 1990

*WORLDWIDE REFINISHING SYSTEMS, INC.
P. O. Box 3146
Waco, Texas 26207

Description of Operation: Refinishing specialists of bathtubs and bath fixtures including antique leg tubs and unique sinks. We can change the color of an entire bathroom including the tile. We also refinish fiberglass benches (fast food restaurants), chip repair on new and used fixtures. We refinish most other surfaces and market a line of bath and kitchen accessories.

Number of Franchisees: Over 200 in 30 States.

In Business Since: 1970

Equity Capital Needed: $11,000

Financial Assistance Available: None

Training Provided: 5 day intensive classroom and on-the-job training. Also includes training video tapes and TV commercials.

Managerial Assistance Available: Complete backup and support system via the telephone for technical and marketing advice. Complete advertising and bookkeeping program.

Information Submitted: May 1990

COSMETICS/TOILETRIES

ALOETTE
345 Lancaster Avenue
Malvern, Pennsylvania 19355
John E. Defibaugh

Description of Operation: Distribution of high quality cosmetics through sales representatives conducting shows in customers' homes. Recent acquisitions will enable the company to vertically integrate and produce its own products.

Number of Franchisees: 66 in 33 States, and 41 in Canada, United Kingdom, Australia, New Zealand, Bahamas.

In Business Since: 1978

Equity Capital Needed: $60,000; $10,000 cash downpayment, balance financed.

Financial Assistance Available: Franchisor has provided financing of franchise note.

Training Provided: Extensive training provided in areas of sales, recruiting, operations, and financial accounting.

Managerial Assistance Available: Sales training manuals and videotapes available. Accounting manual and journals. District set-up allows for technical assistance and support. Regional and national meetings held throughout the year.

Information Submitted: May 1990

CASWELL-MASSEY
121 Fieldcrest Avenue
Edison, New Jersey 08818
Peter Hsu

Description of Operation: Caswell-Massey, the oldest chemists and perfumers in America, was founded in 1752. It is the source for high quality toiletry and personal care items. From its historical register are still made the colognes loved by George Washington and Dolly Madison. With all its products, Caswell-Massey pays attention to product packaging, creating beautiful variegated designs that are representations of its image.

Number of Franchisees: 20 in 12 States including company-owned.

In Business Since: 1976

Equity Capital Needed: $150,000

Financial Assistance Available: None at this time.

Training Provided: 1 week intensive training, refresher training during the initial set-up and on-site training.

Managerial Assistance Available: Complete retail management staff, which consists of the director, associate director and administrative assistant, are available to assist and direct franchisees in all aspects of operating a retail store.

Information Submitted: June 1990

ELIZABETH GRADY FACE FIRST, INC.
One West Foster Street
Melrose, Massachusetts 02176
John P. Walsh, Executive Vice President

Description of Operation: With emphasis on individual consultation and clinical analysis, treatments by professional estheticans and a prescribed home care program, Elizabeth Grady Face First's goal has always been to promote the healthiest skin for all people. Our commitment to serve the best interests of our customers is reflected in the quality of our complete line of products, many of which are specifically developed for Elizabeth Grady salons.

Number of Franchisees: 13 franchises, 14 company-owned stores available for purchase as franchises.

In Business Since: 1974

Equity Capital Needed: Franchise fee of $16,000. $10,000 approximate total investment.

Financial Assistance Available: No, but we will provide assistance in securing third party financing.

Training Provided: Everything you need to know to operate is included in our training program. The tuition is included in your franchise fee. Furthermore, one of our representatives will work with you for 1 week during your first month of operation. Franchisees will also receive an operations manual covering all areas of importance.

Managerial Assistance Available: Training includes periodic updates on all industry trends, new products and services, as well as new advertising and promotional techniques. In addition, franchisee will be provided with total ongoing supervision and support in the form of periodic visits by our experienced staff to consult with your staff on all aspects of operations. Other assistance provided on as needed basis.

Information Submitted: April 1990

*"i" NATURAL COSMETICS NUTRIENT COSMETIC, LTC.
355 Middlesex Avenue
Wilmington, Massachusetts 01887
Robert Greenberg, Chairman

Description of Operation: Unique cosmetic and beauty service shop primarily located in regional malls, offering a complete skin care and cosmetic line that includes more than 350 products. Shops offer the following services: make-up styling, skin care analysis, color consulting, nail sculpturing and manicure, facials, waxing and ear piercing. Products are based on natural ingredients and are exclusively offered in "i" natural shops.

Number of Franchisees: 100 plus shops

In Business Since: 1970

Equity Capital Needed: No franchise fee or royalties. Total capital required, approximately $40,000 to $90,000 for inventory, start-up expenses, shop improvements and working capital.

Financial Assistance Available: "i" natural may provide assistance securing funding for new locations and financing may be available when existing shops are purchased or through landlord contributions.

Training Provided: "i" natural provides an on-site training for owners and their staff that includes operations, management, merchandising and sales. Training consultants typically re-visit new shops within 6 weeks of opening for further training. Additional training available and includes manuals, product up-dates, on-site visits and regional and national conventions.

Managerial Assistance Available: "i" natural offers expertise in real estate, architecture, construction, equipment, initial and ongoing training, store opening, advertising and promotions, marketing, insurance and operational issues.

Information Submitted: April 1990

JUDITH SANS INTERNATIONALE, INC.
3853 Oakcliff Industrial Court
Atlanta, Georgia 30340
Judith Sans, President

Description of Operation: A total "Judith Sans Total Image" makeover center with skin care, body care, hair care, private label manufacturer (cosmetics) and complete skin care cosmetic line for the ethnic market, traded under the name "Women of Color Inc." Complete start-up packages available.

Number of Franchisees: 45 in 13 States plus distributors that approximate 820 plus over 1,400 private label accounts throughout the country in various beauty salons, department stores, boutiques, etc., and in several foreign countries. "Women of Color" retail line for the ethnic market is mall marketed throughout the United States.

In Business Since: 1969, franchising, distributoring, private label 1978.

Equity Capital Needed: $40,000 to $70,000 for distributors. No minimum order for private label.

Financial Assistance Available: None

Training Provided: 14 days intensive training provided by franchisor, distributor at company's training school in Atlanta, Georgia. Comprehensive, technical, administrative manuals, and recordkeeping, advertising assistance, and quarterly fresh-up training, site location and layout help provided. Field personnel start-up, on-site help, and periodic evaluation.

Managerial Assistance Available: Continuous

Information Submitted: May 1990

SYD SIMONS COSMETICS, INC.
2 East Oak Street
Chicago, Illinois 60611
Jerome Weitzel, President

Description of Operation: Syd Simons Cosmetics offers a unique, completely equipped makeup and skin care studio for the sale of a complete line of cosmetic products and accessories as well as related services. The package includes all furniture, fixtures, studio supplies, opening inventory, decorating, brochures and advertising and promotional materials.

Number of Franchisees: 5 in Illinois

In Business Since: Retailing 1940, franchising 1972.

Equity Capital Needed: Approximately $60,000

Financial Assistance Available: Franchisor will assist franchisee in obtaining business loan from appropriate lending institution.

Training Provided: Syd Simons Cosmetics provides basic 60 day training period in makeup and skin care as well as studio operations and business procedures at the franchisor's home office. Additional on-site training conducted periodically.

Managerial Assistance Available: Syd Simons provides continual managerial, legal, financial and promotional guidance in accordance with the needs of the franchisee, as well as assistance in sales areas.

Information Submitted: April 1990

DENTAL CENTERS

AMERICAN DENTAL COUNCIL, INC.
15760 Ventura Boulevard
Suite 1030
Encino, California 91436
Martin M. Cooper, President

Description of Operation: Dental referral service providing free referral to private-practice general dentist or orthodontist in local area. Panel consists of at least 25 private dental practices, composed of dentists who wish to gain more patients by bonding together, pooling advertising (TV, newspaper) funds, and creating a total marketing program.

Number of Franchisees: 2 in California and 1 in Michigan

In Business Since: 1980

Equity Capital Needed: $75,000

Financial Assistance Available: None

Training Provided: Ongoing

Managerial Assistance Available: Assistance with creation of dental panel by putting on group meetings and involvement with personal sales followup. Providing of complete operational handbook and hands-on assistance with such details as staffing, office procedures, patient relations, dental law and ethics. Furnishing of turnkey advertising program, including actual commercials, ongoing media buying and placement, marketing strategy, publicity, etc.

Information Submitted: April 1990

DENTAL HEALTH SERVICES
4014 Gunn Highway
Suite 258
Tampa, Florida 33614
George Linsey, Chief Executive Officer

Description of Operation: Traditional dental offices in high traffic locations. DHS is popularly priced and advertised. We provide complete management services, bookkeeping, laboratory advertising, etc.

Number of Franchisees: 16

In Business Since: 1981

Equity Capital Needed: $50,000 (working capital and franchise fee)

Financial Assistance Available: We arrange financing.

Training Provided: Extensive and ongoing—we train all individuals in our business systems.

Managerial Assistance Available: DHS provides ongoing assistance to its franchisees. We are responsible for new advertising campaigns, implementation of new profit centers, aid in professional hiring, purchasing, etc.

Information Submitted: June 1990

DENTAL POWER INTERNATIONAL
5530 Wisconsin Avenue
Suite 735
Chevy Chase, Maryland 20815
Merle Baboyian, President

Description of Operation: Dental Power is a profitable, nationally recognized personnel placement and consulting network serving the dental community exclusively. Each office uses professional, proven methods of operations, sophisticated and innovative advertising and marketing techniques, and is staffed by former members of the dental office team. Services include temporary and permanent staffing, seminars and workshops, in-office consulting and placement of associates and "locum tenens."

Number of Franchisees: 30 in the U.S. and Canada.

In Business Since: 1984 (prototype, Dental Power of Washington, in business since 1974).

Equity Capital Needed: Approximately $30,000 including franchise fee.

Financial Assistance Available: Yes

Training Provided: Consultation and assistance available by telephone or personal visit. Updates on advertising and video-taped updates on recruitment, seminars, and new services ongoing. Review and analysis of financial statements quarterly.

Managerial Assistance Available: Consultation and assistance available by telephone or personal visit. Updates on advertising, recruitment, seminars, and new services ongoing. Review and analysis of financial statements quarterly.

Information Submitted: June 1990

JONATHAN DENTAL INC.
5909 Baker Road
Minnetonka, Minnesota 55345
Dan Racine, President

Description of Operation: Jonathan Dental is a franchisor of independently owned, traditional fee-for-service dental practices located in high traffic retail settings. Jonathan provides franchisees a full realm of services including site selection, construction materials, staffing assistance, training, practice management consulting, quality assurance, marketing and advertising, and a comprehensive computerized business system.

Number of Franchisees: 12 in Minnesota

In Business Since: 1980

Equity Capital Needed: $14,500

Financial Assistance Available: None

Training Provided: 3-5 days initial training for franchisee, managing dentists, and business manager encompassing personnel and dental business systems.

Managerial Assistance Available: Heavy on-site assistance in practice management during the first operating year, tapering to 4-6 days per year thereafter.

Information Submitted: June 1990

NU-DIMENSIONS DENTAL SERVICES
1196 Palisade Avenue
Fort Lee, New Jersey 07024

Description of Operation: Nu-Dimensions Dental Centers are comprehensive, consumer-oriented, group dental practices, operating 7 days and 5 evenings a week, and utilizing sophisticated business systems appropriate for high-volume dental practices. Fee structure is less than prevailing community averages, but practices are not discount-oriented.

Number of Franchisees: 9 in New Jersey and New York (excludes company-owned units)

In Business Since: 1978

Equity Capital Needed: $250,000

Financial Assistance Available: Franchisor is able to introduce qualified prospective franchisees to major regional banks with which successful banking relationships have long been established.

Training Provided: Formal training program is one month prior to opening, plus 75 days after opening; ongoing technical assistance is also provided throughout franchise relationship.

Managerial Assistance Available: Nu-Dimensions provides a complete managerial and business systems format for its franchisees and provides technical assistance as an ongoing component of its management services throughout the duration of the franchise. This includes, but is not limited to, marketing and advertising services, financial controls and managerial systems support, operational guidance, group purchasing arrangements, organizational collaboration on systems improvement, and general updating of all business procedures as improvements become indicated.

Information Submitted: June 1990

DRUG STORES

DRUG CASTLE FRANCHISES, INC.
810 East High Street
Springfield, Ohio 45505
Dale A. Obracay, Director of Franchising

Description of Operation: High volume, low margin, deep discount drug stores.

Number of Franchisees: 5 in Ohio, 2 in Indiana, and 1 in Florida

In Business Since: 1984

Equity Capital Needed: $600,000

Financial Assistance Available: Counsel and introduction to banking sources and governmet programs

Training Provided: Initially—30 days, balance of franchise agreement—on demand.

Managerial Assistance Available: Initially—30 days, balance of franchise agreement—on demand.

Information Submitted: June 1990

DRUG EMPORIUM, INC.
7760 Olentangy River Road
Suite 207
Columbus, Ohio 43235
Pat Hiller, Vice President-Franchising

Description of Operation: Drug Emporium is a high-volume, low-margin retail drug store that carries a broad line of health and beauty aids, cosmetics, greeting cards, and a full service pharmacy.

Number of Franchisees: 113 in 20 States plus 84 company-owned

In Business Since: 1977

Equity Capital Needed: $600,000

Financial Assistance Available: Guidance only

Training Provided: 200 hours training in Columbus; manuals are furnished with documentation of start-up and operations including forms needed for operation function.

Managerial Assistance Available: Assistance is constant and predicated on the fact that our income starts after the franchisee is successful.

Information Submitted: June 1990

*HEALTH MART, INC.
1220 Senlac Drive
Carrollton, Texas 75006
Bruce Kneeland, Vice President

Description of Operation: Health Mart will provide franchises with substantial assistance in the operational and merchandising aspects of operating a full line drug store which includes private label products.

Number of Franchisees: 628 stores in 23 States

In Business Since: 1982

Equity Capital Needed: $5,750 to $55,750—existing operation, $145,000 to $192,000—new operation

Financial Assistance Available: Fixturing, signage and decor are available on a lease basis.

Training Provided: The H/M training department provides intensive 3 day managerial training seminars, 1 day intensive clerk seminars, a monthly training newsletter, various video training programs, and a complete retail operations manual. The H/M district manager provides in-store training at the time of store set-up and ongoing training during the monthly store visits.

Managerial Assistance Available: Assistance is provided during the initial store set-up phase and ongoing throughout the franchise. Assistance is provided in the areas of trade area analysis, site selection, lease negotiation, finance negotiations, fixturing, design, decor, signage, store layout, merchandising product selection, planograming, pricing, in-store promotion, advertising, personnel selection and training, inventory control and basic store operations.

Information Submitted: June 1990

*MEDICAP PHARMACIES, INC.
10202 Douglas Avenue
Des Moines, Iowa 50322
Calvin James, Vice President-Franchise Development

Description of Operation: Medicap Pharmacies are convenient and low cost professional pharmacies. They typically operate in a 800-1000 square feet location with 80 to 90 percent of the business being the filling of prescriptions. Providing over the counter medically oriented products is 10 to 20 percent of the business.

Number of Franchisees: 79 in 12 States

In Business Since: 1971

Equity Capital Needed: $30,000

Financial Assistance Available: On behalf of the franchisee our assistance includes preparation of growth projections and capital needs as well as the actual presentation of the program to the lending institution.

Training Provided: A minimum of 3 days in the Des Moines area provides 3 days of classroom situation and 1 day in several Medicap Pharmacies with on-the-job experience. Training covers all aspects of operation from bookkeeping and cash register procedures to proper handling of patients and employees. A complete procedures manual is fully discussed.

Managerial Assistance Available: A full management training course is provided by Medicap Pharmacies, Inc. In addition to the initial 3 days in the Des Moines area, continuing training and guidance are provided through periodic store visits by home office personnel. Periodic seminars, workshops and equipment exhibits are held. Much of the annual 3 day convention is devoted to technical and managerial assistance.

Information Submitted: April 1990

*MEDICINE SHOPPE INTERNATIONAL, INC.
1100 North Lindberg Boulevard
St. Louis, Missouri 63132
Jerome F. Sheldon, President

Description of Operation: Retail prescription and health care centers, emphasizing prescriptions, OTC items and professional health care programs. The format includes major emphasis on the pharmacist/manager being an integral part of the health care delivery team in the store's market area. Approximately 90 percent of the sales volume is generated by prescriptions, with the remainder being over-the-counter drugs, Medicine Shoppe brand label products, and health care related items.

Number of Franchisees: 821 in 48 States

In Business Since: 1970

Equity Capital Needed: $92,000, which includes fee, fixtures, supplies, inventory and opening promotion.

Financial Assistance Available: Franchisor provides financial assistance up to 80 percent of the cost of the franchise, or guidance in dealing with commercial and SBA lenders, leasing packages, etc.

Training Provided: Intensive 1 week training seminar at corporate headquarters with direct instruction by all department heads. Two days or longer at store location during store opening. Franchisor also conducts district, regional and national meetings for the continued training of franchisee.

Managerial Assistance Available: Substantial assistance is given in all of the following key areas: site selection, lease negotiations, store layout, fixturing, personnel selection and training, opening procedures, purchasing guidelines and sales and expense, and an operations report. Stores have individual operations representatives who work closely with the manager/owner in the monthly analysis of sales, gross profit, expenses and other salient areas. Heavy emphasis is given to public relations efforts, advertising and marketing programs at all times.

Information Submitted: April 1990

SNYDER DRUG STORES, INC.
14525 Highway #7
Minnetonka, Minnesota 55345
William J. Vidmar, Vice President/
Wholesale/Pharmacy Operations

Description of Operation: Full line wholesaler of health and beauty aids, drugs, and general merchandise from its 363,000 square feet company-owned warehouse. It wholesales to approximately 200 independent retail drug store operators and operates 62 company-owned stores. There is no franchise fee.

Number of Franchisees: 200 in Iowa, Michigan, Minnesota, South Dakota, Illinois and Wisconsin plus 62 company-owned stores.

In Business Since: 1928

Equity Capital Needed: Equity plus loan availability to $300,000

Financial Assistance Available: Company assists operator in developing bank and SBA credit.

Training Provided: While most of Snyder independent retail operators are pharmacists or individuals with retail experience, training in a company-owned store can be provided.

Managerial Assistance Available: Complete new store assistance from market survey, site selection, store fixturing and merchandise layout. Continuous management counseling by experienced store operations personnel, year round advertising and promotional program.

Information Submitted: April 1990

EDUCATIONAL PRODUCTS/SERVICES

*BARBIZON INTERNATIONAL, INC.
950 Third Avenue
New York, New York 10022
B. Wolff, President

Description of Operation: Barbizon operates modeling and personal development schools for teenage girls, homemakers, and career girls. The schools also offer a male modeling program, acting course, and make-up artistry, and sell Barbizon cosmetics. We are the largest organization in this field.

Number of Franchisees: 91 in 40 States

In Business Since: 1939

Equity Capital Needed: $25,000-$50,000

Financial Assistance Available: Franchisee can finance 50 percent of franchise fee with franchisor. Total franchise fee is $19,500 to $35,000.

Training Provided: Intensive 1 week training program for franchisee and his/her director at corporate office. Extensive on-site field visits at franchisee's location by home office staff during first 6 months. Periodic staff visits and conferences at home office thereafter on a continuing basis.

Managerial Assistance Available: In addition to initial training indicated above, Barbizon makes available continuing staff programs, sales aids, new programs, brochures, direct mail pieces, etc.

Information Submitted: April 1990

BETTER BIRTH FOUNDATION, INC.
739 Main Street
Stone Mountain, Georgia 30083
Brenda Seagraves, President

Description of Operation: Better Birth Foundation offers unique courses in family centered child birth preparation for expectant couples, and post partum classes for new mothers and infants. Better Birth Foundation is presently designing additional classes for expectant couples, families and children.

Number of Franchisees: 4 in Georgia and 1 in Colorado.

In Business Since: 1981

Equity Capital Needed: $19,000

Financial Assistance Available: $15,000 franchise fee. The balance is for working capital; there is no financing available through the Better Birth Foundation.

Training Provided: Intensive 15 module educational home study program. An additional 1 week intensive training program at Better Birth's home office, which would include team teaching, practice teaching with supervision and training for the general business operation of the franchise.

Managerial Assistance Available: Better Birth provides continual management with manuals of operation, forms, etc. Better Birth Foundation works closely with franchisees to assist in ongoing training, to maintain a high degree of service and professionalism.

Information Submitted: June 1990

THE CAROLE RIGGS DANCE STUDIOS
116 Bateman Bridge Road
Forest, Virginia 24551
Carole Riggs Harris, President

Description of Operation: Instructional system, largely aimed at children and young adults, which offers to the public, including but not limited to, the teaching of dance, motor development skills, modeling, karate, and musical programs.

Number of Franchisees: 3 company-owned in Virginia

In Business Since: 1966

Equity Capital Needed: $19,900

Financial Assistance Available: No financial assistance provided. Fee paid in two installments.

Training Provided: Franchisee must stay 1 week at corporate headquarters to be trained in operations and procedures. Franchisee may bring 1 additional person. Advisory service with corporate headquarters.

Managerial Assistance Available: Continual service for length of franchise. Complete operational manual also records, cassettes and videos on operations and syllabus.

Information Submitted: May 1990

ELS INTERNATIONAL, INC.
5761 Buckingham Parkway
Culver City, California 90230
Jerry D. Loudenback, President

Description of Operation: ELS International, Inc., is offering franchises to operate ELS International Language Schools for the teaching of English as a Second Language in foreign countries. ELS International is related to ELS Language Centers, which owns and operates 22 language centers.

Number of Franchisees: 19 in Japan, Korea, Thailand, Peru, Taiwan, Spain and Indonesia, plus 22 company-owned in 16 States and the United Kingdom, plus 3 joint-venture schools in Brazil.

In Business Since: 1961

Equity Capital Needed: $150,000-$300,000

Financial Assistance Available: No financing is available from franchisor or its affiliates.

Training Provided: Prior to franchisee's opening, franchisor will conduct a minimum 8 day training session at franchisor's headquarters. A "start-up" kit is provided that includes curriculum guides, tests, course syllabi and outlines. Franchisor will also conduct a 5 day training session at franchisee's premises prior to opening. Franchisor will conduct an additional 5 day on-the-job training session at franchisee's premises approximately 6 months after the franchisee commences.

Managerial Assistance Available: ELS International provides continued support throughout the term of the franchise by conducting professional seminars for franchisee's teachers, providing updated curriculum guides and manuals for professional English courses and a communication system with each franchisee. Franchisor will also provide each franchisee with its operations manual, which sets forth franchisor's unique program of English

language instruction. Franchisor's designated representatives will visit each language school at least 2 times per year to inspect the operations and assist the franchisee.

Information Submitted: June 1990

EXECUTRAIN CORPORATION
1000 Abernathy Road
Suite 400
Atlanta, Georgia 30328

Description of Operation: ExecuTrain, the nation's leading personal computer training franchise, offers exclusive franchise opportunities in the $44 billion training industry. ExecuTrain has trained well over 100,000 business people on how to use Lotus 1-2-3 and other popular computer programs.

Number of Franchisees: 31

In Business Since: 1984

Equity Capital Needed: At least $75,000 cash available.

Financial Assistance Available: None

Training Provided: General manager training (1 week), trainer training (1 week per trainer), sales training (3 days per sales person), accounting system training (3 days), and management information system training (2 days).

Managerial Assistance Available: Conferences (2 times a year), phone support (toll free), on-site visits and newsletters.

Information Submitted: April 1990

GODDARD EARLY LEARNING CENTER
381 Brooks Road
King of Prussia, Pennsylvania 19406
Jill Panetta

Description of Operation: Goddard Early Learning Centers has begun to franchise a chain of high quality child care facilities to meet one of the most challenging problems facing millions of American families in the 1990s. The same expertise that has made MAACO Enterprises, Inc., a giant in the franchising world is being combined with experts in the field of child care to search for a corps of men and women with the skills and talents to build a child care chain with a competitive edge on other services throughout the country.

Number of Franchisees: 5 plus 2 company-owned units in 3 States.

In Business Since: 1986

Equity Capital Needed: $30,000-$40,000. Total investment $100,000-$140,000.

Financial Assistance Available: Yes

Training Provided: Training provided in all phases of operating the franchise.

Managerial Assistance Available: Complete managerial assistance available.

Information Submitted: April 1990

*GYMBOREE CORPORATION
577 Airpost Blvd., #400
Burlingame, California 94010
Bob Campbell, Director of Franchise Sales

Description of Operation: Gymboree, a quality developmental play program, offers weekly classes to parents and their children, age 3 months to 4 years, on custom-designed equipment for infants, toddlers and preschoolers. The program is based on sensory integration theory, positive parenting, child development principles, and the importance of play.

Number of Franchisees: Over 292 Gymboree centers in operation (including 5 company-owned). Franchises have been granted to over 146 franchisees covering market plans for the development of over 408 centers in 35 States, Australia, France, Israel, Mexico, and Taiwan.

In Business Since: 1976

Equity Capital Needed: $8,000-$18,000 fee per site depending on number of sites. Approximately $9,000 per site for equipment and supplies; $4,000-$6,000 working capital.

Financial Assistance Available: None

Training Provided: All franchisees attend a 9 day training seminar with a follow-up visit to their location(s) after opening and once a year thereafter. Regional training programs are held on an ongoing basis.

Managerial Assistance Available: There is an annual seminar for ongoing training. All franchisees are visited annually. Phone contact regularly.

Information Submitted: April 1990

HUNTINGTON LEARNING CENTERS, INC.
660 Kinderkamack Road
Oradell, New Jersey 07649
Thomas Anderson, Franchise Director

Description of Operation: Individualized instruction is provided for school-aged children and adults in remedial and speed reading, study skills, spelling, phonics, math, and SAT preparation. Prior to admission, each student receives an educational evaluation. During a parent conference, recommendations are made regarding the type and degree of help needed. The system of diagnosis and conferencing incorporates an educationally sound assessment of skills with a professional presentation. This presentation is designed to "sell" the parents on the importance of the center in their child's academic life.

Number of Franchisees: 16 company-owned centers in New York, New Jersey and Pennsylvania and over 83 franchised centers in 27 States.

In Business Since: 1977

Equity Capital Needed: From $70,000 to $100,000

Financial Assistance Available: No financing arrangements are offered by the franchisor.

Training Provided: Intensive 2 week initial training program covering educational and testing materials; phone call training to get parents to bring the child for testing; initial conference procedures to help parents help the child and to keep the student enrolled; management systems for the center's efficient operation; quality control procedures. Follow-up on-site training is also conducted.

Managerial Assistance Available: Franchisor provides franchisee with the management and administrative systems to minimize time spent on non-productive miscellaneous administrative matters. To aid in the center's efficient operation, seasoned professionals are available to provide additional advice and assistance over the phone or in person. In addition, periodic visits to each center are planned in advance. Franchisor provides statistical tools to compare franchisee's performance to an over-all average. This statistical information permits franchisor to review each center for possible weaknesses, and to schedule additional problem-solving visits.

Information Submitted: April 1990

INSTITUTE OF READING DEVELOPMENT
FRANCHISING CORP.
4470 Redwood Highway
San Rafael, California 94903
Paul Cooperman, President

Description of Operation: The Institute of Reading Development (IRD) offers several programs of speed reading and comprehension training for college students, professional persons, and junior high and senior high school students. The programs are marketed solely to institutions, such as corporations, universities, and public and private schools, municipal governments and professional associations. They are endorsed by a number of major California universities, and were developed by IRD's founder and president, Paul Cooperman, who is the author of the widely acclaimed book on the decline of academic achievement of American students, *The Literacy Hoax* (Fall 1978, William Morrow and Company).

Number of Franchisees: 3 in California

In Business Since: 1971

Equity Capital Needed: $55,000

Financial Assistance Available: None

Training Provided: IRD will supply extensive and continuous training in 3 areas: marketing, management, and reading instruction. The initial training consists of a 5 week session for franchisee at IRD's home office.

Managerial Assistance Available: IRD will supply franchisee with all marketing and instructional materials (including training manuals for all jobs), bookkeeping forms, and a cost accounting/sales analysis system. IRD will also supply continuous training and supervision in all phases of marketing and reading instruction, including training in new marketing and instructional programs as they are developed. This is an extraordinary opportunity for someone with a strong marketing/sales background who wants to work in private education.

Information Submitted: June 1990

*JOHN ROBERT POWERS FINISHING, MODELING
& CAREER SCHOOL WORLD HEADQUARTERS
9 Newbury Street
Boston, Massachusetts 02116
Barbara J. Tyler, Executive Vice President

Description of Operation: John Robert Powers School offers finishing, self-improvement, drama, modeling, executive grooming, fashion merchandising, interior design, make-up arts, TV acting/drama, flight attendants, pre-teen and communications in today's world to women and men of all ages. Classes are held year round—day and evening.

Number of Franchisees: 70 in 26 States and Singapore; Manila, Philippines; Jakarta, Indonesia; Bangkok, Thailand; Sidney and Adelaide, Australia; and Japan.

In Business Since: 1923

Equity Capital Needed: $25,000

Financial Assistance Available: None

Training Provided: 3 weeks of teaching and administrative training plus semi-annual seminars.

Managerial Assistance Available: We provide managerial and technical assistance during the life of the franchise by visiting field personnel. Accounting assistance is provided by home office personnel. Conferences are held during the year.

Information Submitted: May 1990

KID'S TIME, INC.
5250 West 73rd Street
Edina, Minnesota 55435
Red Campbell and Sue Johnson

Description of Operation: A supervised, drop-in play center for children between the ages of 18 months and 12 years.

Number of Franchisees: 2 and 2 corporate-owned stores.

In Business Since: 1981

Equity Capital Needed: $85,000

Financial Assistance Available: None

Training Provided: Manager training program—required.

Managerial Assistance Available: Training/orientation; complete operations manual provided; ongoing consultation; regular visits by district manager.

Information Submitted: May 1990

KINDERDANCE INTERNATIONAL, INC.
2150 Atlantic St., P. O. Box 510881
Melbourne Beach, Florida 32951
Bernard Friedman, Vice President

Description of Operation: "Education through Dance." A homebased dance/gymnastics/motor development program designed for boys and girls, ages 2-5. Preschoolers learn basics of ballet, tap, modern dance, gymnastics, blended with vocabulary, numbers, colors, shapes. A full service program allows franchisees to teach in local nursery schools, day care centers, similar settings.

Number of Franchisees: 16 franchisees, 22 units in 11 States.

In Business Since: 1979

Equity Capital Needed: $7,000 total, includes $5,000 franchise fee.

Financial Assistance Available: None

Training Provided: An intensive 7 day training program is provided at company headquarters in Melbourne Beach, Florida, in all aspects of the business for quick start-up in local area and quick return on investment. Training includes a complete operations manual, initial start-up supplies, dancewear, video tapes, cassette tapes, classroom and on-site instruction with preschoolers.

Managerial Assistance Available: Kinderdance provides a follow-up visit to franchisee's area by company personnel, free accounting systems, toll-free hotline, newsletters, discounted insurance, discounted hotel rates while training, annual conventions, continuing education, complete line of marketing, advertising, and public relations tools, site selection assistance, grand opening procedures.

Information Submitted: April 1990

LI'L GUYS 'N' GALS DAYCARE INTERNATIONAL, INC.
10850 North 90th Street
Scottsdale, Arizona 85260
Tom Trollope, President/CEO

Description of Operation: Preschool daycare for corporate and neighborhood locations.

Number of Franchisees: 2 company-owned outlets just commencing franchising.

In Business Since: 1987

Equity Capital Needed: $100,000 total investment.

Financial Assistance Available: Financing is available.

Training Provided: Start-up assistance, operational support and a 10 day training session are provided.

Managerial Assistance Available: Ongoing

Information Submitted: April 1990

MAC TAY AQUATICS, INC.
P. O. Box 753
Champaign, Illinois 61824-0753
Karen N. Taylor, President

Description of Operation: Mac Tay Acquatic Schools are known nationally as a unique self-motivating approach to swimming instruction. Mac Tay is a full comprehensive learn-to-swim program for all ages from infants to adults, as well as programming for the special populations. Mac Tay Aquatic Schools were designed by a professional educator, based upon flexible teaching techniques and approaches. Mac Tay Aquatics, Inc., will help with site selection, and lease negotiation, and provide an affordable liability insurance carrier and an extensive training program.

Number of Franchisees: 4 in Indiana and Illinois plus 1 company-owned.

In Business Since: 1974, franchising since 1985

Equity Capital Needed: In order to obtain and/or commence the franchise operation, must pay $20,000. The total initial investment in the franchise is $25,900-$29,300.

Financial Assistance Available: Financing available to qualified buyers.

Training Provided: 2 week intensive training course, which includes classroom work, observation, discussion and "hands-on" training course, is held at home location in Illinois. A manual is provided that serves as a reference for procedures, techniques and business details.

Managerial Assistance Available: Mac Tay Aquatics, Inc., will be involved in initial media coverage, grand opening procedures and follow-up consultation. Ongoing assistance in advertisement, business aspects, monthly newwsletters, telephone hotlines and regularly scheduled seminars are also part of the Mac Tay Aquatics Franchise.

Information Submitted: April 1990

MODEL MERCHANDISING INTERNATIONAL, LTD.
111 East 22nd Street
New York, New York 10010
Fernando Casablancas, President

Description of Operation: MMI franchises the John Casablancas Modeling and Career Centers. MMI, a subsidiary of Elite Model Management, offers a complete franchise package that includes course programs, operations manuals, advertising and promotion material and audio visuals, ongoing guidance, and a promotional/placement link with Elite, the world's leading model agency group.

Number of Franchisees: 93 throughout the world

In Business Since: 1980

Equity Capital Needed: $22,000-$88,000 (depending on type of franchise and location)

Financial Assistance Available: The franchise fee is $6,000 to $27,000 (depending on population and type), with terms offered. A conversion franchise with existing premises and cash flow may require only promotional outlay to establish itself as a John Casablancas Center. A center starting from scratch will require working capital through breakeven. details on request.

Training Provided: Offered at other centers in New York and at the new franchise's place of business (1 week minimum) with regular visits by MMI and Elite personnel.

Managerial Assistance Available: Service and management guidance, market information, merchandising material, model recruitment, advertising and promotional material and events, plus new programs and audiovisual updates are provided by MMI on an ongoing basis.

Information Submitted: June 1990

PEE WEE WORKOUT
Cardiac Carr Co. (Parent Company)
5568-A Bramble Court
Willoughby, Ohio 44094
Margi Carr

Description of Operation: Exercise program for children.

Number of Franchisees: 16

In Business Since: 1986

Equity Capital Needed: $1,000-$3,000

Financial Assistance Available: None

Training Program: Video based training program.

Managerial Assistance Available: Home office support, advertising materials, marketing and administrative guides.

Information Submitted: May 1990

PERKINS FIT BY FIVE, INC.
1606 Penfield Road
Rochester, New York 14625
Betty Perkins-Carpenter, President

Description of Operation: Athletically oriented pre-school program for children 2-1/2 to 5 years. The fundamental approach to instruction is through development of physical skills as the key to the acquisition of self-confidence, social interaction, tolerance, self-discipline, and verbal-conceptual understandings. The above purpose is accomplished through a revolutionary new idea in pre-school education, using unique teaching techniques, special equipment, and unusual activities. Exercises, music, and basic motor skills are but some of the tools of instruction, which is success oriented, heavily flavored with kindness, consideration, respect, and love.

Number of Franchisees: 1 in Maryland, 2 in New York, and 1 in Pennsylvania, not including company-owned

In Business Since: 1969

Equity Capital Needed: $35,000-$40,000 fee per site depending on number of sites, approximately $6,000 per site for equipment and supplies.

Financial Assistance Available: Financial assistance is not provided.

Training Provided: All franchisees attend a 2 week training program. Follow-up visits to their location(s). Also additional training in Rochester, New York, as needed on ongoing basis.

Managerial Assistance Available: All franchisees are visited once annually. Phone contact as needed, written communications monthly.

Informatoin Submitted: May 1990

PLAYORENA, INC.
125 Mineola Avenue
Roslyn Heights, New York 11577
Fred Jaroslow, Executive Vice President

Description of Operation: Playorena is a recreational and exercise program for children 3 months to 4 years old who attend weekly sessions with a parent. Activities and equipment are custom designed and time tested for the rapidly shifting stages of motor development. Program is based on learning through natural play.

Number of Franchisees: 64 in 6 States

In Business Since: 1981

Equity Capital Needed: From $14,000 to $7,000 fee per site depending on number of sites. Approximately $8,000 per site for equipment. Additional working capital required.

Financial Assistance Available: Up to 50 percent of franchise fee may be financed by qualified applicants.

Training Provided: 8 day training program encompassing the business as well as program aspects of Playorena. Upgrading and refresher training on a continuing basis.

Managerial Assistance Available: Complete manuals provided. On-site visits by management. Seminars and franchisee meetings. Ongoing bulletin service. Public relations assistance. Marketing direction and advice.

Information Submitted: May 1990

PRIMARY PREP INC.
1601 Forum Place
Suite 802
West Palm Beach, Florida 33401
Pauline A. McKee

Description of Operation: Pre-school educational system with written curriculum. Franchisor is committed to a quality learning/educational environment. Barbara J. Wallis, Director of Training and Curriculum Development, holds a masters degree in curriculum development. Complete equipment package, operations manual. Turnkey. Regional areas available.

Number of Franchisees: 15 in Florida plus 1 company-owned

In Business Since: 1984

Equity Capital Needed: $60,500 plus working capital.

Financial Assistance Available: WIll arrange for assistance in developing a loan package to present to a financial institution.

Training Provided: 1 week training at our training center. At grand opening, the training director will come to your school for 1 week to assist in set-up and training your personnel. Training program incorporates cognitive, physical, social and emotional development. Complete operations manual included.

Managerial Assistance Available: Monitoring, management and educational consulting last for the life of the franchise (which is perpetual) on both a regular and an as needed basis.

Information Submitted: May 1990

PRIMROSE SCHOOL FRANCHISING CO.
5131 Roswell Road, NE
Marietta, Georgia 30062
Paul Erwin, President
Jo Kirchner, Executive Vice President

Description of Operation: Quality educational child care with proven curriculum and lesson plans for infants through kindergarten.

Number of Franchisees: 12 in 2 States plus 3 company-owned units.

In Business Since: 1982

Equity Capital Needed: $80,000-$100,000; includes franchise fee of $48,500.

Financial Assistance Available: Assist in finding financing.

Training Provided: Thorough in-house and on-site training. Comprehensive operations manual with lesson plans and monthly package. Ongoing support from skilled corporate staff.

Managerial Assistance Available: See above.

Information Submitted: April 1990

SANDLER SYSTEMS, INC.
P. O. Box 183
2005 Greenspring Valley Road
Stevenson, Maryland 21153
David Sandler, President

Description of Operation: The franchise being offered consists of the right to operate a business devoted to a distinctive style of training persons in the fields of management consulting, leadership development and sales techniques; and also the methods of teaching such subjects through seminars and workshops including programs known as the Sandler Selling System and Systematic Sales Management and other programs to be offered in the future.

Number of Franchisees: 67 in USA

In Business Since: 1983

Equity Capital Needed: $20,000 minimum

Financial Assistance Available: The total investment of $20,000 pays for inventory, training, administrative expenses, and opening costs. Franchisor does not offer any financing arrangements to franchisee.

Training Provided: Franchisor provides regular, periodic training every 90 days, held during business hours at franchisor's principal office in Baltimore. The training program consists of 2 full days, and includes such techniques, expertise, and trade secrets as developed by the franchisor. The training program is mandatory. Periodic newsletters, bulletins, phone consultations will be made available to franchisee.

Managerial Assistance Available: Sandler Systems provides continual assistance for the life of the franchise, and a sales support manager is assigned to each franchisee to work directly with him to answer any technical questions. Sandler Systems sponsors meetings of franchisees to discuss marketing ideas, present new material, etc., in order to maintain high standards of motivation.

Information Submitted: June 1990

SPORTASTIKS INC.
2091 Watterson Street
Champaign, Illinois 61821
Bev Mayasaki, President

Decription of Operation: A children's fitness and gymnastics training center for children from 18 months to 18 years. Pre-school motor development program, recreational class program, accelerated program that leads into competition. Each program is designed so each child feels success, builds confidence and cordination.

Number of Franchisees: 13 in Illinois, Missouri, Indiana, Washington, South Carolina and Virginia

In Business Since: 1979

Equity Capital Needed: Minimum investment $100,000. Maximum investment will depend on demographic requirements and individual needs.

Financial Assistance Available: Equipment leasing available depending on analysis of financial statement.

Training Provided: 24 months of ongoing training includes 6 week correspondence course, complete with videos, 10 day training at national headquarters in Champaign and 22 month ongoing training by phone and visitation.

Managerial Assistance Available: Sportastiks will train each franchisee in daily operations of their business. We will also train a master coach for each facility to assist in daily operations and to provide the gymnastics knowledge necessary to operate a Sportastiks franchise. The owner-operator needs no previous gymnastics experience.

Information Submitted: June 1990

*SYLVAN LEARNING CORPORATION
2400 Presidents Drive
Montgomery, Alabama 36103-5605

Description of Operation: Diagnostic testing and prescriptive programs in reading, math and other curriculum for children and adults. Individualized instruction by certified teachers using proven learning materials and Sylvan innovative educational techniques.

Number of Franchisees: 475 in 47 States, and 4 Canadian Provinces

In Business Since: 1979

Equity Capital Needed: $85,000. Total investment $90,000-$125,000.

Financial Assistance Available: Equipment financing.

Training Provided: 2 weeks initial training in methods of instruction and business plan.

Managerial Assistance Available: Continual franchisee operational and service support.

Information Submitted: May 1990

*TELLER TRAINING DISTRIBUTORS, INC.
440 Ual Building
2033 Sixth Avenue
Seattle, Washington 98121
David Lonay, President

Description of Operation: Teller Training Distributors, Inc., owns and franchises post-secondary proprietary schools (Teller Training Institutes) specializing in the training of persons for entry-level positions in the banking industry. The student completes 80 hours of instruction that includes training on all standard banking machines, computer training, and all methods and procedures necessary to begin work with minimal orientation. The course is approved and accredited for 5 credits by the American Institute of Banking. Graduates are given ongoing placement assistance until employed. Placement rates are very high. Exclusive franchise territories are available to persons who will be personally involved in the operation of the franchise.

Number of Franchisees: 15 in 11 States

In Business Since: 1971

Equity Capital Needed: Up to $25,000 in addition to franchise fee which varies by territory.

Financial Assistance Available: Franchisor will assist franchise owner in obtaining financing.

Training Provided: No prior experience required. Up to 1 month at corporation headquarters for franchise owners in administration, marketing, financing, hiring, recruiting, and placement. Up to 1 month at corporation headquarters for head instructor in instruction methodology and curriculum. Periodic meetings of all franchise-owners provides exchange of current and new methodology in all phases of the business.

Managerial Assistance Available: Franchisor will provide the franchisee with continual support and assistance. Included in franchisor services are (1) aid in selection of school location; (2) aid in

negotiating a favorable lease; (3) provide information and research requirements for city, county, and state licenses; (4) selection of office furniture, school equipment, and supplies; (5) establishment of an advertising program and schedule including prepared print advertisements and television commercials; (6) establishment of an operations budget; (7) assistance in employing and training employees; and (8) accounting and recordkeeping through the corporation's computer. In addition to the continual communication between the franchise-owner and the franchisor by telephone, and the continued furnishing of information through the mail, visits, a detailed operations manual as well as other reference manuals and guides. There is always available to the franchise-owner someone at corporation headquarters to assist in any area that is required.

Information Submitted: May 1990

TGIF VOCATIONS
P.O. Box 828
Old Lyme, Connecticut 06371
Joanne Kobar, President

Description of Operation: Training program for nannies and other in-home help for the private family. Various curricula including 14-week, evening, and correspondence courses, graduating certified nannies and/or governesses to help today's parents find the quality childcare so badly needed. Future plans include courses for other home care fields. Placement of these graduates can be accomplished through the other TGIF franchises, TGIF People Works. Dual franchise ownership is available at a reduced combination fee.

Number of Franchisees: 2

In Business Since: 1982, franchising since 1990

Equity Capital Needed: $15,000-$25,000 franchise fee plus $10,000-$50,000 equity and/or collateral necessary for start-up.

Financial Assistance Available: None

Training Program: Week-long all-expenses-paid training at prototype school in New England; visitation to site prior to actual opening.

Managerial Assistance Available: Step-by-step guidance in obtaining site, necessary state licensing, hiring faculty and staff, and recruiting students. Ongoing support through our experts in franchising, nanny school curriculum, and management information systems. A start-up kit of marketing and operational materials.

Information Submitted: April 1990

TRAVEL PROFESSIONALS INSTITUTE, INC.
10172 Linn Station Road
Suite 360
Louisville, Kentucky 40223
James C. Vernon, President

Description of Operation: Travel Professionals Institute offers and sells franchises which provide professional educational training and services for individuals seeking a career in the travel industry. Our team has over 15 years experience in travel franchising and travel school operations.

Number of Franchisees: 1

In Business Since: 1989

Equity Capital Needed: $61,000

Financial Assistance Available: None

Training Provided: We assist in all phases of start up. Curriculum includes 140 hours, 100 of which are spent in hands-on computer training. The curriculum is updated monthly. Directors are trained in placement techniques. The Institute also offers continuing educational program and industry seminars to those professionals already in the industry. The Institute offers continuous training and assistance to all affiliates.

Managerial Assistance Available: For a period of 5 days the affiliate is trained by the Institute in all aspects of the operation. This includes participation in classes in progress, training in the curriculum and instructional methods and training in office opening and operations procedures. All affiliates receive numerous manuals and proven guidelines for their personal use in the operation of their business.

Information Submitted: March 1990

THE TRAVEL TRADE SCHOOL, INC.
7921 Southpark Plaza
Suite 105
Littleton, Colorado 80120
Adonna L. Hipple, President

Description of Operation: Educational institutions which are individually owned and operated and prepare students for a career in the travel industry. Franchisor provides complete start-up assistance, including site selection, marketing, and state approval for operating a school, guidelines for advertising, equipment and furniture needs and training for directors and instructors.

Number of Franchisees: 5 in Colorado including company-owned.

In Business Since: 1975

Equity Capital Needed: $17,000 in addition to franchise fee that varies by territory.

Financial Assistance Available: Franchisee must be able to handle their own financing.

Training Provided: Start-up assistance and continuing assistance throughout duration of franchise. Assistance in obtaining state licenses, certification and approval assistance in setting up office system, recordkeeping, recruitment, enrollment and continuing education program. Training of director and guidelines for hiring instructors (testing), complete curriculum and guide and all teaching materials.

Managerial Assistance Available: Technical assistance throughout duration of relationship with franchisor. Advertising co-operation, revision of teaching materials, printing of catalogue and materials, workshops to up-date skills and implement changes, training of new personnel (director and instructors). Maintain quality control and train in methods to monitor success.

Information Submitted: June 1990

WEIST-BARRON, INC.
35 West 45th Street
New York, New York 10036
Bob Barron

Description of Operation: Teaching the performance of commercials to adults and children, both in TV and radio. Also teaching soap opera technique to actors. Classes in newscasting, auditioning techniques for musical comedy, classes in sitcom technique, classes in performing musicals and comedy and remedial acting classes.

Number of Franchisees: 6 in Georgia, Pennsylvania, California and Massachusetts.

In Business Since: 1958

Equity Capital Needed: $20,000

Financial Assistance Available: None

Training Provided: Training sessions on the premises conducted by the franchisor for all classes to be in curriculum. Expenses paid by franchisee. Once a year visits to hold seminars and re-training sessions. Paid for by franchisee. Money made by seminars held by franchisee.

Managerial Assistance Available: All the consultation in our New York studios required by franchisee.

Information Submitted: June 1990

EMPLOYMENT SERVICES

*AAA EMPLOYMENT FRANCHISE, INC.
4910K Creekside Drive
Clearwater, Florida 34620
Stacy Madhu, Franchise Operations Director

Description of Operation: AAA Employment Franchise, Inc., offers a highly ethical and professional service to both applicants and employers. AAA offices do not limit themselves to specialized areas of employment. Full service is available—executive to domestic placement—both temporary and permanent employment. The low-discount placement fee of only 3 weeks salary has proven to be in great demand for the past 33 years. Coast-to-coast, border-to-border territories available on a first to qualify basis.

Number of Franchisees: 40 in 19 States plus 85 company-owned offices in 4 States.

In Business Since: AAA Employment, Inc.—1957; AAA Employment Franchise, Inc.—1977.

Equity Capital Needed: Down payment depends on size of territory selected (minimum $4,000—maximum $15,000) and approximately $4,000 (includes office space, furnishings, office supplies, and licensing).

Financial Assistance Available: Once down payment is made, the balance of the fee is paid $50 per week until paid off.

Training Provided: The franchisor's staff will provide the franchisee with an intensive 2 week training program at the corporate headquarters in St. Petersburg, Florida. Additional on-the-job training will be conducted in the field for the franchisee and employees. A representative from the home office will spend the first week of operation in the franchisee's office to offer assistance. Seminars are held semi-annually to keep franchisees updated on new ideas and techniques.

Managerial Assistance Available: The staff of the franchisor will provide the franchisee with continual support and assistance. Some of the services provided by the franchisor are 1) aid in selecting a prime location, 2) aid in negotiating a lease, 3) providing information and research requirements for city, county and State licenses, 4) selection of office furniture and supplies, 5) establishing an advertising schedule, 6) establishing a budget schedule, 7) hiring and training employees, and 8) recordkeeping. In addition to the continual communication between the franchisee and franchisor by phone, and the continued furnishing of information through the mail, visits will be made periodically in the field by a representative of the corporation. The franchisee will also be provided with a detailed operations manual as well as other reference guides. Every effort will be made by AAA Employment Franchise, Inc.

Information Submitted: April 1990

*ADIA PERSONNEL SERVICES
64 Willow Place
Menlo Park, California 94025
Ronald C. Picco, Vice President, Franchise Operations

Description of Operation: ADIA Personnel Services, Inc., is principally engaged in providing a full-service temporary help franchise to independently owned franchisees, who furnish office, clerical, word processing, sales, marketing and industrial personnel to clients on a temporary, as needed basis. The franchise is offered to qualified start-up and existing business owners. ADIA has both company-owned and franchised operations in major markets throughout the United States and is part of an international organization based in Lausanne, Switzerland, with over 800 offices worldwide. The franchise offered includes permanent place, in addition to temporary services. The ADIA System provides the franchisee with research, marketing programs, advertising techniques, materials, publicity methods, awards programs, accounts receivable financing and billing systems, temporary employee benefits programs, management reports and management and staff training. For further information call (800) 366-ADIA, or in California, (415) 324-0696 collect.

Number of Franchisees: 124 franchisees plus 178 company operated offices in 33 States and the District of Columbia

In Business Since: 1957

Equity Capital Needed: $70,000 plus, inclusive of $17,500 initial franchise fee. Initial capital required also depends on whether the franchise is for an established or start-up operation.

Financial Assistance Available: ADIA finances 100 percent of the temporary employees' payroll and accounts receivable financing for 90 days. In addition, ADIA participates in the franchise's local advertising through a co-operative advertising plan which funds up to 50 percent of local costs for pre-approved programs. In addition, ADIA may assist applicants in locating other sources of financing for capitalization. ADIA does not finance directly any portion of the initial franchise fee or other costs.

Training Provided: ADIA provides initial training to the franchisee in 3 phases, coinciding with the opening of the franchisee's office. Initial orientation in operations is provided through manuals, branch observation, and video programs. The second phase, sales and management, is conducted at the U.S. headquarters in the San Francisco area. The training program involves 5 days of intensive instruction in ADIA sales and office management techniques. The third phase of initial training involves on-site support and implementation of programs and systems during the first 2 weeks that the franchisee opens for business, and includes instruction and guidance for both the franchisee and his or her staff. Ongoing training is provided through field support, national meetings, written publications, and field consultation throughout the franchise relationship.

Managerial Assistance Available: Ongoing consulting services and managerial guidance are provided on a regular basis. In addition to initial training, ADIA maintains headquarters and field staff proficient in the entire industry spectrum. These resources are available to each franchisee, offering advice and assistance in such areas as management, marketing, sales, operations, administration, computer information, training, office lay-out and design, legal affairs, insurance, government regulations, finance, purchasing, word processing, employee benefits, public relations, and advertising. Regularly scheduled visits are conducted to assist the franchisee in establishing objectives and to review progress, as well as to ascertain additional services to be provided by ADIA to focus support on areas of specific need.

Information Submitted: April 1990

ANY SITUATION, INC.
Box 340
Bala Cynwyd, Pennsylvania 19004
Helen Tucker

Description of Operation: Franchisor of nanny placement offices that provide long-term and short-term child care in the clients' home.

Number of Franchisees: 1 plus 1 company-owned unit.

In Business Since: 1985, franchising since 1989

Equity Capital Needed: Cash requirements $21,500-$26,500.

Financial Assistance Available: Contact company.

Training Provided: 8 days' minimum training in company's headquarters, assistance from then on.

Managerial Assistance Available: Complete support system through operations manual and continuing advice from the headquarters. Any Situation offers franchisees its expertise in all phases of day-to-day operations including pre-opening hiring and training, marketing and advertising, recordkeeping, selection and training of nannies, all systems.

Information Submitted: April 1990

*ATLANTIC PERSONNEL SERVICE SYSTEMS, INC.
4806 Shelly Drive
Wilmington, North Carolina 28405
Lorraine G. Taylor, Vice President, Marketing

Description of Operation: Premanent job placement, targeting entry level to middle management positions.

Number of Franchisees: 6 in North Carolina and South Carolina. Soliciting new franchisees in other Southeastern States.

In Business Since: 1985

Equity Capital Needed: $14,500-$24,500

Financial Assistance Available: None

Training Provided: 1 week training (classroom, corporate headquarters) and 1 week additional training (on-site).

Managerial Assistance Available: Automatic periodic visitation by corporate operations consultants and specific visitation on request. Financial and bookkeeping forms, business cards, letterhead and envelopes. Periodic franchise meetings and seminars.

Information Submitted: June 1990

BAILEY EMPLOYMENT SYSTEM, INC.
51 Shelton Road
Monroe, Connecticut 06468
Sheldon Leighton, President

Description of Operation: Profitable, nationally scoped, placement techniques augmented with a centralized, electronically computerized, data retrieval system. Centrally filed applicants and centrally filed job specifications, registered by individual Bailey Employment System offices, allow all franchisees a constant pool of qualified applicants and employers with which to work at all times. Bailey offers extensive training in the use of the intelligent computer Bailey provides to each franchisee. This computer permits instant retrieval of valuable candidate and/or company data in order for Bailey offices to hold a competitive advantage.

Number of Franchisees: 15 in 3 States

In Business Since: 1960

Equity Capital Needed: $40,000

Financial Assistance Available: If desired, purchase price may be financed at going bank rates.

Training Provided: Complete training in the profitable operation of a Bailey Employment Service office is given to each franchise operator before a new office is opened for business. Our training courses may be attended again and again by the franchise operator and his or her staff at their convenience. Additional training in advanced techniques of professional placement is offered 52 weeks a year. All such additional training is free of charge to all franchise operators and personnel. Conventions are offered at least 4 times a year to insure continued interoffice cooperation, camaraderie and profits.

Managerial Assistance Available: Every conceivable service to insure the owner a profitable return on his or her investment is offered.

Information Submitted: April 1990

BAKER & BAKER EMPLOYMENT SERVICE, INC.
P. O. Box 364
3 Jackson
Athens, Tennessee 37303

Description of Operation: Franchising of employment service agencies for small towns of 20,000 population and city metropolitan area.

Number of Franchisees: 8 in 3 States

In Business Since: 1967

Equity Capital Needed: $10,000 to $20,000 dependent on location, plus $2,500 working capital.

Financial Assistance Available: Yes

Training Provided: Comprehensive training course before opening and additional periodic on-the-job training at the franchise location.

Managerial Assistance Available: Selection of suitable location, a nationally aimed public-relations program and instructions and materials for obtaining maximum publicity in local advertising media, all forms required for the first 12 months of operation, an established accounting system, national placement tele-system operating between offices, assistance in interpreting State laws and complying with license regulations. Trained assistance on call at all hours on any agency problem.

Information Submitted: June 1990

BUSINESS & PROFESSIONAL CONSULTANTS, INC.
3255 Wilshire Boulevard
Suite 1732
Los Angeles, California 90010
W. J. LaPerch, President

Description of Operation: Executive search, recruitment and placement of managerial and executive talent at the professional level. Covers engineering, banking, insurance, accounting, finance, data processing, sales, marketing, and an employment agency as executive recruiters. The ideal franchise owner will come from industry at the middle to senior management level, will be degreed or equivalent (an advanced degree is desirable), will be people-oriented, will work well as part of a national team, and yet be capable of individual accomplishment and leadership. An additional facet of this franchise is the inclusion of a professional level temporary service to serve the same customer base and thus be able to satisfy all of the customer's needs. The company finances and handles all details of payroll and billing for the franchisee, so no large amount of payroll capital is required.

Number of Franchisees: 3 in California

In Business Since: 1961

Equity Capital Needed: $10,000 franchise fee

Financial Assistance Available: Will finance portion of franchise fee at no interest.

Training Provided: An initial 2 week program at the home office to cover the basics of executive search, hiring and training of staff personnel, operational and accounting procedures and market penetration. This is followed by an on-site training program of 1 full week at the franchisee's location, and by further field visits by home office training personnel.

Managerial Assistance Available: Continuous on an as needed basis and may consist of seminars, field visits, refresher training at franchisor's home office, and constant communication.

Information Submitted: April 1990

CAREER BLAZERS
590 Fifth Avenue
New York, New York 10036
Peter Bell, Director of Franchising

Description of Operation: Franchising of employment service agencies.

Number of Franchisees: 4 franchisees, 7 branches

In Business Since: 1949

Equity Capital Needed: $15,000-$18,000 franchise fee, plus $94,000-$120,650 for capital requirements.

Financial Assistance Available: None

Training Provided: Formal 2-week intensive training at corporate headquarters followed by in-field training and ongoing continuing education.

Managerial Assistance Available: Comprehensive management training program includes opening assistance, recruitment, operations, sales and marketing, advertising and promotions, and ongoing management consultation.

Information Submitted: April 1990

*CAREER EMPLOYMENT SERVICES, INC.
1600 Stewart Avenue
Westbury, New York
Howard Fader, Vice President, Marketing

Description of Operation: Career Employment Services, Inc., offers a unique franchise opportunity for entrance into the temporary help industry using its nationally registered name Temp Force in all States other than Georgia, Texas and Minnesota, where it operates as Temp Staff, supported by a comprehensive program of providing training, payroll funding, promotion and all bookkeeping functions.

Number of Franchisees: 47 in 24 States

In Business Since: 1962

Equity Capital Needed: $87,000-$117,000

Financial Assistance Available: None

Training Provided: The franchisor offers a formal 2 week training program at its training center.

Managerial Assistance Available: Ongoing support and training by way of periodic visits by a field service representative and fully computerized statistical management reports for ongoing analysis and consultation by home office with owner.

Information Submitted: May 1990

*DIVISION 10
535 Fifth Avenue - 33rd Floor
New York, New York 10017
Collin Gaffney, Director of Franchise Development

Description of Operation: Permanent and temporary recruitment and placement of individuals in the financing, accounting, EDP and office clerical skills. Company povides 5 weeks training, computer software, direct mail campaign, site location assistance, office layout and designs, training manuals and videos, operations manual and camera ready forms package.

Number of Franchisees: 15 coast to coast.

In Business Since: 1979

Equity Capital Needed: Approximately $40,000-$80,000, includes franchise fee.

Financial Assistance Available: Financing available.

Training Provided: 5 weeks: 3 corporate, 2 field.

Managerial Assistance Available: Ongoing telephone, newsletters, conferences, advisory councils, management memos and management reports.

Information Submitted: April 1990

*DUNHILL PERSONNEL SYSTEM, INC.
1000 Woodbury Road
Woodbury, New York 11797

Description of Operation: Dunhill Personnel System is an international company offering 3 different franchises in personnel services. The Full Service franchise is recruitment and search for management and professional personnel on a national level, the Office Personnel franchise specializes in the high demand area of executive and legal secretaries, word processing operators and other office personnel job classifications, and the Temporary Service franchise contracts out office and light industrial staff for both short- and long-term assignments.

Number of Franchisees: 268

In Business Since: 1952

Equity Capital Needed: The Full Service franchise requires minimum capital of $50,000, exclusive of personal needs. The Office Personnel combines O/P with the Temporary Service franchise, depending on the size or scope of the operation, requires $53,000 to $116,000. These amounts include the down payment of the franchise fee.

Financial Assistance Available: Dunhill System will finance up to 60 percent of the franchise fee over a 4 year period, commencing 10 months after opening at 8 percent interest.

Training Provided: Dunhill Personnel System provides intensive, continuous and updated training. The initial training provides 2 weeks of hands-on training in New York covering the search and placement cycle and the managerial aspects of the business. Extensive follow-up training is continuously provided on a regional and national basis. Motivational training and special industry training in the form of workshops and seminars are provided for franchisees and their consultants.

Managerial Assistance Available: Follow-up support is provided through our qualified field representatives, both in the franchisee's office and through constant telephone contact. Audio visual programs and resource material for in-house training are also available.

Information Submitted: May 1990

*EXPRESS SERVICES, INC.
6300 NW Expressway
Oklahoma City, Oklahoma 73132
Tom Gunderson, Franchise Director

Description of Operation: Express is a national corporation with more than 140 offices in 24 States. With 3 distinct divisions, the franchised offices provide clients with temporary help, permanent placements, and executive recruitment. Express Temporary Service supplies office, clerical, word processing, marketing, technical, and light industrial temporaries for short-term needs or long-term growth. Express Personnel Service provides qualified permanent employees for entry level through management positions. Robert William James & Associates, the management recruiting division, offers a professional approach to executive search. Together, the 3 divisions of Express give total, guaranteed personnel service. Acquired franchise service corporation in 1986 (15 offices).

Number of Franchisees: 141 in 24 States

In Business Since: 1983

Equity Capital Needed: $12,000-$15,000 franchise fee per office, plus start-up capital (approximately $80,000). Initial investment depends upon whether operation is established or a start-up.

Financial Assistance Available: Temporary payroll is 100 percent financed by Express and accounts receivable are financed for 60 days. Express also participates in a local franchise advertising plan that is funded according to the franchisee's sales.

Training Provided: An intensive 2 week training class is provided initially, followed by on-site visits by a traveling training director. Regional seminars, an annual company-wide meeting, and an ongoing supply of publications and training materials complete the program. A tape library is also available to franchise owners for in-service programs and individual use.

Managerial Assistance Available: Express supplies complete operations manuals, all forms, marketing brochures and promotional programs, advertising campaigns, and general PR help. Computer payrolling, client billing, and management consulting are included in the system. Field personnel are available for on-site help in planning and implementation of the Express program after initial training is completed.

Information Submitted: May 1990

FIVE STAR TEMPORARIES, INC.
1415 Elbridge Payne
Chesterfield, Missouri 63017
A. H. Harter, Jr., President

Description of Operation: We provide temporary personnel to businesses, factories, and municipalities. Personnel provided includes secretaries, typists, clerical workers, and also engineers as well as general laborers.

Number of Franchisees: 3 in Missouri, 1 in Indiana

In Business Since: 1981

Equity Capital Needed: Maximum of $60,000.

Financial Assistance Available: There is no franchise fee.

Training Provided: 2 months concentrated training at franchisee and franchisor location. Manuals are provided plus follow-up training and assistance for 2 years.

Managerial Assistance Available: Complete assistance in every aspect of the operations including sales, accounting, legal office management and general management. There is also a buy-back agreement at the option of the franchiser.

Information Submitted: April 1990

F-O-R-T-U-N-E FRANCHISE CORPORATION
655 Third Avenue
Suite 1805
New York, New York 10017
Rudy Schott, President

Description of Operation: F-O-R-T-U-N-E Personnel Consultants offers a quality middle management/executive recruiting service, using unique, proven methods of operation to achieve its present status of industry leadership. F-O-R-T-U-N-E's reputation is highlighted by its professional service, innovative marketing concepts and sophisticated system of exchange of applicants and job orders, together with an excellent program of support for its franchise offices.

Number of Franchisees: 60 in 22 States

In Business Since: 1973 as F-O-R-T-U-N-E Franchise Corporation.

Equity Capital Needed: $60,000

Financial Assistance Available: $30,000 is the minimum franchise fee; additional funds are required to meet pre-opening expenses and working capital, which in aggregate should be between $20,000 and $35,000. This amount will vary by the size of the office and number of personnel employed.

Training Provided: Intensive 15 day training program is required. 10 days are conducted for the owner at F-O-R-T-U-N-E home office on business fundamentals and management controls; 5 days are spent on location by F-O-R-T-U-N-E executives training franchise owner and staff. Continued training is available at home office and on field visits. The franchisor prides itself on its personal committment to ongoing training and support for each new owner and his/her staff.

Managerial Assistance Available: F-O-R-T-U-N-E provides ongoing management assistance in the areas of franchise controls, exchange programs for applicants and companies and daily operational support. Communication is maintained by regular telephone contact, workshops, bulletins, newsletters, national conventions and on-site visits. Innovative techniques to improve quality and profitability of the F-O-R-T-U-N-E offices are continual.

Information Submitted: April 1990

GEROTOGA ENTERPRISES, INC.
211 Park Avenue
Scotch Plains, New Jersey 07076
Audrey Hull

Description of Operation: A permanent professional, technical and clerical employment service under the names "Gerotoga" and "Plusmates," as well as temporary help service, under the name of "Apoxiforce," specializing in clerical and industrial temporaries.

Number of Franchisees: 10 in New Jersey

In Business Since: 1960

Equity Capital Needed: $25,000 (includes franchise fee and office set-up), plus approximately $10,000 operating capital for first 3 months.

Financial Assistance Available: None

Training Provided: Prior to opening of business, company will provide 3 weeks training at corporate headquarters, training and assistance is also provided the licensee and his personnel at the licensee's office. Operations and training manuals and training aids provided.

Managerial Assistance Available: Company provides printing and operating forms sufficient to do business for 90 days, continuous follow-up and support and field trips to licensee's office. Company will assist and/or advise the complete set-up of office, advertising, accounts, and hiring and training of initial personnel. Meetings and seminars are conducted to improve expertise and efficiency.

Information Submitted: June 1990

GILBERT LANE PERSONNEL SERVICE
221 Main Street
Hartford, Connecticut 06106
Howard Specter, President

Description of Operation: Gilbert Lane Personnel Service offers a broad based employment recruiting system that specializes in middle-management and professional level placement with quotas and concentration on engineering and high technology recruitment.

Number of Franchisees: 7 in 5 States, including company-owned.

In Business Since: 1957

Equity Capital Needed: $40,000 minimum

Financial Assistance Available: Investment would include franchise fee and pre-opening expenses to include rent deposit, utility deposit, advertising, legal fees, etc. Additionally, $15,000-$20,000 recommended for use as operating capital. Company will give consideration to making financial arrangements.

Training Provided: The owner/manager is required to attend an intensive 2 week pre-opening training session at the company's home office. Additional training is conducted at franchisee's office for both himself and his staff at the time of opening. The operation is then closely monitored, including staff visits, until effectively operating.

Managerial Assistance Available: Gilbert Lane provides continuous guidance and assistance in all areas of agency management. Interchange job openings and applicants throughout the Gilbert Lane network. Annual franchise manager's meetings, issuance of training tapes and operating manuals are part of ongoing program.

Information Submitted: June 1990

THE HAYES GROUP, INC.
3020 East Camelback Road
Suite 367
Phoenix, Arizona 85016
David Hayes, Director of Franchising

Description of Operation: An executive recruiting service designed to start out in your home or executive suite with minimum capital outlay. The Hayes system requires no ongoing royalties or territorial restrictions: grow where and when you want at no additional cost. The system makes available affiliates, research, marketing, advertising techniques and a complete operations manual along with an ongoing consulting program.

Number of Franchisees: 3 and 1 company-owned

In Business Since: 1974

Equity Capital Needed: Franchise fee is $10,500

Financial Assistance Available: Franchise fee includes training operating manual and video training library for a completely automated office, utilizing home space or an executive suite to minimize any long-term expense commitment until the business requires employees.

Managerial Assistance Available: Same as above

Information Submitted: April 1990

HERITAGE PERSONNEL SYSTEMS, INC.
4926 Windy Hill Drive
Raleigh, North Carolina 27609
Robert A. Hounsell, Director of Franchising

Description of Operation: Full service, across the board professional personnel service, from entry level positions to top executives in all job categories on a company-paid fee basis, offering both advertising and recruiting services with marketing emphasis on a national basis.

Number of Franchisees: 3 in North Carolina and Tennessee

In Business Since: 1974; began franchising in 1977

Equity Capital Needed: $10,000-$30,000 initial franchise fee, plus approximately $3,000 start-up costs.

Financial Assistance Available: Possibility of company-financing of up to 50 percent of franchise fee, and advice and consultation in obtaining other sources of financial assistance.

Training Provided: 2 weeks at company headquarters, 1 week in franchisee's office, continuous consultancy and assistance thereafter.

Managerial Assistance Available: Continuous assistance to franchisee in advertising, marketing, hiring and training of staff, accounting, legal, office expansion and new job market development. Close cooperation in the system's "management by objectives" procedures is maintained by phone, mail and personal visits.

Information Submitted: June 1990

*JOBMATE AFFILIATED COMPANIES, INC.
232 Highway 51 North
P. O. Drawer 959
Ridgeland, Mississippi 39158
Thurman L. Boykin, President

Description of Operation: A JobMate franchisee provides total payroll processing plus cafeteria plan flexible benefits to small business clients through a unique lease-back method. Clients tender one check per pay period covering all employee pay and benefits. JobMate is America's first national franchise in employee leasing.

Number of Franchisees: 1 in Pennsylvania, 1 in Mississippi, and 1 in Georgia

In Business Since: 1986, franchising since 1989

Equity Capital Needed: $35,000, plus $10,000 start-up

Financial Assistance Available: The company will assist the franchisee in applying for financing. The company does not make loans to franchisees.

Training Provided: Intensive 1 week comprehensive training in all aspects of operation of an employee leasing company including computer and manual functions.

Managerial Assistance Available: JobMate franchisees are provided operations manuals as well as management oversight at all times on an on-call basis.

Information Submitted: April 1990

LLOYD PERSONNEL CONSULTANTS
10 Cuttermill Road
Great Neck, New York 11021
Merrill Banks, President

Description of Operation: A highly respected national placement firm. Major areas of specialization are in sales, sales management and marketing staff personnel in the computer, communications, and office products field. Other areas of national specialty are insurance, office services, and graphics. A professional office services temporary operation known as Lloyd Creative Temps is a sister company that is also available.

Number of Franchisees: 2 in New York and New Hampshire

In Business Since: 1971, franchising since 1986.

Equity Capital Needed: $25,000 franchise fee plus $5,000 start-up cost, plus living expenses.

Financial Assistance Available: Yes, payment terms available.

Training Provided: The initial training provided to new franchisee consists of a combination of 15 days in franchisor's office and in the new franchisee's office. The initial training consists of a comprehensive program of management training, including leadership responsibilities, planning, both monetary and performance, personnel selection, retention, compensation and responsibilities, client relations, marketing and advertising techniques, accounting, bookkeeping and financial matters, as well as training in all phases of the actual activities of a placement counselor involved in the recruiting and interviewing of applicants, the solicitation of job orders, the making of referrals and the effecting of placements. After the initial training, additional training is provided on an as needed and requested basis.

Managerial Assistance Available: Assistance begins with site selection, office layout, equipment purchase, and complete office set up including all forms and necessary printing. Franchisor or representative will be on-site for opening of franchise office for the purpose of continued education and rendering assistance. A daily telephone contact program covering everyday operation will take place for as long as franchisee deems necessary. This daily assistance program will be insulated with a written manager's operational guide as well as a situation answer guide to questions.

Information Submitted: June 1990

*MANAGEMENT RECRUITERS INTERNATIONAL, INC.
1127 Euclid Avenue
Suite 1400
Cleveland, Ohio 44115-1638
Alan R. Schonberg, President

Description of Operation: Search and recruiting service business under the names of Management Recruiters, Sales Consultants. OfficeMates/5, and CompuSearch. Also refer to the listing under Sales Consultants International.

Number of Franchisees: 583 offices (including company-owned offices) in 45 States, the District of Columbia and Puerto Rico.

In Business Since: 1957

Equity Capital Needed: Minimum $35,500 to $62,400 depending on location.

Financial Assistance Available: None

Training Provided: The franchisor's staff will provide the licensee with an intensive initial training program of approximately 3 weeks conducted at the franchisor's corporate headquarters in Cleveland, Ohio, plus an initial on-the-job training program of approximately 3 additional weeks conducted in the licensee's first office. In addition to the above, the franchisor's staff will assist and advise the licensee in (a) securing suitable office space and the negotiation of the lease for same, (b) the design and layout of the office, (c) the selection of office furniture and equipment and the negotiation of the purchase or lease agreement for same, and (d) the establishment of a suitable telephone system for the licensee's office.

Managerial Assistance Available: The licensee is provided with a detailed operations manual containing information, procedures and know-how for operating the business, account executive, accounting and administrative assistant's manuals. In addition, the licensee receives a VCR/color TV set plus franchisor's complete video training film series (21 cassettes), and a 90 day supply of all necessary operating forms, brochures, etc. The franchisor will furnish the licensee with continuing advice, guidance and assistance through national and regional meetings, seminars, correspondence, video training films, and telephone and personal instruction with respect to the licensee's personnel placement service operations and procedures and their improvement and revision.

Information Submitted: April 1990

MTS, INC.
Box 456
Harrogate, Tennessee 37752-0456
Harold Huff

Description of Operation: A temporary service agency specializing in the placement of general labor, skilled labor, office personnel, management, engineers, and high tech personnel.

Number of Franchisees: 9 plus 8 company-owned

In Business Since: 1963

Equity Capital Needed: $20,000 minimum, franchise fee $15,000.

Financial Assistance Available: Up to 60 percent.

Training Provided: 1 week training.

Managerial Assistance Available: Ongoing advice and assistance.

Information Submitted: April 1990

THE MURPHY GROUP
1211 West 22nd Street
Oak Brook, Illinois 60521
William A. Murphy, President

Description of Operation: Murphy Employment Service offers a unique full service private personnel placement service concentrating on the placement of administrative, executive, sales, professional, secretarial and general office personnel. All offices are currently integrated with a unique computerized interoffice communications system for the exchange of job orders and candidates.

Number of Franchisees: 8 in Illinois and Florida

In Business Since: 30 years

Equity Capital Needed: Franchise fee of $15,000 and $25,000 available capital.

Financial Assistance Available: None

Training Provided: For Illinois franchisees only, placement consultant training is conducted at the corporate office, primarily classroom in nature, consisting of 5 or more half day sessions. This is followed up with 24 half hour instructional audio tapes covering all facets of actual activities of the personnel consultant, plus a series of video tapes with a thorough analysis of interviewing and marketing. In addition, franchisee will receive periodic analysis of operating statistics. All franchisees in Illinois and other States are furnished with a complete set of training manuals and tapes, and an operations manual. They are also provided with continual management service for the life of the franchise in such areas as operations, analysis and advertising.

Managerial Assistance Available: Manager's training consists of 12 half day sessions over a minimum of 6 days that cover basic management and leadership training, budgeting, all facets of personnel functions from a management perspective, marketing, advertising, client relations, and training as well as networking.

Information Submitted: April 1990

NETREX INTERNATIONAL
A Division of NRS INC.
5420 LBJ Freeway
Suite 575
Dallas, Texas 75240
Frank A. Cooksey, President

Description of Operation: Contingency and retainer executive recruiting/search specializing only in data processing, accounting, finance, engineering, sales, sales management, and general management. Netrex International is known as the "National Network for Recruiting Specialists." Each office is owned and staffed by executives whose business background has been in the industry which they specialize in. Netrex International's success has been established by developing systems that provide a real opportunity for an individual to "control their own destiny" utilizing those proven systems and established computerized client and candidate referral system.

Number of Franchisees: Newly developed

In Business Since: 1989

Equity Capital Needed: $60,000 to $80,000, depending on location.

Financial Assistance Available: Yes

Training Provided: Intensive training program of 2 weeks at the corporate headquarters in Dallas, Texas. Using the latest audio visual training techniques in the industry, including video tapes, training/operation manual, reference guides and client/candidate information. Netrex International provides training in all aspects of the recruiting and executive search business, including specialized training for owner-managers and account executives. Also, all account executives employed during the lifetime of the franchise, are trained in-house by Netrex International. On the job training is conducted by home office representatives to provide continuing training through a program of weekly telephone and periodic visits. In addition, Netrex International conducts bi-annual training seminars and conferences. Netrex International will assist and advise the licensee in (1) office site selection and lease negotiation, (2) office layout and furniture selection, (3) selection of computer equipment system, and (4) account executive recruitment. In summary, Netrex International will provide its network franchisees with training, resources and guidance to operate a medical sales management and marketing executive recruiting business.

Managerial Assistance Available: Continuing support through daily, weekly, monthly phone consultation and periodic management visits covering all aspects of the medical recruiting business. In addition, Netrex International provides collection assistance of licensee's accounts receivable and detailed analysis of all phases of their operation. Netrex International also provides national advertising and marketing support programs.

Information Submitted: April 1990

*NORRELL TEMPORARY SERVICES, INC.
3535 Piedmont Road, N.E.
Atlanta, Georgia 30305
Stan Anderson, Regional Vice President of Franchise Sales

Description of Operation: Temporary help industry catering to all segments of business. Vertical marketing programs designed for the banking, insurance, financial services and office automation industries. Unique facilities staffing concept to address clients' changing personnel needs. Uses a consultive approach to the temporary help industry.

Number of Franchisees: 141 in 40 States plus 189 units company-owned.

In Business Since: 1963

Equity Capital Needed: $50,000-$80,000, no up-front franchise fee.

Financial Assistance Available: Payroll financing and accounts receivable financing.

Training Provided: Initially, both field training and 5 day classroom courses are provided. Continuing classroom training and seminars in the franchisee's area are provided quarterly. Cassette tapes, manuals and other written programs are available for each individual franchise office.

Managerial Assistance Available: Field-dedicated regional managers and district managers assist in making sales calls with the franchisee, teaching proper pricing, assisting in recruiting, etc. Norrell supplies computer payrolling, customer billings, operations manuals, forms, brochures, national advertising and direct mail promotion.

Information Submitted: April 1990

THE OLSTEN CORPORATION
1 Merrick Avenue
Westbury, L.I., New York 11590
Robert J. Lemenze, Assistant Vice President

Description of Operation: A national public company operating branch, franchise and licensed offices. Provides temporary office and industrial personnel for as long as needed by businesses, government, industry and institutions.

Number of Franchisees: 105 franchise offices and 90 licensed offices.

In Business Since: 1950

Equity Capital Needed: $40,000 minimum, includes working capital required to cover start-up costs and general operating expenses plus living expenses. No up-front money.

Financial Assistance Available: Temporary payroll funded by The Olsten Corporation.

Training Provided: Comprehensive on-the-job training and field training as well as periodic visits covering every phase of business operations.

Managerial Assistance Available: Full operating manuals, forms, printed sales material and basic supplies provided at no charge. In addition, provides continuous, ongoing assistance in all facets of the business including technical assistance, insurance, marketing, sales, advertising and other areas of temporary help. National sales leads also supplied whenever possible.

Information Submitted: April 1990

*PERSONNEL POOL OF AMERICA, INC.
Personnel Pool Division
2050 Spectrum Boulevard
Fort Lauderdale, Florida 33309
John J. Marquez, Director, Market Development

Description of Operation: International firm providing temporary help services to commercial, industrial and governmental clients. Personnel services include clerical, word/data processing, marketing, telemarketing, para-legal, para-technical, light industrial and industrial work skills. Franchise opportunities available nationwide.

Number of Franchisees: Franchisees, 156, company-owned, 80.

In Business Since: 1946

Equity Capital Needed: $50,000-$65,000 including working capital to cover start-up costs and general operating expenses, plus living expense.

Financial Assistance Available: Temporary employee payroll, taxes and insurance funded by Personnel Pool.

Training Provided: 2 weeks at company's corporate service center in Ft. Lauderdale; includes owner/management training in financial, back office and sales/marketing, plus 2 weeks on-the-job training at franchisee's office. Owner and staff training ongoing via seminars, regional training, teletraining, video and audio training programs.

Managerial Assistance Available: Dedicated franchise operations director assists and consults owner on all facets of operating the business including sales, advertising, insurance, legal, risk management, market development, data processing, finance, national accounts and recruitment.

Information Submitted: May 1990

PLACE MART FRANCHISING CORP.
PLACE MART/EDP SEARCH
277 Fairfield Road
Fairfield, New Jersey 07004
M. B. Kushma, President

Description of Operation: Employment agency specializing in the data processing industry.

Number of Franchisees: 2 in New Jersey

In Business Since: 1962

Equity Capital Needed: $40,000-$50,000

Financial Assistance Available: None

Training Provided: Intensive training at corporate office from 3 to 6 weeks, then follow-up training at franchisee's location. Periodic systematic supervisory follow-up.

Managerial Assistance Available: Continuous training and supervision from field personnel, seminars, training sessions, newsletters, new ideas and systems constantly introduced. Periodic franchise meeting discussing policies and administrative problems and exchange of ideas for mutual help.

Information Submitted: April 1990

RETAIL RECRUITERS INTERNATIONAL, INC./
SPECTRA PROFESSIONAL SEARCH
100 Foxborough Boulevard
Foxboro, Massachusetts 02035
Jacques J. Lapointe, President

Description of Operation: Personnel placement service business under the names of Retail Recruiters, and Spectra. Specializing in middle to upper level management placement and executive search. Strong co-brokering system within organization.

Number of Franchisees: 34 in 16 States

In Business Since: 1969

Equity Capital Needed: $60,000-$75,000 depending on location.

Financial Assistance Available: None

Training Provided: Complete training in all aspects of operation. Intensive 3-4 weeks training of new franchisee and new employees of initial franchise. Training at home office and at new franchisees first office. Continuous and follow-up training as needed. Assist in securing suitable office space, help negotiate lease, design layout of office, and selection of proper office furniture and equipment and proper telephone system.

Managerial Assistance Available: Company provides detailed training manual and video tapes that contain information and know-how for operating personnel business. We will provide continuing advice, guidance and assistance through meetings, personal visits on a continuous basis to insure proper operation of business.

Information Submitted: April 1990

ROMAC & ASSOCIATES, INC.
183 Middle Street
P. O. Box 7469 DTS
Portland, Maine 04112
Richard C. Sandler, Director of Sales/Marketing

Description of Operation: Romac & Associates is a network of offices that provides personnel placement services to clients in need of professionals in the areas of corporate accounting, public accounting, data processing, finance and banking. The offices are staffed by executives whose business background is in the fields which they serve. Romac's reputation for success is based on its strict adherence to confidentiality, to the interaction of the offices within the organization, and to a guarantee backed by refunds.

Number of Franchisees: 41 in 24 States

In Business Since: 1966

Equity Capital Needed: $150,000 (depending on market area)

Financial Assistance Available: Yes

Training Provided: All franchisees participate in an intensive training program in the corporate office at which time all phases of the business operation are covered. Follow-up training is conducted at the local office.

Managerial Assistance Available: Interoffice jobs and candidate referrals are maintained through our exclusive electronic mail ROMNET system. Continuous training and support, training sessions, SM seminars, newsletters, and training manuals are provided, as well as preparation and assistance with advertising, marketing, recruiting and screening, and help with financial and accounting procedures. Group plans for insurance and employee benefits, fee schedules, cooperative advertising, etc., are continually updated and maintained.

Information Submitted: April 1990

ROTH YOUNG PERSONNEL SERVICE, INC.
500 Fifth Avenue
New York, New York 10017
Collin Gaffney, Director of Franchise Development

Description of Operation: For 25 years Roth Young has excelled in executive recruitment and placement of individuals in the food hospitality, health , manufacturing and finance industries.

Number of Franchisees: 28 coast to coast

In Business Since: 1964

Financial Assistance Available: Financing available.

Training Provided: Initial training of 2 weeks at home office, 1 week at licensee's office. Further training as determined by licensor.

Managerial Assistance Available: Management reports, newsletters, telephone communications, franchise and advertising councils, meetings, seminars and conferences.

Information Submitted: April 1990

*SALES CONSULTANTS INTERNATIONAL
A Division of MANAGEMENT RECRUITERS
INTERNATIONAL, INC.
1127 Euclid Avenue, Suite 1400
Cleveland, Ohio 44115-1638
Alan R. Schonberg, President

Description of Operation: An opportunity to join an organization involved solely in searching and recruiting of sales managers, salesmen, saleswomen, sales engineers, and marketing people.

Number of Franchisees: 167 offices (including company-owned offices) in 40 States and the District of Columbia

In Business Since: 1957

Equity Capital Needed: $35,500 to $62,400 depending on location.

Financial Assistance Available: None

Training Provided: The franchisor's staff will provide the licensee with an intensive initial training program of approximately 3 weeks conducted at the franchisor's corporate headquarters in Cleveland, Ohio, plus an initial on-the-job training program of approximately 3 additional weeks is conducted in the licensee's first office. In addition to the above, the franchisor's staff will assist and advise the licensee in (a) securing suitable office space and negotiation of the lease for same, (b) design and layout of the office, (c) selection of office furniture and equipment and the negotiation of the purchase or lease agreement for same, and (d) establishment of a suitable telephone system for the licensee's office.

Managerial Assistance Available: The licensee is provided with a detailed operations manual containing information, procedures and know-how of operating the business, account executive, accounting, and an administrative assistant's manual. In addition, the licensee receives a VCR/color TV set plus franchisor's complete video training film series (21 cassettes), and a 90 day supply of all necessary operating forms, brochures, etc. The franchisor will furnish the licensee with continuing advice, guidance and assistance through national and regional meetings, seminars, correspondence, video training films, and telephone and personal instruction with respect to the licensee's personnel placement service operations and procedures and their improvement and revision.

Information Submitted: April 1990

*SANFORD ROSE ASSOCIATES INTERNATIONAL, INC.
265 South Main Street
Akron, Ohio 44308
Doug Eilertson, Executive Vice President

Description of Operation: SRA provides a responsive executive search service that is effective at virtually all levels in an organization. SRA uses its data base of candidates and custom computer software to allow each office to make glove fit matches with client openings without sacrificing personal relationships. Professionalism is SRA's watchword.

Number of Franchisees: 90

In Business Since: 1959

Equity Capital Needed: $50,000 minimum

Financial Assistance Available: Yes

Training Provides: Current program is approximately 14-15 intensive 8 hour days in addition to a minimum of 10 days of follow-up training. This includes classroom as well as "hands-on" work. Extensive training manuals and audio and visual tapes are furnished to each licensee. Regular training courses are also furnished on a no charge basis to the licensee's employees at any time.

Managerial Assistance Available: Sanford Rose Associates provides a complete time tested system for executive search. SRA provides an effective system of sharing of candidate resumes and jobs that results in significant shared revenues between offices. Custom computer software further enhances office operation. Complete computerized financial statements are rendered monthly to each office. Field operations personnel meet with owners on a routine and requested basis. Sales contests, seminars, and other recruiter incentives are regularly used by Sanford Rose Associates.

Information Submitted: May 1990

SCINETICS CORP
One Ramada Plaza
Suite 7021
New Rochelle, New York 10801
Louis G. Cornacchia, President, Electronic Engineer

Description of Operation: Scinetics is a full service temporary hi-tech personnel company providing industry with state of the art engineering support, computer programmers, technicians, designers, CAE, CAD capabilities and other scientific disciplines. The founder of the franchise has owned and operated 2 corporations providing primary engineering and other temporary support personnel. The franchise is offered to qualified start-up and existing business owners. Scinetics finances 100 percent of all temporary support personnel payroll, and provides all back office support for payroll documentation taxes, invoicing, etc. Scinetics makes available marketing, research client support, creative advertising, all support manuals, temporary employee benefits, continuing employee educational materials, newsletter, staff training, national accounting and franchisor-franchisee group events. For further information call (914) 576-6530 collect.

Number of Franchisees: 2 in New York

In Business Since: Collins Consultants International, Ltd. 1967, Charger Tech Services, Inc., 1974. Both still in business and to be joined to Scinetics as company-owned operations. Scinetics Corp., August 1987.

Equity Capital Needed: $46,500-$66,500. Franchise fee of $10,000 included in initial capital required.

Financial Assistance Available: Negotiable, will finance portion of franchise fee at no interest.

Training Provided: An initial 2 week program at central home facility. Training includes use of training manuals developed by Scinetics. Franchisor will provide continued training at franchisee office and continuing field support by franchisor professional staff. Seminars, national meetings, newsletters and other publications will be provided in the future for continuous support in all special areas to meet future continuing changing disciples evolving in the temporary support industry.

Managerial Assistance Available: Scinetics will augment, on a national scale, techniques using data-based systems allowing immediate-access capabilities by our franchisees to current ongoing engineering and scientific data. Candidate availability, industry information both economic and technical, military and industrial contract awards, and other current data will also be provided via newsletters and bulletins for creating a competitive edge. Scinetics is a highly disciplined organization with a unique concept of the professional approach.

Information Submitted: May 1990

*SNELLING AND SNELLING, INC.
Executive Offices
Snelling Plaza
4000 South Tamiami Trail
Sarasota, Florida 33581

Description of Operation: Snelling and Snelling franchisees, depending on location, experience and inclination of owner, range in size from 1-15 or more employees. Their fields of placement and recruiting range from highly specialized services in areas such as data processing, engineering, marketing, accounting, finance, oil and gas, etc., to the general areas of secretarial, office and clerical, sales, administrative, and technical.

Number of Franchisees: Over 480 in U.S. and Brazil.

In Business Since: 1951

Equity Capital Needed: $50,000 to $105,000

Financial Assistance Available: None

Training Provided: Video tapes covering virtually every aspect of the profession are backed up by detailed training manuals for each position in the franchise. Initial training consists of 2 weeks at home office in Sarasota, Florida, for owner(s) and staff. The franchisor is available for counseling and at the present time national marketing consultants travel throughout the United States offering additional management advice, assistance, and training.

Managerial Assistance Available: Pre-opening aid selection, lease negotiation, phone systems, furniture selection, etc., provided by staff at home office.

Information Submitted: June 1990

*STAFF BUILDERS INTERNATIONAL
1981 Marcus Avenue
Lake Success, New York 11042
Ed Teixeira, Vice President of Franchising Division

Description of Operation: There are 2 franchise programs: (1) Health Care franchise provides supplemental staffing and home care services to private individuals, hospitals, nursing homes and other health care facilities; (2) Personnel Services provides temporary and permanent placement personnel, secretaries, word processors, bookkeepers, clerks and light industrial help.

Number of Franchisees: 35 in 24 States

In Business Since: 1961

Equity Capital Needed: $50,000-$100,000

Financial Assistance Available: Company will introduce to finance sources. Field payable and accounts receivable are funded by franchisor.

Training Provided: 2 weeks in classroom and 1 week at location.

Managerial Assistance Available: Staff Builders will provide computerized office and grand opening advertising campaign. Regional managers visit locations on a regular basis to provide sales and operational assistance.

Information Submitted: April 1990

*TALENT FORCE TEMPORARIES
2970 Clairmont Road
Atlanta, Georgia 30329

Description of Operation: Provides full service temporary help to businesses.

Number of Franchisees: 3, plus 12 company-owned.

In Business Since: 1976

Equity Capital Needed: $7,500-$17,500 franchise fee and $58,000-$120,000 operating capital, depending on market.

Financial Assistance Available: Dependent on qualifications.

Training Provided: 2 weeks opening training and continuous assistance and training at branch level.

Managerial Assistance Available: Complete support system from site selection, office layout, design criteria, pre-opening hiring, marketing, advertising and accounting training. Ongoing sales and operations guidance via dedicated franchise staff and other company executives.

Information Submitted: April 1990

TEMPS & CO.
245 Peachtree Center Avenue
2500 Marquis One Tower
Atlanta, Georgia 30303
A. R. French, Director of Marketing

Description of Operation: Temporary and permanent placement service specializing in clerical and office automation.

Number of Franchisees: 11 franchises, 13 company-owned offices.

In Business Since: 1972

Equity Capital Needed: Requires $50,000 to $90,000 working capital.

Financial Assistance Available: Franchisor funds temporary payroll and accounts reeivable.

Training Provided: 2 weeks of initial training provided. Ongoing training is available.

Managerial Assistance Available: In addition to funding payroll and receivables, franchisor provides site selection, lease negotiation, computer software, advertising support and ongoing consultative management support.

Information Submitted: April 1990

TGIF PEOPLEWORKS
P. O. Box 828
Old Lyme, Connecticut 06371
Joanne Kobar, President

Description of Operation: Search service for domestic in-home help. We act as matchmaker between private families and applicants looking to work as nannies, eldercare companions, and housekeepers, etc. We offer affordable fees to appeal to the average-income family. Can be operated from home in most States. Works with TGIF Vocations recruiting potential students who can then be employed through this employment service nationwide. Dual franchise ownership is available at a reduced combination fee.

Number of Franchisees: 15 locations including company-owned.

In Business Since: 1982, franchising since 1986.

Equity Capital Needed: $8,500 franchise fee plus $4,700 start-up costs.

Financial Assistance Available: None

Training Provided: 3 day all-expenses-paid training at either site or home office.

Managerial Assistance Available: Continuous support and guidance with home office network of franchisees; monthly informational newsletter and constant updating of new innovations and expanded services to the franchisees; beneficial sister-franchise TGIF Vocations can provide trained employees for job placement.

Information Submitted: April 1990

TIME SERVICES, INC.
6422 Lima Road
Fort Wayne, Indiana 46818
Bruce Bone, President

Description of Operation: A midwestern corporation with company-owned and franchised offices offering a full line of temporary help in the office clerical and light industrial fields and contract help in the technical fields.

Number of Franchisees: 1 in Ohio

In Business Since: 1982

Equity Capital Needed: $75,000 to $100,000

Financial Assistance Available: Payroll and accounts receivable are financed by franchisor.

Training Provided: Up to 3 weeks of formal classroom and field training are provided. Ongoing support services include regularly scheduled visits by our field operations professionals, toll free "action" line, monthly communications, quarterly business development seminars and profit/loss consultation.

Managerial Assistance Available: Managers work in the franchise office and in the field with sales calls on a regularly scheduled basis. Continuous planning, advertising material and copy counsel and marketing assistance are provided. Management also provides periodic visits and seminars to supplement the training programs.

Information Submitted: May 1990

TODAYS TEMPORARY
18111 Preston Road
Suite 800
Dallas, Texas 75252
Jennifer Allen, Franchise Marketing Coordinator

Description of Operation: Franchisor operates a full-service, high-quality office clerical temporary employment service, a business in which franchisor's founders have over 20 years experience collectively.

Number of Franchisees: 25 in 11 States

In Business Since: 1982

Equity Capital Needed: No franchise fee, $80,000 to $125,000 working capital to cover start-up and operating expenses.

Financial Assistance Available: Temporary payroll and accounts receivable financing.

Training Provided: Initial training involves a minimum of 3 weeks intensive classroom and field training on all aspects of sales, operations, and management of franchisor's temporary service. Quarterly training seminars along with periodic in-market visits by field coordinators provide franchisees with continued training in all aspects of business operations.

Managerial Assistance Available: Franchisor provides a comprehensive set of manuals detailing start-up, operations and sales procedures. In addition, assistance is provided for temporary recruiting, yellow page advertising, site selection, business development, insurance, and budgeting. Franchisor also provides direct mail and national account leads.

Information Submitted: April 1990

TRC TEMPORARY SERVICES, INC.
100 Ashford Center
North 100
Atlanta, Georgia 30338

Description of Operation: Franchise opportunity with one of the finest temporary help firms in the country. Business is the placement of temporary workers with clients, in the areas of clerical, secretarial, word processing, marketing and light industrial skills.

Number of Franchisees: 20 in 11 states.

In Business Since: 1980

Equity Capital Needed: $75,000-$125,000 of working capital.

Financial Assistance Available: No financial assistance toward working capital. However, franchisor finances temporary help payroll, credit and collections, taxes, insurance, supplies, and field training.

Training Provided: Pre-opening training, formal training for sales, operations and management, 5 days each course. Within 6 weeks of opening, 30 man days of training at the office site. Ongoing communications, newsletter, seminars.

Managerial Assistance Available: 10 days after closing, 3 man days of management consultation. 5 man days per quarter, spent in each office. Ongoing monitoring.

Information Submitted: June 1990

UNIFORCE TEMPORARY PERSONNEL, INC.
1335 Jericho Turnpike
New Hyde Park, New York 11040
John Fanning, President/CEO

Description of Operation: A publicly held, national temporary personnel service company that offers a complete line of services to business, industry and government in the following areas: general and automated office, marketing, accounting, technical, legal, records management, hospitality and light industrial. In addition to supplying basic temporary personnel services, Uniforce specializes in project staffing, providing large groups of temporaries for long-term special assignments.

Number of Franchisees: 108 in 34 States

In Business Since: 1962

Equity Capital Needed: Approximately $75,000, which includes an initial licensing fee of $15,000. The remaining capital is needed for general operating expenses. Regional franchises available with an initial licensing fee of $25,000. Additional capital of approximately $100,000 is necessary for general operating expenses. Licensees maintain full equity and 100 percent control.

Financial Assistance Available: Temporary employees payroll financing and financing of accounts receivable without any interest charge—ever! Multi-million dollar liability insurance and bonding protection on all temporary personnel fully provided by headquarters. Fifty percent of the licensing fee may be financed through promissory notes at current interest rates.

Training Provided: No prior experience is necessary. Owner will spend 1 week of training at the company's home office training center. Using the latest state-of-the-arts audio-visual training techniques, including video tapes and role-playing, Uniforce will provide training in all phases of temporary help operations, including specialized training for owner-managers, in recruiting temporary employees and all sales and marketing functions. In addition, on-site video training is provided for all staff positions. On-the-job training is conducted by a home office field service representative assigned to the franchisee's office to provide ongoing guidance through a program of telephone contact and periodic on-site visits, enhanced by operational support by one of 3 regional Uniforce offices. In addition, Uniforce conducts a series of regional conferences and seminars for owners and their staffs, as well as an annual national conference and training seminar.

Managerial Assistance Available: From the start, expert assistance is provided in marketing, training and recruiting to allow for true turnkey operation. Assistance in initial selection of site and layout of office, negotiation of lease, selection of furniture and equipment and telephone systems. A continuous free supply of all forms and materials necessary for the operation of the Uniforce business: manuals, guides, monthly updates, unlimited phone consultation and periodic management visits. In addition, Uniforce prepares and finances the temporary help payroll, billing and accounts receivable, and provides detailed computer analyses to each office on all phases of the temporary help operation. Bimonthly management guidance tapes are provided along with the support by the home office staff. Audio and visual training tapes provided at no charge. Uniforce also provides marketing support, including all necessary promotional materials, along with local and national advertising and public relations programs to insure year-round visibility of the Uniforce name.

Information Submitted: April 1990

UNI/SEARCH, INC.
P.O. Box
Waterbury, Connecticut 06762
Peter Allvin, President

Description of Operation: Uni/Search is a regional franchised professional employment service with 5 offices principally concerned with the placement of clerical and middle management personnel. A unique job exchange system provides for maximum utilization of the resources of the network. New franchisees would benefit most from being located within reasonable proximity to existing offices in Connecticut.

Number of Franchisees: 5 in Connecticut

In Business Since: 1968

Equity Capital Needed: Franchise cost is $10,000. The only additional money needed is for working capital and varies depending on location, size of office, personal needs of franchisee, etc.

Financial Assistance Available: Up to $2,500 of the franchise fee may be financed by the franchisor. Franchisee must be willing to incur all of the start-up costs plus 6 months working capital.

Training Provided: Formal training of franchisee prior to start-up date is usually 2 weeks in length, depending on previous experience of franchisee. Training is usually in the form of one-on-one discussions on all subjects relevant to the management of a private employment agency, and follows closely the training guidelines provided by the National Association of Personnel Consultants, Post-start-up training is continuous through formal meetings, lectures, on-site review of operations, etc.

Managerial Assistance Available: A complete range of managerial assistance is available from site selections, advertising and public relations, legal, accounting, and of course relevant placement techniques. After start-up most assistance is provided on as needed basis.

Information Submitted: June 1990

WESTERN TEMPORARY SERVICES, INC.
301 Lennon Lane
P. O. Box 9280
Walnut Creek, California 94598
A. Terry Slocum, Vice President, Corporate Development

Description of Operation: Western operates over 350 offices in the United States and overseas, both company-owned and franchised. We provide a full line of temporary personnel services, including clerical office support, industrial, marketing, technical, medical/dental, pharmacy and Santa/Photo.

Number of Franchisees: 110 in 31 States

In Business Since: 1948

Equity Capital Needed: Initial franchise fee based on population, ranging from $10,000 to $25,000 for most cities, plus sufficient working capital to cover initial operating and living expenses.

Financial Assistance Available: Western finances the temporary payroll and accounts receivable completely. Western also provides a special start-up incentive for the franchised operation for the first 6 months, and offers additional incentives for volume thereafter.

Training Provided: Western provides initial training in 3 phases: 1) 1 week of operational and sales classroom training at corporate headquarters; 2) 2-3 days supervised hands-on experience in an operating field office; and 3) 2 days on-site training and orientation after the new franchise office has opened. Ongoing training through annual workshops is also made available.

Managerial Assistance Available: Western supplies complete operating manuals to all franchisees, and provides an experienced manager for on-site sales and operational assistance during training. In addition, franchisees receive ongoing management and technical assistance, which includes field meetings, publications, training tapes, sales bulletins, sales leads and referrals, public relations and direct mail assistance, promotional events, accounting support, credit and collection assistance, and national advertising. Western's corporate staff is always available for advice and consultation.

Information Submitted: April 1990

EQUIPMENT/RENTALS

*APPARELMASTER, INC.
2786 East Crescentville Road
West Chester, Ohio 45069
George E. Beetz, Sales Manager

Description of Operation: Offers unique business service for drycleaning, laundry, linen supply, and formal wear establishments with interest toward turnkey operations. Includes detailed instruction and on-site training in how to utilize existing trial uniforms, dust control, and career apparel rental. Other services and benefits include optional data processing invoicing, accounting and inventory control, ongoing seminars and workshops, training schools, and garment and emblem supply.

Number of Franchisees: 10 in 38 States

In Business Since: 1971

Equity Capital Needed: License of $17,000

Financial Assistance Available: None

Training Provided: Ongoing

Managerial Assistance Available: Operation and other manuals provided. Managerial and technical assistance provided on every aspect of the industry for life of franchise.

Information Submitted: July 1990

*COLORTYME, INC.
501 Dallas Highway
Dallas, Texas 75751
Saundra Blackwell, Franchise Administration
Wayne Atchison, Vice President–Development

Description of Operation: ColorTyme franchised stores provide a specialized inventory of rental products such as televisions, audio-video equipment, appliances, and furniture to consumers under a rent-to-own program.

Number of Franchisees: 495 in 41 States

In Business Since: 1979, franchising since 1982

Equity Capital Needed: $83,400-$162,500, depending on location.

Financial Assistance Available: ColorTyme Financial Services, Inc., a wholly owned subsidiary of ColorTyme, Inc. offers financing for all approved products. Existing franchisees who execute a franchise for an additional store may finance the initial franchise fee.

Training Provided: Prior to the opening of a ColorTyme store, the franchisor will provide 2 weeks of classroom instruction for franchisee and manager at franchisor's headquarters in Athens, Texas, or other designated location, and an additional 1 week of on-the-job training at a designated training center. Additionally, managerial and multi-store operators seminars are available at no cost.

Managerial Assistance Available: Assistance is provided in site selection, store design, personnel training and product selection. Continuing assistance inculudes advertising, merchandising business analysis, forms and documents for daily operation, and a copy of the confidential operating manual and various training seminars. The ColorTyme support staff includes all officers of the company who are readily available to assist franchisees in any manner required.

Information Submitted: April 1990

GRAND RENTAL STATION
P.O. Box 1510
Butler, Pennsylvania 16003-1510
Tom Hazel, General Manager

Description of Operation: Licensed, nationally registered general rental program offered by Servistar Corporation to its owner/members (over 3800) and to related business entrepreneurs. By taking advantage of its co-op buying leverage, the company can offer members products and services at advantageous pricing. As a buying co-op any profit realized, after deducting operating costs, is shared with its owner members. Unique state-of-the-art store design included in program.

Number of Franchisees: 150 in 27 states.

In Business Since: 1910

Equity Capital Needed: $50,000-$75,000

Financing Assistance Available: 3-5-7 year fixed term financing for highly rated accounts.

Training Provided: 4 day in-store hands-on training provided within reasonable distance of business location. Exposure and participation in all operational aspects of a general rental business are included. Training on specific product lines also available from company or supplier/vendor.

Managerial Assistance Available: Complete managerial assistance is provided both on and off premise during start-up and initial opening period. Ongoing consulting and management assistance is available via phone from various departments at company headquarters, or on-site when requested.

Information Submitted: April 1990

HOUSE OF RENTALS
3545 Motor Avenue
Los Angeles, California 90034-0725
R. Feinstein, President

Description of Operation: House of Rentals stores will feature a full line of home electronics, major appliances, and furniture rentals. All items will be available for short-term rentals, rent-to-own or outright cash purchase. Stores will be comprised of 12 departments, party, home/office, electronics, major appliances, home furnishings, children and baby, home health care, small appliances, musical instruments, camping/leisure time, auto sound and home theater.

Number of Franchisees: 1 company-owned

Equity Capital Needed: $50,000

Financial Assistance Available: None

Training Provided: Training will be accomplished using company-owned stores or franchise-owned stores. Ongoing assistance will be provided in the areas of accounting, financing, advertising, inventory selection and purchasing, store operations and procedures.

Managerial Assistance Available: Ongoing in all phases of operation.

Information Submitted: April 1990

MARBLES MUSIC & VIDEO
3545 Motor Avenue
Los Angeles, California 90034-0725
R. Feinstein, President

Description of Operation: Marbles Music & Video stores will feature a full line of home entertainment items that are for rent or sale. Each store will contain pre-recorded video movies, audio cassettes and CD for sale, also television sets, VCRs, Camcorders, Nintendo decks and cartridges. Marbles is the total home entertainment store, and is unique as there are very few stores that rent total entertainment. These stores will feature $.99 cents on most movie rentals. New releases will be $1.99. When people have "nothing to do at night" we want them to think of Marbles, where they will find everything they want for an evening's entertainment at home.

Number of Franchisees: 3 in California

In Business Since: 1989

Equity Capital Needed: $50,000

Financial Assistance Available: None

Training Provided: Training will be accomplished using company-owned stores or franchise-owned stores. Ongoing assistance will be provided in the areas of accounting, financing, advertising, inventory selection and purchasing, store operations and procedures.

Managerial Assistance Available: Ongoing in all phases of operation.

Information Submitted: April 1990

MILITARY RENT-ALL, INC.
3545 Motor Avenue
Los Angeles, California 90034-0725
R. Feinstein, President

Description of Operation: Military Rent-All stores have been serving the needs of the military market for over 20 years, operating on or near major bases throughout the Unites States. The customer is provided with the ability to rent or rent-to-own items such as TVs, stereos, VCRs, washer/dryers, refrigerators, microwaves and household furniture on a short-term basis. Military Rent-All was the first to provide this service with a national scope, and today is the largest in the country.

Number of Franchisees: 20 plus 4 company-owned

In Business Since: 1968

Equity Capital Needed: $50,000

Financial Assistance Available: None

Training Provided: Training will be accomplished using company-owned stores or franchise-owned stores. Ongoing assistance will be provided in the areas of accounting, financing, advertising, inventory selection and purchasing, store operations and procedures.

Managerial Assistance Available: Ongoing in all phases of operation.

Information Submitted: April 1990

*MR. MOVIES, INC.
6566 Edenvale Boulevard
Eden Prairie, Minnesota 55346
William H. Kaiser, President
Teri Moody, Director of Franchising

Description of Operation: Mr. Movies is one of the nation's fastest growing chains of video cassette rental stores. The stores boast an attractive decor and service representatives help insure expertly merchandised stock. Market research department selects location and provides in-depth market analysis on an individualized basis. Point of sale computer system gives store owner vital stock information.

Number of Franchisees: 60 in Minnesota, Iowa, Wisconsin, and Massachusetts.

In Business Since: 1985

Equity Capital Needed: $70,000 to $150,000

Financial Assistance Available: No financing is available in-house at this time. Mr. Movies will assist in preparing loan applications.

Training Provided: Extensive training program including 40 hours of in-store training, 8 hours of computer training, and 8 hours of purchasing and operations training.

Managerial Assistance Available: Franchisee receives "recommended buy" list each month. Service representatives visit stores on a quarterly basis. Operational consultants, computer troubleshooters, and title selection advisors are available via toll-free number. Franchisees' computer data is analyzed by franchisor monthly. Advertising and promotional material, store supplies, and some pre-recorded video cassettes can be obtained from Mr. Movies warehouse.

Information Submitted: April 1990

NATION-WIDE GENERAL RENTAL CENTERS, INC.
1684 Highway 92 West
Suite A
Woodstock, Georgia 30188
I. N. Goodvin, President

Description of Operation: Nation-Wide General Rental Center operates a full-line consumer-oriented rental center including items for the contractor and do-it-yourself home owner—items, such as baby equipment, camping supplies, contractors' equipment and tools, concrete tools, carpenters tools, invalid needs, lawn and yard tools, mechanics' tools, painters' equipment, moving needs, party and banquet needs, plumbers' tools, sanding machines, trailer hitches, household equipment and local trucks and trailers. Building required is 1,800 to 3,000 square feet with outside fenced storage area, good traffic flow and parking for 6 to 10 cars.

Number of Franchisees: 196 in 38 States

In Business Since: 1976

Equity Capital Needed: $25,000 plus $7,500—$10,000 working capital. No franchise fees.

Financial Assistance Available: With the down payment of $25,000, franchisee will get $98,500 worth of equipment and opening supplies. The balance can be financed over 5 years with local banks—company assistance to qualified applicants. No franchise or royalty fees; down payment goes toward equipment cost. All risk liability, conversion, group health, accident and life insurance coverage available to franchisee. We also have a buy back agreement and exclusive area agreement.

Training Provided: On-the-job training for 5 full days at no charge to the franchisee. Training covers everything you need from familiarization with and maintenance of equipment, accounting computerized system, advertising and promotion, purchasing add on equipment, rental rates, insurance, inventory control and operation manual covering much more.

Managerial Assistance Available: Consultation on location and market feasibility studies; assistance in securing and negotiation building lease; a monthly computerized financial report giving balance sheet/income statement, and a list of all equipment in inventory with a month rental income per item. A rate guide book giving rental rates for each item and for your area. One hundred percent financing for growth inventory or new equipment. Franchisees can buy all their equipment at 3 to 10 percent over cost, which offers great purchasing power and discounts to each store owner. Buy back agreement gives you full credit on equipment. At the grand opening we will be there to help establish the franchisee in the community. We also mail 9,000 promotions to every home around a new center at grand opening time.

Information Submitted: April 1990

PCR PERSONAL COMPUTER RENTALS
2557 Route 130
Cranbury, New Jersey 08512
Dan Bayha or Joe Laudisdo, Vice President,
Franchise Development

Description of Operation: Business oriented rental center operated from office space. Each outlet provides short-term microcomputers and peripherals to all segments of the business community. Owners stress value added customer service and cater to the needs of the client including free delivery, installation and maintenance, extensive training and personal support.

Number of Franchisees: 49 in 8 States plus 1 company-owned unit.

In Business Since: 1983

Equity Capital Needed: $40,000 to $50,000.

Financial Assistance Available: None

Training Provided: Minimum 2 week comprehensive training for owner-operator and assistant manager. Additional week available (optional) to strengthen hardware, software knowledge.

Managerial Assistance Available: After initial training, ongoing support and training are provided for the term of the franchise agreement. Complete manuals, forms and instructions are furnished. In addition, franchisees will be informed of new products with evaluations, price changes, and improved software and hardware to market. A continuous research and development program will thoroughly test and evaluate products before they are recommended. Ongoing advertising will serve to create awareness of franchise and develop preference level.

Information Submitted: April 1990

REMCO FRANCHISE DEVELOPMENT CORP.
P. O. Box 720259
Houston, Texas 77272
Sam Love, Vice President, Franchising

Description of Operation: Rental, sales, and service of name brand television, stereo, video, and major appliances with rental ownership options. Over 70 company stores in 17 States.

Number of Franchisees: 109 in 29 States

In Business Since: 1969

Equity Capital Needed: $75,000-$250,000 (includes franchise fee).

Financial Assistance Available: Financing arranged through major lending institution for inventory requirements.

Training Provided: Comprehensive 3 week training program in Houston for store managers that includes classroom teaching. On-the-job training in a Remco store for a minimum of 6 weeks. Major training areas are sales management, credit management, administrative management, and store management. Special 3 day training seminar for investors. Continued weekly training in the form of printed material and video tapes.

Managerial Assistance Available: Company representatives provide regular on-site assistance in all phases of operations. A complete and highly detailed set of operational policies and procedures is provided to each franchise. All marketing and advertising programs are administered by the corporate office.

Information Submitted: June 1990

RENAPPLI OF AMERICA, INC.
1600 South Grand Avenue East
Springfield, Illinois 62703
Lou R. Messervy, President

Description of Operations: Rent-to-own-appliances TVs, stereo, VCRs, furniture, computers, satellites. Store consists of 2,000-3,000 square feet, must have off-store parking potential, unlimited—any town 4,000 population or more.

Number of Franchisees: 6 in Illinois and Iowa

In Business Since: 1972

Equity Capital Needed: $60,000

Financial Assistance Available: Contact with National Finance Company. Normally 80 percent of inventory.

Training Provided: Originally, 1 week—(home office)—1 week in field continues throughout agreement.

Managerial Assistance Available: Training and procedure manual, audio, video training films, computer home, software, updated as needed. Profit and loss statements, balance sheets are provided monthly, comparisons with all stores showing products rented, time rented, average income per unit, etc.

Information Submitted: June 1990

TAYLOR RENTAL CORPORATION
(Subsidiary of THE STANLEY WORKS)
P. O. Box 8000
1000 Stanley Drive
New Britain, Connecticut 06050

Description of Operation: General equipment rental center. Taylor stores carry products, tools and equipment for yard and garden, carpet and floor care, do-it-yourself projects, plumbing, automotive, contractors and builders, paint and wallpaper, moving, banquets and special occasions.

Number of Franchisees: 239 in 35 States

In Business Since: 1963

Equity Capital Needed: Total investment of $267,000 of which $90,000 is in liquid assets.

Financial Asssistance Available: No financial assistance available.

Training Provided: Intensive 2 week training session at a company-owned store. Ongoing counseling and advice from your regional director. Annual convention/trade show and business seminars.

Managerial Assistance Available: See above.

Information Submitted: April 1990

YARD CARDS INC.
2940 West Main Street
Belleville, Illinois 62223
Michael Hoepfinger, President

Description of Operation: Yard Cards specializes in the rental of 8' high wooden greeting cards to be placed in yards as well as indoors to recognize special occasions. This can be an excellent opportunity for an add-on business for a florist, balloon business, cake decorating business, or party supply business, as well as an independent business operated from your home.

Number of Franchisees: 22 plus, company-owned in 11 States.

In Business Since: 1983, franchising since fall of 1986

Equity Capital Needed: $5,000-$15,000

Financial Assistance Available: None

Training Provided: Training is provided at the office of franchisor and will not be longer than 3 days. Attendance is optional, and at the expense of franchisee. A complete, detailed operations manual is provided.

Managerial Assistance Available: Ongoing assistance is provided by Yard Cards personnel. This includes all phasis of operation, and is provided readily at the request of franchisee. Complete, detailed operations manual is provided, and includes updates as they occur.

Information Submitted: April 1990

ZM VIDEO RENTAL, INC.
3501 Chateau Boulevard
Suite C-102
Kenner, Louisiana 70065
Tony Hojjat

Description of Operation: Fast growing and aggressive video rental stores of movies and equipment. We offer professional ongoing support and group purchasing benefits.

Number of Franchisees: 22 in Louisiana and Mississippi

In Business Since: 1984

Equity Capital Needed: $70,000-$110,000

Financial Assistance Available: Financing is available but must have 1/2 equity.

Training Provided: The initial training is at our training center for 1 week. Classroom and in-store.

Managerial Assistance Available: Field training at locations during opening and ongoing consulting.

Information Submitted: April 1990

FOOD—DONUTS

DAWN DONUT SYSTEMS, INC.
G-4300 West Pierson Road
Flint, Michigan 48504
Bill Morin, Director of Franchising

Description of Operation: A Dawn Donut shop offers donuts, baked goods, coffee and other beverages, and other food items for sale on a retail basis, and each shop can be a production base for wholesale business as well. Most shops developed since the mid-1970s also offer a major brand of gasoline and a "convenience" grocery store. (Those shops generally require 22,000 square feet of property and a 2,400 square foot building.) A Dawn Donut shop can be a perfect addition to an existing retail gasoline and/or convenience store operation. In some cases, the initial Dawn Donut shop can produce product for "satellite" units. For multi-unit operators the company offers a Special Territorial Expansion Plan (STEP). Dawn Donut does require a seating package in all units, but a more efficient seating package can be used with existing gasoline and/or convenience stores.

Number of Franchisees: 42 with 56 units in Michigan

In Business Since: 1956

Equity Capital Needed: Minimum of $50,000.

Financial Assistance Available: Franchisor prefers franchisees obtain their own financing. However, franchisor will assist in arranging financing, and in some cases will finance qualified franchisees.

Training Provided: Franchisees and/or their designated representatives must successfully complete the Dawn Donut Training Program, which is conducted at a designated Dawn Donut Shop. The curriculum includes instruction on operations, merchandising, marketing, and business functions that the franchisor considers essential to operate a Dawn Donut Shop successfully.

Managerial Assistance Available: Initial site selection assistance provided, and franchisor must approve site. Franchisor maintains a continuing advisory relationship with franchisees, including consulting in the areas of marketing, merchandising and general business operations.

Information Submitted: May 1990

DIXIE CREAM FLOUR COMPANY
P. O. Box 180
St. Louis, Missouri 63166
Attention: Franchise Director

Description of Operation: Franchised privately owned donut and coffee shops, with both walk-in and drive-thru stores. Retail and wholesale selling of over 50 varieties of freshmade yeast raised and cake donuts, as well as coffee and other beverages.

Number of Franchisees: 42 in 11 States

In Business Since: 1929

Equity Capital Needed: Franchise and training fee $5,000. No overrides, royalties or percentages. Equipment cost $15,000 to $40,000.

Financial Assistance Available: None

Training Provided: As part of the franchise fee, we have an extensive hands-on, in-shop training program of approximately 2 weeks duration. Our company technicians work with you in your shop during this period. A comprehensive training manual is provided for production assistance. Additionally, information concerning new products, as well as pertinent new ideas in helping your donut shop operate as efficiently as possible, are available from our St. Louis office.

Managerial Assistance Available: Continuous communication by correspondence, direct toll-free phone and in-store visits by qualified home office personnel. There is also a procedures manual provided for everyday use in your donut shop. This manual, along with our technical assistance, will help each franchise attain its ultimate goal of profit and success.

Information Submitted: May 1990

THE DONUT HOLE
Rt. 1, Box 704
Dickinson, North Dakota 58601
Guy Moos, Director of Franchising

Description of Operation: Franchised and company-owned shops with sit-down and take-out service with over 50 varieties of donuts and muffins, plus decorated cakes and tortes, cookies, pastry items, beverages, and the original Birthday Donut. The majority of products are delivered to The Donut Hole shops on a regular basis from a central production facility in a frozen dough stage. Franchisor owns and operates the production facility, assuring consistent quality of products to all franchise outlets. Products are then baked or fried daily in each shop to guarantee freshness. All shops required to build or remodel to uniform specifications and standards.

Number of Franchisees: 15 The Donut Hole franchised stores located in North Dakota, South Dakota, and Montana, plus 2 corporate-owned shops in Dickinson, North Dakota, which are also used for franchisee training.

In Business Since: Owners have operated independent bakeries since 1955; opened first The Donut Hole store in 1976; began selling franchises in 1979.

Equity Capital Needed: $35,000 to $40,000

Financial Assistance Available: Franchisor will assist franchisee in arranging financing through local lending institutions.

Training Provided: Franchisor requires that franchisee attend an intensive 3 week training program at our home office and at a designated The Donut Hole shop. Our company technicians will train you in every aspect of business operations, including food preparation, merchandising, marketing, administrative, and organizational procedures. Franchisee must satisfactorily complete this training before being permitted to open his/her shop.

Managerial Assistance Available: Franchisor assists in site selection, pre-opening, and grand opening activities. Franchisee receives comprehensive operational and procedures manuals, with ongoing updates on new products and procedures. Ongoing communications and support are provided by a monthly newsletter, an annual 2 day seminar and awards program, and a support services representative who visits each store on a regular basis throughout the year, working with the franchisee to improve his/her knowledge of store operations. Home office provides marketing and advertising assistance, and outside contract accounting services are available.

Information Submitted: April 1990

*DONUT INN INC.
6355 Topanga Canyon Boulevard
Suite 403
Woodland Hills, California 91367-2185

Description of Operation: Franchised donut and coffee shops—drive-in and walk-in units. Retail selling of more than 80 varieties of donuts, pastries, cookies and muffins, bagels, and croissants. Drinks are primarily coffee, milk, orange juice, and other non-alcoholic beverages. We offer individual franchises or territory (areas) franchises. We encourage growth through qualified individuals and groups with our sub-franchisor program.

Number of Franchisees: 36 plus 3 company-owned in California.

In Business Since: 1975

Equity Capital Needed: Franchise fee: $20,000. Equipment package approximately $45,000 to $65,000.

Financial Assistance Available: We finance up to 75 percent of the equipment package to qualified franchisees.

Training Provided: 3-4 weeks of concentrated training in all phases of the business in our training facility. Continuous updating and retraining as needed, on the newest and most innovative concepts and equipment. 1 week training in your store upon opening.

Managerial Assistance Available: We provide a comprehensive recipe and procedure manual that guides the franchisee in the every day operation relating to product and quality control, service, sales, bookkeeping, inventory, ordering, marketing, etc. Whenever the franchisee has a question or needs advice on anything relating to their Donut Inn shop, there is a 24-hour a day, 7-day a week, hot line.

Information Submitted: May 1990

DONUTLAND USA, INC.
5265 Rockwell Drive, N.E.
Cedar Rapids, Iowa 52402

Description of Operation: Franchised and company-owned specialty food shops with sit-down, take-out and drive-thru service. Over 65 varieties of donuts and donut-related products are sold retail and wholesale. Each shop serves product that is prepared fresh daily. Deli-sandwiches, soup and salad are also served.

Number of Franchisees: 18 plus 3 company-owned in Illinois, Iowa, North Dakota, Wisconsin and Nebraska.

In Business Since: 1964

Equity Capital Needed: Franchise fee $25,000. Total package, excluding real estate, $140,000 approximately.

Financial Assistance Available: Assistance in securing financing is provided.

Training Provided: 6 week training program is provided in Cedar Rapids, Iowa, corporate headquarters. The source includes training in production, operations, labor relations, accounting and financial management.

Managerial Assistance Available: Site selection and pre-opening assistance is provided. Throughout the term of the franchise, ongoing assistance is provided in accounting, marketing and operations.

Information Submitted: June 1990

DONUT MAKER
99 Cambridge Street
Charlestown, Massachusetts 02129
James DeVellis, Treasurer

Description of Operation: Retail coffee, donut, muffin stores.

Number of Franchisees: 17 in Massachusetts and New Hampshire

In Business Since: 1978

Equity Capital Needed: $60,000-$75,000

Financial Assistance Available: None

Training Provided: Intensive 5-6 weeks of training in all aspects of operating a donut shop. These include manufacturing of products, financial equipment maintenance, personnel and customer service.

Managerial Assistance Available: Franchisor will assist franchise for 2 weeks on a full-time basis at opening of new store and any additional expertise necessary to make operator operationally sound. Complete manual of operations is provided.

Information Submitted: June 1990

DONUTS GALORE, INC.
107 East Glenside Avenue, Suite E
Glenside, Pennsylvania 19038

Description of Operation: Franchised and company-owned coffee and donut shops with drive-in, walk-in units and shopping mall units. Retail selling of more than 50 varieties of donuts, cookies, muffins, brownies, macaroons, cupcakes, cookies and other bakery products, soup, hotdogs, coffee and other beverages. Donut products are centrally made, frozen and shipped to shops on regular basis. No bakers required on premises. Donut Shop consulting services available for private enterprise.

Number of Franchisees: 3 (1 company) in Pennsylvania and New Jersey.

In Business Since: 1955

Equity Capital Needed: Franchise fee $15,000; working capital approximately $16,000; equipment package approximately $50,000 plus. Consultation fee $5,800 and up depending upon services required.

Financial Assistance Available: We will assist franchisee in securing financing. No franchise fees for consulting services.

Training Provided: 1 week training program consisting of practical instruction in our stores.

Managerial Assistance Available: Continuous operational assistance is available. The company helps in quality control, new products programs, and marketing programs for all shops.

Information Submitted: May 1990

*DUNKIN' DONUTS OF AMERICA, INC.
P. O. Box 317
Randolph, Massachusetts 02368
Lawrence W. Hantman, Senior Vice President

Description of Operation: Franchised and company-owned coffee and donut shops with drive-thru and walk-in units. Sales of over 52 varieties of donuts, munchkin donuthole treats, muffins, cookies, brownies, and related bakery items, at retail, along with soup, coffee and other beverages. Franchises are sold for individual shops and, in selected markets, multiple license agreements may be available. Franchisor encourages development of real estate and building by the franchisee, subject to approval of Dunkin' Donuts of America, Inc. Franchisor also develops locations for franchising and for company supervisions.

Number of Franchisees: 1,714 units in 39 States, Canada, Japan, the Philippines, Thailand, Bahamas, Korea, Singapore, Colombia, Venezuela, Chile, Brazil, Indonesia, Saudi Arabia and Taiwan.

In Business Since: 1950

Equity Capital Needed: Franchise fee, $27,000 to $40,000, depending on geographical area and whether franchisee owns or controls the real estate. Working capital, approximately $18,000.

Financial Assistance Available: Financing assistance for real estate acquisition and development. Equipment and sign financing assistance is available to qualified franchisees.

Training Provided: 6 weeks training course for franchisees at Dunkin' Donuts University in Braintree, Massachusetts, consisting of production and shop management training. Initial training of donutmakers and managers for franchises and retraining are carried out at Dunkin' Donuts University without additional charge.

Managerial Assistance Available: Continuous managerial assistance is avaiable from the district sales manager assigned to the individual shop. The company maintains quality assurance, research and development and new products programs. The franchisee-funded marketing department provides marketing programs for all shops. The marketing programs are administered by a field marketing manager who develops plans on a market basis.

Information Submitted: June 1990

FOSTER'S DONUTS, INC.
Suite 3J
4685 East Industrial Street
Simi Valley, California 93063
Linda Horn, Franchise Broker

Description of Operation: The Foster's Donuts shop franchise is a retail donut shop usually located in a neighborhood shopping center and sublet to the franchisee by Foster's. The shop sells a complete assortment of Foster's Donuts freshly baked on the premises every day and a complimentary variety of hot and cold beverages. Each franchise offers take-out service and some counter seating and is fully equipped to bake and sell donuts. Area franchises available for development in selected areas.

Number of Franchisees: 55 units in California

In Business Since: 1971

Equity Capital Needed: $35,000

Financial Assistance Available: Franchise fee of $35,000 must be in cash. Foster's will finance the equipment package.

Training Provided: The Foster's Donuts training program includes no less than 10 days of pre-opening training covering all phases of Foster's Donuts shop operation, including donut baking, equipment operation, product merchandising, and business management. This is followed by 10 days of in-shop training and supervision at the franchisee's shop when it opens, during which the franchisee will operate the shop under the guidance of a Foster's field representative.

Managerial Assistance Available: Foster's provides ongoing managerial and technical assistance by having a field representative available for telephone consultation every weekday between 9 am and 5 pm; field representatives also visit the franchise location regularly to check on shop operations and are available for trouble-shooting and problem solving. All shop bookkeeping and tax return preparation is done by Foster's. Foster's also provides the franchisee a confidential operating manual containing technical and managerial advice, forms, guides, directions, and operating tips and techniques and conducts periodic refresher courses, seminars, and other educational programs and continuous market and product research.

Information Submitted: June 1990

JOLLY PIRATE DONUT SHOPS
3923 East Broad Street
Columbus, Ohio 43213
Nick Soulas, President

Description of Operation: Retail sales of donuts, cookies, brownies, baked goods, and coffee and soft drinks.

Number of Franchisees: 15 in 3 States

In Business Since: 1961, franchising since 1970.

Equity Capital Needed: $40,000 minimum, depending on ability to finance.

Financial Assistance Available: None

Training Provided: 6 weeks to 3 months on-the-job, learning product preparation and shop management, in an operating shop.

Managerial Assistance Available: 2 weeks in-store training for manager, bakers and crew at opening. Periodic visits by company personnel to consult and advise, and as requested by phone.

Information Submitted: June 1990

*MISTER DONUT OF AMERICA, INC.
P. O. Box 317
Randolph, Massachusetts 02308
Ralph Gabellieri, President

Description of Operation: Franchised doughnut and coffee shops—drive-in and walk-in units. Retail selling of more than 55 varieties of doughnuts, baked goods and nonalcoholic beverages, primarily coffee. Located on well traveled streets, near schools, churches, shopping centers, amusements and entertainment. Each shop produces its own doughnuts in its own kitchen.

Number of Franchisees: Over 500 in USA and 2 countries.

In Business Since: 1955

Equity Capital Needed: Franchise fee $25,000. Cost of real estate and building are responsibility of franchisee, but location is subject to Mister Donut's approval.

Financial Assistance Available: None

Training Provided: Continuous professional 4 weeks training program, consisting of practical as well as classroom training at company school in St. Paul, Minnesota.

Managerial Assistance Available: An area representative is permanently located at company expense in each area of the United States and Canada for managerial assistance to franchise operators. The company maintains a quality control service as well as a research and development department, marketing and advertising services to assist franchise owners. Location analysis, lease negotiation and assistance with building design and construction are also provided by Mister Donut personnel.

Information Submitted: June 1990

SOUTHERN MAID DONUT FLOUR COMPANY
3615 Cavalier Drive
Garland, Texas 75042
Doris Franklin, Vice President

Description of Operation: Southern Maid offers a tailored to order operation for each prospect. We have available all technical, managerial, and business information. Southern Maid sells all brands of donut equipment. We consider our flour blends of the finest quality for the price. Franchises are available nationwide.

Number of Franchisees: 65 in Texas, Kansas, Louisiana, Arkansas, and Florida.

In Business Since: 1937

Equity Capital Needed: A 50 percent down payment is required before equipment is ordered. Franchise fee is $5,000.

Financial Assistance Available: None

Training Provided: In-shop technical training for period necessary (time varies with each operation).

Managerial Assistance Available: Continuous advisory information is available.

Information Submitted: April 1990

SPUDNUTS
A Division of U.S. DESIGN SYSTEMS, INC.
742 Hampsnipe Road
Suite B
Westlake Village, California 91361

Description of Operation: Spudnuts offers franchisees a unique and established product for a retail donut shop. The store is approximately 1,800 square feet and includes drive-thru service whenever possible. The exterior image of the building has a brand new look that blends in any area.

Number of Franchisees: 28 in 9 States including 4 company-owned stores.

In Business Since: 1939

Equity Capital Needed: $20,000 franchise fee

Financial Assistance Available: Franchisees to arrange their own financing. Franchisor will assist in arrangements.

Training Provided: 4 weeks of in-depth training are provided plus additional training in the new franchised shop at the time of opening. Training includes making Spudnuts unique products, hiring of personnel, record keeping, promotional and advertising concepts, production controls, quality control, and marketing ideas and concepts.

Managerial Assistance Available: Spudnuts assistance continues for the length of the franchise agreement. Spudnuts knowhow manual will be revised on a continual basis. Field support will visit shops and assist franchisee with complete operation of shops and introduce new products developed from their research and development department.

Information Submitted: April 1990

TASTEE DONUTS, INC.
5600 Mounes Street
Harahan, Louisiana 70123
Joe Santopadre

Description of Operation: Tastee Donuts, Inc., offers investment and career opportunities to both multiple unit and single unit licensees. Our concept is to provide a large variety of fresh, high quality donuts, baked goods, and small hamburgers with excellent coffee and other beverages, either to take-out, sit-down or drive-thru, in both free-standing and shopping center locations.

Number of Franchisees: 52 in 3 States

In Business Since: 1965

Equity Capital Needed: Total investment about $165,000.

Financial Assistance Available: None

Training Provided: Intensive 6 week training course covering all aspects of production and shop management. The course is taught at the Tastee Donuts training school in New Orleans, Louisiana.

Managerial Assistance Available: Continuous managerial assistance is available from regional supervisors. Advertising and marketing assistance is provided through licensee supported programs.

Information Submitted: June 1990

THE WHOLE DONUT FRANCHISE SYSTEMS, INC.
894 New Britain Avenue
Hartford, Connecticut 06106-3921
Frank S. Gencarelli, President

Description of Operation: Each store averages 1,700-1,800 square feet with drive through and walk-in units. The Whole Donut sells donuts, pastries, muffins and cookies along with coffee and soft drinks. Some stores have a deli where sandwiches, soups and salads are served. Most stores are open 24 hours a day.

Number of Franchisees: 38 in Connecticut, Massachusetts, New Hampshire, Rhode Island and Vermont.

In Business Since: 1953, started franchising in 1984

Equity Capital Needed: $60,000 cash, which includes the $25,000 franchise fee. $75,000 financed. $10,000 working capital. Excluding cost of real estate and buildings which must be approved by The Whole Donut.

Training Provided: 5 to 6 weeks training course in Hartford, Connecticut. Instructions in product preparation, marketing, customer service, hiring, employee training, inventory control, recordkeeping, and other supervisory skills. Instruction is continued at franchisee's location before and immediately after opening for business.

Managerial Assistance Available: Company representatives are at your side assisting you in setting-up and operating your store. The company provides marketing and advertising services to franchisees, along with continued product line evaluation and selection.

Information Submitted: June 1990

*WINCHELL'S DONUT HOUSE
16424 Valley View Avenue
La Mirada, California 90637
Chuck Tortorice

Description of Operation: Winchell's is an established and highly recognized retail donut shop chain that offers a large variety of donuts, brownies, croissants, muffins, cookies and related bakery items, as well as coffee and other beverages. Retail units are normally free standing or strip shopping center, walk-in and drive-thru locations.

Number of Franchisees: 617 company-owned and 84 franchised locations in 13 Western States. Also, 34 locations in Japan, Korea, Philippines and Guam.

In Business Since: 1948

Equity Capital Needed: $55,000 minimum with the ability to secure financing for the remaining portion of investment. (Initial franchise fee $25,000-$30,000.)

Financial Assistance Available: Franchisees to arrange own financing. Winchell's provides a list of approved lenders.

Training Provided: A comprehensive 6 week franchisee training course where you'll receive extensive instruction from the production of donuts to retail sales management, as well as personal development and communication. Additional training and supervision by a qualified company representative for approximately 7 days during store opening.

Managerial Assistance Available: Franchisee will receive operations support through effective operating methods, systems and procedures that begins at the grand opening and continues with periodic store visits throughout the term of the franchise. Also marketing support, developed by qualified professionals, through high impact advertising materials and promotions, and Winchell's television and radio advertising, as well as research and development of new products and sales building promotions.

Information Submitted: June 1990

FOOD—GROCERY/SPECIALTY STORES

ALPEN PANTRY, INC.
1748 Independence Boulevard
Suite C-6
Sarasota, Florida 33580
John Hartnett

Description of Operation: Retail specialty food stores located primarily in major regional shopping malls featuring gourmet foods, domestic and imported cheeses, sausages, wines and "deli board" gourmet sandwiches.

Number of Franchisees: 10 in 8 States

In Business Since: 1975

Equity Capital Needed: Approximately $75,000 plus leasehold improvements.

Financial Assistance Available: Assistance in obtaining local bank financing.

Training Provided: Prior to opening, 2 week course in product knowledge, sales techniques, merchandising, promotional calendar, inventory control and managing a successful business.

Managerial Assistance Available: Ongoing program of communication by bulletins, phone and store visits, annual convention, and sales seminars.

Information Submitted: June 1990

AMERICAN BULK FOOD
22451 Michigan Avenue
Dearborn, Michigan 48124
Martin Benson or Jeff English

Description of Operation: American Bulk Food is a bulk food grocery store that stocks over 1,100 gourmet, exotic, ethnic, natural, diet and sugar-free products in bulk. Items are displayed in clear plastic bins that allow the consumer to see the colors and quality and smell the aromas of the food. The consumer may buy as much or as little as needed, which makes buying exciting, fun, practical and economical.

Number of Franchisees: 10 plus 2 company-owned in Michigan.

In Business Since: 1983

Equity Capital Needed: $120,000-$200,000

Financial Assistance Available: Financing available to qualified applicants.

Training Provided: Training covers all aspects of bulk food market operations, which include sanitation, inventory procedures, quality control, shelf life control, pricing strategies, ordering and product selection, display and signage, market environment control, advertising and promotion, ongoing owner staff training in the above, and many other areas.

Managerial Assistance Available: Ongoing support program 52 weeks a year, newsletter, field consultant, technical and operating trainers, regular visits by field consultants, ongoing research and development programs, seminars and meetings. Access to centralized buying from corporate warehouse.

Information Submitted: June 1990

ATLANTIC RICHFIELD COMPANY
am/pm MINI MARKET FRANCHISE
1055 West 7th Street
Los Angeles, California 90051-0570
Thomas L. Everett, Manager
am/pm Franchise Marketing

Description of Operation: The "am/pm" mini market franchise is a system for retail grocery store and fast food services and the identification, layout, and operation of retail grocery and fast food stores identified principally by the service name and service mark "am/pm," featuring the sale of prepackaged foods, fast foods, beverages, sundries and convenience store goods.

Number of Franchisees: 731 as of February 1990 in 5 States

In Business Since: 1979

Equity Capital Needed: $126,500 through $568,000 excluding the cost of acquiring or leasing the real estate and excluding any deposits and any investment required in connection with other businesses conducted from the premises.

Financial Assistance Available: None

Training Provided: 8 to 12 weeks training including basic bookkeeping, accounting, sales promotion, inventory control and retail and management techniques.

Managerial Assistance Available: Complete managerial assistance from franchisor includes the personalized service of an am/pm franchise representative, sales manager, and franchise manager at the field level with assistance from a headquarters staff to create new program and manage sustaining advertising and sales promotion techniques. Additionally, complete manuals detailing systems, forms, accounting and inventory service, and marketing techniques are also provided to the franchisee.

Information Submitted: April 1990

AUGIE'S, INC.
1900 West County Road C
St. Paul, Minnesota 55113
Ray Augustine, President

Description of Operation: Industrial catering. Special equipped trucks to serve hot foods to workers on-the-job.

Number of Franchisees: 54 in Minnesota

In Business Since: 1958

Equity Capital Needed: $5,000, some instances less.

Financial Assistance Available: Weekly payment on amount due.

Training Provided: Approximately 1 week training in driving and sales.

Managerial Assistance Available: Same as above.

Information Submitted: June 1990

BALBOA BAKING COMPANY
4686 University Avenue
San Diego, California 92105
Fabian Stebenski

Description of Operation: We make quality bread, specializing in sourdough loaves and rolls. Franchising in the San Diego area only.

Number of Franchisees: 6 in California

In Business Since: 1970

Equity Capital Needed: $100,000

Financial Assistance Available: Will help in financing if franchisee is fully qualified.

Training Provided: Training for packers and drivers. Packers—slicing and packing bread for following day. Drivers—learn routes. Customer promoting—restaurants, delis and markets.

Managerial Assistance Available: Balboa provides continual management service for the life of the franchise in areas such as bookkeeping, advertising and inventory control. Complete manuals of operations, forms and directions are provided. District and field managers are available to work closely with franchisee and assist in solving problems. Balboa sponsors meetings and conducts marketing and product research to maintain high Balboa consumer acceptance.

Information Submitted: June 1990

BARNIE'S COFFEE & TEA COMPANY, INC.
340 North Primrose Drive
Orlando, Florida 32803
B. Philip Jones, Jr., President

Description of Operation: Barnie's is a gourmet coffee and tea store selling imported whole bean coffees, bulk and packaged teas, related accessories, and cupped coffee, espresso, cappuccino and specialty baked goods for take out. Store units are located in premiere regional mall locations.

Number of Franchisees: 26 in Florida, Alabama, Georgia, Illinois, and Tennessee.

In Business Since: 1980, incorporated in 1982 (43 company-owned stores).

Equity Capital Needed: $150,000-$200,000 (including debt capital).

Financial Assistance Available: No financial assistance is available. The franchisor does help coordinate presentation of loan package to lending institutions.

Training Provided: 5 day orientation at home office. Franchisee and staff participate in initial store set-up. Grand opening week with company, in-store supervision. Detailed operations manual provided.

Managerial Assistance Available: During first year visits by franchise operations department. Three franchisee meetings per year for duration of franchise agreement. Access to central buying power and distribution through warehouse. Ongoing participation in store with promotions and new product introduction.

Information Submitted: April 1990

BLUE CHIP COOKIES, INC.
124 Beale Street
4th Floor
San Francisco, California 94105
Matt Nader, CEO

Description of Operation: Retail gourmet fresh cookies.

Number of Franchisees: 26 in California, Arizona, Colorado, New Mexico, Ohio, Texas and Minnesota.

In Business Since: 1983

Equity Capital Needed: $90,000-$115,000

Financial Assistance Available: None

Training Provided: All aspects from making the cookie dough to mixing, baking, selling and marketing. 2-3 weeks of training for franchisee and/or management.

Managerial Assistance Available: As needed and when needed for the life of the franchise. Building and architectual design, layout, equipment specs and purchasing.

Information Submitted: June 1990

LE CROISSANT SHOP
dba BLUE MILL ENTERPRISES CORP.
227 West 40th Street
New York, New York 10018
Robert Le Lamer, President
Jacques Pelletier, Vice President

Description of Operation: Retail facilities selling authentic French baked croissants, pastries, breads, salads, soups, beverages and other baked and cooked products.

Number of Franchisees: 16 plus 6 company-owned in New York

In Business Since: 1981, offering franchises since 1984

Equity Capital Needed: $125,000 to $300,000

Financial Assistance Available: None

Training Provided: 4 weeks training in baking and sales

Managerial Assistance Available: Operational and managing assistance provided throughout the term of the contract.

Information Submitted: April 1990

*BOARDWALK FRANCHISE CORPORATION, INC.
T/A THE BOARDWALK PEANUT SHOPPE
10th Street and Boardwalk
P.O. Box 749
Ocean City, New Jersey 08226
Leo Yeager III, President

Description of Operation: Retail nut and candy shoppe. Featuring "hot" roasted peanuts, freshly prepared nuts and popcorn, dried fruits, health mixes and seeds, chocolates, candy, and gift packages.

Number of Franchisees: 4 plus 2 company-owned

In Business Since: 1972

Equity Capital Needed: Total investment ranges from $94,500-$132,000. This includes a $12,000 franchise fee. Additional working capital and deposits of $15,000 may be required.

Financial Assistance Available: No. Franchisor will assist in preparation of a loan package.

Training Provided: A policies manual is issued and enhanced by a 1 week training program. This on-the-job training provides exact specifications for producing quality products, marketing strategies, management and administrative systems.

Managerial Assistance Available: Start-up assistance provided in opening locations as well as ongoing support. Through a call-line, a franchisee can contact the franchisor with a problem or question. Franchisees will receive updates on the latest trends and promotional strategies. There is also periodic field supervision.

Information Submitted: June 1990

*BULK INTERNATIONAL
755 West Big Beaver Road
Suite 1600
Troy, Michigan 48010
Leonard A. Daitch

Description of Operation: Bulk International is the franchisor of Mister Bulky's Foods and Johvince Bulk Food stores. Bulk International offers turnkey franchises of retail bulk food markets. Each store is between 1,600 and 2,600 square feet, and is located in strip malls or regional malls. These markets are unique as they offer over 1,000 bulk food items to consumers, with the opportunity to buy a pinch or a pound, and in most cases, at considerable savings over normal grocery markets. The products are merchandised out of plexigas bins, and an extremely attractive presentation acts as a strong incentive to the consumer. Items merchandised are dried fruits and nuts, candies, spices, grains and cereals, pastas, peas and beans, large assortment of flours, sugars, spices of the world, extracts, cake mixes, baking supplies, baking ingredients, and related giftware.

Number of Franchisees: 51 in 14 States

In Business Since: 1983

Equity Capital Needed: $75,000 minimum

Financial Assistance Available: A total investment of between $130,000 (low) to $250,000 (high) is required to open a bulk food franchise on a turnkey basis. This includes the franchisee fee, all fixturing and equipment, shelving, two computerized checkout counters, signage package, and approximately $35,000 of start-up inventory. This figure also includes an estimation for leasehold improvement, first and last month's rent and initial advertising and insurance costs. The franchisor does no direct financing, but will provide the franchisee with assistance to obtain financing, and if the franchisee's credit and security are acceptable, lending institutions will generally advance 50 percent of the required capital.

Training Provided: The franchisor provides assistance in site selection and lease negotiation. Franchisor provides approximately 3 weeks of training for manager, owner, and staff, comprised of 2 weeks prior to store opening at franchisee's location or other designated location, and 1 week of training reinforcement after store has opened. Ongoing supervision is part of the franchisor's program. Training methods include operating manuals, hands-on training, cashier manuals, employee handbook specifically dealing with care and control of handling foods in bulk, and retail merchandising.

Managerial Assistance Available: Bulk International provides continual supervision through store visits, newsletters, and area meetings, to ensure that the franchisee is kept up to date on seasonal merchandise, new products, new ideas, and new merchandising techniques.

Information Submitted: April 1990

*BUNS MASTER BAKERY SYSTEMS CORP.
6505 East Mississauga Road North
Mississauga, Ontario, Canada L5N 1A6
Jon Mallinick, Franchise Manager (United States)

Description of Operation: Buns Master Bakery is a unique self-service, bake-on-premises bakery that offers distinctive quality breads, buns, rolls and other bakery products at factory prices. All bakeries use the same formula and all are required to have the same name, logo, decor, product bins and product mix.

Number of Franchisees: 6 in Washington, Ohio, Michigan and Arizona. 116 in Canada

In Business Since: 1979 in the U.S.A.; 1976 in Canada

Equity Capital Needed: Minimum $75,000

Financial Assistance Available: None

Training Provided: An initial training program that consists of participating in the day-to-day operation of another Buns Master Bakery for 2 to 5 days prior to opening his/her own bakery is offered to the franchisee. In addition, for the first 14 days of operation of the franchisee's bakery, a technical trainer teaches the franchisee and his staff the Buns Master Bakery system's methods of preparing and merchandising products, and standard operating practices, methods and procedures.

Managerial Assistance Available: The franchisor assists the franchisee in site selection, lease negotiations, bakery layout, preparing financial information for financing, purchasing the required equipment package, initial training, initial advertising and promotion, continuing advertising and promotion, product mix and product development.

Information Submitted: April 1990

CHEESECAKE, ETC.
400 Swallow Drive
Miami Springs, Florida 33166
Bill Wolar, Jr., Vice President, Franchise Director

Description of Operation: Cheesecake, Etc. offers franchise owners a sound profit potential in the ever-increasing specialty dessert industry. Each unit is beautifully decorated for eat-in or take-home retail business. The wholesale market allows for outstanding long-term growth. All varieties and flavors of cheesecake, gourmet chocolates and many other specialty desserts. A simple "pour and bake" system; other desserts supplied ready-to-serve.

Number of Franchisees: 4 in 3 States

In Business Since: 1974

Equity Capital Needed: None

Training Provided: 7 days at home office and on-site support for opening. Extensive operations manual from baking to customer relations to wholesale selling.

Managerial Assistance Available: Assistance with site selection, design of unit, lease negotiations, advertising materials and continual home office support.

Information Submitted: May 1990

CHEESE SHOP INTERNATIONAL, INC.
14819 Inwood
Dallas, Texas 75244

Description of Operation: Retail sale of fine cheese, gourmet foods, related gift items and wines where permissible. Typically located in a shopping center or on main street of better suburban communities.

Number of Franchisees: 50 in 16 States

In Business Since: 1965

Equity Capital Needed: $50,000-$100,000

Financial Assistance Available: None

Training Provided: 4 weeks; 5 days per week actually working in an existing Cheese Shop under the direction of a company expert.

Managerial Assistance Available: In addition to the training we provide an expert to help during the grand opening week. On a continuous basis we accept collect phone calls to plan and advise on all purchases necessary to run the business. This service includes discussing the following as applies to various suppliers: availability of product, freshness, specials, quality, next arrivals, trucking routes, air freight, costs, etc. It also includes recommending where to place a given order for a certain product at that particular time. This service is optional and typically done on a weekly basis. We also organize promotions, designed to increased sales. Continuous supervision and advice in all phases of retail operations is available.

Information Submitted: June 1990

CHEZ CHOCOLAT
P.O. Drawer 11025
Winston-Salem, North Carolina 27116

Description of Operation: Retail candy and nut shops selling domestic and imported products. Operated primarily in kiosk and store locations in regional malls.

Number of Franchisees: 32 stores in 12 states plus 1 company-owned.

In Business Since: 1972

Equity Capital Needed: Estimated costs include complete turnkey, franchise fee, and inventory, Kiosks range from $30,000—$135,000. In-line stores range from $65,000-$150,000.

Financial Assistance Available: None. Outside financing only. Some internal financing available under certain circumstances.

Training Provided: Regional supervisors and field operations managers train franchisees in their respective locations for a time depending on past retail experience.

Managerial Assistance Available: Field operations managers set up and open stores providing in-depth initial training. Afterwards, regional supervisors visit locations as needed to assist in maximizing operations, marketing new, seasonal, and holiday merchandise. Regional meetings are held for operations seminars and holiday product shows in advance of major holidays.

Information Submitted: April 1990

*THE COFFEE BEANERY, LTD.
G-3429 Pierson Place
Flushing, Michigan 48433
JoAnne Shaw, President

Description of Operation: Specializes in gourmet coffee and tea, selling coffee by the pound and cup, bulk and packaged tea, related accessories. Stores are located in major malls.

Number of Franchisees: 31 stores in 6 States.

In Business Since: 1976

Equity Capital Needed: Net worth of $200,000.

Financial Assistance Available: A total investment of $95,000 to $196,000 is required to open a Coffee Beanery, Ltd. on a turnkey basis. Included would be franchise fee, fixturing, shelving, signage, inventory and some working capital. Franchisor does no direct financing but will provide qualified franchisees assistance in obtaining financing.

Training Provided: 1 week in corporate office, 1 week in company-owned store, and 2 weeks in franchise store. Training manuals include employee manual, management manual and product training manual. Training may include product, inventory control, bookkeeping, daily operations and much more.

Managerial Assistance Available: Assistance available by store visits, training meetings, newsletters, phone, access to group buying through central distribution, a complete monthly marketing program, research and development for new products and marketing techniques.

Information Submitted: April 1990

THE COFFEE MERCHANT
Box 2159
Sand Point, Idaho 83864

Description of Operation: The Coffee Merchant is a specialty retail store providing an exceptional variety of the world's best coffees, fine teas and related accessories.

Number of Franchisees: 3 in California, 3 in Iowa, 1 in Illinois, 1 in Idaho, 1 in Kansas and 1 in Ohio

In Business Since: 1979

Equity Capital Needed: $95,000 to $135,000 dependent on store size, location and construction need.

Financial Assistance Available: The franchisor will assist the franchisee in applying to local banks for financing.

Training Provided: The prospective franchisee is trained for a 2 week period in a company store with emphasis placed on merchandising and accounting skills.

Managerial Assistance Available: The franchisor provides ongoing managerial assistance and has available accounting services for the franchisee.

Information Submitted: April 1990

COFFEE, TEA & THEE
c/o Specialty Retail Concepts, Inc.
P. O. Drawer 11025
Winston-Salem, North Carolina 27116

Description of Operation: Gourmet coffee and tea specialty shops located within enclosed shopping malls.

Number of Franchisees: 14 in 15 States, plus 5 company-owned.

In Business Since: 1979

Equity Capital Needed: $85,000 to $125,000

Financial Assistance Available: No financial assistance available. However, franchisor is available for consultation with lenders.

Training Provided: Initial training of staff (normally 1 to 2 weeks) and periodic visits thereafter.

Managerial Assistance Available: Initial training at same time staff training takes place. Periodic visits by operations staff thereafer.

Information Submitted: April 1990

COLONIAL VILLAGE MEAT MARKET FRANCHISE CORP.
Manoa Shopping Center
Office #4
Harbertown, Pennsylvania
Stanley Kadash

Description of Operation: Each store is approximately 4,000 square feet with ample store front parking. Our meats are displayed in self-service cases for volume purposes. Our meat rooms are visually displayed to the customers for their inspection. All stores have a full service deli line with a full or limited line of grocery and product. Our reputation is built on giving our customers quality, cleanliness, service and variety of competitive prices.

Number of Franchisees: 15 in Pennsylvania, New Jersey and Delaware

In Business Since: 1968

Equity Capital Needed: $50,000 to $100,000

Financial Assistance Available: Financial assistance is limited. Third party financial institutions will provide partial financing to acceptable franchisee. Franchisor, in certain situations, may finance all or part of franchisee's equipment requirement.

Training Provided: Prospective franchisee should have at least 5 years managerial experience in retail food industry with working knowledge of meats. Sixteen hours of class training with 2 weeks of in-store training are recommended and sometimes required.

Managerial Assistance Available: We provide ongoing management services for the life of the franchise in all areas of internal and external store operations. Complete manuals of store operations, forms and directions are provided. Field managers are available in all regions to work closely with franchisees and visit stores.

Information Submitted: June 1990

CONVENIENT FOOD MART, INC.
World Headquarters
9701 West Higgins Road
Suite 850
Rosemont, Illinois 60018
Richard Harper, President

Description of Operation: Grocery stores are 2,400 to 3,600 square feet in size with ample parking. Stores are open 365 days a year from 7:00 am until midnight. Stores stock complete lines of top name national brand merchandise normally stocked in a chain supermarket (except fresh red meat requiring cutting at store level). CFM franchises regional territories to a franchisor under a licensing agreement who, as an independent contractor, in turn franchises stores to individuals. The regional franchisor selects locations, negotiates with investors to build the store, and takes a long-term lease, subleasing same to CFM owner-operators. There are 48 licensed franchisors (some with multiple franchises) operating in parts or all of 38 States and Canada. Information about open areas and franchisors for any State may be obtained from national office.

Number of Franchisees: Over 1,500 throughout the United States, 2 countries.

In Business Since: 1958

Equity Capital Needed: Varies by regional franchisor.

Financial Assistance Available: Varies by regional franchisor.

Training Provided: Program includes planning, hiring, purchasing, merchandising, advertising, and business management. Easily implemented cash and inventory controls are also taught. Additional training at franchisee's store at time of opening.

Managerial Assistance Available: Continuous communication by bulletins, correspondence, direct phone, in-store visits by qualified personnel, and ongoing training sessions are conducted.

Information Submitted: June 1990

*COOKIE FACTORY OF AMERICA
651 East Butterfield Road
Suite 503
Lombard, Illinois 60148
Contact: Director of Franchising

Description of Operation: Specialty bake shop featuring premium quality cookies, decorated cookies, muffins, cinnamon rolls, pecan rolls, croissants and other popular baked goods. Some locations offer a light cafe menu featuring fresh-made sandwiches, salads and soups.

Number of Franchisees: 35 in 16 States

In Business Since: 1974

Equity Capital Needed: Subject to franchisee's financial status.

Financial Assistance Available: CFA will assist franchisee in preparing financing requests and plans. Also, the franchisee will be referred to lenders familiar with CFA's financing criterion.

Training Provided: CFA provides comprehensive in-store training covering product preparation, store operations, merchandising.

Managerial Assistance Available: Upon request CFA will assist with site selection, store design, store construction and store opening.

Information Submitted: April 1990

THE COOKIE STORE
c/o SPECIALTY RETAIL CONCEPTS
P. O. Drawer 11025
Winston-Salem, North Carolina

Description of Operation: Cookies, cookie cakes, brownies, frozen yogurt, and related items.

Number of Franchisees: 12 in 6 States, plus 1 company-owned.

In Business Since: 1982

Equity Capital Needed: $75,000 to $100,000

Financial Assistance Available: No financial assistance available. However, franchisor is available for consultation with lenders.

Training Provided: Initial training of staff (normally 1 week) and periodic visits thereafter.

Managerial Assistance Available: Initial training at same time staff training takes place. Periodic visits by operations staff thereafter.

Information Submitted: April 1990

CRUISERS SHOP AROUND
DRIVE THRU FOOD STORE
619 Divesadero Street
Fresno, California 93701
George Pratt

Description of Operation: Walk-in N roll-in, the ultimate in convenience food stores.

Number of Franchisees: 1 company-owned in California

In Business Since: 1987, franchising started in 1989

Equity Capital Needed: $60,000-$120,000. Investor multi-units also available.

Financial Assistance Available: None

Training Provided: 2 weeks detail orientation.

Managerial Assistance Available: Managerial assistance via operations manual.

Information Submitted: April 1990

*DAIRY MART CONVENIENCE STORES, INC.
240 South Road
Enfield, Connecticut 06082
Leonard F. Crogan, Vice President

Description of Operation: Dairy Mart Convenience Stores, Inc., operates retail convenience stores in southern New England and the Midwest. Dairy Mart/Lawson stores are open 7 days a week from 18 to 24 hours per day depending on location. Stores average approximately 1,800 to 2,000 square feet in size. Dairy Mart/Lawson typically provides the physical location and all equipment necessary to operate a convenience store.

Number of Franchisees: 167 in 6 States

In Business Since: 1957

Equity Capital Needed: Minimum of $15,000

Financial Assistance Available: No direct financial assistance is provided by franchisor. However, franchisor will make banking contract and assist franchisee in obtaining bank financing.

Training Provided: Typically, a 2 week training period is provived, primarily at the store location.

Managerial Assistance Available: After the initial training period, regular store visits are made by Dairy Mart area supervisors. Dairy Mart also sponsors periodic meetings covering various aspects of store management including personnel, merchandising, and theft prevention.

Information Submitted: June 1990

DIAL-A-GIFT, INC.
2265 East 4800 South
Salt Lake City, Utah 84117
Clarence L. Jolley, President

Description of Operation: National gift wire service (like florists). National delivery of fancy gift baskets—fresh fruit, gourmet foods, cheeses, wines and champagne, decorated cakes, bouquets of balloons, steaks, smoked ham, turkey and salmon.

Number of Franchisees: 115 in 28 States

In Business Since: 1980

Equity Capital Needed: $15,000

Financial Assistance Available: None

Training Provided: Intensive 3 days training at home office.

Managerial Assistance Available: Perpetual assistance.

Information Submitted: June 1990

FOOD-N-FUEL, INC.
4366 Rollins Hill Road West
Arden Hills, Minnesota 55112
Edward Bird, General Manager

Description of Operation: Retail grocery and gasoline.

Number of Franchisees: 80 in Minnesota, Wisconsin, Iowa, North Dakota and South Dakota.

In Business Since: 1978

Equity Capital Needed: $250,000-$500,000

Financial Assistance Available: None

Training Provided: 1 week prior to opening store, ongoing thereafter.

Managerial Assistance Available: Ongoing

Information Submitted: June 1990

LAURA CORPORATION
dba FRONTIER FRUIT & NUT COMPANY
3823 Wadsworth Road
Norton, Ohio 44203
Alex E. Marksz, Vice President

Description of Operation: The Frontier Fruit & Nut Company offers a unique retail store operation in regional malls featuring the retail sales of bulk dried fruits, nuts, candies and gifts.

Number of Franchisees: 6 franchisees, 58 locations in 6 States and Canada.

In Business Since: 1977

Equity Capital Needed: $25,000 minimum

Financial Assistance Available: None

Training Provided: On-site training by full-time Frontier Fruit & Nut employee at time of opening.

Managerial Assistance Available: Frontier provides continual assistance for the life of the franchise in such areas as bookkeeping, advertising and inventory control. Complete manual of operations, product knowledge, forms and directions are provided.

Information Submitted: April 1990

GIULIANO'S DELICATESSEN & BAKERY
1117 East Walnut Street
Carson, California 90746
John E. Kidde, President

Description of Operation: Specialty store consisting of a full service delicatessen offering 125-150 imported and domestic meats and cheeses; kitchen with an extensive take-out menu; catering; bread and pastry bakery; gourmet grocery; and extensive selection of imported and domestic wines and beers.

Number of Franchisees: 6 in California

In Business Since: 1953

Equity Capital Needed: Total package including building, leasehold improvements, inventory, initial franchise fee and working capital is between $500,000-$600,000. Equity capital initially required is approximately $150,000.

Financial Assistance Available: Franchisor does not provide direct financial assistance, although it is very active in assisting in securing attractive and reasonable terms for its franchisees. Franchisor will act as lessee and sublet to franchisee to assist in securing the best location at an attractive rate. Franchisor extends attractive credit terms on all purchases by franchisee from its central commissary.

Training Provided: 2 to 2 1/2 months initial training program before commencement of operation.

Managerial Assistance Available: Ongoing assistance from franchisor includes site visitations by company representative; classes and training sessions for new products, merchandising, personnel and hiring practices; complete corporate advertising program, etc. Franchisor provides an operations manual, bookkeeping system and promotional assistance.

Information Submitted: April 1990

GLASS OVEN BAKERY
1640 New Highway
Farmingdale, New York 11735
Robert G. Emmett, President

Description of Operation: Retail bakery/cafe where all baked goods are baked directly in view of the customers. One can choose to enter into the retail bakery or combine the retail bakery with the concept of a fast-food service as well. A complete and diversified line of baked goods is offered for sale. The company was purchased by a national franchisor with the intent to develop a nationwide network of franchised units.

Number of Franchisees: 30 in 6 States

In Business Since: 1977

Equity Capital Needed: Franchise fee $19,500. Total investment required will vary dependent upon location, cost of renovations at said location and extent and cost of equipment.

Financial Assistance Available: Financing may be available through lending institutions and leasing companies.

Training Provided: 2 week training program in management, operations, recordkeeping, employee relations, scheduling, bookkeeping, ordering and other aspects of managing and operating a bakery or a bakery/fast-food business. A company representative will be available on location for 40 hours to assist in grand opening and to work with the owner and employees in helping get the business started.

Managerial Assistance Available: Information on new products, new systems, updated equipment information, advertising and continued guidance and support provided by franchisor.

Information Submitted: June 1990

GLORIA JEAN'S COFFEE BEAN CORP.
120 West College Drive
Arlington Heights, Illinois 60004
Edward C. Kvetko, President

Description of Operation: Gloria Jean's Coffee Bean Stores offer for retail sales approximately 64 types of bulk gourmet coffees, teas, coffee and tea related supplies, equipment, accessories and gifts, and most stores carry beverages, including coffee, tea, cappuccino and espresso, for on-the-premises and "to go" consumption. Some stores carry cookies, pastries and baked goods. The stores are generally located in high traffic, high density regional shopping centers and require between 800 to 1,000 square feet of space. The franchisor's affiliate currently leases locations and sublets them to franchisees.

Number of Franchisees: 72 Stores including company-owned stores located in Illinois, Missouri and Minnesota.

In Business Since: 1979

Equity Capital Needed: Initial store costs average approximately $185,000, depending on premises, equipment and inventory, of which two-thirds may typically be financed by a prospective franchisee.

Financial Assistance Available: Qualified franchisees will be referred to a third party for financing assistance.

Training Provided: All new franchisees and managers are required to complete the Gloria Jean's Coffee Bean Store training program. The program comprises 10 business days of intensive instruction at the Gloria Jean's Coffee Bean Franchising Corp. corporate offices as well as at neighboring retail stores. The course covers such topics as product knowledge, equipment use and care, store operations and procedures, sales training, merchandising and in-store training.

Managerial Assistance Available: Gloria Jean's Coffee Bean provides an operations manual to all franchisees containing specifications, standards and operating procedures necessary in the management of a Gloria Jean's Coffee Bean Store. In addition, Gloria Jean's Coffee Bean provides refresher training programs, offers advice and assistance on store operations and merchandising, and assists franchisees in obtaining store brands and other approved brands.

Information Submitted: April 1990

*GREAT EARTH VITAMIN STORES
175 Lauman Lane
Hicksville, Wyoming 11801
Harvey Kavecz

Description of Operation: Great Earth Vitamin stores offer an extensive line of the highest quality vitamin and mineral products, sold at competitive prices by well-trained vitamin specialists. The typical store is 600 square feet.

Number of Franchisees: 160 stores in 16 States

In Business Since: 1971

Equity Capital Needed: Franchise fee $20,000, opening fee $7,500; product inventory, leasehold improvements, equipment, supplies and operating capital typically are an additional $60,000 to $80,000.

Financial Assistance Available: Willing to carry note on a portion of franchise fee for qualified license applicants.

Training Provided: 4 weeks of extensive training in product knowledge, retail sales, systems and procedures, advertising, promotion, and management of the business.

Managerial Assistance Available: Great Earth International (as franchisor) provides assistance in store site selection, lease negotiation, leasehold improvement supervision, and grand opening. Field representatives provide ongoing assistance in hiring and training of your personnel, and communicating new product and promotion information on a regular basis. A library of video tapes is also maintained for continuing education in all aspects of the business.

Information Submitted: June 1990

HAM SUPREME SHOPS
P. O. Box 07009
Detroit, Michigan 48207
Dominic Bonanno, President

Description of Operation: Specialty shop featuring the Supreme Spiral Sliced Honey-Glazed Ham, sold while or half. Whole smoked turkeys, barbecued ribs, canadian bacon, all fully cooked and ready to eat. Six outstanding overstuffed sandwiches, plus deli, offering party trays, homemade soups, salads, and other speciality items.

Number of Franchisees: 16 in 4 States

In Business Since: 1986

Equity Capital Needed: $100,000 minimum capital; not including leasehold improvements, total investment, $140,000-$170,000.

Financial Assistance Available: None

Training Provided: 5 day classroom and hands-on training at corporate headquarters and company-owned store, plus on-site training during and after opening with continual support. Full marketing program, operations and food preparation manuals provided along with ongoing assistance.

Managerial Assistance Available: Continuous as long as the franchise is in operation.

Information Submitted: April 1990

HEAVENLY HAM
8800 Roswell Road
Suite 135
Atlanta, Georgia 30350
R. H. (Hutch) Hodgson, President

Description of Operation: Heavenly Ham is a high quality specialty food store specializing in spiral sliced, fully baked, honey and spiced glazed hams. Heavenly Ham also sells smoked turkey, bacon, and fully cooked barbecued ribs and smoked pork chops plus a variety of condiments. All stores concentrate on high quality food products, convenience and customer service.

Number of Franchisees: 30 with 37 stores in 17 States

In Business Since: 1984

Equity Capital Needed: $100,000

Financial Assistance Available: Heavenly Ham does not provide any direct financing to franchisees. However, it does provide assistance in obtaining financing by helping the franchisee in preparing his proposal for bank financing and meeting with potential lenders.

Training Provided: Up to 1 week training course at company headquarters. On-site training prior to opening plus ongoing managerial assistance. Manuals, public relations, sales and promotional strategies, accounting and operations assistance.

Managerial Assistance Available: Heavenly Ham provides assistance in store site selection, lease negotition, store plans tailored to location, and store opening. Field service personnel make regular visits. Newsletter, advertising and promotional materials, etc.

Information Submitted: April 1990

*HICKORY FARMS OF OHIO, INC.
1505 Holland Road
Maumee, Ohio 43537
Franchise Services

Description of Operation: Retail stores selling packages and bulk specialty food featuring the Hickory Farms Beef Stick Summer Sausage, a variety of imported and domestic cheeses, candies and other related food products under the Hickory Farms label. Locations are usually situated in regional shopping centers. The service and operation are under direct supervision of home office on a continuing basis.

Number of Franchisees: 99 franchise stores, 134 company stores in 43 States

In Business Since: 1959

Equity Capital Needed: $180,000 plus leasehold improvements, inventory and other expenses described in UFOC.

Financial Assistance Available: None. Capital requirements vary by location.

Training Provided: 1 week at home office in planning, purchasing, stocking and merchandising, advertising and business operation. Two weeks prior to opening a new store, company assists in the direct opening of the store.

Managerial Assistance Available: Continuous communication by bulletins, correspondence, direct phone, in-store visits by qualified home office personnel, annual national convention and interim regional meetings and training sessions are conducted.

Information Submitted: April 1990

HIS ROYAL HIGHNESS DUMPLIN'S
112 East Center Street
Sikeston, Missouri 63801
LaDona DeKriek or David York

Description of Operation: A specialty bake shop serving homemade baked goods, salads, sandwiches, homemade bread and dinner rolls. The upscale bake shop also serves diet entrees and diet desserts.

Number of Franchisees: 9

In Business Since: 1987

Equity Capital Needed: $75,000 to $150,000

Financial Assistance Available: None

Training Provided: 2 weeks prior to opening.

Managerial Assistance Available: Full ongoing support.

Information Submitted: April 1990

IN 'N' OUT FOOD STORES, INC.
19215 West Eight Mile Road
Detroit, Michigan 48219

Description of Operation: Convenience food stores with or without gasoline sales.

Number of Franchisees: 53 in Michigan

In Business Since: 1976

114

Equity Capital Needed: Approximate average $60,000 and $75,000.

Financial Assistance Available: The total investment required is from $110,000 to $200,000. Initial fee $15,000. A down payment can range from $60,000 to $75,000 depending on store circumstances. Financing assistance is available through company.

Training Provided: When a 3 day initial evaluation program is passed, then a 1 week pre-opening training in a local store is provided by franchisor.

Managerial Assistance Available: Through field reps and other personnel, advisory assistance is provided for the life of the franchise in the following areas: accounting, security, merchandising, advertising and inventory control. Also a complete manual of operation is provided. In 'N' Out sponsors franchisee meetings with results of market and product research and emphasis on high consumer acceptance.

Information Submitted: June 1990

JAKE'S TAKE N' BAKE PIZZA, INC.
620 High Street
San Luis Obispo, California 93401
Willis Reeser, President

Description of Operation: The selling of unbaked pizzas, salads, cookie dough, soft drinks and ice cream novelties.

Number of Franchisees: 17

In Business Since: 1984, first franchisee 1986

Equity Capital Needed: Approximately $35,000 to $45,000

Financial Assistance Available: None

Training Provided: 2 weeks of comprehensive training in all aspects of operation provided to one management personnel per store to be opened.

Managerial Assistance Available: Site selection, equipment lists, preliminary drawings on store, inventory lists and specifications, opening procedures manual, 5 day in-store training when new location opens, operations manual, ongoing supervision for the operation of the business.

Information Submitted: April 1990

JO-ANN'S NUT/HOUSE
P. O. Drawer 11025
Winston-Salem, North Carolina 27116

Description of Operation: Retail candy and nut shops, selling domestic and imported products. Operated primarily in kiosk and store locations in regional malls.

Number of Franchisees: 52 stores in 18 States

In Business Since: 1972

Equity Capital Needed: Estimated costs include complete turnkey, franchise fee, and inventory. Kiosks range from $30,000-$100,000. In-line stores range from $65,000-$150,000.

Financial Assistance Available: None. Outside financing only. Some internal financing available under certain circumstances.

Training Provided: Regional supervisors and field operations managers train franchisees in their respective locations for a time depending on past retail experience.

Managerial Assistance Available: Field operations managers set up and open stores providing in depth initial training. Afterwards, regional supervisors visit locations as needed to assist in maximizing operations, marketing new, seasonal and holiday merchandise. Regional meetings are held for operations seminars and holiday product shows in advance of major holidays.

Information Submitted: April 1990

JOHNNY QUIK FOOD STORES, INC.
7955 North Cedar Avenue, Suite 104
Fresno, California 93710
Ernie Beal

Description of Operation: Franchise convenience stores with gasoline and an extensive fast food program.

Number of Franchisees: 21

In Business Since: 1985

Equity Capital Needed: $100,000-$125,000

Financial Assistance Available: None

Training Provided: 45 hour training program in all phases of operations.

Managerial Assistance Available: Corporate representative calls on each franchisee weekly.

Information Submitted: April 1990

JR. FOODMART
440 North Mill Street
P. O. Box 3500
Jackson, Mississippi 39207
Jack Parker, Vice President, Franchise Sales

Description of Operation: Junior Food Mart Convenience Stores. Stores licensed on a multi-store basis or a single location. All stores are three dimensioned: groceries, fast foods and self-service gasoline. Major concentration and future development geared to rural communities.

Number of Franchisees: 450 units in 20 States

In Business Since: 1919

Equity Capital Needed: Multi-store license: $110,000 needed for inventory, equipment and working capital; initial territory franchise fee is $35,000. Single license: $60,000 needed for inventory and working capital; initial franchise fee is $10,000.

Financial Assistance Available: None; company finds locations, secures leases and constructs buildings.

Training Provided: Operations and food service personnel provide pre-opening assistance, in-store training, pre-opening merchandising, equipment set-up, store operations, vendor and distribution contracts and grand opening assistance. New franchisees are required to attend training school, plus management information systems training.

Managerial Assistance Available: Ongoing and periodic evaluations performed.

Information Submitted: May 1990

KATIE MCGUIRE'S OLDE FASHIONED PIE SHOPPE
17682 Sampson Lane
Huntington Beach, California 92647
Byron Stiegemeyer, Franchise Development

Description of Operation: Old fashioned, home style, pie and bake shop. Typically located in shopping centers and utilizing space of 1,200 to 1,500 square feet. Stores are able to operate without experienced employees as all of the products are produced at a central location.

Number of Franchisees: 19 in California

In Business Since: 1982

Equity Capital Needed: $85,000-$150,000

Financial Assistance Available: None

Training Provided: Complete training program including all operations, accounting and management.

Managerial Assistance Available: Ongoing technical assistance by a professional staff through the term of the franchise agreement.

Information Submitted: May 1990

*KID'S KORNER FRESH PIZZA, INC.
P. O. Box 9288
Waukegan, Illinois 60079-9288
Kathleen Gulko, Vice President

Description of Operation: Custom made pizza you take home to bake.

Number of Franchisees: 30 in Wisconsin, Minnesota, Illinois, Georgia and Louisiana.

In Business Since: 1977

Equity Capital Needed: Approximately $30,000 to $40,000 including franchise fee, equipment and inventory.

Financial Assistance Available: None—company can assist in preparing financial presentations for use with lenders.

Training Provided: On-site training at home office and outlet site. Help with site selection, equipment selection, and decor and layout.

Managerial Assistance Available: Help with advertising, promotion, seminars, bookkeeping, and product research.

Information Submitted: April 1990

LE MUFFIN PLUS
P. O. Box 888760
Atlanta, Georgia 30356
Albert Brull, President

Description of Operation: Gourmet muffin, cookie, coffee shoppe, catering to high volume foot traffic market.

Number of Franchisees: 18 including company stores in USA and Canada.

In Business Since: 1985

Equity Capital Needed: Variable depending upon size, scope and location.

Financial Assistance Available: None

Training Provided: Comprehensive training program in franchisee's shoppe, including but not limited to shoppe opening, detailed baking and preparation instruction, materials acquisition, personnel and systems management.

Managerial Assistance Available: Complete site selection, lease negotiation, design service, and continual management assistance and product development.

Information Submitted: April 1990

LI'L PEACH CONVENIENCE FOOD STORES
101 Billerica Avenue
North Billerica, Massachusetts 01862
Francis X. Kearns, President

Description of Operation: Li'l Peach offers fully equipped and stocked convenience food stores averaging approximately 1,800-2,400 square feet. All stores are open 7 days a week, most from 7:00 am until 12 midnight.

Number of Franchisees: 42 plus 2 company-owned in Massachusetts

In Business Since: 1972

Equity Capital Needed: Minimum of $8,000

Financial Assistance Available: Financial assistance is available toward purchase of the store inventory. The franchisor does not extend financial assistance in regard to the initial investment.

Training Provided: In-store training totaling 3 weeks in one of our special training stores and in the new franchisee's own store.

Managerial Assistance Available: Continual management service in such areas as accounting, payroll preparation, loss prevention. All manuals and forms are provided. Li'l Peach works closely with its franchisees through regularly scheduled visits by field representatives.

Information Submitted: June 1990

LOGAN FARMS HONEY GLAZED HAMS
10001 Westheimer #1040
Houston, Texas 77042
Pink Logan, President

Description of Operation: Gourmet meat stores specializing in sales on honey glazed, spiral sliced hams. Also sells groumet rib eye roast, pork loins, chicken breast, smoked turkeys, spiral sliced boneless hams, spiral sliced honey glazed turkey breast,

smoked sausage, bacons, cheesecakes, a variety of honey mustard and preserves. Stores also have a deli department making a variety of subway sandwiches and po-boys.

Number of Franchisees: 9 stores in 4 States including 2 company-owned.

In Business Since: 1984

Equity Capital Needed: $250,000

Financial Assistance Available: None

Training Provided: 2 weeks on procedures and techniques in manufacturing and marketing the products, manuals provided for advertising and market programs, recordkeeping and inventory control.

Managerial Assistance Available: During first week of franchise's opening, franchisor or employee at location for opening assistance. Franchisor offers continuing services relative to the conduct of franchisee's business.

Information Submitted: April 1990

MRS. EMM'S ALL NATURAL HEALTH FOOD STORES
1907 Greentree Road
Cherry Hill, New Jersey 08003
Al Hirsh, General Manager

Description of Operation: Complete health food store with natural foods, vitamins, bulk foods, natural cosmetics and other nutritional products. We train you in nutrition and in the business with our state-of-the-art intensive training program. Computerized ordering for ease of operation.

Number of Franchisees: 14 stores total; 7 franchises

In Business Since: 1978

Equity Capital Needed: $55,000 cash needed.

Financial Assistance Available: We will assist qualified buyers in securing loans and/or leasing plans.

Training Provided: Intensive 4 week training program in home office as well as in franchisee's own store. Continuous training and strong support even after franchise store is open. We train you completely in nutrition and in business operations.

Managerial Assistance Available: Continuous ongoing support includes operations, marketing, advertising and nutrition support.

Information Submitted: April 1990

*MRS. POWELL'S CINNAMON ROLLS
500 Franklin Village Drive
Suite 106
Franklin, Massachusetts 02038
Julie A. Woodworth

Description of Operation: On premises baking of fresh cinnamon rolls, gourmet sandwiches, muffins, soups, salads and related homemade products. Products are unique, fresh, wholesome and served in a fun, clean, courteous atmosphere.

Number of Franchisees: 54 in 23 States

In Business Since: 1984

Equity Capital Needed: $125,000-$170,000

Financial Assistance Available: Assistance with bank financing information.

Training Provided: Complete training including both corporate schooling and on-site training.

Managerial Assistance Available: Assistance with lease negotiations, design and blueprints. Complete set of production and operations manuals.

Information Submitted: April 1990

MOUNTAIN MAN NUT & FRUIT CO.
10338 South Progress Way
P. O. Box 160
Parker, Colorado 80134
David D. Conner, President

Description of Operation: Route sales of nuts, dried fruit, trail mixes, candies and homemade chocolates sold directly to the consumers at their place of employment. Products are not sold in stores, but rather delivered on a route schedule to office buildings and other businesses. 300 different products in take home size bags weighing 1 lb. each. NOT vending or Honor snacks.

Number of Franchisees: 235 in 26 States, 1 in Oregon, and 1 company-owned in Colorado.

In Business Since: 1977, franchising since 1984.

Equity Capital Needed:

Financial Assistance Available: We do not provide financial assistance.

Training Provided: 2 weeks prior to grand opening in franchisee's plant, theoretical and practical training in all areas of plant operation including food preparation and packaging, scheduling, quality control, and equipment maintenance. The operation manual is complete and should be used as a master reference for management.

Managerial Assistance Available: Full assistance is given in all phases of operation from site selection, plant design, equipment selection, management training, bookkeeping and administrative procedures, inventory control, ordering, marketing assistance, sales seminars and ongoing supervision for the day to day operation of the business.

Information Submitted: April 1990

MY FAVORITE MUFFIN
15 Engle Street
Suite 302
Englewood, New Jersey 07631
John Sterns

Description of Operation: Specialty baked goods, gourmet muffins and mini muffins, over 120 varieties from a unique recipe and privately labeled gourmet coffee and frozen yogurt.

Number of Franchisees: 15 franchises, 1 company store.

In Business Since: 1987

Equity Capital Needed: $140,000-$300,000 total investment.

Financial Assistance Available: Will assist.

Training Provided: 2 weeks training at company store, 1 week on-site.

Managerial Assistance Available: Ongoing

Information Submitted: June 1990

T F M CO.
dba OKY DOKY FOOD MARTS
1250 Iowa Street—P. O. Box 300
Dubuque, Iowa 52001
John F. Thompson, President

Description of Operation: Stores average from 1,200 square feet to 4,000 square feet—convenient parking required—open daily 7 a.m. to 11 p.m.—inventory selected for maximum turnover—equipment and building may be leased. Regional franchises now available to qualified individuals. Renovating gas stations or other existing good locations our specialty. No franchise fees charged on gas.

Number of Franchisees: 21 in Iowa, Wisconsin and Illinois. Company operations presently centered in the tri-state region of Iowa, Illinois and Wisconsin. However, other regional franchises are available.

In Business Since: 1947

Equity Capital Needed: Minimum $15,000 plus $25,000.

Financial Assistance Available: None

Training Provided: On-job training at home office or on site is required before franchisee is considered. This is at no expense to franchisee.

Managerial Assistance Available: Expertise always available at home office upon request.

Information Submitted: April 1990

*THE ORIGINAL GREAT AMERICAN CHOCOLATE CHIP COOKIE COMPANY, INC.
4685 Fredrick Drive
Atlanta, Georgia 30339
Arthur S. Karp, President

Description of Operation: Retail cookie stores primarily in major regional malls nationwide.

Number of Franchisees: Over 300 franchised units

In Business Since: 1977

Equity Capital Needed: $30,000; total investment is between $100,000-$125,000.

Financial Assistance Available: None

Training Provided: Complete training is provided in all operations of a cookie store.

Managerial Assistance Available: Managerial assistance is provided as long as necessary.

Information Submitted: June 1990

PAPA ALDO'S INTERNATIONAL, INC.
9600 S.W. Capital Highway
Portland, Oregon 97219
John A. Gundle, President

Description of Operation: Take-out pizza. Fresh unbaked pizza to be baked at home.

Number of Franchisees: 85 in 6 States.

In Business Since: 1981

Equity Capital Needed: $15,000-$25,000

Financial Assistance Available: None

Training Provided: 2 weeks total—1 week at corporate company store, 1 week in franchisee's store.

Managerial Assistance Available: Ongoing field support.

Information Submitted: June 1990

RICH PLAN CORPORATION
P. O. Box 224
Utica, New York 13503
Thomas R. Steinback, President

Description of Operation: Home food service, largest private labeler of premium frozen foods and appliances directly sold to the home.

Number of Franchisees: 20 franchises

In Business Since: 1946

Equity Capital Needed: $100,000

Financial Assistance Available: None

Training Provided: Full training provided.

Managerial Assistance Available: Ongoing support.

Information Submitted: April 1990

SAV-A STEP FOOD MART, INC.
4265 Roosevelt Avenue
Louisville, Kentucky 40213
Joseph Pierce, President

Description of Operation: Grocery-convenient type. Floor space approximately 2,000 square feet. Open 8 am til midnight, 7 days a week. Franchisee owns all equipment and inventory and leases building from parent firm. Regional franchises available in most States.

Number of Franchisees: 6 in Indiana and Kentucky and 19 company stores.

In Business Since: 1973

Equity Capital Needed: $40,000

Financial Assistance Available: Help with securing bank loans.

Training Provided: 4 to 6 weeks in-store training.

Managerial Assistance Available: Site selection, equipment installed. On-job training, consistent supervision, accounting service that includes monthly P & L. Sales and tax reports, payroll and paying weekly invoices. Marketing merchandising and promotions. Self-service gasoline.

Information Submitted: June 1990

6-TWELVE CONVENIENT MART, INC.
18757- N. Frederick Road
Gaithersburg, Maryland 20879
James Davis, Franchise Coordinator

Description of Operation: Large "upscale" convenience store featuring groceries, complete line of fast foods and beer and wine where permitted.

Number of Franchisees: 12 in Maryland and Virginia

In Business Since: 1984

Equity Capital Needed: $80,000-$100,000

Financial Assistance Available: In Mid-Atlantic area franchisors may lease site from owner/landlord and sublease to franchisee.

Training Provided: 3 weeks of management training and 1 week operation training in store.

Managerial Assistance Available: Ongoing assistance by operational consultants.

Information Submitted: April 1990

*THE SOUTHLAND CORPORATION
2828 North Haskell Avenue
Dallas, Texas 75204
Tom Kanawyer, Franchise Director

Description of Operation: Convenience grocery stores (7-Eleven).

Number of Franchisees: 3,064 in 20 states plus District of Columbia.

In Business Since: 1927, franchised operations since 1964.

Equity Capital Needed: Total investment required: The costs of a store's inventory and cash register fund average $38,806 and $773 respectively. The cost of all necessary business licenses, permits, and bonds is approximately $500. The franchise fee is computed for each store as follows: The initial franchise fee for a store that has not been continuously operated for the preceding 12 calendar months is an amount equal to 15% of the previous calendar year's annualized average per store month gross profit (excluding gross profit from gasoline) for all stores located within the district in which the franchised store is or is to be located. If the store has been continuously operated for at least the preceding 12 calendar months, the franchise fee is an amount equal to 15% of that store's gross profit (excluding gross profit from gasoline) for the immediately preceding 12 calendar months.

Minimum Initial Investment: The minimum initial investment required includes the franchise fee, the amount of the cash register fund, and a portion of the cost of the initial inventory and of business licenses, permits, and bonds. Except where a franchisee transfers from one 7-Eleven Store to another, the franchisee is required to provide, in cash, as a portion of the cost of the inventory, a down payment of the greater of $12,500 or an amount equal to the average weekly sales of the store for the prior 12 month period or such shorter time as the store has been open.

Financial Assistance Available: The remainder of the investment in the inventory and of the cost of business licenses and permits may be financed with Southland, as well as the franchisee's continuing purchases and operating expenses.

Training Provided: 2 weeks in local training store and 1 week in a regional training center are provided.

Managerial Assistance Available: Continuing advisory assistance is provided by field consultants and other 7-Eleven personnel. 7-Eleven has been a member of the International Franchise Association (IFA) since beginning franchised operations.

Information Submitted: June 1990

*SWISS COLONY STORES, INC.
1 Alpine Lane
Monroe, Wisconsin 53566
James N. Liermann, President

Description of Operation: Retail stores offering popularly priced, high quality domestic and imported cheeses, sausage, European style pastries, candy, specialty foods, gifts, and a food service sandwich, deli and bakery program.

Number of Franchisees: 75 stores in 35 States

In Business Since: 1964

Equity Capital Needed: Approximately $100,000 plus leasehold improvements.

Financial Assistance Available: None

Training Provided: 7 day mandatory, thorough training at home office in Monroe, Wisconsin, plus 2 weeks in-store training covering all phases of store operation, management and retailing. Advanced programs with incentives also available

Managerial Assistance Available: Continuous supervision in-store at intervals by highly qualified company personnel.

Information Submitted: April 1990

T. J. CINNAMONS, LTD.
1010 West 39th Street
Kansas City, Missouri 64111
William Teel, Vice President

Description of Operation: T. J. Cinnamons operates and franchises retail bakery operations. These bakeries specialize in cinnamon-related bakery products. Bakeries range from 700 square feet to 1,200 square feet and are located in major shopping malls and strip centers. Units are open 7 days per week, approximately 12-14 hours per day.

Number of Franchisees: About 400 in 40 States and Canada

In Business Since: 1985

Equity Capital Needed: Varies by territory, but a minimum of $100,000-$150,000.

Financial Assistance Available: None.

Training Provided: Intensive 12-day mandatory training course is required for each person who will be responsible for the overall day-to-day management of a bakery. This course is held in Kansas City and is tuition-free. A T. J. Cinnamons trainer goes to help open the first 2 bakeries opening in each territory for a 4-day period at each bakery.

Managerial Assistance Available: Assistance includes ongoing managerial, operations, and bakery consultation. Our vice president/real estate assists with real estate contracts, lease consultation, etc. Complete manuals and specifications for opening and operating a bakery are provided as is assistance in using this material. Advertising and marketing guidance is provided. T. J. Cinnamons also conducts ongoing market research into new products and monitors quality standards of the franchise operations.

Information Submitted: June 1990

TOM'S FOODS INC.
900 Eighth Street
P. O. Box 60
Columbus, Georgia 31994
Al Davis, Vice President - Distributor Development
Charles Gosa, Director - Distributor Franchise Development

Description of Operation: Route distribution of snack food products through national accounts, independent accounts, and vending accounts.

Number of Franchisees: 330 in 46 States

In Business Since: 1925

Equity Capital Needed: $7,500 to $100,000

Financial Assistance Available: Assistance in financing through outside financial institutions.

Training Provided: On-the-job training plus classroom training provided, accounting procedures, merchandising, and marketing training.

Managerial Assistance Available: Home office, field sales organization, advertising materials and promotions.

Information Submitted: April 1990

---

*U.S.A. TREATS
230 Davidson Avenue
Somerset, New Jersey 08873

Description of Operation: Treats stores offer over 100 varieties of fresh-from-the-oven muffins, cookies and other specialty items. Delicious quality products that also appeal to the tastes and needs of diet- and nutrition-conscious Americans. Easy to bake.

Number of Franchisees: 14 plus 152 in Canada.

In Business Since: 1977, franchising since 1979

Equity Capital Needed: Full investment $50,000-$125,000.

Financial Assistance Available: None

Training Provided: No baking experience necessary, full training is provided.

Managerial Assistance Available: Ongoing managerial assistance.

Information Submitted: June 1990

VIE DE FRANCE CORPORATION
(dba VIE DE FRANCE BAKERY & CAFE)
8201 Greensboro Drive
Suite 1200
McLean, Virginia 22102
Jeffrey I. Newman, Vice President, Restaurant Development

Description of Operation: Cafeteria-style food service in an upscale dining environment featuring a freshly baked full-line bakery and specialty prepared soups, salads, sandwiches, and light entrees.

Number of Franchisees: 60 units (1 franchised and 59 company-owned).

In Business Since: 1972

Equity Capital Needed: Approximately $200,000 of the $700,000 to $850,000 investment. The company will not make loans to franchisees. Franchisee fee is $25,000 for the initial unit and $20,000 for each additional unit.

Financial Assistance Available: None

Training Provided: The franchisee will be trained in all areas of operation. Full details provided in the Disclosure Document.

Managerial Assistance Available: Operating manuals, forms, and procedures as well as site review, equipment, and food specifications. The company provides ongoing supervision for the operation business for a 4 percent royalty. New product introductions, marketing assistance, and administrative guidelines are available.

Information Submitted: April 1990

---

*WHITE HEN PANTRY, INC.
660 Industrial Drive
Elmhurst, Illinois 60126
James O. Williams

Description of Operation: A White Hen Pantry is a convenience food store of approximately 2,500 square feet. There is generally up-front parking for 10 to 15 cars. Stores are usually open 24 hours (some operate a lesser number of hours) 365 days a year. Product line includes a service deli, fresh bakery, fresh produce, and a wide variety of the most popular staples. White Hen Pantry stores are franchised to local residents who become owner/operators of this "family business."

Number of Franchisees: 365 in Illinois, Wisconsin, Indiana, Massachusetts and New Hampshire

In Business Since: 1965

Equity Capital Needed: $20,000-$25,000 (varies by location)

Financial Assistance Available: Total investment averages $41,300-$48,000. Investment includes approximately $24,000 merchandise, $5,000 security deposit, $3,000 supplies, $200 cash register fund, and $10,000 training and processing fee. A minimum investment of $20,000 is required. Financial assistance available.

Training Provided: Classroom and in-store training precede store opening. Follow-up training provided after taking over store. Detailed operation manuals are provided.

Managerial Assistance Available: This is a highly organized and comprehensive program. Other services provided include merchandising, accounting, promotions, advertising, and business insurance (group health and plate glass insurance are optional). Store counselor visits are regular and frequent.

Information Submitted: June 1990

WYOMING ALASKA COMPANY
Box 26
Woods Cross, Utah 84087
Reuel T. Call

Description of Operation: Trailside General Store, 2,400 square feet unit for general merchandise, fast food, solarium seating and gasoline canopy.

Number of Franchisees: 4 in Utah, Arizona and Montana.

In Business Since: 1979

Equity Capital Needed: $300,000-$500,000 depending on land costs.

Financial Assistance Available: Franchisor may co-sign on approved sites. Company may furnish equipment, which amounts to about one third of total investment.

Training Provided: Classroom and in-store training. A required continuing program conducted with personnel and employees from some 20 company-operated stores.

Managerial Assistance Available: Assistance in managing your people, serving the public, inventory control, keeping a clean store and clean yard. Also assistance on the computer in the small store.

Information Submitted: May 1990

ZARO'S AMERICA'S HOME BAKERY
138 Bruckner Boulevard
Bronx, New York 10454
Melton Carl

Description of Operation: A full-line bakery including hot and cold drinks, frozen yogurt, bagels with spreads. Bakery items are prepared in commissary and shipped frozen and baked off in front of consumer. Items include muffins, croissants, pastries, layer cakes, bread, rolls, bagels, etc.

Number of Franchisees: 6 plus 9 company-owned in New York, New Jersey and Connecticut.

In Business Since: 1935

Equity Capital Needed: $100,000 cash. Equity capital approximately $350,000 depending on size and condition of store.

Financial Assistance Available: Assistance offered by introduction to bank.

Training Provided: 4 to 5 weeks training in our plant, in company stores and an additional 2 weeks in franchisee's store after opening. Training includes baking off procedures, merchandising, and operating a Zaro's Bakery.

Managerial Assistance Available: Continuous assistance by phone and by periodic visits our operations manager. Merchandising aids are available for all occasions.

Information Submitted: June 1990

ZIP FOOD STORES, INC.
1200 West 15th Avenue
Gary, Indiana 46407
E. T. Eskilson, President

Description of Operation: Zip stores are approximately 2,500 square feet in size with adjacent parking. Depending on location, open 12-15 hours per day, 7 days per week. Zip provides the building and equipment on leases with renewed options to its franchise operator. Products are name brand merchandise and most stores have delis and fast food accommodations.

Number of Franchisees: 12 in Indiana (Limited to Northwest Indiana.

In Business Since: 1970

Equity Capital Needed: $12,000 minimum

Financial Assistance Available: Franchisee is required to purchase store inventory of approximately $30,000. $9,000 of the $12,000 minimum capital will be applied to inventory purchase. Franchisee can arrange own financing or Zip, Inc., will finance balance if credit references are acceptable.

Training Provided: 1 week to 10 days of full-time training on site with experienced supervisor to acquaint operator and his personnel with policies and procedures.

Managerial Assistance Available: Continuous management services provided. All bookkeeping, inventory control, payroll and related services provided at central office for all stores. Monthly profit and loss statements provided on request or suggestion of franchisor.

Information Submitted: June 1990

FOODS—ICE CREAM/YOGURT/CANDY/ POPCORN/BEVERAGES

ALL AMERICAN FROZEN YOGURT SHOPS
4800 S.W. Macadam Avenue, Suite 301
Portland, Oregon 97201
Tom Ramsey, Director of Franchise Sales

Description of Operation: A specialty frozen dessert retailer featuring premium frozen yogurt treats, ice cream and other food items targeted to the ever-increasingly health conscious consumer. The majority of our shops are located in shopping malls. There are a total of 15 company-owned shops.

Number of Franchisees: 4 in 4 States (total of 9 franchise units).

In Business Since: 1986

Equity Capital Needed: $40,000 to $50,000 range.

Financial Assistance Available: Will assist franchisees by recommending sources of financing.

Training Provided: New franchisee will be trained at company-owned shops and when new franchise location opens. Ongoing assistance during term of franchise agreement.

Managerial Assistance Available: Continuous assistance from our operations staff with current updates to the franchise operations manual. Franchise program is designed to allow an inexperienced franchisee to be in the frozen yogurt business.

Information Submitted: April 1990

*BASKIN-ROBBINS, INCORPORATED
31 Baskin-Robbins Place
Glendale, California 91201
Jim Earnhardt, President, B-R USA, CO.

Description of Operation: High quality, multi-flavored, hand dipped retail ice cream store. Franchisor normally selects site, and negotiates a lease; the store is completely equipped, stocked and

brought to a point where it is ready to open. The complete store is then sold to a qualified individual under a franchise after intensive training.

Number of Franchisees: Over 3,000 stores in 895 cities throughout the United States, Canada, Japan and Europe.

In Business Since: 1945

Equity Capital Needed: Approximately $50,000 plus, depending on retail location.

Financial Assistance Available: Yes

Training Provided: A complete training program is provided plus on-the-job training in operating store under the guidance of experienced supervisors.

Managerial Assistance Available: Continuous merchandising program, accounting procedures, business counsel, and insurance program (source optional).

Information Submitted: April 1990

*BEN & JERRY'S HOMEMADE INC.
Box 240, Route 100
Waterbury, Vermont 05676
Fred Loger, Director of Retail Operations

Description of Operation: Ben & Jerry's offers a super premium ice cream parlor and scoop shop, featuring 47 flavors, sundaes, fountain sodas, and fresh squeezed juices.

Number of Franchisees: 82 in 18 States

In Business Since: 1978

Equity Capital Needed: Approximately $75,000.

Financial Assistance Available: None

Training Provided: Extensive 1 week mandatory training course scheduled for manager/franchisees. Bookkeeping and office procedures, hands-on operation/waiting on customers, quality and portion control.

Managerial Assistance Available: On-site pre-opening assistance by field personnel for store set-up, hiring and employee training. Refresher training by field representative is available upon request.

Information Submitted: April 1990

*BRESLER'S INDUSTRIES, INC.
999 East Touhy Avenue, Suite 333
Des Plaines, Illinois 60018
Howard Marks, Director of Franchise Development

Description of Operation: Multi-flavor specialty ice cream and yogurt shops—featuring ice cream cones, hand-packed ice cream, soft serve yogurt, complete soda fountain and made-to-order ice cream specialty items.

Number of Franchisees: Approximately 300 in 30 States

In Business Since: 1962

Equity Capital Needed: Approximately $40,000.

Financial Assistance Available: At present, total investment of approximately $90,000 to $105,000 required plus working capital. Franchisee may obtain own financing, or at his request franchisor will attempt to obtain third party financing for qualified applicant.

Training Provided: Classroom and in-store training comprising a minimum of 3 weeks duration.

Managerial Assistance Available: Franchisor assists franchisee in all aspects of shop operation, recordkeeping, advertising, and promotion and selling techniques. Manuals of operations and counseling are provided. Area licensees and home office field personnel are available to visit stores regularly.

Information Submitted: May 1990

*BRIGHAM'S
30 Mill Street
Arlington, Massachusetts 02174
Clark Merrill, Director of Franchising

Desciption of Operation: Family restaurant featuring Boston's #1 premium ice cream and frozen yogurt.

Number of Franchisees: 42 total, including 1 in New York, the remainder in Massachusetts.

In Business Since: 1914

Equity Capital Needed: Between $300,000-$500,000

Financial Assistance Available: None

Training Provided: Approximately 3 to 6 weeks, on-site and at headquarters.

Managerial Assistance Available: Store directors (consistent and ongoing assistance). Chain-wide advertising. Site selection and lease negotiation assistance also provided.

Information Submitted: April 1990

BRODY'S YOGURT COMPANY
106 NW 33rd Court
Gainesville, Florida 32607
John Chambers

Description of Operation: Frozen yogurt and fresh fruits retail.

Number of Franchisees: 21

In Business Since: 1983

Equity Capital Needed: $80,000-$130,000

Financial Assistance Available: None

Training Provided: 1 week management and operations training at headquarters, plus additional training in franchisee's shop.

Managerial Assistance Available: Franchise service personnel available to assist franchisee.

Information Submitted: April 1990

THE CALIFORNIA YOGURT COMPANY
162 S. Rancho Santa Fe Road
Suite F-50
Encenitas, California 92024
Jim Swickard, President

Descripton of Operation: The California Yogurt Co. is now offering its sparkling hi-tech look stores as a franchise. The stores offer 10 flavors of fresh frozen yogurt daily, 30 toppings and a variety of specialty yogurt items.

Number of Franchisees: 3 company-owned stores in California and 5 franchise stores plus 27 in Norway and Japan.

In Business Since: 1982

Equity Capital Needed: $60,000-$75,000.

Financial Assistance Available: Franchisor will assist the franchisee in applying for financial assistance. The company does not make direct loans to the franchisee.

Training Provided: Complete training is provided at the franchisor's training school. The training includes all phases of the stores operation, including equipment maintenance, bookkeeping, inventory control, employee management, and customer relations. An additional 5 day training will be provided in the franchisee's store prior to opening.

Managerial Assistance Available: The California Yogurt Co. franchisees are provided with a confidential operations manual which provides detailed information on all aspects of the CYC system. Site selection, equipment purchase and grand opening activities are also provided by the franchisor.

Information Submitted: April 1990

CARBERRY'S HOMEMADE ICE CREAM FRANCHISE SYSTEMS, INC.
42 Rose Street
Merritt Island, Florida 32953
Stephen R. Carberry

Description of Operation: Carberry's Homemade Ice Cream Parlours offer a complete range of ice cream operation from manufacturing to sale. Carberry's caters to children of all ages.

Birthday parties and field trip showing children how Carberry's makes ice cream are our specialties. Master franchise territories available throughout the United States.

Number of Franchisees: 6 in Florida

In Business Since: 1980

Equity Capital Needed: $75,000-$95,000

Financial Assistance Available: None

Training Provided: 5 days of training at Carberry's training facility in Merritt Island, Florida. 2-5 days training at franchisee's new location.

Managerial Assistance Available: Sales management, cost control, training manual provided. Field supervisors make periodic in-store inspections and assist in any way they can.

Information Submitted: June 1990

CARTER'S NUTS, INC.
47-15 36 Street
Long Island City, New York 11101
Robert Rogal, Marketing Director

Description of Operation: Retail nut outlets—containing a full variety of all the world's nuts and dried fruits—where all nuts are freshly roasted every day on the premises. Freshly made popcorn, potato chips, plantain chips, freshly roasted coffee and tea, and a full line of fresh-exotic fruits. Mobile truck units are also available.

Number of Franchisees: 3 in New York

In Business Since: 1976

Equity Capital Needed: $35,000

Financial Assistance Available: 50 percent of equipment for stores. 90 percent for mobile truck units.

Training Provided: 100 page operations manual is provided by franchisor to franchisee and an intensive in-store work program of 2 weeks is required. Two weeks assistance is provided upon opening of franchisee's store.

Managerial Assistance Available: Managerial assistance in purchasing and hiring.

Information Submitted: May 1990

*CARVEL CORPORATION
201 Saw Mill River Road
Yonkers, New York 10701
Gia Bocciarelli

Description of Operation: Retail ice cream shops, featuring both hard and soft ice cream, manufactured by the store owner in the shop for on and off premises consumption. Specializing in full-line of ice cream (36 flavors, 60 varieties) for all occasions. Also cakes and dessert items. Locations include free standing, shopping center, and inner city types.

Number of Franchisees: Over 650 stores operating in 18 States (not including international).

In Business Since: Carvel franchising ice cream stores since 1948. In business since 1934.

Equity Capital Needed: Approximately $60,000-$70,000.

Financial Assistance Available: Yes

Training Provided: 19 day training period covering all facets of store operation and complete standard operating procedure manual, plus assistance in opening store.

Managerial Assistance Available: Continuous in-field counseling covering merchandising, quality control, advertising, promotion, and annual area educational seminars.

Information Submitted: June 1990

DIPPER DAN ICE CREAM SHOPPES & SWEET SHOPPES
DIPPER DAN, INTERNATIONAL, INC.

P.O. Box 47068
St. Petersburg, Florida 33743
Leo L. LaBonte, Executive Vice President

Description of Operation: 5 unique concepts, each focusing its marketing on retailing 32 delicious ice cream flavors from cones to mile-high sundaes. In addition to ice cream, our "basic" unit features a food program, cookies and candy. The "basic plus" shoppe also features gourmet popcorn and fudge, both made on premises. There are two "upscale" type shoppes, one which features a secondary line in hand-cut doughnuts and the other a full bakery operation, truly a total sweet shoppe. New for 1987, a unique concept whereby ice cream is merchandised along with a full muffin program. Space requirements vary between 900 to 1,800 square feet, depending on concept.

Number of Franchisees: Over 400 in 13 States, Japan, and Taiwan.

In Business Since: 1955, franchising since 1963

Equity Capital Needed: Approximately $70,000 to $100,000, depending on concept and geographic area.

Financial Assistance Available: None

Training Provided: A complete and comprehensive program on every facet of shoppe operations conducted at location.

Managerial Assistance Available: The shoppe owner is continuously assisted in all phases of merchandising and shoppe operations. Special services rendered to assisting lease negotiations; customized mechanical blueprints provided.

Information Submitted: June 1990

*DOUBLE RAINBOW FRANCHISES, INC.
275 South Van Ness Avenue
San Francisco, California 94103
Leslie Cass

Description of Operation: Double Rainbow Gourmet Ice Cream has been voted Best in the USA over 75 brands in the Great American Lick Off. The complete line of all natural super premium ice creams is displayed in a unique dessert cafe concept featuring award-winning architecture. An extensive assortment of gourmet cakes, pastries, coffees is also sold.

Number of Franchisees: 30 franchises in California plus 3 company-owned parlors.

In Business Since: 1976, franchising since 1983.

Equity Capital Needed: Total investment for a typical dessert cafe is $100,000-$150,000. Equity required depends on franchisee's financial strength.

Financial Assistance Available: Franchisor assists in guiding franchisees to third party financing sources.

Training Provided: 2 week training program for owner-operators begins in corporate headquarters in San Francisco. Training includes all phases of the parlor's operation—inventory control, customer relations, personnel training, equipment maintenance. The program continues with hands-on experience in an established parlor followed by special support during the franchise opening week.

Managerial Assistance Available: Double Rainbow, backed by 10 years' experience operating its own ice cream parlors, offers the franchisee practical advice and support through a continuous program of management assistance. The program includes merchandising and promotion techniques and computerized management control systems. A complete operations manual is provided. In addition to the above, the franchisor's staff will assist and advise the franchisee in securing a suitable location, negotiating the lease, and shopping for the equipment and supplies. Customized architectural blue-prints are provided.

Information Submitted: June 1990

EMACK AND BOLIO'S ICE CREAM AND YOGURT
FOR THE CONNOISSEUR
P. O. Box 703
Brookline, Massachusetts 02147
Robert Rook, President

Description of Operation: Emack and Bolio's Ice Cream and Yogurt for the Connoisseur is a gourmet ice cream and yogurt company. Ice cream and hard no fat frozen yogurt are manufactured by the company and sold retail by the retailer. The guiding principle behind the company is to produce super premium ice cream and no fat hard frozen yogurt in exotic flavors. Flavor selections change weekly. The ice cream and yogurt are served in hand rolled gourmet cones as well as cups, sundaes, etc. Ice cream and yogurt cakes are also profitable items for shop owners.

Number of Franchisees: 10 in Massachusetts and 1 in New Jersey.

In Business Since: 1975

Equity Capital Needed: Initial investment $75,000—$125,000.

Financial Assistance Available: None

Training Provided: A training program is scheduled in company-owned store in Boston.

Managerial Assistance Available: Emack and Bolio's provides operational support for the life of the franchise.

Information Submitted: May 1990

ERNIE'S WINE & LIQUOR CORP.
P. O. Box 525
Rutherford, California 94573
Jim Altoff

Description of Operation: Retail liquor, beer and wine stores.

Number of Franchisees: 40 in California (only)

In Business Since: 1938

Equity Capital Needed: $120,000

Financial Assistance Available: None

Training Provided: A complete program is provided that includes pre-opening training and on-the-job training.

Managerial Assistance Available: Limited; see training provided.

Information Submitted: June 1990

FILTERFRESH CORPORATION
Trimex Building, Route 11
Mooers, New York 12958
Leslie Allan, Franchise Sales Manager

Description of Operation: Hi-tech office coffee service using a patented single-cup coffeemaker. Filterfresh brews coffee by-the-cup from fresh ground coffee in seconds. Choice exclusive territories are available. The franchise provides access to patented equipment, detailed training in sales and service, ongoing support and supply services.

Number of Franchisees: 24

In Business Since: 1986, franchising since 1987

Equity Capital Needed: $100,000-$250,000 total investment.

Financial Assistance Available: Assistance in securing financing on equipment purchases.

Training Provided: Training consists of an initial 8 day session on technical training, sales, data processing, purchasing and inventory control, staffing, marketing, cash and financial control, and management.

Managerial Assistance Available: During the first week of franchisee's opening, franchisor provides at least one employee at franchisee's location for opening assistance. Franchisor offers continuing services relating to the conduct of franchisee's business.

Information Submitted: April 1990

FLAMINGO'S FROZEN YOGURT, INC.
9549 Montgomery Road
Cincinnati, Ohio 45242
John J. Granito, Director of Franchising

Description of Operation: Flamingo's unique approach goes far beyond that of the average frozen yogurt store. Step into a Flamingo's and experience an ambience not duplicated in the industry. While some are just selling frozen yogurt as a commodity, Flamingo's is marketing a concept of gourmet enjoyment with their focus on fun and quality in an obviously superior presentation.

Number of Franchisees: 53 in 8 States

In Business Since: 1987

Equity Capital Needed: $122,500-$205,500

Financial Assistance Available: Does not offer direct financing but will assist with referrals to potential financial institutions.

Training Provided: Comprehensive 2 week training. Site evaluation and leasing assistance. Store layout and design. Accounting and control systems. Year round advertising program including pre-opening and grand opening promotions. New product development.

Managerial Assistance Available: Continuous support.

Information Submitted: April 1990

FOREMOST SALES PROMOTIONS, INC.
5252 North Broadway
Chicago, Illinois 60640

Description of Operation: Foremost is a marketing and consulting service for (1) experienced retail liquor store owners already in business; (2) inexperienced retail liquor store owners who purchase existing stores; and (3) both experienced and inexperienced people who open new retail liquor stores. The service includes but is not limited to information on operating a successful retail package liquor store such as site selection, store layout, inventory control, accounting methods, advertising, merchandising, sales promotion and Liquor by Wire service. Each store operates within the laws of the State in which it does business.

Number of Franchisees: Over 105 in Illinois and Florida. More than 2,000 retail stores affiliated through Foremost Liquor by Wire Network and Foremost National Network of Independent Liquor Dealers.

In Business Since: 1949

Equity Capital Needed: Approximately $100,000 to $350,000.

Financial Assistance Available: Available to qualified people.

Training Provided: See Managerial Assistance

Managerial Assistance Available: As package liquor store consultants, full scale assistance is available pertaining to all the information needed to operate a successful package liquor store.

Information Submitted: April 1990

FRESHENS PREMIUM YOGURT
2849 Paces Ferry Road
Suite 750
Atlanta, Georgia 30339

Description of Operation: Premium yogurt concept with other yogurt related toppings/products.

Number of Franchisees: 192 in 35 States with 2 company-owned stores.

In Business Since: 1984

Equity Capital Needed: Approximately $150,000 for a single store franchise, includes franchise fee, furniture and equipment, leasehold improvements, grand opening advertising, initial inventory and working capital.

Financial Assistance Available: Assist in preparation of pro formas.

Training Provided: 2 week initial training including classroom and in-store session. Student/teacher ratio averages 4 students/teacher. Ongoing training for existing franchisees and their management team. Assistance also supplied for new store opening. Field workshops on food cost control, labor management, turnover, financial reports.

Managerial Assistance Available: Field services and field operations on call at all times. Field services handle all product and distribution issues. Field operations assist with development and execution of business plan. Personally visit with each franchisee on ongoing basis to analyze results and assist in identifying and implementing necessary improvements.

Information Submitted: April 1990

FROSTY FACTORY INTERNATIONAL, INC.
1600 Furman
Ruston, Louisiana 71270
Dolph Williams, President

Description of Operation: The franchise offered consists of the right to sell frozen alcoholic and nonalcoholic beverages in a retail store using recipes and machines provided by franchisor in an approved location under the proprietary mark Frosty Factory.

Number of Franchisees: 4 in Louisiana

In Business Since: 1985

Equity Capital Needed: $150,000 minimum.

Financial Assistance Available: Part of the franchise fee may be financed for a year period. The remaining amount must be provided by franchisee or it may be financed by an outside source.

Training Provided: A 1 week training period is provided by franchisor at a company-owned store. Store opening training is provided by franchisor at franchisee's outlet.

Managerial Assistance Available: As a service, we offer help with detailed drawings, specifications and site location. We also provide training programs and operational assistance, which includes hi-tech electronic cash registers, interfaced with an in-house micro-computer. By using these required components, the owner is provided with management reports, such as daily, weekly, and monthly sales analysis reports, labor productivity reports and inventory variance reports.

Information Submitted: June 1990

FRUSEN GLADJE FRANCHISE, INC.
200 Bulfinch Drive
Andover, Massachusetts 01810
Michael Newport

Description of Operation: Ice cream manufacturer and franchisor of ice cream stores.

Number of Franchisees: 12 in 5 States

In Business Since: 1981

Equity Capital Needed: $75,000

Financial Assistance Available: We consult with franchisees regarding financing of project costs by independent financial institutions.

Training Provided: Intensive training in all phases of ice cream store operations.

Managerial Assistance Available: Managerial assistance is provided in all areas of store operations.

Information Submitted: June 1990

THE FUDGE CO.
103 Belvedere Avenue
Charlevoix, Michigan 49720
R. L. Hoffman, President
Dennis Crain, Vice President, General Manager

Description of Operation: The Fudge Co. is a retail fudge store. An important part of the operation is cooking in copper kettles, and creaming (forming) done on large marble slabs. Only natural ingredients are used and combine with the showmanship of making fudge to provide a unique, enjoyable and profitable retail operation. Each store requires 400 to 600 square feet. Fudge Co. provides all equipment. Franchisee leases or purchases its own building, with guidance from the Fudge Co. also includes cookie franchise, baking and selling fresh chocolate chunk and a variety of six other cookies. Either franchise can be purchased separately.

Number of Franchisees: 7 in 6 States and Virgin Islands, plus 1 company-owned stores.

In Business Since: 1978, franchising since 1982

Equity Capital Needed: Resort area includes all equipment, training, 3 month starting inventory; cost—$35,000 to $42,000. Regional mall store—equipment, training, 3 month inventory; cost—$75,000 to $85,000.

Financial Assistance Available: None, franchise fee $12,500.

Training Provided: Franchisor trains and educates franchisees 2 to 3 weeks in its home office in Dallas, Texas. Upon opening of franchisee's store, franchisor's general manager supervises and trains personnel for 7 to 14 days.

Managerial Assistance Available: Fudge Co. provides managerial service including inventory control, advertising and assistance for day-to-day operations during the life of the franchise. Franchisor provdes all necessary forms and documents for daily operation. Provides information regarding new products and how to prepare and merchandise said products. Franchisor provides personnel to visit franchisee's outlet to assist in solving problems of cooking and day-to-day operations.

Information Submitted: April 1990

GASTON'S, INC.
1880 Los Altos Drive
San Mateo, California 94402
Douglas D. Gaston, President

Description of Operation: Gaston's Ice Cream of San Francisco offers a wide selection of ice cream delicacies and fountain items for take out. There are over 100 flavors of ice cream all developed by its founder Doug Gaston. The ice cream is made fresh daily on the premises.

Number of Franchisees: 30 in California and 2 in Indonesia, 1 in Singapore

In Business Since: 1976

Equity Capital Needed: Approximately $120,000 depending on location and type of store.

Financial Assistance Available: The company will assist the franchisee in applying for financing. The company will not make direct loans to franchisee.

Training Provided: Gaston's training program will consist of a 3 week training period. The franchisee will be trained in manufacturing, preparing all ice cream delicacies and fountain items, accounting, inventory control, store management, employee management, customer relations, and other additional areas.

Managerial Assistance Available: Gaston's franchisees are given a confidential manual which gives in detail the complete operations of a Gaston's Ice Cream Shop. Gaston's is available at all times to the franchisee to offer assistance in all problems the franchisee may have.

Information Submitted: June 1990

J. L. FRANKLIN & CO.
dba GELATO AMARE
11504 Hyde Place
Raleigh, North Carolina 27614
John L. Franklin, President

Description of Operation: Gelato Amare stores feature over 45 flavors of delicious all natural frozen yogurt, most of which have no fat and no cholesterol! Many of our yogurt flavors are also sugar-free! To appeal to as large a target market as possible, most of our stores also feature over 100 flavors of outstanding Italian style superpremium low fat, low calorie ice cream made right in the store. Since all of the ice cream is made in the store, franchisees are not subject to price increases on ice cream manufactured by a franchisor and remain in better control of their own costs and distribution. Many stores also serve light salads and sandwiches tailored to the store's specific marketing area. Each

store makes its own cones and serves decorated yogurt and ice cream pies and cakes as well as sundaes, smoothies, shakes, Hurricanes, lite fruit bowls and many other delicious treats. In addition, over 30 delectable toppings are offered for customer enjoyment.

Number of Franchisees: 10

In Business Since: 1983

Equity Capital Needed: $40,000-$50,000 of $90,000-$135,000 total investment.

Financial Assistance Available: Total assistance in preparation of business presentations to banks, lending institutions, etc.

Training Provided: 2-3 weeks intensive training for owners and all management in company-owned retail store. Continuing training in franchisee store.

Managerial Assistance Available: Full assistance is provided in site selection, lending institution presentations, management training, store design, equipment selection, store opening and personnel and administrative procedures. Continuing assistance includes advertising, public relations, market research and new product development. A 24-hour-a-day telephone hotline is available to answer questions as they arise.

Information Submitted: April 1990

*GELATO CLASSICO FRANCHISING, INC.
369 Pine Street, Suite 900
San Francisco, California 94104
Janet Willis, Director of Franchising

Description of Operation: Gelato Classico Italian ice cream manufactures a complete line of Italian ice cream, sorbetto, and yogurt and supplies these products to its franchisees who retail to the public. Franchisees are part of nationwide program for franchised shops.

Number of Franchisees: 43 franchise locations plus 2 company-owned stores in 11 States

In Business Since: 1976

Equity Capital Needed: $50,000 per shop

Financial Assistance Available: No financial assistance provided by franchisor.

Training Provided: Intensive 2 week program prior to opening, and additional training in franchisee's shop during first 5 days at opening. Complete operations manual also provided.

Managerial Assistance Available: In addition to above, franchisor visits periodically to provide in-shop assistance. Other assistance provided on as needed basis.

Information Submitted: April 1990

GORIN'S HOMEMADE ICE CREAM AND
SANDWICHES
158 Oak Street
Avondale Estates, Georgia 30002
Robert Solomon, President

Description of Operation: Upscale homemade ice cream and sandwich shop featuring gourmet ice cream and a wide selection of grilled deli sandwiches.

Number of Franchisees: 32 in Georgia, North Carolina and Alabama.

In Business Since: 1981

Equity Capital Needed: $35,000-$50,000, total investment of $100,000-$150,000.

Financial Assistance Available: Lease equipment assistance available.

Training Provided: 3-4 weeks of comprehensive training in all aspects of operation for 3 management personnel per store to be opened.

Managerial Assistance Available: Site selection, equipment lists, preliminary drawings on store, inventory lists and specifications, ongoing supervision for the operation of the business.

GOURMET POPPING CORN COMPANY
formerly VIC'S CORN POPPER
11213 East Circle, Suite B
Omaha, Nebraska 68137

Description of Operation: Small retail stores (500 square feet to 1,500 square feet) with old-fashion decor that feature pre-packaged gourmet white hulless popped popcorn, caramel and cheese popcorn, plus soft drinks and old-fashion ice cream. Products are also sold off premises in wholesale outlets. A companion mail order popcorn gift business also run out of retail locations. Emphasis is on quality, taste, value and convenience.

Number of Franchisees: 60 franchised and 12 company-owned stores in 12 States.

In Business Since: 1980 under this corporate name, but recipes used go back 50 years.

Equity Capital Needed: Contact company for full information.

Financial Assistance Available: None. Franchisees required to have adequate net worth to qualify.

Training Provided: Separate training courses offered to both owners and operators. Training conducted in model training stores and on-site. Pre-opening store training also provided.

Managerial Assistance Available: Regular consultation and assistance. Detailed operating manuals are provided on each facet of the operation. Company makes available promotional and advertising materials.

Information Submitted: May 1990

THE GREAT MIDWESTERN ICE CREAM CO.
209 North 16th Street
P. O. Box 1717
Fairfield, Iowa 52556
Jamie Robert Vollmer, Director Franchise Development

Description of Operation: Great Midwestern Ice Cream Company Stores are premium dessert shops featuring 32 flavors of ice cream, fresh croissants, and deluxe coffees. Great Midwestern Ice Cream, voted the Best Ice Cream in America by People Magazine, is a superpremium, 16 percent buttterfat product using all natural ingredients. We are presently working with Barn'rds Old Fashion Roast Beef sandwich restaurants to combine their excellent, made from scratch sandwich, soup and salad menu with our world famous ice cream dessert system. The stores are approximately 2,000 square feet, seat 40-50 people in an upscale environment of warm, beautiful colors.

Number of Franchisees: 9 in Iowa, Nebraska, Missouri, Kansas and Illinois.

In Business Since: 1979

Financial Assistance Available: Great Midwestern has been given the authority by a bank to qualify applicants for financial assistance. This program is available only to those who, with aggressive Great Midwestern participation, have been unable to secure financing through a lending institution in their market area. Representatives from Great Midwestern will consult with the applicant and visit local bankers and SBA officials.

Training Provided: You will be required to spend 4 to 8 weeks in an operating restaurant for hands-on experience in restaurant operations, food production and systems accounting. The operation manual is thorough, organized and highly usable as ready reference for management.

Managerial Assistance Available: Operating staff will be available for assistance to insure systems disciplines, quality food and service to customers. All members of the support staff including all officers of the company are always available to assist the franchise in their development.

Information Submitted: April 1990

*HEIDI'S FROGEN YOZURT SHOPPES, INC.
200 Bulfinch Drive
Andover, Massachusetts 01810
Michael Newport

Description of Operation: All Heidi's are located in high traffic quality centers and malls. The menu selection and unique store design make it possible to offer a limitless choice of flavors daily. All products are developed from low-fat, or non-fat, low-calorie, soft serve frozen yogurt. All shoppes are custom-designed with ceramic tile, oak, custom wallpaper, and premium quality equipment.

Number of Franchisees: 61 in 5 States plus 5 company-owned.

In Business Since: 1982

Equity Capital Needed: $80,000 per shoppe.

Financial Assistance Available: Heidi's consults with franchisees regarding financing of project costs by independent financial institutions.

Training Provided: A comprehensive, hands-on training course is provided for owners and managers, and the franchisee also receives training guides and manuals for the shoppe's employees. 1 week of training is spent in a corporate training facility, and for your second week trainers come to you to assist in your first week of business.

Managerial Assistance Available: The franchisor provides technical assistance with all equipment placed in the field. The staff of the franchisor will be providing a substantial amount of follow-up management support and quality control service to the franchisee. The franchisee is also endorsed by Heidi A. Miller, President and Co-Founder of the franchise, fashion model, actress, and the national bodybuilding champion.

Information Submitted: June 1990

*I CAN'T BELIEVE IT'S YOGURT
5005 LBJ Freeway
Suite 700
Dallas, Texas 75244

Description of Operation: Our business is serving soft-serve frozen yogurt in cones, sundaes, parfaits and shakes. Our ICBIY "Softie" ® frozen yogurt is a special recipe we manufacture ourselves to ensure the highest of quality and innovation.

Number of Franchisees: 286 franchise locations, 9 company-owned locations.

In Business Since: 1977

Equity Capital Needed: Total investment approximately $150,000. Equity capital varies due to location and franchisee financial strength.

Financial Assistance Available: Not available at this time.

Training Provided: Shortly before the opening of a franchise store, a 10 day training school will be conducted. A maximum of 2 people representing each franchise store can attend. This school will cover our success formula, accounting and bookkeeping procedures, operations, staffing, cost control, and the basics of management.

Managerial Assistance Available: Our company has an ICBIY Franchise Consultant who is a resource person for trouble shooting in all areas of store operation and is readily available for managerial and technical assistance. Such assistance and supervision will be provided in the following ways: mail, phone contacts, visits, conferences, newsletters, clinics and seminars. These methods will remain in effect for the duration of the business partnership between ICBIY and its franchise owners.

Information Submitted: April 1990

THE ICE CREAM AND YOGURT CLUB
THE ICE CREAM CLUB, INC.
278 South Ocean Boulevard
Manalapan, Florida 33462
Richard Draper, President

Description of Operation: Retail ice cream and yogurt parlors featuring homemade ice cream, yogurt and fat free, sugar free frozen desserts.

Number of Franchisees: 10

In Business Since: 1982, franchising since 1984

Equity Capital Needed: $85,000

Financial Assistance Available: None

Training Provided: Complete operation manual, 1 week pre-opening training and 3 days in your new store upon opening.

Managerial Assistance Available: Continued support through regular visits from management personnel.

Information Submitted: April 1990

ICE CREAM CHURN, INC.
P. O. Box 1569
Byron, Georgia 31008
Wendell Parker, President

Description of Operation: Ice Cream Churn establishes an ice cream parlour with 28 flavors of dip ice cream, milk shakes, sundaes and banana splits in a current operating business such as convenience stores, delis, and bakeries. A unit for malls and a new 14'x36' modular unit designed for smaller markets and metropolitan markets are also available.

Number of Franchisees: 75 locations in 35 States

In Business Since: 1978—Franchising since 1981

Equity Capital Needed: (1) Individual franchises for existing locations, $3,500-$5,000, (2) Modular concept franchises, $24,000-$30,000.

Financial Assistance Available: Available for all phases of operation by franchisor.

Training Provided: Complete training of all regional agents who are responsible for the franchise's individual stores training. An agent works with locations on regular visits.

Managerial Assistance Available: Ice Cream Churn furnishes each franchisee with all training, equipment, inside and outside signs, promotions and incentives programs for managers.

Information Submitted: June 1990

I LOVE YOGURT CORP.
12770 Coit Road
Suite 1115
Dallas, Texas 75251
Robert J. Schultz, Vice President/Developments

Description Operation: Gourmet frozen yogurt and sandwich shoppes.

Number of Franchisees: 8 in Kansas, Texas and Louisiana

In Business Since: 1980

Equity Capital Needed: $84,000-$135,000

Financial Assistance Available: None, but will assist in securing.

Training Provided: 1 week intensive training at home office and 1 week in-store training at time of opening.

Managerial Assistance Available: Management and operational assistance provided to all franchisees. Computerized accounting system for store evaluation and complete simplified advertising and marketing program.

Information Submitted: April 1990

ISLAND FREEZE FRANCHISE SYSTEMS, INC.
2222 Kalakaua Avenue
Suite 1200
Honolulu, Hawaii 96815
Bonnie J. Thorsby

Description of Operation: Island Freeze features Dolewhip frozen dessert, the non-dairy, fruit based, soft-serve which has no cholesterol and is low in calories. The attractive small unit sells Dolewhip frozen dessert in cones and cups as well as in shakes and smoothies. Master franchises are also available.

Number of Franchisees: 2 company-owned locations.

In Business Since: 1986

Equity Capital Needed: $39,500 to $114,000

Financial Assistance Available: None

Training Provided: Training is comprehensive and hands-on. In person site approval; 1 week training in Honolulu in all aspects; complete manuals and materials; and a training team to visit your site to assist in opening the business are all part of the total training package.

Managerial Assistance Available: Management assistance is continually provided by franchisor personnel via personal visits, correspondence and telephone.

Information Submitted: April 1990

ISLAND SNOW HAWAII
P. O. Box 364
Kailua, Hawaii 96734
James J. Kodama, President
Lisa M. Sinai, Vice President

Description of Operation: Hawaiian theme dessert shaved ice, gourmet ice cream, yogurt and logoed sportswear.

Number of Franchisees: 8 in Hawaii

In Business Since: 1981

Equity Capital Needed: $50,000-$100,000

Financial Assistance Available: None

Training Provided: The training covers operation and maintenance of the shaved ice machine, preparation of the syrup where applicable, inventory control and storage, customer service, sanitation and pest control, employee hygiene, computerized accounting system, procedures, marketing and other miscellaneous subjects pertinent to the operation of an Island Snow Hawaii shop. Generally, the training time covers approximately 20 hours, but the training time may vary depending on the trainee's ability to master the subjects being taught.

Managerial Assistance Available: Ongoing

Information Submitted: April 1990

*J. HIGBY'S YOGURT TREAT SHOPPES
11030 White Rock Road
Suite 210
Rancho Cordova, California 95670
Steve Kircher, President

Description of Operation: Over 60 flavors of fresh frozen yogurt. Also serve ice cream and a variety of fresh baked cookies, "walk-away sundaes," yogurt fruit salads, hot "Higby Dogs," drinks and other related items.

Number of Franchisees: 32 in 4 States

In Business Since: 1983

Equity Capital Needed: Varies as to location and franchisee.

Financial Assistance Available: Franchisor will assist with third party financing.

Training Provided: A minimum of 2 weeks at the corporate training center and franchisee's store.

Managerial Assistance Available: Management and operational assistance provided to all franchisees. Computerized accounting system for store evaluation and complete simplified advertising and marketing program.

Information Submitted: June 1990

KARMELKORN SHOPPES, INC.
P. O. Box 35286
Minneapolis, Minnesota 55435
John Hydwke, Vice President

Description of Operation: Karmelkorn Shoppes make and sell Karmelkorn popcorn candy, popcorn, popcorn confections, a variety of kitchen style candies and related snack food items. New shoppes range in size from 400 to 650 square feet and are mostly located in major shopping centers. Business hours are those established by the shopping center with minor variations. In most cases, the company accepts the primary lease liability and sublets to the owner-operator.

Number of Franchisees: 205 in 44 States

In Business Since: The original Karmelkorn Shoppe was established in 1929

Equity Capital Needed: $75,000 to when standard financing is available.

Financial Assistance Available: The total investment in a Karmelkorn franchised shoppe varies according to construction costs. Most shoppes in 1986 ranged from $90,000 to $150,000. The company assists franchisee in applying for his original financing upon request.

Training Provided: A national training center at the Minneapolis office of Karmelkorn Shoppes, Inc., is built as a model Karmelkorn Shoppe to simulate working conditions during training. The 5 day curriculum is designed for new and existing franchisees, as well as their shoppe managers and key employees. Grand opening assistance is provided by a company representative.

Managerial Assistance Available: The franchisee receives and is instructed in the use of an operating manual, which is supplemented by business newsletters that provide updates and operational information. Management and supervisory services are provided for the life of the franchise, and include periodic supervision by training supervisors, annual conference with business, product and advisory seminars, assistance in obtaining sources of supply and equipment, promotional material, and assistance in planning promotion programs.

Information Submitted: June 1990

*KILWINS CHOCOLATES FRANCHISE
355 North Division Road
Petoskey, Michigan 49770
Wayne Rose, President

Description of Operation: Franchise Kilwins Chocolate and Ice Cream Shoppes. These stores sell Kilwins handmade chocolates. fudge and homemade ice cream.

Number of Franchisees: 24 in 8 States

In Business Since: 1981

Equity Capital Needed: $70,000 to $150,000 for turnkey operation.

Financial Assistance Available: $20,000 franchise fee. Financing not available from franchise company.

Training Provided: The training program is designed to last 10 business days and will cover all the basic aspects of the retail confectionary business including how the candy and ice cream are manufactured, how they are packaged, and sales techniques along with other techniques for operating the franchisee's business.

Managerial Assistance Available: Regular reports of improvements in business methods developed by franchisor and other franchisees, the services of franchisor's advertising department to assist franchisee in planning local advertising and, on franchisee's request, the personal assistance and counsel of a qualified representative of franchisor.

Information Submitted: April 1990

*LARRY'S ICE CREAM AND YOGURT, INC.
14550 McCormick Street
Tampa, Florida 33625
Dante Moscone, President

Description of Operation: Larry's Ice Cream and Yogurt serves only the award-winning Larry's Ice Cream. Parlours emit an atmosphere of "yesteryear" offering customers homemade ice cream in cones, sundaes, shakes and malteds, sodas, and cakes and pies. Larry's has received the Award of Excellence from the National Ice Cream Retailers Association, Larry's was named Best Chocolate Ice Cream at the Fountainbleau Chocolate Festival, and is featured in the book, *The Very Best: Ice Cream and Where to Find It* by Carol Robbins and Herb Wolff.

Number of Franchisees: 50 parlours located in 3 States.

In Business Since: 1981

Equity Capital Needed: Minimum $72,000-90,000 investment for complete turnkey operation. Distributorships also available with investments varying according to regional areas desired.

Financial Assistance Available: Franchisor cannot provide financing in developing new parlours.

Training Provided: A comprehensive traning program is provided in an established parlour and is completed in the franchisee's parlour upon opening. Ongoing technical support is provided for the duration of the franchise agreement through a regularly updated operations manual, franchisee meetings and seminars, and a monthly newsletter.

Managerial Assistance Available: (1) The corporate marketing department provides brand awareness and identity through advertising, publicity, and promotions. This department also assists individual franchisees with their particular marketing needs. (2) The corporate operations department works with parlours on a regular basis to improve profitability. (3) Franchisee representatives meet monthly with the company president and executive vice president to maintain lines of communication between franchisees and franchisor.

Information Submitted: April 1990

LOVE'S YOGURT AND SALADS
1830 Techny Court
Northbrook, Illinois 60025
Robert Silverstein, President

Description of Operation: Love's Yogurt and Salads offers a unique soft serve frozen yogurt and salad bar concept. The emphasis is toward healthy quality foods with prepared salads made daily, in addition to soups, chili, baked potatoes with toppings, and freshly baked muffins. Personalized service is our specialty.

Number of Franchisees: 11 including 3 company-owned in Illinois and Indiana.

In Business Since: 1987

Equity Capital Needed: $20,000 franchise fee, total investment $200,000.

Financial Assistance Available: Financial assistance available up to $50,000 to qualified applicants. Assistance in preparing bank preparations to secure up to 100 percent financing.

Training Provided: Complete franchise training and assistance including site selection, lease negotiations, customer relations, personnel, marketing, operational and technical training, continuing operational support. The franchisee training program is 2 weeks, plus additional on-site training.

Managerial Assistance Available: Managerial operations are covered in the franchisee training program with on-site programs, complete manual, and assistance from operation specialists.

Information Submitted: April 1990

MALIBU MAGIC FRANCHISING CORP.
1 Hartfield Boulevard
Suite 204
East Windsor, Connecticut 06088
Robert S. Zunick, Director of Franchise Development

Description of Operation: Full line of frozen yogurt treats featuring 45 flavors of no fat and no cholesterol frozen yogurt with 20 calories per ounce. Also serve cookies, hot beverages, cold beverages, complete fountain menu and take-home desserts.

Number of Franchisees: 7 in 5 States

In Business Since: 1989

Equity Capital Needed: Approximately $55,000.

Financial Assistance Available: Leasing program is available.

Training Provided: A complete training program is provided to all franchisees. The store's staff is trained prior to the opening of the store.

Managerial Assistance Available: Ongoing assistance is provided in all phases of the store's operation. An operations supervisor visits each store on a periodic basis.

Information Submitted: April 1990

MARBLE SLAB CREAMERY, INC.
3100 South Gessner
Suite 230
Houston, Texas 77063
Linda Taylor, Franchise Sales

Description of Operation: Retail ice cream stores featuring super premium quality ice cream, cones baked fresh daily, fresh frozen yogurt, frozen pies, cakes, cookies and brownies. Ice cream is custom designed for customer on frozen marble slab (patent pending) and made daily in the store. Open 7 days a week.

Number of Franchisees: 24 in Texas, and Louisiana

In Business Since: 1983

Equity Capital Needed: $30,000

Financial Assistance Available: None

Training Provided: 10 days training in the company's training facility in Houston, Texas. 6 additional days of training at franchisee's store (3 days before opening, 3 days after opening). Ongoing technical assistance is provided, operations, manual and franchisee meetings.

Managerial Assistance Available: Marble Slab Creamery, Inc., maintains an ongoing business relationship with its franchisees, with assistance available in all phases of store operations. A complete operations manual is provided to all franchisees. Company field personnel visit stores on a regular basis to insure that operating standards are being followed and to insure the consistency of operations throughout the franchise system. Marble Slab Creamery, Inc., constantly updates advertising programs and evaluates new products for its franchised locations.

Information Submitted: April 1990

M.G.M. LIQUOR WAREHOUSE INTERNATIONAL, INC.
1124 Larpenteur Avenue West
St. Paul, Minnesota 55113

Description of Operation: Retail, off-sale liquor store, specializing in fine wine, spirits and beer. Standard store size 5,000 to 8,000 square feet. Franchises currently available in Minnesota, South Dakota, Wisconsin, California, Arizona.

Number of Franchisees: 21 franchise units in Minnesota, and 1 franchise unit in Wisconsin, 1 in South Dakota, and 2 in Arizona.

In Business Since: 1970

Equity Capital Needed: Total package price exclusive of building $210,000 to $350,000, including franchise fee.

Financial Assistance Available: Financing available at local banks—not available from franchisor.

Training Provided: Company-operated management training school providing extensive and detailed instruction in store operation, management, and administration for franchisees, management, or both. Instore training.

Managerial Assistance Available: Operational and merchandising assistance is provided as needed through the headquarters office.

Information Submitted: June 1990

MS. MUFFET'S YOGURT SHOPS
P. O. Box 447
Wrightsville Beach, North Carolina 28480
Bernie Pisczek, Vice President

Description of Operation: Upscale frozen yogurt shops with both inside and drive-thru service, featuring 9 different flavors (from a selection of over 50) plus over toppings. Also serve 15 specialty items, such as Fruit 'N Yogurt Salad, Lickety Split, etc. Concept features in-store flavoring of product, which requires less inventory and easier shop management. 80 percent of flavors are no fat and no cholesterol. Sugar free unflavored mix is also available.

Number of Franchisees: 32 shops in 6 States

In Business Since: 1985, and franchising since 1989

Equity Capital Needed: $85,000 to $130,000 (includes $17,500 franchise fee).

Financial Assistance Available: None directly, but will assist in the preparation of loan packages.

Training Provided: 2 weeks total, 1 week at corporate headquarters and 1 week on-site. Three training manuals with periodic updates also included.

Managerial Assistance Available: In addition to training, we monitor franchisee operations on a weekly basis and assist where necessary. Our methods are especially helpful to absentee owners who require special assistance in overseeing their operation.

Information Submitted: June 1990

MISTER SOFTEE, INC.
901 East Clements Bridge Road
P. O. Box 313
Runnemede, New Jersey 08078
James F. Conway, Vice President and General Manager

Description of Operation: Retailing soft ice cream products from a mobile unit, a complete dairy bar on wheels. Dealer is given a franchised area to operate. Mister Softee, Inc., maintains a supply department plus a service and parts department. Franchisees are supported with a merchandising, promotional, and advertising program.

Number of Franchisees: 860 in 20 States

In Business Since: 1956

Equity Capital Needed: $22,000

Financial Assistance Available: Financing can be arranged for qualified individuals.

Training Provided: Franchisee is trained on his mobile unit in his franchised area for 1 week in merchandising, route planning, operation of the mobile unit, sanitation and maintenance.

Managerial Assistance Available: Area representative visits franchisee for continuing assistance periodically and suggests improvements when needed. Standard operating procedure manual, service manual, accounting ledgers. Inventory control forms are provided to each franchisee.

Information Submitted: June 1990

NATURALLY YOGURT/SPEEDSTERS CAFE
One Annabel Lane, Suite 207
San Ramon, California 94583
Sheldon Feinberg, Vice President

Description of Operation: Naturally Yogurt is a quality, fresh frozen yogurt operation. Clean, high-tech graphics in a unique presentation offering a wide range of toppings, sundaes, shakes, smoothies and other specialty items. Speedsters is an expanded menu concept in keeping with today's yuppie movement, offering fresh salads, homemade soups, baked potatoes and a complete yogurt presentation that leads up to the tag line "Fun, Fast, First Class."

Number of Franchisees: 12

In Business Since: 1983

Equity Capital Needed: Subject to franchisees' financial status.

Financial Assistance Available: None

Training Provided: 2 weeks in company-owned store.

Managerial Assistance Available: Ongoing support, site selection, lease negotiation.

Information Submitted: April 1990

NIBBLE-LO'S
5300 West Atlantic Avenue
Delray Beach, Florida 33484
Michael L. Slope, Director of Franchising

Description of Operation: Nibble-Lo's features a delicious, healthful, fat-free, cholesterol-free frozen dessert that rivals the taste of premium ice cream. Unlike other frozen desserts currently on the market, Nibble-Lo's is made from 98 percent skim milk. The unique traffic pattern, variety of novelty items, and marketing concept creates a year-round business with take-home products accounting for 45 percent of sales since the dessert can be frozen without the threat of freezer burn or loss of taste and texture.

Number of Franchisees: 5 franchise locations, plus 1 company-owned store.

In Business Since: 1988

Equity Capital Needed: $35,000-$50,000. Total investment of $110,000-$150,000.

Financial Assistance Available: Company will assist the franchisee in applying for financing.

Training Provided: Complete, hands-on training is provided for owners and managers for 2 weeks at the corporate office, and 1 additional week is spent with franchisee at their store during the first week of operation. Franchisee also receives training guides and manuals for the employees at their store.

Managerial Assistance Available: Nibble-Lo's provides ongoing management support and technical assistance.

Information Submitted: April 1990

NIELSEN'S FROZEN CUSTARD
NFC MANAGEMENT CORPORATION
P. O. Box 731
Bountiful, Utah 84010
Doug Nielsen, Director of Marketing
Jeff Dunford, Franchise Development

Description of Operation: Nielsen's Frozen Custard is proud to bring back the goodness and taste of an old-fashioned ice cream product. Our frozen custard is made fresh every few hours right in the store. Our secret recipe, specially designed patented freezing machine, and concern for quality all result in the rebirth of the smooth real dairy taste that America loves.

Number of Franchisees: 5 plus 4 company-owned in 5 States.

In Business Since: 1981

Equity Capital Needed: Franchise fee $12,500. Total investment $70,000 to $90,000.

Financial Assistance Available: None

Training Provided: Nielsen's training personnel will instruct you and your people during the build-out of your store at our training facility. You will receive a Nielsen's "know-how book" which covers everything from the design and operation of the machine to the recipes and finished products. We also cover accounting procedures, employee management, customer relations, and much more.

Managerial Assistance Available: The people at NFC will make final site approval, supply state-of-the-art marketing ideas, develop special advertising materials to cover from ground breaking to grand opening, provide an ongoing flow of new advertising ideas, and supply a store design package that includes store layout, construction specifications, menu board ideas and information, major and miscellaneous equipment lists, and sign design requirements.

Information Submitted: June 1990

THE NUT KETTLE
68895 Perez Road
Cathedral City, California 92234
Keith Culverhouse, Chairman

Description of Operation: The Nut Kettle Candy Kitchen specializes in original recipe popcorn confections, fudge, chocolate specialties and freshly roasted nuts of the highest quality. All are prepared in the on-view kitchen that's part of the retail store. Famous all over the country for the superior taste and flavors. Sold under private labels in such leading department stores as Neiman Marcus, I. Magnin, Jacobson's and Macy's. Tremendous repeat popularity and unlimited gift potentials.

Number of Franchisees: 3 plus 1 company-owned.

In Business Since: 1968

Equity Capital Needed: $130,000-$170,000 (including $20,000 franchise fee) depending on location.

Financial Assistance Available: None

Training Provided: Training at company store plus on-location pre-opening of store.

Managerial Assistance Available: Continuous assistance on as needed basis.

Information Submitted: April 1990

THE NUT MAN CO., INC.
47 Heisser Lane
Farmingdale, New York 11735
David Goldberg, Vice President

Description of Operation: Direct retail distribution of a wide variety of prepackaged gourmet nuts, candy, trail mixes and gifts to the final consumer at his place of work. This is not a retail store; the franchisee works out of his home and uses his vehicle to visit his customers. The franchisor provides all products including a constant flow of new products for the franchisee to sell.

Number of Franchisees: 7 in New York

In Business Since: 1979, began franchising 1989.

Equity Capital Needed: Approximately $7,500, total investment, $11,000.

Financial Assistance Available: None

Training Provided: 1 week of training in-house and in the field.

Managerial Assistance Available: Franchise training manager available to work with franchisees as needed.

Information Submitted: April 1990

THE PEANUT SHACK OF AMERICA, INC.
c/o SPECIALTY RETAIL CONCEPTS, INC.
P. O. Box 11025
Winston-Salem, North Carolina 27116

Description of Operation: Specialty nut and candy shops located within enclosed shopping malls.

Number of Franchisees: 106 in 24 States and Puerto Rico, plus 7 company-owned.

In Business Since: 1975

Equity Capital Needed: $50,000-$125,000

Financial Assistance Available: No financial assistance available. However, franchisor is available for consultation with lenders.

Training Provided: Initial training of staff (normally 1 to 2 weeks) and periodic visits thereafter.

Managerial Assistance Available: Initial training at same time staff training takes place. Periodic visits by operations staff thereafter.

Information Submitted: April 1990

PENGUIN'S PLACE, INC.
325 East Hillcrest
Suite 130
Thousand Oaks, California 91360
Mr. Doug Frank, Director of Franchising

Description of Operation: Penguin's Frozen Yogurt master franchisor. Penguin's sells its proprietory frozen yogurt. It is a quick serve, convenience restaurant with 36 different toppings and 30 flavors of yogurt served in a clean, black and white, contemporary environment. Yogurt cakes, pies, and gourmet coffee add to the offering.

Number of Franchisees: 114 in 5 States plus 9 company-owned.

In Business Since: 1983, franchising 1984

Equity Capital Needed: An ability to finance an investment of $180,000-$200,000 or a minimum net worth of about $350,000 is required.

Financial Assistance Available: We do not provide financial assistance for any part of the store costs.

Training Provided: A 3 week program consisting of a 2 week training in a designated training center; a 5 day classroom program, and 1 week spent in 2 or 3 stores with the chain's most successful managers.

Managerial Assistance Available: Continuous managerial and technical assistance when needed.

Information Submitted: May 1990

PERKITS YOGURT, INC.
434 Bigsby Creek Road
Cleveland, Tennessee 37311
Director, Franchise Development

Description of Operation: Soft frozen yogurt shops.

Number of Franchisees: 35 in 15 States

In Business Since: 1985

Equity Capital Needed: Approximately $100,000.

Financial Assistance Available: Up to 80 percent through various lending sources.

Training Provided: 1 to 2 weeks on premises.

Managerial Assistance Available: Continual support in all areas of growth.

Information Submitted: April 1990

PHANNY'PHUDGE EMPORIUMS
1525-A West Orange Grove Avenue
Orange, California 92668
John F. Peace, President

Description of Operation: A non-preparation specialty store selling chocolates, coffee/tea and machines, fresh desserts, food gift baskets with Phanny's labels, etc.

Number of Franchisees: 5 in California

In Business Since: Franchisor established 1957, franchising since 1985

Equity Capital Needed: Approximately $25,000-$100,000. Total investment will vary between $45,000-$225,000 depending upon Emporium size.

Financial Assistance Available: Provides franchisee with assistance in locating financing sources.

Training Provided: 3 weeks of comprehensive training for owner and manager. Training covers all aspects of operational procedures, bookkeeping, employee training, advertising and promotion and management techniques.

Managerial Assistance Available: Prior to opening field coordinator spends 1 week at location assisting franchisee. Continuous ongoing marketing and field support.

Information Submitted: June 1990

*POPCORN PLUS, INC.
4277 Transport Street Unit C
Ventura Marina, California 93003
Alden Jay Glickman, Franchise Director

Description of Operation: Retail sales of gourmet popcorn, country fudge, gifts and also mail order division and commercial sales.

Number of Franchisees: 5 including company-owned in California

In Business Since: 1984

Equity Capital Needed: $10,000 to $20,000

Financial Assistance Available: None

Training Provided: Yes

Managerial Assistance Available: Bi-monthly lists, operations manual, test kitchen, new product development, etc. Full technical assistance and bookkeeping assistance.

Information Submitted: April 1990

ROCKY MOUNTAIN CHOCOLATE FACTORY, INC.
P. O. Box 2408
Durango, Colorado 81302
Franklin E. Crail, President

Description of Operation: Sale of gourmet chocolate and other premium confectionery products.

Number of Franchisees: 67 in 20 States

In Business Since: 1981

Equity Capital Needed: $90,000-$120,000

Financial Assistance Available: Corporation does not provide financing but does assist in acquiring financing.

Training Provided: 1 week intensive training in Durango, 1 week training in respective store.

Managerial Assistance Available: Continual support in marketing, merchandising, finance, etc.

Information Submitted: April 1990

SMOOTHIE KING, HOME OF THE MUSCLE PUNCH
2725 Mississippi Avenue
Suite 7
Metairie, Louisiana 70003
Richard R. Leveille, Franchise Consultant

Description of Operation: Nutritional fruit formulas that are low in calories and have no cholesterol or saturated fat (over 20 varieties) as well as gain-weight formulas. Our formulas are made with only the finest natural ingredients. Full line of vitamin, protein, and diet supplements and all the latest trends in sports nutrition.

Number of Franchisees: 6 in Louisiana

In Business Since: 1973, franchising since 1988

Equity Capital Needed: $40,000-$79,000 total investment

Financial Assistance Available: None

Training Provided: Full training provided.

Managerial Assistance Available: Assistance provided in all aspects of business.

Information Submitted: April 1990

STEVE'S HOMEMADE ICE CREAM, INC.
200 Bulfinch Drive
Andover, Massachusetts 01820
Michael Newport

Description of Operation: Steve's offers the highest quality super premium ice cream in over 50 flavors yet still maintaining the old fashion store look.

Number of Franchisees: 100 franchise owned stores.

In Business Since: 1974

Equity Capital Needed: 10 percent of total investment of $75,000.

Financial Assistance Available: Steve's consults with franchisees regarding financing of project costs by independent financial institutions.

Training Provided: A 1 week training program is provided at a company training store in all phases of store operation.

Managerial Assistance Available: Ongoing operational assistance will include visits by an operations representative to monitor quality control and store appearance. Complete manuals of operations, advertising, and promotion are provided. Other services include site approval, store design, approved suppliers, cooperative advertising assistance, ongoing proven menu enhancements and the availability of a unique equipment package.

Information Submitted: June 1990

*SWENSEN'S ICE CREAM COMPANY
200 Bulfinch Drive
Andover, Massachusetts 01810
Michael Newport

Description of Operation: Swensen's Ice Cream Stores offer the complete range of ice cream operations from manufacture to sale. Each "store sells" its own ice cream from manufactured secret formulas developed by the firm's founder, Earl Swensen, who has been in the ice cream business in San Francisco since 1948. Franchisees purchase their supplies from independent suppliers. Swensen's stores vary from 250 to 4,000 square feet and are complete turn-of-the-century ice cream parlors, featuring marble tables and soda fountain, tufted booths, Tiffany-style lights and oak woodwork and furnishings. Swensen's stores engage in the retail sale of ice cream, fountain products, and ice cream novelties made to Swensen's specifications. Many stores also offer a sandwich menu.

Number of Franchisees: 275 in 35 States and 16 countries.

In Business Since: 1963

Equity Capital Needed: $120,000 minimum; equity capital requirements may vary depending on size of the store.

Financial Assistance Available: Swensen's consults with franchisees regarding financing of project costs by independent financial institutions.

Training Provided: Training consists of a 4-week program in Swensen's training facility in Phoenix, Arizona, where franchisees learn ice cream making, preparation of fountain items, ice cream specialty and other items, food preparation, store operation, accounting, store maintenance, inventory control and all other aspects of the operation of a Swensen's Ice Cream Store. Extensive operations manuals provided and training films available.

Managerial Assistance Available: In addition to initial training, complete operations manuals and forms are provided. Franchisees are periodically provided with new flavor recipes and related promotional material. Swensen's maintains full-time operations and product personnel who regularly visit stores to assist franchisees. Franchisees submit monthly operating statements to Swensen's home office.

Information Submitted: June 1990

TCBY ENTERPRISES, INC.
dba "TCBY" YOGURT
1100 TCBY Tower
425 West Capitol Avenue
Little Rock, Arkansas 72201
Herren Hickinbotham, President
Roger Harrod, Vice President, Franchise Sales

Description of Operation: Frozen yogurt and yogurt related treats.

Number of Franchisees: Over 1,700 locations from coast to coast and in Canada, the Bahamas, Taiwan, Malaysia, Singapore, and Japan.

In Business Since: 1981

Equity Capital Needed: $102,000-$182,000

Financial Assistance Available: No financing available on first two stores.

Training Provided: 10 day intensive training program at home office (personnel, accounting, operations) and 1 week in-store training at time of opening.

Managerial Assistance Available: Ongoing assistance in all phases of operations is provided. Services include site approval, store design, complete manuals of operations, approved suppliers and equipment packages. Additionally, field supervisors make periodic in-store inspections to monitor store appearance and quality control and offer ongoing support.

Information Submitted: April 1990

TOPSY'S INTERNATIONAL INC.
221 West 74th Terrace
Kansas City, Missouri 64114
Robert Ramm, President

Description of Operation: Topsy's Popcorn Shoppes are engaged in the sale of popcorn, caramel corn, gift canisters, caramel apples, fudge, ice cream, and confectionery items, along with soft drinks.

Number of Franchisees: 9 who have 15 shoppes in 2 states (company-owned and franchised). Some franchisees have been in business in excess of 20 years.

In Business Since: 1966

Equity Capital Needed: $100,000 plus license.

Financial Assistance Available: None

Training Provided: Topsy's offers a 5-day training program in an actual shoppe. The training program includes information necessary to operate a Topsy's Popcorn Shoppe, including recipes, food preparation, quality standards, employee training, proper use of accounting forms and business practices.

Managerial Assistance Available: Topsy's approves the site selected for the franchise location, and provides basic layout plans for the franchisee to adapt to the space available. An operations manual, reporting methods and procedures for accounting, and advice with respect to purchasing and selection of suppliers are furnished. Topsy's provides a representative for 4 working days to assist the franchisee during opening of the shoppe. Additional training available. Topsy's provides advice and consultation with respect to operation of the shoppe and administers the national advertising fund.

Information Submitted: July 1990

WHIRLA WHIP SYSTEMS, INC.
9359 "G" Street
Omaha, Nebraska 68127
Duke Fischer, Director of Marketing

Description of Operation: The custom blending of vanilla and chocolate ice cream or yogurt with the customer's choice of candy bars, fruits, cookies, nuts or candy. Done in seconds at the point of sale.

Number of Franchisees: 108 in 17 States and Washington, D.C., Canada, Japan, Australia, Singapore, Korea, Malaysia, Puerto Rico, Venezuela and all of Europe.

In Business Since: 1981

Equity Capital Needed: $13,000 to $80,000.

Financial Assistance Available: None

Training Provided: Initial training 3 days, continued training as needed.

Managerial Assistance Available: Initial training 3 days, opening assistance as needed, continued assistance as needed.

Information Submitted: April 1990

*WHITE MOUNTAIN CREAMERY
1576 Bardstown Road
Louisville, Kentucky 40205
Charles G. Ducas, Director of Franchising

Description of Operation: On-site production of super-premium ice cream, frozen yogurt and bakery.

Number of Franchisees: 27 stores in 8 States, 2 company-owned stores and 130 stores committed in 132 States.

In Business Since: 1982

Equity Capital Needed: $75,000 and ability to acquire financing.

Financial Assistance Available: None

Training Provided: 12 days, 4 classroom and 8 in-store training at the corporate headquarters.

Managerial Assistance Available: Franchisees are provided with thorough training in all aspects of the business. Services provided include site selection assistance, demographic investigation and information, new product research and development; construction, pre-opening and grand opening assistance; complete equipment package assistance; franchise marketing and advertising system; 4 detailed manuals covering product production, store management, customer service and store construction and development. Franchise field service personnel periodically assist each franchise partner. Continued support and ongoing assistance.

Information Submitted: April 1990

THE YOGURT STATION
618 West Arrow Highway
San Dimas, California 91773
Patricia Beaty

Description of Operation: Retail frozen yogurt and treats shops.

Number of Franchisees: 7

In Business Since: 1981

Equity Capital Needed: $50,000

Financial Assistance Available: Referral only.

Training Provided: Training is provided.

Managerial Assistance Available: Full support.

Information Submitted: April 1990

*ZACK'S FAMOUS FROZEN YOGURT, INC.
3420 Severn - P. O. Box 8522
Metairie, Louisiana 70011-8522
Ken F. Kreeger, Franchise Director

Description of Operation: Zack's is a manufacturer, retailer, and franchisor in the frozen yogurt industry. Each retail shop offers cups, cones, sundaes, banana splits, milkshakes, smoothies, etc., all made with frozen yogurt.

Number of Franchisees: 200 plus 400 under construction.

In Business Since: 1977

Equity Capital Needed: $110,000

Financial Assistance Available: Advice and counsel as to where and how funds may be obtained. No direct financial assistance provided.

Training Provided: Initial training is of 1 week duration at company headquarters. Ongoing training provided at franchisee's location.

Managerial Assistance Available: Franchisees are provided with in-depth training re: shop management, employee relations, inventory control, accounting, product preparation, and a thorough familiarization with all aspects of the business.

Information Submitted: May 1990

FOODS—PANCAKE/WAFFLE/PRETZEL

ELMER'S PANCAKE & STEAK HOUSE, INC.
11802 Southeast Stark Street
P. O. Box 16595
Portland, Oregon 97216
Herman Goldberg, President

Description of Operation: Full service family restaurant, serving breakfast, lunch and dinner.

Number of Franchisees: 17 plus 10 company-owned in 6 States.

In Business Since: 1960

Equity Capital Needed: Minimum $150,000

Financial Assistance Available: Financial assistance is not available.

Training Provided: Training at company location in Portland, Oregon, and at franchisee's site.

Managerial Assistance Available: Annual management seminar, ongoing consultations, on-site visitations, newsletters, training manuals.

Information Submitted: June 1990

*INTERNATIONAL HOUSE OF PANCAKES
RESTAURANTS
6837 Lankershim Boulevard
North Hollywood, California 91605
Richard K. Herzer, President

Description of Operation: Full service family restaurant serving breakfast, lunch, dinner, snacks and desserts including a variety of pancake specialties and featuring cook's daily special. Wine and beer served in some locations.

Number of Franchisees: 461 in 36 States, Canada and Japan

In Business Since: 1958

Equity Capital Needed: Varies depending on location.

Financial Assistance Available: None

Training Provided: 4-6 weeks of classroom and on-the-job instruction. Continued training available.

Managerial Assistance Available: Franchisor provides opening supervision, regular visits and assistance from field coordinators. Complete manual of operations specifies how each menu item is prepared and served, and how the business is to be operated profitably.

Information Submitted: June 1990

*LE PEEP RESTAURANTS, INC.
4 West Dry Creek Road
Suite 201
Littleton, Colorado 80120
Tony Doyle, Senior Vice President, Franchise Development

Description of Operation: Le Peep is an upscale breakfast, lunch and dinner restaurant, specializing in creative omelettes, frittatas, pancakes, and sandwiches. We offer full table service in a relaxing atmosphere. Our restaurants are open from 6:30 am to 2:30 pm, Monday-Friday, and 7:00 am to 2:30 pm Saturday and Sunday.

Number of Franchisees: 37 in 17 States

In Business Since: 1981

Equity Capital Needed: Range $300,000-$400,000

Financial Assistance Available: None

Training Provided: Le Peep provides 9 weeks of comprehensive training in all aspects of restaurant operations for 3 management personnel per restaurant to be opened.

Managerial Assistance Available: Le Peep provides real estate site selection assistance; the preliminary drawings of each restaurant; construction assistance; approved vendors for equipment and food; marketing assistance and grand openings and ongoing promotional activities; and operational consultations for all phases of an ongoing business.

Information Submitted: June 1990

PANCAKE COTTAGE FAMILY RESTAURANTS
P. O. Box 1909
North Massapequa, New York 11758
Chris Levano, Vice President/Franchise Development

Description of Operation: Pancake Cottage Family Restaurants are full service restaurants, specializing in pancake and waffle specialities. Famous for our breakfast, we also offer a large variety for lunch and dinner. Established in 1965 and a franchise system since 1971, future plans call for aggressive expansion.

Number of Franchisees: 21 in New York

In Business Since: 1971

Equity Capital Needed: $150,000 in liquid down payment with an overall investment ranging from $550,000 to $1,500,000 (approximately).

Financial Assistance Available: No direct financing is available from the franchisor, but guidance is offered.

Training Provided: The franchisor will conduct a training program encompassing the major aspects of owning and operating a Pancake Cottage Family Restaurant. Training will take place approximately 3 months prior to the opening of the restaurant. The term of the program will vary slightly, depending on the prior experience of the candidate. In most cases training will run no less than 2 months.

Managerial Assistance Available: A complete operations manual is provided on loan to all franchisees. District managers provide continual supervision of the restaurant's operation. There is a franchise advisory council, as well as regular quarterly meetings of all franchisees and the franchisor.

Information Submitted: April 1990

*PERKINS RESTAURANTS, INC.
6075 Poplar Avenue
Suite 800
Memphis, Tennessee 38119-4709
Phil Joseph, Director Franchise Development

Description of Operation: 24 hour, family-style restaurant with moderately priced menu items.

Number of Franchisees: 377 in 35 States

In Business Since: 1957

Equity Capital Needed: Estimated initial investment ranges from $959,000 to $1,500,000; equity required varies depending upon lender's requirements. Estimated initial cash investment would be $250,000.

Financial Assistance Available: Financial personnel available for consultation and assistance.

Training Provided: Franchisee and management training in company-owned, operated restaurant for 4-6 weeks. Opening team at restaurant to assist in training of staff for 3 weeks.

Managerial Assistance Available: Provide designs, plans and specifications for construction, furnishing, equipping restaurant. Advice, consultation and specifications for purchasing food supplies and uniforms. Provide core menu with specifications. Marketing and advertising programs. Quality assurance inspections to ensure compliance with standards of operation. Ongoing operations consultation.

Information Submitted: April 1990

VICORP RESTAURANTS, INC.
Selling: VILLAGE INN FRANCHISES
400 West 48th Avenue
Denver, Colorado 80216
Maxine Crogle. Director/Franchise Services

Description of Operation: Village Inn restaurants are family oriented, offering moderately priced menu items for all meal periods with emphasis on breakfast served all day.

Number of Franchisees: 36 in 20 States

In Business Since: 1958

Equity Capital Needed: $100,000, not including real estate and equipment.

Financial Assistance Available: None

Training Provided: Recommended 10-14 weeks management training for general manager and kitchen manager's positions, plus ongoing program of instruction.

Managerial Assistance Available: Provides consultation and supervision in the areas of marketing, operations and purchasing. Also, provides training staff for new restaurant openings, operating manuals and industry updates.

Information Submitted: April 1990

WAFFLETOWN U.S.A. LTD.
3 Koger Center
Norfolk, Virginia 23502
Tim Mathas

Description of Operation: Table service 1-1/4" Belgian waffles, pancakes, eggs, omelettes, sandwiches, entrees, family style restaurant.

Number of Franchisees: 8 in Virginia

In Business Since: 1981

Equity Capital Needed: $75,000 to $125,000 based on type of unit.

Financial Assistance Available: None

Training Provided: All personnel trained 2 week period.

Managerial Assistance Available: Continuous technical assistance.

Information Submitted: April 1990

FOODS—RESTAURANTS/DRIVE-INS/ CARRY-OUTS

*A & W RESTAURANTS, INC.
17197 North Laurel Park Drive
Suite 500
Livonia, Michigan 48152
Franchise Sales Dept.

Description of Operation: Quick service restaurant featuring world famous A&W Root Beer, hamburgers, hot dogs and "coney dogs," grilled chicken sandwiches, curly fries and onion rings. The restaurant can be free-standing with a drive-thru window or a mall location, ranging in size from 500 square feet to 3,000 square feet. Conversions of existing restaurants are considered on a case-by-case basis.

Number of Franchisees: 636 in 41 States plus 67 international.

In Business Since: 1919—Franchising since 1925

Equity Capital Needed: $150,000-$250,000 depending on financing.

Financial Assistance Available: No direct financial assistance is available at this time.

Training Provided: A minimum 3 week mandatory initial training course is provided for the franchisee (or a member of franchisee's management staff) before the restaurant opens for business. Refresher courses and seminars are also available periodically. A VHS video tape training library is also provided.

Managerial Assistance Available: In addition to training, the franchisee is provided pre-opening and opening assistance in staffing, equipment procurement and layout, purchasing and distribution, advertising and promotions, as well as periodic visits by field representatives.

Information Submitted: May 1990

ACROSS THE STREET RESTAURANTS OF AMERICA, INC.
United Founders Tower
Suite 300
Oklahoma City, Oklahoma 73112

Description of Operation: Family charcoal hamburger restaurant specializing in 1/4 pound hamburgers in 12 varieties, spaghetti, steaks, shrimp, telephone order system, Americana decor. Atmosphere above other fast food systems and just under a supper club theme.

Number of Franchisees: 8 in 3 States

In Business Since: 1964

Equity Capital Needed: $90,000 plus

Financial Assistance Available: Franchisor wil counsel franchisee in obtaining a loan.

Training Provided: Franchisor provides 14 days of training for franchisee's management at training center in Oklahoma City concerning all phases of operation: food preparation, cooking, make-up, procedures, etc. Franchisor's training personnel sent to franchisee's restaurant to assist for 10 days during restaurant opening.

Managerial Assistance Available: A.I.A. building plans and specifications provided to franchisee. Aid in site selection. Operations manual including policies, procedures, recipes, forms, etc.

Information Submitted: June 1990

ALL-V'S, INC.
26 West Dry Creek Circle
Suite 390
Littleton, Colorado 80120
Kenneth K. Cox, President

Description of Operation: Quick service, primarily hot sandwiches freshly and individually prepared for each customer. 44 sandwiches from Italian cold cuts, steak, pastrami and sausage, etc.

Number of Franchisees: 4 in Colorado

In Business Since: 1973

Equity Capital Needed: $100,000-$160,000

Financial Assistance Available: Yes

Training Provided: Minimum training 4 weeks before the franchisee's unit opens, consisting of all food preparation, management, inventory, handling co-workers, bookkeeping, budget and monetary control. A representative of All-V's, Inc., will spend 2 weeks in franchisee's unit, or more, if needed, to assist in opening of store.

Managerial Assistance Available: Training for at least 4 weeks in management, inventory, training, food preparation, bookkeeping and monetary control. Ongoing

Information Submitted: May 1990

AL'S BAR BQ, INC.
AL'S CHICAGO'S 1 ITALIAN BEEF
22 West 140 North Avenue
Glen Ellyn, Illinois 60137
Terry G. Palelli, President

Description of Operation: Fast food, Italian beef, sausage and hot dogs.

Number of Franchisees: 3 in Illinois

In Business Since: 1985

Equity Capital Needed: $110,000

Financial Assistance Available: None

Training Provided: 6 weeks in all phases of operation.

Managerial Assistance Available: Continual management service for the life of the franchise.

Information Submitted: May 1990

THE AMERICAN CAFE
7911 Braygreen Road
Laurel, Maryland 20707
Regis Robbins, Director of Franchising

Description of Operation: Full service casual dining restaurant and gourmet deli.

Number of Franchisees: 14 company-owned

In Business Since: 1971

Equity Capital Needed: $600,000-$1,000,000

Financial Assistance Available: None

Training Provided: 8 week training program plus 2 week opening team.

Managerial Assistance Available: Ongoing field consultants.

Information Submitted: April 1990

ANDY'S OF AMERICA, INC.
P. O. Box 24720
Little Rock, Arkansas 72221-4720

Description of Operation: Fast food restaurant featuring a complete breakfast with fresh biscuits and cooked-to-order eggs. A variety of quality sandwiches and related items. Salad and baked potato bars. Andy's own delicious frozen yogurt completes the menu.

Number of Franchisees: 2 stores plus 14 company stores.

In Business Since: 1977

Equity Capital Needed: Approximately $50,000

Financial Assistance Available: None

Training Provided: A 5 week training program including 2 week in-store orientation and 3 week training school in company.

Managerial Assistance Available: Building and equipment plans and specifications, complete operations sytsem and manual. National accounts buying power, ongoing training and supervision programs. Business forms and financial control systems available. In-house advertising agency available to franchisees.

Information Submitted: June 1990

APPETITO'S, INC.
5517 North 7th Avenue
Phoenix, Arizona 85013
Richard L. Schnakenberg, Chairman and President

Description of Operation: Appetito's, Inc., is a fast service Italian restaurant. The average store size is 1,800 square feet, although restaurant sizes range from 900 square feet to 3,000 square feet and are in-line, in shopping centers or stand alone buildings. The menu consists of hot and cold submarines, pizza by the slice or pie, salads and hot dinners of spaghetti, lasagna and ravioli. The company stresses quick service including drive through, take-out and delivery, cleanliness and high quality food products. Total turnkey operation. Selling individual restaurants and multiple unit territory franchises.

Number of Franchisees: 19 plus 1 company-owned

In Business Since: 1974

Equity Capital Needed: $40,000 to $50,000

Financial Assistance Available: Equipment financial package.

Training Provided: Minimum of 160 hours of training at company facility in Phoenix, Arizona, for franchisee's managers and assistant managers.

Managerial Assistance Available: Operations, training, maintenance, accounting and financial planning. Company provides grand opening package, multi-franchise territory package, central advertising and promotion.

Information Submitted: June 1990

APPLEBEE'S
2300 Main Street
Suite 900
Kansas City, Missouri 64108
Stuart Wagner

Description of Operation: Applebee's is positioned as a neighborhood pub, where consumers can obtain a high value experience through attractively priced food and alcoholic beverages. The principles of fast food (convenience, quality and service, coupled with limited time and money) can be applied to an adult consumer.

Number of Franchisees: 131

In Business Since: 1983

Equity Capital Needed: $4,000,000 net worth and $500,000 liquid assets.

Financial Assistance Available: None

Training Provided: Training is provided for general manager, kitchen manager and franchisee's restaurant managers in operations training facility for such period of time as franchisor shall deem reasonably necessary, and shall complete that course to franchisor's reasonable satisfaction.

Managerial Assistance Available: Applebee's basically provides management training, preopening assistance, ongoing and follow-up assistance. Additionally, they help find site locations, and offer assistance with purveyors for purchasing; marketing programs and format assistance provided.

Information Submitted: June 1990

*ARBY'S, INC.
Ten Piedmont Center, Suite 700
3495 Piedmont Road, Northeast
Atlanta, Georgia 30305
Jim Squire, Group Vice President/Franchising

Description of Operation: Fast food restaurant specializing in roast beef sandwiches.

Number of Franchisees: 500 in U.S. and internationally; 2,291 stores open as of January 31, 1990.

In Business Since: 1964

Equity Capital Needed: Minimum of $100,000 plus (assuming land and building are leased) and ability to acquire financing.

Financial Assistance Available: No direct assistance—however, Arby's will guide franchisees in obtaining financing.

Training Provided: Training to include classroom and in-store training. 2 week owner and 6 week operator training.

Managerial Assistance Available: Manuals, advice and counseling available covering all aspects of Arby's operation.

Information Submitted: May 1990

ARKANSAS TRAVELER BAR-B-Q, L.P.
c/o ARKANSAS TRAVELER RESTAURANTS, INC.
347 Lively Boulevard
Elk Grove, Illinois 60007
Wayne Samuel Kurzeja, Director of Franchise Development
David M. Bassett, President

Description of Operation: Arkansas Traveler Bar-B-Q offers both modular buildings with drive-up windows and full service barbecue restaurant operations featuring naturally smoked meats, ribs, chicken, beef, pork and other regional menu items using the 30-year old award winning Bassett family recipes. Store size from 600 square feet to 2,500 square feet.

Number of Franchisees: None yet as of November 1989.

In Business Since: B&B Bar-B-Q was established in 1960, which is Arkansas Traveler Bar-B-Q's original store in Fayetteville, Arkansas. Arkansas Traveler Bar-B-Q, L.P. and Arkansas Traveler Restaurants, Inc. was established in 1989.

Equity Capital Needed: Amounts vary depending upon structural locale, etc. Contact company for full particulars.

Financial Assistance Available: None at this time.

Training Provided: New franchisees required to undergo intensive 2 phase, on location training program lasting 5 weeks; assistance thereafter through manuals and seminars.

Managerial Assistance Available: Assistance from day one. Complete support system from location finding, design criteria, equipment and product specifications, pre-opening hiring and training, advertising, marketing and sales promotion, inspection, retraining, uniforms, and accounting systems. Periodic visits to store by key personnel on a continuous basis as well as ongoing operational guidance.

Information Submitted: April 1990

ARTHUR TREACHER'S, INC.
5121 Mahoning Avenue
Youngstown, Ohio 44515
James R. Cataland, President

Description of Operation: Offers franchises for the operation of Arthur Treacher's Fish & Chips Restaurants. Arthur Treacher's Fish & Chip Restaurants have a fast food format located in free-standing buildings and presently concentrating efforts in the food court concept in shopping malls. All restaurants project the Arthur Treacher image. Franchisee offers all items on the standard menu, which features seafood and chips specialties, and also includes such items as chicken, soup, sandwiches and other complements.

Number of Franchisees: 75 franchise units plus 14 company-owned units in 12 States and Canada

In Business Since: 1969

Equity Capital Needed: Franchise fee $15,000. Capital requirement $85,000-$125,000 for food court unit.

Financial Assistance Available: None

Training Provided: An initial training program for franchisee and managers of approximately 4 weeks is conducted at an Arthur Treacher's restaurant selected by the franchisor. A minimum of 4 days in class training. Franchisee is provided with an operations manual and other approximate materials at the training session. Franchisee is required to satisfactorily complete the course prior to opening a restaurant. Continuous training is available and sometimes required.

Managerial Assistance Available: There is no tuition charge for the initial training course; however, franchisee must bear the cost of room and board, travel and other personal expenses. Arthur Treacher's at all times makes available to the franchisee advice with regard to the management and operation of a restaurant. It also makes available to a franchisee changes and improvements in its menu, products, food preparation techniques and business methods.

Information Submitted: April 1990

ASTOR RESTAURANT GROUP, INC.
740 Broadway
6th Floor
New York, New York 10003
Charles Leaness, Vice President, Franchise Development

Description of Operation: Limited menu operation featuring "America's Best Dressed Sandwich" and marketing concept. Cooking, eat-in and take-out units. Also features 3 and 6 food party sandwiches and customized catering for special occasions.

Number of Franchisees: 350 in 17 States

In Business Since: 1964

Equity Capital Needed: $37,900

Financial Assistance Available: Total investment ranges from $70,000-$100,000. Company may assist with the arrangement of financing.

Training Provided: 1 week classroom training in our Atlanta office and 80 hours in-store training includes on-the-job training in sandwich preparation, purchasing, inventory control, cost controls, financial statements and advertising.

Managerial Assistance Available: Continuous managerial assistance for the duration of the franchise provided by area and regional representatives. Areas of assistance include manage-

135

ment, menu pricing, cost of sales, inventory control, problem solving and advertising/marketing. Operation, construction and advertising manuals provided. Monthly newsletter.

Information Submitted: April 1990

AURELIO'S PIZZA FRANCHISE LTD.
18162 Harwood Avenue
Homewood, Illinois 60430
Joseph M. Aurelio, Director

Description of Operation: Aurelio's Pizza restaurants engaged in the retail sale of pizzas, sandwiches and liquid refreshments. Options for sit-down restaurant or a carry-out type of operation. Franchisees are independent owners.

Number of Franchisees: 28 in Illinois, Indiana, and Minnesota plus 5 company-owned stores.

In Business Since: 1959

Equity Capital Needed: $130,000-$400,000

Financial Assistance Available: Assistance in obtaining financing and advice.

Training Provided: 72 hour training program for start-up. Continuous training as desired/required.

Managerial Assistance Available: Continuous assistance and advice as required/desired for all phases of operations during life of contract.

Information Submitted: June 1990

BACALLS CAFE FRANCHISES, INC.
Suite 200
6118 Hamilton Avenue
Cincinnati, Ohio 45224

Description of Operation: Bacalls is a comfortable, neighborhood-oriented, full service restaurant and bar, seating between 100 and 125. The design of each unit is tailored to the individual community, yet each location uses the standardized strengths of the Bacalls system.

Number of Franchisees: 4 in Ohio and Florida

In Business Since: 1982

Equity Capital Needed: $50,000 minimum

Financial Assistance Available: A total minimum investment of $165,000 will be needed to open a Bacalls Cafe. No direct financing is offered. However, full assistance is average to complete presentations for financial institutions or government agencies offering financing.

Training Provided: All franchisees, and if they choose, 2 other employees, must attend and successfully complete 4 weeks of training at the company headquarters.

Managerial Assistance Available: An operational specialist works with the franchisee during the first month of operation. A Bacalls operations manual covering all facets of the business is provided and updated as needed. A field representative regularly visits each unit to consult with the franchisee and offer useful advice and counsel on such system elements as identity, quality, customer convenience, product information, advertising, record keeping, training, communication, and incentives.

Information Submitted: May 1990

BAGEL NOSH, INC.
247 West 12th Street
New York, New York 10014

Description of Operation: Manufacturing of bagels and sale of delicatessen meats, salads, smoked fish on bagels—no bread used—light hot meals—health salads—cafeteria style with average unit seating 100.

Number of Franchisees: 35 in 14 States

In Business Since: 1973

Equity Capital Needed: $100,000 cash including $25,000 franchise fee.

Financial Assistance Available: $275,000 needed to build and equip a Bagel Nosh. Equipment leasing available to qualified individuals—franchisee may select own bank or SBA.

Training Provided: 6 to 8 week mandatory in-store for training under supervision of company instructors for all owners, managers and personnel that franchisee wishes trained.

Managerial Assistance Available: Bagel Nosh provides continual management service for term of agreement in quality controls. Company supervisors work closely with franchisees and visit all units on regional basis. Operational manuals are provided for all phases of Bagel Nosh operations and standards.

Information Submitted: June 1990

BALDINOS GIANT JERSEY SUBS, INC.
760 Elaine Street
Hinesville, Georgia 31313
William H. Baer, President

Description of Operation: 20 hot and cold submarine sandwiches. Rolls baked on premises twice daily. Quality ingredients are sliced fresh as ordered on every sub. Everything is done in full view of the customer(s).

Number of Franchisees: 17 in Georgia, North Carolina and South Carolina and 6 company units in Georgia

In Business Since: 1975

Equity Capital Needed: $75,000-$10,000 franchise fee.

Financial Assistance Available: Equipment leasing and financing programs available to qualified investers. $130,000 minimum investment.

Training Provided: Complete training—30 days. On-site training team at opening. Continuous classes offered at our training center.

Managerial Assistance Available: For duration of agreement: follow-up supervision, periodic on-site inspections and assistance and continuous update of technical data and operations manual.

Information Submitted: April 1990

BARN'RDS INTERNATIONAL
307 First National Bank Building
Council Bluffs, Iowa 51501
Samuel B. Marvin

Description of Operation: Fast food restaurant specializing in baked, natural, lite foods featuring beef, ham, turkey, chicken, cod, salads, soup and chili.

Number of Franchisees: 9 in 6 States

In Business Since: 1980

Equity Capital Needed: $40,000-$80,000 depending on the size and location of restaurant.

Financial Assistance Available: Complete counseling service.

Training Provided: Initial training period—4 weeks technical and people skills. Store opening assistance—2 weeks technical and people skills.

Managerial Assistance Available: Continuous in all phases of operation.

Information Submitted: June 1990

BARRO'S PIZZA, INC.
401 North LaCadena Drive
Colton, California 92324
Larry R. Polhill, President
John C. Martinez, Vice President/Franchising Director

Description of Operation: Making and selling of pizza, sandwiches and other complementary items. Beer and wine at our larger eat-in locations.

Number of Franchisees: 40 in California, Arizona, Colorado, and Illinois.

In Business Since: 1969

Equity Capital Needed: $25,000

Financial Assistance Available: Equipment leasing and equipment packages.

Training Provided: 2 weeks to 1 month training.

Managerial Assistance Available: Owner's manual and on-the-job training. Operation is simplified. Training is required as an on-the-job process.

Information Submitted: April 1990

BEEFY'S, INC.
107 Music City Circle
Suite 305
Nashville, Tennessee 37214
Charles R. Montgomery, President
Ron Jones, Director of Operations
Ed Griswold, Director of Franchise Services

Description of Operation: Double drive-thru restaurants with walk-up window and picnic tables, specializing in quality 1/4 lb. hamburgers, grilled chicken sandwiches, crispy fries and soft drinks at reasonable prices. Unique building design using modular or on-site construction. Area development and single unit franchises available.

Number of Franchisees: 9 company-owned and 22 franchised totaling 31. Units located in 7 States. Planned additional growth nation-wide.

In Business Since: 1984

Equity Capital Needed: $40,000-$190,000

Financial Assistance Available: Through third party.

Training Provided: 3 weeks comprehensive training conducted in Nashville, Tennessee, plus minimum 4 days additional assistance during first month of new operation with periodic store visits.

Managerial Assistance Available: Managerial and technical assistance provided for site selection, building design, site layout, equipment purchases and sources of supplies. Complete set of operational and general manuals covering restaurant operations, quality standards, financial controls, etc.

Information Submitted: April 1990

BENIHANA OF TOKYO
8685 N.W. 53rd Terrace
P. O. Box 020210
Miami, Florida 33152
Michael W. Kata, Director of Licensee Operations

Description of Operation: Benihana is a Japanese style steakhouse featuring teppanyaki cooking. All meals are prepared on the same table around which guests are seated. Each table seats eight, leaving room for a skilled chef to do slicing, seasoning and cooking in full view of everyone.

Number of Franchisees: 11 in 8 States and 3 foreign countries.

In Business Since: First company-owned restaurant opened 1964, first franchise restaurant opened 1970.

Equity Capital Needed: $550,000

Financial Assistance Available: A total investment of at least $1,500,000 is necessary to build and open a free standing Benihana restaurant. A substantial portion of this cost can normally be financed, depending on the franchisee's financial soundness. However, Benihana does not provide any financing to its franchisees.

Training Provided: An intensive 12 week training course is available for all restaurant management staff. An intensive 8 to 12 week training course is available for all chefs. All training is performed at a company restaurant under the supervision of a full-time Benihana employee.

Managerial Assistance Available: Benihana provides free consultation for the life of the franchise in all phases of the restaurant operation including bookkeeping, inventory control and menu de-

velopment. Complete manuals of operations, forms, recipes are provided. District and field managers are available in different regions to work with each franchisee if requested.

Information Submitted: March 1990

BENNETT'S PIT BAR-B-QUE
6635 South Dayton
Suite 330
Englewood, Colorado 80111
James W. Conway, Franchise Director

Description of Operation: Full service and limited service Bar-B-Que restaurants featuring real hickory smoked barbeque in a fast paced, friendly, family atmosphere.

Number of Franchisees: 8 franchised units and 8 company-owned units.

In Business Since: Incorporated 1984. Began franchising in April 1989.

Equity Capital Needed: $250,000 net worth and $100,000 liquid.

Financial Assistance Available: None

Training Provided: 4 to 8 weeks at training center, plus 1 to 2 weeks initial on-site training.

Managerial Assistance Available: Site approval, lease negotiations, construction management are available on fee basis.

Information Submitted: April 1990

*BIG BOY INTERNATIONAL
4199 Marcy
Warren, Michigan 48091
Attention: Ron Johnston

Description of Operation: Full service, family style restaurant featuring a high quality American menu including Big Boy's famous breakfast, soup, salad and fruit bars at moderate prices. The restaurants are open 7 days a week from 6 a.m. until 1 a.m.

Number of Franchisees: 70 franchisees operating over 760 Big Boy restaurants in 28 States, Canada, and Japan.

In Business Since: 1938

Equity Capital Needed: Applicants must have a net worth of $450,000, of which $150,000 is in liquid assets, plus franchise fee of $25,000 per unit.

Financial Assistance Available: None

Training Provided: Intensive training conducted at Big Boy International headquarters in Warren, Michigan. Unit owner management training encompasses, pre-opening hiring, training, opening procedures, operating management and cost controls.

Managerial Assistance Available: Full resources of the Elias Brothers Restaurants, Inc., Big Boy Division in marketing, procurement, personnel, operations, training, maintenance, accounting, design and construction.

Information Submitted: May 1990

BIG ED'S HAMBURGERS FRANCHISE SYSTEMS
P. O. Box 20370
Oklahoma City, Oklahoma 73156
Ed Thomas, President

Description of Operation: Family restaurant specializing in hamburgers.

Number of Franchisees: 14 in Oklahoma and Kansas plus 5 company-owned.

In Business Since: 1964, franchising since 1982

Equity Capital Needed:

Financial Assistance Available: None

Training Provided: 3 weeks management and operations prior to opening. Training of employees prior to opening (approximately 4 days) and supervision/training during first days open (4-8 days as needed).

Managerial Assistance Available: Big Ed's provides continuing consultation throughout the term of the contract. Short-term workshops are provided to upgrade and improve operational skills. Areas included are bookkeeping, cooking procedures, supervision of employees, marketing skills and more. Operations consultants make periodic visits to aid in helping franchisee maintain procedures consistent with established procedures.

Information Submitted: June 1990

BJ'S KOUNTRY KITCHEN
600 West Shaw, Suite 160
Fresno, California 93704
Gary Christy

Description of Operation: Kountry Coffee Shop operating 6 a.m. to 2 p.m. that bustles! Shorter hours and a single shift give you more time to do it right, as well as monitor the performance of others. Breakfast and lunch (especially breakfast) mean lower food cost with biscuits and gravy, omelets, hamburgers, and sandwiches, good 'ole basic food served quickly, simply, economically, with real hustle and bustle!

Number of Franchisees: 12

In Business Since: 1981

Equity Capital Needed: $55,000 to $100,000 plus.

Financial Assistance Available: Partial financing or lease available, subject to credit approval. Cost includes franchise fee and site acquisition.

Training Provided: We train the beginner to become a pro by keeping our operation simple. Franchisee plus 2 employees get a 2 week classroom and on-site program which offer the technique and training to BUSTLE, including full operations, advertising, record-keeping, personnel and management. Full manuals and follow-up support.

Managerial Assistance Available: Franchise office staffed with full-time management for assistance.

Information Submitted: April 1990

*BOARDWALK FRIES
8307 Main Street
Ellicott City, Maryland 21043
Jack Czicsek, Vice President, Franchising & Leasing

Description of Operation: Fast food—french fries, fried veggies, bar-b-que sandwiches, stuffed potatoes, and fries, served with toppings of cheese or gravy, sold with sodas.

Number of Franchisees: 71 in 19 States and Washington, D.C.

In Business Since: 1981

Equity Capital Needed: Initial franchise fee with down payment on location—total to amount to between $110,000 and $190,000.

Financial Assistance Available: Through commercial lending institution.

Training Provided: 12 days training.

Managerial Assistance Available: 5 days, longer if necessary.

Information Submitted: April 1990

*BOBBY RUBINO'S USA, INC.
900 N.E. 26th Avenue
Ft. Lauderdale, Florida 33304
Frank Galgano

Description of Operation: Bobby Rubino's Place for Ribs is a full service restaurant specializing in barbequed ribs and chicken. Each store is approximately 7,600 square feet.

Number of Franchisees: 14 plus 9 company-affiliated in Florida, Pennsylvania, New York, New Jersey, Illinois, Canada, California, and Indiana.

In Business Since: 1978

Equity Capital Needed: $500,000 plus

Financial Assistance Available: None

Training Provided: 28 day intensive management training program at home office and in home market restaurants for key people. Two to 5 weeks training on-site from pre-opening until all franchisees and staff are comfortable with the system.

Managerial Assistance Available: Continual management for the life of the franchise in bookkeeping, advertising (franchisor controls a flat 2 percent of annual gross). Complete operation manuals, forms and materials are provided. Excellent marketing support.

Information Submitted: June 1990

BOBBY'S KASTLE, INC.
10547 Collins Street
Suite B-5
Tarzana, California 91356
Robert Solner, President

Description of Operation: Fast food deli serving breakfast, lunch, dinner specially in 7 oz. Hot Corned Beef sandwich - $3.49, 1 lb. Bobby Burger - $3.99,,Fresh Roasted Gourmet Coffee - 35 cents. Breakfast special at $1.49 - 2 eggs (any style), toast, potatoes and coffee.

Number of Franchisees: 2 plus 2 company-owned.

In Business Since: 1984

Equity Capital Needed: Varies, $100,000-$300,000.

Financial Assistance Available: Franchisee must obtain own financing.

Training Provided: Training in one of our restaurants in cooking service, purchasing and bookkeeping, usually for 3 weeks or until company and licensee are sure of licensee's readiness to open his/her own restaurant.

Managerial Assistance Available: Company continues to counsel franchisee in advertising, merchandising and quality control.

Information Submitted: April 1990

*BOJANGLES' OF AMERICA, INC.
c/o BOJANGLES' CORPORATION
P. O. Box 240239
Charlotte, North Carolina 28224-8837
Eric M. Newman, Vice President

Description of Operation: Bojangles' is a quick-service food operation featuring Cajun Style cooking, offering Cajun and Southern Style fried chicken, homemade biscuits and a variety of chicken sandwiches. Bojangles' has 153 restaurants in 11 States. The units offer a 3-plus meal opportunity for the consumer. All products are fresh and prepared at each location. The majority of the loctions are free-standing facilities offering 54 to 84 seats and drive-through windows.

Number of Franchisees: 28 in 11 States (128 franchise units)

In Business Since: 1977

Equity Capital Needed: Approximately $150,000.

Financial Assistance Available: Bojangles' provides no financing.

Training Provided: 5 weeks management training.

Managerial Assistance Available: Continuous service from our field service department. Real estate site selection assistance, equipment purchasing assistance. Product evaluation continuously. Complete marketing program for advertisement.

Information Submitted: May 1990

*BONANZA RESTAURANTS
8080 North Central Expressway
Suite 500
Dallas, Texas 75106-1666
Ken Myres, Director, Franchise Development

Description of Operation: Franchisor of Bonanza Restaurants.

Number of Franchisees: 615 in 43 States, Canada, and Puerto Rico

In Business Since: Bonanza International, Inc. from 1966 to October 1983; Bonanza restaurants since 1983

Equity Capital Needed: Amounts vary depending on structural locale, etc. Contact company for full particulars.

Financial Assistance Available: Contact company

Training Provided: 5 days training in company classrooms plus minimum of 30 days on-the-job training. 5 to 7 days spent in unit by company representative and/or representative of area developer if applicable.

Managerial Assistance Available: Continuous guidance by all company personnel when and as needed; calls via telephone and in person on continuous basis during life of license agreement. Special visits in person when and as conditions required.

Information Submitted: June 1990

BOWINCAL INTERNATIONAL, INC.
421 Virginia Street West
Charleston, West Virginia 25302
Buford Jividen, President

Description of Operation: Bowincal offers franchises for its family fast-food restaurants featuring "simply delicious" olde fashioned hot dogs and Bowincal soft-serve ice cream. Each store is free standing or store-front (most remodelled existing structures), with approximately 1,100-1,500 square feet. Bowincal provides a complete set of specs and drawings for the standardized equipment and decor.

Number of Franchisees: 11 in West Virginia

In Business Since: 1973

Equity Capital Needed: $25,000

Financial Assistance Available: A total investment of $55,000 to $75,000 is required to open a Bowincal franchise. The $25,000 cash required represents the franchise fee of $9,500, down payments on equipment and remodeling, security deposits, licenses and opening inventory. Bowincal provides no financing.

Training Provided: 10 day training program at the company training center and Bowincal opening crew spends 2 weeks training franchisees and opening inventory. Bowincal provides no financing.

Managerial Assistance Available: Bowincal offers franchisees its expertise in all phases of day-to-day operations, including employment, training, systems, advertising and sales promotion, inspection, retraining, uniforms and accounting systems.

Information Submitted: June 1990

BOY BLUE OF AMERICA, INC.
10919 West Janesville Road
Hales Corners, Wisconsin 53130

Description of Operation: Franchising of soft serve, and limited menu stores. Territory franchises available.

Number of Franchisees: 12 stores in Wisconsin

In Business Since: 1963

Equity Capital Needed: Over $60,000

Financial Assistance Available: Boy Blue of America, Inc., will assist the operator in finding sources of financing and will assist in the preparation of the necessary financial statements.

Training Provided: The operator is required to complete a 2 week training program and pass all the tests connected with the course.

Managerial Assistance Available: Semi-annual advertising meetings and profit seminars for the franchisees.

Information Submitted: May 1990

BOZ HOT DOGS
770 East 142nd Street
Dolton, Illinois 60419
Don Hart, President
Harry Banks, C.B.

Description of Operation: Fast food carry-out—no grills or fryers. All steamtable operations. Limited menu.

Number of Franchisees: 27 in Indiana and Illinois plus 6 company-owned.

In Business Since: 1969

Equity Capital Needed: $50,000

Financial Assistance Available: None

Training Provided: New franchisee trained on location for 1 month, assistance from then on.

Managerial Assistance Available: Assistance from day one; stands are checked weekly for freshness and cleanliness.

Information Submitted: April 1990

BREADEAUX PISA
Frederick Avenue at 23rd Station
P. O. Box 158 Fairleigh Station
St. Joseph, Missouri 64506
Jerry G. Banks, Director of Franchise Development

Description of Operation: High quality pizza outlet. Operating throughout the Midwest in small to large towns. Extensive menu, Buy one, Get one free pizzas, quality products. Operate in 800 to 1,800 square feet existing buildings and strip centers.

Number of Franchisees: 98

In Business Since: 1985

Equity Capital Needed: $20,000 to $40,000 cash. Total investment range $65,000 to $100,000. Including equipment, remodeling, franchise and other start-up costs.

Financial Assistance Available: Possible equipment leasing.

Training Provided: 2 weeks extensive at headquarters. 1 week on location at opening. Ongoing support, training and assistance.

Managerial Assistance Available: Design, site selection, marketing, accounting, services, general management consultation.

Information Submitted: April 1990

BRIDGEMAN'S RESTAURANT, INC.
6009 Wayzata Boulevard, Suite 113
St. Louis Park, Minnesota 55416
Steve Lampi, Vice President/General Manager
John P. Taft, Franchise Development

Description of Operation: Bridgeman's operates a chain of family style restaurants offering moderately priced, high quality food in an attractive and comfortable setting. Bridgeman's features products in our famous ice cream specialty treats and desserts.

Number of Franchisees: 24 units located in Minnesota and Wisconsin including company-owned. Strategic expansion plans including the surrounding 5 State area, Minnesota, Wisconsin, Iowa, North Dakota and South Dakota.

In Business Since: 1967

Equity Capital Needed: $90,000-$150,000 minimum and the ability to obtain additional financing of $50,000-$125,000. Bridgeman's will work directly with owner/operator on planning and costs involved in a restaurant conversion to a Bridgeman's Original Ice Cream Restaurant.

Financial Assistance Available: Franchisee to obtain franchising.

Training Provided: 9 week training program with 3 weeks intensive on-site training. Pre-opening restaurant staff selection and training assistance. Post-opening support and supervision from district manager.

Managerial Assistance Available: Complete set of restaurant operation manuals. District managers provide ongoing support, training and monthly field inspections. Bridgeman's staff and district managers are constantly available to assist in ongoing restaurant operations and will readily assist on a daily basis to help solve any problems that may surface. Franchisee meetings are held on a monthly basis.

Information Submitted: April 1990

BROWNS CHICKEN
377 East Butterfield Road
Lombard, Illinois 60148
Frank Portillo, Jr.

Description of Operation: Combination sit down/carry-out restaurants. Specialty "chicken."

Number of Franchisees: 120 (including 30 company-owned) in Midwest and Florida.

In Business Since: 1965

Equity Capital Needed: $100,000 to $150,000 and ability to obtain financing on an additional $100,000 to $350,000.

Financial Assistance Available: Franchisees must obtain their own financing.

Training Provided: 6 weeks training school plus continual training on an inspection basis or request from franchisee.

Managerial Assistance Available: Training school, monthly field inspections, special assistance upon request, annual franchise seminar and spring and fall advertising meetings.

Information Submitted: April 1990

BUBBA'S BREAKAWAY FRANCHISE SYSTEMS, INC.
2738 West College Avenue
State College, Pennsylvania 16801
Joseph I. Shulman, Executive Vice President,
Franchise Development

Description of Operation: Bubba's Breakaway offers the franchisee a unique opportunity in the area of home delivery of subs and cheesesteaks. Quality, variety and free delivery are the fundamentals stressed in each store unit. A complete menu of sandwiches, cheesesteaks, pierogies, tacos, chips, salads, and soups are offered to the public through free home delivery.

Number of Franchisees: 20 in 6 States plus 4 company-owned.

In Business Since: 1981

Equity Capital Needed: $28,500 minimum

Financial Assistance Available: A total investment of approximately $70,000 is necessary to open a Bubba's Breakaway store unit. Bubba's Breakaway Franchise Systems, Inc., provides no direct financing. However, the corporation will assist the franchisee in securing outside financing through the franchisee's own sources or one suggested by the franchise corporation.

Training Provided: Intensive, 21-day, mandatory training course is scheduled for all new franchisees and their personnel. 14 days are conducted at the home office school and at corporately owned stores; 7 days at franchisee's store unit under the supervision of full-time Bubba's Breakaway Franchise Systems, Inc. employees.

Managerial Assistance Available: Bubba's Breakaway Franchise Systems, Inc., provides continual management service for the life of the franchise in such areas as recordkeeping, advertising, inventory control and store operations. A complete manual of operations, forms, directions and advertising is provided. District operations managers are available in all regions to work closely with franchisees and visit stores regularly to assist in solving problems. Bubba's Breakaway sponsors a franchise advisory council and conducts marketing and product research to maintain high Bubba's Breakaway consumer acceptance.

Information Submitted: June 1990

*BURGER KING CORPORATION
P. O. Box 520783 (CMF)
M3#5N
Miami, Florida 33152
Keas Kondraschow, Vice President, Franchise Affairs

Description of Operation: Limited menu restaurants specializing in hamburgers. The company's operating philosophy is to consistently serve quality food, reasonably priced with fast courteous service in clean, pleasant surroundings.

Number of Franchisees: More than 6,035 restaurants, including approximately 994 company operated units, located in all 50 States, Puerto Rico, and 28 international markets.

In Business Since: 1954

Equity Captial Needed: For markets where the land and building will be developed by the franchisee, a net worth of $500,000 is required, of which $300,000 must be in cash or liquid assets. For markets where the land and building will be developed by Burger King and leased to the franchisee, a net worth of $250,000 is required, of which $170,000 must be in cash or liquid assets.

Financial Assistance Available: Franchisees must arrange their own financing, which can usually be obtained from local banks and national finance or leasing companies.

Training Provided: Preopening training consists of a comprehensive restaurant operations training program at market training centers and operating restaurants, and a management course at Burger King University in Miami, Florida.

Managerial Assistance Available: Restaurant development, operations, marketing, human resource, accounting and training. Operations, equipment and accounting manuals are loaned to the franchisee.

Information Submitted: June 1990

BUSCEMI'S INTERNATIONAL
30362 Gratiot Avenue
Roseville, Michigan 48066
Anthony Buscemi

Description of Operation: Fast food—pizza, submarines, steak sandwiches. Dine in, carry out, drive thru window.

Number of Franchisees: 26 in Michigan including 4 company-owned.

In Business Since: 1975

Equity Capital Needed: $60,000-$80,000

Financial Assistance Available: None

Training Provided: 4 week training program at operating location.

Managerial Assistance Available: 2 week in-store training by supervisor, company policy book and operating manual.

Information Submitted: June 1990

CAJUN JOE'S
325 Bic Drive
Milford, Connecticut 06460
Donald G. Fertman, Franchise Director

Description of Operation: Premium fried or roasted chicken available with "Hot" or "Mild" seasoning. Cajun-style side orders include beer-batter onion rings, chicken gumbo, fried okra, corn-on-the-cob, and fresh baked buttermilk biscuits and corn muffins. Take-out facilities in all units and seating available in many. Simple, low-cost operation.

Number of Franchisees: 35 in 12 States and Canada.

In Business Since: 1985

Equity Capital Needed: Approximately $45,000. Total investment: $57,900 to $94,100.

Financial Assistance Available: Equipment leasing available depending on analysis of financial statements.

Training Provided: Cajun Joe's provides 2 weeks of comprehensive classroom and practical training at Cajun Joe's headquarters for store owners and store managers. The classroom curriculum includes training in location selection, store construction, accounting procedures, management theory as well as instruction in business analysis, product formulas and control mechanisms specific to Cajun Joe's. In addition to classroom study, practical training is provided in one of the local Cajun Joe's stores to develop skills in sandwich making along with the day-to-day operation and management of a successful Cajun Joe store.

Managerial Assistance Available: During store construction, which takes between 20 to 60 days, managerial and technical assistance is provided for each franchisee by a development agent and an office coordinator assigned to handle his/her file. Areas covered in this assistance include site selection, store design and layout, interior construction, equipment purchasing, arrangement of suppliers and initial inventory ordering. When a store is scheduled to open, a development agent is available to help oversee the operation and provide back-up support for the store owner in areas of employee training and successful operational procedure. After store opening, periodic inspections and field visits are conducted in each unit by the assigned development agent. Continual office support is made available to each franchisee through frequent contact with one's assigned coordinator. The coordinator development agent system for service provides continual assistance and support for each franchisee through the life of the franchise (20 years). Weekly, a newsletter, comprised of articles written by department heads, is sent to all franchisees. With receipt of this newsletter, all franchisees are kept continually apprised of new company policies and developments across the country. Also included in this publication are sections dealing with store management. Ongoing assistance in advertising is provided by the franchise advertising fund, which is directed by a board of directors comprised of 11 store owners elected by the franchisees.

Information Submitted: April 1990

*CALIFORNIA SMOOTHIE
1700 Route 23
Wayne, Wisconsin 07470
Richard Pineles, President

Description of Operation: Limited menu "healthy foods" featuring California Smoothies frozen yogurt with unlimited toppings, quiche, pita lites, salads, soup, and other fresh juice beverages. Typically located in mall food courts or in-line stores between 500 and 1,200 square feet.

Number of Franchisees: 10 in 6 States

In Business Since: 1973

Equity Capital Needed: Investment between $129,000 and $197,000 total.

Financial Assistance Available: Franchisor does not provide financing but will assist franchisee in preparing package for presentation to financing institutions.

Training Provided: Minimum of 8 days in company store and home office plus 2 weeks with opening team on franchisee's premises. Longer training available at no additional cost to franchisee if requested by franchisee.

Managerial Assistance Available: In addition to preopening training, franchisor provides assistance with supplier selection, employee training, complete design and construction, equipment selection, and ongoing supervision through franchisor's regional operations managers for the entire term of the initial agreement (typically 10 years).

Information Submitted: June 1990

CAP'N TACO SYSTEM
P. O. Box 415
North Olmsted, Ohio 44070
Ray Brown

Description of Operation: Mexican theme oriented fast food.

Number of Franchisees: 3 company-owned units.

In Business Since: 1976

Equity Capital Needed: Approximately $100,000.

Financial Assistance Available: None

Training Provided: Yes

Managerial Assistance Available: Yes

Information Submitted: April 1990

*CAPTAIN D'S—A GREAT LITTLE SEAFOOD PLACE
1727 Elm Hill Pike
Nashville, Tennessee 37210
Attention: Jeffrey L. Heston, Executive Director,
Franchise Development

Description of Operation: Quick service seafood restaurant with drive-thru service.

Number of Franchisees: 263 units in 23 States

In Business Since: 1969

Equity Capital Needed: $100,000 liquid

Financial Assistance Available: Franchisor does not provide financing but will assist franchisee in preparing package for presentation to financial institutions.

Training Provided: A 4 to 7 week formal training and management course is required for all new franchisees or their managers and is conducted by qualified instructors at the franchisor's training facilities. Supervision and training at franchisee's location during initial start-up period is provided.

Managerial Assistance Available: Franchisor provides advisory services on areas of financing, real estate, site selection, construction, equipment, advertising, accounting, purchasing, training, opening and ongoing technical and operational support.

Information Submitted: April 1990

CAPTAIN TONY'S PIZZA, INC.
2990 Culver Road
Rochester, New York 14622
Michael J. Martella, President

Description of Operation: Pizza and pasta take-out, delivery and dine-in; variety menu.

Number of Franchisees: 17 internationally

In Business Since: 1985

Equity Capital Needed: $55,000-$250,000

Financial Assistance Available: None

Training Provided: Up to 3 weeks training.

Managerial Assistance Available: None

Information Submitted: April 1990

CARBONE'S PIZZERIA
680 East 7th Street
St. Paul, Minnesota 55106
Thomas Carbone, President

Description of Operation: Family restaurant specializing in pizza and Italian food.

Number of Franchisees: 14 in Minnesota and Wisconsin

In Business Since: 1953—franchising since 1967

Equity Capital Needed: $150,000

Financial Assistance Available: No direct financial assistance is provided.

Training Provided: 4 weeks including on-the-job training and opening assistance.

Managerial Assistance Available: Ongoing assistance in advertising and other business aspects. Periodic visits and guidance as needed.

Information Submitted: April 1990

*CARL KARCHER ENTERPRISES, INC.
1200 North Harbor Boulevard
Anaheim, California 92803
Frank Karcher, Vice President of Franchising

Description of Operation: Carl Karcher Enterprises operates a chain of fast food restaurants that offers moderately priced, high quality food in attractive and comfortable surroundings. A diversified menu features hamburgers, specialty sandwiches, salad bar, dessert items and breakfasts.

Number of Franchisees: 78 plus 394 company-owned in California, Arizona, and Nevada

In Business Since: 1956

Equity Capital Needed: $250,000 net worth of which $175,000 must be in liquid assets from non-borrowed funds.

Financial Assistance Available: Interim financing for land and construction with third party commitment to assume franchisor's position.

Training Provided: 1 week of classroom and an additional 9 weeks of in-restaurant training at CKE corporate headquarters in Anaheim, California.

Managerial Assistance Available: Site selection, real estate construction and orientation course, prior to opening. Opening assistance. Thereafter, CKE will provide franchise operations personnel to assist the franchise operator during the entire term of the franchise.

Information Submitted: June 1990

CASA OLE' RESTAURANT & CANTINA
1050 Edgebrook, Suite 4
Houston, Texas 77034
Herb Rihn, Director, Franchise Development

Description of Operation: Casa Ole' Restaurants and Cantinas feature a Mexican restaurant that appeals to the family trade as well as the business person. Quality products and service at a moderate price are what we have built our reputation on. Although Tex-Mex is our specialty, we also feature some traditional "Old Mexico" as well as "California style" entrees. A full service restaurant from 4,000-5,000 square feet that seats an average of 180.

Number of Franchisees: 18 franchised units and 18 company-owned units.

In Business Since: 1973

Equity Capital Needed: $150,000. Must be able to obtain financing for land, building and equipment.

Financial Assistance Available: None

Training Provided: Complete on-the-job training provided: 6 weeks minimum, preferably 12 weeks. Training covers all aspects of the business: operational procedures, bookkeeping, employee training, advertising, promotion and management techniques.

Managerial Assistance Available: In addition to pre-opening and opening assistance, Casa Ole' provides continual management service in such areas as marketing, quality control, cost control and operations. Franchisee assistants are available to assist in any problem areas.

Information Submitted: April 1990

*CASSANO'S, INC.
1700 East Stroop Road
Dayton, Ohio 45429-5095
Richard O. Soehner, Senior Vice President

Description of Operation: Cassano's, Inc., a wholly owned subsidiary of SHAKAR Corporation (privately held), operates and franchises Cassano's Pizza and Subs, specializing in the sale of pizzas, subs and beverages. The business specializes in eat-in, delivery and carry-out services. There are 59 operating units.

Number of Franchisees: 12 in 4 States including Ohio, Kentucky, Missouri, and Illinois

In Business Since: 1953

Equity Capital Needed: $150,000 net worth with $100,000 in liquid assets. Total investment (excluding building and land) approximately $128,000 to $258,000.

Financial Assistance Available: No direct financing, but third party commitments available with no franchisor guarantees.

Training Provided: 4 weeks in unit/classroom in home office facility. Ongoing training provided.

Managerial Assistance Available: Ongoing assistance for all facets of the business—regular visits and consultation from franchisor's field representatives.

Information Submitted: April 1990

CATFISH SHAK, INC.
309 Courthouse Road
Gulfport, Mississippi 39507
Greg Malone

Description of Operation: Seafood restaurant franchise with rustic decor, featuring farm raised catfish, cajun style dishes and country cooking.

Number of Franchisees: 1 in Texas and 1 company-owned in Mississippi.

In Business Since: 1982

Equity Capital Needed: $850,000-$1,000,000

Financial Assistance Available: None

Training Provided: 4-6 weeks training at headquarters.

Managerial Assistance Available: Provide manuals, training program at headquarters, periodic visits as needed by field representatives.

Information Submitted: June 1990

CHEESE VILLA
INTERNATIONAL SERVICES COMPANY, LTD.
One Bowen Place
126 East Sixth Street, Suite 301
Cincinnati, Ohio 45202
Carlton C. Perin, President

Description of Operation: Non-cooking, limited menu food service for on-premise consumption and carry-out. Deli-style sandwiches featured plus gourmet soups, salads, desserts and soft serve yogurt. Primary locations are in downtown high traffic areas, major office buildings and commercial retail plazas. Format breakfast items. Typical hours of operation 7 am to 6 pm and limited Saturday operation depending upon location.

Number of Franchisees: 9 franchises in 5 States

In Business Since: 1975

Equity Capital Needed: $30,000 to $70,000 depending on total cost of project and strength of your financial statement. Total cost can range from $100,000-$300,000.

Financial Assistance Available: No direct financing provided. Assistance is provided in preparing presentations to lending institutions. SBA guaranteed loans have been obtained for several Cheese Villas.

Training Provided: 1 week of home study, 2 weeks of training in a Cheese Villa shop. Training includes stocking, food preparation, store management, advertising and promotion. One week prior to opening a supervisor handles receipts of inventory, stocking of store, and grand opening preparations. Supervisory personnel on hand during first week of opening.

Managerial Assistance Available: Location evaluation, lease negotiation, grand opening allowance, and continuing assistance. Inspection, financial and administration consultation, and protected operating territory. Communication by correspondence, telephone and visitation.

Information Submitted: May 1990

*CHELSEA STREET PUB
c/o RANKEN INC.
8802 Shoal Creek

P. O. Box 9989
Austin, Texas 78766
Norman Crohn, President

Description of Operation: Chelsea Street offers a quick service, seated restaurant, in an English Pub atmosphere, serving food, liquor, beer, and wine. The pub features giant, deli style sandwiches, super salads, gourmet hamburgers, and Southwest style meals, full bar, featuring fancy, alcoholic drinks, with live entertainment nightly after the mall closes. All locations are in regional malls.

Number of Franchisees: 9 plus 12 company-owned in Texas, New Mexico, Louisiana, Florida and Tennessee.

In Business Since: 1973

Equity Capital Needed: $350,000

Financial Assistance Available: Total investment is approximately $350,000.

Training Provided: Mandatory 45 day intensive training program including 15 days in Chelsea Street's home office school plus 30 days in on-the-job supervised training encompassing every phase of running a successful Chelsea Street Pub.

Managerial Assistance Available: Chelsea Street provides both technical and managerial assistance throughout the life of the franchise. Chelsea Street will supply site selection and build a complete pub as well as assist in opening the unit plus training all personnel. Continued assistance in advertising, supply, purchasing, entertainment.

Information Submitted: May 1990

CHICAGO'S PIZZA, INC.
1111 North Broadway
Greenfield, Indiana 46140
Robert L. McDonald

Description of Operation: Pizza, sandwiches, salad bar.

Number of Franchisees: 10 in Indiana.

In Business Since: 1979

Equity Capital Needed: $80,000 to $200,000

Financial Assistance Available: None

Training Provided: Complete 4 week opening, 2 weeks on site after opening and quarterly inspection.

Managerial Assistance Available: Consult in all areas.

Information Submitted: April 1990

*CHICKEN DELIGHT OF CANADA, LTD.
395 Berry Street
Winnipeg, Manitoba
Canada R3J 1N6
Otto Koch, President
Robert J. Ritchie, Director of Marketing

Description of Operation: Inside dining and/or carry-out and delivery restaurant plus catering; some units also have drive-through windows. All facilities feature chicken, shrimp, fish, BBQ ribs and pizza. Area franchises also available.

Number of Franchisees: 100 in 4 States, Canada, Trinidad and the Bahamas

In Business Since: 1952

Equity Capital Needed: $101,000 to $275,000 (exclusive of land costs), depending on size of unit, and ability to acquire additional financing.

Financial Assistance Available: None directly.

Training Provided: On-the-job training that includes all phases of operations.

Managerial Assistance Available: Continual assistance in all phases of operations.

Information Submitted: April 1990

CHILI GREAT CHILI, INC.
215 West Franklin Street
Suite 307
Monterey, California 93940
Vernon W. Haas, President

Description of Operation: Restaurant, original chili, vegetarian chili, and new hothead chili, served in one hundred ways. Salad bar, beer and wine.

Number of Franchisees: 2 in California

In Business Since: 1984

Equity Capital Needed: $35,000

Financial Assistance Available: Yes

Training Provided: 1 month training provided in all aspects of operations.

Managerial Assistance Available: Turnkey operation

Information Submitted: April 1990

CHURCH'S FRIED CHICKEN, INC.
1333 South Clearview
Jefferson, Louisiana 70121
William A. Copeland, Senior Vice President
Terrel A. Rhoton, Vice President

Description of Operation: Fast food restaurant.

Number of Franchisees: 300 in 36 States plus 800 company-owned.

In Business Since: 1952

Equity Capital Needed: Varies

Financial Assistance Available: None

Training Provided: Store and classroom training in a CFC Management Development Center for 4 weeks.

Managerial Assistance Available: Real estate/construction consultant assistance during site selection and construction of all stores. Operations field consultant assistance during opening of all new stores and duration of the store thereafter.

Information Submitted: June 1990

CIRCLES INTERNATIONAL NATURAL FOODS, INC.
310 Bay Ridge Avenue
Brooklyn, New York 11220
John Fahy, Franchise Manager

Description of Operation: Large menu with mixed ethnic specialities from all over the world and inexpensive gourmet fish and chicken dishes. Baked goods on premises and natural beverages.

Number of Franchisees: 8 in New York

In Business Since: 1976

Equity Capital Needed: Over $260,000 to open a store.

Financial Assistance Available: None

Training Provided: 2 weeks in home store and 2 weeks in franchisee's store.

Managerial Assistance Available: Daily checks on operations, 5 days. Ongoing development.

Information Submitted: June 1990

C. J. CARYL'S INTERNATIONAL, INC.
One Meridian Plaza
10585 North Meridian, Suite 245
Indianapolis, Indiana 46290
Dr. Haikaz A. Stephan

Descripion of Operation: Restaurant, fast food (chicken and fish, cooked with no oil or fat, process patented).

Number of Franchisees: 7 in U.S.A. and 1 in Japan

In Business Since: 1985, franchising started 1989.

Equity Capital Needed: $70,000 cash with leased equipment, otherwise $150,000 in cash.

Financial Assistance Available: None

Training Provided: Yes

Managerial Assistance Available: Yes

Information Submitted: April 1990

CLASSIC QUICHE CAFE
330 Queen Anne Road
Teaneck, New Jersey 07666
Michael W. Malloy, Chief Executive Officer

Description of Operation: Cafe with 25 varieties of quiche, and soups. Twenty varieties of salads and sandwich specials.

Number of Franchisees: 2 plus 1 company-owned.

In Business Since: 1988

Equity Capital Needed: $50,000-$90,000

Financial Assistance Available: None

Training Provided: 2 weeks in company store; field consultants provide continuing guidance and assistance at all times.

Managerial Assistance Available: Unit manager works with each franchisee to promote successful marketing and new menu ideas.

Information Submitted: April 1990

COCK OF THE WALK
115 Page Point Circle
Durham, North Carolina 27703
Steve Owens, President

Description of Operation: Cock of the Walk is a restaurant concept which serves mainly catfish fillet in a rustic style family restaurant.

Number of Franchisees: 10 in 7 States

In Business Since: 1977

Equity Capital Needed: Franchise costs $18,000 to $25,000 plus enough to get financing for $400,000 to $750,000 depending on size and area.

Financial Assistance Available: Franchisee is to arrange own outside financing.

Training Provided: 1 week training at restaurant of our choice for owner or manager and 2 or 3 key personnel and cooks. 1 week opening assistance in all phases of the operation, or longer if required.

Managerial Assistance Available: Manuals for construction and materials to be used, operational manual for bookkeeping, forms, day-to-day operation, cooking, pre-mix and recipes. A field representative is available to assist in solving problems. At least one annual meeting for franchisees plus training for any new products.

Information Submitted: June 1990

COLONEL LEE'S ENTERPRISES, INC.
3080 East 50th Street
Vernon, California 90058
Colonel John C. Lee, President

Description of Operation: Specialty fast service restaurant offering limited menu of individually prepared Mongolian barbeque of beef, lamb, pork and turkey meats and a variety of vegetables, Colonel Lee's special sauces and other complementary items. Emphasis is on efficient service with inside seating service. Restaurant is operated under the trade name of Colonel Lee's Mongolian Bar-B-Q. The concept and menu line date back to beyond the 13th century in ancient China.

Number of Franchisees: 4 in California

In Business Since: 1967, franchise operation began in 1976.

Equity Capital Needed: $165,000 to $195,000 and ability to acquire financing.

Financial Assistance Available: None

Training Provided: 20 days on-the-job training mandatory. Complete operational manuals and handbook provided.

Managerial Assistance Available: Regular visits by field supervisors. Advertising program, accounting system, management training provided by home office throughout the operation of the business. Advice and consultation with home office available on request.

Information Submitted: April 1990

CONFUCIUS SAYS
38901 MacArthur Boulevard, Suite 200
Newport Beach, California 92660
Don Beauregard, President

Description of Operation: A fast service food operation that specializes in home delivery of Chinese food. Quality is stressed with a limited menu and every dish cooked fresh to order. a Computerized "One Number" central ordering system keeps ordering quick, easy and efficient.

Number of Franchisees: 9 in operation with aggressive expansion in 1990-91.

In Business Since: 1986

Equity Capital Needed: $110,000-$150,000

Financial Assistance Available: None

Training Provided: 21 days intensive training in company's training center and in a functional restaurant. Follow-up training in franchisee's unit by area developer or company representative as required.

Managerial Assistance Available: Complete support system from location finding, layouts, design criteria, equipment and product specifictions, to pre-opening hiring and training. Further support in analyzing computerized reports, accounting, advertising and day-to-day operations.

Information Submitted: April 1990

CORN DOG 7, INC.
P. O. Drawer 907
Hughes Springs, Texas 75656
L. Ray McKinney, President

Description of Operation: Limited menu restaurants specializing in corn dogs and fresh lemonade. The company's mission statement is to promote pride in Corn Dog 7 and one's self by striving to provide the highest quality products with the best customer service.

Number of Franchisees: 98 (including 50 company-owned)

In Business Since: 1978

Equity Capital Needed: $90,000-$100,000

Financial Assistance Available: None

Training Provided: Intensive, mandatory training course is scheduled for all new franchisees and their personnel.

Managerial Assistance Available: As much technical assistance as is needed for as long a period as is necessary.

Information Submitted: April 1990

COTTAGE INN PIZZA
508 East Williams
Ann Arbor, Michigan 48104
John Roumanis

Description of Operation: Pizza delivery.

Number of Franchisees: 14 franchise-owned and 8 corporate-owned.

In Business Since: 1948

Equity Capital Needed: $25,000 cash. $100,000-$120,000

Financial Assistance Available: None

Training Provided: Yes, in-store prior to opening, and continuing education thereafter.

Managerial Assistance Available: Supervisor assistance in area. Special assistance as needed.

Information Submitted: June 1990

*COUNTRY KITCHEN INTERNATIONAL, INC.
Carlson Parkway, P. O. Box 59159
Minneapolis, Minnesota 55459-8203
Frank Steed, President and Chief Executive Officer

Description of Operation: Sit-down service restaurant; family type, full-line menu offering home style cooked meals; modestly priced. 16-24 hour operation; high quality oriented; breakfast, lunch, dinner. Country pub and meeting room modules available.

Number of Franchisees: 255 in U.S. and 2 Provinces in Canada, and 1 in Japan; 240 under development.

In Business Since: 1939

Equity Capital Needed: $75,000 plus

Financial Assistance Available: No direct financing available, but possible third party financing.

Training Provided: Classroom and on-the-job training, plus 1 to 2 weeks training during opening.

Managerial Assistance Available: Complete operations and marketing manuals, special menu service, programming advertising, purchasing programs, training up-dates, seminars, conventions, research and development, franchise committee meetings, and consulting services.

Information Submitted: May 1990

*COUSINS SUBMARINE SANDWICH SHOP SYSTEMS, INC.
N93 W16112 Megal Drive
Menomonee Falls, Wisconsin 53051
David K. Kilby, Vice President

Description of Operation: Uniquely developed submarine sandwich operation with 18 years expertise. Volume oriented, fast service concept in an upscale in-line strip or free standing location, some with drive-up windows. Outstanding fresh baked bread, and the finest quality ingredients go into our hot and cold subs, delicious soups and garden fresh salads. New franchising opportunities for a select group of single and multi-unit franchise owners.

Number of Franchisees: 28 in 2 States plus 38 company-owned units.

In Business Since: 1972

Equity Capital Needed: $50,000-$100,000 liquid.

Financial Assistance Available: 1/2 area development fee up front, SBA source, equipment package leasing sources.

Training Provided: Assessment center which enables us to evaluate managerial and supervisory strengths and weaknesses. Store building seminar for site selection, lease negotiation and construction, 20 days hands-on training, plus 10 days opening assistance and training. National and local store marketing support. Operations visits monthly or more if required.

Managerial Assistance Available: Initially Cousins provides design criteria and resource manual, franchise manual, operations manual, real estate site selection manual, sandwich making manual, modular video training program and recommended supplier list. Additionally, Cousins provides ongoing seminars and training both in the store and corporate sponsored seminars and training classes. A corporate area representative meets with each franchise location management 3 or more times per month to maintain communication and assist in problem solving.

Information Submitted: April 1990

COZZOLI PIZZA SYSTEMS, INC.
555 N.E. 15th Street
Suite 33-D
Miami, Florida 33132
Merrill I. Lamb, President

Description of Operation: Regional mall in line or food court units. We now ship a complete equipment package for an individual to go into business anywhere in the world. 750 to 1,200 square feet.

Number of Franchisees: 51 in 9 States and Guatemala.

In Business Since: 1951

Equity Capital Needed: $40,000 cash—cost of units $60,000 to $125,000 depending on size.

Financial Assistance Available: Complete financial assistance above the minimum amount of $40,000.

Training Provided: 2 weeks in existing store and at least 1 week in his/her store under supervision. Training center is in Miami, Florida.

Managerial Assistance Available: We are available on any problem for as long as he/she wishes.

Information Submitted: May 1990

CREATIVE CROISSANTS
ST. CLAIR DEVELOPMENT, INC.
3111 Camino Del Rio North, Suite 1100
San Diego, California 92108
Gretchen Schoonover

Description of Operation: Creative Croissants franchises offer a unique blend of fresh and nutritious gourmet fast foods in a comfortable and creative atmosphere. Freshly baked breads, rolls, muffins and croissants served hot from the oven, select international coffees and cappuccino, garden fresh tossed salads, pastas, gourmet hot filled croissant sandwiches at reasonable prices, and in a beautiful French-style cafe with a very European flair make up a Creative Croissants franchise.

Number of Franchisees: 28

In Business Since: 1981

Equity Capital Needed: $85,000-$100,000

Financial Assistance Available: None

Training Provided: 1 week in company-owned store and 1 week in franchisee's location.

Managerial Assistance Available: Complete support system available, from site location, design criteria, layouts, equipment and product specifications, to pre-opening training. Continued support after opening.

Information Submitted: May 1990

CUCOS INC.
3009 25th Street
Metairie, Louisiana 70002
C. B. Walker II, Vice President, Franchise Development

Description of Operation: Cucos is a high quality, casual, upscale Mexican restaurant, specializing in "fresh" Sonoran-style cuisine. Cucos' food is never pre-cooked. We have no microwaves in our restaurants and the only thing we want in our freezer is our ice cream. We know of no other Mexican restaurant chain that serves higher quality or fresher ingredients than Cucos. Taste the fresh approach to fine Mexican dining at Cucos.

Number of Franchisees: 14 franchisees operating 20 restaurants in 11 States.

In Business Since: 1981

Equity Capital Needed: Between $200,000 and $300,000 estimated.

Financial Assistance Available: None. Cucos estimates that the capital requirements will range between $430,000 to $775,000 excluding real estate.

Training Provided: A 10 week comprehensive management training program must be completed before restaurant opening. In-restaurant training is provided by Cucos prior to restaurant opening.

Managerial Assistance Available: Cucos provides continued assistance and training throughout the term of the franchise agreement. A regional supervisor periodically visits each restaurant. Each franchisee receives a set of operations manuals, along with assistance in site selection, marketing and advertising, food and equipment procurement, design and architectural services, staffing and training.

Information Submitted: April 1990

DAIRY BELLE FREEZE DEVELOPMENT COMPANY, INC.
570 Valley Way
Milpitas, California 95035
Steven H. Goodere, Executive Vice President

Description of Operation: Fast food restaurant featuring a complete line of soft-serve products, hamburgers, fries, specialty sandwiches, and much more.

Number of Franchisees: 17 in California

In Business Since: 1957

Equity Capital Needed: Depends upon the demographics of the area, landlord's requirements, and franchisee's financial statement.

Financial Assistance Available: Franchisor does not provide a finance program.

Training Provided: A minimum of 2 weeks training in company-owned stores. In-store assistance for additional time, as necessary.

Managerial Assistance Available: Continued assistance in all phases of the Dairy Belle restaurant operation, including food preparation, cost controls, marketing, accounting, insurance, new product development, purchasing programs, in-store inspections and evaluations, employee development, and customer service educational information.

Information Submitted: May 1990

DAIRY CHEER STORES
2914 Forgey Street
Ashland, Kentucky 41101
W. H. Culbertson

Description of Operation: Fast food, sandwiches, chicken, fish, soup, beans, soft-serve and hard ice cream and serve yourself desserts, salad bar. Available for most States.

Number of Franchisees: 10

In Business Since: 1949

Equity Capital Needed: $5,000 franchise fee, building $85,000; equipment $70,000 and signs $18,000, approximately.

Financial Assistance Available: Local bankers are usually very helpful.

Training Provided: On-the-job training before and after opening.

Managerial Assistance Available: Instructions in technical operations, inspections, advertising, formulas and recipes.

Information Submitted: June 1990

*DAIRY ISLE CORPORATION
P. O. Box 273
Utica, Michigan 48087
David K. Chapoton, President
Shirley Chapoton, Corporate Secretary

Description of Operation: Soft ice cream stores and fast food operation.

Number of Franchisees: 42 in 7 States

In Business Since: 1942

Equity Capital Needed: Minimum $35,000

Financial Assistance Available: Dairy Isle Corporation does not provide direct financing to franchisees at the present time. However, it does provide assistance in obtaining financing, such as assisting the franchisee in preparing his proposal for bank financing and meeting with potential lenders.

Training Provided: 3 days or more depending on individuals being trained plus calls during the operating season.

Managerial Assistance Available: Operations of unit and follow-up promotional ideas and equipment purchasing.

Information Submitted: June 1990

DALY FRANCHISE COMPANY
800 Ann Arbor Road
Plymouth, Michigan 48154
Rita Grace

Description of Operation: Daly restaurants feature a full service, moderately priced menu including breakfast, lunch and dinner items, featuring our "gourmet Dalyburger," foot long "Daly Dog" and "Daly-Maid" ice cream.

Number of Franchisees: 6 in Michigan

In Business Since: 1948

Equity Capital Needed: $30,000 and up.

Financial Assistance Available: None

Training Provided: 2 weeks at company-owned store and 3 weeks at franchisee's store.

Managerial Assistance Available: Continuous technical assistance.

Information Submitted: June 1990

DAMON'S FRANCHISE CORP.
(DAMON'S THE PLACE FOR RIBS)
P. O. Box 6747
Hilton Head, South Carolina 29938
Attention: Franchise Agent

Description of Operation: Sit-down family style restaurant with cocktail lounge. Featuring BBQ ribs, shrimp, and chicken, steaks, seafood and sandwiches. Approximately 5,000-8,000 square feet. Number of seats 130-180. Either free standing building or shopping center store. Can convert existing restaurant.

Number of Franchisees: 32 in 13 States, 8 company-owned stores.

In Business Since: 1979

Equity Capital Needed: $300,000-$400,000

Financial Assistance Available: None

Training Provided: 8 weeks required for operations personnel.

Managerial Assistance Available: Damon's provides continual management service for the life of the franchise in areas such as operations, advertising and cost control. Complete manuals of operations, recipes and systems are provided. Field managers are available to work closely with franchises and visit stores regularly.

Information Submitted: April 1990

DEL TACO RESTAURANTS, INC.
Corporate Headquarters and Regional Operations
400 Northcreek, Suite 700
3715 Northside Parkway, N.W.
Atlanta, Georgia 30327
Eugene A. Kray, Chief Financial Officer

Description of Operation: Quick service restaurants specializing in moderately priced Mexican-style and American-style food in a distinctive, attractive, casual setting.

Number of Franchisees: 18

In Business Since: 1967

Equity Capital Needed: $20,000 franchise fee.

Financial Assistance Available: None

Training Provided: Completion of 6 week manager training program required; 11 day on-site employee training and assistance during opening period.

Managerial Assistance Available: Ongoing in all phases of operation.

DENNY'S INC.
P. O. Box 25320
Santa Ana, California 92799-5320
Director of Franchise Development

Description of Operation: Full service family restaurants.

Number of Franchisees: 200 plus

In Business Since: 1953

Equity Capital Needed: Franchise fee: $35,000

Financial Assistance Available: None

Training Provided: Store opening, 1 week prior to opening and 2 weeks after.

Managerial Assistance Available: Manager training 4 weeks.

Information Submitted: April 1990

DIAMOND DAVE'S TACO CO., INC.
1929 Keokuk Street
Iowa City, Iowa 52240
Stanley White, President

Description of Operation: The sale of fast food Mexican restaurants and their services. Also the sale of liquor where feasible.

Number of Franchisees: 30 in Iowa, Illinois, Wisconsin, Missouri and Indiana.

In Business Since: 1978

Equity Capital Needed: $125,000 to $225,000

Financial Assistance Available: Partial financing of equipment.

Training Provided: Full training in food preparation, food service, management and bookkeeping. Training 1 to 2 weeks.

Managerial Assistance Available: Ongoing

Information Submitted: June 1990

DIETWORKS OF AMERICA, INC.
1236 Brace Road
Suite C
Cherry Hill, New Jersey 08034
Leonard S. Torine, President

Description of Operation: Reduced calorie, gourmet, full service restaurants complete with retail department. Emphasis on fresh, quality contemporary cuisine. Average unit 2,000 square feet with 60-70 seats. We provide training and turnkey operation. Very timely concept. We have interest in going national with territories and individual units.

Number of Franchisees: 10 in New Jersey

In Business Since: First unit 1975; Dietworks of America formed 1982.

Equity Capital Needed: Total investment $150,000-$200,000—cash required depends on franchisee.

Financial Assistance Available: Possible guidance or assistance depending on financial background of franchisee.

Training Provided: Complete training in all phases of operation, 4-8 weeks at our training unit (New Jersey).

Managerial Assistance Available: Continuous ongoing management and support—new methods, recipes, technical assistance, marketing, etc.

Information Submitted: June 1990

*DINO'S/CRUSTY'S U.S.A., INC.
19215 West 8 Mile Road
Detroit, Michigan 48219
John E. Ray, President

Description of Operation: Crusty's Pizza offers one concept. This concept consists of a carry-out and delivery pizza unit which was the foundation for Crusty's overall success. All products are the best quality obtainable.

Number of Franchisees: 200 in 14 States

In Business Since: 1961

Equity Capital Needed: Total investment is in the range of $55,000 to $250,000, depending on number of units.

Financial Assistance Available: Total investment, depending on location, from $50,000-$150,000. Will direct but will not guarantee financing through normal banking channels. Referral is made to developers who will develop locations for qualified franchisees.

Training Provided: Franchisees are required to attend a training program for a minimum of 300 hours, which includes on-the-job training in designated units. The training includes all phases of the business with continuing assistance to open the franchised unit.

Managerial Assistance Available: Franchise relations personnel are on call if needed and will visit all locations on a regularly scheduled basis.

Information Submitted: June 1990

*DOG N SUDS RESTAURANTS
2804 Del Prado Boulevard
Cape Coral, Florida 33904
Franchise Department

Description of Operation: Retail sale of hot dogs, related food products and premium draft root beer.

Number of Franchisees: 17 in 8 States

In Business Since: 1953

Equity Capital Needed: $75,000 to $200,000

Financial Assistance Available: None

Training Provided: Yes, in all phases of operation.

Managerial Assistance Available: Ongoing

Information Submitted: April 1990

*DOMINO'S PIZZA, INC.
3001 Earhart Road
P. O. Box 997
Ann Arbor, Michigan 48105
Deborah S. Sargent, National Director of Franchise Services

Description of Operation: Pizza carry-out and delivery service.

Number of Franchisees: Approximately 1,000 in the United States and 19 foreign countries.

In Business Since: 1960

Equity Capital Needed: $83,000 to $194,000.

Financial Assistance Available: Domino's Pizza does not directly provide financing but can refer to lending institutions who will consider providing financing to qualified franchisees.

Training Provided: Potential franchisees must complete the company's current training program, which shall consist of both in-store training and classroom instruction.

Managerial Assistance Available: Domino's Pizza only franchises to internal people, and the kinds and duration of managerial and technical assistance provided by the company are set forth in the franchise agreement.

Information Submitted: May 1990

DOSANKO FOODS, INC.
440 West 47th Street
New York, New York 10036
T. Yamamori, President

Description of Operation: Dosanko Restaurants operate Japanese fast service food restaurants serving moderately priced menu. Emphasis on quick, efficient service, high quality and freshly cooked food, and cleanliness. The standard menu consists of four varieties of Japanese soup and noodles, dumplings, stir-fried noodles with beef and crisp-fried noodles with beef smothered in sauteed vegetables, Japanese style fried chicken, and assorted beverages.

Number of Franchisees: 7 plus 4 company-owned in New York and New Jersey. Company also has 1,200 franchisees plus 25 company-owned units in Japan.

In Business Since: 1975

Equity Capital Needed: $150,000 minimum and ability to acquire outside financing of $150,000 to $20,000.

Financial Assistance Available: None

Training Provided: 2 week training course in Dosanko Restaurant. 1 week course to study accounting procedures in Dosanko.

Managerial Assistance Available: Technical assistance on special kitchen equipment which is not available tin the United States as well as for special seasoning. Operations, training, maintenance, accounting and equipment manuals provided. Company makes available promotional advertising material plus field representative consultation and assistance.

Information Submitted: June 1990

*DRUTHER'S INTERNATIONAL, INC.
P. O. Box 4999
Louisville, Kentucky 40204
Thomas L. Hensley, President

Description of Operation: Fast food restaurant.

Number of Franchisees: 102 in 7 States plus 54 company-owned units.

In Business Since: 1963

Equity Capital Needed: $50,000 plus or less depending on franchisee's financial capabilities.

Financial Assistance Available: Assistance in acquiring equipment loan or lease, joint venturing opportunities for qualified candidates.

Training Provided: Development training program—5 weeks—combined unit and classroom work at special training unit—follow-up visits at franchisee's unit by training director during next 25 weeks and continued visits by area supervisor.

Managerial Assistance Available: Continued assistance regarding operations and accounting through field and office staff.

Information Submitted: June 1990

DUCHESS WORLDWIDE, INC.
125 Bruce Avenue
Stratford, Connecticut 06497
Bernard Lavin, President of the Franchise Division

Description of Operation: Fast food restaurants.

Number of Franchisees: 12 company-owned

In Business Since: 1956, franchising since 1990.

Equity Capital Needed: $25,000 initial franchise fee.

Financial Assistance Available: None

Training Provided: Full training provided in all phases of operation.

Managerial Assistance Available: Ongoing

Information Submitted: June 1990

EL CHICO CORPORATION
12200 Stemmons Freeway
Suite 100
Dallas, Texas 75234
Wes Jablonski, Vice President, Corporation Development/Franchise

Description of Operation: El Chico Restaurants are full-service, mid-priced Mexican restaurants with bar facilities. Store sizes approximate 5,100 square feet to 6,000 square feet, requiring 45,000 square feet to 50,000 square feet of land adequate to accommodate building, signage and parking for 100-110 cars. Units operate 7 days per week, 10-12 hours daily. Product quality, customer service, menu variety, and product presentation key elements of business. Many items are unique and proprietary.

Number of Franchisees: 28 in Texas, Louisiana, Arkansas, Mississippi, Oklahoma, Kentucky, Tennessee and Alabama.

In Business Since: 1940

Equity Capital Needed: $80,000 net worth—$300,000 liquid.

Financial Assistance Available: None

Training Provided: Intensive 10-week training in designated training unit of franchisor. Required: 2 management representatives of franchise for full term of training, which includes O.J.T. training in operations, service, product and administration.

Managerial Assistance Available: Ongoing franchise service for term of license, including franchise consultant, field service visitation program, standards maintenance, progress monitoring, periodic training updates offered, marketing materials available, access to corporate accounting system and operations manual, forms and newsletter services.

Information Submitted: June 1990

EL TACO RESTAURANTS
7870 Florence Avenue
Downey, California 90241

Description of Operation: Mexican food drive-thru restaurants—inside seating for 50 people. 20 percent of the business through the drive thru.

Number of Franchisees: 7 in 2 States

In Business Since: 1959

Equity Capital Needed: $150,000 cash required

Financial Assistance Available: None

Training Provided: 6 weeks in-store training.

Managerial Assistance Available: None

Information Submitted: June 1990

ENTERTAINMENT ONE
1900 Yorktown
Suite 400
Houston, Texas 77056
Chuck Badrick

Description of Operation: Entertainment One is presently offering its concept: Studebaker's, a 50's and 60's bar/diner serving alcoholic drinks of all kinds including beer and wine. A limited late night snack menu is offered. Sites can be free-standing or in shopping malls located in city or suburban areas.

Number of Franchisees: 12 in 9 States including company-owned.

In Business Since: 1982

Equity Capital Needed: $300,000 and up depending on operators ability to finance.

Financial Assistance Available: Franchisee is responsible for land, building and equipment.

Training Provided: Training at corporate office.

Managerial Assistance Available: The company provides ongoing assistance on a regular basis for the management, operational and promotional program.

Information Submitted: June 1990

ESTEBAN INTERNATIONAL, INC.
903 Marquette Avenue South
Minneapolis, Minnesota 55402
R. Stephen Tanner, Chairman
Richard Tourand, President

Description of Operation: Mexican full service with liquor, family atmosphere and mid-priced menu.

Number of Franchisees: 2 in Minnesota plus 5 company-owned.

In Business Since: 1976

Equity Capital Needed: $190,000 cash

Financial Assistance Available: None

Training Provided: 8 weeks full on-site training for staff with manuals. Complete training of restaurant operations with updating of training on an ongoing basis.

Managerial Assistance Available: Accounting-statements, manuals and various materials, franchise director for guidance, full access to upper level management for support (operational), and sound/profitable business ideas.

Information Submitted: June 1990

*EVERYTHING YOGURT INC./BANANAS
Franchise Division
304 Port Richmond Avenue
Staten Island, New York 10302
Richard Nicotra, Chairman

Description of Operation: Everything Yogurt restaurants are fast service retail operations featuring soft frozen yogurt sundaes and shakes, salads, quiche, hot and cold vegetable entrees, assorted pasta salads, fresh squeezed fruit juices and related healthful food and beverage items.

Number of Franchisees: Over 300 plus 5 company-owned.

In Business Since: 1976, offering franchises since 1981.

Equity Capital Needed: $56,000, total investment $175,000-$225,000.

Financial Assistance Available: No company financing offered. Administrative assistance offered by company in providing necessary information to local banks for financing.

Training Provided: 2 week initial training program provided at company headquarters and at other stores in chain. Additional on-site training at franchisee's store for one week prior to opening. Follow-up training provided on a continuing basis as directed by company.

Managerial Assistance Available: Operational and merchandising assistance provided as needed through headquarters office. Area representatives visit franchisees for continuing assistance, periodically suggesting improvements when needed. Comprehensive operations manual provided.

Information Submitted: June 1990

FAJITA JUNCTION, INC.
9801 McCullough
San Antonio, Texas 78216
Gerry Telle, President

Description of Operation: Fast food Mexican restaurant.

Number of Franchisees: 9

In Business Since: 1983

Equity Capital Needed: $17,500

Financial Assistance Available: None

Training Provided: Training provided in all aspects of operations.

Managerial Assistance Available: Ongoing, full support.

Information Submitted: April 1990

RANDALL ENTERPRISES, INC.
dba FAMILIES ORIGINAL SUBMARINE
SANDWICHES
5376 Tomah Drive #204
Colorado Springs, Colorado 80918
Randall Smith, President

Description of Operation: Families delivers a menu of 27 basic submarine sandwiches with complementary salads, soups, chili, desserts, and other specialties. Breakfast menu available in some shops. Success is based on unique methods of portion control using Families recipes and formulas, emphasizing nutritional quality and quantity of product delivered in a fast service take-out or sit-down setting. Shop size is 1,000 to 2,500 square feet and can be incorporated in a Shoppette or in a free-standing facility depending on site availability and business potential. Shops are open 12 hours per day, 7 days per week. Families offers tailored cost-effective design and special equipment package resulting in a relatively low initial capital investment.

Number of Franchisees: 31 in Colorado, Indiana, South Dakota, and New Mexico.

In Business Since: 1972

Equity Capital Needed: Approximately $55,000-$60,000 will provide franchise fee, equipment, fixtures, inventory, start-up capital, etc., depending on the extent of necessary or desired leasehold improvements or property ownership.

Financial Assistance Available: Families will assist franchisee in developing projections and proposals for financing agencies, including SBA, and may meet with such representatives on your behalf, but provides no financial assistance as such.

Training Provided: A mandatory 80 hour training period for each of 2 persons is conducted in Colorado Springs or at a place approved by the franchisor. The course for owners and managers covers the entire operation including necessary accounting, record keeping, marketing, advertising, and personnel management. Also covered are food preparation, sandwich making, and the use and maintenance of standard equipment. Additional instruction for owners, managers, and subordinate personnel will be provided during the opening and grand opening of franchisee's shop.

Managerial Assistance Available: Ongoing training, education, and assistance are provided regularly during the lifetime of the franchise agreement. The franchisee will be kept abreast of new developments in company and industry-wide advertising and marketing techniques as well as economic trends that affect profits. Franchisor will conduct periodic quality control surveys and evaluation of shop operations, to include monthly financial management, costs, profits, use of personnel, governmental reporting, continuing education, and other pertinent areas of concern.

Information Submitted: June 1990

FAT BOY'S BAR-B-Q FRANCHISE SYSTEMS, INC.
1550 West King Street
Cocoa, Florida 32922

Description of Operation: Fat Boy's Bar-B-Q Franchise Systems offers franchises in one of the country's most successful barbeque restaurants. The restaurant serves breakfast, lunch and dinner based on a complete menu. Seating ranges from the 64 seat to the 197 seat restaurant with optional banquet facilities.

Number of Franchisees: 27 franchised, 1 company and family-owned.

In Business Since: 1958

Equity Capital Needed: $100,000-$150,000

Financial Assistance Available: Company will provide full bank and credit references to assist franchisee in obtaining his/her own outside financing. Assist in acquiring financing through established contacts.

Training Provided: Intensive in-restaurant training program. No prior restaurant experience necessary. Will completely train franchisee in operation of restaurant from cooking to purchasing and bookkeeping in an existing Fat Boy's. Training will continue until company and franchisee feel confident of franchisee's readiness for success in opening his/her own restaurant. Mandatory 400 hours.

Managerial Assistance Available: In addition to the complete training program, company will send a start-up team to each grand opening to aid the franchisee in both the kitchen and floor areas. Bookkeeping service is provided if requested. Company continually assists in all aspects of operation from promotion through menu pricing and purchasing. Establishes national purchasing accounts and provides distribution through a national distributing company. All secret recipes and cooking knowledge are passed on to the franchisee. Quality control is maintained on a regular basis throughout the chain.

Information Submitted: June 1990

FATBURGER, INC.
9229 Sunset Boulevard
Suite 718
Los Angeles, California 90069
Franchise Director

Description of Operation: Fast food hamburger stand started over 35 years ago. The high quality custom burger and the homemade chili have established a very successful customer following. The meat is the best fresh beef available and the meat patties are hand made. Food is made to order for each customer. Grill is visible for customer to view food preparation.

Number of Franchisees: 25 in California, 21 franchised and 4 company-owned.

In Business Since: 1952

Equity Capital Needed: $120,000-$175,000

Financial Assistance Available: $30,000 of the franchise fee may be financed.

Training Provided: Training up to 1 week at the franchisor's location. Supervision at the franchisee's store for up to 2 weeks, for opening.

Managerial Assistance Available: The franchisee and manager will be trained for up to 1 week at a company store. A company supervisor will be at the franchisee's store for up to 2 weeks of supervision.

Information Submitted: April 1990

FLAP JACK SHACK, INC.
3980 U.S. 31 South
Traverse City, Michigan 49684
Virginia Burley, President

Description of Operation: Food service restaurant (family type operation).

Number of Franchisees: 3 in Michigan plus 4 company-owned in Michigan and Florida.

In Business Since: 1975

Equity Capital Needed: $500,000 plus. Call franchisor for prospectus and franchise offering circulars.

Financial Assistance Available: None

Training Provided: Provide classroom and on-the-job training for 7 employees of the franchise owner. Such training to be at one of the Flap Jack Shack restaurants owned by the franchisor located in Traverse City, Michigan. Provide opening assistance starting 7 days prior to the franchise owner's opening, and continuing until 30 days thereafter, as needed.

Managerial Assistance Available: Make available to the franchise owner or individual group advice, consultation and assistance, rendered by personal visit or telephone, as the franchisor may deem necessary and appropriate. General manager and an assistant or kitchen manager shall be able to receive assistance from 7 days prior to franchise owner opening, and continued for 17 days thereafter. Continuous help and assistance by consultation thereafter. Handbooks and employee manuals are furnished to franchise owner.

Information Submitted: June 1990

FLUKY FRANCHISE SYSTEMS INTERNATIONAL, INC.
6821 North Western Avenue
Chicago, Illinois 60645
Jack Drexler, President

Description of Operation: Fast food restaurants.

Number of Franchisees: 5 in Illinois

In Business Since: 1929

Equity Capital Needed: $50,000 to $300,000

Financial Assistance Available: None

Training Provided: 1 month in company store and 2 months in franchisee's store.

Managerial Assistance Available: 2 months full supervision at franchisee's store.

Information Submitted: April 1990

FOSTERS FREEZE INTERNATIONAL, INC.
1052 Grand Avenue, Suite C
Box 266
Arroyo Grande, California 93421
Cliff Hiatt, President & CEO
Contact: Dennis Poletti, Director Franchise Development

Description of Operation: Fosters Freeze International, Inc., is a franchisor of the unexcelled Fosters Freeze soft serve desserts plus a variety of high quality food items.

Number of Franchisees: 190 in California, 2 in Arizona and 1 in Manila, the Philippines.

In Business Since: 1946

Equity Capital Needed: Estimated initial investment to commence operation of the franchised business may be $340,000 to $750,000. This includes the initial franchise fee of $40,000. The continuing franchise license fee is 4 percent of gross sales and the sales promotion fee is 3 percent of gross sales.

Financial Assistance Available: Fosters Freeze International's support team will assist in the location of financing for the franchisee.

Training Provided: Training is provided at corporate headquarters located in Arroyo Grande, California, and at company stores for franchisees and their managers.

Managerial Assistance Available: Assistance provided in the areas of menu, private label products, advertising, store openings, operations manuals, regular systemwide meetings, ongoing communications and support staff to give continued support to the franchisee.

Information Submitted: June 1990

FOUR STAR PIZZA FRANCHISING CORPORATION
Parent Company: CUTCO INDUSTRIES, INC.
P. O. Box 1370
301 Franklin Farms Road
Washington, Pennsylvania 15301
George Chavel, President

Description of Operation: Four Star Pizza specializes in the free home delivery of their special recipe pizza. Each pizza is made to order from the finest quality ingredients, and is delivered to the customer's door within 30 minutes. In addition to pizza and non-alcoholic beverages, many units offer specialty sandwiches. Fresh dough is made daily in the store along with fresh cut meats and vegetables.

Number of Franchisees: 100 in 10 States

In Business Since: 1981

Equity Capital Needed: $85,000 to open store (including franchise fee), $40,000 liquid. Franchise fee: $9,000. Bloc franchise fee. 3 or more stores, $5,000 per store.

Financial Assistance Available: For qualified applicants.

Training Provided: A minimum 24 day training program is provided for franchisees. This training includes classroom and in-store training.

Managerial Assistance Available: Support in store development, site selection, lease negotiation, store design, and marketing, as well as ongoing operational support by our franchise liaison personnel.

Information Submitted: April 1990

FOX'S PIZZA DEN INC.
3243 Old Frankstown Road
Pittsburgh, Pennsylvania 15239
James R. Fox, President

Description of Operation: Small home town pizza den operation. Open 7 days a week, 8 hours per day. Specializing in professional home delivery service. Ideal size 500 to 800 square feet. Ideal for home town individuals to work in business in their home town. Own and operate its own commissary and trucks. Private labeling on all food products.

Number of Franchisees: 120 in Western Pennsylvania, Ohio, Maryland, West Virginia, Virginia and New York.

In Business Since: 1971

Equity Capital Needed: $40,000

Financial Assistance Available: Will assist in bank financing in local towns.

Training Provided: 10 days of training

Managerial Assistance Available: Fox's Pizza Den, Inc., provides continual management service for the life of the franchise in such areas as bookkeeping, advertising, inventory control. Complete manuals of operations, forms, and directions are provided. District and field managers are available in all regions to work closely with franchisees and visit stores regularly.

Information Submitted: May 1990

FRANKIE'S FRANCHISE SYSTEMS, INC.
643 Lakewood Road
Waterbury, Connecticut 06704
Frank Caiazzo, President

Description of Operation: Fast food restaurants called Frankie's Family Restaurants offers a variety of cooked to order foods, specializing in hot dogs with a variety of toppings. Also seafood, hot oven grinders, and hamburgers.

Number of Franchisees: 8 plus 4 company-owned in Connecticut and Florida

In Business Since: 1934—started franchising in 1978

Equity Capital Needed: $35,00-$60,000

Financial Assistance Available: None

Training Provided: Complete training is provided at a company store for franchisee and store managers.

Managerial Assistance Available: Continuous assistance and supervision are provided. Franchisee is given an operations manual for all phases of operation.

Information Submitted: June 1990

FUDDRUCKERS, INC.
dba DAKA INTERNATIONAL
Two Lakeside Office Park
P. O. Box 4040
Wakefield, Massachusetts 01880

Description of Operation: Fuddruckers, Inc., operates and franchises restaurants that specialize in high-quality, upscale hamburgers cooked to order and that emphasize fresh ingredients and moderate prices in a self-serve atmosphere. The key menu items are the 1/2 and 1/3 pound hamburgers; however, the menu also includes rib-eye steak sandwiches, hot dogs, wurst, chicken sandwiches, taco salad, french fries, pinto beans, grilled onions, cookies, brownies, soft drinks and ice cream. Each restaurant has a condiment bar where customers may add lettuce, tomatoes, onions, pickles, relish, sauerkraut, melted cheese and barbeque sauce to their sandwich. All of the restaurants serve beer and wine and many serve other alcoholic beverages. Each restaurant has a butcher shop in which fresh beef is cut and ground daily and a bakery in which hamburger buns, cookies and brownies are baked daily. Each restaurant has an indoor dining area from which diners may observe the preparation of hamburgers and other foods, as well as an additional dining area under a yellow awning simulating a patio motif, and many restaurants have outdoor patios. The size of the prototypical restaurant is approximately 6,600 square feet.

Number of Franchisees: There are 73 franchised restaurants in 27 States and Canada, Mexico, Argentina, and Turkey. Franchisor is currently franchising and developing restaurants in foreign markets such as Europe, Japan and Australia.

In Business Since: 1979

Equity Capital Needed: $350,000 in liquid assets.

Financial Assistance Available: Franchisees bear all costs involved in development, construction and operation of their restaurant.

Training Provided: 6 week comprehensive training for 3 to 4 of franchisee's managers. Also provide experienced opening crew for 4 days before and 4 days after opening to assist in training franchisee's employees. Continuing inspections and evaluations of franchisee's restaurant made during the year.

Managerial Assistance Available: Franchisor will provide assistance in evaluation of sites proposed by franchisee, standard set of plans and specifications for adaptation to franchisee's site, updated confidential policies and procedures opening, periodic financial analyses or reports, and continuing advice and consultation regarding restaurant operation.

Information Submitted: May 1990

FUZZY'S, INC.
P. O. Box 151
Madison, North Carolina 27025
Fred H. Nelson, Senior Vice President

Description of Operation: A fast food Bar-B-Q restaurant with sit down/drive-thru service. The standard menu consists of chopped/sliced Bar-B-Q sandwiches, plates, trays, Fuzzy burger, hush puppies, French fries, home made banana pudding and assorted beverages.

Number of Franchisees: 2 in North Carolina

In Business Since: 1954—Fuzzy's, Inc. since 1978

Equity Capital Needed: Approximate initial investment—$150,000 cash minimum with sufficient net worth.

Financial Assistance Available: None

Training Provided: 2 weeks of on-the-job training at one of our company operated stores. 2 weeks of supervision at franchisee's outlet by a full-time representative from Fuzzy's, Inc., to assist in solving problems.

Managerial Assistance Available: Continuous assistance in areas such as quality control, inventory, advertising, etc. Operations manual provided. An ongoing inspection program designed to evaluate the individual store and advise in the physical and technical aspects of the operation.

Information Submitted: June 1990

GALLUCCI PIZZERIA INC.
2845 N.W. Highway 101
Lincoln City, Oregon 97367
Sharon Gallucci Wright, President

Description of Operation: Pizzeria, also serving soup, 40 item salad bar, sandwiches, and frozen yogurt. Restaurants have game room and giant TV. Take-out and un-cooked pizzas also sold.

Number of Franchisees: Company-owned units plus 1 franchised.

In Business Since: 1974, franchising since 1988

Equity Capital Needed: Minimum $150,000

Financial Assistance Available: None

Training Provided: Franchisee is fully trained, then receives frequent field inspections, special assistance upon request and franchisee meetings.

Managerial Assistance Available: Operations manual loaned to each franchisee. Site selection, marketing and all types of management assistance are provided.

Information Submitted: May 1990

GIFF'S SUB SHOP FRANCHISE SYSTEM, INC.
634 Eglin Parkway
Ft. Walton Beach, Florida 32548
Lance H. Arnette

Description of Operation: Custom-made submarine sandwiches; specializing in steak subs.

Number of Franchisees: 16 in Florida

In Business Since: 1977

Equity Capital Needed: $25,000-$35,000

Financial Assistance Available: None

Training Provided: 1 week at corporate headquarters and 1 week on location.

Managerial Assistance Available: Giff's provides ongoing assistance to all outlets. We help set up bookkeeping, inventory and opening equipment.

Information Submitted: May 1990

GIORDANO'S ENTERPRISES
308 West Randolph
Chicago, Illinois 60606
John Apostolou

Description of Operation: Acclaimed for Chicago's best pizza and originators of famous stuffed spinach pizza. Giordano's also serves famous stuffed sandwiches, stuffed pasta and a wide variety of salads, other products and desserts.

Number of Franchisees: 24 in Illinois and Iowa plus 8 company-owned.

In Business Since: 1974—franchising since 1980

Equity Capital Needed: Minimum $100,000 to $150,000.

Financial Assistance Available: Will assist in finding financing.

Training Provided: 6 weeks complete training course at one of the company-owned restaurants for the franchisee and their personnel. Two week supervised help on the opening of franchisee's outlet.

Mangerial Assistance Available: Provides management training, kitchen training, cooperative advertising, manual of operation and employee's handbook. Field supervision is available to fully assist in all problem areas. Meetings are held to discuss marketing, restaurant operation and product quality.

Information Submitted: June 1990

*GODFATHER'S PIZZA
9140 West Dodge Road
Omaha, Nebraska 68114
Bruce Cannon, Director of Franchise Development

Description of Operation: Godfather's Pizza offers franchises for the development and operation of Godfather's Pizza restaurants. Specializing in high quality pizza with thick crust and plentiful toppings, each restaurant sells a variety of pizza products, salads, beverages, and sandwiches in some locations. Average Godfather Pizza units are approximately 3,000 square feet in size, and are located in or near major shopping areas. Most restaurants offer a combination of dine-in, take-out, and delivery service.

Number of Franchisees: 62 operating 317 units in 379 States and 171 company-owned restaurants.

In Business Since: 1973

Equity Capital Needed: $200,000 minimum net worth, excluding personal property, $100,000 of which is in cash or liquid assets.

Financial Assistance Available: None

Training Provided: All training programs offered by Godfather's Pizza are provided free of charge, excluding transportation and accommodation expenses. Training consists of several comprehensive elements, including a 5 day owner's orientation providing new franchisees with a basic understanding of restaurant operations. Also offered is a 5 week operator's training program. This program is conducted in a Certified Training Restaurant designated by Godfather's Pizza and acquaints new operators with all aspects of operations management. A wide variety of videotapes and audio/visual presentations are available for training other franchise personnel.

Managerial Assistance Available: The franchisor assigns each franchisee a regional franchise manager to provide assistance to the franchisee in operation matters. The franchisor's field marketing staff all provides marketing support in the development of new products and enhancement of existing products.

Information Submitted: April 1990

GOLDEN CHICKEN FRANCHISES
3810 West National Avenue
Milwaukee, Wisconsin 53215
Bryan Bloom

Description of Operation: Fast food offering both carry-outs and home delivery. Specializing in chicken, pizza and seafood. Open minimum of 6 days per week for 7 hours each day. Each store requires approximately 800 square feet of space. Franchisee provides own space and equipment. Stores are located in store fronts and preferably strip shopping centers.

Number of Franchisees: 15 in Wisconsin and Minnesota plus 1 company-owned.

In Business Since: 1959

Equity Capital Needed: $3,500 for franchise fee plus net cost for equipment and setup.

Financial Assistance Available: A total investment of approximately $30,000 is needed. Franchisor does no financing but will assist franchisee in securing sources. Primary source of financing has been leasing company. Franchisee puts up $6,000 for franchise fee, lease and security deposits and working capital. Balance usually financed over 60 month period.

Training Provided: Franchisee must spend 7 days at a company store. Franchisor spends 14 days with franchisee in his own unit after opening.

Managerial Assistance Available: Golden Chicken provides continual management service for the life of licensing agreement in such areas as bookkeeping, advertising and promotions. Franchisor visits stores a minimum of once a year, sponsors meetings of franchisees and keeps franchisee informed of new products and promotions via news letters.

Information Submitted: June 1990

*GOLDEN CORRAL FRANCHISING SYSTEMS, INC.
5151 Glenwood Avenue
Raleigh, North Carolina 27612
Larry I. Tate, Vice President, Franchising

Description of Operation: Franchisor of Golden Corral Family Steakhouse Restaurants. Golden Corral is the largest operator of company-owned Family Steakhouse Restaurants in the world. Golden Corral was founded in 1973 and opened over 400 company-owned Steakhouse Restaurants before franchising its first location.

Number of Franchisees: 12 in 11 States

In Business Since: 1986

Equity Capital Needed: $110,000-$225,000

Financial Assistance Available: None for new franchise locations. Assistance varies for conversion of company-owned locations.

Training Provided: 2 weeks classroom training and 8 weeks on-the-job training in the managerial training program will be completed approximately 8 weeks prior to opening.

Managerial Assistance Available: We provide extensive training program, operations manual, supplemental training program and accounting forms and procedures, building plan and specifications, national purchasing program, marketing and promotions assistance, new product development and testing.

Information Submitted: April 1990

GOLDEN FRANCHISING CORPORATION
4835 LBJ Freeway
Suite 525
Dallas, Texas 75244
Mark S. Parmerlee, President

Description of Operation: Golden Franchising Corporation is a franchisor of Golden Fried Chicken fast food restaurants, specializing in quality fried chicken and appropriate side orders. A typical restaurant requires 2,000 square feet and a drive-thru window.

Number of Franchisees: 31 operating 69 restaurants in Texas, Oklahoma and Arkansas.

In Business Since: 1967

Equity Capital Needed: Minimum liquid net worth is $75,000. Typical restaurant costs under $400,000 including land, building, equipment, and working capital.

Financial Assistance Available: None

Training Provided: Pre-opening training and opening support.

Managerial Assistance Available: GFC provides continuous support for the life of the franchise, including pre-opening assistance, marketing programs, negotiation of national purchase contracts, operations manuals, regular visits by field personnel, and product, equipment, and market research.

Information Submitted: March 1990

GOLDEN SKILLET INTERNATIONAL, INC.
P. O. Box 35286
Minneapolis, Minnesota 55439
Glenn Lindsey, Executive Vice President

Description of Operation: Golden Skillet International, Inc., operates and franchises a chain of fast food restaurants featuring a unique fried chicken. Restaurants are free-standing with country kitchen decor. Golden Skillet promotes friendly and courteous service, high standards of restaurant cleanliness, and top quality food products. The fried chicken cooking process and cooker are patented. Golden Skillet is a subsidiary of International Dairy Queen, Inc.

Number of Franchisees: Over 71 in 7 States, Puerto Rico and Japan.

In Business Since: 1963

Equity Capital Needed: The franchise fees are $25,000 for plan A plus $15,000 for initial sales promotion. All prospective franchisees must meet certain financial requirements.

Financial Assistance Available: Qualified franchisees may purchase equipment on a conditional sales contract over a 5 year payment period with the required down payment.

Training Provided: Franchisees are required to complete a 2 week scheduled first phase training session in basic operations. Support training, second phase, by operations department at franchisee's new restaurant.

Managerial Assistance Available: Golden Skillet provides full-range support services including real estate consultation, building plans and specifications, equipment training, maintenance, accounting, marketing. The company provides an operations manual, marketing handbook, plus field representative consultations and assistance.

Information Submitted: April 1990

GOLDIE'S RESTAURANTS INC.
8332 East 73rd Street South
Tulsa, Oklahoma 74133
Richard K. Harkey, Vice President Franchising

Description of Operation: Goldie's Restaurants Inc. operates and franchises Goldie's Patio Grill Restaurants. Goldie's are full service limited menu family restaurants serving primarily charbroiled, cooked to order 1/3 lb. burgers seasoned with Goldie's special spices. Charbroiled chicken breast sandwiches and dinners are also offered along with charburger steak dinners, rib eye and strip steak dinners and Goldie's country gravy.

Number of Franchisees: Goldie's has 5 franchisees operating 7 restaurants in 3 States. There are 7 company-owned locations also.

In Business Since: 1962

Equity Capital Needed: An ability to finance an investment of $100,000-$300,000.

Financial Assistance Available: None

Training Provided: 6 weeks intensive training for managers and cooks in company-owned location. 4 days training for all crew members prior to opening. Operations personnel will be on-site for 2 to 4 weeks after opening.

Managerial Assistance Available: Goldie's offers ongoing assistance in operations and marketing. Operations personnel will make visits to franchisee's restaurant to insure QSC standards are met and to assist in problem solving. Goldie's is available at all times to the franchisee to offer assistance in any related problems the franchisee may have.

Information Submitted: April 1990

GOLD STAR CHILI, INC.
5204 Beechmont Avenue
Cincinnati, Ohio 45230
Raymond P. Peterson, Franchise Manager

Description of Operation: Gold Star Chili is a specialty restaurant, featuring our chili. The single item menu concept assures the highest quality control, at the same time permitting a high volume of sales with a minimum of employees. Locations are free standing (2,100 square feet), or in mall food courts (450 to 600 square feet).

Number of Franchisees: 77 in Ohio, Kentucky, Florida, and Missouri

In Business Since: 1964

Equity Capital Needed: $12,000 franchise fee, equipment approximately $50,000.

Financial Assistance Available: None

Training Provided: On-the-job training provided for operations personnel for a minimum of 2 weeks.

Managerial Assistance Available: Site location, equipment layout, consulting assistance for installation of equipment, opening—specialized field consultant up to 1 week, advertising and promotional materials and continuing unit inspection.

Information Submitted: June 1990

GOOD EARTH CORPORATION
23945 Calabasas Road
Suite 107
Calabasas, California 91302
E. R. Wilson, President

Description of Operation: The Good Earth Corporation offers restaurant franchises which sell health-oriented foods, substantially free of preservatives, artificial flavors and colors.

Number of Franchisees: 15 in California

In Business Since: 1986

Equity Capital Needed: Approximately between $579,000 and $775,000

Financial Assistance Available: None

Training Provided: The following positions are required to pursue and complete the franchisor's operations training course: franchisee and/or general manager, 1 assistant manager, 1 kitchen manager and 1 baker. This course lasts approximately 1 month.

Managerial Assistance Available: Franchisor will make available to the franchisee names of approved suppliers; consultation on-site adaptation equipment; opening supervision and consultation at the franchisee's premises during not less than 30 days; standard chart of accounts, cashier's training systems and portion control systems; marketing research and advice; recipes, food preparation instructions; also additional services, facilities, rights and privileges used in the program will be made available from time to time.

Information Submitted: June 1990

GRAND RESTAURANT CORP.
2025-D Leestown Road
Lexington, Kentucky 40511
James Hoff, Franchise Director

Description of Operation: Grand Junction Hamburger Stations offer both the consumer and franchise investor a system of fast food at affordable prices. The small, double-drive-thru facilities require low investment for land, building and up-keep, thereby allowing the consumer to enjoy quality fast food at prices approximately 25 percent less than those of major franchisors', limited menu.

Number of Franchisees: 7

In Business Since: Established in 1984

Equity Capital Needed: Cash investment: $60,000-$150,000.

Financial Assistance Available: None

Training Provided: 3 weeks at headquarters.

Managerial Assistance Available: Yes

Information Submitted: April 1990

*GRANDY'S, INCORPORATED
997 Grandy's Lane
Lewisville, Texas 75067
Franchise Department

Description of Operation: Fast food chicken restaurant.

Number of Franchisees: 89 units in 19 States

In Business Since: 1973

Equity Capital Needed: $750,000-$900,000

Financial Assistance Available: No financial assistance available through Grady's, Inc.

Training Provided: 5 weeks, 6 days a week, classroom and on-the-job training in all facets of the restaurant. 6 day overview course of study available for owners and their executive officers.

Managerial Assistance Available: Complete line of operational training, real estate construction and marketing services.

Information Submitted: April 1990

GREENSTREETS NATIONAL CORPORATION
72 Garden Drive
Burnsville, Minnesota 55337
Gordon Weber, President

Description of Operation: Hamburger grill and bar.

Number of Franchisees: 3 in Minnesota

In Business Since: 1982

Equity Capital Needed: $50,000-$150,000

Financial Assistance Available: None

Training Provided: 1 month initial training plus ongoing in all phases of operation.

Managerial Assistance Available: 1 month initial managerial assistance plus ongoing.

Information Submitted: April 1990

HACIENDA FRANCHISING GROUP, INC.
HACIENDA MEXICAN RESTAURANTS
3302 Mishawaka Avenue
South Bend, Indiana 46615
Dean Goodwin, Vice President
Gary White, Director of Franchise Development

Description of Operation: The Hacienda Mexican Restaurants are high volume Mexican full service restaurants and lounges. Menu pricing and portions reflect a commitment to a strong price/value relationship.

Number of Franchisees: 2

In Business Since: 1978

Equity Capital Needed: Varies by location, generally $100,000-$200,000.

Financial Assistance Available: None

Training Provided: Hacienda Franchising Group, Inc., provides an intensive 4 week training course for the franchisee and an approved manager at Hacienda's home office, including hands-on experience at a local operation. Training is also provided at the franchisee's location for initial staff 1 week before opening and for at least 2 weeks after opening.

Managerial Assistance Available: Hacienda Franchising Group, Inc., provides management services long after the restaurant opens. Operations manuals, site selections, training guides, advertising assistance, and field support are all at the franchisee's disposal. Field representatives are available to work closely with franchisees and visit restaurants to assist in solving problems.

Information Submitted: April 1990

HAPPY JOE'S PIZZA & ICE CREAM PARLORS
2705 Commerce Drive
Bettendorf, Iowa 52722
Lawrence J. Whitty, President and Chairman of the Board

Description of Operation: Happy Joe's Pizza & Ice Cream Parlors specialize in delivery, take-out, and catering to families and feature superb pizza and premium quality ice cream creations. Family appeal is emphasized with birthday party celebrations a house specialty.

Number of Franchisees: 56 in 7 States and Cairo, Egypt.

In Business Since: 1972

Equity Capital Needed: Approximately $80,000-$500,000

Financial Assistance Available: None

Training Provided: Extensive on-the-job training, including all facets of the operation, lasting up to 30 days.

Managerial Assistance Available: Complete assistance and supervision in opening the business and an ongoing program of managerial and operational training and assistance from field supervisors. Additional assistance in advertising and promotion is also available.

Information Submitted: May 1990

HAPPY STEAK COMPANIES, INC.
2246 East Date Avenue
Fresno, California 93706
Randy Brooks, Vice President

Description of Operation: Family style budget steakhouse.

Number of Franchisees: Happy Steak, Inc. (28), Perko's, Inc. (41) in California and Nevada.

In Business Since: 1969

Equity Capital Needed: $95,000

Financial Assistance Available: None

Training Provided: Complete on-the-job restaurant training prior to opening—then as needed.

Managerial Assistance Available: Minimum monthly scheduled visits of 4 hours.

Information Submitted: June 1990

*HARDEE'S FOOD SYSTEMS, INC.
1233 North Church Street
Rocky Mount, North Carolina 27801-1619
Roger Attanas, National Director
of Franchise Sales

Description of Operation: Hardee's offers its customers one of the most diverse product offerings in the industry, ranging from a strong breakfast menu to thick and juicy burgers, specialty sandwiches, garden fresh salads, beverages, and desserts.

Number of Franchisees: 2,072 in 40 States and 9 foreign countries, 1,038 company-owned restaurants.

In Business Since: 1961

Equity Capital Needed: $500,000 net worth (excluding personal residence), $150,000 liquid assets.

Financial Assistance Available: None

Training Provided: Hardee's provides 6 weeks training for the owner and the management staff.

Managerial Assistance Available: Hardee's provides continued supervision on a scheduled basis, to include franchise development, real estate, construction, distribution, equipment, advertising direction, complete operating manual, continued advice and counseling.

Information Submitted: April 1990

HARTZ KRISPY CHICKEN
dba HARTZOG, INC.
14409 Cornerstone Village Drive
Houston, Texas 77014
Milton Lambert, President

Description of Operation: Hartz Krispy Chicken is a fast food operation maintaining excellence of quality and providing the utmost in customer service. Krispy fried chicken the main menu item. Side orders include potato salad, cole slaw, french fries, and corn on the cob. All food is served in an Early American atmosphere or may be taken out.

Number of Franchisees: 32 franchisees in Texas, Mississippi, Alabama and Georgia operating 47 locations.

In Business Since: 1972

Equity Capital Needed: $200,000 not including land and building. Acquisition of real estate is a franchisee responsibility.

Financial Assistance Available: None. Franchisee is responsible for obtaining all financing.

Training Provided: Hartz requires at least 200 hours training at the franchisee's expense. Training facilities are provided by Hartz in Houston, Texas. Assistance and guidance, but not labor, is supplied during pre-opening stages.

Managerial Assistance Available: Hartz personnel continuously inspect and oversee franchise stores in order to maintain uniformity and quality. Discourse and correspondence are maintained with franchisees on a daily basis.

Information Submitted: June 1990

HEAVENLY HOT DOGS, INC.
2804 Del Prado Boulevard
Cape Coral, Florida 33904

Description of Operation: Retail sale of all beef vienna hot dogs, served Chicago style, related food products, and premium draft root beer. Outlets specially designed to be owned, operated or to employ the physically handicapped.

Number of Franchisees: 3 company-owned outlets, franchisees in Colorado, North and South Carolina, Chicago-area, and Illinois.

In Business Since: 1985

Equity Capital Needed: $55,000-$200,000

Financial Assistance Available: None

Training Provided: Yes

Managerial Assistance Available: Yes

Information Submitted: April 1990

HENNY O'ROURKES
7516 Heatherwood Lane
Cincinnati, Ohio 45244
Jeff Osterfeld

Description of Operation: Henny O'Rourkes serves "Just Chicken, Just Right." We specialize in a variety of sandwiches, nuggets and salads. Store locations include regional shopping malls and any special large scale retail centers.

Number of Franchisees: 2

In Business Since: 1988

Equity Capital Needed: $96,000-$160,000

Financial Assistance Available: None

Training Provided: 2 weeks of training in all phases of operation in Cincinnati, Ohio.

Managerial Assistance Available: We provide grand opening assistance and monthly ongoing support on an as needed basis.

Information Submitted: April 1990

HIGH WHEELER ICE CREAM PARLOUR/RESTAURANT
5192 William Street
Kalamazoo, Michigan 49009

Description of Operation: Large turn-of-the-century, family-oriented ice cream parlour restaurants, featuring an extensive ice cream creation menu and over 45 flavors of ice cream, gourmet hamburgers, lunches and dinners. Further enhanced by an old-fashioned candy and bake shoppe where fudge, chocolates, candies, brownies, cookies and breads are made in view of the customers.

Number of Franchisees: 4 plus 2 company-owned.

In Business Since: 1975, franchising in 1986

Equity Capital Needed: $100,000, total investment $1,000,000

Financial Assistance Available: Available to qualified prospects.

Training Provided: 8 week full training in all aspects of operation at company headquarters.

Managerial Assistance Available: Complete ongoing managerial support.

Information Submitted: April 1990

HUBB'S PUB
P. O. Box 279
Altamonte Springs, Florida 32701
Fran Ungar

Description of Operation: Pub restaurant with a specialty in draft imported beer (30 kinds) and deli sandwiches.

Number of Franchisees: 4 in Florida

In Business Since: 1983

Equity Capital Needed: Minimum $75,000

Financial Assistance Available: Will help secure financing.

Training Provided: Required 3 weeks, optional 3 weeks added.

Managerial Assistance Available: Constant

Information Submitted: April 1990

*HUDDLE HOUSE, INC.
2969 East Ponce De Leon Avenue
Decatur, Georgia 30030
Douglas Kley, Executive Vice President

Description of Operation: 24 hour convenience restaurant, full service, featuring breakfast, steaks, seafood items and sandwiches.

Number of Franchisees: 101 in 10 States

In Business Since: 1964

Equity Capital Needed: $48,613-$498,643

Financial Assistance Available: None

Training Provided: 30 days of classroom and hands-on experience in training unit; 10 days to 2 weeks on-site training during pre-opening and early stages of opening period.

Managerial Assistance Available: Training, site selection and construction specifications and assistance, continuous supervision, central food distribution center purchasing, restaurant equipment and supplies, operation manuals, daily accounting forms; franchise field consultants work closely with owner/operators to solve problems and promote profits.

Information Submitted: April 1990

THE HUNGRY HOBO
5306—23rd Avenue
Moline, Illinois 61265
Ray Pearson, Vice President-Sales

Description of Operation: Fast food restaurant specializing in deli sandwiches. We also bake our own bread. Sell 6 food party sandwiches and cater party buffet trays. Baked potatoes and taco salads.

Number of Franchisees: 8 and 10 company-owned in Illinois and Iowa

In Business Since: 1969

Equity Capital Needed: $55,000 to $100,000

Financial Assistance Available: Legal assistance in negotiating a loan.

Training Provided: On-the-job training in sandwich making, portion control of meats and cheeses. Cost controls, advertising, purchasing, inventory control, financial statements—2 weeks.

Managerial Assistance Available: Start-up crew provided for the opening of new location until new employees are properly trained. Weekly reports, monthly financial statements and other records monitored by franchisor. Scheduled and unscheduled visits to franchisee on a monthly basis.

Information Submitted: June 1990

INTERNATIONAL DAIRY QUEEN, INC.
P. O. Box 35286
Minneapolis, Minnesota 55435
John Hyduke, Vice President, Franchise Development

Description of Operation: International Dairy Queen, Inc., is engaged in developing, licensing and servicing a system of franchised retail stores that offer a selected menu of soft dairy products, hamburgers and beverages marketed under Dairy Queen, Brazier and Mr. Misty trademark.

Number of Franchisees: There are currently over 5,177 Dairy Queen and Dairy Queen/Brazier stores located in all 50 States and 12 foreign countries.

In Business Since: The soft serve dairy product was first offered to the public in 1938 with the first Dairy Queen store being opened in 1940. In 1962 certain territorial operators formed International Dairy Queen, Inc., by contributing their respective Dairy Queen territorial franchise rights.

Equity Capital Needed: The franchise fees are $30,000. All prospective franchisees must meet certain financial requirements.

Financial Assistance Available: Qualified franchisees may purchase equipment on a conditional sales contract over a 5 year payment period with the required down payment.

Training Provided: International Dairy Queen, Inc.'s national training center in Minneapolis, Minnesota offers an intensive 2 week training course to all new and existing franchisees. The course covers sanitation, sales promotion, inventory control and basic functions of management. The company also offers new franchisees the services of a special opening team that assists operators in opening their new Dairy Queen or Dairy Queen/Brazier store.

Managerial Assistance Available: International Dairy Queen, Inc., maintains an operations specialty division in addition to regional and district managers, who provide continuing assistance involving store operation, product quality, customer convenience, product development, advertising, financial control, training, communication and incentives. A research and development department is engaged in developing new products, cooking methods and procedures. Sales promotion programs are conducted through newspapers, radio, television and billboards.

Information Submitted: June 1990

INTERNATIONAL SHORT STOP, INC.
720 Brazos
Suite 1210
Austin, Texas 78701
Jay Caldwall, Director of Franchising

Description of Operation: Short Stop sells franchises for the operation of drive-thru restaurants featuring the sale of high quality hamburgers, French fries and soft drinks.

Number of Franchisees: 45 in Texas, Florida, Louisiana, North Carolina, Missouri, and New Mexico.

In Business Since: 1984

Equity Capital Needed: $180,000 per store

Financial Assistance Available: None

Training Provided: 30 day training school

Managerial Assistance Available: Pre-opening assistance, operating assistance, site selection and training programs.

Information Submitted: April 1990

IRVINGS FOR RED HOT LOVERS
3330 Old Glenview Road
Suite 3
Wilmette, Illinois 60091
Andrew Greenspan

Description of Operation: Irvings For Red Hot Lovers offers a wide variety of menu items which are all made to order. Menu includes hot dogs, hamburgers, polish sausage, italian beefs, charbroiled chicken, baked potato, salads, and our special cheddar fries to name a few. We are a fast service oriented operation with an upscale look and menu. Store size varies from 1,200 to 3,000 square feet.

Number of Franchisees: 5 plus 9 company-owned

In Business Since: 1975

Equity Capital Needed: $45,000-$65,000, total investment $155,000-$185,000.

Financial Assistance Available: None

Training Provided: A 4 week training program prior to opening. 2 week training during grand opening.

Managerial Assistance Available: Site selection, lease negotiation, architectural outlines, buildout, equipment specifications, training, confidential operations manual, grand opening training, ongoing supervision and inspection of operations.

Information Submitted: April 1990

ITALO'S PIZZA SHOP, INC.
3560 Middlebranch Road, N.E.
Canton, Ohio 44705
Italo P. Ventura

Description of Operation: Italo's Pizza franchise is designed for small investors. Any store over 900 square feet can be turned into a profit making operation. For the next 2 years Italo's Pizza Shop, Inc., is concentrating expansion only in Ohio.

Number of Franchisees: 10 and 3 company-owned in Ohio

In Business Since: 1966, franchising since 1975

Equity Capital Needed: $12,000

Financial Assistance Available: A total investment of $62,250 for carry-out only and about $95,500 with dining room. Franchisee must provide outside financing.

Training Provided: Intensive 2 months on-the-job training in our main location, 2 weeks of assistance at the time of opening, and continuing assistance as needed.

Managerial Assistance Available: Italo's Pizza provides continual assistance and recommendations in any area. Forms and manuals are provided for the smooth performance of the business. Weekly or monthly visits by franchisor to help solve any problem and continued assistance by phone for any emergency.

Information Submitted: April 1990

*JACK IN THE BOX FOODMAKER, INC.
9330 Balboa Avenue
P. O. Box 783
San Diego, California 92112
William Thelen, Division Vice President, Franchise Development

Description of Operation: Jack in the Box is a popular fast food chain in the Western States with hamburgers as a mainstay, but best known for the variety in menu. The first to have remote-entry drive-through ordering, five years ago Jack in the Box also revolutionized the fast food menu from "hamburger and fries" to bacon cheeseburgers, chicken supreme sandwiches, breakfasts, Mexican food, and salads to go. Jack in the Box is offering a unique chance to buy existing restaurant units in many major market areas. This assists new franchisees to become knowledgeable in the fast food business quickly. Also offered are new-store development possibilities and some exclusive territory agreements. Jack in the Box is searching for the experienced businessperson who wants multiple store ownership.

Number of Franchisees: Over 217 locations. The company operates 665 restaurants, all west of the Mississippi.

In Business Since: 1951

Equity Capital Needed: Existing restaurants: $140,000 liquid assets minimum; much higher net worth required to construct new units and obtain development rights.

Financial Assistance Available: Existing restaurant: The cost of a unit is estimated to be in the range of $275,000-$400,000 excluding the land and building. Franchisee will be required to invest 40 percent of actual investment at the onset of the venture. New restaurants: Franchisees are required to have adequate net worth to obtain land, building and equipment. Foodmaker prefers any needed financing be obtained from outside sources in both instances.

Training Provided: Comprehensive 8 weeks field training program in 4 major cities plus 3 days classroom time in San Diego. Within 6 months after taking over restaurant, franchisee will be required to return to San Diego for 1 week of advanced management training.

Managerial Assistance Available: Franchise operations consultants are available in the field to work closely with franchisees and visit stores regularly to assist in solving problems.

Information Submitted: June 1990

JAKE'S INTERNATIONAL, INC.
1204 Carnegie Street
Rolling Meadows, Illinois 60008

Description of Operation: Jake's International is a franchised pizza operation. Emphasis is on high quality food, cleanliness and efficient service in the carry-out and delivery food industry. Pub type operations with full dining rooms and cocktail lounges are also available.

Number of Franchisees: 22 in Illinois

In Business Since: 1962

Equity Capital Needed: $78,500 minimum and the ability to acquire financing.

Financial Assistance Available: Equipment leasing if elected by the franchisee and if qualified.

Training Provided: Minimum of 200 hours in actual operations. Additional management training is provided on-the-job and throughout the duration of the franchise.

Managerial Assistance Available: Training, operations management, on-site field consulting and quality control assistance and market available promotional advertising material. Access to central commissary, if desired.

Information Submitted: April 1990

JERRY'S SUB SHOP
15942 Shady Grove Road
Gaithersburg, Maryland 20877
Kathleen L. McDonald

Description of Operation: The chain is famous for its "over-stuffed" subs and pizza. The self-service concept is placed in high volume, high traffic locations in very pleasant, up-scale surroundings; beer and wine complement the menu.

Number of Franchisees: 70 in 5 States and Washington, D.C.

In Business Since: 1954

Equity Capital Needed: $19,500 franchise fee and approximately $50,000 additionally for deposits, etc.

Financial Assistance Available: Assistance in loan preparation as well as contacts to particular SBA programs that franchise qualifies for.

Training Provided: Extensive training both in classroom as well as unit operation. Follow-up training in franchisee's own site is also provided.

Managerial Assistance Available: When a new store opens, Jerry's places a start-up team of trained supervisors in the store to help with the opening. The franchisor then has site supervisors visit the store twice a month, more if necessary, to assist the franchisee in running an efficient operation.

Information Submitted: April 1990

JIMBOY'S TACOS
JIMBOY'S MARKETING, INC.
3112 "O" Street, Suite 2
Sacramento, California 95816
George Heath, Vice President, Franchise Development

Description of Operation: Jimboy's Marketing, Inc., offers franchises in California and Nevada. Mexican restaurants serving a limited menu for both in-house dining and take-out orders.

Number of Franchisees: 27 units in California and Nevada.

In Business Since: 1977

Equity Capital Needed: $150,000

Financial Assistance Available: No financing is available from franchisor at this time.

Training Provided: Operations manual is provided to franchisee, in-store training followed by ongoing assistance to the franchise through periodic store inspections and visits. Continuous promotional and advertising campaigns.

Managerial Assistance Available: See above.

Information Submitted: April 1990

JO ANN'S CHILI BORDELLO, INC.
2652 Atlantic Boulevard
Jacksonville, Florida 32207
Leonard Doctors, President

Description of Operation: A specialty restaurant serving 15 varieties of gourmet chili, gourmet hamburgers, plus a selection of fancy sandwiches in an operation designed to run with a minimum of labor and food costs.

Number of Franchisees: 10 in Florida, Nevada and Arizona

In Business Since: 1981

Equity Capital Needed: $60,000-$150,000

Financial Assistance Available: Franchisees to provide their own financing.

Training Provided: Training at franchisee site, 2-3 weeks and home office.

Managerial Assistance Available: Training at franchisee site and home office.

Information Submitted: June 1990

JOHNNY ROCKETS
1145 Gayley Avenue
Los Angeles, California 90024
Carl Jeffers, Franchise Director

Description of Operation: Johnny Rockets is a retro diner with a bold contemporary flair. Each store is approximately 900-1,500 square feet and houses a 20-28 stool counter. Stores are open 13 to 15 hours daily, 7 days a week. A lean, well defined menu is maintained. In addition to regular Johnny Rockets 900 to 1,500 square feet there is also a new Johnny Rockets designed especially for malls using 600 square feet. This mall Johnny Rockets requires $150,000.

Number of Franchisees: 11 in California, Illinois and Georgia and 1 in Tokyo.

In Business Since: 1986

Equity Capital Needed: $250,000 minimum

Financial Assistance Available: None

Training Provided: Intensive 30 day mandatory training course is scheduled for all new franchisees and their personnel. Training program is conducted at the home office school and on-site at the company store.

Managerial Assistance Available: Johnny Rockets provides continual management service for the life of the franchise in such areas as operations, inventory control, promotion and/or advertising. Complete manuals of operations, forms, and directions are provided. Field managers are available in all regions to work closely with franchisees and visit stores regularly to assist in solving problems.

Information Submitted: April 1990

JOYCE'S SUBMARINE SANDWICHES, INC.
1527 Havana Street
Aurora, Colorado 80010
David Meaux, President

Description of Operation: Fast food franchise consisting of submarine and deli sandwiches, soup, chili, salad bar, soft drinks, snacks and desserts. Operates in 1,000-1,500 square feet leased space. Open 7 days per week.

Number of Franchisees: 41 in Colorado, Montana, Nebraska, and Wyoming.

In Business Since: 1971

Equity Capital Needed: $25,000 minimum down payment for turnkey store operation.

Financial Assistance Available: The total cost of a Joyce's Sub Shop operation is $50,000. $25,000 is required for a down payment. Joyce's Submarine Sandwiches, Inc., will carry back note for balance of $25,000 to acceptable persons with good credit references. Franchisee has option to arrange own outside financing.

Training Provided: Joyce's Subs provides 3 weeks free, intensive training for up to 2 persons at company-owned training store. Franchisee trained in menu preparation, inventory ordering and portion control, customer and employee relations, expense control, and fast food marketing techniques.

Managerial Assistance Available: Periodic monitoring of store operations by Joyce's corporate staff to assure product quality control, hygiene, customer relations, inventory and portion control, expense control, marketing techniques, and development of advertising and promotion programs. Joyce's provides complete training manual and conducts periodic owners' meetings to assist in problem solving and assure quality in its operations.

Information Submitted: April 1990

JRECK SUBS, INC.
P. O. Box 6
Watertown, New York 13601
H. Thomas Swartz, President

Description of Operation: Sit-down and carry-out of submarine sandwiches in all stores. Stores vary in size and volume depending on market area.

Number of Franchisees: 60 in New York

In Business Since: 1967

Equity Capital Needed: $50,000 plus

Financial Assistance Available: Franchisor will aid in securing outside financing in an advisory role.

Training Provided: 3 weeks of intensive in-store training, including sandwich preparation, store management, bookkeeping, personnel management and operational procedures.

Managerial Assistance Available: Marketing, advertising, operational assistance on a continuous basis.

Information Submitted: April 1990

JR.'S HOT DOGS INTERNATIONAL
1661 North Swan
Suite 100
Tucson, Arizona 85712
Roy Vander Wall

Description of Operation: Carry-out and sit-down fast food. Hot dogs, chili dogs, cheese dogs, beef sandwiches, cold drinks, French fries and Polish sausage.

Number of Franchisees: 23 in 2 States plus 4 company-owned.

In Business Since: 1969

Equity Capital Needed: $75,000-$125,000

Financial Assistance Available: None

Training Provided: Complete on-the-job and classroom training.

Managerial Assistance Available: We will assist in site selection, hiring, set-up of new location, and overall operation for the first few weeks of operation.

Information Submitted: June 1990

J-SYSTEMS FRANCHISING, INC.
3134 Lehigh Street
Allentown, Pennsylvania 18103
Harold G. Fulmer, President

Description of Operation: J's Steaks and Subs is a fast food submarine sandwich shop featuring steak sandwiches, a variety of cold and hot subs, salads, and side orders for eat-in or take-out.

Number of Franchisees: 34 in Pennsylvania, New Jersey and New York.

In Business Since: 1968

Equity Capital Needed: $50,000 minimum

Financial Assistance Available: None

Training Provided: Training program is held 2 weeks prior to opening covering all aspects of the operation. A J's representative will spend 2 weeks, or more as needed, at the franchisee's premises to facilitate opening.

Managerial Assistance Available: Provide ongoing training and supervision of franchisee's unit. Provide to franchisee advancements and new developments through the operating manual, bulletins, and other promotional material. J-Systems will administer and direct a national advertising fund for group advertising.

Information Submitted: April 1990

J. T. MCCORD'S RESTAURANTS
1701 North Greenville
Suite 900
Richardson, Texas 75081
Howell Kemp

Description of Operation: J. T. McCord's is a full service restaurant and bar that specializes in "gourmet style hamburgers," assorted finger foods, and a variety of sandwiches and dinners. It is medium priced dining in a casual atmosphere with large quantities of tasty food.

Number of Franchisees: 5 including company-owned in Texas.

In Business Since: 1978

Equity Capital Needed: $350,000 estimated

Financial Assistance Available: The capital requirements to open a J. T. McCord's will vary depending on local real estate values and costs to either purchase or lease the facility. Flagship estimates the total capital requirements will range between $500,000 and $1,500,000. Flagship does not provide any financing.

Training Provided: A comprehensive training program must be completed by all members of management. A minimum of 8 weeks is spent at the company training store in Dallas, Texas. Hourly training is also provided in the restaurant by the franchisor, prior to restaurant opening.

Managerial Assistance Available: J. T. McCord's continues to provide assistance to each franchisee throughout the term of the agreement. A regional manager visits each restaurant periodically to assist in operations. Each franchisee receives a set of operations manuals and constant assistance in areas of marketing, menu development, food and equipment procurement, real estate, architectural services, staffing and training.

Information Submitted: June 1990

K-BOB'S, INC.
5757 Alpha Road
Suite 716
Dallas, Texas 75240
Vice President of Development

Description of Operation: Family western style steakhouse, full sit down service, steaks, salad wagon, chicken, fish, hamburgers and Mexican. Each restaurant is approximately 4,000 to 6,000 square feet.

Number of Franchisees: 61 in Texas, Oklahoma, New Mexico, Kansas, Colorado and Arizona.

In Business Since: 1966

Equity Capital Needed: $100,000 to $200,000, estimated based on location and whether remodeled or new construction.

Financial Assistance Available: None

Training Provided: 6 to 8 weeks of management training, standard building plans and equipment package, site selection and marketing analysis. On-site opening assistance, 2 weeks. Continual operational assistance.

Managerial Assistance Available: Continual operational assistance.

Information Submitted: April 1990

*KEN'S PIZZA
4441 South 72nd East Avenue
Tulsa, Oklahoma 74145
Dan Brand

Description of Operation: The Ken's Pizza concept entails an integrated system using an attractive free-standing building with a drive-thru window, a unique limited menu and a simplified operating concept. Taken all together, the system combines a profitable menu with confortable table service format. Ken's Pizza is owned by Ken's Restaurant Systems, Inc., which has been in business for 23 years.

Number of Franchisees: 26 locations plus 30 company-owned in 11 States.

In Business Since: 1961

Equity Capital Needed: Initial franchise fee—$20,000. Land, building and equipment must be financed by franchisee.

Financial Assistance Available: None

Training Provided: Training program provided in Tulsa, Oklahoma, training restaurant. Program is extensive and follows a formal management training manual. Time required varies between 4-15 weeks depending on capabilities and previous experience of franchisee.

Managerial Assistance Available: 3 full-time employees travel among franchise stores offering operational assistance, further training and inspections. Company regularly conducts new product and training seminars in its Tulsa facilities. All franchisees are invited to these seminars.

Information Submitted: June 1990

*KETTLE RESTAURANTS, INC.
dba KETTLE RESTAURANTS
P. O. Box 2964
Houston, Texas 77252
Philip W. Weaver, Director of Franchise

Description of Operation: Full service 24-hour family restaurants.

Number of Franchisees: 111 in 71 States (95 company-owned)

In Business Since: 1968

Equity Capital Needed: $139,000

Financial Assistance Available: None

Training Provided: On-the-job training from 2 to 16 weeks.

Managerial Assistance Available: Managerial instruction given during the normal on-the-job training. Technical assistance given by franchisor to key personnel prior to opening for business and after opening until the operation stabilizes. Periodic visits thereafter, approximately every quarter or more often if deemed necessary or requested.

Information Submitted: June 1990

*KFC CORPORATION
P. O. Box 32070
Louisville, Kentucky 40232
Walter J. Simon, Vice President, Franchising,
Domestic

Description of Operation: Sale of Colonel Sanders' Kentucky Fried-Chicken and related products.

Number of Franchisees: 762 in all States except Montana and Utah, and 230 Internationally.

In Business Since: March 1964 (purchase of Kentucky Fried Chicken, Inc., which was begun in 1952 by Colonel Harland Sanders).

Equity Capital Needed: Variable. Applicants are required to have liquid assets of at least $200,000 and should have a minimum net worth of $500,000. $20,000 initial franchise fee. Land, building and equipment must be financed by franchisee.

Financial Assistance Available: Commercial sources available based on franchisee's own merits. KFC is committed to providing franchising and some financing opportunities to qualified minority applicants who are owner/operators with previous retail business experience and funds available to invest in their own business.

Training Provided: Required of all new franchisees and recommended for key employees, 12 day training seminar covering proper store operation including management, accounting, sales, advertising, catering and purchasing. Ongoing training provided in areas of customer service, general restaurant management and quality control. Also available, sales hostess instruction and seminars for instruction on specific KFC programs and equipment such as the automatic cooker. Franchisees are also provided with confidential operating manual.

Managerial Assistance Available: Engineering assistance regarding best suited building, blueprints, recommended floor plan lay-out, placement of selected equipment, field services assistance including store opening, periodic visits to assist in matters dealing with daily store operation, and quality control standards; corporation offers regional and local seminars and workshops.

LAMPPOST PIZZA
3002 Dow Avenue, Suite 320
Tustin, California 92680
Tom Barro, President

Description of Operation: Family style pizza restaurant serving Italian food, appealing to families and large groups.

Number of Franchisees: 72 in California.

In Business Since: 1976

Equity Capital Needed: $250,000 ($75,000 cash minimum)

Financial Assistance Available: Assistance in seeking financing is provided.

Training Provided: Management and employee training for 30 days located at company headquarters and company-owned restaurants.

Managerial Assistance Available: Assistance by management staff and field representatives in site selection, financial assistance, restaurant start-up, staffing, cost control, marketing and advertising.

Information Submitted: April 1990

LANDIS FOOD SERVICES, INC.
210 Carnegie Center
Princeton, New Jersey 08540
Mitchell Landis, President

Description of Operation: Landis Food Services, Inc., is the franchisor of seven operating Mexican full service restaurants. Our Marita's Cantina dinnerhouses serve Mexican favorites such as tostadas, fajitas, grilled fish dishes, chimichangas, and other specialties in a well developed, casual atmosphere. Our Cantina, or lounge, offers many Mexican beers, over 17 types of tequila, large frozen Margaritas, and red and white sangria.

Number of Franchisees: 10 in New Jersey, Pennsylvania

In Business Since: 1977

Equity Capital Needed: Pre-opening costs range from $125,000 to $375,000, of which past franchisees have been able to borrow up to 70 percent.

Financial Assistance Available: Franchisor, although not providing financial assistance, will consult with franchisee on possible avenues of financing.

Training Provided: Training is as follows: franchisee and/or manager will train at existing locations until proficient in the Marita's Cantina operating system. Then, upon opening of franchisee's restaurant, the field supervisor will remain in the restaurant for up to two weeks. Additional help is available as required.

Managerial Assistance Available: Franchisor will instruct franchisee as to Marita's operating systems including the computerized register system, sales recording, employee timekeeping and payroll, food and beverage inventories, in addition to consulting on employee hiring, training, staffing, scheduling, and advertising and promotion. Franchisor will also consult with franchisee on site selection, lease negotiation, interior and exterior design, and equipment purchasing.

Information Submitted: May 1990

LAROSA'S, INC.
5870 Belmont Avenue
Cincinnati, Ohio 45224
Stewart A. Smetts, Franchise Director

Description of Operation: A full service, full menu, Italian style family restaurant especially known for pizzas. Most locations offer beer and wine.

Number of Franchisees: 40 in Ohio and Kentucky

In Business Since: 1954—franchising began in 1967

Equity Capital Needed: $50,000 minimum

Financial Assistance Available: Prospective franchise owner must secure own financing.

Training Provided: Mandatory training for franchise owner in a corporate facility. Management and supervisory personnel to be trained in corporate facility at franchisee's expense—duration of training depends on the experience and capabilities of the personnel.

Managerial Assistance Available: An opening supervisory crew trains employees for 1 week prior to opening and stays approximately 2 weeks after opening. After the first 6 months, franchise operations personnel spend a day at all locations approximately once every 30 days.

Information Submitted: April 1990

LEE'S FAMOUS RECIPE COUNTRY CHICKEN
1727 Elm Hill Pike
Nashville, Tennessee 37210
Attention: Jeffrey L. Heston, Executive Director,
Franchise Development

Description of Operation: Sit down/take out chicken restaurant.

Number of Franchisees: 233 franchised units in 18 States

In Business Since: 1965

Equity Capital Needed: $100,000 liquid

Financial Assistance Available: Franchisor does not provide financing but will assist franchisee in preparing package for presentation to financial institutions.

Training Provided: A 5 week formal training and management course is required for all new franchisees or their managers, and is conducted by qualified instructors at the franchisor's training facilities. Supervision and training at franchisee's location during initial start-up period is provided.

Managerial Assistance Available: Franchisor provides advisory services on areas of financing, real estate, site selection, construction, equipment, advertising, accounting, purchasing, training, opening and ongoing technical and operational support.

Information Submitted: April 1990

LIFESTYLE RESTAURANTS, INC.
17 West 32nd Street
New York, New York 10001
Scott J. Kriger, Senior Vice President -
Director of Operations

Description of Operation: Lifestyle Restaurants, Inc., owns and operates restaurants throughout the Eastern Seaboard. Our restaurants are best known for their dining package, consisting of a complete dinner with unlimited salad and shrimp, plus beer, wine, and sangria, and have a loyal following attracted by good food at excellent value.

Number of Franchisees: 15 in 6 States

In Business Since: 1969

Equity Capital Needed: Initial $125,000

Financial Assistance Available: None

Training Provided: We train owners, managers and staff. We provide marketing, advertising, promotions, assistant purchasing, and cost project analysis.

Managerial Assistance Available: Consult and assist managers in making restaurants as profitable as possible.

Information Submitted: April 1990

LINDY-GERTIE ENTERPRISES, INC.
8437 Park Avenue
Burr Ridge, Illinois 60521
Joseph P. Yesutis

Description of Operation: A sit-down restaurant featuring two famous products in one attractive food service operation. Lindy's Chili was established in 1924 and is the oldest chili parlor in Chicago featuring its unique famous chili. Gertie's Ice Cream was established in 1901 and features old-fashioned ice cream creations. The franchise package offers a thoroughly modern, attractively designed restaurant, equipment operational support, and a complete operations manual to each franchisee.

Number of Franchisees: 9

In Business Since: 1985

Equity Capital Needed: $50,000 in liquid equity and the ability to finance $90,500 or more depending on the size and location of the business property.

Financial Assistance Available: None

Training Provided: We will train you and your managers in a comprehensive program lasting up to 6 weeks. This training will take place at a Lindy's Chili/Gertie's Ice Cream Restaurant or other location we designate. We also offer opening assistance at your site.

Managerial Assistance Available: Lindy-Gertie Enterprises provides ongoing quality control assurance through field operations management. Marketing and advertising programs are implemented in conjunction with the franchisees.

Information Submitted: April 1990

*LITTLE CAESAR ENTERPRISES, INC.
2211 Woodward Avenue
Detroit, Michigan 48201
Gary Jensen

Description of Operation: Little Caesars is the world's largest carry-out pizza chain in the country and the third largest pizza chain overall. Aggressive expansion plans provide investors with an excellent opportunity for growth and profit.

Number of Franchisees: 2,747 franchised and 655 company-owned as of March 31, 1990.

In Business Since: 1959

Equity Capital Needed: Approximately $120,000-$160,000.

Financial Assistance Available: Third party financing available.

Training Provided: Little Caesars Human Resource Center provides all necessary training. The initial intensive training program includes classroom and in-store sessions. Classes are provided for all levels of management.

Managerial Assistance Available: Little Caesars corporate staff of professionals provides its franchisees with ongoing managerial assistance for all phases of operations.

Information Submitted: June 1990

*LITTLE KING RESTAURANT CORPORATION
11811 'I' Street
Omaha, Nebraska 68137
Rebecca R. Bishop, Director of Franchise Development

Description of Operation: The Little King Restaurant Corporation operates and directs a successful chain of company- and franchised-owned submarine/deli-style sandwich and pizza outlets. Emphasis is on fresh-foods-fast, with the products being prepared directly in full view of the customers from the freshest of ingredients, fresh bread baked on the premises, and a special 300 calorie or less "lite menu." Product quality, customer service, and store cleanliness are the standards of the Little King operation for over 20 years.

Number of Franchisees: 69 units in 16 States plus 32 company-owned outlets.

In Business Since: 1968—franchising began in 1978

Equity Capital Needed: $65,000-$125,000 (approximate) single restaurant. Area development program available to qualified candidates.

Financial Assistance Available: Equipment lease programs available through non-affiliated sources.

Training Provided: Total 4 weeks. 2 week course in company headquarters, Omaha, Nebraska, which includes in-store and classroom studies of operations, managerial methods, accounting

procedures, marketing techniques. 2 weeks training and supervision are provided by field representatives in franchisee's restaurant prior to and during initial opoening.

Managerial Assistance Available: Field representation and consultation is provided at franchisee's restaurant quarterly, in addition to weekly communications, verbal and written materials. Company provides promotional and marketing ideas and concepts to franchisee's through monthly marketing report. Each facet of the operation is supported by detailed manuals.

Information Submitted: April 1990

LONDON FISH N'CHIPS, LTD.
306 South Maple Avenue
South San Francisco, California 94080

Description of Operation: Fast food service for both eat in and take out.

Number of Franchisees: 41 in California

In Business Since: 1967

Equity Capital Needed: $78,000

Financial Assistance Available: None

Training Provided: In shop training and in company shop training. Direct supervision in franchisee shop as needed.

Managerial Assistance Available: Help with bookkeeping. Advise on new methods and products and selling procedures for duration of franchise. Provide periodic inspection and instruction as needed.

Information Submitted: June 1990

*LONG JOHN SILVER'S, INC.
JERRICO, INC.
P. O. Box 11988
Lexington, Kentucky 40579
Eugene O. Getchell, Vice President, Franchising
Chip Hardy, Director, Franchise Sales

Description of Operation: Fast food restaurants: self-service-carry-out or seating in a wharf-like atmosphere. Menu includes fish and fries. Shrimp, clams, chicken, hush puppies, cole slaw, desserts, sea salads and a variety of hot and cold beverages.

Number of Franchisees: 476 franchised plus 1,007 company-owned.

In Business Since: Founder started in 1929. Parent company, Jerrico, Inc., incorporated in 1946. Long John Silver's started 1969.

Equity Capital Needed: Contact company for full information.

Financial Assistance Available: None: franchisees required to have adequate net worth to obtain real estate and equipment on their own.

Training Provided: 7 weeks formal training course for management.

Managerial Assistance Available: Continuous training and supervision program in all phases of management through training academy, field supervisors and home office personnel.

Information Submitted: April 1990

LOVE'S RESTAURANTS
568 East Lambert Road
Brea, California 92621
Ronald C. Mesker, President

Description of Operation: Complete full service restaurant featuring barbecued ribs, beef, pork, chicken, steak, seafood and salads. Love's is a medium priced lunch and dinner house located in the Western United States. Love's Restaurants also offer late evening suppers and cocktail lounge service. Breakfast now being served at some locations.

Number of Franchisees: 21 franchised units plus 2 company-owned in California.

In Business Since: 1948

Equity Capital Needed: Varies as to location.

Financial Assistance Available: None

Training Provided: Formal training as required by individual franchisee.

Managerial Assistance Available: Franchisor provides opening supervision, assists in hiring of personnel plus regular visits and assistance from field coordinators. Complete manual of operations specifies how each menu item is prepared and served, how the business may be operated effectively.

Information Submitted: April 1990

MACAYO MEXICAN RESTAURANTS, INC.
4001 North Central
Phoenix, Arizona 85012
Stephen C. Johnson, President

Description of Operation: Full service Mexican restaurants with lounges.

Number of Franchisees: 12 company-owned in Arizona and Nevada.

In Business Since: 1940

Equity Capital Needed: $300,000

Financial Assistance Available: None

Training Provided: 3-6 weeks for management training course, and at store location 2-3 weeks for hands on supervision.

Managerial Assistance Available: Manuals. 6 week training for general management at Phoenix, Arizona unit. Lodging and transportation provided by franchisee. Opening team for 2 weeks at initial opening, and monthly supervisory trips to monitor store.

Information Submitted: May 1990

MAID-RITE PRODUCTS, INC.
3112 University Avenue
Des Moines, Iowa 50311
John Gilotti, President

Description of Operation: Fast food—limited menu sandwich type operation with take-out or sit-down—suitable in towns of population 2,000 to 2 million. Restaurant in free-standing buildings, strip malls or shopping centers.

Number of Franchisees: 160 in 18 States

In Business Since: 1928

Equity Capital Needed: $50,000-$85,000 average. Varies with size of operation, site and location, including initial franchise fee, equipment package, signs, opening inventory and working capital. Leasehold improvements or construction costs will vary with site and size.

Financial Assistance Available: None

Training Provided: On-the-job training and class-room—operations manual on food preparation, personnel management and cost control.

Managerial Assistance Available: Continuing assistance by some office personnel in regard to operation, operations manual, recommended floor plan layout, product development cooking methods, bookkeeping and architectural services available when requested, ongoing assistance in advertising.

Information Submitted: June 1990

MANCHU WOK
400 Fairway Drive
Suite 106
Deerfield Beach, Florida 33441
John Deknatel

Description of Operation: Chinese fast food.

Number of Franchisees: 50

In Business Since: 1980

Equity Capital Needed: $200,000 to $250,000

Financial Assistance Available: None

Training Provided: Training provided in all operations of franchise.

Managerial Assistance Available: Ongoing

Information Submitted: April 1990

MARCO'S, INC.
dba MARCO'S PIZZA
5254 Monroe Street
Toledo, Ohio 43623
Pasquale "Pat" Giammarco, President
Kenneth R. Switzer, Director of Administration

Description of Operation: Marco's Pizza offers premium quality pizza and hot submarine sandwiches for carryout and delivery. Their emphasis on high quality, conscientious service and strong brand image has enabled them to become the leading pizza company in northwest Ohio and southeast Michigan.

Number of Franchisees: 24 located in northwest Ohio and southeast Michigan, plus 17 company stores.

In Business Since: 1978

Equity Capital Needed: $80,000 to $125,000 total, including initial franchise investment; equity needed depends on franchisee's financing capabilities.

Financial Assistance Available: Marco's, Inc., does not provide direct financing to franchisees at the present time. However, it does provide assistance in obtaining financing such as assisting the franchisee in preparing his/her proposal for bank financing and meeting with potential lenders.

Training Provided: Minimum of 2 months and up to 4 months, depending on the rate of progress of the franchisee. Prior food service experience preferred.

Managerial Assistance Available: Ongoing business consulting and specialized training are provided in the store and also in regional meetings. Each franchisee receives personal advertising support and assistance and in-depth policy and procedure manuals covering both food preparation and business management.

Information Submitted: April 1990

MAVERICK FAMILY STEAK HOUSE, INC.
1104 West Reynolds
Springfield, Illinois 62702
Russ Hruby

Description of Operation: Semi-cafeteria style family steak house.

Number of Franchisees: 4 company owned stores in Illinois plus 2 franchises in 2 States.

In Business Since: 1983

Equity Capital Needed: Approximately $100,000 to $150,000.

Financial Assistance Available: No direct financial assistance.

Training Provided: Training on-the-job at company-owned stores and training facility. Supervision prior to and during opening.

Managerial Assistance Available: Continuous assistance when and as needed. Operations manuals furnished and updated. Special training and visits in person as conditions require.

Information Submitted: April 1990

*MAZZIO'S PIZZA
4441 South 72nd East Avenue
Tulsa, Oklahoma 74145
Dan Brand

Description of Operation: Mazzio's Pizza concept is an integrated concept that features a high value pizza product. Mazzio's restaurants are primarily free-standing buildings, but include in-line shopping center locations or remodeled existing buildings. Mazzio's Pizza is owned by Ken's Restaurant Systems, Inc., which has been in business since 1961.

Number of Franchisees: 117 locations plus 77 company-owned in 13 States.

In Business Since: 1916

Equity Capital Needed: Variable, depending on size and location.

Financial Assistance Available: None

Training Provided: Intensive, mandatory training for key personnel. Training could be up to 5 weeks at company's location. Training is under the direction of franchisor and is formalized in nature.

Managerial Assistance Available: Continual management supervision. Specifications as to operations, food preparation, food specifications, accounting, advertising. Complete manual of operations is provided and field supervision is conducted by franchisor to assist franchisee.

Information Submitted: June 1990

NEW BOSTON CHICKEN, INC.
230 Western Avenue, Suite #502
Boston, Massachusetts 02134
Charles A. Cocotas, President

Description of Operation: New Boston Chicken, Inc., operates a chain of retail food establishments under the service mark Boston Chicken. The company's product strategy is aimed at emerging consumer demand for poultry and other wholesome, freshly prepared foods. The menu features rotisserie chicken, hot vegetables, deli-salads, soups and baked goods. The company's retail format emphasizes takeout service, capitalizing on significant increases in the at-home market. In addition to its company-owned operations, New Boston Chicken grants franchise licenses for both individual outlets and multi-unit area development. A minimum of 1,450 square feet is needed (if no seats). The setting is an upscale environment of warm, beautiful colors with traditional styling.

Number of Franchisees: 18

In Business Since: 1988

Equity Capital Needed: $317,360-$491,000

Financial Assistance Available: None

Training Provided: A comprehensive, hands-on 3 week training course is provided for owners and managers. Training includes a confidential operations manual and covers the daily operations of a store including inventory management, food cost control, advertising, scheduling, food production, employee recruitment and training.

Managerial Assistance Available: Boston Chicken will provide managerial assistance as requested. The operations department has multi-years in the food service industry. Members of the support staff are always available to assist the franchisees in their development. A continuous process to improve and advance the techniques at Boston Chicken is always a priority and franchisees are solicited to contribute to this development through an advisory council.

Information Submitted: April 1990

NEW ENGLAND SEAFOOD
15 Engle Street
Suite 302
Englewood, New Jersey 07631
John Sterns

Description of Operation: Offers a variety of fresh seafood cooked to order. The menu includes fresh fish, clams, scallops, shrimp, steamed lobsters, steamers, fried vegetables, homemade onion rings, chowders and salad rolls.

Number of Franchisees: 3 company stores

In Business Since: 1986

Equity Capital Needed: $140,000-$190,000

Financial Assistance Available: Will assist.

Training Provided: 2 weeks at company store, 1 week on-site assistance.

Managerial Assistance Available: Yes

Information Submitted: June 1990

NEW MEIJI FRANCHISE CORPORATION
1620 West Redondo Beach Boulevard
Gardena, California 90247

Description of Operation: A fast food oriental restaurant serving hot food items in combinations or in individual portions in addition to a wide variety of sushi (Japanese style raw fish and rice).

Number of Franchisees: 16 in California

In Business Since: 1976

Equity Capital Needed: $100,000 to $120,000

Financial Assistance Available: None

Training Provided: 3 weeks intensive training for the franchisee and personnel in management, hot food and sushi preparation. Complete set of manuals is provided in addition to hands-on training.

Managerial Assistance Available: Franchisee will receive information regarding site selection, store design and equipment specifications. Opening week assistance in addition to periodic visits will provide managerial and technical assistance in advertising, merchandising and quality control. Franchisor helps in advertising and promotion, continuous research and develop new food items and combinations.

Information Submitted: June 1990

NEW ORLEANS' FAMOUS FRIED CHICKE
OF AMERICA, INCORPORATED
P. O. Box 700
Greenwood, Mississippi 38930

Description of Operation: New Orleans Famous of America, Inc., is a fast food operation that s specially seasoned chicken and biscuit breakfast. N also sells many side orders like baked beans, cole sl potatoes, gravy and onion rings.

Number of Franchisees: 22 in Mississippi, Tenness and Idaho plus 20 company-owned.

In Business Since: 1974, franchising since 1979

Equity Capital Needed: $50,000 plus cost of land and

Financial Assistance Available: None

Training Provided: 4-8 weeks training for manager or ope in classroom and on-the-job training at New Orleans Famous F Chicken's Management Institute in Columbus, Mississippi.

Managerial Assistance Available: We provide operation manuals. Every franchise is inspected frequently to insure that the continued quality is maintained. All franchises are constantly informed on new products and techniques to improve their productivity and profitability. Bookkeeping and accounting services available.

Information Submitted: June 1990

NEW YORK BURRITO
7901 East Bellview Avenue
Suite 240
Englewood, Colorado 80111
Robert Palmer

Description of Operation: New York Burrito is a Southwestern style "no cook concept" fast food operation. Basic food products are delivered to the store pre-cooked and quick frozen using the cryovac cook chill system. The products are warmed, put into the steam line and each customer order is prepared individually. The food is fresh, tasty, wholesome and consistent in taste and quality.

Number of Franchisees: 7 plus 2 company-owned.

In Business Since: 1988, franchising since April 1990.

Equity Capital Needed: $35,000 plus working capital of $6,000.

Financial Assistance Available: Average total investment for a New York Burrito Restaurant is $65,000 plus working capital of $6,000 and first month's rent. The company, upon an initial down payment of $35,000, will build out and equip the restaurant. The balance of $30,000 will be financed by the company for 4 years at 8 percent simple interest. The franchisee will have to provide his/her own financing for the initial $35,000 and working capital.

Training Provided: Company provides pre-opening training at franchisee's restaurant or other designated restaurant by company personnel. Ongoing seminars are conducted by franchisor as deemed necessary by the franchisor.

Managerial Assistance Available: Complete operations manual provided that details product preparation, cost controls, and other key areas. Advisory services available through seminars and on-site inspections and reviews.

Information Submitted: August 1990

NOBLE ROMAN'S INC.
333 North Pennsylvania, Suite 808
Indianapolis, Indiana 46209
John West, Vice President

Description of Operation: Noble Roman's is a restaurant business specializing in 4 types of pizzas, salads, and sandwiches for on premises and off premises consumption.

Number of Franchisees: 90 in Midwest as of March 1989.

In Business Since: 1972—franchising since 1972.

Equity Capital Needed: Franchise fee $12,500; approximately $250,000 to $450,000 for total package.

Financial Assistance Available: None

Training Provided: Training is provided at a company training center. The standard training period is approximately 4 weeks for candidates with a restaurant background.

Managerial Assistance Available: Managerial, technical and marketing assistance provided.

Information Submitted: April 1990

NORTH'S FRANCHISING CORPORATION
1016 North Riverside Avenue
Medford, Oregon 07501
John F. North, Jr., President

Description of Operation: NRI is a unique, buffet style restaurant chain. The restaurants vary in size from approximately 6,000 square feet to 12,000 square feet, with approximately 125 parking spaces. The restaurants are open 7 days a week and serve lunch and dinner, except Sunday, on which day dinner only is served.

Number of Franchisees: 14 in California, Idaho, Oregon and Washington plus 8 company-owned.

In Business Since: 1959

Equity Capital Needed: $100,000 minimum

Financial Assistance Available: None

Training Provided: Extensive 60 day mandatory training program, which covers all aspects of restaurant operation, with additional on-site supervision by company personnel during the initial opening, plus extensive follow-up during the first few months of operation.

Managerial Assistance Available: NRI provides continual management service for the life of the franchise on a minimum of once a quarter visit to outlet. All accounting and payroll functions are done by the home office. Complete operations, accounting and employee manuals are provided; district management personnel are available to work closely with franchisees and to visit outlets on a regular basis to assist in solving problems. NRI sponsors meetings and work shops for the franchisees and their management personnel.

Information Submitted: June 1990

NUGGET RESTAURANTS
4650 Brightmore Road
Bloomfield Hills, Michigan 48013
Gordon R. Eliassen, President

Description of Operation: Short order—full menu restaurant.

Number of Franchisees: 10 in Michigan

In Business Since: 1962

Equity Capital Needed: $60,000

Financial Assistance Available: None

Training Provided: Training is provided as necessary.

Managerial Assistance Available: Managerial and technical assistance is provided when needed.

Information Submitted: May 1990

*NUMERO UNO FRANCHISE CORPORATION
8214 Van Nuys Boulevard
Panorama City, California 91402
Ronald J. Geiet, President

Description of Operation: Pizzeria full menu-full service restaurant.

Number of Franchisees: 55 in California

In Business Since: 1973

Equity Capital Needed: $100,000-$125,000 cash minimum. Total investment $200,000-$300,000.

Financial Assistance Available: None

Training Provided: 4 weeks extensive training.

Managerial Assistance Available: Continuous and ongoing.

Information Submitted: April 1990

O! DELI
65 Battery Street
San Francisco, California 94111
Mike Kiiek, Director of Franchising

Description of Operation: O! Deli offers quality sandwiches, salads, breakfast and desserts at fast food prices. Customers are primarily working people during working hours, with O! Deli's often open only 5 days per week. O! Deli quality and value build a loyal repeat clientele. Catering and delivery are used. O! Deli's are approximately 1,000 square feet.

Number of Franchisees: 21

In Business Since: 1985

Equity Capital Needed: $35,000-$50,000

Financial Assistance Available: O! Deli assists franchisees, when requested, in preparing business plans and obtaining financing.

Training Provided: O! Deli provides 2 weeks training in an operating O! Deli. O! Deli staff provides training and assistance during franchisee store opening week. An extensive operations manual covers portion control, hiring and training, financial controls, and food preparation.

Managerial Assistance Available: O! Deli helps with site selection, lease negotiation, restaurant layout, discounts on equipment and food purchases, and training in operations management and control. Ongoing assistance involves frequent contact with O! Deli operations people to fine tune your operation, analyze sales trends and help the business prosper.

Information Submitted: May 1990

THE OLDE WORLD CHEESE SHOP
3333 South Pasadena Avenue
South Pasadena, Florida 33707
Robert Ross, President

Description of Operation: The Olde World Cheese Shop offers a unique family restaurant that has designed gourmet sandwiches using our own breads and dressings. In addition, we serve our own unique omelets and appetizers. We are open 7 days a week for breakfast, lunch and dinner.

Number of Franchisees: 9 plus 1 company-owned in Florida

In Business Since: 1975

Equity Capital Needed: $450,000-$1,000,000 total investment.

Financial Assistance Available: We will assist the franchisee in arranging the balance of the investment with our bank or the Small Business Administration. Our total turnkey cost is approximately $450,000 for a line unit and $1,000,000 for a free standing restaurant.

Training Provided: We have a mandatory 12 week training course at our headquarters in South Pasadena, Florida. During these 8 weeks the franchisee is trained by our specialists in every facet of our operation. We then go with franchisees and assist them in the opening of their new store.

Managerial Assistance Available: The Olde World Cheese Shop provides management service for the entire life of the franchise in all areas of operation. Complete operation manuals, visits by our staff regularly, and a monthly newsletter are provided. We are always available to help the franchisee with any problems. The Olde World Cheese Shop conducts constant research for new products and new marketing techniques.

Information Submitted: June 1990

*OLGA'S KITCHEN LICENSING, INC.
1940 Northwood Drive
Troy, Michigan 48084
Robert H. McRae, Vice President-Franchise Operations

Description of Operation: Specialty restaurant, table service at moderate prices, featuring The Olga, with secret recipe bread, cooked fresh to order.

Number of Franchisees: 55 in operation and 15 franchised.

In Business Since: Olga's Kitchens in operation since 1976. Franchising since January 1984.

Equity Capital Needed: Approximately $100,000 to $150,000 (providing that financing is obtainable) with total investment ranging from $450,000 to $650,000 depending on size and type of outlet.

Financial Assistance Available: None

Training Provided: Comprehensive PRO training program of approximately 5-6 weeks duration at our Detroit area training center, and restaurant opening assistance of approximately 2 weeks.

Managerial Assistance Available: Our specialists will provide recommended locations or location evaluations, store development and employee training for opening the restaurant. After start-up the operation will continue to benefit from our follow-up systems. We can supply services in areas such as operations, quality control, advertising, marketing, insurance, bookkeeping and cost analysis.

Information Submitted: April 1990

1 POTATO 2, INC.
5640 International Parkway
New Hope, Minnesota 55428
Theodore L. Priem, President

Description of Operation: 1 Potato 2, Inc., offers a wide selection of baked potato entrees that range from seafood to steak to a generous selection of vegetable toppings. The company also supplies a number of French fried potato products, such as potato skins and French fries. These products are all prepared fresh in full view of the customer at the time of each order.

Number of Franchisees: 65 franchisees in 25 different States and 2 in Japan.

In Business Since: 1979

Equity Capital Needed: Approximately $125,000 depending on the location size.

Financial Assistance Available: Company will assist the franchisee in applying for financing. The company will not make loans to franchisees.

Training Provided: 1 Potato 2's training program will consist of a 3 to 5 week training period depending on the franchisee's food experience. The franchisee will receive complete training in all aspects of the operations manual, including accounting, inventory control, store management, employee management, customer relations and other additional areas.

Managerial Assistance Available: Full assistance is provided in site selection, lending institutions presentations, management training, store design, equipment selection, store opening and personnel and administrative procedures. These areas are all defined in a very well documented and detailed operational procedures manual that is provided to each franchisee. Field management personnel located in regional offices across the United States are available on a 24 hour basis to answer questions that may arise.

Information Submitted: April 1990

ORANGE BOWL CORPORATION
227 N.E. 17th Street
Miami, Florida 33132
Leonard Turkel, President

Description of Operation: A bright, colorful snack bar designed exclusively for operation in shopping centers, having the advantage of a limited menu offering popular food products such as pizza, hot dogs, hamburgers, soft ice cream and fruit drinks.

Number of Franchisees: 40 nationwide

In Business Since: 1965

Equity Capital Needed: Approximately $50,000 to $60,000—total cost $95,000 to $135,000.

Financial Assistance Available: The franchisor does not directly offer any financing to the franchisee; however, it does assist the franchisee in securing bank financing and/or SBA guaranteed financing.

Training Provided: 2 weeks of on-the-job training and orientation at the franchisor's training center for the franchisee, his designee or manager.

Managerial Assistance Available: Complete turnkey opening provided, with continual home office and area assistance in every aspect of store operations, promotions, and store review.

Information Submitted: April 1990

*ORANGE JULIUS OF AMERICA
P. O. Box 35286
Minneapolis, Minnesota 55435

Description of Operation: Specialty drinks and hot dogs.

Number of Franchisees: 708 plus 1 company-owned.

In Business Since: 1926, franchising since 1930.

Equity Capital Needed: Total investment $143,000-$170,000

Financial Assistance Available: 50 percent of franchise fee over a 5 year period.

Training Provided: Complete training in all aspects of operating a franchise.

Managerial Assistance Available: Ongoing managerial assistance is provided.

Information Submitted: June 1990

OREAN THE HEALTH EXPRESS
1320 North Vine
Hollywood, California 90028
Orean C. Thomas III, President

Description of Operation: Vegetarian fast food take-out.

Number of Franchisees: 1 unit

In Business Since: 1984

Equity Capital Needed: Liquid assets, minimum $100,000.

Financial Assistance Available: None

Training Provided: Complete training provided.

Managerial Assistance Available: Ongoing support.

Information Submitted: April 1990

THE ORIGINAL WIENER WORKS, INC.
8290 Hubbard Road
Auburn, California 95603
Harold G. Ackerman, President

Description of Operation: The Original Wiener Works is a unique fast food sit down restaurant that serves 49 different hot dogs, 6 hamburgers and over 50 different domestic and imported beers. One of the other unique products sold is fresh cut French fries. Each unit is decorated like an old hot dog restaurant. Size of units vary from 1,200 square feet to 1,500 square feet. Units are open 7 days a week from 11 a.m. until 10 p.m. The company provides site selection, plans, bookkeeping system and advertising assistance.

Number of Franchisees: 1 plus 1 company-owned in California.

In Business Since: 1983

Equity Capital Needed: $87,500 to 93,000

Financial Assistance Available: Although company provides no financing, the Original Wiener Works, Inc., will provide help in compiling and presenting loan package to various financial institutions.

Training Provided: Extensive 3 weeks hands-on training at a training store prior to opening of franchisee's unit. 1 week or more as needed after unit is opened.

Managerial Assistance Available: The Original Wiener Works, Inc., provides extensive ongoing help with bookkeeping, management, food cost control, advertising, employee relations and all other aspects of the business that relate to the continuing success of the franchisee and the unit.

Information Submitted: June 1990

O'TOOLE'S FOOD GROUP OF AMERICA, INC.
585 Aero Drive
Buffalo, New York 14225
Michael F. Donnelly, Vice President, Operations

Description of Operation: A service restaurant/pub-style neighborhood gathering place.

Number of Franchisees: 85 plus in Canada; 9 in the United States.

In Business Since: 1983

Equity Capital Needed: $200,000

Financial Assistance Available: None

Training Provided: Classroom and hands-on training of 6 to 12 weeks.

Managerial Assistance Available: Operating policies and procedures, menu development, quality assurance, food costing programs, hiring, training, advertising, marketing and promotions.

Information Submitted: April 1990

PACIFIC TASTEE FREEZ, INC.
556 North Diamond Bar Boulevard
Suite 104
Diamond Bar, California 91765
Lowell Meyer, President
Loy Coon, General Manager

Description of Operation: Fast food drive-in restaurant featuring hamburgers, Mexican food, ice cream and beverages.

Number of Franchisees: 34 in California and Oregon.

In Business Since: 1955

Equity Capital Needed: Approximately $120,000-$180,000 plus land and building.

Financial Assistance Available: Equipment financing and/or leasing assistance available.

Training Provided: 4 weeks in actual store.

Managerial Assistance Available: Duration of franchise, assistance through field representation.

Information Submitted: April 1990

PAPACHINOS FRANCHISE CORPORATION, INC.
PAPACHINOS RISTORANTE & PIZZA RESTAURANTS
7940 Silverton Avenue, Suite 103
San Diego, California 92126
Stephen O. Slamon, Vice President

Description of Operation: Papachinos Ristorante & Pizza Restaurants are full service, family-style Italian restaurants, serving pizza, pasta, sandwiches, desserts and beverages, at moderate prices. Papachinos has achieved a loyal customer following through careful attention to quality in every aspect of the operation. It all starts with painstaking recipe development. Customers know quality when they taste it, so Papachinos gives it to them in the form of the best and freshest ingredients available, along with a near extinct care in preparation techniques. Not only do people respond to quality, they also respond to quantity. Serving up extra-large portions of pizza and pasta has become one of the restaurants' trademarks.

Number of Franchisees: 2 to open in late 1990, plus 2 company stores.

In Business Since: Franchising since May 1988, company restaurants open since 1978.

Equity Capital Needed: Approximately $300,000 total needed, of which approximately one-half ($150,000) is required in cash.

Financial Assistance Available: None

Training Provided: Each franchisee and up to 2 designated managers must complete an intensive 2 week training program at one of the company restaurants that includes both classroom sessions and on-the-job training. Individual instruction is given in all aspects of the business from opening the restaurant in the morning to closing at night. The training program includes food preparation, customer service and relations, employee relations, financial management and control, merchandising and advertising, equipment maintenance and more. Each franchisee is provided with a "Confidential Operations Manual" that covers every aspect of the business in great detail.

Managerial Assistance Available: Upon opening of the restaurant, one of our managers is assigned to your store for a 1 month period. During this initial period of operations the manager will help the franchisee with every detail of managing the restaurant. Thereafter, a representative of the franchise company will visit the restaurant about every 2 weeks to meet with the owner to assist in reviewing operating results and to offer suggestions for possible improvements.

Information Submitteed: April 1990

PARIS CROISSANT NORTHEAST CORP.
670 Point Road
Little Silver, New Jersey 07739
Gaston A. Schmidt

Description of Operation: French cafe bakery.

Number of Franchisees: 4 in Connecticut

In Business Since: 1984

Equity Capital Needed: $150,000

Financial Assistance Available: None

Training Provided: 3 weeks in all phases of operation

Managerial Assistance Available: Managerial and technical assistance up to 30 days during first year.

Information Submitted: June 1990

PASQUALE FOOD COMPANY, INC.
19 West Oxmoor Road
Birmingham, Alabama 35209

Description of Operation: Prepare and serve to the public pizza, pasta, and a line of Italian-style sandwiches. Meat, bread and pizza doughs are manufactured and baked under strict quality control complete with chemist and laboratory.

Number of Franchisees: 60 plus 1 company-owned in 13 States.

In Business Since: 1955

Equity Capital Needed: Approximately $70,000 $100,000.

Financial Assistance Available: None

Training Provided: Initial 2 weeks training and periodically thereafter.

Managerial Assistance Available: Managerial and technical assistance provided.

Information Submitted: April 1990

THE PASTA HOUSE COMPANY FRANCHISES, INC.
1924 Marconi
St. Louis, Missouri 63110
John Ferrara, President

Description of Operation: Our concept is to offer the public delicious Italian foods, with a complete menu of gourmet pastas, appetizers, salads, sandwiches, soups, deserts, pizzas, etc., for the family at affordable prices. 80 percent of gross income from food, 20 percent from beer, wine and liquor.

Number of Franchisees: 13 plus 10 company-owned in Missouri, Illinois, Tennessee, and Florida.

In Business Since: 1967

Equity Capital Needed: $45,000 franchise fee. Total costs exceed $500,000.

Financial Assistance Available: Franchisor does not finance any portion of the total investment.

Training Provided: 12 to 14 weeks of basic training for key personnel covering all aspects of the business plus kitchen, dining room and bar training. 2 to 4 weeks of on-the-job-site store opening training.

Managerial Assistance Available: Managerial assistance in basic training (13 weeks), store opening training (3 weeks), financial packaging, site selection, furniture, fixtures, equipment, architectural design, decor and construction. Ongoing support, audits and reviews, public employee surveys, advertising assistance, and menu additions and testing and expansion or resale assistance.

Information Submitted: June 1990

PENGUIN POINT FRANCHISE SYSTEMS, INC.
P. O. Box 975
Warsaw, Indiana 46580
W. E. Stouder, Jr., Vice President

Description of Operation: Fast food restaurants.

Number of Franchisees: 1 in Indiana

In Business Since: 1949

Equity Capital Needed: $125,000

Financial Assistance Available: None

Training Provided: 6 weeks training in company-owned training store and 2 weeks assistance during opening.

Managerial Assistance Available: Continuing support in operation including bookkeeping, inventory and labor cost control, advertising and technical assistance.

Information Submitted: June 1990

PENN STATION STEAK & SUB
7516 Heatherwood Lane
Cincinnati, Ohio 45244
Jeff Osterfeld

Description of Operation: Penn Station is an upscale submarine shop that focuses on preparing its food—subs, salads, fresh baked bread, fresh squeezed lemonade and fresh-cut French fries—right before the customer's eyes. We have a proven track record with double digit sales increases in mall and strip center locations alike.

Number of Franchisees: 8 in 2 States

In Business Since: 1985

Equity Capital Needed: $96,000-$160,000

Financial Assistance Available: None

Training Provided: 2 weeks of training in all phases of operation in Cincinnati, Ohio.

Managerial Assistance Available: We provide grand opening assistance and monthly ongoing support on an as needed basis.

Information Submitted: April 1990

*PEPE'S, INCORPORATED
1325 West 15th Street
Chicago, Illinois 60608
Robert C. Ptak, President
Mario Dovalina, Jr., Secretary

Description of Operation: Pepe's, Incorporated franchises Pepe's Mexican restaurants. The restaurants are a combination carry-out and family dining. A full menu of Mexican meals is our specialty. Most restaurants offer beer and wine. Seating capacity is from 75-150 seats.

Number of Franchisees: 52 in Illinois, and Indiana.

In Business Since: 1967

Equity Capital Needed: $75,000-$200,000

Financial Assistance Available: A total investment of $150,000-$350,000 is necessary to open a Pepe's Mexican Restaurant. This is for the cost of remodeling, purchasing equipment and signs, paying deposits on utilities and insurance, and payment of franchise fee.

Training Provided: A new franchisee is required to train for a period of 4 weeks at one of our existing restaurants.

Managerial Assistance Available: Pepe's Incorporated provides continuing management service during the entire franchise period in the areas of quality control, advertising, inventory control, and new product development. A manual of operations and menu preparation is provided.

Information Submitted: April 1990

PETER PIPER PIZZA
2321 West Royal Palm Road
Phoenix, Arizona 85021
John Baillon, Director Franchise Sales

Description of Operation: Peter Piper Pizza operates and directs a system of family pizza restaurants, offering "great pizza, about half the price." Menu is limited to pizza, salads, soft drinks, and beer. Approximately 50 percent carry out, no delivery.

Number of Franchisees: 11 with 73 units plus 39 company-owned restaurants in 9 States.

In Business Since: 1973

Equity Capital Needed: $150,000 minimum.

Financial Assistance Available: Total investment ranges from $325,000 to $500,000 for a suitable shopping center location, leasehold improvements, furniture, fixtures, and equipment. Franchisor does not provide funding but will assist in locating sources.

Training Provided: Franchisee and/or manager must complete minimum 2 week training session conducted at the national training center and corporate restaurants in Phoenix, Arizona.

Managerial Assistance Available: Store opening assistance provided plus ongoing support in operations and marketing. Operations, training, and marketing manuals are provided for continual reference.

Information Submitted: April 1990

THE PEWTER MUG
1406 West 6th, Suite 400
Cleveland, Ohio 44113
Stanley Morganstern

Description of Operation: English pub and restaurant, serving luncheon and dinner.

Number of Franchisees: 8 in Ohio

In Business Since: 1962

Equity Capital Needed: Approximately $375,000, depending on location.

Financial Assistance Available: Limited

Training Provided: Training of all personnel in parent restaurant in Cleveland and on premises by training staff.

Managerial Assistance Available: Assistance given in lease negotiations, general contracting, hiring of employees and co-ordination of kitchen and bar operation. We have our own man on premises 1 week before opening and 1 week after opening.

Information Submitted: June 1990

PEWTER POT, INC.
P. O. Box 1267
Salem, New Hampshire 03079-1138
Bruce R. Butterworth, President

Description of Operation: Pewter Pot Family Restaurants, we believe, offer a more "total experience" than any similar chain in the country. Pewter Pot offers a warm, early American atmosphere with real wood, carpeting and hand painted murals, and a varied menu of high quality foods, including main courses, endless omelettes, hearty breakfasts, all-American sandwiches, and bounteous desserts. Plus an extra measure of hospitality served up New England style.

Number of Franchisees: 9 plus 7 company-owned in Massachusetts, and Connecticut.

In Business Since: 1964

Equity Capital Needed: Approximately $100,000.

Financial Assistance Available: A total investment of approximately $350,000 is needed to build and equip a Pewter Pot Family Restaurant. Pewter Pot does not finance any of the package.

Training Provided: Intensive 6 week mandatory training course is scheduled for all new franchisees and their manager. This course is conducted at the home office school and on-site company store under the supervision of a Pewter Pot supervisor.

Managerial Assistance Available: Pewter Pot Family Restaurants provide continual management services for the life of the franchise in such areas as operations, menu planning, advertising, inventory control, and food cost control.

Information Submitted: June 1990

PHILADELPHIA STEAK & SUB COMPANY
1700 Route 23, Suite 120
Wayne, New Jersey 07470
Richard Pineles, President

Description of Operation: Limited menu featuring Philly-style cheesesteak and submarine sandwiches, primarily located in regional shopping malls in either food court or in-line adaptations. Store size is between 600 and 800 square feet.

Number of Franchisees: 8 in 5 States plus 11 company-owned.

In Business Since: 1977

Equity Capital Needed: Total investment about $175,000.

Financial Assistance Available: Franchisor does not provide financing but will assist franchisee in preparing package for presentation to lending institutions.

Training Provided: Minimum 8 days in company operated store and home office plus 2 weeks with opening team in franchisee's premises.

Managerial Assistance Available: In addition to pre-opening training, franchisor assists with selection of suppliers, complete design and construction, equipment selection, employee training, and ongoing regional supervision through company supervisors for the entire duration of the agreement (typically 10 years).

Information Submitted: June 1990

PIETRO'S PIZZA PARLORS, INC.
407 Cernon Street
Vacaville, California 05688

Description of Operation: Family style restaurant—pizza, Italian dinners, open 7 days a week 11 am to 12 pm.

Number of Franchisees: 6, plus 1 company-owned in California.

In Business Since: 1960

Equity Capital Needed: $75,000 to $150,000 depending on size of operation.

Financial Assistance Available: None

Training Provided: 8 weeks and then whatever is necessary.

Managerial Assistance Available: Continuous service as needed.

Information Submitted: June 1990

PIONEER TAKE OUT CORPORATION
7301 Topanga Canyon Blvd., Suite 200
Canoga Park, California 91303
Charles Denise

Description of Operation: Pioneer provides a unique fast food service operation featuring an exciting variety menu. In addition to its gold medal winning golden fried chicken there's Pioneer crispy chicken, Pioneer oven baked chicken, Pioneer's famous chicken chili, as well as fish fillets, home baked biscuits, all the great side dishes, and for dessert, fresh baked chocolate chip cookies. There's even a brand new building design that needs only a smidgen of land to offer drive-thru service or on-premise dining. When you talk about getting it all together—you talk Pioneer Chicken!

Number of Franchisees: 156 in California, Hawaii and Arizona including company-owned.

In Business Since: 1961

Equity Capital Needed: $65,000 to $175,000

Financial Assistance Available: Pioneer does not provide direct financing; however, we have a list of sources from whom financing is available for franchise fees, equipment, signs, and even land and building if desired.

Training Provided: 10 weeks intensive and complete training program: 3 weeks on-the-job training in special training units, 2 weeks management training, 2 weeks management internship and 3 weeks in your restaurant when it opens. Our training program is college accredited.

Managerial Assistance Available: Pioneer Take Out Corporation provides continuous management services for the life of the license in such areas as bookkeeping, advertising, quality, service, food preparation and control. Complete manuals of operations, food preparation and field marketing are provided. Field coordinators work closely with licensees; and visit stores regularly to assist in solving problems. Pioneer conducts licensee seminars and market and product research to maintain high volume, profitable locations.

Information Submitted: June 1990

PIZZA CHALET FRANCHISE CORPORATION
P. O. Box 7100
Redlands, California 92374
Donald F. Frisbie, President

Description of Operation: Pizza parlor done in a Swiss decor with family dining.

Number of Franchisees: 18 in California

In Business Since: 1972

Equity Capital Needed: $150,000

Financial Assistance Available: Assist in getting loans from bank.

Training Provided: In-store training 6 weeks.

Managerial Assistance Available: Ongoing managerial and technical assistance.

Information Submitted: June 1990

PIZZA FACTORY INC.
P. O. Box 989
49430 Road 426
Oakhurst, California 93644

Description of Operation: Family style restaurant (dine in or take out) serving pizza (hand tossed the old fashioned way), pasta, sandwiches, beer/wine.

Number of Franchisees: 57 locations in 7 States plus 3 company-owned.

In Business Since: 1979; franchising since 1984

Equity Capital Needed: $90,000-$120,000 depending on location and type of store. Franchise fee $20,000 plus $2,500 training fee, royalty 3 percent, advertising 1 percent.

Financial Assistance Available: Equipment financing available.

Training Provided: 325 hour training required (minimum) at a designated Pizza Factory training facility. Training fee $2,500.

Managerial Assistance Available: Site location selection, lease negotiations, construction/equipment inspections, quarterly inspections by field consultant, advertising support, owner's manual, regional meetings, annual convention. Continual assistance from corporate offices as needed.

Information Submitted: April 1990

*PIZZA INN, INC.
2930 Stemmons Freeway
P. O. Box 660193
Dallas, Texas 75266-0193

Description of Operation: Pizza Inn is a $265 million company that operates and franchises over 600 pizza restaurants in 30 States and 5 foreign countries. The vertically integrated company has its own distribution company that supplies every item essential to the successful operation of a Pizza Inn. The 2,990 square feet, 125 seat free-standing Inns feature dine in, take out and home delivery capabilities. Two classes of franchises are offered: (1) full service Pizza Inns with optional delivery and (2) home delivery Pizza Inns that feature pizza, pastas, and salads, the two popular take away and home delivery foods.

Number of Franchisees: 180 franchisees.

In Business Since: 1959

Equity Capital Needed: $75,000 liquidity and $150,000 net worth per Inn.

Financial Assistance Available: None

Training Provided: A highly structured 5 week training program consists of video, classroom and hands-on training. Each new unit is equipped with a learning center for hourly employees. Opening assistance is provided by certified trainers using a state-of-the-art video hourly operations training program. Ongoing training is provided by literally hundreds of seminars conducted at convenient locations each year. The company believes the training program is among the best in the restaurant industry.

Managerial Assistance Available: Development stage management assistance is provided for site selection and construction. A professional operations specialist offers periodic on-site support. Manuals are furnished covering all basic functions including operations, marketing and advertising, personnel, real estate and construction, accounting, management and production skills development. Voluntary one-stop shopping at competitive prices is available with weekly delivery from company-owned distribution centers.

Information Submitted: April 1990

PIZZA MAN "HE DELIVERS"
6930-1/2 TuJunga Avenue
Los Angeles, California 91605
Vance E. Shepherd, President

Description of Operation: Pizza Man offers a fast food home delivery operation. Each store is approximately 1,000 square feet, does 80 percent of its business in home delivery, and is open 7 days a week, 12 noon to midnight. Limited menu, low rent leases, turnkey operation.

Number of Franchisees: 61 in California

In Business Since: 1973

Equity Capital Needed: $75,000

Training Provided: Complete training given, 30 days mandatory for franchisee with 4 or more weeks available. All training at no charge to franchisee. Training at Hollywood, California. Training for franchisee's employees given at franchisee's outlets.

Managerial Assistance Available: Pizza Man provides continual management assistance for the life of the franchise. Complete operation manuals, bookkeeping forms and direction are provided. Supervisor visits stores regularly to assist franchisee. Pizza Man provides advertising and promotional designs and research.

Information Submitted: April 1990

PIZZA PIT INVESTMENT ENTERPRISES, INC.
dba PIZZA PIT
4253 Argosy Court
Madison, Wisconsin 53714
Kerry P. Cook, Vice President and Director

Description of Operation: Pizza Pit restaurants feature free, fast and hot home delivery of pizza and sandwiches and catering, with optional inside seating, pizza-by-the-slice and salads.

Number of Franchisees: 8 plus 12 company-owned in Wisconsin and Iowa.

In Business Since: 1969

Equity Capital Needed: $109,280-$236,240

Financial Assistance Available: None

Training Provided: 4-6 week course covering all aspects of the operation of a Pizza Pit unit.

Managerial Assistance Available: Managerial and technical assistance is provided continuously from 60 days prior to opening and throughout the life of the unit. Marketing and training support is continuous and periodically updated via on-site visits and regular interactive communication.

Information Submitted: April 1990

PIZZA RACK FRANCHISE SYSTEMS, INC.
2130 Market Avenue North
Canton, Ohio 44714
William Cundiff, President

Description of Operation: Operate and franchise pizza, French bread pizza, chicken and submarine sandwich carry-outs, with delivery. Franchise is designed for small investors. Stores are designed with a Victorian atmosphere for family dining or carry-out.

Number of Franchisees: 15 Stores in Ohio

In Business Since: 1975

Equity Capital Needed: $36,000-$45,000

Financial Assistance Available: Assistance with bank presentation.

Training Provided: A new franchisee is required to train for a period of 6 weeks at one of our existing stores.

Managerial Assistance Available: Pizza Rack provides continuing management service during the entire franchise period in the areas of quality control, advertising, inventory control and new product development. A manual of operations and menu preparation is provided.

Information Submitted: June 1990

PIZZAS BY MARCHELLONI
1051 Essington Road
Suite 130
Joliet, Illinois 60435
Hass Aslam

Description of Operation: Pizza delivery, carry-out and dine in.

Number of Franchisees: 8 plus 8 company-owned.

In Business Since: 1986

Equity Capital Needed: $33,000-$112,000

Financial Assistance Available: None

Training Provided: 14 days training in all aspects of operation.

Managerial Assistance Available: Ongoing

Information Submitted: April 1990

PIZZERIA UNO
100 Charles Park Road
W. Roxbury, Massachusetts 02110
William F. Suessbrick, Jr., Vice President,
Development

Description of Operation: A Pizzeria Uno Restaurant and Bar is a full-service restaurant with a complete bar serving a variety of menu items and featuring Chicago's original deep-dish pizza. There are over 36 units throughout the world.

Number of Franchisees: 29 in 15 States, Washington, D.C., England, Australia and New Zealand plus 16 company-owned.

In Business Since: 1979

Equity Capital Needed: Fully capitalized, it costs approximately $1,250,000 to open a 5,000 square foot restaurant.

Financial Assistance Available: None

Training Provided: Intensive 7 week program in Boston.

Managerial Assistance Available: Quarterly visits to all units by company field consultants. Detailed operations manuals are provided along with supplementary manuals on marketing, recipes, etc.

Information Submitted: June 1990

PLUSH PIPPIN RESTAURANTS, INC.
31620 23rd Avenue, South
Suite 318
Federal Way, Washington 98003

Description of Operation: Family-oriented restaurants specializing in freshly-baked pies of over 30 varieties. Also have full line of ice cream and fountain favorites, making a Plush Pippin the place "where dessert becomes the main course."

Number of Franchisees: 11 plus 8 company-owned units in Oregon, Washington, Idaho, Minnesota, Colorado and Hawaii.

In Business Since: 1974

Equity Capital Needed: $100,000 minimum and ability to acquire financing.

Financial Assistance Available: None

Training Provided: A minimum of 14 weeks of on-the-job training and instruction is required in the preparation and merchandising of Plush Pippin and in the procedures to be followed in operation and managing a Plush Pippin Restaurant.

Managerial Assistance Available: Continuous management assistance for the life of the franchise in such areas as management, bookkeeping, menu pricing, and food costing. Operations manuals, recipes, forms and directions are provided. Computerized accounting with financial statements available also for a reasonable monthly fee.

Information submitted: June 1990

PO FOLKS, INC.
P. O. Box 17406
Nashville, Tennessee 37217
John A. Scott, President and CEO

Description of Operation: Full service family restaurants with country cooking and down home atmosphere.

Number of Franchisees: 129 in 21 States

In Business Since: 1975

Equity Capital Needed: $500,000 plus

Financial Assistance Available: None

Training Provided: 4 month manager training in restaurants that also includes a 2 week classroom training course at corporate headquarters. Also 4 days prior and 2 weeks after opening of each restaurant.

Managerial Assistance Available: Inspection and advice during term of the franchise agreement. Co-operative purchasing available through distributors. Regular meetings with franchise advisory committee. Annual franchise meeting.

Information Submitted: April 1990

*PONDEROSA STEAKHOUSES
Division of METROMEDIA STEAKHOUSES, INC.
P. O. Box 578
Dayton, Ohio 45401
Edward J. Day, Director, Franchise
Sales/Administration

Description of Operation: Modified self-service steakhouse restaurant, open 7 days a week for lunch and dinner, featuring a reasonably priced menu including the Grand Buffet, beef, seafood and chicken entrees.

Number of Franchisees: 340 units (plus 397 company-owned units) in 34 States and 8 countries.

In Business Since: 1965

Equity Capital Needed: Over $125,000 plus $500,000 net worth.

Financial Assistance: Franchisor helps identify through outside sources.

Training Provided: 5 weeks of training in field, then 1 week at headquarters, then 3 additional weeks in the field.

Managerial Assistance Available: Complete operations manual detailing methods of scheduling labor, maintenance of equipment, training of employees, hiring practices, ordering supplies and recording and controlling expenses. Field consultants and field marketing staff provided on regular basis to help resolve operational problems. Seminars held to give advertising, promotional, and other managerial support to franchisee.

Information Submitted: April 1990

PONY EXPRESS PIZZA
931 Baxter Avenue
Louisville, Kentucky 40204
Kenneth Lamb, President

Description of Operation: Pizza delivery chain.

Number of Franchisees: 16 in Kentucky and Indiana.

In Business Since: 1982

Equity Capital Needed: $2,500 minimum

Financial Assistance Available: Relative to location selection and financial stability.

Training Provided: Area supervisor provides complete training in the art of pizza making and business related paperwork for all new franchisees and their personnel.

Managerial Assistance Available: Pony Express provides continual management service for the life of the franchise in such areas as bookkeeping, advertising, food cost and inventory control. Complete manuals of operation, recipes, paperwork forms and directions are provided. Area supervisors are available in all regions to work closely with franchisees and visit stores regularly to assist in solving problems.

Information Submitted: June 1990

*POPEYES FAMOUS FRIED CHICKEN AND BISCUITS
International Headquarters
One Popeyes Plaza
1333 South Clearview Parkway
Jefferson, (New Orleans) Louisiana 70121
William A. Copeland, Senior Vice President-Franchise Division
Terrel A. Rhoton, Vice President

Description of Operation: Fast food operations specializing in sales of specially seasoned products, conducting business from single units with drive-thru and sit-down facilities.

Number of Franchisees: 640 in 40 States plus 120 company-owned units.

In Business Since: 1972

Equity Capital Needed: Approximately $150,000 per unit with $1,000,000 net worth.

Financial Assistance Available: None

Training Provided: 7 weeks.

Managerial Assistance Available: Accounting, operational, marketing, advertising and real estate.

Information Submitted: June 1990

PORT OF SUBS, INC.
100 Washington street
Suite 200
Reno, Nevada 89503
Patricia Larsen, President

Description of Operation: Port of Subs, Inc., is a submarine sandwich restaurant operation. Sandwiches are made-to-order with highest quality ingredients. Typical stores are approximately 1,200-1,500 square feet and seat 30-35 people. Simplicity of operation and efficiency are cornerstones of the Port of Subs system. A nautical theme with blue, yellow and white interiors presents a crisp, clean environment.

Number of Franchisees: 41 (plus 7 company-owned units) in Arizona, California, Nevada and Washington.

In Business Since: 1975

Equity Capital Needed: $35,000-$50,000

Financial Assistance Available: A total investment of $120,000 is estimated for a Port of Subs franchise. Port of Subs, Inc., assists potential franchisees in preparing documents for financing and maintains relationships with several banking institutions. Port of Subs, Inc., does not provide any internal financing.

Training Provided: Port of Subs, Inc., provides a mandatory, intensive 16-day training course that will give the skills, the knowledge and the confidence franchisee needs to manage the business effectively and efficiently. Training is conducted at corporate headquarters and at a company-owned store location and covers all material aspects of the operation of a Port of Subs franchise.

Managerial Assistance Available: Port of Subs, Inc., provides franchisees with reference manuals, business forms, purchasing power, accounting service (optional), and the benefits of creative advertising campaigns. Port of Subs, Inc., also provides opening assistance during the initial opening for at least 5 days, and provides guidance in creating an attention-getting grand opening. Ongoing support includes monthly visits by representatives who will provide new updates, merchandising concepts, idea exchanges and two-way communication. The corporate staff is always available between visits to provide assistance.

Information Submitted: May 1990

PUB DENNIS INTERNATIONAL, INC.
329 Park East Drive
Woonsocket, Rhode Island 02895
Jerry Buck, Director of Franchising

Description of Operation: Pub Dennis is a full service family style restaurant. Our restaurant system is a distinctive, highly competitive operation featuring steak, seafood, chicken, daily specials, a children's menu and a Sunday (only day) breakfast buffet. The restaurants are approximately 5,000 square feet, seating 180, set in a standardized, unique free standing building. The decor includes distinctive carousel horses, natural oak and lots of brass.

Number of Franchisees: 13 in Rhode Island and Massachusetts

In Business Since: 1983

Equity Capital Needed: $250,000 to $350,000 plus ability to acquire financing for an additional $350,000 to $600,000 depending on location.

Financial Assistance Available: Franchisee obtains own financing. Advice available.

Training Provided: Training at corporate headquarters and nearby Pubs. A minimum of 4 weeks training for franchisee. A minimum of 8 weeks training for the franchisee's 2 senior managers. Ongoing assistance on all aspects of the business.

Managerial Assistance Available: The company provides ongoing assistance on a regular basis for the management and operation of the Pub Dennis. Operations and equipment manuals provided.

Information Submitted: May 1990

PUDGIES PIZZA FRANCHISING, INC.
524 North Main Street
Elmira, New York 14901
Francis J. Cleary

Description of Operation: New York and Sicilian style pizza and a variety of hot and cold submarine sandwiches, burgers, French fries and standard soft drinks. 3,000 square feet free standing units with 72 and 82 seats and drive-in window. Pudgies is presently considering expansion into other Northeastern States under multi-unit development agreements.

Number of Franchisees: 36 units in New York and Pennsylvania plus 1 in South Carolina.

In Business Since: 1963, started franchising in 1973.

Equity Capital Needed: $125,000, excluding building and leasehold improvements; minimum capital requirements—$50,000.

Financial Assistance Available: No direct financing available. Pudgies does, however, assist in the preparation of the financing application and the structuring of the bank presentation. Company also makes available, to qualified franchisees, a list of potential developers who have expressed interest in investing in leasehold improvements.

Training Provided: 6 week program of classroom and in-store instruction at the company's schooling facilities in Elmira, New York.

Managerial Assistance Available: Pudgies has an ongoing inspection program designed to evaluate the individual store and advise as to physical and technical aspects of the operation. Pudgies also has a continued product development program and test-markets various related products for chain-wide introduction to the menu.

Information Submitted: April 1990

173

QUIZNO'S INTERNATIONAL, INC.
190 East 9th Avenue
Suite 190
Denver, Colorado 80203
Boyd R. Bartlett, Vice President

Description of Operation: Fast food franchise shops offering Classic Subs made of the finest, freshest ingredients. Quizno's compliments the Classic Subs with a unique salad and dessert menu.

Number of Franchisees: 31 in 2 States

In Business Since: 1981

Equity Capital Needed: Minimum of $40,000 (depending on location).

Financial Assistance Available: Financial assistance provided to qualified franchisees.

Training Provided: Franchisees complete a comprehensive training program in company store prior to franchise opening.

Managerial Assistance Available: Management representatives spend first 2 weeks assisting new franchisees in shops. Comprehensive operations manual provided with appropriate adjustments made to keep manuals updated. Operation hours response service available to franchisees to call for advice and problem solving.

Information Submitted: April 1990

RANELLI FRANCHISE SYSTEMS, INC.
dba RANELLIS DELI AND SANDWICH SHOPS
2134 Warrier Road
Birmingham, Alabama 35208
Frank A. Ranelli, President

Description of Operation: Ranellis is a deli and sandwich shop operation specializing in deli type sandwiches and pizza. Feature product is a 16" Poboy called a Richman. Also featured is homemade lasagna served every Thursday. Stores have a specialty grocery section as well as a by-the-pound deli case.

Number of Franchisees: 8 in 3 States

In Business Since: 1949, started franchising in 1979.

Equity Capital Needed: $7,500 franchise fee.

Financial Assistance Available: Total investment is approximately $40,000-$65,000 including franchise fee. Franchisor offers no financial assistance.

Training Provided: 2 weeks in company unit, 1 week at location. Continuing assistance with problems thereafter.

Managerial Assistance Available: Operations manual provided, and assistance with problems. Continuing inspections to avert problems.

Information Submitted: June 1990

RAX RESTAURANTS, INC.
1266 Dublin Road
Columbus, Ohio 43215
Robert W. Bafundo, Vice President/Franchising Operations

Description of Operation: Rax Restaurants, Inc., is headquartered in Columbus, Ohio. Rax Restaurants serve a wide menu, featuring sandwiches, salad bar, and baked potatoes with toppings. The Rax Restaurant is an upscale concept in menu and building design.

Number of Franchisees: 355 franchise stores and 135 company-operated units in 29 States and in Canada.

In Business Since: 1978

Equity Capital Needed: $100,000 plus net worth for lease.

Financial Assistance Available: None

Training Provided: Currently a 5 week program: 3 weeks of in-resturant training, beginning with production and service training, and basic management functions; 2 weeks of classroom training, focusing on supervisory skills and administration.

Managerial Assistance Available: Rax provides initial standard specifications and plans for the building, equipment, furnishings, decor, layout and signs, together with advice and consultation concerning same. Franchise area supervisors offer guidance and assistance beginning in the early stages of planning. A variety of company resources is available to franchisees in areas such as marketing, development and purchasing. Company training instructors are provided to train employees several days prior to opening, and remain in store 2 days after opening.

Information Submitted: April 1990

RED ROBIN INTERNATIONAL, INC.
9 Executive Circle, Suite 190
Irvine, California 92714
Madison Jobe, Vice President, Franchise

Description of Operation: Casual dining, full service restaurant and bar. Red Robin features gourmet burgers, steak, chicken, pasta, pizza and signature salads, and for dessert, delectable ice cream delights. America's Master Mixologists serve both potent concoctions and non-alcoholic "mocktails."

Number of Franchisees: 60 restaurants in 12 States and 2 provinces of Canada.

In Business Since: 1969

Equity Capital Needed: $300,000 $500,000

Financial Assistance Available: No direct financing. Red Robin will provide franchisee with lists of potential sources of lease/financing and potential investors.

Training Provided: Initial 10-12 weeks on-the-job training in corporate operations. Certain operations, training, and standards manuals, forms and other tools for operating the ongoing restaurant.

Managerial Assistance Available: Provide initial support and standard specifications for building, equipment, furnishings, decor, signage and purchasing for all goods used in the restaurant. Provide ongoing support in marketing, human resources, operations, training, real estate development and menu development. Regional franchise manager will make regular visits to the restaurant as well as direct the training team prior to and during the restaurant opening.

Information Submitted: May 1990

*RITZY'S AMERICA'S FAVORITES
1946 Old Henderson Road
Columbus, Ohio 43220
Franchise Sales Department

Description of Operation: Upscale decor, premium quality food and ice cream restaurant characterizing the soda shop or road side diner of the 1940s era. Featuring fresh grilled hamburgers, coneys, chicken, light menu.

Number of Franchisees: 57 in 12 States

In Business Since: 1980

Equity Capital Needed: $250,000

Financial Assistance Available: None

Training Provided: 3 weeks initial, then ongoing training for "refresher."

Managerial Assistance Available: Periodic visits to franchised store for advice and update. Assistance with training, operations, expansion planning.

Information Submitted: June 1990

*ROCKY ROCOCO CORPORATION
340 West Washington Avenue
Madison, Wisconsin 53703
Thomas R. Hester

Description of Operation: Pizza restaurant providing full dining, carry-out, drive-thru, delivery service and featuring pizza by the slice.

Number of Franchisees: 70 units including company-owned in Illinois, Iowa, Minnesota, Wisconsin, Colorado, Ohio, and Florida.

In Business Since: 1974

Equity Capital Needed: $75,000

Financial Assistance Available: None

Training Provided: 6 week manager training, combination of classroom and in-restaurant, various 1-2 day seminars.

Managerial Assistance Available: Continuous business assistance in areas such as real estate, construction, operations (from restaurant opening to regular visits), marketing, finance, and quality assurance.

Information Submitted: April 1990

ROLI BOLI
15 Engle Street
Suite 302
Englewood, New Jersey 07631
John Sterns

Description of Operation: Specialty sandwich operation, French bread dough stuffed with a variety of 25 different fillings and baked fresh to order.

Number of Franchisees: 3 franchises, 2 company-owned

In Business Since: 1987

Equity Capital Needed: $140,000-$190,000

Financial Assistance Available: Will assist.

Training Provided: 2 weeks at company store, 1 week on-site assistance.

Managerial Assistance Available: Ongoing

Information Submitted: June 1990

*ROMA CORPORATION
10,000 North Central Expressway
Suite 900
Dallas, Texas 75231
Dale Ross, Vice President, Franchise Development

Description of Operation: Tony Roma's is the largest dinnerhouse specializing in barbecue ribs and chicken along with famous onion ring loaf. We have a special niche in the industry with great price/value relationship, high quality food products and full bar service. Also offering take out and delivery.

Number of Franchisees: 121 in 18 States and 6 countries.

In Business Since: 1972 under private ownership, corporation since 1976.

Equity Capital Needed: $600,000-$900,000

Financial Assistance Available: None; Roma Corporation does not lend or guarantee the financial responsibilities of its franchisees.

Training Provided: Training of general manager and kitchen manager. Training program lasts 6 weeks. Refresher courses are available.

Managerial Assistance Available: Training program held in company-owned stores. In-store supervision and assistance offered before and after opening.

Information Submitted: April 1990

ROUND TABLE FRANCHISE CORPORATION
655 Montgomery Street
San Francisco, California 94111
Robert S. Veeneman, Vice President of Franchise Sales

Description of Operation: Round Table Pizza franchises are restaurants offering a distinctive atmosphere serving a superior pizza product, sandwiches, hamburgers, salads and beverages. Appealing to a broad spectrum of the public, we're known as "The Last Honest Pizza."

Number of Franchisees: Over 517 restaurants in 12 States.

In Business Since: Round Table originated in 1959, began franchising in 1962.

Equity Capital Needed: $320,000 ($100,000 cash minimum).

Financial Assistance Available: Assistance in seeking financing is provided.

Training Provided: Extensive 4 week training course required at our training facility in Culver City, California. Cost of training included in initial investment.

Managerial Assistance Available: Headquarters staff and field representatives provide comprehensive assistance and direction in site generation, financial assistance, restaurant start-up, staffing, cost control, maintenance, sanitation and quality control, local and regional marketing and system-wide advertising.

Information Submitted: April 1990

ROYAL GUARD FISH & CHIPS, INC.
4 Apple Tree Drive
Stamford, Connecticut 06905
Henry R. Parente, President, Franchising

Description of Operation: Fish and chips, etc., self-service seating or take-out.

Number of Franchisees: 3 in Connecticut, 1 in New York and 2 company-owned.

In Business Since: 1970

Equity Capital Needed: Contact company for full information.

Financial Assistance Available: None

Training Provided: 4 weeks company shop training.

Managerial Assistance Available: Bookkeeping, etc. Complete operation is supported by company manuals.

Information Submitted: April 1990

S.A.F. CALIFORNIA/LETTUCE PATCH
333 Bristol Street
Costa Mesa, California 92626

Description of Operation: Salad bar restaurant.

Number of Franchisees: 4 in California

In Business Since: 1976

Equity Capital Needed: $200,000 to $250,000

Financial Assistance Available: Total financial assistance available after extensive training program (approximately 1 year).

Training Provided: A franchisee will work in a new or existing unit, training in all phases of operation for approximately 1 year or until he has proven he can totally run the operation.

Managerial Assistance Available: Total assistance both managerial and technical for duration of franchise agreement.

Information Submitted: June 1990

SALADALLY RESTAURANTS, INC.
Suburban Square
Coulter Avenue & St. James Street
Ardmore, Pennsylvania 19003
Steve Byer

Description of Operation: Lite, healthy food with full service.

Number of Franchisees: 7

In Business Since: 1978

Equity Capital Needed: $150,000

Financial Assistance Available: None

Training Provided: Complete training in all aspects of operation.

Managerial Assistance Available: Site selection, start-up and ongoing.

Information Submitted: April 1990

SBARRO, INC.
763 Larkfield Road
Commack, New York 11725
Mario Sbarro, President

Description of Operation: Italian style restaurant chain, featuring pizza, calzone, sausage rolls, and other Italian specialty items.

Number of Franchisees: 76 in 13 States

In Business Since: 1977

Equity Capital Needed: $250,000-$750,000

Financial Assistance Available: None

Training Provided: 4 weeks training in all phases of operating a Sbarro restaurant.

Managerial Assistance Available: Managerial and technical assistance is given during training.

Information Submitted: June 1990

SCHLOTZSKY'S, INC.
200 West 4th Street
Austin, Texas 78701

Description of Operation: Limited menu sandwich shop concept featuring unique sandwiches served on daily fresh baked bread, also salads and soup.

Number of Franchisees: 224 in 14 States plus 23 company-owned.

In Business Since: 1971

Equity Capital Needed: Approximately $110,000.

Financial Assistance Available: Shlotzsky's, Inc., does not offer any financing arrangements.

Training Provided: Pre-opening training program in company-owned stores addressing all operational aspects of sandwich production and store management.

Managerial Assistance Available: Supply complete and detailed operations manual covering every aspect of shop operations. Immediate response to all significant operational problems encountered by licensee. Diagnostic business reviews and quality controls subject to check on a regular and consistent basis. Established elected-franchisee committee interfaces on a regular basis with Schlotzsky's, Inc.

Information Submitted: June 1990

SCOTTO MANAGEMENT CORPORATION
1895 Greentree Road
Cherry Hill, New Jersey 08003
John Scotto

Description of Operation: Sales of pizza by slice or by pie, Italian style sandwiches, specialty dishes.

Number of Franchisees: 50 Nationwide

In Business Since: 1977

Equity Capital Needed: $180,000-$209,000 approximately.

Financial Assistance Available: Scotto Management Corporation does not offer any financing arrangements nor does it recommend any particular financing institution.

Training Provided: Provide pre-opening training program at a Scotto Pizza Restaurant that would include food preparation, special recipes, advertising promotion, hiring and training of personnel and bookkeeping procedures. It is anticipated that the training program will be approximately 6 weeks.

Managerial Assistance Available: Assist licensee in selecting location and negotiating lease. Prepare and provide initial plans for building, equipment, furnishings, decor and signs, together with advice and consultation concerning them. Provide opening supervision with regard to promotion, merchandising, marketing and special techniques.

Information Submitted: June 1990

*SEAFOOD AMERICA
645 Mearns Road
Warminster, Pennsylvania 18974

Description of Operation: Seafood America is a retail seafood carry-out franchise. Approximately 1,600 square feet are needed to operate a Seafood America carry-out. The site may be located in either a viable shopping center or a free-standing building.

Number of Franchisees: 20 franchisees in Pennsylvania and New Jersey.

In Business Since: 1971

Equity Capital Needed: $60,000, total $150,000.

Financial Assistance Available: No financing assistance available.

Training Provided: A 2 phase traning program. The first takes place over a period of 6 to 8 weeks and requires 15 to 20 hours a week in an existing Seafood America restaurant. The second phase is post-opening and includes further training of franchisee and initial employees at franchisee's actual location lasting usually 6 weeks, with trainers gradually diminished during this period.

Managerial Assistance Available: Seafood America Franchise, Inc., provides a wide range of services designed to help the franchisee. These include one-time services such as site and building development as well as ongoing services such as purchasing, training, marketing and equipment engineering when needed. The company maintains trained employees to answer questions and lend assistance when needed.

Information Submitted: April 1990

SEAWEST SUB SHOPS, INC.
One Lake Bellevue Drive, Suite 107
Bellevue, Washington 98005
Jim Iseman, President

Description of Operation: Limited menu submarine sandwich; the franchise takes a flat fee of $2,000 year one; $3,000 year two; $4,000 years 3 through 10; no percentage royalty.

Number of Franchisees: 96 all franchised

In Business Since: 1980, franchised since 1985.

Equity Capital Needed: Minimum $15,000 cash.

Financial Assistance Available: Franchisees must obtain their own financing.

Training Provided: 2 weeks at regional office or Seattle, regional developer in market before a franchise is sold.

Managerial Assistance Available: Ongoing assistance.

Information Submitted: April 1990

SERGIO'S INTERNATIONAL, INC.
Suite 212
16 Broadway
Fargo, North Dakota 58102
Randy Thorson

Description of Operation: Franchising Mexican restaurants.

Number of Franchisees: 4 in Wisconsin and North Dakota

In Business Since: 1981

Equity Capital Needed: Varies from $145,000 to $220,000 per restaurant depending on the nature of the financing.

Financial Assistance Available: None

Training Provided: Franchisee and kitchen manager must attend a formal training program provided at a corporate store and normally lasting from 10 to 30 days.

Managerial Assistance Available: All types of managerial and technical assistance are provided by the franchisor to franchisee, including but not limited to training, marketing, accounting, quality control, site selection assistance, etc.

Information Submitted: June 1990

*SHAKEY'S INCORPORATED
651 Gateway Boulevard
Suite 1200
South San Francisco, California 94080
Stan Oliveira

Description of Operation: Shakey's new look is a turn of the century motif featuring stained glass, Tiffany lamps, hanging plants and natural woods. Customer dining areas have raised levels to create a comfortable atmosphere for the entire family. Menu features thick, thin and super pan pizza, chicken, sandwiches, pasta, salad bar, domestic and imported beers, wine and soft drinks. Shakey's is currently developing shopping center locations, conversion of existing structures as well as free standing restaurants.

Number of Franchisees: Over 400 in the United States, Canada, Mexico, Japan, the Phillippines, Guam, Singapore, Taiwan, West Indies, Malaysia and Thailand.

In Business Since: 1954

Equity Capital Needed: Varies—$400,000 working capital.

Financial Assistance Available: None

Training Provided: Complete training consisting of classroom and in-restaurant curriculum provided. Training at company facilities for a period of 3 weeks and grand opening assistance.

Managerial Assistance Available: Shakey's provides continual management service in such areas as marketing, quality control, and operations. Complete operating manuals are provided. Regional managers and dealer consultants work closely with franchisees and visit restaurants to assist in any problem area. Franchisees meet generally 2-3 times a year to exchange views and opinions with Shakey's advisory staff. Shakey's also provides site selection counseling and assistance in prototype plans and specifications and sources for FF&E.

Information Submitted: June 1990

SHONEY'S RESTAURANTS–AMERICA'S DINNER TABLE
1727 Elm Hill Pike
Nashville, Tennessee 37210
Attention: Jeffrey L. Heston, Executive Director
Franchise Development

Description of Operation: Full service family restaurant featuring original breakfast bar.

Number of Franchisees: 409 franchised units in 21 States.

In Business Since: 1959

Equity Capital Needed: $150,000 liquid

Financial Assistance Available: Franchisor does not provide financing but will assist franchisee in preparing package for presentation to financial institutions.

Training Provided: A 4 to 7 week formal training and management course is required for all new franchisees or their managers; and is conducted by qualified instructors at the franchisor's training facilities. Supervision and training at franchisee's location during initial start-up period is provided.

Managerial Assistance Available: Franchisor provides advisory services on areas of financing, real estate, site selection, construction, equipment, advertising, accounting, purchasing, training, opening and ongoing technical and operational support.

Information Submitted: April 1990

*SHOWBIZ PIZZA TIME, INC.
dba ShowBiz Pizza Place and Chuck E. Cheese
4441 West Airport Freeway
Irving, Texas 75062
Franchise Sales

Description of Operation: Are entertainment centers featuring life-sized animated floor shows; a menu of quality pizza, deli sandwiches and salad bar; plus games and rides for the entire family.

Number of Franchisees: 130 company-owned units and 127 franchised units.

In Business Since: Parent company 1980, franchising 1981.

Equity Capital Needed: $300,000

Financial Assistance Available: None

Training Provided: Instruction for managers and electronic specialists is provided at ShowBiz Pizza Time in Irving, Texas. Training in all phases of entertainment center operations is accomplished through classroom lectures, group exercises, and hands-on teaching.

Managerial Assistance Available: Site selection counseling and assistance; prototype plans; on-site opening assistance and supervision at franchisee's expense; installation of animated entertainment components at franchisee's expense; specifications and sources for FF & E; continuing advisory assistance on the operation of the franchised restaurant; periodic evaluation of the restaurant and of the products sold and used in its operation.

Information Submitted: April 1990

SIR BEEF, INC.
P. O. Box 15162
Evansville, Indiana 47716
Jon K. Fink, President

Description of Operation: Fast food restaurant with British atmosphere. Inside seating for 90 with a drive-up window. Limited menu with roast beef a feature item (55 percent of sales is roast beef). Fresh meat, not a processed loaf, roasted on site continually. Full salad bar, 15 different varieties of sandwiches, 18 side order varieties (baked potatoes, desserts, onion rings, etc.).

Number of Franchisees: 2 in Indiana

In Business Since: 1967

Equity Capital Needed: $150,000

Financial Assistance Available: None

Training Provided: Minimum 6 weeks on-job training needed.

Managerial Assistance Available: Field consultant works in unit with management to insure that the operation manual, which details system, procedures and control, is being followed.

Information Submitted: April 1990

*SIRLOIN STOCKADE INTERNATIONAL, INC.
Nine Compound Drive
Hutchinson, Kansas 67502
Judy Froese, Director of Franchise Development

Description of Operation: Sirloin Stockade family steakhouses feature a selection of top quality steaks, chicken and fish, served quickly and attractively, and a self-service salad bar, hot food and dessert bar, at affordable prices. Restaurant facilities are free standing buildings of 6,300-7,800 square feet, seating 240 to 320 persons. Approximately 1 acre of land is required.

Number of Franchisees: 64 units plus 6 company-owned units in 12 States.

In Business Since: Sirloin Stockade restaurants since 1966; Sirloin Stockade International, Inc., since 1984.

Equity Capital Needed: $100,000 minimum; must be able to obtain financing for land and building.

Financial Assistance Available: SSI estimates the total capital requirements to open a Sirloin Stockade franchise will range between $750,000 and $1 million, depending on the cost of real estate and the method of financing for improvements and equipment. Sirloin Stockade International provides no financing.

Training Provided: A comprehensive 6-week training program in all phases of operation is provided for store management at a company training facility. The franchisee receives a complete set of confidential operation manuals, including recipes and food prep procedures, employee training, marketing and equipment manuals.

Managerial Assistance Available: In addition to pre-opening assistance, SSI provides ongoing training, education and assistance during the lifetime of the franchise agreement. Regular visits by SSI operation field consultants offer assistance in solving field problems, conduct quality control surveys and evaluate store operations. Franchisees are informed of new development in the company and the industry, as well as techniques to improve productivity and profitability. A nation-wide marketing program is administered by the Franchise Marketing Advisory Council. Competitive food prices with weekly delivery are offered from the product distribution center.

Information Submitted: April 1990

SIR PIZZA INTERNATIONAL, INC.
15311 N.W. 60th Street
Miami Lakes, Florida 33014

Description of Operation: A full service or take-out and delivery pizza chain offering pizza, pasta, sandwiches, salads, and dessert. Video tape available detailing operations and support.

Number of Franchisees: 398 in 7 States and 5 countries

In Business Since: 1958

Equity Capital Needed: $105,000-$145,000

Financial Assistance Available: Will provide assistance in securing financing.

Training Provided: Complete on-the-job training program provided. Training covers all aspects of the business: operational procedures, bookkeeping, employee training, advertising and promotion and management techniques, menu selection.

Managerial Assistance Available: Comprehensive support for all franchisees includes assistance in site selection, store layout and design, equipment specifications, marketing, training, ongoing support, research and development.

Information Submitted: May 1990

SIZZLER STEAK-SEAFOOD-SALAD
12655 West Jefferson Boulevard
Los Angeles, California 90066
James S. McGinnis, Vice President, Franchise Development

Description of Operation: Moderately priced, self-service, limited menu restaurants featuring steaks, seafood and salads; emphasis on quick, convenient meals.

Number of Franchisees: 450 franchised and 205 company-owned, U.S. and foreign combined.

In Business Since: 1959

Equity Capital Needed: Net worth in excess of $1 million; minimum cash required $300,000. Multi-unit restaurant experience required.

Financial Assistance Available: None

Training Provided: 13 weeks in a certified training unit; 1 additional week at corporate office.

Managerial Assistance Available: Sizzler Steak-Seafood-Salad provides continued field and management services for life of the franchise in areas of marketing, advertising, and training of key personnel, accounting, purchasing, restaurant management and scheduled training schools and seminars. The Sizzler Restaurant Management Guide, a confidential plan for successful management, is provided each new licensee. Field representatives contact periodically to review progress and help institute new policies and procedures to improve service, sales and profits.

Information Submitted: April 1990

SKINNY HAVEN, INC.
2710 East Regal Park Drive
Anaheim, California 92806

Description of Operation: Restaurants that cater to special diets in a healthy way of eating.

Number of Franchisees: 7 in California, Texas and Arizona plus 6 company-owned.

In Business Since: 1970

Equity Capital Needed: Depends on type and size of unit.

Financial Assistance Available: None

Training Provided: 4 to 8 weeks—dependent on franchisee's previous experience.

Managerial Assistance Available: Daily assistance in all phases from start to approximately 2 weeks after opening. District managers are available thereafter for any assistance required.

Information Submitted: June 1990

*SKIPPER'S, INC.
14450 N.E. 29th Place
Suite 200
Bellevue, Washington 98007
Bob Taft, C.O.O.

Description of Operation: Skipper's offers a limited menu of fish, shrimp, oysters, clams, chicken, salad bar, salads, and clam chowder in a casual, quick service, moderately priced restaurant with a fisherman's wharf motif. Approximately 2,100 square feet of restaurant, with beer and wine, open 7 days a week. Currently we have a total of 215 restaurants open.

Number of Franchisees: 30

In Business Since: 1969

Equity Capital Needed: $75,000-$100,000 and ability to acquire outside financing depending on location, and if property is leased or purchased.

Financial Assistance Available: None

Training Provided: 8 weeks of classroom and in-restaurant training at specified Skipper's training restaurants. Further training will be provided at the opening of the franchisee's new restaurant. This program is designed for the individual with no restaurant background.

Managerial Assistance Available: Skipper's, Inc., will provide representatives who will visit a franchisee's restaurant periodically for inspections and assistance in the areas of operations, cost control, marketing, accounting, real estate and construction. Franchisee will be supplied with complete sets of manuals of operations, all necessary forms, standard specifications and building plans, site selection assistance, marketing support and purchasing support.

Information Submitted: June 1990

SKOLNIKS, INC.
10801 Electron Drive
Suite 308
Louisville, Kentucky 40299
Larry Baresel, Director of Franchise Administration

Description of Operation: Skolniks Bagel Bakery Restaurants offer a delicatessen style menu of fresh foods served on bagels, which are baked on-site, together with a streamlined service system to cut traditional service time and increase sales.

Number of Franchisees: 10

In Business Since: 1981

Equity Capital Needed: Subject to franchisee's financial status.

Financial Assistance Available: None

Training Provided: 5 weeks of intensive restaurant operations and management training are provided by the company for 2 people together with operation and management manuals. Grand opening team is provided prior to opening to assist in training crew and opening.

Managerial Assistance Available: Site selection, construction, lease negotiation, marketing/advertising and accounting. Director of franchise operations visits each franchisee on regular basis to review/assist operations and store.

Information Submitted: April 1990

SKYLINE CHILI, INC.
109 Illinois Avenue
Cincinnati, Ohio 45215
Bill Kagler, President

Description of Operation: Manufacturer of chili and franchisor of restaurants serving a limited menu specializing in chili related food products.

Number of Franchisees: 52

In Business Since: 1949

Equity Capital Needed: $30,000-$150,000 depending on nature of intended site.

Financial Assistance Available: None

Training Provided: 5 week in-depth training program consisting of 4 weeks on-the-job training (in company stores) and 1 week management workshop.

Managerial Assistance Avaialble: Comprehensive management training program, restaurant opening assistance, and periodic quality assurance reviews, and updates on techniques, equipment, etc.

Information Submitted: June 1990

*SONIC INDUSTRIES, INC.
120 Robert S. Kerr Avenue
Oklahoma City, Oklahoma 73102
Robert P. Flack, Vice President of Corporate
Development

Description of Operation: Fast food drive-in restaurant specifically designed for speed of service and freshness of food. Emphasis on hamburgers, hot dogs, onion rings.

Number of Franchisees: 924 plus 91 company-owned in 22 States

In Business Since: 1959

Equity Capital Needed: $38,000 to $68,000, includes $15,000 franchise fee.

Financial Assistance Available: None

Training Provided: Franchisor requires classroom and on-location training and provides management seminars and periodic updates on new techniques and profit making.

Managerial Assistance Available: Specifically designed and tested equipment; certain expertise in site selection; quality control recommendations and testing of food products; requirements of proper training, chain-wide inspection program. Helps to provide voluntary chain-wide advertising programs and purchasing co-ops. Sonic Industries, Inc., provides time-tested managerial and technical assistance to each franchise with the ultimate goal of profit and success.

Information Submitted: June 1990

SONNY'S REAL PIT BAR-B-Q, INC.
3631 S.W. Archer Road
Gainesville, Florida 32608
Frank K. Scharf, Jr., Director of Marketing/Franchise
Sales

Description of Operation: Sonny's Real Pit Bar-B-Q, Inc., offers a licensing program for the South's most successful and finest barbeque restaurants. Family dining, including lunch specials and diet plates, a 40 item salad bar, children's menu, catering and take-out service are also available. Seating ranges from 80 up to 200 plus.

Number of Franchisees: 80 currently open. Area of operations incude Florida, Georgia, Alabama, North Carolina, Mississippi, Louisiana and Kentucky.

In Business Since: 1968, licensing since 1977.

Equity Capital Needed: Net worth of approximately $350,000 (excluding primary residence) with a minimum liquidity of $150,000. The franchise fee is $35,000.

Financial Assistance Available: None

Training Provided: In one of our restaurants licensee will be fully trained in all departments (cooking, service, purchasing and bookkeeping), usually 400 man-hours or until company and licensee are sure of licensee's readiness to open their own restaurant.

Managerial Assistance Available: In addition to manager training we also train assistant manager or head cook for additional 150 hours in kitchen operation. Additional services available under the system for the franchisee is central purchasing, field operations evaluation, field training, initial store opening, newsletter, regional and national meetings. Advertising and marketing assistance is also available on an ongoing basis to current franchisees.

Information Submitted: April 1990

SOUP AND SALAD SYSTEMS, INC.
2645 Financial Court
Suite A
San Diego, California 92117
Don Boensel, President

Description of Operation: Owner and operator of Soup Exchange restaurants. These are modern self-service soup, salad, bakery, and dessert bar operations that offer a wide variety of fresh, healthful, high quality foods in an upscale dinner-house dining environment. Size ranges from 5,000 to 10,000 square feet and seating from 175 to over 300 with patios. Average meal price is $6.00 to $6.50 in an all-you-can-eat format; a 60 item salad bar, 6 fresh soups per day, and freshly baked muffins, breads and pastries are featured, along with fresh fruits.

Number of Franchisees: 12 in 5 States

In Business Since: 1978, including predessors.

Equity Capital Needed: $150,000 to $300,000 depending on location.

Financial Assistance Available: Assistance in preparation of forecasts and plans for securing financing through leasing and loan arrangements. Direct loans or equity seed financing are also available in some limited special circumstances.

Training Provided: Intensive training of up to 5 key personnel for 60 days at one of the existing Soup Exchange locations is a requirement for each franchise location.

Managerial Assistance Available: A complete and comprehensive operating manual is provided, along with a library of training video segments for each of the job functions in a Soup Exchange restaurant. Assistance is also provided for site analysis and selection, lease/purchase analysis and negotiation, design and construction of the facility, recruitment, interview, and hiring of the initial work crew, and the presence of an on-site supervisor for at least 1 week before and 1 week after the scheduled opening. In addition, ongoing guidance and direction as well as on-site assistance are provided through area representatives via visits twice per month at each franchise store; these are supplemented by daily accumulation of sales, labor, and food cost data from each franchise location through a modern point-of-sale data acquisition system linked to a home office computer.

Information Submitted: April 1990

SPINNER'S PIZZA
910 KCK Way
Cedar Hill, Texas 75104
Dick Pryor

Description of Operation: Spinner's Pizza provides management expertise to enable you to operate a pizza delivery and take-out business in a proven and profitable manner. The system includes a two for the price of one marketing system backed up by the finest ingredients and best equipment available. Operates from 1,000 square foot space with approximately 12 employees. A simple menu consisting of large or small pizza and a sub sandwich (three varieties).

Number of Franchisees: 40

In Business Since: 1984

Equity Capital Needed: Cash requirements $35,000 to $65,000 depending on whether you lease or purchase equipment package.

Financial Assistance Available: Equipment leasing program available, plus assistance in finding sources of financing.

Training Provided: Franchisee/operator receives practical, on-site training of up to 500 hours at company store in Dallas, Texas. Trainee must complete certification test at end of training.

Managerial Assistance Available: Ongoing assistance and support with site selection, lease negotiation, equipment leasing or purchase, advertising and marketing.

Information Submitted: April 1990

THE STEAK ESCAPE
ESCAPE ENTERPRISES, INC.
1265 Neil Avenue
Columbus, Ohio 43201
Kennard M. Smith, Chairman

Description of Operation: The Steak Escape typically operates in 600 to 900 square feet located in retail mall food courts or in specialty retail projects. We specialize in fresh grilled sandwiches and fresh-cut French fries. Outstanding performance record and industry reputation.

Number of Franchisees: 64 in 20 States and 2 countries.

In Business Since: 1982

Equity Capital Needed: Total investment approximately $180,000 to $230,000

Financial Assistance Available: None

Training Provided: Management training—4 to 6 weeks and store opening training—3 weeks.

Managerial Assistance Available: Store planning and design. Architectural drawing development. Ongoing weekly and monthly support with regard to all aspects of store operations.

Information Submitted: May 1990

STEAK-OUT FRANCHISING, INC.
8210 Stephanie Drive
Huntsville, Alabama 35802
David Martin, President

Description of Operation: The home and office delivery of char-broiled steak and chicken dinners, with freshly prepared salads and baked potato. The menu also offers other related char-broiled items as well as beverage and dessert. A Steak-Out facility is usually located in a strip shopping center or on-street store front with good vehicular visibility.

Number of Franchisees: As of July 1, 1990, 12 multi-unit franchise owners operating 18 Steak-Out facilities in 14 cities throughout the South and Southwest, with approximately 50 additional units contractually committed to open within the next 24 months. In addition, 3 corporate units are currently operating in Huntsville, Alabama.

In Business Since: 1987

Equity Capital Needed: The start-up capital required to open a Steak-Out unit ranges from approximately $70,000 to $100,000 depending on the size of the facility, which determines the amount of equipment and leasehold improvements.

Financial Assistance Available: The franchisor provides no financial assistance. However, a substantial part of the initial investment may be obtainable by qualified applicants through third party sources.

Training Provided: The franchisor provides intense classroom and on-the-job training at its headquarters training facility for 6-8 weeks. In addition, further training is given at the owners' franchised premises.

Managerial Assistance Available: The franchisor provides an ongoing managerial assistance program through periodic visitations by its field personnel. This assistance includes quality control improvement, profit and loss evaluation, personnel recruitment, and other operational matters.

Information Submitted: July 1990

STEWART'S RESTAURANTS, INC.
114 West Atlantic Avenue
Clementon, New Jersey 08021
Michael W. Fessler, President

Description of Operation: Drive-in restaurants, with or without dining room, with car-hop service.

Number of Franchisees: 51 in 5 States

In Business Since: 1924

Equity Capital Needed: $50,000-$75,000

Financial Assistance Available: Land acquisition is franchisee's responsibility.

Training Provided: Complete on-the-job training program provided. Training covers all aspects of the business: operational procedures, bookkeeping, employee training, advertising and promotion and management techniques, menu selection.

Managerial Assistance Available: Regional managers continue to counsel dealer in advertising, merchandising and quality control for the life of the franchise. Parent company helps with local advertising and promotion.

Information Submitted: April 1990

STRAW HAT COOPERATIVE CORPORATION
dba STRAW HAT PIZZA
6400 Village Parkway
Dublin, California 94568
Jack T. Wood, President & CEO

Description of Operation: Eat in-take out-delivery of 3 kinds of pizza (original/pan/sourdough), salad bar, soft drinks, sandwiches, beer and wine.

Number of Franchisees: 80 restaurants

In Business Since: 1969

Equity Capital Needed: $80,000-$450,000

Financial Assistance Available: None

Training Provided: 4 week training program.

Managerial Assistance Available: Ongoing

Information Submitted: April 1990

STUCKEY'S CORP.
2135 Wisconsin Avenue, N.W.
Suite 403
Washington, D.C. 20007
Charles Rosencrans, Vice Chairman

Description of Operation: A one-stop center for the traveler on the interstates and main U.S. highways. Specializing in unique pecan candies, a broad-based food service program, restaurant seating, novelties, gifts, and souvenirs, gasoline service and sparkling clean restrooms. Open 7 days per week, approximately 12-14 hours per day.

Number of Franchisees: 117 in 25 States

In Business Since: 1931

Equity Capital Needed: Amount varies dependent upon individual situation. Determined during discussions.

Financial Assistance Available: Limited—dependent upon individual situation.

Training Provided: 3 week program in zone training stores. This includes business operation procedure, bookkeeping procedures, management techniques, on-the-job experience in our local shoppe and concepts and procedures of the administrative functions of the corporate office. Periodic regional meetings for continuous updating on procedures and operations are held.

Managerial Assistance Available: Managerial and technical assistance is provided in site location, site preparation and building construction. Company representatives also visit units periodically for inspection and assistance in all phases of the business. Home office personnel are always available to assist the franchisee in all areas of the business. A complete accounting and retail auditing service is available at a nominal monthly fee. Stuckey's sponsors meetings of franchisees and meets with the franchise advisory board. A newsletter is also sent to all franchisees.

Information Submitted: April 1990

STUFF 'N TURKEY
15 Engle Street
Suite 302
Englewood, New Jersey 07631

Description of Operation: Specialty deli operation featuring home cooked turkey and glazed ham. A unique healthy and home cooked approach.

Number of Franchisees: 7 franchises, 7 company stores.

In Business Since: 1986

Equity Capital Needed: $140,000-$190,000

Financial Assistance Available: Will assist.

Training Provided: 2 weeks at company store, 1 week on-site

Managerial Assistance Available: Ongoing

Information Submitted: June 1990

STUFT PIZZA FRANCHISE CORPORATION
26875 Calle Hermosa
Capistrano Beach, California 92624
Bill Boie, Vice President, Franchise Development

Description of Operation: Stuft Pizza operates 3 company stores and has an additional 29 franchises. This chain's award winning pizza features fresh dough, hand-formed and tossed to develop a fine and tender crust. Incorporating a special sauce and the finest cheeses available, Stuft Pizza selects vegetables fresh each day and uses only the choicest meats. This outstanding pizza can be enjoyed in a relaxed and pleasant atmosphere, suitable for all ages.

Number of Franchisees: 27 in California and 2 in Oregon

In Business Since: 1976

Equity Capital Needed: $105,000 to $500,000

Financial Assistance Available: Franchisee obtains own financing.

Training Provided: Training includes 2 weeks intensive management and operation experience in existing store plus full-time consultant first 5 days of operation on new franchise. Continuing advisory services provided including consultation on promotions, business problems and analysis of business.

Managerial Assistance Available: Stuft Pizza will provide, at no charge to franchisee, assistance in site selection, business format, operations manual, standardized recordkeeping techniques, and continuing consultation services.

Information Submitted: May 1990

SUB & STUFF SANDWICH SHOPS, INC.
Suite 412, First National Center
Hutchinson, Kansas 67501
Louis Stoico, President, CEO

Description of Operation: Specialty sandwich shop operation including Italian style submarine sandwiches and steak sandwiches.

Number of Franchisees: 6 in Kansas

In Business Since: 1977

Equity Capital Needed: $60,000-$100,000

Financial Assistance Available: No.

Training Provided: 3 week comprehensive on-the-job management training program in one of franchisor's units prior to store opening. Pre-opening and opening week assistance in training part-time employees.

Managerial Assistance Available: Ongoing operational assistance and appraisal. Location selection and lease negotiation assistance. Store development guidance and standard building plans for free-standing units. Operative and advertising manuals. Guidance and assistance in all aspects of advertising and promotion. Ongoing product review and new product testing.

Information Submitted: June 1990

SUB STATION II, INC.
P. O. Box Drawer 2260
Sumter, South Carolina 29151-2260
Richard W. Reid, Vice President

Description of Operation: Sub Station II sandwich shops offer a variety of over 25 submarine sandwiches. We have developed an efficient method of preparing each sandwich to the customer's request. Emphasis is on high quality food and cleanliness.

Number of Franchisees: 93 in 11 States

In Business Since: 1975, first franchise began opration in January of 1976.

Equity Capital Needed: Minimum of $65,000

Financial Assistance Available: Provides franchisee with financial counseling and assistance in locating financing sources.

Training Provided: Owner/operator must complete a minimum of 7 consecutive full days at a designated training unit. A representative of the training department is avaiable for a period of up to 7 days prior to opening to assist with installation of equipment and decor and 7 days after opening to assist in training additional staff and follow-up on the progress of the trainee.

Managerial Assistance Available: Operations, maintenance, equipment, public relations, and food safety manual is provided. Also availble is promotional and advertising material and field representation, consultation and assistance.

Information Submitted: June 1990

*SUBWAY
325 Bic Drive
Milford, Connecticut 06460
Donald G. Furtman, Franchise Director

Description of Operation: Freshly prepared foot-long specialty sandwiches (submarines) and salads. Present menu includes 10 varieties of hot and cold sandwiches. No grilling is involved other than in a microwave oven. All stores have a take-out service and many stores have eat-in facilities. Stores are open late 7 nights per week. All franchisees make freshly baked bread and whole wheat bread.

Number of Franchisees: 4,400 in 50 States, Washington, D.C., Canada, Puerto Rico, Bahrain, the Bahamas, and Australia

In Business Since: 1965 (franchising since 1974)

Equity Capital Needed: Approximately $35,000. Total investment $39,900 to $67,900.

Financial Assistance Available: Equipment leasing available depending on analysis of financial statements.

Training Provided: Subway provides 2 weeks of comprehensive classroom and practical training at Subway headquarters for store owners and store managers. The classroom curriculum includes training in location selection, store construction, accounting procedures, and management theory as well as instruction in business analysis, product formulas and control mechanisms specific to Subway system. In addition to classroom study, practical training is provided in one of the local Subway stores to develop skills in sandwich making along with the day-to-day operation and management of a successful Subway store.

Managerial Assistance Available: During store construction, which takes between 20 and 60 days, managerial and technical assistance is provided for each franchisee by a development agent and an office coordinator assigned to handle their file. Areas covered in this assistance include site selection, store design and layout, interior construction, equipment purchasing, arrangement of suppliers and initial inventory ordering. When a store is scheduled to open, a development agent is available to help oversee the operation and provide back-up support for the store owner in areas of employee training and successful operational procedure. After store opening, periodic inspections and field visits are conducted in each unit by the assigned development agent. Continual office support is made available to each franchisee through frequent contact with one's assigned coordinator. The coordinator development agent system for service provides continual assistance and support for each franchisee through the life of the franchise (20 years). Weekly, a newsletter comprised of articles written by department heads is sent to all franchisees. With receipt of this newsletter all franchisees are kept continually apprised of new company policies and developments across the country. Also included in this publication are sections dealing with store management. Ongoing assistance in advertising is provided by the franchise advertising fund, which is directed by a board of directors comprised of 11 store owners elected by the franchisees.

Information Submitted: April 1990

*TACO BELL CORPORATION HEADQUARTERS
17901 Von Karman Avenue
Irvine, California 92714
Attention: Manager, Franchise Development

Description of Operation: Taco Bell is the nation's largest operator and franchisor of fast service Mexican food restaurants with over 3,100 units operating in over 40 States, as well as internationally. Franchised restaurants total 1,250 to date.

Number of Franchisees: 350 in 47 States

In Business Since: 1962 (franchising since 1965)

Equity Capital Needed: Minimum requirement of $1,000,000 net worth, $250,000 of which needs to be liquid assets.

Financial Assistance Available: None provided.

Training Provided: 150 hour restaurant orientation is part of the initial orientation program. After qualifying, training is a four-step process beginning with a pre-opening 2 to 6 week intensive training program for the franchise owner and manager. Additional training programs for management personnel are held at division training centers during the course of the year, with crew training programs available.

Managerial Assistance Available: Real estate orientation and site selection assistance are provided. An operations professional assist in the opening of the restaurant. Ongoing consultation is provided as required.

Information Submitted: May 1990

TACO CASA INTERNATIONAL, LTD.
P. O. Box 4542
Topeka, Kansas 66604
James F. Reiter, President

Description of Operation: Taco Casa International, Ltd., is the operator and franchisor for Taco Casa restaurants. Taco Casa is a fast food Mexican restaurant featuring a limited menu and quick, courteous service in an attractive atmosphere. Taco Casa International, Ltd., operates both free-standing and enclosed mall locations. Normal operating hours are from 11 am to 12 midnight, 7 days a week.

Number of Franchisees: 20 in 8 States plus 2 company-owned.

In Business Since: 1963

Equity Capital Needed: The total franchise package is approximately $85,000, which includes equipment, inventory, start-up costs, starting capital, plus leasehold improvements.

Financial Assistance Available: May assist in methods for arranging financing.

Training Provided: An initial 2 weeks for new licensees at our training school. One week assistance upon opening the new unit. Complete operations manual provided to unit. Continuous counseling and assistance with routine inspections by company representative. Monthly newsletter updating current events in Taco Casa and restaurant industry.

Managerial Assistance Available: Open line for licensee's inquiries and assistance. Perusal of weekly reports by Taco Casa headquarters and appraisal given. Routine inspections and assistance by company representatives. Bulletins concerning important legislation. Continuing research in products and procedures. Assistance in advertising. Regional or national advertising when minimum level of units makes it possible.

Information Submitted: April 1990

TACO GRANDE, INC.
P.O. Box 780066
Wichita, Kansas 67278
John Wylie, President

Description of Operation: Mexican limited menu restaurants.

Number of Franchisees: 15 plus 9 company stores in 5 States.

In Business Since: 1960

Equity Capital Needed: $250,000 to $45,000 minimum cash requirement.

Financial Assistance Available: None

Training Provided: 4 to 6 weeks in company store.

Managerial Assistance Available: Operations manual, training manual and franchise development guidelines manual provided. Consultation on operations, marketing, real estate, construction and menu development.

Information Submitted: April 1990

*TACO JOHN'S INTERNATIONAL
808 West 20th Street
Cheyenne, Wyoming 82001
Harold Holmes and James F. Woodson

Description of Operation: Taco John's is a fast food, carry-out, limited menu, Mexican food operation. Restaurants are between 800 and 2,200 square feet. The locations can be free-standing, in line or a food court. Most units have drive-thrus where available.

Number of Franchisees: 447 in 31 States

In Business Since: 1969

Equity Capital Needed: $70,000 minimum

Financial Assistance Available: A minimum total investment of $150,000 is necessary to open a Taco John's unit. The ideal method of financing is at a local bank, and Taco John's International is available to provide background information, projections, references, etc., to the bank to enable them to make a decision on the loan. A number of SBA loans have been obtained and a few units have been leased. If the franchisee desires to lease the building and equipment, Taco John's has sources available for them to contact.

Training Provided: An intensive 15 day mandatory training course is scheduled for all franchisees or their managers in Cheyenne, Wyoming. The training consists of a combination of classroom and actual production at an operating Taco John's unit.

Managerial Assistance Available: Taco John's International provides technical and managerial assistance through the life of the franchise. When the new Taco John's is open, we provide opening personnel for approximately 1 week thereafter, and periodic calls by Woodson-Holmes field personnel; complete manuals of operation, forms, and directions are provided and are continually updated. In addition, advertising materials are provided periodically, a monthly newsletter gives operating tips and general information, and regional and national meetings are held throughout the year and provide additional assistance.

Information Submitted: April 1990

THE TACO MAKER, INC.
P. O. Box 9519
Ogden, Utah 84409
Gil L. Craig, President
Wayne P. Webster, Jr., Executive Vice President

Description of Operation: Mexican fast food, American style, franchising. Great menu, inside seating and drive-thru window, quick service, quality products.

Number of Franchisees: 82 in 18 States and Puerto Rico, Saudi Arabia and Panama.

In Business Since: 1977 (with 18 years in other Mexican fast food under different names).

Equity Capital Needed: $60,000 to $75,000 minimum

Financial Assistance Available: Open for discussion.

Training Provided: 30 day training. Great store opening program with marketing.

Managerial Assistance Available: Continual ongoing follow-up in advertising, research and development; operational and other. Pre-opening and grand opening detail assistance.

Information Submitted: April 1990

TACO MAYO FRANCHISE SYSTEMS, INC.
10405 Greenbriar Place
Suite B
Oklahoma City, Oklahoma 73159
Randy Earhart, President

Description of Operation: Taco Mayo is a fast food Mexican restaurant with an ever increasing broad range of customers. All of our products are prepared fresh daily with only the finest ingredients. We have recently completed construction of our new 2,000 square foot prototype building designed to provide our customers with pleasant inside dining and a fast, efficient drive-thru service.

Number of Franchisees: 35 franchise units plus 20 company units in Oklahoma, Texas, Arkansas, Kansas, and New Mexico.

In Business Since: 1978

Equity Capital Needed: $80,000 to $300,000

Financial Assistance Available: None

Training Provided: We offer an extensive, comprehensive training program of approximately 6 to 8 weeks that is designed to familiarize each individual with basic operational skills necessary to operate a successful operation.

Managerial Assistance Available: To provide a continuing advisory service including, but not limited to, consulting on franchisee's promotional, business or operational problems. To provide analysis of franchisee's sales, marketing and financial data. To provide franchisee informational bulletins on sales, marketing developments and suggested operational techniques.

Information Submitted: May 1990

*TACO TICO, INC.
7610 Stemmons Freeway
Suite 600
Dallas, Texas 75247
Director of Licensing

Description of Operation: Taco Tico, Inc., is engaged in the business of operating and granting licenses to operate high quality, limited menu, Mexican style fast food restaurants.

Number of Franchisees: 41 units in 7 States (plus 75 company-operated units).

In Business Since: 1962

Equity Capital Needed: Over $50,000.

Financial Assistance Available: No direct financial assistance is available. Company may, however, be able to direct franchisee to prospective financing sources or assist in preparing financial presentations to lending institutions or investors.

Training Provided: A pre-opening training course is conducted in a designated restaurant by a company training instructor.

Managerial Assistance Available: Complete operation manual detailing product preparation, quality control, cost control and other key areas. Field assistance to help resolve operational problems. Advisory service available on all functional areas of the business.

Information Submitted: June 1990

*TACO TIME INTERNATIONAL, INC.
3880 West 11th Avenue
P. O. Box 2056
Eugene, Oregon 97402
Jim Thomas, Vice President, Franchise Development

Description of Operation: Taco Time® is a dynamic leader in the Mexican fast-food business. Outstanding food products feature quality fresh ingredients and exciting menu items. New 1,800 square foot solarium or 1,950 square foot tile roof prototype units are highly efficient and attractively designed to encourage high volume sales and low break-even point. High quality food and new product development have made Taco Time® a favorite in the United States, Canada, Japan, Venezuela, and the United Arab Emirates.

Number of Franchisees: 292 in the United States, 101 in foreign countries and 19 company-owned.

In Business Since: 1959

Equity Capital Needed: Approximate initial investment: $129,000 to $203,000 (exclusive of leasehold improvements and land and building costs).

Financial Assistance Available: No financing by franchisor, its agents, or affiliates, but some packaging assistance and resource referrals are available.

Training Provided: Taco Time International, Inc., conducts an extensive 5 week training program at its corporate headquarters in Eugene, Oregon. The program is taught in two phases. Phase I focuses on co-worker skills and Phase II teaches management and administrative skills. Taco Time International, Inc.'s pre-opening team assists in the actual store opening, followed by continued support.

Managerial Assistance Available: Franchise operations personnel conduct in-store visitations and facility inspections periodically. Trouble-shooting and pre-opening assistance for new stores are additional services provided. Franchisees are kept up-to-date through bulletins, training seminars, and conventions. Research and development on new products is a continuing process carried on at corporate headquarters. Computer software for accounting and food cost explosion programs are also available for franchisee purchase.

Information Submitted: April 1990

TASTEE FREEZ INTERNATIONAL, INC.
8345 Hall Road, P. O. Box 162
Utica, Michigan 48087
David K. Chapoton, President
James Brasier, Vice President

Description of Operation: Year-round fast food services family restaurants and seasonal ice cream stores. The menu includes a variety of foods, such as the Tastee Burger family, Tastee Crisp Chicken family, fish and salad bar. Also features the complete line of Tastee-Freez soft ice cream desserts plus new homemade premium ice cream. Seeking individuals or investor groups capable of multi-unit as well as single unit development in reserve market areas.

Number of Franchisees: Over 400 throughout 38 States and overseas.

In Business Since: 1950

Equity Capital Needed: Total investments for restaurant equipment and license run from $55,000 to $125,000, which does not include sales tax if applicable, or operating capital and food inventory.

Financial Assistance Available: T.F.I. does not provide direct financing to franchisees at the present time. However, it does provide assistance in obtaining financing, such as assisting the franchisee in preparing his proposal for bank financing and meeting with potential lenders.

Training Provided: Training course for all new licensees conducted at company training center and/or licensee's own store. Source covers managerial, accounting, promotional, food preparation and operational phases under actual operating conditions. Continuous in-field counseling thereafter, covering merchandising, quality control, advertising and promotion by company regional store supervisors.

Managerial Assistance Available: Regional territorial franchisees and/or State supervisors continue to counsel licensee in cost controls, new operational methods, advertising, merchandising and quality control. In addition, company conducts national convention once each year for all licensees to exchange ideas on merchandising, advertising, management and new food preparation methods.

Information Submitted: May 1990

TEXAS TOM'S, INC.
11918 Mar-Bec Trail
Independence, Missouri 64119
Tom Nigro, President

Description of Operation: We offer a wide variety of food items on the menu and homemade recipes. Both sit-down and carry-out service are available and also call-in service. We also feature several "basket" combinations, unique to the fast food industry. Western decor.

Number of Franchisees: 9 in Missouri and Kansas

In Business Since: 1953

Equity Capital Needed: $50,000

Financial Assistance Available: Company assists qualified applicants in arranging financing. Assistance in obtaining equipment financing, equipment lease, sign lease and specifications.

Training Provided: 3 weeks in-store traning. Company also will send qualified representative after store opens for 2 weeks (minimum).

Managerial Assistance Available: Provide assistance in site selection, building financing, lease negotiations, accounting referral, and continuous advisory assistance. Also, inspection of premises and advertising aids.

Information Submitted: June 1990

TIPPY'S TACO HOUSE, INC.
P. O. Box 665
Winnsboro, Texas 75494
W. L. Locklier, President

Description of Operation: Fast food to take home—using drive-thru and inside seating—Mexican food.

Number of Franchisees: 17 in 6 States

In Business Since: 1967

Equity Capital Needed: Cash and credit, approximately $106,000 plus.

Financial Assistance Available: None

Training Provided: Pre-opening training on location at operating unit and opening week training.

Managerial Assistance Available: Continuing assistance by personal visitations, letters, bulletins, telephone.

Information Submitted: May 1990

*TOGO'S EATERY
M.T.C. MANAGEMENT INC.
900 East Campbell Avenue, Suite 1
Campbell, California 95008
Ross Woodard, Vice President

Description of Operation: Fast food sandwiches.

184

Number of Franchisees: 126 in California, 1 in Oregon and 1 in Texas.

In Business Since: 1977

Equity Capital Needed: $90,000 to $160,000

Financial Assistance Available: None

Training Provided: 2 weeks on-site with periodic follow-up.

Managerial Assistance Available: Purchasing, cost control, sanitation, product development, promotion, and general management for the life of the franchise.

Information Submitted: April 1990

TUBBY'S SUB SHOPS, INC.
34500 Doreka Drive
Fraser, Michigan 48026
John G. Yatros, Senior Vice President of Franchising

Description of Operation: A unique fast food concept serving 25 varieties of submarine sandwiches competitively priced. Sandwiches offered consist of steak, burger, ham and traditional Italian meats. All sandwiches are custom made to order either cold or grilled, using only high quality ingredients. Customer services offered are sit-down, drive-thru and call-in with some stores offering a delivery service. Area franchises currently available.

Number of Franchisees: 60 in Michigan, 1 in Florida, 1 in Illinois (to open summer, 1990), 1 company-owned.

In Business Since: 1968

Equity Capital Needed: Cash and credit, approximately $97,500 to $251,500.

Financial Assistance Available: None

Training Provided: 150 hours minimum of comprehensive training for franchise owners, which includes indoctrination in all upper management functions, plus orientation in every phase of store operation at an operating unit.

Managerial Assistance Available: Continual accessibility to company headquarters. Development of public, employee and community relations, services of company supervisor in assembling an opening staff for unit operation, plus others.

Information Submitted: May 1990

2 FOR 1 PIZZA ENTERPRISES
736 East Lincoln
Orange, California 92665
John T. Murray, President

Description of Operation: 2 for 1 Pizza Company, take-out and delivery pizza. With buy 1 and get 1 free offer always in effect. We require approximately 1,100 square feet with ample store front parking and open 12-14 hours per day.

Number of Franchisees: 19 franchised and 24 units company-owned in California, South Carolina and Hawaii.

In Business Since: 1982

Equity Capital Needed: $35,000

Financial Assistance Available: A total or $70,000 is necessary to open a 2 for 1 Pizza Co. franchise. We offer assistance in locating lenders.

Training Provided: 6 weeks in training store.

Managerial Assistance Available: Location and construction assistance, store supervision, bookkeeping, and QSC supervision.

Informatin Submitted: June 1990

UNCLE TONY'S PIZZA & PASTA FAMILY RESTAURANT
Suite 27
1800 Post Road
Warwick, Rhode Island 02886
Edward A. Carosi, President

Description of Operation: Family style Italian restaurant, dining room and take-out service.

Number of Franchisees: 8 in Massachusetts and Rhode Island.

In Business Since: 1970

Equity Capital Needed: Approximately $60,000.

Financial Assistance Available: Preparation of bank proposals and SBA applications.

Training Provided: Will be trained in every phase of the Uncle Tony's systems; training will be both classroom and on-the-job for about 3 months.

Managerial Assistance Available: Ongoing assistance in day-to-day operations and administration.

Information Submitted: May 1990

VISTA FRANCHISE, INC.
1911 Tuttle Creek Boulevard
Manhattan, Kansas 66502
Bradley C. Streeter, President

Description of Operation: Fast food operation specializing in quality hamburgers and dairy items.

Number of Franchisees: 7 in Kansas

In Business Since: 1964

Equity Capital Needed: Total capital needed—$150,000 equipment, $250,000 building.

Financial Assistance Available: Possible building lease available.

Training Provided: Initial training program 3 months. Continuous training available as needed.

Managerial Assistance Available: All necessary work methods, building plans, accounting, and training procedures available.

Information Submitted: June 1990

*WARD'S INTERNATIONAL, INC.
P. O. Box 870
Hattiesburg, Mississippi 39403
Kenneth R. Hrdlica, President

Description of Operation: Fast food restaurant with high food quality. Standard menu consists of hamburgers, chili dogs, chicken nuggets, fries, shakes, root beer in frosted mugs and breakfast menu.

Number of Franchisees: 53 in 4 States

In Business Since: 1978

Equity Capital Needed: Cash and financing needed, $250,000-$325,000 depending on building and land costs.

Financial Assistance Available: None

Training Provided: 4 week in-store training for management personnel. Pre-opening and grand opening staff support. Continuous operational, marketing, and cost control analysis from area franchise consultants.

Managerial Assistance Available: Regular visits by Ward's field consultants, employee training, new merchandising techniques, financial reviews, and seminars; other support personnel are available for consultation upon request.

Information Submitted: April 1990

*WENDY'S INTERNATIONAL, INC.
P. O. Box 256
4288 West Dublin-Granville Road
Dublin, Ohio 43017
Franchise Sales and Development Department

Description of Operation: Fast service restaurant with quality food. Limited menu centered around fresh-cooked 1/4 pound hamburgers, chili, breast of chicken sandwich, hot stuffed baked potatoes, and salad bar, featuring dining rooms and "pick-up" window.

Number of Franchisees: 2,459 units plus 1,034 company restaurants located throughout the United States, Bahamas, Belgium, Canada, England, France, Germany, Japan, Luxembourg, Malaysia,

Netherlands, Puerto Rico, Spain, Switzerland, Australia, Italy, South Africa, Singapore, Korea, Mexico, Philippines, Guam, and the Virgin Islands.

In Business Since: 1969

Equity Capital Needed: $600,000-$1,300,000 total investment.

Financial Assistance Available: None. Total investment varies.

Training Provided: Intensive 14 week in-restaurant and classroom structured program for new owners.

Managerial Assistance Available: Provide manuals, field service, and consultation at regular intervals to provide support and insure compliance with company standards.

Information Submitted: June 1990

WESTERN SIZZLIN, INC.
17090 North Dallas Parkway
Dallas, Texas 75248
Michael J. Stack, President & CEO

Description of Operation: Semi-cafeteria style family steak house.

Number of Franchisees: 490 in 30 States, Canada and Japan

In Business Since: 1962

Equity Capital Needed: $250,000 liquid assets and $750,000 total net worth.

Financial Assistance Available: No direct financial assistance.

Training Provided: Training for new franchisees is an intensive 8 week training program followed by a 1 week classroom course.

Managerial Assistance Available: Regional management consultants visit franchise restaurants on a frequent basis.

Information Submitted: April 1990

WESTSIDE DELI, INC.
2420 Grand River Avenue
Williamston, Michigan 48895
Martin Dunleavy, Marketing Director

Description of Operation: A variety of options are available, from take-out to seating inside and drive thrus—featuring a large sandwich, sweet shop and pizza menu.

Number of Franchisees: 35 in Michigan

In Business Since: 1981

Equity Capital Needed: $80,000-$120,000, if building and equipment are leased and franchisee credit sufficient.

Financial Assistance Available: None

Training Provided: It is mandatory that franchisee spend 2 weeks plus in-training at company designated location. Applicant must pass corporate criteria or franchise will be denied.

Managerial Assistance Available: Baking, cooking of all menu items, store management, bookkeeping, advertising, custom controls, marketing and personnel management.

Information Submitted: May 1990

*WHATABURGER, INC.
4600 Parkdale Drive
Corpus Christi, Texas 78411
Joseph A. Middendorf

Description of Operation: Fast food restaurant with dining room and drive through facilities featuring four sizes of made-to-order hamburgers. Also serve fish and chicken sandwiches, fajita taco plus breakfast menu. Most units open 24 hours. Emphasis on quality.

Number of Franchisees: 434 units operating in Sunbelt States, including company operations. Franchises being offered in Texas, New Mexico, Arizona, Oklahoma, Arkansas, Louisiana, Mississippi, Tennessee, Alabama, Georgia, and Florida.

Equity Capital Needed: Minimum $150,000 cash. Total investment per unit is $600,000-$900,000 (depending on the location).

Financial Assistance Available: None

Training Provided: Instruction on all phases of restaurant operations—4 to 8 weeks.

Managerial Assistance Available: Ongoing operational, real estate, marketing, and administrative assistance provided throughout the term of the franchise.

Information Submitted: April 1990

WIENER KING SYSTEMS, INC.
1201 Bushkill Street
Easton, Pennsylvania 18042
Richard Dennis

Description of Operation: Fast food restaurant specializing in hot dogs and chili. Also features hamburgers. Seating capacity for 38 or 80 people depending on size of unit.

Number of Franchisees: 18 in 9 States and multiple unit franchisee in Singapore.

In Business Since: 1970

Equity Capital Needed: $50,000 to $80,000

Financial Assistance Available: Development based on individual's net worth.

Training Provided: It is mandatory that franchisee spend 2 weeks plus in training at company designated location.

Managerial Assistance Available: Continuous assistance provided throughout the term of franchise agreement. Each unit is visited periodically by a consultant to assist in maximizing income and by the quality department to assure maintenance of high uniform standards.

Information Submitted: June 1990

WIENERSCHNITZEL INTERNATIONAL, INC.
4440 Von Karman Avenue
Newport Beach, California 92660

Description of Operation: Fast food restaurant specializing in hamburgers and hot dogs. Drive thru service plus patio or inside seating.

Number of Franchisees: 275 in 11 Southwestern States

In Business Since: 1961

Equity Capital Needed: $60,000-$180,000

Financial Assistance Available: Does not generally guarantee or assist in financing; however, consultation and referrals are available.

Training Provided: 6 weeks of in-store and classroom training required. New store training team and ongoing seminars and workshops available.

Managerial Assistance Available: Continuous ongoing consultation, periodic restaurant inspections, marketing and operational consultation.

Information Submitted: April 1990

WINNERS CORPORATION
5995 Barfield Road
Atlanta, Georgia 30328
Rus Umphenour

Description of Operation: Winners Corporation is a 170 unit chain of Mrs. Winner's Chicken House with interior dining area designed to provide a comfortable, soft atmosphere appointed with live plants. The restaurants are open for all 3 meal occasions, offering a variety of breakfast items, whipped potatoes, hash browns, baked beans, country gravy, and strawberry shortcake.

Number of Franchisees: 42 in 8 States

In Business Since: 1971

Equity Capital Needed: $100,000-$200,000

Financial Assistance Available: None.

Training Provided: The required training program consists of a 200 hour comprehensive course both in classroom and on-the-job experience.

Managerial Assistance Available: In addition to assistance in site selection, the company provides opening supervision, frequent operational assistance, marketing assistance, and support "kits" in accounting and operations functions. Single unit and multi-unit operations are considered.

Information Submitted: May 1990

WOODY'S BAR-B-Q FRANCHISE SALES, INC.
1626 Atlantic University Circle
Jacksonville, Florida 32207-2227
J. W. Mills

Description of Operation: Limited menu restaurants specializing in bar-b-q beef, pork, ribs, chicken and turkey.

Number of Franchisees: 18 restaurants, including 7 company operated units, located in 3 States.

In Business Since: 1980

Equity Capital Needed: $14,000 to $250,000

Financial Assistance Available: Franchisees must obtain their own financing.

Training Provided: Pre-opening training mandatory; consists of 30 to 60 days in operating restaurants in all of the key positions from food preparation to store management. In-store accounting and labor controls systems plus operations manuals are provided along with instruction classes, one on one.

Managerial Assistance Available: Yes, complete support system including location finding, design layouts, equipment and product specifications, pre-opening hiring and training. Periodic inspections, retraining and guidance by area supervisor.

Information Submitted: April 1990

*WSMP, INC.
P. O. Box 399
Claremont, North Carolina 28610
Frank D. Knowles, Director of Development

Description of Operation: Western Steer—Mom 'N' Pop's, Inc., operates family style restaurants as well as fast service steak houses and fish restaurants. The company also franchises Western Steer Family Steakhouses. There are presently 47 company-owned units and 174 franchised units, the most popular franchise being the fast service steak houses operated under the tradename Western Steer Family Steakhouse.

Number of Franchisees: 130 Western Steers in 13 States and 42 company-owned Steers.

In Business Since: 1970

Equity Capital Needed: $160,000-$240,000

Financial Assistance Available: Franchisor will offer trained assistance to franchisee to put together total franchise package. Franchisor does not offer direct financial assistance.

Training Provided: Franchisor will train managers, cooks, meat slicers and all other personnel necessary for staffing franchised unit.

Managerial Assistance Available: Western Steer provides extensive and continual assistance to franchisee in all areas of restaurant operation including, but not limited to, bookkeeping, inventory control, purchasing, operations manuals and constant field supervision.

Information Submitted: April 1990

YOUR PIZZA SHOPS, INC.
1177 South Main Street
North Canton, Ohio 44720
John Purney, Jr., President

Description of Operation: Carry-out, dining room operation with salad bar and or smorgasbord available.

Number of Franchisees: 20 in Ohio, Arizona and Florida.

In Business Since: 1949

Equity Capital Needed: $40,000-$60,000

Financial Assistance Available: None directly but source information available.

Training Provided: 1 month training in one of our operating shops, then training in franchisee's own shop until we feel franchisee can handle his/her own operation.

Managerial Assistance Available: We are always available to our franchisees if they have any problems or questions of any kind, be it legal, accounting, managerial or operational, for as long as they remain franchisees.

Information Submitted: June 1990

ZIPPS DRIVE THRU, INC.
393 North Euclid
St. Louis, Missouri 63108
Robert W. Gontram, President

Description of Operation: Double drive-thru hamburger system offering a limited menu of quality food at low prices and speed of service.

Number of Franchisees: 20 company units and 13 franchise units.

In Business Since: 1987

Equity Capital Needed: Total unit costs vary from $400,000 to $560,000.

Financial Assistance Available: None

Training Provided: The operator is required to complete a 2 week training program.

Managerial Assistance Available: Complete support from site location through opening crew training and assistance. Periodic visits and operations review. Operations manual is loaned to franchisee.

Information Submitted: April 1990

GENERAL MERCHANDISING STORES

*BEN FRANKLIN STORES, INC.
BEN FRANKLIN CRAFTS, INC.
500 East North Avenue
Carol Stream, Illinois 60188

Description of Operation: Ben Franklin Stores is a franchisor and wholesaler of general merchandise nationwide. Ben Franklin Crafts is the largest franchisor and wholesaler of crafts in the continental United States. The franchisee operates a private business with the advantages of chain-store buying, merchandising and promotional expertise, and with a nationwide reputation of professional service to the public.

Number of Franchisees: 1,055 franchised outlets.

In Business Since: 1877; in franchising since 1925.

Equity Capital Needed: $150,000-$300,000 cash start up; $600,000-$1,000,000 total investment.

Financial Assistance Available: The company will assist the franchisee in obtaining bank financing through local and regional commercial lending institutions.

Training Provided: The new franchisee is required to attend either 1 or 2 weeks of in-store training at one of our training stores.

Managerial Assistance Available: Assistance is available in site selection, lease negotiations, sales promotion and all phases of operation by regular visits of trained field and headquarters personnel.

Information Submitted: April 1990

*COAST TO COAST STORES
501 South Cherry Street
Denver, Colorado 80222

Description of Operation: Retail total hardware store that features national brands plus private-level merchandise structured in 11 basic departments: hardware, electrical, plumbing, automotive, sporting goods, housewares/giftwares, materials, and lawn/farm/garden supplies. Stores are designed to be dominant in their markets.

Number of Franchisees: 920 in 35 States

In Business Since: 1928

Equity Capital Needed: $70,000 to $150,000, depending on store size. Equity investment is secured by inventory and fixtures; there is no initial payment for the franchise. There is a monthly franchisee fee of $100. Entire investment goes for inventory and store operations.

Financial Assistance Available: Franchisee normally furnishes half the initial capital needed; the company's division finance manager and district managers help negotiate additional term financing through local community sources.

Training Provided: New store owners attend a training school (with sessions, lodging and meals at company expense) that thoroughly covers all phases of store operations. Project and district managers help new store owner with layout, display, set-up and grand opening; thereafter, district manager makes continuing visits to give store owner additional training and counsel. This assistance is part of an ongoing program for the store owner.

Managerial Assistance Available: So that the store owner can devote his time to building his business, Coast to Coast offers a wide range of services that eliminate many tedious details. These services include complete bookkeeping and tax accounting, layout and display ideas to maximize inventory turnover, inventory control, pre-printed price tickets, electronic order entry system, group insurance program, sales circulars and merchandising helps, two merchandising meetings a year, training clinics, and continuing advice and assistance from the district manager and other store-operations personnel. Many of these are furnished without charge.

Information Submitted: April 1990

HEALTH AIDS/SERVICES

AMERICAN PHYSICAL REHABILITATION NETWORK, INC.
4050 Talmadge Road
P. O. Box 8864
Toledo, Ohio 43623-0864
Richard R. Leffler, Chairman

Description of Operation: Complete business system for out-patient physical therapy service—free standing clinic.

Number of Franchisees: 5 in Ohio including company-owned

In Business Since: 1958, franchising since 1987

Equity Capital Needed: $25,000 for franchise; $25,000 for EDP system; $25,000 to $50,000 for working capital.

Financial Assistance Available: None

Training Provided: 2 weeks initial, 1 week annually thereafter.

Managerial Assistance Available: Monthly site visits, prototype contractual arrangements, interpretation of medical regulations and preparation of cost reports. Management consultation and all general accounting (financial statement preparation).

Information Submitted: June 1990

BODY BEAUTIFUL BOUTIQUE
6041 Mt. Mariah
Memphis, Tennessee 38115
Liz or Bob Anderson

Description of Operation: Personal care figure salon using European body wrap, nutritional weight loss, passive exercise toning tables, and European facials and skin care.

Number of Franchisees: 6 in Tennessee and Mississippi

In Business Since: 1984

Equity Capital Needed: $36,000

Financial Assistance Available: None

Training Provided: Intensive 5 day instruction in all areas of operation.

Managerial Assistance Available: For life of contract, continuing development of new ideas and methods, area training and sales seminars, advertising advice for local markets.

Information Submitted: June 1990

BODY CONCEPTS, INC.
d/b/a BODY BASICS WEIGHT MANAGEMENT
CENTERS
14483 - 62nd Street No., Building B
Clearwater, Florida 34620

Description of Operation: A Body Basics Weight Management Center franchise is a center to assist people towards weight loss and weight maintenance. The program is designed around normal grocery store foods, on-site low impact exercise, body fat analysis to monitor true fat loss, coupled with a vitamin supplement and nutritional tracking system to monitor the foods consumed. Private and group counseling is a major asset toward over-weight rehabilitation. Body Basics follows the guidelines set by the American Medical Association and the American Dietetic Association.

Number of Franchisees: 2

In Business Since: 1990

Equity Capital Needed: $19,500 plus working capital of $10,000 to $15,000.

Financial Assistance Available: None at this time.

Training Provided: All new franchisees undergo 1 week classroom training at the corporate office in Florida followed by on-site grand opening assistance. Operations, training and counselor manuals are provided. In addition, concentrated training in diet management, consultation, sales and management skills.

Managerial Assistance Available: Each franchisee is supported in every phase of his/her business: 1) Ongoing business and financial consultation. The corporate office monitors progress of each center on sales, goals, advertising, et cetera, ensuring that each center is meeting or exceeding the national averages. 2) Instant computer support via modem hook-up, 3) 800 hotline, to answer any questions or concerns, and 4) Advertising placed regionally and more.

Information Submitted: June 1990

CLAFLIN HOME HEALTH CENTERS
486 Silver Spring Street
Providence, Rhode Island 02904
Richard A. Westlake, President

Description of Operation: Claflin Home Health Centers are designed specifically to serve the needs of the home health care market. They are an integral part of their communities. Personnel are professionally trained in all aspects of the field. Products available for sale or rental in a Claflin Home Health Center include durable medical products such as wheelchairs and hospital beds, surgical and medical supplies, respiratory and physical therapy equipment, and self-care items. All are of the highest quality available.

Number of Franchisees: 6 in Rhode Island and Massachusetts

In Business Since: 1982

Equity Capital Needed: Franchise fee $25,000, total investment $150,000.

Financial Assistance Available: None

Training Provided: Thorough, in-depth traning is vital to the success of our franchise program. Our training staff, comprised of experts in the many aspects of running a Claflin Home Health Center, will guide you through 3 weeks of intensive training in our model store. We will cover such areas as hiring and training your

staff, developing controls and projections, buying procedures, professional sales techniques, bookkeeping methods, and personnel management.

Managerial Assistance Available: Continual management service is provided.

Information Submitted: June 1990

COMMUNIDYNE, INC.
636 Anthony Trail
Northbrook, Illinois 60062
Roger Gerber, President

Description of Operation: Coin-operated diagnostic machines: alcohol breath analyzers, hearing screeners, vision screeners.

Number of Franchisees: 17 in 8 States

In Business Since: 1986

Equity Capital Needed: $5,000

Financial Assistance Available: None

Training Provided: Video, written, seminars.

Managerial Assistance Available: Yes

Information Submitted: March 1990

*DIET CENTER, INC.
220 South 2nd West
Rexburg, Idaho 83440
General Manager of Franchise

Description of Operation: The Diet Center business includes administration of the 5-phase Diet Center Weight Control Program through private, daily counseling and weekly classes, and sales of various vitamin, food, and nutritional products, generally under the Diet Center brand name. The Diet Center organization has grown, since its inception, to become the number-one franchised weight-control program in North America. With more than 2,200 locations throughout the United States and Canada, Diet Center continues to expand the scope of its organization to meet the needs of today's market.

Number of Franchisees: There are over 2,315 in all States of the United States and in Canada

In Business Since: 1972

Equity Capital Needed: Initial franchise fee is $12,000 U.S. and $24,000 U.S. (includes starter kit, complete training program, necessary equipment, and franchise rights in exclusive territory). Minimum $10,000 additional operating capital essential.

Financial Assistance Available: None

Training Provided: A 1-week training seminar is provided to prepare operators for responsibilities of administering the Diet Center program and running a Diet Center business. Included in the seminar are courses providing instruction in every aspect necessary to the successful operation of a Diet Center.

Managerial Assistance Available: In addition to refresher courses provided at counselor training school at the corporate headquarters, continuing education is conducted throughout the year at regional counselor-training seminars across the country and at annual international Diet Center conventions. Counselors and franchisees are also informed of new information through the monthly publications of the AdVantage magazine, the franchisee forum newsletter, and the Diet Center newsletter.

Information Submitted: June 1990

THE DIET WORKSHOP, INC.
Ten Brookline Place West
Suite 107
Brookline, Massachusetts 02146
Rennie Shepen

Description of Operation: The Diet Workshop offers weight control support to members attending one of its three divisions: FlexiGroups, Quick Loss Clinics, and Workplace. In its group weight control classes it offers diet, nutrition, behavior modification and mild toning exercises and related weight control products such as vitamins, low-calorie dried food, diet salad dressing and other nutritious items as well as diet related literature.

Number of Franchisees: 30 in 18 States

In Business Since: 1965

Equity Capital Needed: A minimum of $86,000

Financial Assistance Available: None

Training Provided: New franchises receive training at the national offices and regular follow-up and advice during the initial start-up period.

Managerial Assistance Available: A franchise receives ongoing support through regular mailings and seminars concerning promotions, weight related products, motivation and administration.

Information Submitted: April 1990

DOCTORS & NURSES WEIGHT CONTROL CENTERS, INC.
1600 North Palafox Street, Suite B
Pensacola, Florida 32501
David L. Owens

Description of Operation: Medically supervised weight loss and control.

Number of Franchisees: 30 centers in 7 States

In Business Since: 1987

Equity Capital Needed: $31,400-$57,500 (includes franchise fee).

Financial Assistance Available: None

Training Provided: Yes

Managerial Assistance Available: Yes

Information Submitted: April 1990

*FORMU-3 INTERNATIONAL, INC.
4790 Douglas Center N.W.
Canton, Ohio 44718
Walter Poston, Vice President - Franchise Development

Description of Operation: We offer unique franchise opportunities throughout the United States in the field of weight loss.

Number of Franchisees: 300 plus in 26 States

In Business Since: 1982

Equity Capital Needed: $32,000

Financial Assistance Available: None

Training Provided: Franchisee training consists of 3 day owner's training, 4 day managers class, and 5 day owner/employee training class, plus 1 week grand opening assistance.

Managerial Assistance Available: Monthly area meetings, seminars, ongoing 5 day employee training classes held at corporate headquarters and in the field and 4 day manager training classes held at corporate headquarters. Corporate personnel assistance available.

Information Submitted: May 1990

*FORTUNATE LIFE WEIGHT LOSS CENTERS
P. O. Box 5604
Charlottesville, Virginia 22905
Thomas Beslin, President

Description of Operation: The Fortunate Life Center is a supervised weight control program. The program is scientifically based and focuses on the key ingredients of successful weight control—controlling caloric intake, modifying behavior and working with a committed individual. The program is unique within the weight control industry.

Number of Franchisees: 67 in 15 States

In Business Since: 1984; JenDale, Inc., purchased franchise in June 1986.

Equity Capital Needed: $6,000 plus working capital and initial franchise fee.

Financial Assistance Available: None

Training Provided: 3-5 days extensive marketing and clinical training.

Managerial Assistance Available: Physician and consulting dietician at home office. Marketing and clinical training updates provided through field visits and conventions.

Information Submitted: June 1990

GENERAL NUTRITION FRANCHISING, INC.
921 Penn Avenue
Pittsburgh, Pennsylvania 15222
James E. Sallcross, General Manager

Description of Operation: General Nutrition is committed to becoming the leading provider of products, services, and information in the self-care and personal health enhancement markets.

Number of Franchisees: 30 franchisees, 43 locations.

In Business Since: 1939, franchising since 1988

Equity Capital Needed: Varies.

Financial Assistance Available: Yes

Training Provided: Approximately 3 weeks training: 1 week at corporate headquarters in Pittsburgh, Pennsylvania and 2 weeks in store/on site (prior to grand opening and afterwards). Newsletters, video tapes and manuals provided for business management.

Managerial Assistance Available: Continuous support includes field rep's assistance in volume purchasing, advertising and promotions.

Information Submitted: April 1990

HEALTHCARE RECRUITERS INTERNATIONAL, INC.
5420 LBJ
Suite 575
Dallas, Texas 75240
Frank A. Cooksey, President

Description of Operation: Contingency and retainer executive recruiting/search specializing only in medical sales, marketing, management, and administrative positions plus physician recruitment positions. HealthCare Recruiters is known as the "National Network for Health Care Professionals." Each office is owned and staffed by executives whose business background has been in the healthcare industry only. HealthCare Recruiters International's success has been established by developing systems that provide a real opportunity for an individual to "control their own destiny" using those proven systems and established "computerized client candidate referral system."

Number of Franchisees: 35 in 28 states

In Business Since: 1983

Equity Capital Needed: $60,000 to $80,000—Depending on location.

Financial Assistance Available: Yes

Training Provided: Intensive training program of 2 weeks at the corporate headquarters in Dallas, Texas, using the latest audio visual training techniques in the industry, including video tapes, training/operation manual, reference guides and client/candidate information. HealthCare Recruiters provides training in all aspects of the recruiting and executive search business, including specialized training for owner-managers and account executives. Also, all account executives employed during the lifetime of the franchise are trained in-house by HealthCare Recruiters International. On-the-job training is conducted by home office representatives to provide continuing training through a program of weekly telephone and periodic visits. In addition, HealthCare Recruiters International conducts bi-annual training seminars and conferences. HealthCare Recruiters International will assist and advise the licensee in (1) office site selection and lease negotiation, (2) office layout and furniture selection, (3) selection of computer equipment system, and (4) account executive recruitment. In summary, HealthCare Recruiters will provide its network franchisees with training, resources and guidance to operate a medical sales management and marketing executive recruiting business.

Managerial Assistance Available: Continuing support through daily, weekly, monthly phone consultation and periodic management visits covering all aspects of the medical recruiting business. In addition, HealthCare Recruiters International provides collection assistance of licensee's accounts receivable and detailed analysis of all phases of their operation. HealthCare Recruiters International also provides national advertising and marketing support programs as well as target account solicitation by headquarters personnel.

Information Submitted: April 1990

HEALTH CLUBS OF AMERICA
Box 4098
Waterville, Connecticut 06714
Gregg Nolan, Franchise Director

Description of Operation: Health and slenderizing salons with separate facilities for men and women.

Number of Franchisees: 18 in Connecticut, New York and New Jersey.

In Business Since: 1961

Equity Capital Needed: Minimum of $35,000, depending on equipment.

Financial Assistance Available: Financing may be arranged through Horizons of America, Inc., parent company.

Training Provided: 1 week management training in main office in New York. At least 3 weeks of day-to-day operational training at own club.

Managerial Assistance Available: Company is always available for counseling.

Information Submitted: May 1990

HEALTH FORCE
1600 Stewart Avenue, Suite 700
Westbury, New York 11590
Michael Ward, Franchise Director

Description of Operation: Company provides staff relief in hospitals and nursing homes, and home health care for the elderly and convalescents. Company funds weekly outside payroll for nurses, aides and homemakers. Company handles receivables and billings, in turn freeing franchisee for marketing.

Number of Franchisees: 39 in 13 States

In Business Since: 1960

Equity Capital Needed: Total investment, $102,000-$137,000.

Financial Assistance Available: Unlimited funding of weekly temporary payroll and partial financing of franchise fee.

Training Provided: 2 weeks home office, 1 week franchisee's office, periodic field service throughout the year, plus ongoing help as needed.

Managerial Assistance Available: Aid in surveying the market, setting rates, site selection, training of permanent staff. A complete set of oprations manuals. Field servicing throughout the year. Computerized operating systems and processing of payroll and receivables. Franchisor does all billing to accounts, provides continual back-up services including administrative and marketing assistance.

Information Submitted: May 1990

HOMECARE HELPING HAND, INC.
Subsidiary of PHARMACEUTICAL INNOVATORS, LTD.
116 Franklin, P. O. Box 308
West Union, Iowa 52175
Ronald Garceau, President
Robert Johnson, Vice President

Description of Operation: Selling and renting of durable medical equipment and supplies to homebound patients, nursing homes, hospitals and medical clinics, plus serving public and private health organizations.

Number of Franchisees: 3 in Iowa

In Business Since: 1983

Equity Capital Needed: $25,000 to $50,000

Financial Assistance Available: None

Training Provided: Intensive 2 weeks training at the home office for all new franchisees and their personnel. Additional training is conducted at the franchisee's place of business as an ongoing educational program and updated.

Managerial Assistance Available: Homecare Helping Hand, Inc., provides continual management service for the life of the franchise in such areas as bookkeeping, computer service, advertising, inventory buying and control, assistance with claims control and marketing of the services. Home office personnel are available per toll free call 24 hours daily and make visits to stores regularly to assists in solving problems. Home office also seeks out the latest in medical equipment by attending national and international buying shows and gives report to franchisees.

Information Submitted: May 1990

JAZZERCISE, INC.
2808 Roosevelt Street
Carlsbad, California 92008

Description of Operation: Jazzercise is a dance fitness program using choreographed dance fitness routines to music. The franchisee must successfully complete a training workshop and be proficient in dance and exercise in order to qualify for a franchise.

Number of Franchisees: 4,000 franchised instructors in the USA plus 29 foreign countries.

In Business Since: 1974

Equity Capital Needed: Approximately $3,000.

Financial Assistance Available: None

Training Provided: A 4 day workshop.

Managerial Assistance Available: Jazzercise provides the services of agents who supervise and assist franchisees in all facets of their business on an ongoing basis.

Information Submitted: June 1990

JENEAL INTENSIVE SKIN CORRECTION AND HEALTH CENTERS
3798 West Chase
Houston, Texas 77042
Dr. Jerry O'Neal, Ph. D., President

Description of Operation: Jeneal is a system of skin correction which utilizes certain methods, techniques and products to provide skin analysis, dietary recommendations and surface exfoliation of the dead cells of the skin and the promotion of rapid reproduction of normal skin cells. This system ultimately results in smooth, blemish-free skin. Jeneal also is a system of superfluous hair removal that uses an organic enzyme.

Number of Franchisees: 13 in 6 States.

In Business Since: 1965

Equity Capital Needed: $15,000-$60,000

Financial Assistance Available: None

Managerial Assistance Available: An intensive 14 day mandatory training course is scheduled for all new franchisees and their managers at Jeneal Corporation offices in Houston, Texas. An additional 7 days of training is conducted at the franchisee's outlet under the supervision of a full-time Jeneal employee (usually the company president).

Information Submitted: May 1990

*JENNY CRAIG INTERNATIONAL, INC.
445 Marine View Avenue, Suite 300
Del Mar, California 29014
Gary Hawk, Vice President/Franchise Development

Description of Operation: Jenny Craig Weight Loss Centres offer clients a safe, guaranteed, easy to live with method of weight loss. Jenny Craig has perfected a program that takes weight off and teaches new lifestyles and eating behavior that help keep it off for a lifetime. The program blends person to person counselling, calorie controlled, nutritionally balanced menus, Jenny's Cuisine, and behavior education.

Number of Franchisees: As of June 1990, 130 franchise centres and 400 company-owned centres in 23 States, Canada, Australia, New Zealand and England.

In Business Since: 1983, franchising since 1987

Equity Capital Needed: $150,000 per centre; most markets require multiple centres.

Financial Assistance Available: None

Training Provided: A comprehensive 6 weeks mandatory training for owners and operations managers, 1 to 2 weeks for centre staff, and continual updates throughout the year.

Managerial Assistance Available: Jenny Craig provides indepth marketing, planning management support and guidance, twice per year in field visits, and continued and comprehensive assistance in daily operation through area managers.

Information Submitted: April 1990

MED-WAY MEDICAL WEIGHT MANAGEMENT
1375 South Voss
Houston, Texas 77057
Jerry O. Cooksey, Executive Vice President

Description of Operation: The Med-Way Medical Weight Management franchise is a proven weight loss program offering sound nutrition, education and behavior modification to the general public. The program is administered by physicians and nurses in a professional, clinical atmosphere. Franchise ownership is available to nurses and non-medical investor owners. Med-Way provides complete assistance with site selection, center layout, personnel selection, training, advertising support and comprehensive ongoing support.

Number of Franchisees: 8 in Texas, 35 additional agreements have been signed. Franchising in other states also.

In Business Since: 1987

Equity Capital Needed: The total capital requirement to get a typical Med-Way Weight Management center open is from a low of $27,000 to $40,000, which includes the franchise fee. Average $36,000.

Financial Assistance Available: Franchisor does not provide financial assistance at this time.

Training Provided: Franchisor provides free training to the franchisee and franchisee's employees at franchisor's headquarters in Houston, Texas. Franchisor will train franchisee's employees at no cost to franchisee for as long as franchisee owns the franchise. The franchisee is responsible for paying all costs of travel, food and lodging to and from Houston, Texas. Franchisor provides 5 days training in Houston and up to 5 days training at franchisee's center.

Managerial Assistance Available: In addition to the above training at franchisor headquarters, franchisor provides ongoing advice and assistance with advertising, promotions, seminars, written advisories, bulletins and meetings at franchise headquarters. Franchisor has staff available during normal working hours to assist all franchisees with routine questions. Franchisor has "Area Nurse Managers" to advise and assist all franchise locations. Franchisor provides all franchisees with an operations manual, supply lists and pre-printed forms lists. Franchisor can supply all items used in each center, but franchisees do not have to purchase anything from franchisor.

Information Submitted: June 1990

NATIONAL HEALTH ENHANCEMENT
SYSTEMS, INC.
3200 N. Central Avenue
Suite 1750
Phoenix, Arizona 85012
Jeffrey T. Zywicki, Vice President of Finance

Description of Operation: National Health Enhancement Systems, Inc., offers health care providers, through a business system, an innovative way of generating additional revenue, through the marketing of health evaluations to prevention-conscious consumers. Its comprehensive medical assessment program, designed to determine the relative health of an apparently well individual, was developed in 1979 by Dr. Edward B. Diethrich, and has evolved into five distinct systems that may be used as stand-alone or complementary products. Each program analyzes life-style, nutritional habits and physical condition as they related to cardiovascular disease risk factor and overall fitness.

Number of Franchisees: 169 in 31 states

In Business Since: 1983, formerly AHI, Limited

Equity Capital Needed: Approximately $22,200, including initial fee.

Financial Assistance Available: In certain situations the initial license fee is payable 1/3 down upon execution of a franchise agreement with the balance (plus interest) due in 12 equal monthly payments. The investment pays for all start-up materials and software product. (Does not include personal computer hardware equipment).

Training Provided: An intensive 4-day mandatory training program held in Phoenix, Arizona; subsequent and follow-up training as often as franchisee requests under the direct supervision of full time NHES employees.

Managerial Assistance Available: National Health provides continual marketing and technical support for the life of the franchise in the administration of the medical assessment and evaluation programs it provides to its franchisees.

Information Submitted: May 1990

*NURSEFINDERS
1200 Copeland Road, Suite 200
Arlington, Texas 76011
Allen Riggs

Description of Operation: Nursefinders is a national supplemental nursing service and home care franchise that provides all classifications of nurses and other nurse specialists as supplemental staff in health care facilities and as private duty staff in both health care facilities and in the home. Each franchise is for an exclusive territory agreed upon by the franchisor and franchisee.

Number of Franchisees: 73 in 32 States

In Business Since: 1975

Equity Capital Needed: $70,000-$180,000

Financial Assistance Available: None

Training Provided: The franchisor provides a 2-week training period for each franchisee at one of its established offices and 2 weeks' additional training at the franchise site before the franchise begins operations. Additional training includes on-site training visits and periodic management workshops.

Managerial Assistance Available: The franchisor assists the franchisee with site analysis and selection and office decor and layout. Regional service directors visit franchise sites at least annually to consult with franchisees about business operations and to offer suggestions for implementing Nursefinders policies and procedures.

Information Submitted: April 1990

*NUTRI/SYSTEM, INC.
Willow Wood Office Center
3901 Commerce Avenue
Willow Grove, Pennsylvania 19090

Description of Operation: Nutri/System Weight Loss Centers offer the consumer a program that features a multi-dimensional approach to weight loss and weight control. The Nutri/System program consists of an exclusive meal plan, nutritional counseling, behavior education, an activity plan and a maintenance program. Nutri/System Weight Loss Centers provide a fast and safe weight loss without the use of drugs, injections, or diet pills.

Number of Franchisees: 1,286 franchise centers in all 50 States, Canada, Australia, and England; 270 company-owned centers.

In Business Since: 1971

Equity Capital Needed: $100,000 minimum.

Financial Assistance Available: None available.

Training Provided: Franchisor provides complete training for franchisees and their staff through on-site instruction, training seminars, and training guides. Operations consultants visit franchise sites to provide continual follow-up supervision.

Managerial Assistance Available: Franchisor provides continual trainings/workshops for managers, multi-center managers (area, regional, and general manager), and marketing managers. Franchisor also provides franchisee with consultation and advice by company's representatives as to the operation and management of the franchise center, informational data and advertising research, and standard accounting and recordkeeping programs and systems developed by the company.

Information Submitted: April 1990

O.P.T.I.O.N. CARE, INC.
1370 Ridgewood Drive, Suite 20
Chico, California 95926
Lee Potts, Vice President of Sales and Marketing

Description of Operation: O.P.T.I.O.N. Care®, a nationwide network of 180 plus offices, providing Home Infusion Therapy and related services for the administration of Total Parenteral Nutrition, antibiotics, analgesics, pain management, chemotherapy and other innovative therapies in the alternative care setting.

Number of Franchisees: 180

In Business Since: This business was started in 1979 by two pharmacists interested in providing quality care in the home setting. On April 5, 1984, O.P.T.I.O.N. Care, Inc., began offering franchises for the establishment of O.P.T.I.O.N. Care® pharmacies.

Equity Capital Needed: Liquid assets, or credit line, for $125,000 to $150,000, excluding personal property. Total investment may range from $150,000 to $400,000.

Financial Assistance Available: None

Training Provided: Each month O.P.T.I.O.N. Care, Inc., offers a comprehensive 2 week training program for all new personnel. Each segment is designed to further skills for operating the O.P.T.I.O.N. Care® office. Training incudes clinical, reimbursement, marketing and legal aspects. In addition, O.P.T.I.O.N. Care, Inc., offers continuing training and support through seminars and new materials developed.

Managerial Assistance Available: O.P.T.I.O.N. Care, Inc.'s support includes clinical, business, marketing and reimbursement specialists who assist in evaluation and problem solving. In addition, there is support available in the form of clinical protocols, national standards of practice, marketing materials, on-site marketing support, seminars, regional meetings, guidelines for working with other health care professionals and newsletters and current educational materials.

Information Submitted: April 1990

OUR WEIGH
3340 Poplar
Suite 136
Memphis, Tennessee 38111
Helen K. Seale, President

Description of Operation: A unique weight control group consisting of 30 minute meetings, behavior modification, exercise, and most important a nutritional diet that allows members to eat what they like and not have to eat foods they don't like. First in the field to introduce "food rewards" and free weekly weigh in upon reaching desired weight.

Number of Franchisees: 5 in Tennessee and Mississippi.

In Business Since: 1974

Equity Capital Needed: $1,500.

Financial Assistance Available: None

Training Provided: 7 to 10 working days training on-the-job at national headquarters. Monthly letter sent to individual franchisees with latest nutritional, advertising, promotions, group leading, personal information.

Managerial Assistance Available: 24 hours a day, 365 days a year open communication with national headquarters executives plus as mentioned above. Constant telephone calls, letters sent and visits to keep franchisees up to date on all aspects of their business.

Information Submitted: April 1990

*PHYSICIANS WEIGHT LOSS CENTERS OF AMERICA, INC.
395 Springside Drive
Akron, Ohio 44313
Franchise Development Department

Description of Operation: A Physicians Weight Loss Center franchise consists of a high volume, medically supervised weight reduction business, offering the consumer a comprehensive professionally supervised program using medical treatment, individualized personal care, counseling, and maintenance. The program consists of a safe, high fiber, low fat diet for weight reduction and control for both men and women with the use of vitamin and mineral supplements, in conjunction with behavior modification counseling and comprehensive maintenance programs.

Number of Franchisees: 396 in 38 States and Canada (36 company-owned).

In Business Since: 1979

Equity Capital Needed: $78,000 to $120,000.

Financial Assistance Available: Yes

Training Provided: Physicians Weight Loss Centers of America provides franchisees with comprehensive educational development programs and technical knowledge in the areas of business management, successful operations of a Physicians Weight Loss Center, record and bookkeeping procedures, marketing, advertising, and staffing of medical and office personnel. Additional instruction is provided in the area of sales and marketing, enrollments, telephone presentations, and motivation. Complete procedures and methods of counseling of clients and the handling of dietary problems are provided as an integral part of the client services.

At Physicians Weight Loss Centers of America, Inc., mandatory attendance of all new franchisees is required for a period of 19 days for initial training.

Managerial Assistance Available: Physicians Weight Loss Centers of America, Inc., provides continued management and technical support in such areas as client treatment, accounting, bookkeeping, multimedia advertising, sales and marketing, inventory control, and motivational and business management. Comprehensive manuals for operation and staffing, behavior modification, and advertising are provided. In addition, regional field service operations personnel work closely with franchisees to analyze and evaluate center operations. Regional and local update seminars and development programs are provided for increased effectiveness and productivity on a quarterly basis.

Information Submitted: April 1990

THE PEGASUS CLINIC, INC.
5580 Peterson Lane
Suite 260
Dallas, Texas 75240
Kirk C. Malicki, President

Description of Operation: Personal, private, one-on-one, fitness and mutritional training. Corporate training, residential training. One-coach-one-client.

Number of Franchisees: 2

In Business Since: 1983

Financial Assistance Available: $5,000 plus good credit background.

Financial Assistance Available: None

Training Provided: 2 months maximum on-site in Dallas, Texas.

Managerial Assistance Available: Continual support 24 hours a day, 7 days a week.

Information Submitted: April 1990

PREGNAGYM
St. Anthony's Ancillary Services
P.O. Box 12588
St. Petersburg, Florida 33733
Rosemary Colombo, Managing Director

Description of Operation: Pregnagym is a medically supervised exercise program designed specifically for pregnant women. Pregnagym requires about 1,200 square feet and the weight based machines are purchased by the franchise. As this is a medically supervised program, the purchaser must be affiliated with a physician or hospital. Pregnagym provides a start-up materials, operational procedures, promotional package and a training program for the staff.

Number of Franchisees: 16 in 8 states

In Business Since: 1984

Equity Capital Needed: Total investment of $90,000 which includes franchise fee of $19,750, $40,000 for equipment, $30,000 for leasehold improvement and signage.

Financial Assistance Available: Leasing of equipment possible.

Training Provided: 3 days of on-site intensive training is provided with an instructor who goes through the assessments and methods of the program. A workbook and video with step by step guidance also is a part of training. Follow-up and consultation available.

Managerial Assistance Available: Policy and procedure manual, camera ready of all forms and operational procedures taught. Telephone consultation available as well as an on-site visit by physician who developed the model of this program. Research continues and as new advances are made, franchises are kept current.

Information Submitted: May 1990

RESPOND FIRST AID SYSTEMS
3850 J. Nome Street
Denver, Colorado 80239
Thomas L. McKevitt, President

Description of Operation: Respond franchisers operate van-oriented, route sales business offering quality first aid and emergency medical supplies, service and training to the commercial market.

Number of Franchisees: 37 outlets in 21 states

In Business Since: 1979

Equity Capital Needed: $25,000

Financial Assistance Available: None

Training Provided: Yes

Managerial Assistance Available: Yes

Information Submitted: April 1990

SLENDER CENTER, INC.
6515 Grand Teton Plaza
Suite 241
Madison, Wisconsin 53719
Jean Geurink, President

Description of Operation: Weight loss consultation. Individualized. No prepackaged foods. Use of 3-Step Breakthrough Program which increases intake at three stages using normal, regular foods for guaranteed loss. Behavior System training called Breakthrough Thinking which personalizes behavior change appropriate for gender/career/lifestyle/weight history. No drugs, no products. Comprehensive program manual provided to all clients. Programs for men, women, adolescents, nursing mothers, vegetarians. Audio cassettes on affirmations, relaxation, exercise and self-esteem. Cookbook.

Number of Franchisees: 34 centers in 6 States

In Business Since: 1979

Equity Capital Needed: $5,000-$10,000 plus franchise fee $12,000-$27,000.

Financial Assistance Available: None

Training Provided: Initial 5 day training at corporate headquarters. Procedure and policy manuals provided to owner and staff without cost.

Managerial Assistance Available: Grand opening assistance for 5 days without fee. Support phone staff available ongoing. All print copy, TV commercials and radio scripts provided. Monthly newsletter, regional meetings, franchise advisory board, annual award convention.

Information Submitted: April 1990

SUTTER MEDICAL MANAGEMENT CO., INC.
1154 Sutter Street
San Francisco, California 94109

Description of Operation: Option I: Turnkey urgent care center. SMMC selects site, does all lease improvements, installs computers, pre-market, and train staff. Option II: Existing clinic. Computerize joint marketing already operating clinic. Infuse capital when needed.

Number of Franchisees: 7 in California

In Business Since: 1984

Equity Capital Needed: Option I: $60,000. Option II: $ 5,000

Financial Assistance Available: Variable

Training Provided: 1 month training.

Managerial Assistance Available: Continuing computer service bureau, payroll, payables, general ledger services and medical peer review.

Information Submitted: June 1990

THIN LIFE CENTERS
151 New World Way
South Plainfield, New Jersey 07080
Lorraine Wurtzel, President

Description of Operation: Thin Life Centers is a medically supervised rapid weight loss facility that deals with the clients psychological, emotional, and physical needs on an individual and group basis. The center is located in a typical medical facility and is currently utilizing the Medifast Program as well as other weight loss programs.

Number of Franchisees: Because of the reorganization, one company-owned franchise exists.

In Business Since: 1977 (parent company Lean Line in business since 1968).

Equity Capital Needed: $15,000 plus franchise fee.

Financial Assistance Available: Assistance in obtaining SBA loan.

Training Provided: Intensive 2 week classroom and clinical experience.

Managerial Assistance Available: Support constantly available.

Information Submitted: May 1990

T.L.C. NURSING, INC.
P. O. Box 767519
Roswell, Georgia 30076-7519
Bill Wimbish, President

Description of Operation: The TLC Nursing Center is a locally owned nurse placement service that arranges nurses, homemakers, sitters, live-ins, etc., catering primarily to the home health care market, but fully capable of furnishing the same to hospitals and institutions.

Number of Franchisees: 10 in Pennsylvania, New Jersey and Georgia.

In Business Since: 1984

Equity Capital Needed: $5,000 to $20,000 plus franchise fee.

Financial Assistance Available: Franchisor will finance up to 25 percent of the franchise fee of $10,000, which includes all material and training necessary to initiate business.

Training Provided: In addition to a complete manual for the business, a trained operator will work with franchisee in a hands-on manner until he is capable of working alone. Additional training is provided later by field people and franchisee may work at an existing center at no charge other than his own expenses.

Managerial Assistance Available: Same as above.

Information Submitted: April 1990

TONING & TANNING CENTERS
c/o FITNESS SYSTEMS, INC.
106 West 31st Street
Independence, Missouri 64055
Glen Henson

Description of Operation: We feature toning tables, tanning beds and isokinetic treadmills, bicycles with a line of isokinetic exercises for muscle toning. The program is designed for all ages of women and men alike. Our centers are priced so they may be adapted to any town of 5,000, to 10,000, or 20,000, as well as the larger communities. Our phone number is 816-254-0805

Number of Franchisees: 300 in 30 States

In Business Since: 1975

Equity Capital Needed: $10,000 and up

Financial Assistance Available: Leasing possible.

Training Provided: 1 week optional in Independence, Missouri, and on-site training when opening at no charge.

Managerial Assistance Available: Total training on all aspects of the business at no charge. Managerial and technical assistance provided in use of all equipment, office forms, bookkeeping, etc.

Information Submitted: April 1990

TOTAL LIFESTYLE CORPORATION
P. O. Box 636
Millington, Tennessee 38083
Dr. Cort McCloud

Description of Operation: Local, franchising Total LifeStyle Centers, physician-owned and directed, and operated by a trained nurse. Offering comprehensive weight-loss care. This includes one-on-one nurse counseling, behavior-modification training, individualized diet and exercise programs, education and motivation, and one year of maintenance once the target weight has been reached. Programs are provided women, men and children, with the average weight loss 18-20 pounds in 6 weeks. No drug injections or pills are used.

Number of Franchisees: 66 in 16 states

In Business Since: 1985

Equity Capital Needed: Initial franchise fee $12,500 for a population area of up to 12,500; $25,000 for a population of up to 25,500. (Fee includes exclusive territory, initial nutritional product order, training, bookkeeping system, marketing and advertising assistance, ongoing visits and monitoring at least monthly, etc.).

Financial Assistance Available: Up to 50 percent of franchise fee.

Training Provided: Complete initial training and continuing advanced seminars on regional basis. Initial training held in Memphis.

Information Submitted: June 1990

TRANSFORM WEIGHT LOSS & WELLNESS CENTERS
27636 Ynez Road, Building L7, Suite 233
Tememula, California 92390
William H. Prouty, Executive Vice President

Description of Operation: A comprehensive wellness resource center providing individual and group programs. A variety of medical diagnostic systems are use to assist customers in fully evaluating their current condition and their progress on one of the specialized programs offered. Unique programs have been developed for use in small to medium sized businesses and organizations. Each center is supported by a network of physicians and healthcare specialists. Centers also serve as training facilities for the independent marketing representatives that operate in the franchise territory.

Number of Franchisees: 5 in California

In Business Since: 1989

Equity Capital Needed: $40,000

Financial Assistance Available: Assistance in obtaining partial financing to qualified individuals.

Training Provided: Intensive home office training course provided plus ongoing training support through regional support training teams. Personal and marketing training also provided through available computer-assisted training programs.

Managerial Assistance Available: District manager works with each franchise to assure maximum market penetration.

Information Submitted: April 1990

UNITED SURGICAL CENTERS
380 Warwick Avenue
Warwick, Rhode Island 02888
Stevan Datz, President

Description of Operation: Home health care—sales and rentals of durable medical equipment and convalescent aids.

Number of Franchisees: 2 in Rhode Island and Massachusetts plus 1 company-owned.

In Business Since: 1973—franchising since 1980.

Equity Capital Needed: $100,000

Financial Assistance Available: None

Training Provided: Hands-on training (in our training school, our store and franchisee's store).

Managerial Assistance Available: Our staff at our location and also at franchisee's. Continual support.

Information Submitted: April 1990

WEIGH TO GO, INC.
2311 205th Street, Suite 103
Torrance, California 90501
Annette Y. Dahlman, Ph.D., President

Description of Operation: Medically supervised weight management program developed exclusively for hospital/clinic operation.

Number of Franchisees: 8 in 5 States

In Business Since: 1983

Equity Capital Needed: $75,000

Financial Assistance Available: Varies

Training Provided: Didactic training for 3 days, on-the-job training monthly.

Managerial Assistance Available: Weigh to Go, Inc., provides complete manuals of operations, forms, programs, and administrative procedures. Continual consultation is provided in areas of marketing, promotion, training, systems and medical updating and research developments. Site representatives work with individual franchisees and maintain close working relationships with staffs. Weigh to Go, Inc., sponsors meetings of franchisees to conduct marketing and product research and update franchisees of recent research developments relating to the Weigh to Live System. Marketing and advertising services are provided and regional programs offered.

Information Submitted: June 1990

WOMEN AT LARGE SYSTEMS, INC.
dba WOMEN AT LARGE FITNESS SALONS
1020 South 48th Avenue
Yakima, Washington 98908
Sharlyne R. Powell, President & C.E.O.

Description of Operation: Well appointed exercise clubs provide a highly professional dance-exercise program directed toward the 35-40 million plus-size women shunned by today's physical fitness industry. These sophisticated, service intensive clubs cater to the fitness, beauty, and self esteem needs of the larger women by offering members a state-of-the-art exercise regime, fitness analysis, wellness system for weight reduction and weight management, support groups, seminars on fashion, wardrobing, hair design, make-up application and image enhancement. Exercise 101 classes teach and educate exercise programming and lifetime commitment to fitness. A full line of workout wear, custom made for larger women under the Women at Large label, is available in the proshop along with the usual athletic gear for an extended profit base.

Number of Franchisees: 25 in 14 States and Canada

In Business Since: 1983, franchising since 1986.

Equity Capital Needed: $45,000-$60,000

Financial Assistance Available: None

Training Provided: Study and body conditioning begin weeks before arrival at home office. Owner arrives 1 week prior to staff for concentrated operations and business training. 5 staff members join the owner for 2 additional weeks of intensive fitness training, body conditioning, choreography memorization, study and testing in areas as diverse as exercise physiology, kinesiology, and external promotions. Video, audio cassettes, written guides, log books, training, and operations manuals provide owner and staff continued means of training and polishing until the Women at Large specialist's arrival 2 days prior to grand opening for final inspection, training and review.

Managerial Assistance Available: New exercise routines and programs with written backups are sent via video tape to keep exercise programming current. Operations specialists are in constant contact with owners via on-site visits and telephone. Regional seminars, national conventions, international aerobic championship meets provide continuing education and advanced training. Corporate newsletters provide a continuous information flow and industry updates.

Information Submitted: April 1990

*WOMEN'S WORKOUT WORLD
5811 West Dempster
Morton Grove, Illinois 60053
Audrey Sedita, President

Description of Operation: Complete women's health and fitness club.

Number of Franchisees: 5 in 3 States

In Business Since: 1968

Equity Capital Needed: $35,0000 initial franchise fee. Approximately $120;000 leasehold improvements. $60,000-$70,000 for equipment.

Financial Assistance Available: None

Training Provided: The franchisee is given a mandatory comprehensive 4 week training program: 2 weeks in a company-owned club and 2 weeks in own club.

Managerial Assistance Available: Franchisee receives complete manuals of operation, forms, advertising, marketing; franchisor provides ongoing management and technical service on a continual basis.

Information Submitted: April 1990

HEARING AIDS

*MIRACLE-EAR
DAHLBERG, INC.
Interchange Tower, Suite 701
600 South County Road 18
St. Louis Park, Minnesota 55426
Dale R. Erickson, Director of Franchising

Description of Operation: The franchisor is in the business of designing, manufacturing, and distributing a complete line of hearing aids and in franchising MIRACLE-EAR Hearing Aid Centers.

Number of Franchisees: 160 in 48 States. 532 retail centers, 1,080 service centers.

In Business Since: 1948

Equity Capital Needed: Approximately $40,000 plus.

Financial Assistance Available: Equipment and fixture leasing available.

Training Provided: 6 week training course in all technical and sales aspects of the hearing aid industry, license application course, advanced technical seminar, and advanced sales seminar.

Managerial Assistance Available: Network of regional managers available at all times to provide ongoing technical and managerial assistance to the franchisee.

Information Submitted: May 1990

HOME FURNISHINGS/FURNITURE— RETAIL/REPAIR/SERVICES

ABBEY CARPET COMPANY
425 University Avenue
Suite 200
Sacramento, California 95825

Description of Operation: Specialty store—retail carpets. Franchises are only available to people already in the retail carpet business.

Number of Franchisees: Over 230 throughout the United States.

In Business Since: 1967

Equity Capital Needed: $5,000

Financial Assistance Available: None

Training Provided: None

Managerial Assistance Available: None

Information Submitted: June 1990

AMITY QUALITY RESTORATION SYSTEMS, INC.
1571 Ivory Drive
P. O. Box 148
Sun Prairie, Wisconsin 53590
George Cash

Description of Operation: Amity offers a unique furniture stripping and restoration system of equipment and chemicals for the stripping and restoration of antiques and furniture. The system to be located in purchaser's rented shop. There are no purchase requirements. No fee, all funds paid are for equipment and merchandise. All chemicals non-flammable. Also sells paint remover, spray equipment and finishes, wholesale to the trade.

Number of Franchisees: 700 in all States except Alaska and Hawaii.

In Business Since: 1971

Equity Capital Needed: $1,800 to $10,000

Training Provided: Training provided at home office for 2 days on use and application. Free consulting advice, conventions, seminars, newsletters. Training includes stripping, finishing and repair.

Managerial Assistance Available: Technical advice provided on restoration, stripping, finishing, repairing, business management.

Information Submitted: April 1990

BOCA RATTAN PREMIUM RATTAN FURNITURE
c/o TMF SYSTEMS, INCORPORATED
127 Mohawk Avenue
Scotia, New York 12302
Richard J. Norelli, Chief Operating Officer

Description of Operation: Boca Rattan premium rattan furniture stores are full business format specialty retail franchise opportunities. Premium rattan furniture, in a variety of styles and finishes, complemented with designer cushions, silk plants and trees, lamps, framed prints and accessories, create an upscale store environment with volume retail pricing. Easy to store and display, Boca Rattan premium rattan furniture does not require a large staff or special inventory management.

Number of Franchisees: 2 in 2 States

In Business Since: 1988

Equity Capital Needed: $135,000-$215,000, $75,000 liquid

Financial Assistance Available: Assistance available in providing lease packages to commercial clients, and in establishing store revolving credit plans.

Training Provided: Each franchisee, plus 2 designees, receives 8 business days of comprehensive training in the Boca Rattan franchise systems. Training includes business software use, hiring employees, marketing and merchandising, furniture maintenance and store decoration. In addition, each franchisee receives 4 days of on-site training at the time of his/her store opening.

Managerial Assistance Available: In addition to site selection and approval and grand opening support, TMF Systems, Inc., will provide franchisees with quarterly newsletters, inter-store inventory transfer liaison, software updates, advertising assistance, new product development, cooperative marketing, site visits, and easy access telephone business assistance.

Information Submitted: April 1990

*CARPETERIA, INC.
28159 Avenue Stanford
Valencia, California 91355

Description of Operation: Franchising and/or operating retail carpet outlets.

Number of Franchisees: 50 in California, Nevada and Washington plus 25 company stores.

In Business Since: 1973

Equity Capital Needed: $150,000 to $500,000, depending on size and scope of operation contemplated.

Financial Assistance Available: Up to $50,000 per unit.

Training Provided: 4-8 weeks depending on prior business and industry training and experience.

Managerial Assistance Available: Managerial and technical assistace is available from the franchisor.

Information Submitted: June 1990

CARPET TOWN, INC.
937 North Citrus Avenue
Hollywood, California 90038

Description of Operation: Floorcovering retail and wholesale.

Number of Franchisees: 18 in California plus 18 company-owned stores.

In Business Since: 1954

Equity Capital Needed: Negotiable

Financial Assistance Available: None

Training Provided: In franchisor's main office in Hollywood, California; in franchisor's warehouse in Hollywood, California; in one or more operating Carpet Town stores. Training program covers both administrative and merchandising matters, and also includes one or more tours of carpet mills; instructors for the training program are key employees of franchisor with 5 or more years of experience. The training is free of charge. Duration: 10-20 full days for franchisees having a basic familarity with retail sales operations; more if not.

Managerial Assistance Available: After the initital training shown above, continued assistance (free of charge) in the following areas: accounting, recordkeeping; inventory control; purchasing; sales; collections; merchandise display; advertising and promotion; price techniques; fiber content, colors and textures; installation; current market trends; etc.

Information Submitted: June 1990

CHEM-CLEAN FURNITURE RESTORATION CENTER
P. O. Box 577
Elmira, New York 14902
Dr. R. G. Esposito, President

Description of Operation: Patented non-water systems for furniture stripping and refinishing.

Number of Franchisees: 77 in 16 states, Canada and Europe.

In Business Since: 1967

Equity Capital Needed: $7,000-$25,000 total required.

Financial Assistance Available: Lease purchase or financing plans available. No royalties; licensee owns all equipment outright. Equipment and solvents covered by U.S. and Canadian patents.

Training Provided: Up to 2 weeks of complete instruction in licensee-owned shop, plus follow-up. Environmental assistance.

Managerial Assistance Available: Complete operating procedures, including technical and managerial techniques. Annual meetings of licensees. Newsletters.

Information Submitted: June 1990

CHEM-DRY CARPET CLEANING
HARRIS RESEARCH, INC.
3330 Cameron Park Drive, #700
Cameron Park, California 95682
Robert Harris, President

Description of Operation: Chem-Dry offers a unique, patented (#4219333) cleaning process utilizing a completely safe, nontoxic solution in conjunction with carbonation. The carbonated cleaner has opened the door for innovative approach to carpet cleaning and franchising. Carpets are guaranteed against damage, are left with no dirt-attracting residues, and generally dry in less than one hour.

Number of Franchisees: 2,406 in 50 States, and 22 countries.

In Business Since: 1977

Equity Capital Needed: $5,000-$12,500

Financial Assistance Available: The down payment pays for equipment and solutions, office supplies, an advertising package, and training. Balance financed by Harris Research, Inc.

Training Provided: A 4 day training program includes on-the-job training where carpet cleaning skills will be taught, as well as the necessary business management aspects. A franchisee, his/her managers or employees may obtain as much additional training as they desire at no charge. Training can also be done by a video tape program that includes a written test.

Managerial Assistance Available: A franchisee, his managers or employees may obtain as much additional training as they desire at no charge.

Information Submitted: May 1990

*CLASSIC CARE OF AMERICA
10190 Belladrum
Alpharett, Georgia 30201

196

Description of Operation: Automated hands-free window washing, carpet, drapery and upholstery cleaning, a three-in-one franchise.

Number of Franchisees: 25

In Business Since: 1987

Equity Capital Needed: Total investment $80,000.

Financial Assistance Available: Some financing available.

Training Provided: Complete hands on 1 week training at National Training Center and 1 week training in field at start-up followed by in-field continued support.

Managerial Assistance Available: Planned field visits by technical and specialty training programs at National Training Headquarters.

Information Submitted: April 1990

DECO HOME STORES, INC.
P. O. Box 1586
Placerville, California 95667
Norman L. McGee, President

Description of Operation: Wallpaper, window covering, paint and carpets.

Number of Franchisees: Over 500

In Business Since: 1983

Equity Capital Needed: $50,000

Financial Assistance Available: None

Training Provided: Limited

Managerial Assistance Available: None

Information Submitted: April 1990

*DECORATING DEN SYSTEMS, INC.
7910 Woodmont Avenue, Suite 200
Bethesda, Maryland 20814
Jim Bugg, President

Description of Operation: The retailing of custom-made draperies, window treatments, floor coverings, wallcoverings, furniture, and other related decorating products. All merchandise sold from samples and catalogues in the customer's home on an appointment basis. Business does not require inventory or a retail store. This is a professional service business with competitive pricing on quality products.

Number of Franchisees: 800

In Business Since: 1970

Equity Capital Needed: Franchise fee of $15,900-$18,900 plus working capital of $4,800 minimum.

Financial Assistance Available: Franchise fee cash. Lease available on ColorVan.

Training Provided: Decorating Den's initial training takes approximately 6 months. It combines classroom work, home study, meetings, seminars, on-the-job experience and an internship with an experienced decorator. Secondary, advanced and graduate training continue throughout the owner's career with Decorating Den. Decorating Den decorators are trained to identify lifestyle, personality, color preferences and a comfortable budget. Emphasis is on the "feeling," the way people live more than historical period stylings.

Managerial Assistance Available: Grand opening preparation and attendance. Planning and sales projection meeting. Post-opening progress checks. Ongoing services in marketing, sales, business operations and business expansion as part of fee.

Information Submitted: June 1990

DIP 'N STRIP, INC.
2141 South Platte River Drive
Denver, Colorado 80223
E. Roger Schuyler, President

Description of Operation: Franchised and company-owned operations providing the household community, antique dealers, furniture refinishers, industrial and commercial accounts in the removal of finishes from wood and metal. Operation requires approximately 2,000 square feet of warehouse space with concrete floor, drain, cold water tap, 220 single-phase power, overhead door, and small office space. The removal is accomplished with a cold stripping formula in chemical solutions. Dip 'N Strip is a federally registered trademark since April 13, 1970. Dip 'N Strip trademark is registered in France, Germany, the Benulux countries, and the United Kingdom.

Number of Franchisees: 214 in 36 States, Canada and 57 in Europe.

In Business Since: 1970

Equity Capital Needed: $12,500—no franchise fee required.

Financial Assistance Available: $3,000 will be financed up to 3 years, simple 10 percent interest, and will be carried by the franchisor for those who qualify.

Training Provided: A complete traning program is provided for 5 days of actual job and office training in all aspects of the business at the franchisee's own location prior to the grand opening. In Europe, the same training is provided at the master licensee pilot location.

Managerial Assistance Available: A complete operations manual and technical assistance is supplied during the training program, and in order to keep the franchisees current on the corporation and other franchisee's activities, a monthly newsletter, Dip 'N Script, is published. All advertising mats, layouts, and slicks are provided without charge to the franchisees on request.

Information Submitted: April 1990

THE DRAPERY FACTORY FRANCHISING CORP.
80 Tanforan Avenue
Suite 10
South San Francisco, California 94080
Vic Brown, Franchise Director

Description of Operation: The Drapery Factory is a retailer of custom window coverings including pleated draperies, sheers, valances, roman shades, austrian shades, balloon shades, swags, lambrequins, bedspreads, dust ruffles, mini blinds, vertical blinds, pleated shades, woven wood shades and duette shades.

Number of Franchisees: 17 in California and Arizona, 2 homeowned.

In Business Since: 1980

Equity Capital Needed: $50,000 includes franchise fee, set-up and operating capital.

Financial Assistance Available: None

Training Provided: 2 week training program plus field training and ongoing support.

Managerial Assistance Available: Clerical training provided at corporate headquarters.

Information Submitted: April 1990

*DURACLEAN INTERNATIONAL
2151 Waukegan Road
Deerfield, Illinois 60015

Description of Operation: On-location cleaning of carpet, rugs, upholstery and drapery fabrics using exclusive, patented processes, plus ceiling cleaning, stain repelling, soil-retarding, static removal, spot removal, mothproofing and minor carpet repair.

Number of Franchisees: 610 in all 50 States, throughout Canada and 20 countries overseas.

In Business Since: 1930

Equity Capital Needed: $14,800 for training and $8,000 for equipment.

Financial Assistance Available: For standard dealership Duraclean will finance balance of cost after $6,900 down payment for qualified applicants. Financing also available for other options.

Training Provided: 1 week resident training school, transportation, tuition, room and board at no cost to new dealers. Also, training with experienced dealer.

Managerial Assistance Available: Advertising, sales promotion, bookkeeping, laboratory services on cleaning and technical spotting. Regional meetings throughout the U.S. and Canada. International conventions.

Information Submitted: June 1990

*EXPRESSIONS
3212 West Esplanade
Metairie, Louisiana 70002
Eric Aschaffenburg, President

Description of Operation: Expressions is a specialty furniture store featuring custom order upholstered furniture. Expressions stores have been developed to maximize sales in a small store using a very limited inventory. This is accomplished by displaying samples of over 100 frame styles for sofas, sofa sleepers, and chairs along with a unique wall display of 500 fabric samples. Customer chooses frame style and fabric and delivery is scheduled within 6 weeks.

Number of Franchisees: 50 in 14 States plus 9 company-owned stores.

In Business Since: 1978

Equity Capital Needed: Approximately $150,000.

Financial Assistance Available: None

Training Provided: Expressions has developed a comprehensive and intensive training program that covers all phases of the furniture industry and in particular the techniques and methodology of running a successful Expressions store. The training program, which is administered by our highly qualified and professional training staff, consists of 6 days at our home office in New Orleans, 1 day at our manufacturing facility in Tupelo, Mississippi, and 1 week at franchise location to include the period of grand opening. An Expressions training manual is provided.

Managerial Assistance Available: Site Selection and Lease Negotiation—Provide site selection guidelines based on traffic count, resident demographics, storefront visibility, and general location layout. Also, assistance in lease negotiations. Merchandising—Design department assists with opening inventory and floor layout with great attention to correlation of fabrics and styles. Ongoing recommendations are made. Advertising—Advertising department furnishes franchisee with effective advertising campaigns and materials. Particular attention is paid to budgeting media selection and advertising material. Financial Analysis—Expressions will review your financial statements on a quarterly basis. Continued Training—Training staff is available with adequate notice to provide review or update training to any personnel. General—Expressions' staff of accountants, designers, sales consultants, advertising and production personnel stand ready to assist at all times.

Information Submitted: June 1990

FABRI-ZONE INTERNATIONAL, INC.
375 Bering Avenue
Toronto, Ontario, Canada M8Z3B1
David Collier, President

Description of Operation: Establish cleaning service franchisees, total service including carpet, upholstery, drapery, ceiling, smoke and fire damage, water restoration, odor removal, and retail product sales.

Number of Franchisees: 15 in 7 States

In Business Since: 1981

Equity Capital Needed: $2,500 to $19,500

Financial Assistance Available: Complete business plan for start-up, territory study, complete program, financing to qualified individuals.

Training Provided: 1 week at corporate office, video tape, and manuals.

Managerial Assistance Available: Complete technical and systems support, advertising and marketing promotions, monthly newsletters, regional seminars, management support, and monthly bulletins.

Information Submitted: April 1990

*FINE DESIGNS, INC.
100 Furniture Parkway
Norwalk, Ohio 44857
William R. Gerken, President

Description of Operation: Custom sofa specialty store offering 400 styles in 1,000 fabrics with 35-day delivery.

Number of Franchisees: 23 stores in 12 States

In Business Since: 1987

Equity Capital Needed: $200,000

Financial Assistance Available: None

Training Provided: Training in sales, service and management.

Managerial Assistance Available: Area representative on site every 2 weeks.

Information Submitted: May 1990

*FLOOR COVERINGS INTERNATIONAL
5182 Old Dixie Highway
Forest Park, Georgia 30050
Joseph R. Lunsford, President

Description of Operation: Floor Coverings International (FCI) is a mobile carpet retail franchise that provides "mill direct" floor covering to residential homes and businesses from coast to coast. Member International Franchise Association.

Number of Franchisees: 103 offices in 38 States, franchises available in remainder of States, Canada and abroad.

In Business Since: 1985

Equity Capital Needed: Total cost of franchise $9,700.

Financial Assistance Available: Yes

Training Provided: Mandatory Carpet College® is the finest in the carpet industry. Total training 1 week at company headquarters.

Managerial Assistance Available: Our franchise includes carpet samples, printing, continual ongoing assistance through upgraded training sessions, monthly newsletters, constant contact with suppliers and manufacturers, and a toll free help line.

Information Submitted: June 1990

THE FLOOR TO CEILING STORE
c/o FCS DISTRIBUTORS, INC.
4909 Highway 52 North
Rochester, Minnesota 55901
Roger Graham, President & CEO

Description of Operation: The Floor to Ceiling Store franchise is a designer showroom of nationally recognized home and office interior products providing decorator and remodeling services in an exciting retail setting.

Number of Franchisees: 45 in 8 Midwestern States plus 2 company-owned.

In Business Since: 1981

Equity Capital Needed: Minimum initial investment $60,000. Total investment ranges from $125,000 to $185,000 depending on store size. Includes an initial franchise fee of $25,000.

Financial Assistance Available: Franchisee normally furnishes 50 percent of the total capital needed. Franchisor will assist in negotiating additional term financing through local community sources. Franchisor also has a dealer finance package available.

Training Provided: Company provides assistance in site development, layout, remodeling, advertising, merchandising and display and accounting. The company also has an ongoing training program both locally and system-wide.

Managerial Assistance Available: Company provides ongoing assistance in store operations, product selection, distribution, advertising, accounting, and group insurance to allow franchisee to concentrate on building his business.

Information Submitted: April 1990

G. FRIED CARPETLAND, INCORPORATED
800 Old Country Road
Westbury, New York 11590
Al Fried, President

Description of Operation: Retail floor covering stores. Stores vary in size from 2,500 feet to 15,000 feet. Smaller stores are purely sample operations. Larger stores show samples and rolls.

Number of Franchisees: 23 in New York, New Jersey, Connecticut and Florida.

In Business Since: Parent corporation—1889. Franchising corporation—1969.

Equity Capital Needed: Cash minimum $15,000 per individual. We suggest two partners in each franchise. In large stores cash requirements would be proportionately more.

Financial Assistance Available: We have been able to arrange loans.

Training Provided: There is no definite training period required. We only want experienced floor covering professionals to apply.

Managerial Assistance Available: Franchisor constantly supervises franchisee's operation.

Information Submitted: June 1990

GROUNDWATER, INC.
3942 North 76th Street
Milwaukee, Wisconsin 53222
Thomas Blaes, Vice President

Description of Operation: Waterbeds and furniture retail store.

Number of Franchisees: 9 in Wisconsin

In Business Since: 1972

Equity Capital Needed: Varies—ranges $40,000

Financial Assistance Available: Co-ordinate bank financing through parent bank.

Training Provided: Varied

Managerial Assistance Available: Whatever is needed.

Information Submitted: June 1990

HILLSIDE BEDDING
700 Havemeyer Avenue
Bronx, New York 10473
Robert Martire, President

Description of Operation: Largest chain of bedding shops offers franchised stores featuring matresses, brass headboards, convertible safas, and most other sleep products. National brand names such as Sealy sold at discount prices.

Number of Franchisees: 72 in New York, New Jersey, Connecticut and Pennsylvania.

In Business Since: 1973

Equity Capital Needed: $39,150-$54,000

Financial Assistance Available: Will assist in obtaining financing.

Training Provided: 1 week of formal classroom training and 1 week with store manager of a company store. 1 week quarterly and 2 day monthly refresher courses available as continuing education.

Managerial Assistance Available: Each region has a local supervisor of operations available at all times. Each month, a vice president of operations visits each store for an entire day to assist owner with problem solving and implementation of new

products and promotional campaigns. Monthly marketing meeting in local areas and quarterly franchise meeting at company headquarters.

Information Submitted: June 1990

INTERNATIONAL HOME MARKETING SYSTEMS, INC.
1450 Mitchell Boulevard
Schaumburg, Illinois 60193
John Beltramo, President

Description of Operation: Buyers club concept whereby members are enabled to purchase home furnishings and related goods and services through the club at dealer's wholesale prices.

Number of Franchisees: 2 in Illinois and 1 in Missouri

In Business Since: Franchisor was incorporated in 1986 and is a wholly owned subsidiary of International Home Marketing, Inc. in 1972.

Equity Capital Needed: Total investment $126,000 to $153,500,, which includes franchise fee of $37,500, showroom display material $12,500, leasehold improvements, office furniture $4,500 to $15,000. Working capital (including insurance and related premiums) $69,000 to $83,500.

Financial Assistance Available: None

Training Provided: Franchisor shall furnish to the initial manager, a training program of such duration as determined by franchisor's sole discretion, based on the initial manager's prior business experience and other relevant factors.

Managerial Assistance Available: Franchisor may, at its sole discretion,, provide from time to time, refresher training programs. Franchisor shall furnish guidance for the operation of the franchised business.

Information Submitted: April 1990

JOHN SIMMONS GIFTS
c/o STS, INC.
36 West Calhoun
Memphis, Tennessee 38103

Description of Operation: Franchised John Simmons and The Shop of John Simmons gift shops. These are retail gift operations specializing in home furnishings and unique gifts. Company also offers its own import operation for incorporation into the franchised stores.

Number of Franchisees: 9 in 5 States

In Business Since: 1960

Equity Capital Needed: $100,000-$135,000

Financial Assistance Available: None

Training Provided: Management training in Memphis 3 to 4 day-cover start to finish of 1 day out of operation. Operating manual is given and highlights are covered. When we supervise setting up of store, we work with personnel in display, sales, and maintenance.

Managerial Assistance Available: We continue to work with franchise by sending a representative from the home office twice a year. We work with franchisee at 2 markets, and talk with each by telephone when needed (as long as the franchise is in effect).

Information Submitted: June 1990

KING KOIL SLEEP PRODUCTS
KING KOIL BEDQUARTERS FRANCHISE DIVISION
770 Transfer Road, Suite 13
St. Paul, Minnesota 55114
Ernest L. Friedman, President

Description of Operation: King Koil BedQuarters offers an opportunity to enter the retail sleep products business with a limited investment and is designed especially for the individual with some prior retail experience, preferably, but not necessarily in the household consumer goods area. The franchisee will be responsible for procuring his own location and commitment to real estate or lease. Inventory requirements are flexible with a minimum King Koil start up inventory of $12,000. King Koil must represent 51 percent or more of the total floor sampling and inventory.

Number of Franchisees: 175 in 22 States and 2 countries

In Business Since: 1982, franchising since 1982.

Equity Capital Needed: $60,000, limited one time franchise fee of $5,000.

Financial Assistance Available: The franchisor has developed an outstanding display package—partially supplied at no cost.

Training Provided: The franchisor has designed exclusive advertising and sales promotion materials including television and radio commercials, newspaper ads, collateral POP material and a sales training manual and marketing manual. Several sales training films will also be available. In addition, new materials will be developed on an ongoing basis. A unique cooperative preplanned advertising program has been developed to maximize penetration. A BedQuarters franchisee will receive continuous sales training, merchandise counseling and long-range promotional planning.

Managerial Assistance Available: A tight system of inventory control will be maintained jointly by King Koil and the franchisee enhanced by the BedQuarters Rapid delivery System. A national advertising program for BedQuarters was initiated in the spring of 1984. In addition to standard nationally advertised King Koil products, the BedQuarters franchise will have exclusive "made by BedQuarters merchandise" available to them.

Information Submitted: April 1990

LANGENWALTER INDUSTRIES, INC.
4410 East LaPalma Avenue
Anaheim, California 92807
Roy Langenwalter, President

Description of Operation: Langenwalter-Harris Chemical Co., Inc., offers a unique carpet and upholstery dye process franchise. A breakthrough in dye chemistry in which the liquid dye is solubilized to produce a stable color. A dye that sets instantly and permanently and allows the dyer to guarantee the color against color fade or lift from cleaning, etc., for 2 years. The dyer can control any color (an array of 18 brilliant colors) with perfect uniformity over extremely large areas of carpet and upholstery. Langenwalter-Harris Chemical Co., Inc., offers two distinct franchises. One is for the businessman who would enjoy providing the dye service for carpet and upholstery. The other is for the entrepreneur who would like to become a sub-franchisor in a region and/or territory wherein he supplies all dye, chemicals and equipment to the dyers. Both franchises now available for marketing overseas.

Number of Franchisees: 243 and 32 sub-franchises in 24 States.

In Business Since: 1972

Equity Capital Needed: $16,500.

Financial Assistance Available: None

Training Provided: An intensive, comprehensive, 5 day mandatory training course. The training program is held in the Langenwalter Dye Concept School facility in Anaheim, California. Franchisor provides testbook, operational and technical manuals.

Managerial Assistance Available: Franchisor provides continual technical, chemical and management update seminars and workshops for all franchisees. A continuous marketing and product research and development program for all franchises.

Information Submitted: April 1990

LAURA'S DRAPERIES & BEDSPREADS SHOWROOM, INC.
2200 Post Oak Boulevard
Suite 515
Houston, Texas 77056
Harold Nedell

Description of Operation: Laura's Draperies & Bedspreads Showrooms, Inc., is a unique retail approach to the custom drapery and bedspread business. "Affordable Elegance" is the idea behind Laura's, with a strong emphasis on service. An inventory of ready-made draperies, bedspreads, and decorator pillows is maintained, but the main thrust of the business is the custom market. Stores are no more than 1,500 square feet and are located in strip centers near major malls, open 6 days a week from 10 a.m. to 6 p.m.

Number of Franchisees: 23 in 7 States

In Business Since: 1986

Equity Capital Needed: Total capital required, $76,000.

Financial Assistance Available: None

Training Provided: 3 weeks in design, fabric selection, management, customer relations, finance, sales and prospecting techniques.

Managerial Assistance Available: Laura's provides continual management service for the life of the franchise in such areas as bookkeeping, advertising, and inventory control. Complete manuals of operations, forms, and directions are provided. Operation managers are available in all regions to work closely with franchisees. Laura's sponsors meetings of franchisees and conducts marketing and product research to maintain high Laura's consumer acceptance.

Information Submitted: April 1990

MODERNISTIC CARPET CLEANING
1271 Rankin
Troy, Michigan 48083
Robert McDonald, President

Description of Operation: Clean carpet, upholstery, draperies, and acoustical ceiling tile.

Number of Franchisees: 2 in Michigan

In Business Since: 1973

Equity Capital Needed: $10,000

Financial Assistance Available: Leasing and possible financial help from local Michigan bank.

Training Provided: 1 week in our shop; training includes video, one-on-one instruction, and in the field training.

Managerial Assistance Available: Complete operational manual; heavy instruction on marketing and telephone. Computer instruction available; bookkeeping available ongoing support 1-800 in Michigan for support over phone. They can come in for additional training at anytime.

Information Submitted: June 1990

*MR. MINIBLIND
17985-F Skypark Circle
Irvine, California 92714
Scott Holt, Vice President, Franchise Sales

Description of Operation: Window covering, sale and installation via mobile vans.

Number of Franchisees: 50 plus 2 company-owned.

In Business Since: 1987, franchising since 1988

Equity Capital Needed: $28,000 total investment.

Financial Assistance Available: None

Training Provided: Complete training program.

Managerial Assistance Available: Managerial assistance is continuously provided.

Information Submitted: June 1990

MURPHY BEDS OF CALIFORNIA, INC.
6904 Miramar Road
San Diego, California 92121
Harry Adler, President

Description of Operation: Murphy Beds of California, Bed Inc., is the exclusive distributor for the trade marked Murphy Bed (concealed metal wall bed) in California. The franchises are retail operations located in strategic areas of California. 1,600 to 2,000 square feet of retail space are required. Murphy Beds of California provides the brand name bed and the custom cabinets that surround the bed.

Number of Franchisees: 6 stores in California including 2 company-owned.

In Business Since: 1984

Equity Capital Needed: $50,000—additional $10,000 needed for start-up costs.

Financial Assistance Available: None. Franchise fee is $50,000. Down payment of $25,000 pays for inventory, sign and carpet. Balance of $25,000 payable upon completion by franchisor of turnkey store. An additional $10,000 needed for start up expenses. There is a 5 percent royalty on all gross sales due franchisor.

Training Provided: Up to 3 months training period either at company stores or on franchise site. Complete how-to manual. Bookkeeping and sales techniques are taught.

Managerial Assistance Available: Original contract calls for a 10 year association with optional renewal clause for another 10 years. Relationship and training are ongoing with all technical assistance provided.

Information Submitted: May 1990

NAKED FURNITURE, INC.
1099 Jay Street
Building 3
Rochester, New York 14611
Peter Judd

Description of Operation: A Naked Furniture store franchise is a specialty retail store selling better quality solid wood ready-to-finish furniture, custom finishing service and custom tailored upholstery.

Number of Franchisees: 50 plus 2 company-owned in 15 States.

In Business Since: 1972

Equity Capital Needed: $50,000 minimum; total package $130,000-$200,000.

Financial Assistance Available: Franchisor will assist in preparing financing proposal for presentation to lending institutions.

Training Provided: Complete operator training and support provided through intensive 1 to 2 week training program as well as full field support on a continuing basis.

Managerial Assistance Available: Naked Furniture, Inc., provides continual management service for the length of the franchise and provides an operations manual, a full bookkeeping package, forms, inventory selection assistance, regional warehousing, advertising and professional floor display plan. Periodic visits from regional field representatives will provide help in every area of store management and operation.

Information Submitted: June 1990

NETTLE CREEK INDUSTRIES, INC.
Peacock Road
Richmond, Indiana 47374

Description of Operation: Home furnishings retail stores specializing in semi-custom-made bedspreads, window treatments and decorative pillows. These are located in high income shopping areas and cater to people that need advice and assistance in interior decorating. The stores are about 1,500 square feet, and feature Nettle Creek products.

Number of Franchisees: 48 in 25 States

In Business Since: 1950

Equity Capital Needed: $50,000 investment including one-time franchise fee of $5,000.

Financial Assistance Available: None

Training Provided: Manuals and operating systems, on-site training of 1 week's duration, in-factory training of 2 to 3 days duration and continuing support and advice after the franchise is opened.

Managerial Assistance Available: Nettle Creek provides bookkeeping systems, complete stationery supplies, advertising materials and operating manuals. Full-time franchise coordinators assist in location research, store layout, set-up, merchandise selection, and co-op advertising. Our entire executive staff is available for consultation.

Information Submitted: June 1990

OFF-TRACK BEDDING
P.O. Box 3240
Providence, Rhode Island 02909
Thomas A. Barron, President

Description of Operation: Retail bedroom furniture showrooms.

Number of Franchisees: 11 in Rhode Island, Massachusetts, Connecticut and New Hampshire including company-owned.

In Business Since: 1980

Equity Capital Needed: $68,000-$99,000, total investment.

Financial Assistance Available: None

Training Provided: 2 weeks on-floor training at an active Off-Track Bedding location. 2 weeks training on-site at the franchised location.

Managerial Assistance Available: All training is ongoing. Site search and selection, complete system of merchandise and operating manuals that are constantly updated. Warehouse distribution center.

Information Submitted: June 1990

*PROFESSIONAL CARPET SYSTEMS, INC.
5182 Old Dixie Highway
Forest Park, Georgia 30050
Joseph R. Lunsford, President

Description of Operation: Professional Carpet Systems is the leader in on-site carpet redyeing, servicing thousands of apartment complexes, hotels, motels, and residential communities. Worldwide services also include carpet cleaning, rejuvenation, repair, water and flood damage restoration, Kool-aid® removal, and "guaranteed odor control" for pet odor removal. "A total carpet care concept." Members American Association of Textile Chemists and Colorists and International Franchise Association.

Number of Franchisees: 394 offices in 47 States; franchises available in remainder of States, Canada and abroad.

In Business Since: 1978

Equity Capital Needed: Total cost of franchise $13,500; franchisor requires $8,500 down, balance financed after the $8,500 down.

Financial Assistance Available: The balance of $5,000 is company financed, using territory as collateral. 6 percent royalty.

Training Provided: 60 hours intensive technical/sales training and 20 hours office and bookkeeping managerial skills. Total training 2 weeks at our company headquarters.

Managerial Assistance Available: Our franchise includes equipment package, supplies, printing, continual ongoing assistance through upgraded training sessions, monthly newsletters, toll free hot lines, and national account acquisition and sales program.

Information Submitted: June 1990

RAINBOW INTERNATIONAL CARPET DYEING AND CLEANING COMPANY
1010 University Park Drive
Waco, Texas 76707
Donald J. Dwyer, President

Description of Operation: Carpet and upholstery dyeing and tinting—carpet and upholstery cleaning, deodorization services, fire and water restoration, fire retardant—fiber guard.

Number of Franchisees: 1,000 in United States, Canada, France, Nassau, St. Croix, Guam, Ireland, Singapore, Taiwan, and Australia.

In Business Since: 1981

Equity Capital Needed: $12,000

Financial Assistance Available: Will finance 70 percent.

Training Provided: 1 week classroom and on-the-job-ongoing training via WATS line—mailing—regional seminars.

Managerial Assistance Available: Continuous back-up and support via toll free telephone number.

Information Submitted: April 1990

REPELE INTERNATIONAL
219 Newbury Street
Boston, Massachusetts 02116
Philip W. Sweeney, Vice President

Description of Operation: Repele International is a service-product company that treats carpets, upholstery, and wall coverings with a proprietary silicone-based fabric finish that protects them against permanent staining. Repele is applied by its licensed fabric technicians. Repele deals with the high end of the residential and commercial marketplace through its unique system of interior designer referrals. The company also markets a complete line of fabric maintenance products.

Number of Franchisees: 10 in California, Texas, Colorado, Florida, New Jersey, New Hampshire and Massachusetts.

In Business Since: 1983

Equity Capital Needed: Varies $15,000-$25,000.

Financial Assistance Available: The company requires a minimum down payment of $7,500 that pays for training, inventory, technical manuals and documentation.

Training Provided: 1 week of intensive training is conducted at the home office; instruction includes on-site application of Repele, technical instructions on fabric finishes, marketing and sales, stain removal and cleaning seminar.

Managerial Assistance Available: Repele provides management, accounting, sales, marketing, and technical assistance for the life of the franchise. The company also conducts periodic seminars for the franchisees. Repele maintains a product research group and a technical advisory service.

Information Submitted: June 1990

*RUG DOCTOR PRO
2788 North Larkin Avenue
Fresno, California 93727
Fred Thompson, National Director

Description of Operation: Carpet upholstery, drapery and specialty cleaning service.

Number of Franchisees: 34 plus 1 company-owned.

In Business Since: 1987

Equity Capital Needed: Equipment packages start at $6,500-$22,000.

Financial Assistance Available: 50 percent financing on franchise fee of $6,000 minimum and up to 90 percent on equipment.

Training Provided: Full training program.

Managerial Assistance Available: Ongoing

Information Submitted: June 1990

*SCANDIA DOWN CORPORATION
2025 First Avenue
Suite 200
Seattle, Washington 98121
Kell Larsen, President

Description of Operation: Scandia Down Shops are full-range bedding shops retailing products such as down comforters and pillows, European linens, wool bed pads, classic brass beds, and contemporary designer beds. The stores range from 500-1,400 square feet. They may, but need not, be located in covered retail shopping malls. Work hours are subject to lease negotiations. Stores must maintain representative samples of all Scandia Down trademarked items. They may stock a variety of bedding-related, non-trademarked items subject to Scandia Down approval. Franchisor participation in lease negotiations, if the franchisee requests.

Number of Franchisees: 66 plus 4 company-owned

In Business Since: 1980

Equity Capital Needed: $8,500-$170,000. Average total investment $235,000.

Financial Assistance Available: Financial assistance available.

Training Provided: Franchisor conducts an intensive 14-day training period at the corporate headquarters. The training is conducted along the outline of the operations manual. In addition, a field representative is provided for the initial 5 days of a new store opening.

Managerial Assistance Available: Scandia Down Corporation provides continuing management services for the life of the franchise in such areas as inventory control, bookkeeping, advertising, continuing marketing research and development, and general store operations. A corporate operations manual guides the full aspects of store operations. District managers and field representatives are available in all regions to work closely with franchisees in all aspects of store operations.

Information Submitted: June 1990

*SERVICEMASTER RESIDENTIAL AND COMMERCIAL CORPORATION
855 Ridge Lake Boulevard
Memphis, Tennessee 38119
Joseph S. Kirday, Director, Market Expansion

Description of Operation: ServiceMaster Residential and Commercial Corporation, a subsidiary of the ServiceMaster Company L.P. offers franchising in On Location Residential Services, Contract Services, Carpet/Upholstery Services, Small Business Contract Services, and On Location/Contract Services in small market, and this encompasses carpet, rug, furniture, smooth-floor surface, housewide cleaning, wall cleaning, disaster restoration, and odor removal in homes and commercial buildings, as well as complete janitorial services.

Number of Franchisees: 4,029 in 50 States and worldwide

In Business Since: 1948

Equity Capital Needed: Initial franchise fee for the On Location franchise is $19,000, including training manuals and aids plus an additional $8,000 for a recommended package of promotional materials, professional equipment, supplies and tools and professional chemicals for a total of $27,000. Initial franchise fee for the Contract Services franchise is $19,000, including manuals and aids plus an additional $9,000 for a recommended package of promotional materials, professional equipment, supplies and tools and professional chemicals for a total of $28,000. Initial franchise fee for the Carpet/Upholstery franchise is $9,200 including training manuals and aids plus an additional $7,500 for a recommended package of professional materials, professional equipment, supplies and tools and professional chemicals for a total of $16,700. Initial franchise fee for On Location/Contract Service in a small market area is $10,000, including training manuals and aids plus an additional $7,500 for a recommended package of promotional materials, professional equipment, supplies and tools and professional chemicals for a total of $17,500. Initial franchise fee for Small Business Contract Service in buildings less than 5,000 square feet is $8,000, including training manuals and aids plus an additional $6,500 for a recommended package of promotional materials, professional equipment, supplies and tools and professional chemicals for a total of $14,500.

Financial Assistance Available: Yes

Training Provided: Comprehensive home study, on-the-job training, set-up training, and classroom training. Continuous training program provided for all licensees.

Managerial Assistance Available: Managerial assistance is available on a continuous basis, from the company and from area based distributors in the field. The company makes available advertising, sales promotions, formal training laboratory services, regional and international meetings.

Information Submitted: June 1990

SIESTA SLEEP, INC.
386 Lindelof Avenue
Stoughton, Massachusetts 02072
Manuel or Alan Glickman

Description of Operation: Retail specialty mattress outlets carrying brand name bedding, brass beds, and related specialty exclusive items.

Number of Franchisees: 5 plus 7 company-owned in Massachusetts and New Hampshire. Two Sleep Specialty Stores.

In Business Since: 1953

Equity Capital Needed: $15,000 to $25,000 or arrange for a turnkey existing and proven shop. Partner often available on financial help.

Financial Assistance Available: Yes

Training Provided: 6 to 8 weeks intensive training plus continuous follow-up supervision plus as needed.

Managerial Assistance Available: Very close contact and sincere assistance.

Information Submitted: June 1990

SLUMBERLAND, INC.
3060 Centerville Road
Little Canada, Minnesota 55117
Kenneth R. Larson

Description of Operation: Slumberland operates retail specialty stores. Slumberland features name brand mattresses, sleep sofas and reclining chairs.

Number of Franchisees: 19 in Minnesota, Iowa, Wisconsin, South Dakota and Nebraska including company-owned.

In Business Since: 1967

Equity Capital Needed: $50,000 to $100,000

Financial Assistance Available: Limited

Training Provided: Extensive training covering marketing, sales and advertising.

Managerial Assistance Available: An ongoing relationship includes marketing assistance, long range planning, site selection, delivery and warehousing.

Information Submitted: May 1990

*SPRING CREST COMPANY, INC.
505 West Lambert Road
Brea, California 92621
Jack W. Long, President

Description of Operation: Spring Crest Drapery Centers retail draperies and other window treatments such as blinds, shades, verticals, drapery hardware and accessories.

Number of Franchisees: 319 in 38 States, Canada, New Zealand, Australia, South Africa, Saudi Arabia, and the United Kingdom.

In Business Since: 1955, franchising since 1968.

Equity Capital Needed: $50,000 for total package.

Financial Assistance Available: Yes

Training Provided: Initital training at headquarters with aditional training at franchise location.

Managerial Assistance Available: Site selection, store design, fixtures and equipment, field staff support, operations manual, regional and national conference, newsletter.

Information Submitted: April 1990

*STANLEY STEEMER INTERNATIONAL, INC.
5500 Stanley Steamer Parkway
P. O. Box 156
Dublin, Ohio 43017
Wesley C. Bates, President

Description of Operation: A complete franchise system for on-location carpet and furniture cleaning, water damage cleanup and odor removal services. Company manufactures patented intruct and portable equipment—maintains complete supplies to provide backup for franchises.

Number of Franchisees: Over 200 in 31 States, plus 19 company operations.

In Business Since: 1947, carpet and furniture cleaning. 1972, manufacturing and franchise sales.

Equity Capital Needed: Variable, minimum $20,000.

Financial Assistance Available: Lease program available on equipment and new truck.

Training Provided: 2 weeks or longer, depending on need at company headquarters. Training conducted by training director with a great amount of OJT with experienced cleaning crews. Periodic review and retraining provided where necessary. All manuals are provided.

Managerial Assistance Available: Bi-monthly newsletter and periodic technical and service bulletins issued. Specific department head help available on an individual basis. A complete advertising department is maintained for franchise support. Annual convention and regional meetings for franchisees. Group liability insurance and major medical and hospitalization insurance programs are available. Continuous research and development for improvement of cleaning methods and equpment.

Information Submitted: April 1990

*STEAMATIC INCORPORATED
1601 109th Street
Grand Prairie, Texas 75050
John Gellatly, Vice President of Franchising

Description of Operation: Steamatic provides 11 diversified cleaning and restoration services for the insurance, commercial and residential market segments. These include air duct cleaning; fire, smoke and water damage restoration; carpet, furniture, ceiling, wall and drapery cleaning; deodorization and decontamination; wood restoration and corrosion control.

Number of Franchisees: 225 (primarily in the United States and Canada).

In Business Since: 1948

Equity Capital Needed: $10,000 to $50,000

Financial Assistance Available: If franchisee qualifies, one-half of franchise fee can be financed through bank in Fort Worth.

Training Provided: Extensive 2 week training course. This includes 1 week of on-location experience in homes and offices, followed by a 1 week mini-business school.

Managerial Assistance Available: Insurance, commercial and residential marketing; advertising; financial management; regional and national seminars; continuous field support services; operational assistance; Steamatic Executive Council and technical bulletins to franchise owners.

Information Submitted: April 1990

STOREHOUSE, INC.
2403-D Johnson Ferry Road
Chamblee, Georgia 30341
Clyde Mynatt, President

Description of Operation: Contemporary home furnishings stores specializing in butcher block tables, custom built sofas, classic design chairs, bedroom furniture, storage systems, and outdoor furniture.

Number of Franchisees: 4 in South Carolina, Texas, Florida and North Carolina plus 23 company-owned stores.

In Business Since: 1969

Equity Capital Needed: Total capital required ranges from $115,000 to $205,000.

Financial Assistance Available: No financial assistance available; however, an inventory repurchase agreement is offered that can be assigned to a lender to assist franchise in acquiring financing.

Training Provided: 1 week in corporate office, 2 weeks in company store and 2 weeks in franchise store.

Managerial Assistance Available: Operating manual and product information manual, site selection, lease negotiation, store design and construction, approximately monthly visits first 6 months, periodic thereafter, monthly advertising program and merchandising program, and merchandise available through company distribution centers.

Information Submitted: June 1990

TOWN & COUNTRY OFFICE & CARPET CARE
2580 San Ramon Valley Boulevard
Suite B-208
San Ramon, California 94583

Description of Operation: State-of-the-art dry extractor carpet cleaning and professional office care.

Number of Franchisees: 90 throughout the United States.

In Business Since: 1971, began franchising in 1986

Equity Capital Needed: $3,000-$10,000

Financial Assistance Available: None

Training Provided: 3-5 days training provided.

Managerial Assistance Available: Continuous managerial assistance available.

Information Submitted: April 1990

UNITED CONSUMERS CLUB
8405 South Broadway
Merrillville, Indiana 46410
Scott M. Powell

Description of Operation: United Consumers Club offers a private service using an alternative to the conventional distribution system, allowing merchandise to be shipped from manufacturers and distributors directly to a local address, thus avoiding the costly expense of the middleman. Each catalog center is approximately 4,000-5,000 square feet and is open 6 days a week. A minimum inventory of brand name merchandise and a wide variety of catalogs representing several hundred manufacturers are available to the membership, allowing easy ordering of furniture, carpeting and appliances.

Number of Franchisees: 77 franchised units in 22 States; 3 company-owned units in Indiana.

In Business Since: 1971

Equity Capital Needed: Approximately $75,000, including working capital.

Financial Assistance Available: A minimum franchise fee down payment of $15,000 is necessary to open a UCC franchise. UCC will finance the balance of the $55,000 franchise fee for qualified candidates.

Training Provided: The UCC provides 4 weeks of initial classroom and on-site training. Major emphasis is placed on understanding and implementing the Club's business plan, operational guidelines and the marketing system to achieve a high level of profitability. A partial transportation allowance, food and lodging are provided to the new franchise owner and one other person.

Managerial Assistance Available: UCC provides continual management service for the life of the franchise in the areas of accounting, sales, personnel, etc. Complete sales and general operation manuals, audio-visual support programs, forms and directives are provided. Field supervision is also available to work with franchisees and conduct marketing and product information seminars.

Information Submitted: April 1990

*WALLPAPERS TO GO
Division of WNS, INC.
P. O. Box 4586
Houston, Texas 77210-4586
Gary K. Akin, Vice President, Franchise Development
Deborah Steinberg, Vice President, Franchise Development

Description of Operation: Wallpapers To Go is the nation's largest chain of retail stores specializing in in-stock wallcoverings and related home decoration products, including coordinated fabrics, window treatments and trim paints. Stores present a distinctively feminine image appealing to women, the primary consumer of residential wallcoverings. Wallpapers To Go targets the do-it-yourselfer with extensive in-store training materials.

Number of Franchisees: 110 plus 14 company-owned throughout the United States.

In Business Since: 1977; franchising since 1986

Equity Capital Needed: Approximately $220,000.

Financial Assistance Available: Assistance in securing SBA loans.

Training Provided: Intensive 5 day classroom training prepares franchisees for the operation of their stores. Field staff assists in store takeover/opening to ensure successful transition.

Managerial Assistance Available: Market research, furnishings, fixtures and equipment. Wallpapers To Go provides assistance with site selection, market research, construction specs, furnishings, fixtures and equipment, merchandising and visual presentation. Field staff work closely with franchisees on an ongoing basis. Franchisees participate in national and regional marketing programs. More than 750 name-brand designer wallcoverings furnished to franchisees through the Wallpapers To Go Distribution Center.

Information Submitted: April 1990

*WASH ON WHEELS-HY-DRY
5401 South Bryant Avenue
Sanford, Florida 32773
George Louser

Description of Operation: Carpet, furniture and drapery cleaning.

Number of Franchisees: 40

In Business Since: 1987

Equity Capital Needed: $5,400

Financial Assistance Available: Financial assistance available to those with good credit. Total investment $16,000.

Training Provided: 5 days intensive training, then constant ongoing manuals, seminars, newsletters, hot lines and direct mail.

Managerial Assistance Available: Ongoing

Information Submitted: April 1990

WFO FRANCHISES
222 Banta Place
Fairlawn, New Jersey 07410
Steve Bromberg

Description of Operation: Retail furniture stores specializing in wall systems, bookcases, audio cabinets, etc.

Number of Franchisees: 26 stores including company-owned in New York and New Jersey.

In Business Since: 1965, franchising since 1984.

Equity Capital Needed: $49,000-$69,000

Financial Assistance Available: None

Training Provided: 2 weeks training on-site in all phases of operation.

Managerial Assistance Available: Ongoing in all aspects of managerial and technical assistance.

Information Submitted: June 1990

*WINDOW WORKS, INC.
2101 N.W. 33rd Street
Suite 300A
Pompano Beach, Florida 33069

Description of Operation: Window Works offers retail stores set-up as showrooms in high-volume shopping plaza. Window Works specializes in the sale and installation of custom interior window treatments. Products include national brands of vertical blinds, mini blinds, interior shutters, drapes, wood blinds and pleated shades. Customers are from the residential and commercial sectors.

Number of Franchisees: 85 in 20 States

In Business Since: 1978

Equity Capital Needed: $70,000. This includes franchise fee, complete store set-up, computer system and software, installation van deposit, first 3 months of advertising.

Financial Assistance Available: None

Training Provided: Training consists of both classroom and in-field instruction. The Window Works training program is designed to give the franchisee complete working knowledge of the product, installation, systems, and operation of business. Training is conducted in Florida and lasts no more than 3 weeks.

Managerial Assistance Available: With extensive computer capability, Window Works International provides detailed monitoring of all areas of franchisee's business, including continuous analysis of sales, margins, marketing, order flow, employee performance, etc. Window Works International also provides complete management service for the life of the franchise.

Information Submitted: May 1990

INSURANCE

AMERICA ONE, INC.
2214 University Park Drive
Okemos, Michigan 48964
Joanne F. Dillman, Vice President of Operations

Description of Operation: America One, Inc., sets up independent insurance agencies for licensed salespeople. Extensive training, licensing with insurance companies, advertising and continuing assistance in marketing, etc., are provided.

Number of Franchisees: 30 in Michigan

In Business Since: 1980

Equity Capital Needed: $12,000

Financial Assistance Available: $6,000 down payment. Balance of $4,000 due upon opening of business.

Training Provided: 12 to 15 days training for franchisee and employees in all aspects of operating an insurance agency. Continuing training in franchisee's office after opening of business. All manuals, forms, etc., provided.

Managerial Assistance Available: America One provides continual management services in areas of bookkeeping, marketing, money management, and advertising, sponsors monthly meetings of franchisees, and does marketing research for additional services that will help franchisees be successful.

Information Submitted: April 1990

*ISU INTERNATIONAL
P. O. Box 2822
San Francisco, California 94126
Thomas Ryan

Description of Operation: An ISU franchise provides a select group of insurance independents with the marketing rights that arise from the strengths and resources of size and industry awareness. It entitles these independent agents to access exclusive insurance products, programs, systems, and company relations.

Number of Franchisees: Over 300 throughout the United States.

In Business Since: 1979

Equity Capital Needed: Initial franchise fee of $3,500.

Financial Assistance Available: None

Training Provided: Formal classroom training, on-premises training in the exclusive ISU/1084 Sales and Marketing System.

Managerial Assistance Available: ISU provides continual management and technical support through the use of a toll-free number. Complete manual of operations is provided. Regional managers are available to work closely with franchisees. ISU organizes regional meetings and yearly national management conferences.

Information Submitted: June 1990

LAUNDRIES, DRY CLEANING/SERVICES

A CLEANER WORLD
ACW MANAGEMENT CORP.
2334 English Road
High Point, North Carolina 27260
Ray W. Edwards, President

Description of Operation: Dry cleaning and shirt laundry featuring drive around service. Selling franchises in the State of North Carolina only.

Number of Franchisees: 29 franchised and 16 company-owned stores in North Carolina, Virginia, Tennessee and Georgia.

In Business Since: 1961

Equity Capital Needed: $50,000

Financial Assistance Available: None

Training Provided: All necessary training provided at a company-owned store.

Managerial Assistance Available: Continuous managerial and purchasing assistance provided. Also complete equipment and maintenance department provided for franchisees.

Information Submitted: June 1990

AMERIVEND CORPORATION
4101 Southwest 73rd Avenue
Miami, Florida 33155
Ralph F. Geronimo, Regional Sales Manager

Description of Operation: Amerivend is an independent factory authorized Maytag distributor—we procure suitable locations in Florida, Georgia and Alabama for the installation of Maytag "JUST LIKE HOME" Coin Op Laundries. Amerivend negotiates the lease, provides mechanical plans and blueprints, and offers factory trained service technicians. These businesses are all independently owned. They pay no royalties, residuals or percentage fees of any kind. Virtually turnkey.

Number of Franchisees: Over 700. Soliciting for Florida, Georgia and Alabama.

In Business Since: 1959

Equity Capital Needed: $25,000-$55,000 depending on total cost.

Financial Assistance Available: Financing for approximately 80 percent of the selling price of the business is presently available. (Lease Purchase Option.)

Training Provided: Amerivend trains our clients re merchandising, store operations, maintenance and bookkeeping.

Managerial Assistance Available: Ongoing throughout the tenure of our clients' business if so desired. We believe we should be available for consultation. Our clients provide outstanding unsolicited testimonials on our behalf because of our attitude toward them.

Information Submitted: April 1990

BRUCK DISTRIBUTING COMPANY, INC.
9291 Arlete Avenue
Arleta, California 91331
Julius Bruck, President

Description of Operation: Eldon Drapery Drycleaning Franchisees: Servicing draperies for both commercial and residential building. 40 percent of business done under name of major department stores.

Number of Franchisees: 45 in 18 States

In Business Since: 1966

Equity Capital Needed: $50,000 to $100,000

Financial Assistance Available: None

Training Provided: Complete production, installation, sales and office procedures. First portion in our training facility. Second portion in franchisee's. We train for as long as franchisee feels is needed.

Managerial Assistance Available: Ongoing program.

Information Submitted: June 1990

*CLEAN'N'PRESS FRANCHISE, INC.
7301 North 16th Street
Suite 101
Phoenix, Arizona 85020
Robert J. Gottschalk

Description of Operation: Clean'n'Press Franchise is a value-priced quality-for-less drycleaner, utilizing a one-price-per-garment approach, positioned about 50 percent below the market. Franchisees can operate multiple stores and their own plant, or individual stores utilizing the cleaning services of the franchisor's plant where applicable.

Number of Franchisees: 85 stores in 8 States

In Business Since: 1982, franchising since 1986

Equity Capital Needed: For a constellation franchise, $100,000 liquid, total approximately $300,000. For a store franchise, $14,000 liquid, total approximately $50,000.

Financial Assistance Available: The franchisor offers no financing but will assist with providing sources.

Training Provided: Franchisor operates a 10 day training school that every franchisee attends in addition to 7 days on-site at grand opening. Complete instruction in business management, marketing, advertising, trade skills is involved.

Managerial Assistance Available: Within the 150 day pre-opening period, we provide assistance in site selection, leasing, equipment purchasing and installation, tenant improvement, ordering supplies, hiring and training of employees, and the initiation of a unique grand opening. Financial analysis, operational assistance, volume purchasing, periodic field visits, and an 800 hot line connection are all part of our ongoing support program.

Information Submitted: April 1990

COIT DRAPERY & CARPET CLEANERS, INC.
897 Hinckley Road
Burlingame, California 94010

Description of Operation: Residential and commercial cleaning services. Cleaning and maintenance of drapery and window coverings, carpets, upholstery, area rugs, fire and water damage restoration, sale of new carpets and window coverings.

Number of Franchisees: 45 throughout the U.S. and Canada

In Business Since: 1950

Equity Capital Needed: $79,000-$200,000

Financial Assistance Available: Assistance available to arrange funding from outside sources.

Training Provided: Initial training at corporate facilities, consisting of management, operational and technical training, complete with manuals. Industry certified technical training done on a regional basis. On-site training by corporate personnel at franchise's location at start-up. Follow-up training avaialble at several corporate facilities.

Managerial Assistance Available: Semi-annual conventions, regional seminars. Continuous managerial and technical assistance. In-house marketing department available to franchisees. Ongoing research and development. Complete computerized operational and financial system. Monthly publication of comparative operational and financial statistical information. Cost bureau. Quarterly newsletter. Video library. Complete manuals and information retention and retrieval system.

Information Submitted: May 1990

*DRYCLEAN-U.S.A., INC.
9100 South Dadeland Boulevard
Suite 1100
Miami, Florida 33156

Description of Operation: Dryclean-U.S.A. has won many plant design awards in the drycleaning industry, based on efficient planning, first-rate equipment, quality work, inviting and attention-getting decor, personal service, attractive packaging, and creative merchandising.

Number of Franchisees: 194 in the United States

In Business Since: 1975

Equity Capital Needed: $50,000-$85,000

Financial Assistance Available: Assistance in financing from financial institutions.

Training Provided: 3 weeks intensive training in franchisor's training school, and 1 week supervisory training upon the opening of the franchisee's store.

Managerial Assistance Available: Dryclean-U.S.A. provides procedural manuals of operation for all franchises. Periodic visits and/or calls are made to assist in any problems and/or questions, and recommendations are made to help retain the high-quality standards Dyrclean-U.S.A. strives for.

Information Submitted: May 1990

*DUDS 'N SUDS
CLEAN DUDS INC.
3401 101st Street, Suite E
Des Moines, Iowa 50322
Philip G. Akin

Description of Operation: Self-serve laundry, snack bar, and cleaning services. We call it "Good, Clean, Fun." A full service laundry that is energy efficient and also has a soda fountain that serves pop, coffee and even beer. It also has a big screen TV, pool table and video games. Approximately 3,000 square feet.

Number of Franchisees: 85 in 27 States

In Business Since: 1983

Equity Capital Needed: $60,000; total system price $80,000

Financial Assistance Available: We have a loan guide and loan proposal that we present to financial institutions. We also work with the SBA. Limited financial assistance available. Equipment lease programs.

Training Provided: On-site training in store during the opening. Also a week training prior to opening at Des Moines, Iowa. Also operations manuals and instructional video tapes are provided.

Managerial Assistance Available: Full promotional and management support, manuals, design and layout of store, all signage, video tapes, financial evaluations, inspections, maintenance program, regional and national franchisor meetings.

Information Submitted: April 1990

EXECUTIVE IMAGE CLEANERS
EXECUTIVE IMAGE CLEANERS, INC.
1333 West 120th Avenue, Suite 222
Denver, Colorado 80234
Chuck Yerbic-Allen Sunset

Description of Operation: Executive Image Cleaners, Inc. (EIC) serves the busy executive and office employee at their place of business. With the ever increasing two income families, time becomes a very important factor in their lives. The office professional can eliminate those extra stops at the local dry cleaners because EIC brings the dry cleaning plant to the employee. EIC is a unique business that features quality, convenience and hand finished garments.

Number of Franchisees: 7 in 3 States

In Business Since: 1988

Equity Capital Needed: Minimum $25,000. Approximate investment $100,000.

Financial Assistance Available: Will assist in finding lenders.

Training Provided: Complete hands-on training on equipment.

Managerial Assistance Available: Detailed administration and operational procedures.

Information Submitted: April 1990

GOLDEN TOUCH CLEANERS, INC.
8237 North Kimball Avenue
Skokie, Illinois 60076
David B. Lieberman, President

Description of Operation: Drycleaning plants.

Number of Franchisees: 9 in Illinois

In Business Since: 1985

Equity Capital Needed: $30,000

Financial Assistance Available: No financial assistance provided other than introducing prospective franchisee to banks familiar with our operation.

Training Provided: Comprehensive training in all phases of operation. Training period lasts up to 1 month.

Managerial Assistance Available: Franchisor is available for assistance during the entire franchise period at no cost to franchisee.

Information Submitted: June 1990

HIS AND HERS IRONING SERVICE, INC.
10841 West 155th Terrace
Overland Parks, Kansas 66221
Kenneth R. Mairs, President

Description of Operation: His and Hers Ironing Service, Inc., offers a unique service business specializing in hand ironing and laundry, with virtually no competition. Residential and commercial customers are served through a pick-up and delivery system.

Number of Franchisees: 3 in Kansas, Missouri, and Tennessee

In Business Since: 1983

Equity Capital Needed: $20,000 to $40,000, which includes franchise fee of $10,000.

Financial Assistance Available: The total investment listed above includes start-up supplies, security deposits, cash fund, licenses, permits, and training for an exclusive territory. Franchisor offers no financial assistance at this time.

Training Provided: Training for 5 days conducted at the franchisor's home office. This training covers office organization, bookkeeping, routes, methods, and promotion. A training manual and instructional video tape are included.

Managerial Assistance Available: On-going assistance is available on a continual basis. Special on-site assistance is available upon request.

Information Submitted: April 1990

LONDON INDUSTRIES INC.
2510 Metropolitan Drive
Trevose, Pennsylvania 19047
Ronald London, President

Description of Operation: Offering complete professional drycleaning plants and coin laundry stores. All stores are custom designed for maximum efficiency and profitability.

Number of Franchisees: 265 in 6 States and Washington, D.C.

In Business Since: 1963

Equity Capital Needed: $35,000 minimum

Financial Assistance Available: Up to 90 percent financing of equipment through financial institutions.

Training Provided: In-house training as required, service clinics.

Managerial Assistance Available: Field inspection and assistance in all phases of management on a continuing basis.

Information Submitted: May 1990

*MARTIN FRANCHISES, INC.
2005 Ross Avenue
Cincinnati, Ohio 45212
Franchise Director

Description of Operation: Comprehensive start-up assistance including locations/site assistance with NDS computerized demographics, mapping capabilities, full plant layout and mechanical drawings, 3 week training program, in-store start-up assistance, equipment shakedown and ongoing local store and marketwide promotional programs, field and operations assistance.

Number of Franchisees: 904 in 49 States and 4 countries.

In Business Since: 1949

Equity Capital Needed: $65,000 start-up cash; $157,000-$230,000 total investment.

Financial Assistance Available: Associated with SBA financial lender and leasing company; however, there is no direct financing.

Training Provided: 3 weeks of comprehensive managerial and technical classroom and in-plant training at Martinizing National Training Center; start-up assistance in franchisee's plant, as well as the comprehensive support listed under "Description of Operation."

Managerial Assistance Available: Supervision and guidance provided by local representative and franchisor.

Information Submitted: April 1990

SOAP OPERA LAUNDRY CENTERS
5757 Corporate Boulevard
Suite 304
Baton Rouge, Louisiana 70808

Description of Operation: Replaces the old style dirty laundromat with a whole new concept of clean, well kept, attended coin laundry offering self-service or drop-off including dry cleaning.

Number of Franchisees: 14 plus 2 company-owned stores. We are presently concentrating on developing Louisiana and Florida.

In Business Since: 1985

Equity Capital Needed: Approximately $50,000 initial investment; total about $200,000.

Financial Assistance Available: Yes

Training Provided: Total training available in procedures, techniques, recordkeeping, all phases of operation. Follow-up on a regular basis.

Managerial Assistance Available: Site selection, marketing, and advertising.

Information Submitted: April 1990

LAWN AND GARDEN SUPPLIES/SERVICES

A-PERM-O-GREEN LAWNS, INC.
P. O. Box 562687
Dallas, Texas 75356-1687
Tommy Isbell, Owner

Description of Operation: A-Perm-O-Green Lawns franchisees provide professional lawn care services (fertilizing, week control, insect and disease control) and tree/shrub care services (fertilizing, insect and disease control) to residential customers.

Number of Franchisees: 2 plus 3 company-owned in Texas and Louisiana.

In Business Since: 1976

Equity Capital Needed: $20,000 minimum

Financial Assistance Available: Financial assistance available to qualified persons.

Training Provided: Technical, sales and managerial training. Bookkeeping service available.

Managerial Assistance Available: Ongoing

Information Submitted: June 1990

BAREFOOT GRASS LAWN SERVICE, INC.
1018 Proprietors Road
Worthington, Ohio 43085
John E. Dunham, Vice President for Franchising

Description of Operation: Barefoot Grass provides professional granular lawn care to residential and commercial lawns. Fertilizers, weed controls, insect controls and disease controls are applied on a scheduled basis following prescribed programs. Enjoyable outdoor work environment.

Number of Franchisees: 30 in 21 States

In Business Since: 1975

Equity Capital Needed: Minimum $25,000.

Financial Assistance Available: None

Training Provided: Technical agronomic training, sales training and business training are provided. Training is conducted at the franchisee's site or at the franchisor's headquarters in Worthington, Ohio, a Columbus, Ohio suburb. Formal introductory training programs last at least 4 days, with follow-up provided as needed.

Managerial Assistance Available: Barefoot Grass provides continuing management services for the duration of the franchise in such areas as computer services, including customer records; bookkeeping, including accounts receivable, payroll; marketing and advertising; purchasing and inventory control. Operating and technical manuals and updates are provided. Forms and supplies are available. Regional managers are available to work closely with franchisees and visit regularly to assist with problem solving and quality control. Barefoot Grass sponsors meetings of branch and franchise managers to maintain high levels of training and performance.

Information Submitted: April 1990

CHEMLAWN SERVICES CORPORATION
8275 North High Street
Columbus, Ohio 43235-1499
Bruce W. Fowler, General Manager, Franchising

Description of Operation: ChemLawn has originated and developed, through extensive time and effort, unique programs for providing lawn care service, consisting of periodic applications of fertilization, weed and insect control materials ("Lawn Care Program") and for providing tree and shrub care service, consisting of periodic applications of fertilization, insect and disease control materials ("Tree and Shrub Care Program") through the use of distinctive types of equipment, supplies, ingredients, business techniques and methods, and sales promotion programs.

Number of Franchisees: 63 in 27 States

In Business Since: 1969, franchising since 1977

Equity Capital Needed: $100,000

Financial Assistance Available: None

Training Provided: Business planning, sales, office, service, equipment, safety, and agronomic. Field training programs provided at no extra charge; these include a leader's guide, video tape and student workbook. Four weeks of training required prior to start-up.

Managerial Assistance Available: Annual technical/agronomic visit and review at location (2 days), annual operations visit and review at location (2 days), annual owners' meeting off location (3 days), annual agronomic training either at or off location (2 days) and annual operations training either at or off location (2 days).

Information Submitted: April 1990

*FASGRAS INTERNATIONAL, INC.
Subsidiary of JOHNSON HYDRO SEEDING CORP.
13751 Travilah Road
Rockville, Maryland 20850
Robert F. Pullliza, Executive Vice President

Description of Operation: Specializes in installing new lawns for builders and erosion control for developers using FASGRAS patented pre-germinated hydro seeding system. Establishes lawns in 3-5 days.

Number of Franchisees: 6 in Maryland and Virginia

In Business Since: 1964, franchising since 1981

Equity Capital Needed: Approximately $30,000.

Financial Assistance Available: None

Training Provided: On-the-job training program is conducted at the home office in Rockville, Maryland. Additional field and management training is provided at franchisee's location on an as needed basis.

Managerial Assistance Available: Continuous throughout the life of the franchise.

Information Submitted: April 1990

GREEN CARE LAWN SERVICE, INC.
3708 8th Avenue North
Birmingham, Alabama 25222
Ronnie L. Zwiebel, President

Description of Operation: Chemical lawn and shrub care programs for southern and transition zone areas. Program of 4 to 6 applications, depending on grass type, assures year round revenues.

Number of Franchisees: 4 in Alabama

In Business Since: 1973

Equity Capital Needed: $30,000

Financial Assistance Available: Long term financing available on equipment, and short-term on some supplies to qualified buyers.

Training Provided: 2 weeks for 2 persons consisting of classroom and on-the-job training at corporate facilities in Birmingham, Alabama. Includes all technical aspects of lawn and shrub care plus application methods and equipment care. All aspects of recordkeeping are covered at this time, also. A week is spent at franchisee's location to assist with start-up.

Managerial Assistance Available: An operating manual is provided for all franchises. Additionally, seminars are held each year for new technical training. Managers' updates are held twice each year to address subjects such as interviewing and hiring, asset management, controlling expenses, etc. Ongoing consultation is available for the term of the agreement.

Information Submitted: June 1990

*LAWN DOCTOR INCORPORATED
P. O. Box 512142 Highway #34
Matawan, New Jersey 07747
Ed Reid, National Franchise Sales Director

Description of Operation: Professional automated lawn services.

Number of Franchisees: Over 300 in 27 States.

In Business Since: 1967

Equity Capital Needed: Minimum of $30,500.

Financial Assistance Available: Yes

Training Provided: Extensive 2 week managerial, sales and technical training at the home office. Technical training for each employee at the home office. Weekly workshops. Management seminars.

Managerial Assistance Available: All necessary initial bookkeeping, advertising, and sales promotional materials supplied. Close follow-up after initial training with service representatives available for both telephone and in-the-field assistance whenever required. Public relations consultation available. Extensive TV advertising campaigns in major markets.

Information Submitted: May 1990

LIQUI-GREEN LAWN CARE CORPORATION
9601 North Allen Road
Peoria, Illinois 61615
B. C. Dailey, President

Description of Operation: Lawn spraying of fertilizer and weed control, plus many additives. Tree spraying, deepfeeding, and injection. Each one is owner operated, consisting of a new 1-ton truck, mounted with 300 and 500 gallon tank with injectors for special products.

Number of Franchisees: 25 in Illinois, Iowa, and Pennsylvania.

In Business Since: 1953

Equity Capital Needed: $10,000

Financial Assistance Available: Possible to qualified persons.

Training Provided: Extensive on-the-job training in technique, material handling, sales and advertising.

Managerial Assistance Available: Liqui-Green sponsors seminars to introduce new ideas, products and advertising ideas. Liqui-Green is staffed with turf and tree experts for counsel to all its franchises.

Information Submitted: April 1990

NITRO-GREEN CORPORATION
2791 F.N. Texas Street
Suite 300
Fairfield, California 94533
Roger Albrecht, President

Description of Operation: Lawn fertilizing, weed control, insect control, disease control for turf. Tree and shrub care.

Number of Franchisees: 39 in 14 States

In Business Since: 1977

Equity Capital Needed: $25,000

Financial Assistance Available: On equipment only.

Training Provided: 10 days training and ongoing. Seminars at various times during the year. Monthly newsletters, toll-free telephone assistance.

Managerial Assistance Available: Bookkeeping and related lawn technology.

Information Submitted: May 1990

*SERVICEMASTER LAWN CARE
855 Ridge Lake Boulevard
Memphis, Tennessee 38119
Dan Kellow, Vice President

Description of Operation: Professional lawn, tree and shrub care for residential and commercial clients.

Number of Franchisees: 175 in USA

In Business Since: 1985

Equity Capital Needed: $10,000 to $12,000

Financial Assistance Available: Up to $15,300 financing through ServiceMaster and leasing arrangements.

Training Provided: Technical agronomic, licensing preparation and marketing training is provided during 6 day academy. On-site training at licensee's business is provided through the regional manager and master franchise coordinator.

Managerial Assistance Available: Continuous support is available throughout the franchise agreement. This support is provided through the master franchise coordinator for the area.

Information Submitted: April 1990

*SPRING-GREEN LAWN CARE CORP.
P. O. Box 908
Naperville, Illinois 60566
Thomas W. Hoter, President

Description of Operation: Professional lawn, tree and shrub care service to residential and commercial customers. Spring-Green uses state-of-the-art equipment and techniques in a modern and rapidly growing industry. Extremely high annual customer renewal plus complete marketing programs help franchisee to realize solid growth. Customer programs generally include 4-6 applications per year.

Number of Franchisees: 137 in 22 States

In Business Since: 1977

Equity Capital Needed: Total initial investment of $17,595 plus $8,000 working capital.

Financial Assistance Available: In addition, a national equipment lease program is available. Assistance is provided in obtaining financing through private sources.

Training Provided: 1 week intensive modular training at beginning of franchise operation with ongoing guidance and support. Periodic instructional meetings as well as seminars are provided at various times during the year. Bi-weekly newsletter and toll-free telephone assistance are available to all franchisees.

Managerial Assistance Available: S-G provides managerial and technical assistance to the franchisees on an ongoing basis. Training manuals as well as various publications are provided for each franchise. Field representatives visit each franchisee on a regular basis to provide assistance in an area where the franchisee may need help. Seminars are also held during the year covering such items as cash flow projections, selling skills and technical assistance. S-G also provides assistance in advertising, marketing and business management, using video and other modern training techniques. For more information call 1-800-435-4051.

Information Submitted: April 1990

SUPER LAWNS, INC.
P. O. Box 34278
Bethesda, Maryland 20817
Ron Miller, General Manager

Description of Operation: Super Lawns offers a modern, profitable, realistic approach to the lawn care service industry. Our automatic method of applying chemicals and seeds while aerating and rolling lawns is fast, easy and efficient. This method reduces labor costs while generating higher gross daily sales per operator.

Number of Franchisees: 23 in Maryland, New Jersey, Virginia and the District of Columbia.

In Business Since: 1976

Equity Capital Needed: From $43,000 plus operating capital of $5,000.

Financial Assistance Available: Limited financing may be available to qualified persons.

Training Provided: Comprehensive training at the home office, in the field and on-the-job. This training includes advertising methods, business systems and accounting, office procedures, sales, turf management and agronomy and general operations.

Managerial Assistance Available: Constant communication and cooperation by parent company to aid franchisee to become a better business person through understanding of advertising concepts, sales, customer relations, bookkeeping, general operations and service industry concepts, quality control, inventory controls, small business management and technical training for as long as required by franchisee. Assistance is only a phone call away.

Information Submitted: June 1990

U.S. LAWNS INC.
2300 Maitland Center Parkway
Suite 116
Maitland, Florida 32751
William H. Neetz, Vice President/General Manager

Description of Operation: Professional commercial landscape maintenance.

Number of Franchisees: 14

In Business Since: 1987

Equity Capital Needed: $25,000 minimum. Total investment $25,000-$50,000.

Financial Assistance Available: None

Training Provided: 1 week at franchise location and 1 week at corporate headquarters.

Managerial Assistance Available: U.S. lawns provides training manuals, marketing videos, protected territories, management training and ongoing assistance and support for all areas of the franchise.

Information Submitted: April 1990

MAID SERVICES/HOME CLEANING/ PARTY SERVICING

*AMERICA'S MAID SERVICE - THE MAIDS
THE MAIDS INTERNATIONAL, INC.
4820 Dodge Street
Omaha, Nebraska 68132
Danielle Bishop

Description of Operation: Your investment accesses you to a multi-billion dollar market positioned for 20 percent annual growth into the 1990s. We've led the way for 10 years with a proven system featuring low investment, up-front cash flow, high customer demand, small inventory with volume discounts on your supply and equipment, total advertising to target your customers and complete management training (featured in USA Today as one of America's top franchise training programs).

Number of Franchisees: 200 in 38 States and 2 countries.

In Business Since: 1980

Equity Capital Needed: Franchise fee $16,900, other capital requirements $20,000 plus.

Financial Assistance Available: Yes

Training Provided: 6 week pre-training counseling. 12 day corporate training (administrative and technical) with complete hands-on computer training. 90 day post-training follow-up.

Managerial Assistance Available: Monthly newsletter, toll-free phone support, regional seminars and annual meetings. Accounting staff, advertising, PR program, tech staff.

Information Submitted: April 1990

CLASSY MAIDS U.S.A., INC.
P. O. Box 160879
Altamonte Springs, Florida 32716-0879
William K. Olday, President

Description of Operation: Classy Maids is a fast growing professional home cleaning service with a proven franchisee training and sales system. Franchise investment includes protected sales territory, classroom type sales marketing, and business training for 2 people at home office for 1 full week. Also, on-the-job training, equipment and supplies, a training film for maids, software for accounting and records. Even a franchisee with no business experience can learn to manage our business after completing our training program.

Number of Franchisees: 22

In Business Since: 1980 and began franchising 1985

Equity Capital Needed: $4,000 to $8,000

Financial Assistance Available: Yes

Training Provided: Complete managerial and operational training starting with 5 day classroom style program covering all facets of sales promotion, advertising, proven methods of getting customers, market study, recruiting profile and know-how, brochures, how to train maids one-to-one and via film, quality control, accounting and recordkeeping, tax and license requirements, pricing for competitive edge, plus management training in all facets of running a well-disciplined cleaning company for profit. Workshops and managerial help on request.

Managerial Assistance Available: Telephone for immediate help, updated training materials, updated programs as developed by franchisor, software availability and consulting services as requested.

Information Submitted: April 1990

DAY'S EASE, INC.
473 Charing Cross Drive
Grand Blanc, Michigan 48439
Sally Tartoni

Description of Operation: A house cleaning service. Four Daisy Girls, insured and bonded, work as a team, thoroughly cleaning a home in less than 2 hours—allowing the lady or the man of the house to have a day of ease.

Number of Franchisees: 3 in Michigan and 1 in Ohio

In Business Since: 1976; active franchising since 1986.

Equity Capital Needed: Franchise fee $7,000.

Financial Assistance Available: A total of $15,000 is recommended. The franchise fee includes equipment, cleaning materials, and training. Company does not provide financial assistance at this time.

Training Provided: Complete training in every aspect of this business that usually takes 5 days to 1 week. This is intense and is done at our home office.

Managerial Assistance Available: We, as the franchisor, will always offer our assistance to the franchisee, as we want them to succeed. Complete manuals, forms and directions are provided. We will work closely with all franchisees in order that all Day's Ease companies uphold the highest of standards. Newsletters, operations systems and seminars will be provided on a regular basis.

Information Submitted: June 1990

DIAL-A-MAID
D. M. Coughlin, Inc.
7531/2 Harry L. Drive
Johnson City, New York 13790
Dennis M. Coughlin, President

Description of Operation: Dial-A-Maid was developed and is headed by Dennis M. Coughlin, who offers over 25 years of experience in the cleaning industry. The service includes both regular clientele and special project cleanings. Maids arrive at each location with all necessary equipment and supplies.

Number of Franchisees: 3 in New York and 3 in Pennsylvania

In Business Since: 1983

Equity Capital Needed: $9,500; additional capital required approximately $10,000-$15,000.

Financial Assistance Available: Franchise fee may be financed.

Training Provided: 1 week at franchisor headquarters, opening assistance, ongoing assistance, and periodic field visits. Manuals and other training materials provided.

Managerial Assistance Available: Continual managerial support for franchisees. Periodic on-site visits by franchisors and 24 hour call line.

Information Submitted: April 1990

EXPRESS MAID
P. O. Box 2500
Williamsport, Pennsylvania 17703

Description of Operation: Franchisor of residential/office cleaning services using the team cleaning concept, whereby a franchisee and two assistants arrive at a home or office, cleaning the property with supplies and equipment that are included in the franchise package. At the time the franchisee requires further consumables, we aid them in locating a local distributorship. Numerous assistance programs are provided to the franchisee to aid in customer satisfaction as well as business operation.

Number of Franchisees: 5

In Business Since: 1988

Equity Capital Needed: Franchise fee, $3,995; additional working capital (depending on advertising needs), $1,000 to $5,000.

Financial Assistance Available: 100 percent on optional van, with no money down.

Training Provided: 5 day training course at national office in Williamsport, Pennsylvania; training manuals to reiterate the course; ongoing field representative support.

Managerial Assistance Available: Available through our field representative program and various other assistance programs.

Information Submitted: June 1990

GUARANTEE GIRLS
6210 Hollyfield Drive
Baton Rouge, Louisiana 70809
Ellen K. Folks, President

Description of Operation: Residential and commercial cleaning. We provide a unique method for cleaning to produce top profits. Training available for carpet cleaning and fire damage clean-up all for the one-time franchise fee.

Number of Franchisees: 3 plus 1 company-owned unit.

In Business Since: 1983

Equity Capital Needed: $17,000-$20,000

Financial Assistance Available: None

Training Provided: 2 weeks training at the home office for up to 2 people. Additional training later for other areas of cleaning at no extra cost. Continued education for all types of cleaning.

Managerial Assistance Available: Management training will be provided during initial 2 week training period. 800 number where someone is always available to answer any problems that may arise. Periodic visits to each location throughout the duration of the contract. Someone from home office staff will assist in grand opening or the first week of business.

Information Submitted: April 1990

HOME CLEANING CENTERS OF AMERICA
11111 West 95th Street, Suite 219
Overland Park, Kansas 66214
Michael J. Calhoon

Description of Operation: Primarily a conventional residential home cleaning service for the two-income family with secondary emphasis on carpet cleaning, window cleaning and small office cleaning. Strong appeal to franchisees who are looking for an individualized business plan that will yield predictable profits.

Number of Franchisees: 12

In Business Since: 1981

Equity Capital Needed: $20,000 to $30,000

Financial Assistance Available: None

Training Provided: 1 week in-house training with follow-up on-site and telephone counsel as indicated.

Managerial Assistance Available: Annual seminars plus on-site visits and telephone communications to help achieve goals.

Information Submitted: April 1990

MAID AROUND THE CLOCK FRANCHISING CO., INC.
P. O. Box 1508
East Greenwich, Rhode Island 02818
David A. Smoller, President

Description of Operation: Providing residential and commercial cleaning and specialty services to aid in home maintenance, such as house, pet and child sitting and party preparation and serving.

Number of Franchisees: 5 including company-owned.

In Business Since: 1987

Equity Capital Needed: $8,500

Financial Assistance Available: Assistance in obtaining bank financing.

Training Provided: Mandatory 2-7 day training depending on needs. If necessary, more time will be given. Training includes operation of the business, financial control, marketing and service techniques, labor deployment, advertising methods and instruction in maintaining professional standards.

Managerial Assistance Available: Continuing advisory service on promotional, business and operational matters.

Information Submitted: May 1990

THE MAID BRIGADE SYSTEMS, INC.
860 Indian Trail Road
Lilburn, Georgia 30247
Don M. Hay, President

Description of Operation: Maid Brigade franchisees provide a high quality residential maid service to households throughout the United States and Canada. Teams of four well-trained, uniformed, bonded, professional maids and their supervisor carry out either regular or special services for our customers.

Number of Franchisees: 104 in States and 98 in Canada

In Business Since: 1979

Equity Capital Needed: Total investment of $33,000 includes everything: franchise fee, training, supplies, equipment, advertising materials, travel costs and all working capital for year one.

Financial Assistance Available: The company will assist in applying for financing, but the company itself does not make loans.

Training Provided: The franchisee's business development officer prepares him/her for the business opening with mailing. Program is conducted at the home office in Atlanta, and followed with on-site start-up assistance.

Managerial Assistance Available: The franchisee's business development officer is in regular contact with him/her by way of visits, regional meetings and telephone. Both the regional and national office contnuously communicate with the franchisee through memos, newsletters, surveys, manual updates and management analysis reports.

Information Submitted: April 1990

MAID EASY INTERNATIONAL
33 Pratt Street
Glastonbury, Connecticut 06033
Patricia Brubaker, President

Description of Operation: Maid Easy is the only residential maid service company that *does not* use the automated team-cleaning concept, but uses a personalized "one person" approach for the ultimate in customer service and satisfaction. Our streamlined operation enables a franchisee to work from the home, with a flexible schedule ideal for anyone wishing to remain at home while pursuing a satisfying and financially rewarding career. The franchise package offers everything the investor needs to be up and running in 30 days.

Number of Franchisees: 3 and 1 company-owned operation.

In Business Since: 1981

Equity Capital Needed: $20,000 to $25,000

Financial Assistance Available: None

Training Provided: 1 week training provided at home office with both pre-training and post-training consultation and assistance.

Managerial Assistance Available: Marketing and advertising promotions, technical seminars and new techniques, newsletters, onoging support and research and development in new customer service areas.

Information Submitted: April 1990

MCMAID, INC.
10 W. Kinzie Street
Chicago, Illinois 60610
Andrew Wright, President

Description of Operation: McMaid offers affordable, efficient residential cleaning services. Our team cleaning concept features uniformed teams of well-trained maids that provide the customer with thorough, highly professional cleaning services.

Number of Franchisees: 4 company-owned units in Illinois, New York and Massachusetts, and 1 franchise unit in Illinois.

In Business Since: 1976 and franchising since 1986

Equity Capital Needed: Equity capital ranges from $10,000-$30,000 and includes the franchise fee.

Financial Assistance Available: McMaid offers financing for part of the franchise.

Training Provided: Prior to the opening of the franchise business, the franchisor will instruct the franchisee in the total management of the business. This will be accomplished during the 7 day training and continuing support programs.

Managerial Assistance Available: McMaid provides continuing managerial assistance through its confidential operating manual, periodic visits by home office personnel, as well as ongoing advisory services in all aspects of the franchise business such as financial controls, marketing techniques, advertising and promotional programs and instruction in maintaining professional standards.

Information Submitted: April 1990

*MERRY MAIDS
11117 Mill Valley Road
Omaha, Nebraska 68154
Bob Burdge/Paul Hogan

Description of Operation: Merry Maids is the largest professional home cleaning service in the nation. With over 500 franchise offices, the company dominates important metropolitan markets. Compared with others, Merry Maids has the strongest business control system, the lowest cost structure on equipment and supplies, the most comprehensive employee recruiting and training tools, highly aggressive marketing and PR programs, and an unmatched depth of corporate office management and staff.

Number of Franchisees: 500

In Business Since: 1980

Equity Capital Needed: Affordable $18,500 franchise fee plus $10,000-$15,000 to cover start-up expenses including office furnishings, required IBM computer and video equipment, and working capital.

Financial Assistance Available: Yes, up to $10,000 of $18,500 franchise fee.

Training Provided: Comprehensive, all-inclusive 5 day training program at Merry Maids' Omaha training center is included in the franchise fee. Curriculum covers all the necessary procedures, program and tools necessary to develop, manage and operate a successful franchise.

Managerial Assistance Available: No one in the industry provides a greater commitment—and ongoing support—to new and established franchise owners. A network of regional coordinators,

a corporate staff and the company's unique "Franchise Buddy System" of established owners all contribute to monitoring, counseling and guiding the growth and success of each Merry Maids franchise operation. Individual support is further enhanced through regional franchise owners' meetings, specialized field seminars and the company's national convention, which is annually attended by more than 80 percent of Merry Maids franchise owners.

Information Submitted: May 1990

METRO MAID HOUSEKEEPING SERVICES, INC.
4336 Gorman Avenue
Englewood, Ohio 45322
Glenn S. Harper, President

Description of Operation: Metro Maid provides customers with uniformed and trained "cleaning technicians." Metro Maid service is either programmed light housekeeping by a team or individuals meeting specific seasonal or personal cleaning needs of residential customers during normal business hours on a regular basis.

Number of Franchisees: 2 in Ohio and Indiana

In Business Since: 1978

Equity Capital Needed: $15,000-$25,000

Financial Assistance Available: None

Training Provided: Initially, either the franchisee or designated manager is given 3 to 5 days home office training. Whether the investor buys a "single" or "multiple" franchise package or is a "present" or "absentee" owner is not important. Metro Maid wants the people responsible for operations to be well trained and capable. Actual on-the-job cleaning, advertising, promotions, banking, bookkeeping, hiring, employee relations, scheduling, and maintenance of equipment and supplies are among the many items to be covered.

Managerial Assistance Available: Follow-up training or simply relearning the basics are available at the home office at any prearranged time at no additional cost to franchisees, except living and traveling costs during the life of the franchise. Answers to day-to-day operating problems are as close as the telephone. Periodically, home office personnel will visit each franchise. Initial start-up equipment and supplies furnished.

Information Submitted: June 1990

MINI MAID SERVICES, INC.
1855 Piedmont Road
Suite 100
Marietta, Georgia 30066
Leone Ackerly, President

Description of Operation: Mini Maid pioneered the residential team cleaning concept in 1973, and has been franchising since 1976, longer than anyone else. We have been cited as one of America's top 101 service companies. Our concept delivers the quality of service desired by today's consumer. Our unique flat rate royalty system, low initial investment and the industry's most comprehensive training program allow our franchisees the industry's best profit opportunity.

Number of Franchisees: 133

In Business Since: 1973—first franchised in 1976.

Equity Capital Needed: $12,000-$20,000

Financial Assistance Available: None

Training Provided: Intensive 5 day headquarters production/administrative training. Complete pre- and post-opening program including additional 55 days at established franchises.

Managerial Assistance Available: Ongoing training, consultation, regional field managers, headquarters staff field visits, toll-free number, regional and national meetings, newsletters, complete supervisory certification programs.

Information Submitted: April 1990

*MOLLY MAID, INC.
707 Wolverine Tower Building
3001 South State Street
Ann Arbor, Michigan 48108
David G. McKinnon, President

Description of Operation: A team of two uniformed maids arrives in a company car with their own cleaning supplies and equipment at the customer's home. Cleaning includes dusting baseboards, pictures, lampshades, knick-knacks, window sills, furniture, fixtures and vacuuming throughout. Kitchen and bathrooms are sanitized, walls are spotcleaned, cabinet fronts and floors professionally washed. All maids are bonded, insured and professionally trained.

Number of Franchisees: 280

In Business Since: Started in Canada in 1978 and licensing in the United States since 1984.

Equity Capital Needed: $16,900 plus approximately $10,000 in start-up costs, along with the ability to support self outside of business for at least 1 year.

Financial Assistance Available: Yes

Training Provided: Prior to the commencement of the Molly Maid business by the franchisee, the franchisor will provide a 5 day training program guiding through methods, procedures, standards and techniques of the Molly Maid system and in the basic marketing, management and bookkeeping system. The training day starts in the early morning and continues through the evening with lectures, discussions, assignments, and actual hands-on training.

Managerial Assistance Available: The franchisor may from time to time hold training seminars, workshops and conferences concerning sales techniques, purchasing, training of personnel, performance standards, advertising and promotion programs and merchandising procedures for the franchisee and the franchisee's managerial staff.

Information Submitted: May 1990

MR. MOM'S INC.
Selling MR. MOM'S MAID SERVICE FRANCHISES
1800 North Main Street
Gainesville, Florida 32609
Lynn I. Davis, President

Description of Operation: Mr. Mom's Maid Service Centers provide residential and office cleaning services on a regular basis using a tested system of delivery by trained men and women. Our unique business name commands attention that results in customer inquiries and higher potential profits. Mr. Mom's philosophy emphasizes a marketing approach to the residential and commercial maid service and cleaning industry founded upon a thorough knowledge of operational requirements.

Number of Franchisees: 2 company-owned stores in Florida

In Business Since: 1987

Equity Capital Needed: Franchise fee up to $15,000 depending on territory, plus $5,000 to $20,000 to cover start-up expenses and working capital.

Financial Assistance Available: None

Training Provided: A 5 day program with Mr. Mom's proven methods along with intensive on-site instruction in accounting, office management, sales and marketing, advertising, purchasing, doing estimates, scheduling your clients, equipment operation, and hands-on cleaning.

Managerial Assistance Available: Ongoing in all phases of operation.

Information Submitted: April 1990

*SERVPRO INDUSTRIES, INC.
575 Airport Boulevard
P. O. Box 1978
Gallatin, Tennessee 37066
Randall H. Isaacson, Executive Vice President

Description of Operation: Multi-profit-center franchise offering carpet, furniture and drapery cleaning. Also, fire and flood damage restoration, janitorial and maid services, carpet dyeing, ceiling cleaning and deodorizing services to residential, retail and commercial clientele.

Number of Franchisees: Approximately 710 in 48 States.

In Business Since: 1967

Equity Capital Needed: Approximately $15,000. Breakeven budget projection provided prior to purchase.

Financial Assistance Available: A total investment of $32,000 is necessary. Servpro will finance 60 percent. Cash discount available.

Training Provided: Servpro provides a complete set of training manuals for documentation. Also, 2 weeks on-the-job with a local general trainer, 10 days at the national training classroom and 2-day franchise start-up training in your franchised area. Also, continuous area and regional seminars, and a national convention.

Managerial Assistance Available: Principles of management and principles-of-success courses. Accounting and cash flow budgeting, sales and sales management. Production management, office procedures, advertising and public relations. Trainers are set up throughout the country to provide ongoing managerial assistance. Monthly newsletter also provided.

Information Submitted: April 1990

*SPARKLING MAID, INC.
7936 East Arapahoel Court
Suite 3300
Englewood, Colorado 80122
Eileen P. Martin, President

Description of Operation: Has a unique system to do home cleaning, "empty move out cleaning" and carpet cleaning.

Number of Franchises: 7 in the state of Colorado

In Business Since: 1987

Equity Capital Needed: $11,500-$12,500

Financial Assistance Available: None

Training Provided: A 4 day comprehensive training program. Airfare, hotel accommodations, and marketing materials are paid for by Sparkling Maid.

Managerial Assistance Available: After initial training, there is an open telephone line provided for assisting the new franciseee.

Information Submitted: April 1991

MAINTENANCE—CLEANING/SANITATION— SERVICES/SUPPLIES

*AMERICLEAN
Americlean Franchising Corporation
6602 South Frontage Road
Billings, Montana 59101
Mark Taverniti, Vice President of Franchise Development

Description of Operation: Disaster restoration services and specialty cleaning.

Number of Franchisees: 105 in 35 States

In Business Since: 1979

Equity Capital Needed: $28,000-$124,000

Financial Assistance Available: Assistance with securing financing through third parties.

Training Provided: 2 week classroom and in-field training. Installation and opening support. Operations manuals, support staff visits and toll-free support line, certified restorer on staff.

Managerial Assistance Available: See above.

Information Submitted: April 1990

AMERICORP
24 Hill Road
Parsippany, New Jersey 07054
Joel Santoro, President

Description of Operation: Commercial and industrial maintenance.

Number of Franchisees: 7 in New Jersey

In Business Since: 1975—franchising since 1980

Equity Capital Needed: $10,000 plus working capital.

Financial Assistance Available: None

Training Provided: Classroom and on-the-job training.

Managerial Assistance Available: Continuous in all operations of the company.

Information Submitted: June 1990

*BIO-CARE, INC.
2105 South Bascom Avenue
Suite 240
Campbell, California 95008

Description of Operation: Bio-Care offers the ideal solution to grease control for the restaurant and food service industry. Environmentally safe bacterial products are used in conjunction with a preventative maintenance program for drain lines and traps. Result: An environmentally safe, cost effective, guaranteed, permanent solution to grease control problems.

Number of Franchisees: 20. Franchise offering established in the summer of 1989.

In Business Since: 1985

Equity Capital Needed: $35,000 investment for one exclusive territory that includes a $15,000 franchise fee, $8,000 for initial equipment and supplies, and $12,000 to cover approximately 4 months of operating expenses.

Financial Assistance Available: None

Training Provided: Full scope training program at our corporate site, including on-location sales follow-up training.

Managerial Assistance Available: Continuous support as long as the franchisee is in operation.

Information Submitted: March 1990

CHEM BROOM INTERNATIONAL INC.
674 Enterprise Drive
Westerville, Ohio 43081
Jim Heid, President

Description of Operation: Chem Broom International, Inc., is a professionally operated cleaning company with the versatility of operating a total cleaning system from floor to ceiling. With the continued support and assistance from the corporate office, Chem Broom franchisees will have a better understanding of how to operate and maintain a well-organized and profitable cleaning company. Computerization is also included in the franchise package to help each franchise operation in ordering chemicals, and supplies and to send information throughout the system.

Number of Franchisees: 2 in 1 States, 1 company operation.

In Business Since: 1988

Equity Capital Needed: Start up $25,000 to $69,000.

Financial Assistance Available: None

Training Provided: 2 weeks in-house, 3 to 5 days at location.

Managerial Assistance Available: Continuous as long as the franchise is in operation.

Information Submitted: April 1990

CHEMAN MANUFACTURING CORPORATION
5679 Monroe Street #208
Sylvania, Ohio 43560
J. Morgan Crossland, President

Description of Operation: The name "CHEMAN" is a combination of two words: "CHEmical" and "MANufacturing." They describe the function of CHEMAN franchisees, which is to manufacture a line of nearly 50 of the most popular, fastest selling and highest profit maintenance and industrial products, which include all types of detergents, waxes, floor and carpet cleaners, glass cleaners, degreasers, bowl cleaners, etc.

Number of Franchisees: 8 in 4 States and Puerto Rico.

In Business Since: 1978 (Parent company, Crossland Laboratories, Inc., in business since 1944.)

Equity Capital Needed: $26,520 minimum

Financial Assistance Available: A total investment of $52,000 to $60,000 is necessary to open a CHEMAN manufacturing business. However, the parent company will finance 49 percent of the total investment on a joint venture arrangement for those who qualify. This permits qualified individuals to get started in this high profit business with an initial investment of only $26,520.

Training Provided: Complete and intensive training is provided in all phases of the business, including the compounding of all products, management, sales and marketing, hiring of personnel, bookkeeping, etc. This training includes a manual of operations and is continuous during the life of the agreement in order to keep owners abreast of new developments, etc., and to assure continued success.

Managerial Assistance Available: CHEMAN provides continual assistance in every phase of the business, with advice and personal assistance in developing new business and adding new and/or improved products, together with the development of new or special products for customers. In short, everything is done to assist all CHEMAN operations to meet constantly changing conditions and develop successful, thriving businesses.

Information Submitted: June 1990

CHEM-MARK INTERNATIONAL
635 East Chapman Avenue
P. O. Box 1126
Orange, California 92668
Darol W. Carlson, President

Description of Operation: Market commercial dishwashing machines, glass washing equipment, filtered air cleaners, cleaning and sanitation products for restaurants and institutions.

Number of Franchisees: 89 in 46 States, Canada, Northern Europe and Singapore.

In Business Since: 1959

Equity Capital Needed: $18,000

Financial Assistance Available: None

Training Provided: 1 week in home office, field help in own territory.

Managerial Assistance Available: Continued managerial and technical assistance.

Information Submitted: April 1990

CLEANSERV INDUSTRIES, INC.
3403 10th Street
Suite 810 - P. O. Box 1700
Riverside, California 92502
Gene Savage

Description of Operation: CleanServ Industries, Inc., has revolutionized the contract cleaning business. With CleanServ, you buy a business, not a job. Join a $15 billion dollar industry! The service industry is the fastest growing of all. Year-round training in contract sales, finance, management, CleanSmart™, BidSmart™, and MarketSmart™, (a lead generation marketing system that is the most comprehensive in the industry) and a toll-free technical hot line.

Number of Franchisees: 14 in California

In Business Since: 1986

Equity Capital Needed: $35,000-$50,000

Financial Assistance Available: Will work with franchisee to obtain direct business.

Training Provided: A 3 week initial training program and on-site training, ongoing support and seminars year-round. Plus a toll free technical hot line to answer questions.

Managerial Assistance Available: Continuous on-site assistance.

InformationSubmitted: May 1990

*COUSTIC-GLO INTERNATIONAL, INC.
7111 Ohms Lane
Minneapolis, Minnesota 55435
Everett C. Smith, President

Description of Operation: The Coustic-Glo concept offers a unique opportunity for an individual to achieve a high degree of financial independence in a virtually untapped industry. The need for ceiling cleaning is all around you in every structure you enter on a daily basis and as a Coustic-Glo franchisee you will be provided with all the equipment, products, chemicals and training necessary to prosper in this field.

Number of Franchisees: 165 throughout the United States, Canada, and Europe.

In Business Since: 1980

Equity Capital Needed: $9,750 to $25,000 dependent upon area assigned.

Financial Assistance Available: None

Training Provided: Each new franchise is provided with a very intensive 2-3 day training program that takes place in their respective exclusive areas under the direct supervision of an experienced franchisee that is brought in from their area to assist in the establishment of the new franchisee's business. Also available to the new franchisee is option of training course provided at home office under direct superivison of home office personnel.

Managerial Assistance Available: The home office of Coustic-Glo International, Inc., provides continual support in all areas of this business. Toll free phones are maintained to give direct and constant access to the home office and assistance with field problems, technical questions, etc. Complete test reports on all products are provided with updating as necessary. A very aggressive national advertising campaign is pursued. Local ad mats and all product identification provided. Complete manuals, forms, and customer lists are supplied each new franchisee. New national accounts are being added and you will have available to you a field man to assist in your area with questions. Company also sponsers meetings of franchisees and continues to maintain market and research and development departments to find further outlets for its products and services.

Information Submitted: June 1990

*COVERALL NORTH AMERICA, INC.
3111 Camino Del Rio North
Suite 1200
San Diego, California 92108
Jack Caughey, Vice President, Franchise Sales

Description of Operation: One of the most successful and fastest growing commercial cleaning franchisors in the world. Coverall provides a turnkey operation including starting customer base, and complete training. Comprehensive janitorial franchise.

Number of Franchisees: 1,050 in 19 States in 3 countries (8 company-owned).

In Business Since: 1985

Equity Capital Needed: $1,700 to $26,000

Financial Assistance Available: Coverall offers 9 starting franchise packages and will finance anywhere from $1,500 to $10,000 of the total price.

Training Provided: Includes operations, marketing and administration training. Classroom and on-the-job training. Average of 2 weeks training conducted by Coverall operation managers.

Managerial Assistance Available: The franchisees enjoy unmatched support from Coverall.

Information Submitted: April 1990

*JANI-KING, INC.
4950 Keller Springs
Suite 190
Dallas, Texas 75248
James Cavanaugh, President
Jerry Crawford, National & International
Marketing Director

Description of Operation: World's largest commercial cleaning franchisor. Franchisees provide professional cleaning programs to commercial and industrial buildings on a long-term contract basis. Franchisees follow proven business plan and benefit from national advertising, excellent references coast-to-coast and support from the industry leader.

Number of Franchisees: 1,500 in the United States and Canada

In Business Since: 1969

Equity Capital Needed: $3,000-$14,500 plus

Financial Assistance Available: A total investment of $6,500 is necessary to start a Jani-King franchise. Jani-King will finance part of the total investment depending on the location desired.

Training Provided: Training is provided for all new franchisees through a designated center. The training is conducted under the supervision of a full-time Jani-King employee.

Managerial Assistance Available: A complete manual of operations, forms and directions are provided for each new franchise. Jani-King also provides continual management service for the life of the franchise, such as contract negotiations, bookkeeping, hiring and training procedures securing new business and public relations. Regional and service managers are available to work closely with franchisees and visit service locations to provide technical advice and assist in solving problems.

Information Submitted: April 1990

JANITIZE AMERICA, INC.
20300 Superior
Suite 190
Taylor, Michigan 48180
Jerry Grabowski, Vice President

Description of Operation: Janitize America is a commercial office cleaning franchise that offers computerized procedures for job estimating, billing, payroll, and much more. Sub-franchisor areas available.

Number of Franchisees: 10 in Michigan, 1 company-owned.

In Business Since: 1988

Equity Capital Needed: $8,500-$17,500

Financial Assistance Available: Some company financing available.

Training Provided: 4 days classroom and 3 days on-the-job. Audio and video program for continued training of your employees.

Managerial Assistance Available: Confidential operations manual provided. Audio and video management tapes provided. Ongoing assistance for the franchisee by the corporate office.

Information Submitted: April 1990

JANUZ INTERNATIONAL LTD.
dba JANUZ MAINTENANCE SYSTEMS
338 West Lexington Avenue, Suite 109
El Cajon, California 92020
Robert A. Erickson, CBSE, President

Descriptin of Operation: Januz Maintenance Systems is a full service company providing maintenance management for property owners and managers. Unique contractor relationship is utilized. Clients receive the best maintenance at a guaranteed cost. Franchisee cost for producing the work is locked in.

Number of Franchisees: 4 franchise locations plus 1 company-owned store in 2 States.

In Business Since: 1986

Equity Capital Needed: Franchise fee: $5,000-$200,000; total investment: $10,000-$35,000

Financial Assistance Available: None

Training Provided: 2 week training, operational and sales manuals, training films, computer survey and bidding programs, newsletters, seminars and continued ongoing support.

Managerial Assistance Available: In addition to above, franchisor visits at least 2 times per year to provide in-shop assistance. Other assistance provided on an as needed basis.

Information Submitted: April 1990

LIEN CHEMICAL COMPANY
501 W. Lake Street
Elmhurst, Illinois 60126
Rick Geu, President

Description of Operation: The Lien Restroom Risk Management System employs original and unique methods for selling and performing a program of continuous infection control in commercial, industrial, retail, and institutional restrooms and for the administration and management of the sale and delivery of such services. Lien's service is performed by a skilled service technician visiting a customer's restrooms at a designated frequency to rejuvenate the quality of the restroom environment and furnish an atmosphere conducive to the health and safety of the restroom user.

Number of Franchisees: 46 franchises in 28 States

In Business Since: 1929

Equity Capital Needed: A minimum of $20,000, which includes a basic $10,000 franchise fee.

Financial Assistance Available: None

Training Provided: Complete training in all facets of franchise operation including management, administration, sales and service. Training includes classroom style, manuals, on-the-job experience, and ongoing consulting assistance. Group training meetings are held periodically on topics essential to successful franchise management.

Managerial Assistance Available: In addition to the above, franchise owner is given assistance during the start-up period of the operation. Ongoing consulting service includes sales, service, financial analysis, pricing, compensation, personnel recruiting and selection, routing, and cost-control.

Information Submitted: June 1990

MR. MAINTENANCE
21401 South Norwalk Boulevard
Hawaiian Gardens, California 90716
Philip A. Syphers, President

Description of Operation: ABC Maintenance development corporation has developed a complete system for providing commercial building maintenance services under the tradename of Mr. Maintenance. The company sales force develops as many customers as are desired by the franchisee. Customers are located in an area chosen by the franchisee. Area sub-franchising rights are available to qualified individuals who wish to sell Mr. Maintenance franchises in selected regions of the country.

Number of Franchisees: 53 plus 13 company-owned units in California.

In Business Since: 1971

Equity Capital Needed: $2,000 to $25,000 (proportional to the $ volume of customers provided)

Financial Assistance Available: Partial financing available.

Training Provided: Complete training is provided which lasts from 3 days to 2 weeks for the service franchisee to 1 month for area sub-franchisors. In either program the training consists of both classroom and field training.

Managerial Assistance Available: The company provides complete ongoing managerial services including computerized bookkeeping systems, billing, collecting, employee referrals; technical advice, sales assistance, company supervision and continuous management counseling. Payroll services, tax deposit and full computerized accounting services are an available option to the franchisee.

Information Submitted: June 1990

MR. ROOTER CORPORATION
P. O. Box 3146
Waco, Texas 76707

Description of Operation: Mr. Rooter has developed improved equipment and marketing materials and techniques in the sewer and drain cleaning business. Each licensee has access to the management skills of generations of master plumbers, the use of five U.S. patent office registered servicemarks and an extensive national advertising program designed to increase business. Mr. Rooter is a step-by-step integrated business system geared for success.

Number of Franchisees: 47 in 15 States

In Business Since: 1968, incorporated 1970

Equity Capital Needed: Initial equipment and supply package is $6,000.

Financial Assistance Available: None by company.

Training Provided: No special training is required prior to owning a franchise.

Managerial Assistance Available: Mr. Rooter corporation maintains a continuous home office advisory service for the lifetime of the agreement. This includes guidance in both managerial and technical aspects of the business. Dealers may take refresher training at any time at their convenience.

Information Submitted: June 1990

NATIONAL MAINTENANCE CONTRACTORS, INC.
1801 130th Avenue Northeast
Bellevue, Washington 98005
Lyle R. Graddon, President

Description of Operation: National Maintenance Contractors is an association of independent janitorial contractors. These contractors purchase a base dollar volume of income from National and are supported, for a fee, by National's administrative services. These services include a guarantee of lost account replacements, bonding, insurance, invoicing, collections, training, etc. Master franchises are now being offered nationwide.

Number of Franchisees: 265 in Washington and Oregon.

In Business Since: 1973

Equity Capital Needed: $1,000 minimum

Financial Assistance Available: Total investment is dependent on the volume of income purchased. National Maintenance Contractors will carry one-half of the investment on a note for 1 year, interest free.

Training Provided: Initial on-the-job training is conducted in franchisee's accounts and optional additional training is handled in periodic classroom seminars.

Managerial Assistance Available: National Maintenance handles nearly all administrative services for life of the franchise. National also has additional staff for filling in for illness or vacations in all areas.

Information Submitted: April 1990

PROFESSIONAL MARINE RESTORATION
3732 West Century Boulevard
Suite 6
Inglewood, California 90303
Brian Pearce, President

Description of Operation: You can enter the yacht and boat restoration industry now with no experience required (although it is valuable). We will train you on over two dozen yacht restoration services that all owners need and want. Utilize American know-how, Swedish craftsmanship and Swiss attention to detail in your own business.

Number of Franchisees: 12 in 3 countries

In Business Since: 1987

Equity Capital Needed: $40,000-$50,000

Financial Assistance Available: To qualified candidates for Master Licenses.

Training Provided: 3 to 5 weeks at the training facility plus 2 to 4 weeks on location.

Managerial Assistance Available: Monthly individual production analysis, advertising recommendations, sales assistance, toll-free hot line to headquarters, etc.

Information Submitted: April 1990

PROFESSIONAL POLISH, INC.
807 Forest Ridge Drive
Suite 106
Bedford, Texas 67022
Sid Cavanaugh

Description of Operation: Professional Polish offers franchises in janitorial and/or lawn maintenance. Professional Polish does all the billing, and collection and maintains account records with total computer support.

Number of Franchisees: One Master Janitorial and Lawn in Wilmington, North Carolina (Professional Polish of North Carolina), One Master Lawn in Fort Worth, Texas, and 14 local Janitorial and Lawn franchises.

In Business Since: 1981

Equity Capital Needed: Local franchise: $3,000 down payment and $500 working capital. Master franchise: $6,000 to $12,000 down payment and $5,000 to $8,000 working capital.

Financial Assistance Available: None

Training Provided: The training consists of 1 week in the following categories: computer understanding, selling accounts, equipment repair and on-the-job training. Our franchises do the managing of their employees and contract requirements, PPI support the franchises with computer data, selling, market, yellow pages, 24 hour answering service, state sales, self-employment (1040E), F.I.C.A. & F.I.T. (941), state unemployment and IRS tax reports and customer relations. Professional Polish training period last 45 days, which enables our local franchises to average monthly billing over $4,000. Master franchises average over $15,000 monthly billing.

Managerial Assistance Available: Professional Polish, Inc., continues supporting the franchises in the following: forms, business cards, stationery, equipment, training employees, presentations and day-to-day operations.

Information Submitted: April 1990

*PROFUSION SYSTEMS, INC.
2851 South Parker Road
Suite 650
Aurora, Colorado 80014
William E. Gabbard, President

Description of Operation: Specializing in repairing, cleaning and redyeing of vinyl, naugahyde, leather, and velour, utilizing technicians and salespersons for total operation. Dash repair and dash covers included. All vinyl repairs guaranteed with lifetime warranty. National accounts established. Franchise fee includes supplies and equipment.

Number of Franchisees: 135 territories in the United States and Canada; 16 in foreign countries.

In Business Since: 1980

Equity Capital Needed: $20,500 minimum

Financial Assistance Available: Yes, for optioned or additional territories.

Training Provided: Comprehensive training provided at company headquarters in Denver, Colorado, for 10 days plus 3 days of field supervision at location of franchise. Technical, managerial, sales all provided.

Managerial Assistance Available: A-Z package. Continual services provided, systems manual, troubleshooting, toll-free hot line for ordering and assistance.

Information Submitted: May 1990

*PROTOUCH MAINTENANCE COMPANY
100 East 20th Street
Kansas City, Missouri 64108
Dain R. Zinn, President

Description of Operation: ProTouch offers a commercial janitorial, carpet cleaning, and window washing franchise operation for owner/operators. ProTouch is based on thirty years of successful commercial cleaning in the mid-west.

Number of Franchisees:

In Business Since: 1959, franchising 1990

Equity Capital Needed: Franchise fee, $15,500, includes all necessary equipment, cleaning supplies, and training.

Financial Assistance Available: Financing available with $7,500 down.

Training Provided: 10 days of training in Kansas City provided. Covers management, sales, and cleaning techniques. 5 days of field training on account sales.

Managerial Assistance Available: Assistance available in all phases of the business including bookkeeping, supervision, sales and cleaning techniques. Also, equipment available at discount prices.

Information Submitted: April 1990

*ROTO-ROOTER CORPORATION
300 Ashworth Road
West Des Moines, Iowa 50265
Paul W. Carter

Description of Operation: Sewer and drain cleaning service.

Number of Franchisees: 650 plus 50 company-owned

In Business Since: 1935

Equity Capital Needed: $7,000 to $60,000

Financial Assistance Available: None

Training Provided: Training available at home office, but most new franchisees prefer training at an operating franchise near their homes.

Managerial Assistance Available: Continued assistance in all phases of operation through field staff, manuals, bulletins, advertising, etc.

Information Submitted: June 1990

SERVICE-TECH CORPORATION
21012 Aurora Road
Warrensville Heights, Ohio 44146
Alan J. Sutton, President

Description of Operation: Service-Tech Corporation's extensive lines of services include air duct cleaning, kitchen exhaust cleaning, vacuum cleaning and industrial oven cleaning to hospitals, restaurants and industrial and commercial customers.

Number of Franchisees: 1

In Business Since: 1960

Equity Capital Needed: $25,000 initial investment/total $55,000-$75,000.

Financial Assistance Available: None

Training Provided: 2 weeks of intensive management training are provided at the home office for 1 or 2 people. Training is also provided at franchiser's location during the opening period.

Managerial Assistance Available: STC provides continuous assistance that includes job training, management, pricing, sales and technical support.

Information Submitted: April 1990

SHADE SHOWER INC.
7820 East Evans Road
Suite 200
Scottsdale, Arizona 85260
Brook Carey, President

Description of Operation: Service commercial and residential customers at their locations; hand-wash mini-blinds, vertical blinds, pleated shades from a Shade Shower WashWagon (patents pending) mobile unit equipped with expandable hanging racks and water treatment system. Also clean interior windows, and with pressure hot water system clean exterior windows and screens. Area franchises and protected territories available.

Number of Franchisees: 5

In Business Since: 1988, franchising since 1989

Equity Capital Needed: $12,500-$16,800

Financial Assistance Available: Franchisee to arrange own financing for purchase price, which includes all tools and equipment. An additional $5,000 of operating capital would be desirable to defray initial operating expenses and for adequate advertising to launch the business.

Training Provided: 1 day training in Scottsdale, Arizona. Optional: One-on-one additional training for as long as required, in Scottsdale.

Managerial Assistance Available: Shade Shower Inc. provides continuing service in advertising, marketing, operations, financial management. Three complete manuals are included. An initial supply of flyers, brochures, doorhangers, forms, stationery, envelopes, business cards, signage and ad slicks of the logo and display ad layouts is provided.

Information Submitted: April 1990

SPARKLE WASH, INC.
26851 Richmond Road
Bedford Heights, Ohio 44146
Wallace Nido, President

Description of Operation: Sparkle Wash, Inc., operates and directs successful international network of mobile power cleaning licensees. These individuals, partnerships, and corporations provide power cleaning services for a diverse market, including truck fleets, mobile and residential homes, commercial, governmental and industrial buildings, and farm machinery, boats, etc. Power cleaning services are provided using the company developed patented mobile cleaning units and marketing programs. Services include washing, waxing, historical restoration, masonry cleaning and sealing, paint and graffitti removal, etc.

Number of Franchisees: 176 in 49 States, Canada, Japan and Austria.

In Business Since: 1965

Equity Capital Needed: $10,000 minimum initial, $37,000-$55,000 total.

Financial Assistance Available: Various financing plans available through company-assisted, GMAC and FMC unit financing plans. Cost includes complete start-up package, mobile equipment, van and training program.

Training Provided: Initial training in equipment operation, maintenance, chemicals, marketing and sales provided at company headquarters or regional offices. In-field training uses licensee's unit and operators. Company representative visits licensee's area to conduct training and generate initial accounts.

Managerial Assistance Available: Company provides regular publications containing up-to-date marketing and technical information. Company also provides computer printouts of truck fleet operators, market surveys, advertising materials, sales and busi-

ness consultation on general or specific needs. Company provides technical assistance programs and periodic regional and international meetings.

Information Submitted: June 1990

UNIMAX BUILDING CLEANING SYSTEM
P. O. Box 2461
Clarksville, Indiana 47131-2461
Attention: Lloyd E. Pate, President

Description of Operation: UNIMAX is a full cleaning service consisting of carpet and janitorial cleaning operations to include fire and floor restoration. Master regional franchises also available with 70 percent financing. Non-franchises also available to the person who would like to use his own name and buy the equipment through us.

Number of Franchisees: 3 plus 2 company-owned

In Business Since: 1986

Equity Capital Needed: $6,000-$10,000

Financial Assistance Available: Up to 55 percent financing through UNIMAX.

Training Provided: 5 days of training at headquarters or we will come to your city.

Managerial Assistance Available: Ongoing assistance with back-up support.

Information Submitted: April 1990

U.S. ROOTER CORPORATION
17023 Batesville Pike
North Little Rock, Arkansas 72116
Troy L. Ratliff, President

Description of Operation: U.S. Rooter sewer and drain cleaning service franchise offers a set of patented sewer machines, accessories, a copyrighted name and service marks, a protected area, a 5 year contract with option to renew at the end of the 5 years.

Number of Franchisees: 10 in California, Louisiana and Arkansas

In Business Since: 1968

Equity Capital Needed: $3,500 minimum

Financial Assistance Available: A minimum of $3,500 will buy the use of 1 set of machines and accessories. Small monthly payments (on a 5 year contract). Both payments based on population or telephone book coverage.

Training Provided: Unless he is already experienced, a franchisee may at his option come to the home office for a minimum of 2 weeks training or more if desired, or to the nearest franchised area.

Managerial Assistance Available: U.S. Rooter Corporation will provide advice, verbal or written, on different modes of advertising, and how to solicit business. We provide a manual of operation.

Information Submitted: April 1990

VALUE LINE MAINTENANCE SYSTEMS
A Division of WESTERN MAINTENANCE COMPANY
3801 River Drive North
Great Falls, Montana 59401
William D. Blackhall

Description of Operation: Value Line Maintenance Systems offers a unique service business, specializing in flexible cleaning programs for supermarkets, large retail outlets and other types of facilities. Franchise areas are protected within the Value Line operations.

Number of Franchisees: 35 in 18 States

In Business Since: 1959, franchising since 1982

Equity Capital Needed: $23,000 minimum

Financial Assistance Available: A total minimum investment of $42,200, consisting of $25,000 franchise fee, $8,800 equipment, $3,000 inventory, $5,400 working capital and miscellaneous, is required. A minimum down payment of $13,000 for franchise fee, plus $10,000 certifiable investment capital, is required. Financing arrangements are available for $12,000 of the franchise fee, and equipment purchases. The inventory can be financed on a 30-60-90-day interest-free payment plan.

Training Provided: An intensive 5 day mandatory training course is scheduled for all new franchisees at the home office. An additional 14 days training is provided in the field, on-site at the franchisee's contracts.

Managerial Assistance Available: Value Line provides continuing management and technical assistance as required for the life of the franchise. An operating guide, employee handbooks, video training tape and many other management aids are provided. Regional marketing representatives are available to assist in marketing and problem solving. Value Line also conducts national and regional marketing and product research. The MASCO Sales Division provides supplies and equipment at specially reduced prices.

Information Submitted: June 1990

*WASH ON WHEELS INDOOR
5401 South Bryant Avenue
Sanford, Florida 32773
George Louser

Description of Operation: Clean acoustical tile/vinyl/painted ceilings and walls.

Number of Franchisees: 35 nationwide

In Business Since: 1986

Equity Capital Needed: $4,900

Financial Assistance Available: Financial assistance available to those with good credit. Total investment $12,750.

Training Provided: 5 days intensive training, then ongoing. Manuals, seminars, newsletters, hot lines and direct mail.

Managerial Assistance Available: Ongoing

Information Submitted: April 1990

*WASH ON WHEELS-WOW
5401 South Bryant Avenue
Sanford, Florida 32773
George Louser

Description of Operation: Mobile power cleaning franchise providing cleaning services for a diverse market, including government, industrial, commercial buildings, residential homes and more.

Number of Franchisees: 52 nationwide

In Business Since: 1965, franchising since 1987

Equity Capital Needed: $7,500-$9,000

Financial Assistance Available: Financial assistance to qualified persons with good credit. Total investment $23,000 to $33,000.

Training Provided: 5 days intensive training, then ongoing. Manuals, seminars, newsletters, hot lines, and direct mail.

Managerial Assistance Available: Ongoing

Information Submitted: April 1990

WEST SANITATION SERVICES, INC.
25100 South Normandie Avenue
Harbor City, California 90710
G. H. Emery, President

Description of Operation: Route odor control and washroom service.

Number of Franchisees: 25 in 8 States

In Business Since: Franchise operations since 1978—wholly owned subsidiary of West Chemical Products Inc., formed in 1882 up to August 1984 when the subsidiary was sold to present owners.

Equity Capital Needed: $9,600 (maximum)

Financial Assistance Available: Franchisor will finance approximately 80 percent of total cost, except inventory and supplies.

Training Provided: Full operational training on-the-job including accounting, administration, customer relations, etc. 1 to 2 weeks duration.

Managerial Assistance Available: Continuous

Information Submitted: April 1990

WINCO WINDOW CLEANING & MAINTENANCE
710 South Gholson
Knoxville, Iowa 50138
David Wolett, Franchise Director

Description of Operation: Winco takes pride in providing uncompromised information, training, and support, enabling opportunity seekers to be in business for themselves, providing services everybody today needs: residential, commercial, hi-rise, industrial, and new construction window cleaning, janitorial services and pest control.

Number of Franchisees: 4 in 3 States

In Business Since: 1977, franchising since 1987

Equity Capital Needed: $3,900. No hidden fees.

Financial Assistance Available: Negotiable

Training Provided: Winco's nationally registered trademark, 3-10 day hands-on training seminar, 6 manuals, along with continuous consultation and support, allow franchisees to be perceived and respected as professionals.

Managerial Assistance Available: Workshop in buyer's area covers business organization, operation, sales, and estimation. Includes training of over 20 revenue sources. Manuals contain more than 700 pages of instruction, personnel development, employee orientation and supervision. Pertinent information essential for a successful business.

Information Submitted: April 1990

MOTELS—HOTELS

AMERICA'S BEST INNS, INC.
1205 Skyline Drive
R.R. #3, Box 1719
Marion, Illinois 62959-7719
Robert N. Brewer, President

Description of Operation: For the establishment, construction, equipping and operation of a high grade economy motel concept.

Number of Franchisees: 23 Inns in Missouri, Oklahoma, Illinois, Kentucky, Texas and Florida, including company-owned.

In Business Since: 1982

Equity Capital Needed: In addition to an initial franchise fee, the franchisee's investment will consist of the cost of the land, buildings, furniture, fixtures, equipment and inventory to conduct the business.

Financial Assistance Available: The franchisor does not intend to offer or provide any financing arrangements directly or indirectly itself or through any affiliated company or agent.

Training Provided: Prior to opening—evaluation and approval of site, specification for existing Best Inns, cost estimates, training of key employees; provide operations manual and employee handbooks, furnish projections. During operations—provide a person on premises for 1 week/semi-annual inspections, recommendations on purchasing, copy of necessary forms and Best Inns approved credit list.

Managerial Assistance Available: See above.

Information Submitted: May 1990

AMERICINN INTERNATIONAL
1501 Northway Drive
P. O. Box 1595
St. Cloud, Minnesota 56302
James J. Graves, C.E.O.
Rodney L. Lindquist, President

Description of Operation: AmericInn International offers a refreshing, warm contemporary concept to the moderately priced luxury budget motel industry. The primary market of the AmericInns has been the travelling commercial guest. With that in mind, AmericInns have tried to present a very upscale, yet comfortable image. AmericInn has a goal of providing moderately priced rooms, yet top quality construction and furnishings.

Number of Franchisees: 24 in Arizona, Illinois, Iowa, Minnesota, and Wisconsin

In Business Since: 1984

Equity Capital Needed: Approximately $250,000.

Financial Assistance Available: Will assist in compiling a loan application. No direct financial assistance is available.

Training Provided: A 1 week training period is provided.

Managerial Assistance Available: Ongoing communication via newsletters and workshops.

Information Submitted: April 1990

CLUBHOUSE INNS OF AMERICA, INC.
7101 College Boulevard
Suite 1310
Overland Park, Kansas 66210-1891
David H. Aull, President

Description of Operation: High quality, garden-style hotel with a "club-like" atmosphere. Included in the room rate is a complimentary, full hot breakfast, plus two hours of complimentary cocktails each evening. 120 to 150 rooms, this is a "cookie cutter type" development and is particularly well known for the warmth between guests and hotel staff.

Number of Franchisees: 12 in 7 states.

In Business Since: 1983

Equity Capital Needed: Approximately 20 percent of construction cost.

Financial Assistance Available: Franchisor will be happy to point out potential financial sources, but will not do the financing itself.

Training Provided: 2 weeks training at ClubHouse Inns' home office, on-site training by ClubHouse Inns of America to basic staff, and ongoing training for all three key employees each year.

Managerial Assistance Available: Quarterly visits and inspections of the property, problem-solving, continuing training as stated above. Full set of operations manuals, ongoing assistance by request.

Information Submitted: May 1990

*COMFORT INNS, QUALITY INNS,
Clarion Hotels & Resorts, SleepInns
QUALITY INNS INTERNATIONAL, INC.
10750 Columbia Pike
Silver Spring, Maryland 20901
Frederick W. Mosser, Executive Vice President,
Franchise Development

Description of Operation: Hotels, resorts, motor inns.

Number of Franchisees: Over 1,300 in the U.S., Canada, Mexico, Europe, and Far East.

In Business Since: 1941

Equity Capital Needed: Variable

Financial Assistance Available: Assistance in preparing and presenting mortgage application.

Training Provided: Orientation program for owners or managers prior to property opening. Employee training programs.

Managerial Assistance Available: Complete operations manuals provided. Continuing seminar programs. Sales and marketing workshops. Property inspections and on-site consultations. Complete management contract services capability.

Information Submitted: April 1990

*COMPRI HOTEL SYSTEMS
410 North 44th Street
Suite 700
Phoenix, Arizona 85008
Kevin W. Holt

Description of Operation: The Compri Hotels is a unique mid-price hotel concept featuring an airline-style club room, four-star quality facilities and a complimentary breakfast and complimentary cocktail reception. The hotels typically range between 150-225 rooms.

Number of Franchisees: 26 in 24 States; 1 in Canada

In Business Since: 1984

Equity Capital Needed: $2,000,000-$5,000,000

Financial Assistance Available: None

Training Provided: Comprehensive training program relating to operating the hotel pursuant to the Compri System standards.

Managerial Assistance Available: Management and technical services provided.

Information Submitted: April 1990

CONDOTELS INTERNATIONAL, INC.
P. O. Box 3196
North Myrtle Beach, South Carolina 29582
Raymond Mann

Description of Operation: Condominium vacation rentals.

Number of Franchisees: 1

In Business Since: 1981

Equity Capital Needed: $25,000 to $75,000

Financial Assistance Available: None

Training Provided: Training provided in all aspects of operation.

Managerial Assistance Available: Ongoing.

Information Submitted: April 1990

COUNTRY HOSPITALITY INNS
Carson Parkway
P. O. Box 59159
Minneapolis, Minnesota 55459-8203

Description of Operation: Limited service motel; modestly priced; residential, cozy theme lodging properties; pool, continental breakfast optional; companion product to Country Kitchen Restaurants.

Number of Franchisees: 13 in the U.S. and Canada; 320 under development.

In Business Since: 1987

Equity Capital Needed: $250,000

Financial Assistance Available: No direct financing available.

Training Provided: Classroom and on-the-job training, plus opening crew at site.

Managerial Assistance Available: Complete operations and marketing manual, consulting services, countryline reservation system, purchasing programs, advertising, training updates, seminars, franchisee meetings.

Information Submitted: May 1990

*DAYS INNS OF AMERICA, INC.
2751 Buford Highway, Northeast
Atlanta, Georgia 30324

Description of Operation: Days Inns of America, Inc., with its Days brand inns, hotels, suites and Daystops, is the third largest hotel brand in the world and the fastest growing in the moderate price segment of the market. Properties are linked by a toll-free computerized reservations system.

Number of Franchisees: An international lodging operator and franchisor, the chain has more than 1,600 hotels open and under development in 50 States, Canada, Mexico, Europe, the Pacific Rim and India.

In Business Since: 1970

Equity Capital Needed: $200,000

Financial Assistance Available: Will assist in preparation of loan applications.

Training Provided: Management training—classroom as well as on-the-job; sales training; reservations systems and front desk operations training.

Managerial Assistance Available: Continual consulting privileges with franchisor's executives. An annual franchise conference is held in Atlanta, Georgia, as well as semi-annual regional meetings. Franchisor will help franchise owners find qualified operating managers. Quarterly quality assurance visitations.

Information Submitted: April 1990

*ECONO LODGES OF AMERICA, INC.
6135 Park Road, Suite 200
Charlotte, North Carolina 28210
Jeff Williams, Senior Vice President,
Franchise Development

Description of Operation: National owner and/or management operator, international franchisor and supplier of Econo Lodges. (Budget and full service budget hotels and motels.)

Number of Franchisees: Over 675 plus 6 company-managed.

In Business Since: 1967

Equity Capital Needed: (a) New construction—one-fourth of total capital investment (could possibly be paid for or with leased subordination land). (b) On conversion of an existing property the equity would be nothing.

Financial Assistance Available: None directly. Indirectly we help obtain mortgage financing. Also have mass purchasing savings to franchisee on furniture and supplies.

Training Provided: Bookkeeping system, site selection, analysis, economics of housekeeping and maintenance, motel inspection periodically by regional operations directors; owner orientation; advertising, marketing and public relations expertise. Will also furnish complete management package if desired. Training provided for owner/managers or managers.

Managerial Assistance Available: As above.

Information Submitted: June 1990

*EMBASSY SUITES, INC.
Suite 1700
222 Las Colinas Boulevard
Irving, Texas 75039
Clyde Culp, President

Description of Operation: Hotels and restaurants.

Number of Franchisees: 55 approved projects in 25 States.

In Business Since: 1983

Equity Capital Needed: Amount would depend upon requirements by prevailing capital markets.

Financial Assistance Available: Lender referrals are made upon request.

Training Provided: Mandatory general manager's training program.

Managerial Assistance Available: Embassy Suites, Inc., does not offer direct managerial assistance but does make available consultation and advise in connection with operation, facilities and marketing.

Information Submitted: May 1990

*FAIRFIELD INN BY MARRIOTT
1 Marriott Drive
Washington, D.C. 20058
Daryl A. Nickel, Senior Vice President,
Franchise Development

Description of Operation: Limited-service economy hotels.

Number of Franchisees: Franchise program initiated in September 1989; anticipated franchise hotel openings in 1990, 1; 1991, 15; and 25 per year thereafter.

In Business Since: 1987

Equity Capital Needed: No minimum required.

Financial Assistance Available: Advisory assistance only.

Training Provided: Initial training program of approximately 6 weeks for franchisee's inn manager and assistant manager; ongoing conferences and seminars.

Managerial Assistance Available: Prototypical plans and layouts; national reservation system; administer a marketing and advertising program; quality evaluation; advisory assistance in management and operations; promotional materials and hotel directories.

Information Submitted: April 1990

FAMILY INNS OF AMERICA, INC.
P. O. Box 10
Pigeon Forge, Tennessee 37863
Kenneth M. Seaton, President

Description of Operation: Motels with optional food and beverage facilities. Specializing in deluxe budget accommodations.

Number of Franchisees: 34 in 8 States

In Business Since: 1971

Equity Capital Needed: Between $100,000 and $250,000 depending on size desired. One to two acres.

Financial Assistance Available: Feasibility studies, plans, guidance and counseling with financial institutions, national contracts for lower construction cost. Investment opportunities through limited partnerships.

Training Provided: Complete training covering all phases of motel business, room renting, restaurant and lounge set-up and planning as long as needed.

Managerial Assistance Available: Guidance and counseling on company policies, complete audit and accounting forms. Complete insepctions by company, annual meetings and other help will be given at any time. Toll free reservation system, national sales force to increase occupancy.

Information Submitted: June 1990

*FRIENDSHIP INNS INTERNATIONAL, INC.
6135 Park South Drive
Suite 304
Charlotte, North Carolina 28210
Abigail Mayer Reece, COO

Description of Operation: Hotel and motel franchising throughout the United States, Canada and Latin America.

Number of Franchisees: 120 in all 50 states.

In Business Since: 1961

Equity Capital Needed: N/A

Financial Assistance Available: None

Training Provided: 5 training seminars—2 days

Managerial Assistance Available: Consulting available in all aspects of hotel-motel industry.

Information Submitted: June 1990

*HAMPTON INNS, INC.
A Promus Company
6800 Poplar Avenue
Suite 200
Memphis, Tennessee 38138
Ray E. Schultz, President

Description of Operation: Franchising and operation of Hampton Inn hotels.

Number of Franchisees: 172 franchise groups, 31 operated by Hampton Inns, Inc. (total of 221 hotels in 37 States).

In Business Since: 1983

Equity Capital Needed: Varies depending on individual project.

Financial Assistance Available: Lender referrals are made upon request.

Training Provided: Mandatory general manager's training program. Optional department head training.

Managerial Assistance Available: Hampton Inns, Inc., does not offer direct managerial assistance but does make available consultation and advice in connection with operation, facilities and marketing. Management contracts available with Hampton Inns, Inc.

Information Submitted: May 1990

*HAWTHORN SUITES
400 Fifth Avenue
Waltham, Massachusetts 02154
Joseph A. McInerney, President

Description of Operation: Hawthorn Suites are limited service all suite hotels geared to meet the needs of the upper/mid-scale extended stay customer and the small meetings market.

Number of Franchisees: 10 open, 4 under construction, and 12 in the planning stage.

In Business Since: 1986

Equity Capital Needed: The total cost of a hotel will vary but is estimated to be in a range of $60,000-$80,000 or more per suite at a Hawthorn Suites Hotel. This includes but is not limited to the cost of plans, permits, building, furniture, fixtures, equipment, initial operating inventories and working capital. The cost of land and other features is additional. Equity requirement is based on the debt equity ratio.

Financial Assistance Available: None

Training Provided: Operational seminars are offered in areas of housekeeping and maintenance, front office, management techniques, marketing and sales throughout the year.

Managerial Assistance Available: Full assistance is provided in site selection, architectural plans and FF&E review. Guidance is provided for pre-opening planning, staffing, training, marketing. Continuing operational consultation is provided. Every property receives a series of manuals on all phases of operations. Our marketing suite program consists of a state-of-the-art 800 number, computerized reservations system, consumer research advertising campaigns, and our Marketing Plus Program.

Information Submitted: April 1990

*HILTON INNS, INC.
9336 Civic Center Drive
Beverly Hills, California 90210
Donald L. Harrell, Executive Vice President

Description of Operation: Subsidiary of Hilton Hotels Corporation for the purpose of franchising hotel properties within the United States.

Number of Franchisees: Over 225 in 44 States

In Business Since: 1965

Equity Capital Needed: 20 percent of cost for land, building and furnishings.

Financial Assistance Available: Referral to lendors who franchise lodging facilities.

Training Provided: Pre-opening training of management and department heads.

Managerial Assistance Available: Quarterly on-site reviews of operation—ongoing communications between regional office and franchise.

Information Submitted: June 1990

*HOLIDAY INNS, INC.
3796 Lamar Avenue
Memphis, Tennessee 38195
Les Willingham, Senior Vice President, System Hotels

Description of Operation: Hotels.

Number of Franchisees: Over 1,400 franchises worldwide plus 176 company-owned.

In Business Since: 1954

Equity Capital Needed: Varies depending on the size of the project.

Financial Assistance Available: None—direct consultation available.

Training Provided: 4 week course at Holiday Inn University and periodic training seminars.

Managerial Assistance Available: Continuing guidance as needed. Franchise district director assistance program.

Information Submitted: April 1990

*HOMEWOOD SUITES HOTEL DIVISION
(of Embassy Suites, Inc.)
3742 Lamar Avenue, 4th Floor
Memphis, Tennessee 38195
Dave Jones, President

Description of Operation: Extended stay hotels.

Number of Franchisees: 30 approved projects in 20 States

In Business Since: 1988

Equity Capital Needed: 20 to 25 percent of total project costs.

Financial Assistance Available: Lender referrals are made upon request.

Training Provided: Mandatory general manager's training program. Optional department head training. Pre-opening hotel-level training.

Managerial Assistance Available: Homewood Suites division does not offer direct managerial assistance but does make available consultation and advice in connection with operation, facilities and marketing.

Information Submitted: May 1990

INNSUITES INTERNATIONAL INNS
AND RESORTS, INC.
7204 North 16th Street
Phoenix, Arizona 85020
Attention: Director Franchise Development

Description of Operation: As a successful long time owner/operator and franchisor in the All-Suite Hospitality Industry, we offer the new property assistance in all phases of development from site selection through opening to include daily operations and accounting procedures. For property conversions we work with franchisee in developing plan to align property with company and All-Suite Industry standards. Our goal is to improve the bottom line of your business without sacrifice of quality of service.

Number of Franchisees: 3 in Arizona, 1 in California plus 5 company-owned operations.

In Business Since: 1980

Equity Capital Needed: Varies with size operation. Minimum, $150,000 cash. Free and clear acceptable land may suffice as equity.

Financial Assistance Available: None

Training Provided: Management required to attend 2 week program at designated corporate facility for classroom and hands-on management training. Designated person representing owner must complete 2 day seminar at corporate office. Training available for all positions of employment if desired.

Managerial Assistance Available: Continuous managerial and technical assistance when needed.

Information Submitted: April 1990

MASTER HOSTS INNS
c/o HOSPITALITY INTERNATIONAL, INC.
1152 Spring Street, Suite A
Atlanta, Georgia 30309
Richard H. Rogers, President

Description of Operation: Franchising and operation of motels for Master Hosts Inns.

Number of Franchisees: 18

In Business Since: 1969

Equity Capital Needed: 30 percent of total cost.

Financial Assistance Available: Assistance is rendered in preparation of mortgage package and introduction to financial institutions.

Training Provided: Field training assistance, management orientation/training given at home office in Atlanta.

Managerial Assistance Available: Management company for the purpose of managing franchised motels.

Information Submitted: April 1990

MIDWAY HOSPITALITY CORPORATION
1025 South Moorland Road
Brookfield, Wisconsin 53005
Peyton A. Muehlmeier, President

Description of Operation: Franchise affiliate of Midway Motor Lodges, et al., operators of motor lodges, restaurants and showroom lounges.

Number of Franchisees: 6 in Indiana, Iowa, Minnesota, Missouri and Wisconsin.

In Business Since: 1963

Equity Capital Needed: 20 to 30 percent of cost of the project.

Financial Assistance Available: Assistance in preparation of mortgage application.

Training Provided: The franchisee's general manager is required to be trained at another Midway Motor Lodge prior to property opening. A continuing education program for lodge management personnel is provided to the franchisee at cost.

Managerial Assistance Available: Operations and construction standards manuals, an institutional advertising program and a reservation system are provided. Property inspections and on-site consultations are made to insure that quality standards are maintained and operating procedures followed. Complete management and accounting services may be contracted separately with affiliated companies.

Information Submitted: June 1990

PRIME RATE, INC.
3335 West St. Germain
Box 1228
St. Cloud, Minnesota 56301

Description of Operation: Moderate, mid-priced type motels.

Number of Franchisees: 5 in Minnesota, South Dakota, Montana and Wyoming plus 3 company-owned.

In Business Since: 1976

Equity Capital Needed: Approximately $220,000-$750,000.

Financial Assistance Available: Consulting assistance available.

Training Provided: 1 to 2 weeks.

Managerial Assistance Available: Management contracts available.

Information Submitted: June 1990

*RAMADA INNS, INC.
345 Park Avenue
31st Floor
New York, New York 10154
Franchise Department

Description of Operation: Hotels and motels.

Number of Franchisees: 518 in the United States and 574 worldwide.

In Business Since: 1959

Equity Capital Needed: A minimum 35 percent of total gross investment.

Financial Assistance Available: None

Training Provided: Field workshops for hotel managers and department heads. Additional specializing training at the Ramada Management Institute.

Managerial Assistance Available: Continual counseling privileges with licensees and corporate executives. Assistance in marketing and in local level sales, as well as guidance in regional sales and promotion effort. Field personnel are available to work with and assist licensees with on-site operations and development problems.

Information Submitted: July 1990

RED CARPET INN
c/o HOSPITALITY INTERNATIONAL, INC.
1152 Spring Street
Suite A
Atlanta, Georgia 30309
Richard H. Rogers, President

Description of Operation: Franchising and operation of motels for Red Carpet Inn.

Number of Franchisees: 120

In Business Since: 1969

Equity Capital Needed: 30 percent of total cost.

Financial Assistance Available: Assistance is rendered in preparation of mortgage package and introduction to financial institutions.

Training Provided: Field training assistance, management orientation/training given at home office in Atlanta.

Managerial Assistance Available: Management company for the purpose of managing franchised motels.

Information Submitted: April 1990

*THE RESIDENCE INN COMPANY
1 Marriott Drive
Washington, D.C. 20058
Daryl A. Nickel, Senior Vice President, Franchise Development

Description of Operation: Extended all-suite hotels.

Number of Franchisees: 105 franchised hotels.

In Business Since: 1975

Equity Capital Needed: No minimum required.

Financial Assistance Available: Advisory assistance only.

Training Provided: Initial training program for franchisee's general manager and sales staff; ongoing conferences and seminars.

Managerial Assistance Available: Prototypical plans and layouts; national reservation system; marketing and advertising program; quality evaluations; advisory assistance in management and operations; promotional materials and hotel directories.

Information Submitted: April 1990

SCOTTISH INNS
c/o HOSPITALITY INTERNATIONAL, INC.
1152 Spring Street
Suite A
Atlanta, Georgia 30309
Richard M. Rogers, President

Description of Operation: Franchising and operation of motels for Scottish Inns.

Number of Franchisees: 143

In Business Since: 1973

Equity Capital Needed: 30 percent of total cost.

Financial Assistance Available: Assistance is rendered in preparation of mortgage package and introduction to financial institutions.

Training Provided: Field training assistance, management orientation/training given at home office in Atlanta.

Managerial Assistance Available: Management company for the purpose of managing franchised motels.

Information Submitted: April 1990

*SHERATON INNS, INC.
Sixty State Street
Boston, Massachusetts 02109
Charles Clark, Vice President,
Director of Franchising

Description of Operation: Franchising subsidiary of Sheraton Corporation is a system of hotels, inns, resorts and all suites worldwide.

Number of Franchisees: 268 in operation in 43 States and 25 in operation in 11 other countries.

In Business Since: 1962

Equity Capital Needed: Approximately 20 to 30 percent of total cost.

Financial Assistance Available: Will assist in preparing mortgage presentation.

Training Provided: Seminars are periodically scheduled around the country and are open to both new and existing franchisees.

Managerial Assistance Available: Professional management assistance by regional directors of operation: various manuals, sales, advertising and marketing guidance, inspections, regional and national meetings.

Information Submitted: May 1990

*SHONEY'S INN
1727 Elm Hill Pike
Nashville, Tennessee 37210
Attention: Jeffrey L. Heston, Executive Director
Franchise Development

Description of Operation: First-class limited service motor hotels.

Number of Franchisees: 56 units in 15 States

In Business Since: 1975

Equity Capital Needed:

Financial Assistance Available: Franchisor does not provide financing but will assist franchisee in preparing package for presentation to financial institutions.

Training Provided: An initial training program is provided for each new franchisee and/or his management team. The program consists of 8 weeks of intensive training at one of 5 locations operated by the Shoney's Lodging Management Company. Training involves all areas of motel operations including front desk, maintenance, housekeeping, lounge and general front office procedures.

Managerial Assistance Available: Franchisor provides advisory services on areas of financing real estate, site selection, construction, equipment, advertising, accounting, purchasing, training, opening and ongoing technical and operational support.

Information Submitted: April 1990

*SUPER 8 MOTELS, INC.
1910 8th Avenue, NE
Aberdeen, South Dakota 57402-4090
Loren Steele, President

Description of Operation: Super 8 Motels, Inc., is a franchisor of "Economy Motels" which offer a full size room with free color TV, direct dial phones and attractive decor.

Number of Franchisees: 672 plus 41 company-owned.

In Business Since: 1972

Equity Capital Needed: $150,000 to $1,000,000 depending on size of motel and arrangements with lender.

Financial Assistance Available: Will assist franchisee in seeking mortgage financing.

Training Provided: Complete management training program is provided, including training films, classroom study, examinations, and on-the-job training.

Managerial Assistance Available: Day-to-day managerial, advertising and accounting services provided. Complete front office procedures and accounting systems are included.

Information Submitted: June 1990

TRUSTHOUSE FORTE HOTELS, INC.
1973 Friendship Drive
El Cajon, California 92020
Jere M. Hooper, Executive Vice President

Description of Operation: Hotels and motels franchising across North America.

Number of Franchisees: 230 in 45 States and worldwide.

In Business Since: 1947

Equity Capital Needed: $500,000 to $1,000,000.

Financial Assistance Available: Will assist franchisee in finding funds.

Training Provided: 2 week training program.

Managerial Assistance Available: Area meetings and seminars are held periodically. Quarterly inspections are standard procedure. Franchise services personnel also render assistance and coordination.

Information Submitted: April 1990

WOODFIN SUITES, INC.
9255 Towne Centre Drive
Suite 900
San Diego, California 92121
Samuel A. Hardage, Chairman

Description of Operation: Woodfin Suites offers a unique all-suite hotel concept. The guest rooms include one to two bedrooms, kitchens and living rooms with fireplace. Suites are fully furnished, including kitchen appliances, televisions, radio, VCR and linens. Common areas include swimming pool and other recreational facilities, a guest laundry room, one or more meeting rooms, guest business center that provides complete secretarial services, and a clubhouse. Typical Woodfin Suites contains 88 to 225 suites with adjacent parking facilities.

Number of Franchisees: 10

In Business Since: 1985

Equity Capital Needed: $1,500,000

Financial Assistance Available: None

Training Provided: General training is required for all general managers hired by franchisee. This training will generally be at another operating hotel designated by franchisor and may be conducted in whole or part at franchisor's offices. Franchisor may require that other employees complete such additional training as directed by franchisor in the areas of marketing and sales, front desk operation, accounting and cash control, housekeeping, maintenance, landscaping and purchasing and inventory control.

Managerial Assistance Available: Woodfin Suites provides management assistance in such areas as accounting, marketing and sales, inventory control and purchasing. Policy and procedures manuals, forms and instructions are provided. Quality assurance evaluations are conducted by Woodfin Suites, Inc., in order to maintain a high standard of quality.

Information Submitted: May 1990

OPTICAL PRODUCTS/SERVICES

AMERICAN VISION CENTERS, INC.
90 John Street, 10th Floor
New York, New York 10038
Dr. Jay Baxter, Vice President, Franchising

Description of Operation: The company franchises and operates American Vision Center retail stores specializing in the sale of eyeglasses, contact lenses and related optical items. They offer a unique operational system as well as related merchandising and advertising programs.

Number of Franchisees: 46 plus 25 company-owned.

In Business Since: 1977

Equity Capital Needed: $25,000

Financial Assistance Available: The total investment in an American Vision Center will run from $75,000 to in excess of $100,000 depending on store size and physical store improvements required.

Training Provided: An intensive training program is provided by the company for all of its franchisees and their personnel. Training in sales, internal procedures, management, product knowledge and financial analysis is conducted at its home office and at a company operated training store.

Managerial Assistance Available: The American Vision Center system provides the support, buying power and merchandising expertise of a major optical chain and provides continuing operational assistance and supervision to its franchised stores. A detailed operations manual is provided and full supervision is available in all areas to work closely with franchisees to solve problems and improve store operations.

Information Submitted: June 1990

D.O.C. OPTICS CORPORATION
19800 West Eight Mile Road
Southfield, Michigan 48075
Richard S. Golden, President

Description of Operation: D.O.C. Optics Corporation operates optical centers staffed by licensed optometrists to provide eye examinations and retailing eye glasses, contact lenses and retail accessories. The company also owns and operates 3 optical laboratories where selected frames are drawn from inventory for fabricating.

Number of Franchisees: 80 company-owned units in 6 States plus 37 franchisees in 4 States and Canada.

In Business Since: 1961

Equity Capital Needed: None

Financial Assistance Available: There is an initial franchise fee of $7,500. Additional costs vary. Contact company for complete information.

Training Provided: Initial intensive training program of up to 2 weeks prior to opening of an office. It consists of instruction in the operation of a D.O.C. retail optometric center, a detailed explanation of D.O.C. systems, and training in clinic management, accounting, sales and marketing techniques.

Managerial Assistance Available: Marketing, site and lease negotiation assistance; standard plans and specifications for the development of a franchise location; pre-opening promotion and advertising support. Detailed operations manuals are provided, as well as advertising programs for a percentage of sales. Additional support includes laboratory services and merchandise purchasing;

annual seminars and optional training programs concerning new products, services, sales and display techniques and guidance related to the proper operation of a D.O.C. clinic.

Information Submitted: June 1990

FIRST OPTOMETRY EYE CARE CENTERS, INC.
31503 Gratiot
P. O. Box 286
Roseville, Michigan 48066
D. M. Borsand, O.D.

Description of Operation: Marketing, advertising, practice management and volume purchasing and participation in industrial eyecare and capture of third party eyecare programs (P.P.O.s), for the professional practicing doctor of optometry.

Number of Franchisees: 35 in Michigan

In Business Since: 1980

Equity Capital Needed: Typical requirements for optometric office.

Financial Assistance Available: Yes

Training Provided: 40 hours at headquarters. Ongoing reinforcement; sales seminars, contact lens, educational, etc.

Managerial Assistance Available: Motivation, in office marketing, para-optometric training, dispensing and sales, contact lens technician training and general management training.

Information Submitted: April 1990

*NUVISION, INC.
2284 South Ballenger Highway
Flint, Michigan 48503
Jonathan Raven, CEO

Description of Operation: NuVision, Inc., markets prescription eyeware, contact lenses, sunglasses and related optical products and accessories. The company also owns and operates a modern ophthalmic laboratory and distribution facility which provides laboratory services and eyecare products to company-operated and franchised offices. In-store Mega-Labs in many locations also provide glasses in about an hour. Optometric services are also provided in all locations.

Number of Franchisees: 47 in Michigan and Indiana. 131 company-owned units.

In Business Since: 1956

Equity Capital Needed: Minimum $50,000.

Financial Assistance Available: Financing of the purchase of existing company-owned locations is available in some situations.

Training Provided: Initial training prior to opening an office consists of a 3-day program designed to teach standardized methods of administrative, merchandising and marketing techniques. Ongoing regular training is also provided.

Managerial Assistance Available: Guidance in connection with methods, sales techniques, procedures, management techniques, services and products, purchasing optical and ophthalmic products, formulating and implementing advertising and promotional procedures for the proper operation of a NuVision office.

Information Submitted: April 1990

OPTOMETRIC EYE CARE CENTER, P.A.
2309 Sunset Avenue
P. O. Box 7185
Rocky Mount, North Carolina 27804
Blair Harrold, O.D.

Description of Operation: With 40 retail locations, OECC is North Carolina's strongest eye care franchise. With an emphasis toward one-hour super optical locations, OECC offers its franchisees dynamic marketing and third-party industrial vision programs. Professional eye examinations and quality eyewear at affordable pricing positions OECC to take advantage of favorable demographics and an aging population.

Number of Franchisees: 28 franchises and 12 corporate offices.

In Business Since: 1976

Equity Capital Needed: $25,000

Financial Assistance Available: Approximately $250,000 is required for opening a one-hour optical franchise. A corporate agent can help arrange financing.

Training Provided: The OECC Training Institute is available to all franchisees. Complete training in financial, technical, and marketing aspects is available for all staff and professional employees. Continuing ongoing education is required.

Managerial Assistance Available: OECC furnishes franchises with all training, equipment, signage, promotions and company benefit programs for doctor and staff.

Information Submitted: April 1990

*PEARLE VISION CENTERS
2534 Royal Lane
Dallas, Texas 75229
Steve Berkman, Vice President-Franchising

Description of Operation: Pearle Vision Centers franchises full-service optical retail outlets.

Number of Franchisees: 425 in 45 States

In Business Since: 1962

Equity Capital Needed: $30,000-$60,000

Financial Assistance Available: Franchisor will provide financing.

Training Provided: Franchisee must be a qualified optician or optometrist with a background in optical management. Franchisor will provide a 3 day orientation program in Pearle Center operations plus optional training programs for franchisees' employees.

Managerial Assistance Available: Franchisor will provide ongoing advice and counsel to franchisee on managerial and technical problems related to the running of a Pearle Vision Center. Franchisor provides advertising support program for a percentage of unit sales and provides marketing support, laboratory services (eyeglass fabrication) and merchandise in accordance with a published price list.

Information Submitted: April 1990

*PROCARE VISION CENTERS, INC.
926 North 21st Street
Newark, Ohio 43055
Dr. Frank Bickle, President

Description of Operation: Retail vision care products.

Number of Franchisees: 18 in Ohio

In Business Since: 1985

Equity Capital Needed: Varies between $30,000 and $200,000.

Financial Assistance Available: Assistance in obtaining financing.

Training Provided: Full training provided.

Managerial Assistance Available: Ongoing support provided.

Information Submitted: April 1990

SINGER/SPECS
1909 Chestnut Street
Philadelphia, Pennsylvania 19103
Alan Singer, President

Description of Operation: Full service vision centers.

Number of Franchisees: 15 in 3 States

In Business Since: 1946

Equity Capital Needed: $79,500

Financial Assistance Available: Yes

Training Provided: 3 step training program, including technical training, management skills, and sales techniques.

Managerial Assistance Available: Singer/Specs provides continual assistance to all franchisees, including monthly meetings that provide updated information.

Information Submitted: June 1990

*SITE FOR SORE EYES OPTICIANS
100 Hegenberger Road
Oakland, California 94621
Paul Licht, President

Description of Operation: 1 hour eye glasses and contact lenses. Each store is approximately 2,000 square feet with on-site lab facilities providing discount eyewear in 1 hour. Stores open to 7 days per week depending on location.

Number of Franchisees: 13 in California

In Business Since: 1979

Equity Capital Needed: $225,000

Financial Assistance Available: None—can assist with local banks.

Training Provided: Training provided for store manager, lab technician, sales people and receptionists. Training is 3 weeks continuous. Training conducted at Site for Sore Eyes training facility at company stores under the direction of full-time trainer.

Managerial Assistance Available: Assistance by phone and on-site for management, technical and sales. Continuous phone consultation and on-site as required. Determined by franchisor, assistance is available Monday through Friday 8:30 a.m. to 6:00 p.m. Other hours by special arrangement. Complete manuals for all operational phases included.

Information Submitted: June 1990

*STERLING OPTICAL
357 Crossways Park Drive
Woodbury, New York 17797
Keith R. Albright, Vice President, Franchising

Description of Operation: Retail optical stores.

Number of Franchisees: 56 plus 200 company-owned.

In Business Since: 1912, franchising since 1987

Equity Capital Needed: $20,000-$50,000. Total investment $200,000-$500,000.

Financial Assistance Available: Financial assistance available.

Training Provided: Full training in operating a optical retail store.

Managerial Assistance Available: Continuous management assistance.

Information Submitted: June 1990

*TEXAS STATE OPTICAL (TSO)
2534 Royal Lane
Dallas, Texas 75229
Mike Simons

Description of Operation: The franchisor (TSO) grants the right to qualified licensed optometrists or experienced opticians to operate a high-quality retail optical dispensing office and an associated optometric office under the proprietary service mark (TSO) which Texas State Optical and such other trademarks, service marks and trade names as Texas State Optical, Inc., may license. The retail dispensing office will sell prescription eyewear, contact lenses, high-quality frames and accessories as may be approved by Texas State Optical, Inc. The franchisee has the right to certain advertising and marketing techniques, business methods, procedures and other expertise supplied by TSO, collectively the "TSO system." Optometric examinations and services are offered at an optometric office adjacent to the retail dispensing office.

Number of Franchisees: 164 plus 82 associates and 25 company-owned.

In Business Since: 1935

Equity Capital Needed: $25,000 to $40,000 depending on qualifications and location.

Financial Assistance Available: TSO has working arrangements with several banks and lending institutions that will provide up to 90 percent financing to qualified, licensed optometrists or experienced opticians. Average total investment for a turnkey TSO franchise including equipment, furniture, fixtures, inventory, signs and leasehold improvements is approximately $125,000 to $175,000, depending on the location.

Training Provided: Initial start-up assistance provided. Optical training programs, including correspondence courses and on-site training, are available to franchisee and employees.

Managerial Assistance Available: Area meetings and seminars are held periodically.

Information Submitted: June 1990

PET SHOPS

DOCKTOR PET CENTERS, INC.
355 Middlesex Avenue
Wilmington, Massachusetts 01887
Leslie Charm, Chairman
Joe Hedl, Director/Franchise Development

Description of Operation: Retail pets, supplies, and pet accessories in regional shopping malls and major strip center locations.

Number of Franchisees: 270 stores in 37 States.

In Business Since: 1966

Equity Capital Needed: Approximately $50,000-$60,000. ($150,000 to $211,000 total investment.)

Financial Assistance Available: Docktor Pet Centers will assist with the preparation and presentation of financing applications; SBA loans available to qualified applicants.

Training Provided: 3 weeks at franchisor's headquarters; subjects covered include store operations, care and maintenance of pets, accounting management, inventory, personnel selection, merchandising, promotions, advertising, etc. Regional and national seminars.

Managerial Assistance Available: Advice on stocking, fixture arrangement, receipt of livestock, maintenance procedures, and profit control, site selection, lease negotiation, store planning, etc. On-the-site advisor guides franchisee during first 2 weeks of operations. Advertising materials, accounting forms and seasonal signs furnished. Consultants make frequent visits to stores to assist franchisees.

Information Submitted: April 1990

LICK YOUR CHOPS, INC.
50 Water Street
South Norwalk, Connecticut 06854

Description of Operation: Lick Your Chops is a complete department store for animals specializing in optimum care and services for the pet.

Number of Franchisees: 4 in Florida, New York, Pennsylvania, and Connecticut plus 2 company-owned.

In Business Since: 1979

Equity Capital Needed: $145,000 turnkey/$25,000 licensing fee.

Financial Assistance Available: None

Training Provided: 1 week training in Westport, Connecticut. Specializing in pet nutrition, retailing, public relations and computer training.

Managerial Assistance Available: Continuous.

Information Submitted: May 1990

*PETLAND, INC.
195 North Hickory Street
P. O. Box 1606

Chillicothe, Ohio 45601-5606
Edward R. Kunzelman, President
Linda H. Heuring, Vice President, Marketing

Description of Operation: Full-service retail pet stores carrying pets and pet supplies, specializing in innovative pet care, housing, and customer education.

Number of Franchisees: 185 plus 2 company-owned stores in the United States, Canada, France and Japan.

In Business Since: 1967

Equity Capital Needed: $40,000-$60,000 depending on store size and location. Total investment $125,000-$300,000.

Financial Assistance Available: Franchisor will assist in preparation of financial presentation package.

Training Provided: Complete classroom at Ohio main office, hands-on in-store training, plus training in franchisee's store. Additional assistance in-store after opening. Ongoing training on specific topics related to business management, livestock care, product knowledge, advertising, and sales.

Managerial Assistance Available: Assistance in merchandising, livestock management, and maintenance procedures. On-site advisor guides franchisee during first week of operation. Advertising manual, ongoing promotion, and standardized accounting and reporting forms furnished. Area field supervisors make regular visits and provide assistance in problem areas. Advertising manual, operations manual, employee training manuals, video tapes, counter reference book, all forms for operations provided.

Information Submitted: April 1990

PET NANNY OF AMERICA, INC.
1000 Long Boulevard
Suite 9
Lansing, Michigan 48911
Rebecca A. Brevitz

Description of Operation: Professional, personalized in-home pet care service. Pet Nanny pet care representatives visit pets in their home while the owner is away, and/or provide midday pet care service to commuters. Pet Nanny also offers other home amenities such as bringing in the mail and newspapers, watering plants and gardens, as well as checking the overall security of the home.

Number of Franchisees: 20

In Business Since: 1983

Equity Capital Needed: Franchise fee: $7,100. Additional capital needed: approximately $2,000 to $4,700.

Financial Assistance Available: Possible in-house financing available based on personal interview.

Training Provided: 4 day training program conducted at company headquarters, including a veterinarian-developed program as well as training for office and personnel management.

Managerial Assistance Available: Pet Nanny provides the ongoing support of professionals from various fields as well as the shared knowledge and diverse talents of other franchisees.

Information Submitted: June 1990

PETS ARE INN, LTD.
27 North Fourth Street
Suite 500
Minneapolis, Minnesota 55401
Harry Sanders-Greenberg, President/Franchising Division

Description of Operation: Pets Are Inn has turned the kennel industry into a cottage industry. We board companion animals and household pets in private homes using senior citizens and retired people as "foster parents." Our system eradicates disease, stress and isolation that often occur with kennel boarding. Our computer program analyzes pet characteristics to find the most compatible home. A thorough knowledge of demographic variables enable us to carefully target our markets to 25 million pet owners throughout the United States.

Number of Franchisees: 25 in 15 States

In Business Since: 1982

Equity Capital Needed: $5,000-$20,000 (including franchise fee).

Financial Assistance Available: None

Training Provided: 4 day intensive training program at headquarters. Includes classroom training (15 hours), in-field placement, computer training, marketing, pricing and scheduling.

Managerial Assistance Available: Ongoing assistance throughout franchise term; includes WATS line, annual convention, newsletter, national advertising, updated procedures, wholesale buying plan on promotional items and pet supplies.

Information Submitted: May 1990

SHAMPOO CHEZ, INC.
1378 Soquel Avenue
Santa Cruz, California 95062
Anne Singer, President

Description of Operation: Self-service dog wash with at least four individual bathing booths equipped with handheld spray nozzles, grooming tables, professional blowdryers, towels and brushes. Quality (natural) pet products as well as professional dog and cat grooming.

Number of Franchisees: 2

In Business Since: 1983

Equity Capital Needed: $55,000-$60,000 is total investment for inventory, equipment, signs, leasehold improvements, start-up expenses and working capital.

Financial Assistance Available: None

Training Provided: On-the-job training at company headquarters (3-5 days). More, if needed. Comprehensive manual of operations, computerized inventory and invoicing system. Assistance with emphasis on advertising and marketing.

Managerial Assistance Available: Management team will help with site selection, and product information, and will be available on an as needed basis, plus periodic personal visits.

Information Submitted: April 1990

PRINTING

AIC INTERNATIONAL
615 Airport Road
Fall River, Massachusetts 02720
Arthur Sansoucy, Chairman and CEO

Description of Operation: ACCU Copy Printing Centers.

Number of Franchisees: 4 including company-owned in Massachusetts and Rhode Island.

In Business Since: 1980

Equity Capital Needed: $37,500

Financial Assistance Available: Lease arrangements. SBA loan application assistance and local bank loan application assistance.

Training Provided: 2 week initial training classes. Ongoing assistance for term of agreement.

Managerial Assistance Available: Technical skills, business management skills, financial management skills and promotional and sales skills.

Information Submitted: June 1990

*ALPHAGRAPHICS PRINTSHOPS OF THE FUTURE
Department Y
3760 North Commerce Drive
Tucson, Arizona 85705
Rodger G. Ford, President

Description of Operation: AlphaGraphics Printshops of the Future operate Electronic Graphic Centers. By taking advantage of advanced technology, we provide quality laser typeset originals, offset printing, high speed duplicating, and binding for professionals and businesses.

Number of Franchisees: 250 in 30 States, plus 9 company stores in Arizona and Texas. Also franchising worldwide.

In Business Since: 1970

Equity Capital Needed: Approximately $65,000-$120,000.

Financial Assistance Available: Total investment is approximately $300,000, with approximately $160,000 financible for a Satellite Center and $180,000 financible for an Electronic Graphic Center. Alternatively, you may qualify for SBA financing of up to 80 percent of the total investment.

Training Provided: 3 weeks of intensive training is provided at company headquarters in Tucson, Arizona, and 1 week in a mature store. There is an additional 10 days of on-site training before and after opening. The curriculum includes LazerGraphics, customer relations, employee relations, equipment operation, planning and budgeting, accounting, marketing and advertising.

Managerial Assistance Available: Ongoing assistance is provided to all franchisees through monthly scheduled visits by field support managers, as well as troubleshooting over our toll-free line, or in person by company executives. National accounts buying plan, monthly merchandising and advertising programs, equipment reviews, up-dated procedures, and annual planning and budgeting are all part of the AlphaGraphics Printshops of the Future support package.

Information Submitted: April 1990

*AMERICAN SPEEDY PRINTING CENTERS, INC.
Corporate Offices
32100 Telegraph Road, Suite 110
Birmingham, Michigan 48010
Vernon G. Buchanan, President

Description of Operation: American Speedy Printing Centers, Inc., offers franchise owners an outstanding profit potential in the fast growing quick printing industry. A center is set up with all the necessary equipment for offset printing, bindery and photo copying as well as all other accessories needed to operate a successful quick printing center. For additional information call 800-521-4002 (in Michigan 800-482-0421; in Canada 800-544-8405).

Number of Franchisees: More than 650 in Unites States, Canada, Japan and England.

In Business Since: 1977

Equity Capital Needed: $40,000 minimum cash requirement.

Financial Assistance Available: Financing available to qualified applicants.

Training Provided: Completion of an extensive 4-week training course that includes bookkeeping and reporting system, equipment operation and maintenance, marketing, pricing, work scheduling and management of employees. Franchisor's representative assists franchisee in his or her location during his or her first week of operation.

Managerial Assistance Available: American Speedy Printing Centers provides a continuing support system to all of its franchisees through the home office as well as several regional offices for the life of the franchise agreement. This includes national conventions, conferences and mini-seminars, advertising; management consultation; employment services; negotiation of national contracts for supply and equipment discounts; equipment, maintenance and repair seminars; sales seminars; press and camera services; technical and supply bulletins; monthly newsletter; and continuing research of new equipment and supplies. The home office staff is available for personal assistance and counseling by telephone and in person.

Information Submitted: June 1990

*AMERICAN WHOLESALE THERMOGRAPHERS, INC.
P. O. Box 777
Cypress, Texas 77429
Patricia Paddy, President

Description of Operation: The American Wholesale Thermographers franchise is a business that offers thermographed (raised letter) printing and attendant services, at the wholesale level. The services and products of the American Wholesale Thermographers Center will be used by retail establishments such as printers, office supply stores, and stationers who will subsequently offer the product to the general public.

Number of Franchisees: 19 in 12 States; also in Canada.

In Business Since: 1982

Equity Capital Needed: Approximately $50,000 minimum.

Financial Assistance Available: Third party financing available.

Training Provided: American Wholesale Thermographers training program encompasses 5 weeks. Two weeks of training are conducted at the corporate headquarters in Cypress, Texas, 2 weeks of training at an operating center and 1 additional week of assistance at the franchisee's AWT Center at the time of opening for business.

Managerial Assistance Available: American Wholesale Thermographers provides continual support service in such areas as operations, advertising, sales, and computer support. Complete manuals of operations, forms, and directions are provided. American Wholesale Thermographers may occasionally hold seminars on subjects of interest to franchisees. Monthly newsletters are issued on various promotional techniques, as well as valuable information about management systems and equipment.

Information Submitted: June 1990

*BUSINESS CARD EXPRESS
2555 South Telegraph
Suite 400
Bloomfield Hills, Michigan 48013
C. S. Derry, Executive Vice President

Description of Operation: Business Card Express is building a network of 100 to 150 fully automated and computerized production facilities to serve the needs of the exploding commercial quick printing market (over 70,000 shops nationwide). Only one Business Card Express will be located in each major market area of 500 printers producing only wholesale thermographed (raised ink) business cards and stationery specialties. Our specialized technology, "captive" market, and simplicity of operation have created a high volume business with outstanding growth potential.

Number of Franchisees: 20 in 9 States

In Business Since: 1982

Equity Capital Needed: $75,000

Financial Assistance Available: BCE will assist franchise owners with collatoral loans and equipment financing. Amounts will be determined by franchise owner's needs and credit history.

Training Provided: Intensive 4 weeks of training: computer opeations, sales and marketing, bookkeeping, typesetting, keylining, proofreading, order processing, stat work, purchasing, inventory, on-site training.

Managerial Assistance Available: Site selection and lease negotiations, layout design, coordinated equipment installation, initial supply packages, research and development of new products, ongoing training and seminars, group insurance packages, one week on-site training, technical bulletins and updates, weekly calls through the first 90 days, 90 day marketing and operational plan of action, computer networking for daily information flow, software updates, national contract pricing for equipment and supplies.

Information Submitted: June 1990

BUSINESS CARDS OVERNIGHT
19 6th Road
Woburn, Massachusetts 01801
Kenneth Hannan, President

Description of Operation: Business Cards Overnight is a wholesale thermographic (raised) printing center. We provide business cards within 24 hours and also do raised printing on stationery and letterheads.

Number of Franchisees: 6 in 5 States

In Business Since: 1980

Equity Capital Needed: $50,000 minimum

Financial Assistance Available: The purchase price of a Business Cards Overnight center is $90,000. An initial $25,000 franchise fee pays for site location, market survey and research, lease negotiation assistance if needed and training of center personnel by franchisor prior to opening of the center. The franchisor has made arrangements with a leasing company for financing for the equipment package of $65,000. Franchisee may obtain his/her own outside financing.

Training Provided: Franchisor will provide franchisee and one other person with training and instruction in the operation and promotion of the center for 5 business days at the home office or other designated site. Also the franchisor will provide an additional 3 weeks (15 business days) training and instruction in the operation of the BCO system and equipment at franchisee's center.

Managerial Assistance Available: Franchisor will provide a continuing assistance program that shall include consulting and assistance by BCO representatives, accounting and marketing assistance, advising the franchisee of new developments and techniques in the thermographic and reproduction industry. In addition franchisor provides a production facility for franchisee to send difficult and/or undesirable work for distributor purposes. Franchisee gets returned completed work for mark-up and resale.

Information Submitted: June 1990

*BUSINESS CARDS TOMORROW, INC.
3000 N.E. 30th Place
5th Floor
Fort Lauderdale, Florida 33306
Robert S. Anderson, Vice President, Franchise
Development

Description of Operation: Business Cards Tomorrow, Inc., is an international franchise organization which offers a wholesale business concept by providing a wide range of quality themographic printing for both commercial and retail printers. Unique to the industry is the specialized service operation—24 hour turnaround for business card printing; 5 business days for other thermographic printing. Free pick-up and delivery are provided with all orders.

Number of Franchisees: 89 in 93 States plus 7 in Canada

In Business Since: 1975

Equity Capital Needed: $95,000

Financial Assistance Available: Initial cash investment $60,000 plus working capital. The initial cash investment of which $35,000 is the franchise fee pays for site location and research, market survey and lease negotiation assistance, training, supervision and assistance provided by franchisor for opening of the center, and general sales and administration expenses of franchisor. The franchisor has made arrangements with finance companies for financing of the equipment package, which is approximately $110,000. Franchisee may obtain his own outside financing.

Training Provided: A mandatory training program is scheduled prior to any center opening. This training is for 2 weeks and consists of equipment orientation and operation, business management and marketing, and sales technique in the thermography industry. In addition, the franchisor will furnish a qualified representative for a period of 10 business days after opening of the center to instruct the franchisee in operation of his center and to aid in the hiring of personnel and to assist in establishing standard procedures.

Managerial Assistance Available: Throughout the term of the agreement, the franchisor shall provide the franchisee with continuous sales, marketing and technical assistance, consultation and advice on operations and procedures, and accounting and administrative guidance. In addition, the franchisor will apprise the franchisee of new developments in the thermographic printing field.

Information Submitted: April 1990

*COPIES NOW
23131 Verdugo Drive
Laguna Hills, California 92653
Kenneth A. Ross, Vice President, System
Development
Richard Lowe, Director, Copies Now

Description of Operation: Full service business communication center. Provides high speed copying, electronic publishing, color reproduction, engineering copying and fax services to small to mid-size businesses.

Number of Franchisees: 65 in 15 States

In Business Since: 1984

Equity Capital Needed: Franchise fee of $27,500, equipment package $37,500 and working capital of $30,000.

Financial Assistance Available: 100 percent financing available on equipment package.

Training Provided: 2 weeks in our University in Laguna Hills, California, for 2 people. Airfare and hotel included. 2 weeks on-site during opening with field representative.

Managerial Assistance Available: Site selection and market survey, floorplanning and design of store, complete starting inventory, monthly mailers, newsletter and advertising repros, resident business management consultant for store, systemwide advertising on CBS Radio, print media and direct mail, regional roundtable training sessions and all pro seminars, national convention and vendor show, ongoing research and development and complete operations, marketing and administrative manuals.

Information Submitted: April 1990

*FRANKLIN'S COPY SERVICE, INC.
135 International Boulevard
Atlanta, Georgia 30303
Hal Collins, President

Description of Operation: Full-service quick printing and office supply stores featuring printing, typesetting, high speed copy reproduction and a complete line of office supplies.

Number of Franchisees: 83 stores in 15 States and Canada.

In Business Since: 1971

Equity Capital Needed: $40,000 to $50,000, which includes working capital.

Financial Assistance Available: Franklin's will assist franchise owner in obtaining bank financing.

Training Provided: 3 weeks and ongoing as necessary.

Managerial Assistance Available: Franklin's provides support to the franchisee in hiring, marketing, advertising, purchasing and receivables control. The franchisor is available for assistance in any area necessary for the operation of the stores.

Information Submitted: May 1990

*THE INK WELL, INC.
2323 Lake Club Drive
Columbus, Ohio 43232
Gerard Ales, Vice President - National Development

Description of Operation: The Ink Well printing centers are positioned in the market to provide high quality printing and related services to the business community through retail printing operations. Our owners benefit from the industry's most experienced management team and an exceptional business system. We offer you complete support: continual training, financial guidance, marketing programs, business management programs and all the other operational support you'd expect from a franchise. Investor opportunities available for regional master franchise expansion program.

Number of Franchisees: 55, plus 1 company-owned.

In Business Since: 1972, franchising since 1981

Equity Capital Needed: $40,000 approximate minimum cash requirement.

Financial Assistance Available: Yes, to qualified prospects through lease programs and SBA loans. Covers the cost of fixtures, equipment, signage. Total investment is $131,800-$167,800.

Training Provided: 2 weeks at national training class at corporate headquarters with a business management, marketing and center operation curriculum augmented with hands-on equipment training. Conducted in a live-store environment. 2 weeks on-site upon opening is followed by seminars and workshops conducted throughout each year by Ink Well staff and outside experts.

Managerial Assistance Available: Annual comprehensive review of center operation with follow-up action plans. Monthly phone contact by assigned franchise services representative, toll free hotline for daily assistance, regional owner meetings, bi-monthly mailings, research and development, personal consultation and owner manuals are all key elements of ongoing management support.

Information Submitted: April 1990

INSTANT COPY
232 West Wayne Street
Fort Wayne, Indiana 46802
John M. Thistlethwaite, Director of Franchising

Description of Operation: Instant copy printing, copying and communications centers, are fully equipped with top of the line equipment and communications hardware to provide full service quick printing and desk top publishing service. Each center utilizes the Instant Copy attitude and Instant Copy guarantee. Typical center is approximately 1,500 square feet.

Number of Franchisees: 5 in Indiana

In Business Since: 1969, franchising began in 1985

Equity Capital Needed: $125,000

Financial Assistance Available: A total investment of $250,000 to $300,000 is necessary to open an Instant Copy Center. Instant Copy provides no financial assistance to the franchisee. Approximately $125,000 in cash is needed if franchisee leases equipment and building.

Training Provided: Complete store operations training for franchisee and employees at the Instant Copy offices for 5 weeks, and 2 weeks on-site training.

Managerial Assistance Available: During store set-up, Instant Copy provides complete facilities preparation assistance, equipment and inventory assistance, as well as opening sales marketing and advertising functions. Ongoing facilities operation analyses, educational seminars, and introduction to new market developments; technical assistance with Instant Copy commercial services plant for business cards, webb press type (high volume) printing, and process printing.

Information Submitted: June 1990

*INSTY-PRINTS, INC.
1010 South Seventh Street
Suite 450
Minneapolis, Minnesota 55415
James H. Kaufenberg, President

Description of Operation: Insty-Prints commercial quick print and copy centers offer high-quality printing services as well as hi-tech pre-press and post-press services. Franchise owners receive a package of services that includes 3 weeks of training, site selection and lease negotiation, store design, comprehensive advertising program, bookkeeping system, pricing and cost ratio programs and continued, long-term management counseling. An equipment and fixture package is provided specific to each location and the needs of the market area. One week's opening supervision is provided in franchise owner's unit and after the unit has been opened for 6 months.

Number of Franchisees: 356 locations in 41 States, Washington, D.C., Puerto Rico and Canada.

In Business Since: 1965

Equity Capital Needed: $88,000 minimum cash requirement.

Financial Assistance Available: A total investment of $132,500 is necessary in order to open an Insty-Prints store. Insty-Prints provides no financial assistance to the franchise owner at this time.

Training Provided: To expedite opening, Insty-Prints provides 1 week of business training at Minneapolis headquarters. This training covers desktop publishing using state-of-the-art Apple Macintosh hardware and software, advertising and marketing systems, sales techniques, job flow systems, bookkeeping, estimating, paper, health and safety on the job, inventory control, the role of the owner and other management skills. 1 week of additional training in the franchise owner's store is offered immediately following the headquarters training. This phase of training provides the franchise owner assistance in putting into practice those systems and programs learned previously. Additional follow-up training is also scheduled at this time.

Managerial Assistance Available: Annual convention seminars and workshops, annual regional workshops, continuing management advice and counsel, instant in WATS telephone communications, continuing advertising and marketing programs, regularly scheduled newsletters/bulletins, informational mailings, national advertising fund.

Information Submitted: April 1990

*KWIK-KOPY CORPORATION
1 Kwik-Kopy Lane
P. O. Box 777
Cypress, Texas 77429
Director—Marketing

Description of Operation: A Kwik-Kopy Center franchise offers a system for production and sale of high quality printing, duplicating, copying, bindery and attendant services on rapid time schedules tailored to meet the customers' desire. The franchise includes volume buying discounts on the purchase of equipment, microcomputer hardware with specialized business systems software, furniture, fixtures and supplies, market research, site selection, negotiation of real estate leases, equipment operation, public relations, sales and advertising programs, start-up assistance, and continued support service in technical and business management problems over the entire 25-year term of the franchise agreement.

Number of Franchisees: Approximately over 1,000 in 42 States, Canada, United Kingdom, Australia, South Africa and Israel.

In Business Since: 1967

Equity Capital Needed: Minimum cash requirement of approximately $40,000-$50,000.

Financial Assistance Available: Third party financing available.

Training Provided: Completion of an intensive 2 week training course is provided by Kwik-Kopy Corporation at its management training center and is required prior to opening a Kwik-Kopy Center. Additional 1 week on-the-job training in the franchise owner's place of business during and after start-up is also provided. Training includes equipment operation, accounting, advertising sales and business methods in Kwik-Kopy Center operations. Pre- and post-training video tapes on business procedures, operation and maintenance of equipment, sales and advertising programs are supplied to each franchise owner.

Managerial Assistance Available: The company provides continued support services to its franchise owners for the term of the franchise agreement, including management counsel, advertising and training of new employees. Assistance and counseling is available to all franchise owners by telephone through nationwide toll-free WATS lines available to all franchise owners.

Information Submitted: June 1990

*MINUTEMAN PRESS INTERNATIONAL, INC.
1640 New Highway
Farmingdale, New York 11735
Roy W. Titus, President

Description of Operation: Minuteman Press International, Inc., offers a unique approach to the instant printing franchise through its full service printing centers. Not only the ability to produce high quality instant printing, but also the versatility of the equipment enable the owners with no previous printing or graphics experience to produce multi-color printing, photostats, overhead visuals and the screening of half-tones. A complete package is offered that includes all the necessary equipment for printing, cutting, folding, padding, collating, stapling, plus the initial supply of ink, film, paper, stationery and promotional materials for marketing. Also included in the package is the research of the proposed area, securing an acceptable location and assistance in the negotiation of the lease as well as overseeing the complete renovations of the location, including the installation of fixtures, signs, furniture and all accessories needed to operate a successful Minuteman Press Full Service Printing Center.

Number of Franchisees: Over 900 in 44 States and Canada

In Business Since: 1973

Equity Capital Needed: Approximately $22,500 to $32,500.

Financial Assistance Available: $94,586 to $116,742 total investment, with financing available through the 3M Company (Minnesota Mining and Manufacturing Company).

Training Provided: There is an intensive 2 week training program held at the Minuteman Press Training Center in Farmingdale, New York, covering all aspects of the business, plus a minimum of 40 hours continued training at the franchisee's own location under home office field supervision. Training covers use of all equipment, advertising, pricing, bookkeeping, sales promotion, counter procedures, inventory, and cost control and general management. The owner is also trained in a marketing program developed by the company, which has been one of the keys to the success of the Minuteman Press franchises.

Managerial Assistance Available: The company has regional offices under the supervision of an officer of the company in Atlanta, Baltimore, Birmingham, Boston, Chicago, Cleveland, Dallas, Denver, Ft. Lauderdale, Los Angeles, Minneapolis, New York, Philadelphia, Pittsburgh, San Francisco, Seattle, St. Louis, and Canada to provide continued support services and guidance to its franchisees, including management, marketing, advertising, and training of new employees. Franchise owners are kept current with results of research and new equipment through periodic meetings and seminars and visits by field representatives who provide assistance as required. Continuous guidance and support are available to all franchise owners through the regional or home office.

Information Submitted: April 1990

*PIP PRINTING
27001 Agoura Road
Agoura Hills, California 91376
Thomas C. Marotto, President/CEO

Description of Operation: World's largest printing franchise. PIP Printing is committed to meet the expanding printing needs in the business market. In addition to black and white and multi-colored printing, PIP stores offer 4-color printing, desktop publishing, typesetting, layout and design, business forms, high-speed duplicating, binding and finishing. Owners are provided a comprehensive opening package, including equipment, initial supplies and marketing materials to promote sales. PIP corporate also assists with the installation of equipment and provides electrical and plumbing specifications.

Number of Franchisees: Over 1,100 locations in 48 States, Washington, D.C., Canada and the United Kingdom.

In Business Since: 1965

Equity Capital Needed: $25,000 down payment, $42,000 working capital plus living expenses.

Financial Assistance Available: Franchisor will finance balance of franchise fee and most equipment for qualified applicants.

Training Provided: 2 weeks of intensive training at PIP's national training center by skilled operations, technical and marketing experts. Training covers the use of all equipment, advertising, marketing, public relations, business management, estimating, recordkeeping, inventory and cost control, sales, customer relations and employee relations. Year-round advanced training programs offered in sales and marketing, personnel management and printing techniques.

Managerial Assistance Available: Immediately following initial training, field support representative spends 1 week assisting with the opening of the store. Ongoing field and marketing support and educational seminars year-round. Biennial conclaves conducted for owners during the even-numbered years.

Information Submitted: April 1990

*THE PRINTHOUSE EXPRESS
2 Pigeon Hill Drive
Suite 510
Sterling, Virginia 22170
Merv Greenwood, Director of Marketing

Description of Operation: Franchising of full service printing and copying centers.

Number of Franchisees: 14 in 2 States

In Business Since: 1987

Equity Capital Needed: Cash requirement: $50,000 to $60,000 with a $150,000 net worth.

Financial Assistance Available: Franchisor will finance part of the franchise fees and will assist with locating a source for equipment package.

Training Provided: 10 day training program at company training center, 80 hours in-store training and support and ongoing training throughout system.

Managerial Assistance Available: Complete support system from day one that includes site locating, lease assistance, and build-out specs. Upon opening, phone and on-site support for day-to-day operations and periodic store visits, both scheduled and unscheduled, for evaluations and recommendations.

Information Submitted: April 1990

*PRINTMASTERS, INC.
370 South Crenshaw Boulevard
Suite E-100
Torrance, California 90503

Description of Operation: PrintMasters, Inc., offers an opportunity for enthusiastic and motivated people to achieve their management and promotional potential in the field of high volume quality instant printing. The Printmaster package includes a complete line of equipment, material and supplies, plus the major items of office furniture required to operate an effective instant printing center.

Number of Franchisees: 101 in California, Arizona and Oregon.

In Business Since: 1976

Equity Capital Needed: Cost of franchise package $109,000. Minimum cash investment $30,000. Working capital $35,000-$40,000.

Financial Assistance Available: Financing available $109,000 (to qualified individuals) on the total package of $109,000.

Training Provided: Technical, managerial and promotional training provided. Minimum of 2 weeks at the franchise training center. Minimum of 2 weeks at the franchisee's location. Managerial and promotional input continues, as well as technical assistance, through quality control visits and direct contact with franchisee. All aspects of owning and operating an instant printing center are covered in detail.

Managerial Assistance Available: Each franchisee undergoes a CPA consultation for the purpose of setting up the center's books and recordkeeping system. The franchisee receives continued management, marketing and promotional guidance and support for the duration of the franchise license agreement. Supply sources, pricing techniques and group purchasing discounts are provided on a constant basis. Periodic quality control visits review current and introduce new technical, managerial and marketing skills and products. PrintMasters emphasizes the need for ongoing interaction between the franchisee and the company headquarters. Direct lines of communication are always open to assist, guide and offer support.

Information Submitted: April 1990

PRINT SHACK
Intracoastal Building, 5th Floor
3000 NE 30th Place
Ft. Lauderdale, Florida 33305

Description of Operation: Print Shack has established itself as the most unique franchise opportunity in the instant printing industry. Our centers market a full range of printed paper products including multi-color work, full typesetting services and related services. Additionally, Print Shack centers offer over 50,000 different advertising specialty products to the same customer base, combining the 3 billion dollar instant printing industry with the 4 billion dollar advertising specialty industry. We offer single store, multi-store and regional opportunities.

Number of Franchisees: 100 in 30 States

In Business Since: 1982

Equity Capital Needed: Franchise fee $30,000, no charge for second franchise; $46,000-$65,000 total cash.

Financial Assistance Available: Financing available for all equipment and a portion of the franchise fee to qualified individuals. SBA also available.

Training Provided: All franchisees receive a full 2 weeks of comprehensive training at our home office in Ft. Lauderdale, Florida, and 2 weeks on location. In addition, training classes are continuous and you may enroll members of your staff or yourself in any ongoing class at no extra charge for the term of the franchise. Instruction covers every aspect of equipment training, marketing, accounting procedures, personnel, advertising, public relations, proper management and systems control.

Managerial Assistance Available: Continuous, ongoing and comprehensive for the life of our agreements. Your success is our success!

Information Submitted: April 1990

*PRINT THREE FRANCHISING INC.
600 Central Avenue
Suite 333
Highland Park, Illinois 60035
Cliff Richler, Vice President, Franchise Development

Description of Operation: Full service electronic printing centers featuring a leading edge desktop publishing system using proprietary laser printing equipment with superior resolution of 1,200 x 600 d.p.i. A high-tech operation with print-link communications, offering instantaneous transmittal of text, data and graphics across the continent.

Number of Franchisees: 175 in 17 States and 2 countries.

In Business Since: 1970

Equity Capital Needed: $50,000

Financial Assistance Available: 100 percent

Training Provided: 3 week comprehensive business training, with 1 week on-site after center opening. Ongoing management and computer training, professional marketing support and periodic business evaluation.

Managerial Assistance Available: All owners are trained in Print Three business operations and customer service techniques. On-site opening assistance, frequent visits, ongoing support and consultation, toll-free operations and technical support hot lines, annual convention, re-training for new staff at no charge.

Information Submitted: April 1990

PRONTO PRINTER
256 Post Road East
Westport, Connecticut 06880
Gerald Marvin, President

Description of Operation: Pronto Printer is a quick printing franchise servicing the printing needs of businesses and organizations. Emphasis is placed on image and professionalism in dealing with our customers, providing offset printing, copying, typsetting, laser printing, and other related services.

Number of Franchisees: 11 in Connecticut and New York

In Business Since: 1969

Equity Capital Needed: $80,000 to $120,000 total to open, including working capital and grand opening advertising.

Financial Assistance Available: Will assist in locating financing.

Training Provided: 3 weeks of training including operating equipment, sales counter procedures, and business procedures. An additional 3 weeks on in-store training during the first 6 months of operation.

Managerial Assistance Available: Ongoing advertising and marketing guidance and materials, educational seminars, and on-site visitation program.

Information Submitted: April 1990

QUIK PRINT, INC.
3445 North Webb Road
Wichita, Kansas 67226
Johnny Tarrant, Senior Vice President

Description of Operation: Quik Print has established itself as an organization with a high standard of customer service and image in mind. A Quik Printing franchise is not only a visible asset in the market place, but also a compliment to the Quik Print Corporation.

Number of Franchisees: 136 franchisee-owned, 66 company-owned in 24 States.

In Business Since: 1963

Equity Capital Needed: Complete franchise package $150,000.

Financial Assistance Available: Financing available to qualified individuals.

Training Provided: 4 to 6 weeks at franchisor's headquarters, plus 2 weeks on-the-job at franchisee's new location.

Managerial Assistance Available: Management services in the area of bookkeeping, advertising, equipment and production techniques.

Information Submitted: June 1990

SIGNAL GRAPHICS PRINTING
848 Broadway
Denver, Colorado 80203
Director of Franchise Development

Description of Operation: Signal Graphics Printing centers offer quick, quality printing and graphics services to the rapidly expanding business communications market. The shops are designed with a familiar "retail" appearance to be visually appealing, and are established in easy-to-find locations. The stores are furnished with the latest technology in high-speed copiers, multi-color-printing presses, darkroom cameras, facsimile (fax) transmission systems, and desktop publishing.

Number of Franchisees: 19 in 6 States

In Business Since: 1982

Equity Capital Needed: $35,000 to $65,000. Total investment $160,000.

Financial Assistance Available: Equipment package financing assistance available to qualified applicants.

Training Provided: 3 weeks of comprehensive training is provided for 2 people at Denver headquarters, followed by 1 week on-site at opening. Training is so thorough that no previous printing experience is required. Subjects include management, operations, personnel, and marketing.

Managerial Assistance Available: Site selection, lease negotiation and store layout. Assistance in purchase and installation of equipment, furniture, fixtures and inventory items purchased through national contracts for maximum discounts. Development of advertising, public relations and promotional programs for your center. Ongoing assistance is provided to all franchisees through visits by support specialists, newsletters and telephone consultation. Continuing support includes sales, marketing and technical assistance and consultation and advice on operations and procedures.

Information Submitted: April 1990

*SIR SPEEDY, INC.
23131 Verdugo Drive
LaGuna Hills, California 92653
Dave Collins, Vice President Franchising

Description of Operation: Sir Speedy, Inc., is a leading franchisor of printing centers, providing full service printing and the highest average gross sales volume per store in the industry. Centers are franchisee-owned, using established system, procedures and techniques. Franchise prackage includes equipment, supplies, signage, graphics, market survey and training programs. Prior printing experience not required.

Number of Franchisees: Approximately 900 in 46 States.

In Business Since: 1968

Equity Capital Needed: Total franchise package is $120,000 plus working capital of $50,000. Initial investment as low as $50,000.

Financial Assistance Available: Financing available for entire package to qualified individuals, excluding working capital.

Training Provided: Total of 4 weeks initial training. This in-depth initial training includes advertising and marketing strategy, bookkeeping and recordkeeping, computer graphic design, shop organization and work flow, pricing, employee relations, and more. Ongoing regional and national seminars and conventions to keep franchisees informed of trends in the industry.

Managerial Assistance Available: In-depth market surveys, site selection, assistance in lease negotiations, national contract purchasing power, marketing and advertising support, accounting system, communication with all franchisees, profit management seminars, equipment evaluations, plus royalty rebate program.

Information Submitted: April 1990

TRANSAMERICA PRINTING, INC.
1286 Citizens Parkway
Suite F
Morrow, Georgia 30260
Patrick Koehler, President

Description of Operation: TransAmerica Printing offers a full service printing operation including a two color press in the initial package necessary for high quality registration work. Experienced pressmen are hired as no training on the press is given or recommended. The franchise package includes assistance in site selection, lease negotiation, store layout, ordering all equipment and supplies and promotional material.

Number of Franchisees: 30 in 11 States.

In Business Since: 1985

Equity Capital Needed: $45,000 plus $30,000 working capital.

Financial Assistance Available: Equipment ($53,000) can be set up on 60 month lease.

Training Provided: Assistance in hiring of pressman and 4 full weeks on-site training after opening. This procedure permits opening in as little as 3 weeks. No training in running the press is given as an experienced pressman is recommended and required for high quality work. Training is concentrated on management and marketing.

Managerial Assistance Available: Following the on-site training of 4 weeks, ongoing assistance is available by phone. Monthly art work for advertising and promotion is made available. Trans-America Printing has quarterly regional seminars on marketing, advertising, financial data and new equipment review.

Information Submitted: April 1990

UNITED PRINTING UNLIMITED, CORPORATION
P. O. Box 3378 - Dept. M
Sarasota, Florida 34230
Jack Swat

Description of Operation: Full service printing centre complete support package. Three weeks of the finest training covering all aspects of the printing business and one more week in your centre. Market research, site selection, lease negotiation and financing. The lowest overhead in the industry.

Number of Franchisees: 6 in 3 States

In Business Since: 1985

Equity Capital Needed: $12,500-$20,000

Financial Assistance Available: None

Training Provided: 3 weeks of extensive hands-on printing and business training.

Managerial Assistance Available: In addition the corporation visits on a 6 month program. Additional assistance provided on as needed basis.

Information Submitted: April 1990

REAL ESTATE

ART FELLER AUCTION AND REAL
ESTATE COMPANY
Garfield Avenue
Box 267
Cissna Park, Illinois 60924
Arthur Feller, Broker

Description of Operation: A real estate franchise where each office is independently owned and operated. Feller Real Estate handles all major advertising, with monthly publicatons of all listings, and all offices work together.

Number of Franchisees: 15 in Illinois and Indiana

In Business Since: 1938—auctioneering, 1982—real estate.

Equity Capital Needed: None—all franchise office work on percentage sold.

Financial Assistance Available: All literature, brochures of all offices and listings of real estate are promoted and advertised throughout area at no cost to franchisee.

Training Provided: Sales meetings held regularly.

Managerial Assistance Available: Sales person visits office when needed to give guidance and advice. District and field managers available to work closely with all franchisees; referrals giving by franchisor.

Information Submitted: June 1990

BELL REALTY
3922 East Florence Avenue
Bell, California 90201
Frank Ortiz, Vice President

Description of Operation: Complete real estate service.

Number of Franchisees: 3 including company-owned in California.

In Business Since: 1959

Equity Capital Needed: None

Financial Assistance Available: None

Training Provided: Franchisor will provide 3 months at the beginning of acquisition.

Managerial Assistance Available: Ongoing

Information Submitted: June 1990

*BETTER HOMES AND GARDENS REAL ESTATE
SERVICE
2000 Grand Avenue
Des Moines, Iowa 50312
Randy Schwager

Description of Operation: A national marketing program licensing the Better Homes and Gardens trademarks to selected real estate firms in assigned exclusive market territories. The variety of programs available to licensees includes a national and local advertising program, a referral service, mortgage origination capability (in states where available), a corporate relocation program, a concurrent licensing program, management seminars, training materials, a home warranty program (in states where available), client promotion materials, a building support program, and the benefits of belonging to a national network of professional real estate firms.

Number of Franchisees: Over 685 in all 50 States

In Business Since: 1978

Equity Capital Needed: The initial joining fee is an applied percentage of the annual residential gross commission income of each firm. The minimum joining fee is $11,000.

Financial Assistance Available: A down payment of 50 percent of the joining fee is due when the contract is executed. The remaining 50 percent is due at the opening date. The opening date is the date that the firm first publicly uses the Better Homes and Gardens marks or 120 days after the effective date of the contract, whichever is earlier.

Training Provided: Better Homes and Gardens Real Estate Service provides a management orientation session for members at Better Homes and Gardens corporate headquarters. In addition, Better Homes and Gardens provides an orientation for the agents of each new firm at its primary office without charge. Better Homes and Gardens provides periodic regional training seminars for the management of its members at reasonable cost.

Managerial Assistance Available: Better Homes and Gardens maintains a service staff with assigned territories to provide each firm with personal contact and consultation on the effective use of the programs. Toll free inbound WATS lines access the service department for improved communication. Regional groups have been established and sponsored by Better Homes and Gardens to provide for periodic meetings of all members in each geographic area to discuss common ideas.

Information Submitted: June 1990

BETTER HOMES REALTY
1556 Parkside Drive
P. O. Box 8181
Walnut Creek, California 94596
Clifford R. Fick, Senior Vice President/CEO

Description of Operation: Better Homes Realty is a network of independently owned and operated real estate offices. A dual-identity program allows brokers to retain their established identity, plus combine with Better Homes Realty brand-name awareness, mass marketing, national relocation services, continuous management and associate training and education programs, and consumer-service preferred treatment programs, including a unique in-house Preferred Financing program. Better Homes Realty is the franchisor of Better Homes Realty.

Number of Franchisees: Better Homes Realty currently has 1,200 associates in over 90 offices.

In Business Since: Founded in Walnut Creek, California, as an all-broker cooperative during the 1960s, Better Homes Realty began franchise expansion in 1974.

Equity Capital Needed: Under the Better Homes Realty franchise agreement, a one-time initial franchise fee of $9,950 allows a franchisee to assume the established Better Homes Realty trademark and support services. A substantial amount of the initial franchise fee is returned to the franchisee in office set-up materials. Service fees are equal to 6 percent of the gross commissions for transactions requiring a real estate license. No additional advertising fees or assessments are charged.

Financial Assistance Available: Franchisor may agree to accept deferred payments totaling $11,190 with a $3,000 down payment and monthly installments of $455.

Training Provided: The Better Homes Realty Institute of Real Estate programs begin with recruitment career nights, and cover a sales training course at no cost to associates, a continuing education program for license renewal credit, and regular management and associate conferences over a 4 to 10 day period.

Managerial Assistance Available: Representatives of the Better Homes Realty business development department make regular visits to Better Homes Realty associate offices to discuss the uses of all business development materials, and to counsel management decisions. Bethome Media, the professionally staffed in-house advertising agency, prepares and produces continuous advertising and marketing campaigns within each regional area.

Information Submitted: April 1990

*BY OWNER, INC.
Lochaven Square, Suite A
North 8884 Government Way
Hayden Lake, Idaho 83835
Jerry L. Wall, President

Description of Operation: BY OWNER franchises feature professional photo property displays in a retail environment, offering marketing and real estate services with no percentage commissions. Our Federally trademarketed BY OWNER logo and franchise locations attract sellers and buyers who want to save thousands of dollars. Franchisee income is derived from very reasonable BY OWNER fees that are based upon services rendered, rather than upon the property's sales price.

Number of Franchisees: 12 in 3 States and Canada.

In Business Since: 1985

Equity Capital Needed: Approximately $15,000, plus cost of franchise, which is currently $16,500.

Financial Assistance Available: BY OWNER, INC. does not offer financing at this time.

Training Provided: Master Franchises: 1 week at corporate headquarters plus on-site follow-up. Unit franchises: 1 week on-site, and follow-up. Training includes computer introduction and application. Ongoing support.

Managerial Assistance Available: Provided by subfranchisor and/or training.

Information Submitted: April 1990

*CENTURY 21 REAL ESTATE CORPORATION
International Headquarters
Century Centre, 2601 S.E. Main Street
P.O. Box 19564
Irvine, California 92713-9564
Vice President, Franchise Sales

Description of Operation: World's largest real estate franchising organization, established to provide a marketing support system for independently owned and operated real estate brokerage offices, offering international advertising, VIP referral system, residential and commercial sales training, management training, national accounts center, client follow-up, and other real estate related services. Insurance, mortgage brokerage, and securities and syndication services are available in selected regions through subsidiary companies in Century 21 Real Estate Corporation. Subsidiary of Metropolitan Insurance Company.

Number of Franchisees: Over 7,000 offices in United States, Canada and Japan.

In Business Since: First offices opened in 1972.

Equity Capital Needed: Cash investment $12,000-$25,000

Financial Assistance Available: Some financing may be available.

Training Provided: The exclusive Century 21 CareerTrak program offers training and accreditation in all major real estate disciplines: office management, investment and residential sales, sales management and relocation services. The program links educational standards with productivity for a system-wide method of motivation and career development.

Managerial Assistance Available: New franchisees attend the international management academy, a 3-1/2 day orientation/management training seminar held in Irvine, California. Other courses offered through the regions include the property management support system, principles of sales management and commercial property series.

Information Submitted: June 1990

CERTIFIED APPRAISAL NETWORK
429 Santa Monica Boulevard
Suite 640
Santa Monica, California 90404
Emile Grauvreau, President

Description of Operation: Real estate appraisal.

Number of Franchisees: 2

In Business Since: 1989, franchising since 1990

Equity Capital Needed: $24,950 total investment

Financial Assistance Available: None

Training Provided: Complete training provided in all operations of the business.

Managerial Assistance Available: Continuous.

Information Submitted: June 1990

COMREAL INTERNATIONAL, INC.
8725 Northwest 18th Terrace
Suite 200
Miami, Florida 33172
Stephen H. Smith, President

Description of Operation: The franchise offered is a format system for operation of a full-service, computerized, commercial real estate brokerage operation including property/asset management, mortgage brokerage, syndication and marketing services.

Number of Franchisees: 6 in Florida

In Business Since: 1983

Equity Capital Needed: $225,000

Financial Assistance Available: None

Training Provided: 1 week for each salesperson and certain staff members; 2 weeks for owners and operators.

Managerial Assistance Available: Continual assistance to franchisee and their staff.

Information Submitted: June 1990

*ELECTRONIC REALTY ASSOCIATES, INC.
4900 College Boulevard
Overland Park, Kansas 66211
Victor Goulet, President

Description of Operation: Electronic Realty Associates, Inc. (ERA), is a membership organization for licensed real estate brokerage firms offering its services and programs for use by its members. ERA grants the use of its registered trademarks and service marks and designs, logos, colors and color patterns, and business methods to its members to promote identification with the products and marketing services of ERA and to permit coordination of advertising programs. ERA members participate in a national referral program, a national advertising program, an equity advance program, and a national residential service contract program. ERA services also include advertising materials, training programs, and management and educational programs for the members' real estate brokerage operations. ERA is the exclusive corporate sponsor from the real estate industry of the Muscular Dystrophy Association (MDA).

Number of Franchisees: Approximately 2,700 franchisees operating from approximately 3,000 offices in the United States, Australia, Guam, Singapore, and Japan as of March 1990.

In Business Since: 1971, and is now a wholly owned subsidiary of ERA Financial Corporation.

Equity Capital Needed: The initial franchise membership fee is $18,900 plus $690 for each branch office. If paid in a lump sum, the initial fee is $16,900 plus $1,690 for each branch office.

Financial Assistance Available: ERA does have a financial assistance program to aid new members in the payment of the initital membership fees. New members who qualify may, upon payment of $5,000, finance $1,300 by payment of $3,500 within 60 days, $3,500 within 90 days, and $6,000 within 120 days. Other financing arrangements may be available from time to time, at the sole option of ERA.

Training Provided: A new member must participate in an orientation training program to familiarize the broker with the ERA services and programs. Other training programs believed by ERA to be beneficial to members and to be important for the full and effective implementation of the ERA system are available.

Managerial Assistance Available: ERA provides continuing management service to members in many areas including training, advertising, insurance, and residential service contract administration. Complete manuals of operations, forms, and directions are provided. ERA representatives are available in all regions to work closely with members and to assist in problem solving. ERA sponsors brokers' councils in each locality and conducts marketing and product research to maintain high ERA consumer acceptance.

Information Submitted: April 1990

GALLERY OF HOMES, INC.
201 South Orange Avenue
Orlando, Florida 32801
Gil DeHamer, Vice President,
National Sales Director

Description of Operation: Gallery of Homes, Inc., franchises existing experienced real estate brokers of good reputation and proven ability and provides national image, referral services, home warranty, recruiting, training and education, national advertising, corporate relocation and in-field service assistance in return for fees as specified in the agreement. Preference is given to brokers with membership in professional real estate organizations. Standards are high. Applicants should contact headquarters' office for information.

Number of Franchisees: 251 offices in the continental United States

In Business Since: 1950

Equity Capital Needed: An existing business plus $9,900.

Financial Assistance Available: Yes

Training Provided: A 4 day orientation program and staff assistance and participation of new franchisees in local council of franchisees. Additional professional courses (sales, management, fiscal control) available.

Managerial Assistance Available: In addition to the above manuals are provided that cover general Gallery of Homes techniques, office layout, referrals and corporate business leads, supplies, catalogues, image program, advertising format guide.

Information Submitted: April 1990

*HELP-U-SELL, INC.
57 West 200 South
Salt Lake City, Utah 84101
Carter Knapp

Description of Operation: Help-U-Sell is a merger of real estate marketing, counseling and traditional real estate. The Help-U-Sell marketing system generates hundreds of buyer and seller leads

for each office without canvassing, farming or holding open houses. The Help-U-Sell counseling method assists home buyers and sellers for a set fee instead of a percentage commission, payable at closing. Help-U-Sell franchisees are real estate brokers and membership in the local multiple listing service is required, where available. This concept provides more benefits to buyers, sellers, brokers and agents than does traditional real estate. It is ideally suited to the changing real estate market. For more information, call 1-800-669-4357 or 1-800-366-1177. Ask for a Franchise Specialist.

Number of Franchisees: 567 in 42 States and Canada

In Business Since: 1976

Equity Capital Needed: Franchise fee is $8,500 and up.

Financial Assistance Available: Terms may be aavailable.

Training Provided: 5 day intensive initial training at corporate headquarters in Salt Lake City. Ongoing support and training through a personal Operations Consultant and through *live* semi-monthly satellite broadcasts.

Managerial Assistance Available: Management consultant assigned to each office.

Information Submitted: May 1990

HER REAL ESTATE, INC.
4656 Executive Drive
Columbus, Ohio 43220
Eleanor B. Bailey, President

Description of Operation: A personalized approach to real estate franchising. The brokers keep their own identity as much as possible for marketing purposes. The identifying marks of the franchisor do not detract or dominate. Franchise owners enjoy "on-location" educational opportunities. Other traditional real estate benefits are offered: an exclusive territory, test-marketed award winning marketing tools and techniques, a superb support program through field representation, continuing education (also "on-location") and other unique educational opportunities.

Number of Franchisees: 35 company and franchised offices in Ohio.

In Business Since: In the real estate industry for over 30 years. Started offering franchises in August 1981.

Equity Capital Needed: Costs of conversion: yard signs, office sign, general office supplies plus the franchise fee. The franchise fees vary with the size and population of the exclusive territory. The minimum franchise fee is $6,900 plus $1,000 for each contiguous county.

Financial Assistance Available: None

Training Provided: Orientation, on-location—ongoing education, continuing education, regional and state-wide programs.

Managerial Assistance Available: The parent company, HER, Inc., is a source for management assistance with 18 managers, relocation division managers, marketing manager and director of career development—all full-time.

Information Submitted: April 1990

HOME MASTER REALTY, INC.
28444 Joy Road
Livonia, Michigan 48150
Christopher L. McDonald, President

Description of Operation: Home Master (a registered trademark) is the "2 percent solution" to satisfy the need of independent real estate brokers of having national name recognition but not siphoning the broker's profit margin for that advantage. State-wide master franchise offered to qualified real estate brokers with good track records in major cities.

Number of Franchisees: 3 in Michigan

In Business Since: 1977

Equity Capital Needed: Net worth of $20,000 for State-wide master franchises.

Financial Assistance Available: Local financing where applicable or terms available with franchisor.

Training Provided: Training for broker and sales associate where applicable.

Managerial Assistance Available: Management training where applicable.

Information Submitted: June 1990

HOMEOWNERS CONCEPT, INC.
3508 W. Galbraith Road
Cincinnati, Ohio 45239
Jeffrey C. Knab, President

Description of Operation: Alternative avenue in selling real estate. Homeowner shows own property and pays flat fee for professional real estate consulting. Homeowners Concept is a corporation in Ohio.

Number of Franchisees: 70 in 18 States

In Business Since: 1982

Equity Capital Needed: $25,000-$30,000—initial fee $9,000.

Financial Assistance Available: Neither the franchisor nor any affiliated persons offer direct or indirect financing to franchisees.

Training Provided: 14 hours on-the-job training.

Managerial Assistance Available: Continuous consulting from franchisor and periodic seminars.

Information Submitted: June 1990

HOMETREND, INC.
P. O. Box 6974
Suite 300
Denver, Colorado 80206

Description of Operation: Hometrend, Inc., is a second generatoin real estate franchisor. In addition to the usual services normally offered, we include a total business management and consulting service to broker-members through a district agent, allow our members to maintain their identity through 50/50 name participation, and provide an incentive service fee program rewarding greater performance. We also provide a computer and computer services as part of our franchise package.

Number of Franchisees: 82 in 8 States.

In Business Since: 1979, acquired by new owner in 1982.

Equity Capital Needed: Master $50,000, broker $12,500.

Financial Assistance Available: Total investment of $12,500 initial fee plus $300 for each branch office. In addition, a cost of approximately $1,500 to convert to our signs, etc. Financing available on an individual basis.

Training Provided: Intensive 2-3 day program to instruct district franchise agent in the operations and selling techniques in operating a franchise. Training conducted at home office in Denver. In addition, member-brokers receive extensive management and sales training through the district agent.

Managerial Assistance Available: Management training, consulting and servicing continues for the life of the district franchise agent and member-broker.

Information Submitted: May 1990

IOWA REALTY COMPANY, INC.
3501 Westown Parkway
West Des Moines, Iowa 50265
Jack McWilliams, Franchise Director

Description of Operation: Training, management assistance, name recognition, advertising insurance department securities. Allows smaller companies in small communities to have large company name recognition, market support materials and management expertise. National referral network offered as part of membership.

Number of Franchisees: 38 in Iowa (restricted to Iowa).

In Business Since: 1980

Equity Capital Needed: Member must be in the real estate business with offices open to the public. There is a franchise fee for membership.

Financial Assistance Available: Assistance in obtaining financing for customers through our local mortgage company and other local companies on purchase of real estate.

Training Provided: Ongoing monthly training for brokers and sales agents includes pre-license, post-license and continuing education classes and seminars.

Managerial Assistance Available: Technical assistance is offered for members through all our department managers and legal staff, including residential, commercial, and farm sales. Rental and property management, closing department securities sales and training department, pre-license and post-license training provided by our staff training department.

Information Submitted: June 1990

KEY ASSOCIATES, INC.
Highway 66, P. O. Box 495
Rockport, Indiana 47635
Donald R. Schulte, President

Description of Operation: Real estate.

Number of Franchisees: 65 in Indiana and Kentucky

In Business Since: 1977

Equity Capital Needed: $5,000

Financial Assistance Available: None

Training Provided: 4 days audio video training at cost.

Managerial Assistance Available: None

Information Submitted: April 1990

REAL ESTATE ONE LICENSING COMPANY
745 South Garfield Avenue
Traverse City, Michigan 49684
Gary L. Pownall, President

Description of Operation: Real Estate One Licensing Company franchises real estate brokers into a network using Real Estate One trademark properties, systems, training methods, and referral programs.

Number of Franchisees: 35 in Michigan

In Business Since: 1972

Equity Capital Needed: Franchise fee is $9,800.

Financial Assistance Available: Yes

Training Provided: Real Estate One provides ongoing seminars and training courses for both brokers and sales associates.

Managerial Assistance Available: In addition to training courses, Real Estate One provides management consultation by visits, telephone, franchise manuals, advertising aids, supplies and forms.

Information Submitted: June 1990

REALTY EXECUTIVES
4427 North 36th Street
Phoenix, Arizona 85018
William Powers, Marketing Director

Description of Operation: The original 100 percent commission concept in real estate. Realty Executives is designed to assist individuals and entities in the development of strong, multi-office companies operating general real estate brokerages using the Realty Executives 100 percent concept as the foundation.

Number of Franchisees: 82 offices in 22 States and 2 in Canada.

In Business Since: 1965

Equity Capital Needed: $15,000 initial fee. Will need minimum of $25,000 for working capital.

Financial Assistance Available: Yes

Training Provided: Intensive 2 day individual instruction, given by national staff, teaching new owners how to operate the Realty Executives 100 percent concept using methods with over 20 years of proven success. A comprehensive operations manual, coupled with the instant accessibility of a national staff, who also administer company-owned offices, provide ongoing assistance. New accounting software is available at additional expense.

Managerial Assistance Available: Unlimited consultation in proven successful accounting procedures, recruiting techniques, clerical hiring, and advertising methods is provided. National and regional meetings cover topics of vital interest to owners. Operation of national referral network and volume purchasing available to our brokers and associates.

Information Submitted: April 1990

REALTY 500
1539 Vassar Street
Suite 101
Reno, Nevada 89502

Description of Operation: A regional marketing program available to select real estate firms, with a variety of educational and functional programs designed to increase production and disseminate the most recent marketing and management methods to our member firms. Examples of programs are Brokers' Council, Quarterly Network meeting, management seminars and retreats. Initial and continual sales training and training aids and client presentation materials all provided at no additional cost to the member. Savings on operating materials (signs, brochures, business cards, stationery, promotional items, etc.) available through corporate volume purchase.

Number of Franchisees: 18 in Nevada

In Business Since: 1979

Equity Capital Needed: $4,500-$5,500

Financial Assistance Available: Yes

Training Provided: Extensive initial sales training for sales associates and management and management retreats are provided (at no charge to member firms).

Managerial Assistance Available: On-site management consultation provided to member firms from the corporate office. Management workshops, seminars, and retreats are also available.

Information Submitted: June 1990

REALTY WORLD CORPORATION
12500 Fair Lakes Circle
Suite 300
Fairfax, Virginia 22033
Jack M. Hoedeman, Senior Vice President

Description of Operation: Realty World Corporation is a full-service network that provides member broker/owners with an international name and image; outstanding ongoing local, regional and national training including courses approved as "equivalent" credit toward the National Association of Realtors® CRS® designation, an international relocation and referral system; a home protection plan; a national advertising and public relations program; errors and omissions insurance; group health insurance; local, regional, and international awards programs; and marketing assistance. Realty World Corporation serves local independent, affiliated broker/owners through its corporate headquarters in Fairfax, Virginia, 6 zone/region offices, and 19 training facilities and service centers across the United States. Franchises are available and information will be furnished on request.

Number of Franchisees: Some 1,800 in North America

In Business Since: 1974 in United States

Equity Capital Needed: No specific equity capital required since generally the franchisee is already engaged in the real estate business. Initial single office franchise fee ranges from $13,900 to $15,900 with lower fees for additional branch offices.

Financial Assistance Available: Yes

Training Provided: Training is supplied to the local franchisee, sales associates and administrative staff on an ongoing basis. Subjects include pre-license training; real estate listing, sales and marketing techniques; commercial real estate; corporate relocation; both introductory and advanced management practices; profitable business planning; financing; developing human potential and other specialized programs.

Managerial Assistance Available: An exclusive RealStart© management program for new broker/owners. Full-time trainers and business management consultants teach and provide ongoing counseling including a special Real Manager business development program. Broker councils in each area provide a communications link to corporate management. Special training is provided for new programs and products.

Information Submitted: May 1990

RED CARPET REAL ESTATE SERVICES, INC.
P. O. Box 85660
San Diego, California 92138
J. T. Morgan, Executive Vice President

Description of Operation: Red Carpet is the "oldest but newest" full service real estate franchise in the United States and Canada. Red Carpet originated real estate franchising in 1966 but has since updated almost every facet of its support and training. We offer a comprehensive training and support program; brokerage management through intensive training and our own computer software; regional and international marketing and television advertising, an international referral network of more than 3,000 affiliated offices; and entrepreneurial opportunities for franchise owners as well as the opportunity for master franchise ownership of geographic regions.

Number of Franchisees: 500 in 21 States in the United States and in Canada.

In Business Since: 1966

Equity Capital Needed: $12,900 initial franchise fee; capital needed varies.

Financial Assistance Available: 50 percent down, financing balance for up to 2 years.

Training Provided: Regional and international training programs for sales representative, manager and broker/owner; training held on an ongoing basis; self-help tapes through advanced training for experienced salespeople.

Managerial Assistance Available: Series of international and regional management training courses backed by management computer software system. Ongoing broker services assistance to aid in recruiting, selecting, training, motivating and managing sales representatives.

Information Submitted: April 1990

RE/MAX INTERNATIONAL
P. O. Box 3907
Englewood, Colorado 80155
Daryl Jesperson, Senior Vice President, Operations

Description of Operation: RE/MAX is an international real estate franchise network. The franchise offered is set up to allow sales associates who join a RE/MAX franchise to receive the highest possible compensation in return for sharing common overhead expenses and certain other fees. RE/MAX offers to its franchisees training programs, a full service relocation company, an R.E.O. (asset management) company, an international insurance franchising outlet, awards banquets, a referral network, advertising research, company publications, educational seminars and an annual convention.

Number of Franchisees: 1,671 opened offices in 49 States and all Canadian Provinces.

In Business Since: 1973

Equity Capital Needed: $15,000 to $25,000 (varies from region to region).

Financial Assistance Available: RE/MAX International provides no financial assistance.

238

Training Provided: Mandatory attendance at the 5 day course in Denver. The course covers tested techniques directed toward the successful implementation of the concept. From organizational establishment and development to retention and recognition: all are examples of course content and the optional semi-annual executive level seminars. In-depth individual management consulting and technical assistance are available upon request.

Managerial Assistance Available: Ongoing consulting services and managerial guidance are provided on a regular basis to all individuals within the system. Each broker-owner is contacted individually through the regional director network to discuss his/her development and any encountered problems. Regional directors are strategically located throughout the United States and Canada and, along with their staff, provide on-site assistance needed by the franchisees. Broker-owner councils and sales advisory councils are developed within each area and provide continuity of effort and consistency in operations throughout the organization.

Information Submitted: April 1990

RENTAL SOLUTIONS, INC.
273 West 500 South, Suite 21
Bountiful, Utah 84010

Description of Operation: Real estate support services assisting in the development of rental, commercial, investment, and property management real estate profit centers for brokerage operations. Use of a "Rental MLS" and "The Associated Commercial Brokers Clearing House" as formats for business growth.

Number of Franchisees: 6 in 5 States

In Business Since: 1983

Equity Capital Needed: $10,000 to $30,000

Financial Assistance Available: Terms available for franchise purchase.

Training Provided: 5 days at headquarters, and 3 annual mandatory symposiums. On-site as available and appropriate.

Managerial Assistance Available: Ongoing support for all aspects of Rental Solutions programs and systems.

Information Submitted: April 1990

STATE WIDE REAL ESTATE, INC.
P. O. Box 297
Escanaba, Michigan 49829-0297

Description of Operation: State Wide Real Estate, Inc., is a national network providing full service real estate franchises to independent real estate brokerage. State Wide provides marketing programs, education systems, full range creative advertising techniques, sales aids, referral programs, monthly and annual sales awards programs, and staff assistance to qualified franchisees. The National Association of Realtors Real Estate residential success series course is integral part of education.

There are two types of franchises available:

1. Master Franchise: Available in selected large areas (States or larger), on a partnership basis with the home office.

2. Office Franchise: Available from the Master franchisee or State Wide Real Estate, Inc., depending on the area in which the franchise will be operated.

Number of Franchisees: 110 throughout Michigan and Wisconsin.

In Business Since: 1944

Equity Capital Needed: $10,000 to $20,000

Financial Assistance Available: State Wide Real Estate, Inc., does not directly provide financial assistance for new franchisees, but will assist the franchisee to locate sources of financial assistance.

Training Provided: All new brokers and sales associates are required to attend a 3 day orientation within 6 months of joining State Wide Real Estate, Inc. Seminars and courses are offered throughout each year on a regional basis. Courses taught in the past include: "Getting Listings Is the Name of the Game," "Legal Awareness and Pitfalls," "Residential Taxation," "Property and Investment Analysis," "Keys to Successful Real Estate Sales," "Business Opportunities," "How to Obtain Commercial Listings," "Agricultural Brokerage," "Tax Planning," and "Nuts and Bolts of Real Estate Financing."

Managerial Assistance Available: In addition to training courses, State Wide Real Estate, Inc., maintains a full corporate staff for consultation by telephone, franchise manuals, a full library of tapes and books, advertising aids provided on a monthly basis, and supplies and forms.

Information Submitted: June 1990

RECREATION/ENTERTAINMENT/ TRAVEL—SERVICES/SUPPLIES

*ASK MR. FOSTER ASSOCIATES, INC.
7833 Haskell Avenue
Van Nuys, California 91406
Kelly Nelson, Chief Operating Officer

Description of Operation: Licensing opportunities to established travel agencies in geographical areas not presently covered by Ask Mr. Foster's 500 plus owned and operated branch offices.

Number of Franchisees: 500 plus in 50 States

In Business Since: 1984 (parent company since 1888)

Equity Capital Needed: None

Financial Assistance Available: None

Training Provided: Initial orientation and ongoing consultation; specific training programs available.

Managerial Assistance Available: Licensee ("Associate") becomes a part of the Ask Mr. Foster branch network and thereby participates in all company marketing programs and proprietary service systems. Licensees have a dedicated company staff to assist them in using company programs to their fullest.

Information Submitted: April 1990

BATTING RANGE PRO
5954 Brainerd Road
Chattanooga, Tennessee 37421-3598
E. K. Magrath, Jr.

Description of Operation: Indoor and outdoor batting ranges with 6 to 9 JUGS Coin Operated Pneumatic Tire, Variable Speed, Baseball and Softball Pitching Machines. A ball is pitched every 6 seconds at a charge of $1.00 for 15 to 20 balls.

Number of Franchisees: 95 in 26 States

In Business Since: 1979

Equity Capital Needed: $45,000 to $90,000, depending on the number of baseball pitching machines installed.

Financial Assistance Available: None

Training Provided: Complete operational kit is provided to instruct operators that will cover most questions asked.

Managerial Assistance Available: Site selection advice, complete batting range construction plans available, assistance in construction planning.

Information Submitted: April 1990

CHAMPIONSHIP MINIATURE GOLF
CMG FRANCHISE SYSTEMS, INC.
P. O. Box 10287
State College, Pennsylvania 16805
Kevin M. Ream, President

Description of Operation: Elaborate miniature golf facilities incorporating beautiful landscaping, boulder mountains, spectacular water features (fountains, waterfalls and streams), realistic challenging hole designs (sandtraps, water hazards, jumps and chutes), 18 or 36 holes with clubhouse and video game room and snack bar.

Number of Franchisees: 6 and 7 independent facilities.

In Business Since: 1984, franchising since 1987

Equity Capital Needed: $150,000 including $5,000 franchise fee.

Financial Assistance Available: None

Training Provided: 3 days training. Training program held at franchisee's facility.

Managerial Assistance Available: Complete design, training course.

Information Submitted: April 1990

CINEMA 'N' DRAFTHOUSE, INC.
2204 North Druid Hills Road
Atlanta, Georgia 30329
John J. Duffy, Owner/Franchise Director

Description of Operation: Motion picture theatres designed in an art deco lounge atmosphere that provides pizza, beer, wine and deli-type food, in addition to being a multi-media facility for seminars and teleconferencing.

Number of Franchisees: 41 in 16 States

In Business Since: 1975

Equity Capital Needed: $15,000 franchise fee, 3 percent royalty fee.

Financial Assistance Available: None

Training Provided: Projection, operation in theatre, bar and restaurant management—2 weeks initial and ongoing refresher courses.

Managerial Assistance Available: Continuous operational assistance in problem solving and promotional direction. Franchisor provides booking service for obtaining films on a weekly basis.

Information Submitted: May 1990

CLUB NAUTICO
5450 NW 33rd Avenue
Suite 106
Fort Lauderdale, Florida 33309
Nino Martini, President

Description of Operation: Powerboat rental operation and boating club. Franchisee maintains a fleet of powerboats and markets club memberships. Members receive preferential rates at all Club Nautico Powerboat Rental Centers.

Number of Franchisees: 62 in 14 States and the Caribbean plus 11 company-owned.

In Business Since: 1986

Equity Capital Needed: $80,000-$120,000

Financial Assistance Available: Equipment leasing.

Training Provided: Pre-opening training and continuing field training.

Managerial Assistance Available: Yes

Information Submitted: April 1990

COMPLETE MUSIC
8317 Cass Street
Omaha, Nebraska 68114
G. E. Maas, President

Description of Operation: Complete Music is the leader in disc jockey entertainment, providing dance music for over 1,000,000 people each year. The uniqueness of this business allows owners, who need not be entertainers, to use their skills in management to hire and book their own Complete Music trained D.J.s for all types of special events.

Number of Franchisees: 76 franchises covering 22 States, plus 1 company-owned location.

In Business Since: 1974, franchising since 1982

Equity Capital Needed: $13,000 for franchise fee, training, materials and supplies. $2,500-$8,000 for lighting and sound equipment.

Financial Assistance Available: Partial assistance available.

Training Provided: Franchisor trains and educates franchisee for 10 days at their home office. During this time, business is generated for the new franchise. Four days of training in franchisee's city is also included.

Managerial Assistance Available: Annual visit to franchisee location plus annual owners' meeting. Video training tapes and manuals are all provided as well as 24 hour access to the franchise office for ongoing support.

Information Submitted: April 1990

CORNER POCKETS OF AMERICA, INC.
P. O. Box 20878
Billings, Montana 59104
George Frank, President

Description of Operation: National franchisor of Doc & Eddy's featuring a restaurant/entertainment concept which includes a "sunny" solarium, casual dining, elevated cocktail lounge, big screen TV, sunken billiard area, darts, custom music system and video dancing featuring Top 40 and modern country music.

Number of Franchisees: 15 in 12 States

In Business Since: 1973

Equity Capital Needed: $75,000-$100,000 with satisfactory financial background.

Financial Assistance Available: None

Training Provided: Approximately 2 weeks of formal training at the corporate office and on-the-job training when the facility is opened.

Managerial Assistance Available: Managerial and technical assistance provided on a continuing basis. Tournament and league organizations and intermittent pocket billiard exhibitions. Pre-designed plans and specifications for standard building, assistance in site selection, construction, opening and grand opening.

Information Submitted: June 1990

CRUISE HOLIDAYS INTERNATIONAL, INC.
4740 Murphy Canyon Road
Suite 200
San Diego, California 92123
David Pava, Vice President, Franchise Marketing

Description of Operation: North America's largest franchisor of cruise-only travel agencies. Complete start-up assistance, use of proprietary software, national advertising and marketing support. Franchisor negotiates volume discounts with major cruise lines. A perfect opportunity in the most profitable segment of the travel industry.

Number of Franchisees: 84 in 21 States and 2 Canadian Provinces.

In Business Since: 1984

Equity Capital Needed: $25,000 franchise fee, $20,000 start-up expenses, and $30,000 working capital, total $75,000.

Financial Assistance Available: None

Training Provided: 2 weeks, conducted in selected port cities nationally, includes ship inspections and cruise.

Managerial Assistance Available: Cruise Holidays provides ongoing management consulting, cruise line negotiation and advisory services. Manuals, forms, data control systems and inventory control guidance are provided. Centralized purchasing of printing supplies is available. Advertising on a regional basis is coordinated by the corporate office.

Information Submitted: April 1990

CRUISE OF A LIFETIME
USA FRANCHISE CORPORATION
237 Park Avenue, 21st Floor
New York, New York 10017
Emilie Galli Zilnicki, Chairman & Founder

Description of Operation: CRUISE OF A LIFETIME USA is a home-based franchise offered on an exclusive county basis. As a franchisee you earn 8 percent (4 percent cash and 4 percent cruise credit) on all topline cruises/products sold from your exclusive county regardless of whether you referred the client, therefore eliminating any payment problems. You are provided with a fax/copier, portable display, camcorder, video library, business cards, letterhead, cruise vacation benefits and your own personalized quarterly magazine. The greatest attributes are that all you have to do is softsell/refer your clients to our national sales center—our specialists will professionally custom-tailor the cruises for your clients.

Number of Franchisees: 7

In Business Since: 1988

Equity Capital Needed: Start-up capital required: $500 to $1,500 depending on market.

Financial Assistance Available: 85 percent financing available offering a low down payment of $1,185.

Training Provided: 1 week classroom training at corporate headquarters and minimum weekend on-board cruise familiarization training.

Managerial Assistance Available: Turnkey support system including national reservation and sales center staffed with highly skilled cruise specialists; national and local advertising campaigns.

Information Submitted: April 1990

CRUISE SHOPPES AMERICA, LTD.
115 Metairie Road
Suite E
Metairie, Louisiana 70005
Bill Worden, CTC/Admiral
Gary P. Brown, Vice Admiral/Franchise
& Associate Development

Description of Operation: Franchisor of cruise-only travel agencies offering initial entry and associate programs for existing travel agencies. Each location is approximately 1,000 square feet with designated motif.

Number of Franchisees: 28 in 15 States

In Business Since: 1985

Equity Capital Needed: Entry level $22,500.

Financial Assistance Available: A total investment of between $87,000 and $93,000 (including working capital) is needed. Some financing available through franchisor.

Training Provided: Intensive 7 day home office training for owner and personnel. Additional on-site training as well as seminars, ship inspections and familiarization cruises.

Managerial Assistance Available: C.S.A. provides continuous managerial services, including marketing and promotional support through its Marketing Center in New Orleans, Louisiana. In addition C.S.A. provides complete operational, sales and marketing manuals.

Information Submitted: April 1990

CRUISES ONLY, INC.
100 First Street
Suite 105
Pittsburgh, Pennsylvania 15222
Gail E. Cortese, President

Description of Operation: Cruises Only, Inc., are retail cruise centers that are service-oriented establishments devoted solely to the sale of retail cruise packages, cruise travel arrangements and other related services. This is an adult market of people in the middle and upper income brackets. A cruise center generally requires 550 square feet of usable commercial space.

Number of Franchisees: 3 in Pennsylvania and Ohio

In Business Since: 1985

Equity Capital Needed: Minimum $15,000

Financial Assistance Available: Minimum total investment of $43,300 is sufficient to open a franchise center. The initial down payment is used to defray expenses for assistance, training and supervision; legal and accounting services; compliance fees; general and administrative expenses; and selling and promotional expenses prior to franchise opening.

Training Provided: The franchisor requires the successful completion of 5 days administrative training for owners and managers, 8 days of sales training and office procedures for sales personnel. Training program to take place at home office site prior to franchise opening.

Managerial Assistance Available: Continual management assistance in accounting, marketing and advertising will be provided throughout the franchise term, plus the updating of operational manuals and procedures together with product knowledge and trends. Also provided will be problem solving on-site assistance and supervision by company coordinators. The franchisor will schedule periodic product seminars and conferences.

Information Submitted: June 1990

EMPRESS TRAVEL FRANCHISE CORPORATION
450 Harmon Meadow Boulevard
P. O. Box 1568
Secaucus, New Jersey 07096-1568
Jack Cygielman, President

Description of Operation: Empress Travel offers a unique retail travel agency operation, in an existing, stimulating, year-round business that gives its participants great pleasure and financial reward. An Empress Travel franchise has full support and assistance at all times from management.

Number of Franchisees: 70 in New York, New Jersey, Connecticut, Pennsylvania, Washington, D.C., Maryland and Virginia.

In Business Since: 1957

Equity Capital Needed: $75,000, including working capital.

Financial Assistance Available: None

Training Provided: Training course for all new franchisees and their personnel at the home office and on-site at company offices; also computer training.

Managerial Assistance Available: Empress Travel provides continual management service with advertising, complete manuals of operations, forms, and directions, etc. Management works closely with franchisees and assists in solving all problems. Empress Travel sponsors meetings of franchisees and conducts marketing research to maintain high Empress Travel consumer acceptance.

Information Submitted: May 1990

FUGAZY INTERNATIONAL FRANCHISE CORP.
555 Madison Avenue
New York, New York 10022
Joan Anderson, Director of Operations

Description of Operation: Full service travel agency.

Number of Franchisees: 42 in 15 States

In Business Since: 1970

Equity Capital Needed: $30,000 and up franchise fee plus $35,000-$40,000 working capital.

Financial Assistance Available: Yes

Training Provided: Fugazy will aid licensee in leasing and furnishing of a travel office, secure necessary approvals from IATA and ARC, and provide trained account executives to establish factors necessary in opening a fully appointed travel agency.

Managerial Assistance Available: Fugazy will assist licensee in recruitment of staff and provide personnel of licensee with training, marketing, sales and advertising handled through corporate office.

Information Submitted: June 1990

GO-KART TRACK SYSTEMS
5954 Brainerd Road
Chattanooga, Tennessee 37421-3598
Jay Grant

Description of Operation: 12 to 15 concession type go-karts that are rented for a 4 to 5 minute ride on approximately 800 foot curved track at a speed of 18-20 mph.

Number of Franchisees: 82 in 20 States

In Business Since: 1972

Equity Capital Needed: $45,000-$70,000

Financial Assistance Available: None

Training Provided: Training on-the-job until operator is completely satisfied he can handle the job. Manager's manual will cover most questions that come up.

Managerial Assistance Available: Site selection, complete track and building layout, and construction planning.

Information Submitted: April 1990

GOLF PLAYERS, INC.
5954 Brainerd Road
Chattanooga, Tennessee 37421
Earl Magrath, President

Description of Operation: Miniature golf courses with very large, colorful, and distinctive figures and caricatures—some animated. Operation under the name Sir Goony Golf.

Number of Franchisees: 49 in 12 States

In Business Since: 1964

Equity Capital Needed: $36,800

Financial Assistance Available: None

Training Provided: Training at home office and on-the-job. Continuing help by personal visits, newsletters and phone calls. A complete operational manager's manual is provided.

Managerial Assistance Available: Course design and construction planning, continuing management service and advice.

Information Submitted: April 1990

GOLF USA
1801 South Broadway
Edmond, OK 73013
Jim Gould, Franchise/Marketing Director

Description of Operation: GOLF USA markets retail golf franchises for individual ownership. Specializing in quality golf equipment, clothing, accessories, supplies and services.

Number of Franchisees: 41 franchises and 39 licensed stores.

In Business Since: 1986

Equity Capital Needed: $75,000 to $150,000

Financial Assistance Available: None

Training Provided: A 1 week training class is mandatory prior to store opening. Classes are held in a workshop type setting and include guest speakers from major manufacturers. Complete computer training and observation of our model stores operations.

Managerial Assistance Available: GOLF USA store operations representative will be on-site with you for approximately 4 days in connection with your store opening. Representative will provide aditional training for franchisee and his staff.

Information Submitted: April 1990

GRAND SLAM USA ACADEMY
115 Post Street
Santa Cruz, Oregon 95060
David Shepard, Franchise Coordinator

Description of Operation: Grand Slam USA Baseball/Softball Academies. Completely automatic batting cages. Instruction in such aspects as hitting, fielding, pitching, etc. Machines are coin or token operated. Will throw baseballs or softballs at push of a button. Pro Shop.

Number of Franchisees: 83 in 32 States

In Business Since: 1976

Equity Capital Needed: $150,000

Financial Assistance Available: None

Training Provided: 3 day training at home office in marketing, business, operations, and technical is mandatory. Complete detailed operations manual given to each trainee.

Managerial Assistance Available: Ongoing with field reps calling on franchisees every 6-8 weeks.

Information Submitted: April 1990

HARTLEY VACATION CENTERS, INC.
508 Reservoir Avenue
Cranston, Rhode Island 02910
Andrew J. Acciaioli, President

Description of Operation: Retail tour operator and vacation and cruise packager.

Number of Franchisees: 5 franchised locations and 5 company-owned locations in Connecticut, Massachusetts and Rhode Island.

In Business Since: 1983

Equity Capital Needed: $30,000-$100,000 depending on location and population served.

Financial Assistance Available: None

Training Provided: 2 weeks: 1 week at an existing Harley Vacation Center and 1 week in new franchisee's unit.

Management Assistance Available: New franchisees are provided with two confidential operations manuals: "Pre-Opening Manual" and "Post-Opening Manual." We also offer continuous management contact and support plus access to our inhouse advertising and marketing firm.

Information Submitted: April 1990

INTERNATIONAL TOURS, INC.
2840 East 51st Street
Second Floor
Tulsa, Oklahoma 74105
Roger H. Jared, Director - Franchise Sales

Description of Operation: The company represents itself as the oldest franchisor of travel agencies in the United States and offers two types of franchises: (1) for new agencies, and (2) for conversion of established agencies. The new start-up franchise package includes 35 key points, i.e., site selection, selection of office manager, bookkeeping system, office forms, operations manuals, open house assistance, budget assistance, advertising and marketing plans, national meetings and seminars, study trips, and representation through a franchisee member Advisory Council. International Travel Institute, a travel agent training school, offers basic knowledge courses for new franchisees and their employees. The school is a subsidiary of the company, and is located in Houston, Texas.

Number of Franchisees: 338 in 42 States

In Business Since: 1970

Equity Capital Needed: $61,000-$131,000

Financial Assistance Available: None

Training Provided: 3 day training session for the owner at the corporate office; 3 day training session for the manager at the corporate office; 7 days on-site management assistance and inhouse training; regional training seminars; national meetings.

Managerial Assistance Available: Complete set of operations manuals for operation of a travel agency; company-owned travel agent training school available for franchisees and their employees; prepare franchisees' applications for conference appointments; find qualified and experienced manager to be employed by franchisee; assist with franchisee's grand opening and advertising plans; availability of 800 number technical assistance program; provide qualified regional directors for on-site and telephone consultation.

LOMMA MINIATURE GOLF
1120 South Washington Avenue
Scranton, Pennsylvania 18505
Gary Knight, Executive Vice President

Description of Operation: The Lomma Miniature Golf Company, the world's oldest and largest designer and builder of miniature golf courses, offers a dynamic non-commodity, easily run, high cash flow recreational business. The modular golf courses are designed for maximum flexibility of layout and the portability allows usage indoors and outdoors for year round revenue.

Number of Franchisees: 5,108 in 50 States and 15 countries around the world.

In Business Since: 1960

Equity Capital Needed: $5,900

Financial Assistance Available: As little as 10 percent down payment is needed and the balance payable up to 5 years. Complete and concise free franchise program with no franchise or royalty fees to pay.

Training Provided: We conduct seminars at our offices for small groups and/or regionally at your location.

Managerial Assistance Available: We supply a detailed manager's guide and operating manual.

Information Submitted: April 1990

MINI-GOLF, INC.
202 Bridge Street
Jessup, Pennsylvania 18434
Joseph J. Rogari, Director of Marketing

Description of Operation: The world's largest builder of pre-fab miniature golf courses. Company's owners have almost 70 years experience in miniature golf. Each operator gets a layout to scale tailor-made for their area. Courses are designed for an unlimited clientele with very animated, moving, flashing, and challenging obstacles. Easy to set up outdoors or indoors. Theme courses available. Courses shipped within 5 days. High cash flow, non-commodity, easy business to run.

Number of Franchisees: 957 in 50 States in 11 countries.

In Business Since: 1981

Equity Capital Needed: $4,000-$19,900

Financial Assistance Available: Cash plan: 10 percent discount; financing: 35 to 50 percent down with 2 years remaining on balance.

Training Provided: Training sessions conducted at home office. Weekends also available.

Managerial Assistance Available: Extensive operator's manual with press releases, promotions, parties, and major tournaments. Support includes periodic follow-up after installation.

Information Submitted: April 1990

PAY N PLAY RACQUETBALL OF AMERICA
23165 Vista Way
Eltoro, California 92630
Charles L. Hohl, President

Description of Operation: Pay N Play Racquetball of America builds convenient, low cost automated racquetball/handball/tennis practice centers that are open to the public 24 hours per day in most locations. There are no memberships, monthly dues, or reservations. Players purchase the amount of court time they want using the automated dollar bill acceptor at each center. Pay N Play provides the building/equipment on long-term lease to franchisees.

Number of Franchisees: 20 in California, Oregon and Washington.

In Business Since: 1978

Equity Capital Needed: $30,000-$60,000 investment.

Financial Assistance Available: Pay N Play Racquetball of America will assist the franchisee in obtaining financing.

Training Provided: An intensive 3 day mandatory training course is scheduled for all new franchisees. All training is conducted in Orange County, California.

Managerial Assistance Available: Pay N Play provides continual management service for the life of the franchise in areas of facility maintenance, advertising, marketing, programming, and bookkeeping. Field managers are available to work closely with franchisee to provide assistance. Pay N Play sponsors meetings of franchisees and conducts marketing and product research to maintain high Pay N Play consumer acceptance.

Information Submitted: April 1990

PUTT-PUTT GOLF COURSES OF AMERICA, INC.
P. O. Box 35237
Fayetteville, North Carolina 28303
Bobby Owens, National Franchise Director

Description of Operation: Franchised miniature golf facilities with standardization of color scheme, construction, and putting surface with elaborate themed courses as designed by Putt-Putt® Golf Courses of America, Inc. Also included are franchises for video game rooms and "Games To Go!"®, which is a video and games rental system operated from the gameroom clubhouse.

Number of Franchisees: Over 400 in 40 States, and 4 foreign countries.

In Business Since: 1954

Equity Capital Needed: $25,000 to $125,000

Financial Assistance Available: No financing provided by company; however, assistance in obtaining financing through banks and SBA is available.

Training Provided: 1 week annually at international convention. Five regional, 2-day seminars each year from March 1st through July 1st. On-site training is available any time at no additional charge from the national training director.

Managerial Assistance Available: Complete computer accounting. Complete manager's manual. Complete promotional program provided including radio, TV, and newspaper advertising, etc., for the duration of the length of the contract.

Information Submitted: April 1990

PUTT-R-GOLF, INC. - SGD COMPANY
Box 5445
Akron, Ohio 44313
Dennis McGregor

Description of Operation: Supply plans and equipment for family fun centers concentrating on miniature golf, baseball batting ranges, slo-pitch softball batting ranges.

Number of Franchisees: 8 in 3 States and Canada

In Business Since: 1952

Equity Capital Needed: $60,000 to $200,000

Financial Assistance Available: Plans, material lists and consulting.

Training Provided: Informal

Managerial Assistance Available: As needed basis.

Information Submitted: April 1990

TRAVEHOST AGENCIES, INC.
8080 North Central Expressway
14th Floor
Dallas, Texas 75206
Tamela Gustafson, Vice President

Description of Operation: Turnkey travel agency.

Number of Franchisees: 41

In Business Since: 1988

Equity Capital Needed: Total investment $60,000-$122,000.

Financial Assistance Available: WIll finance 50 percent of initial fee at prime rate.

Training Provided: Complete training program is provided.

Managerial Assistance Available: Managerial assistance provided in all areas of operating a travel agency.

Information Submitted: April 1990

*TRAVEL AGENTS INTERNATIONAL, INC.
111 Second Avenue, NE, 15th Floor
St. Petersburg, Florida 33731-8905
James A. Sahley, Senior Vice President

Description of Operation: Travel Agents International offers potential franchisees a retail, turnkey, full service travel agency. Travel Agents International's buying power and negotiations with suppliers help franchisees earn overrides and higher commissions.

Number of Franchisees: 353 in 39 States and Canada

In Business Since: 1980, franchising since 1982

Equity Capital Needed: $90,000-$100,000 includes franchise fee and first year working capital.

Financial Assistance Available: None

Training Provided: 3 week initital training program.

Managerial Assistance Available: Assistance provided during start-up, with site location, interior design, reservation system, and personnel. Ongoing support in management, personnel, operations, accounting and sales, and marketing for both corporate and leisure business.

Information Submitted: April 1990

TRAVEL ALL ENTERPRISES, CORP.
28 East Jackson
Suite 408
Chicago, Illinois 60604
Dr. Ibrahim Y. Elgindy, Franchise Manager

Description of Operation: Travel All/shipping all systems of unique and complete transportation services agency, travel, air cargo and freight forwarder on stages. Also offers much higher than normal incentive commissions on many international carriers and much lower cost on air cargo and ocean freight. Provide training, location selection, lease negotiation, assistance in licensing support in operation, cooperative advertising and assistance in marketing.

Number of Franchisees: 2 in Illinois

In Business Since: 1983

Equity Capital Needed: $65,000

Financial Assistance Available: A total investment of $65,000 is needed to open Travel All franchise. Travel may finance franchisee up to $25,000 depending on credit references of franchisee. Franchisee may provide his financing.

Training Provided: Franchisee shall have 2 weeks of training in Chicago, 1 week in Texas on Sabre computers. For travel, 2nd phase air cargo, franchisee will be trained in Chicago for 1 week ocean freight, franchisee will be trained in Chicago for 1 week.

Managerial Assistance Available: Travel provides continual management service for the life of the franchise in such areas as bookkeeping, accounting, marketing, advertising. Complete managing of operations.

Information Submitted: June 1990

TRAVEL BUDDY, INC.
P. O. Box 31146
Minneapolis, Minnesota 55431
Dona M. Risdall, Director of Franchising

Description of Operation: Travel Buddy is a national travel service, offering highly accredited travel Buddy/Assistants for seniors, children, and the slightly handicapped. The service is available to anyone, any age, traveling anywhere in the world.

Number of Franchisees: 8 in Florida, Colorado, Nevada and Arizona.

In Business Since: 1984

Equity Capital Needed: $500 franchise fee plus approximately $250 start-up cost if operating from a home office. Expenses for setting up office outside the home would depend on location and office.

Financial Assistance Available: None provided by franchisor.

Training Provided: A complete and comprehensive training manual is provided with step-by-step instructions to guide the franchisee through preparation, start-up and the operation of their Travel Buddy service. Free ongoing assistance is provided via telephone and correspondence, indefinitely. The staff of the franchisor will be providing a substantial amount of follow-up management support and quality service to franchisee. Franchisee has access to all Buddy files of franchisor.

Managerial Assistance Available: Assistance and supervision will be provided in the following ways: telephone, mail, newsletters, and as our franchise pool expands, seminars will be added to our training itinerary.

Information Submitted: April 1990

TRAVELPLEX INTERNATIONAL
655 Metro Place South
Suite 250
Dublin, Ohio 43017
Darryl Warner, C.E.O.
Scott Wise, Vice President

Description of Operation: Retail travel agency franchise, specializing in business and vacation travel arrangements. This unique franchise has been created by working agency owner-managers. A comprehensive training program is provided for all staff levels. TravelPlex International provides recruitment services and productive office procedures. Franchisees will receive sales and marketing programs designed to attract and maintain customers. Solid operational support provided and effective networking with member agencies.

Number of Franchisees: 9 in 3 States

In Business Since: 1989

Equity Capital Needed: Capital requirement is $70,000-$100,000 depending on location.

Financial Assistance Available: Assistance in obtaining bank financing for qualified applicants.

Training Provided: Consultation provided for site selection, financial and regulatory requirements, sales, marketing, equipment and supplies. Training furnished for agency owners and managers. Continuing assistance in advertising, training and operations.

Managerial Assistance Available: On-site training, office procedures and policies updates and product and service development seminars offered by TravelPlex International. Volume discounts available on supplies and promotional items. Continuing technical and sales support assistance provided.

Information Submitted: April 1990

TRAVEL PROFESSIONALS INTERNATIONAL, INC.
Suite 360
10172 Linn Station Road
Louisville, Kentucky 40223
James C. Vernon, President

Description of Operations: Travel Professionals International, Inc. (TPI) offers franchises to investors interested in establishing or converting travel agencies. TPI services include high-volume negotiations, marketing services and materials, information processing, training, and proprietary travel packages for agency use.

Number of Franchisees: 40 in 16 States

In Business Since: 1983

Equity Capital Needed: $98,700

Financial Assistance Available: None

Training Provided: Managers quarterly, bookkeeping as needed—2 days; outside sales as needed—2 days; owners included in all of the above. Travel Professionals conducts a continuing education program for all franchise employees under the auspices of Dr. Bernard Strenecky, Ph.D.

Managerial Assistance Available: TPI develops all advertising materials, TV, radio, and print for franchisees. TPI provides on-site corporate sales, incentives, and group assistance. In the case of a new agency TPI provides hands on assistance in office development, hiring, bookkeeping, office layouts, and procedures.

Information Submitted: April 1990

TRAVEL FRANCHISE SYSTEM
4350 La Jolla Village Drive
San Diego, California 92122
James W. Hill, President

Description of Operation: An association of independently owned and operated travel agencies located throughout the entire United States, receiving assistance and support through our centralized marketing, advertising, operations, accounting services, training, program, interior design package, and signage.

Number of Franchisees: 104 located throughout the United States.

In Business Since: 1979—merged with TravelMate Corporation in June 1983.

Equity Capital Needed: $77,000, fee included.

Financial Assistance Available: Assistance in securing outside financing.

Training Provided: 1 week of intensive training for owner and manager is provided. Ongoing training provided by field operations staff.

Managerial Assistance Available: Assistance is provided during start-up and on a continuous basis in the areas of management, personnel, agency operations, tour packaging and business account development.

Information Submitted: June 1990

*UNIGLOBE TRAVEL (INTERNATIONAL), INC.
1199 West Pender Street
Suite 900
Vancouver, British Columbia
Canada V6E 2R1
Michael Levy, Senior Vice President

Description of Operation: Uniglobe International is the master franchisor for the Uniglobe system, which is #1 in travel franchising and one of the Top Four travel organizations in North America. Uniglobe is designed to build the profitability of new and existing independent travel agencies. Uniglobe agencies benefit from a common image, professional training, business development assistance and ongoing support services. Uniglobe International has 19 of its 20 regions in operation in less than a 6 year period.

Being a Uniglobe franchisee entitles you to a vast array of services such as national TV advertising, brand image, profitability software programs, ongoing business consultation, one-on-one agency visits for business development counseling, owners and managers meetings, preferred override programs, plus hundreds of hours of training. These services are coupled with the fact that 200 staff members service the 520 plus independently owned and operated agencies. All resources of the regional offices are available to the franchisee.

Number of Franchisees: Over 800 in USA and Canada.

In Business Since: 1980

Equity Capital Needed: Start-up agency $125,000, includes franchise fee and working capital. Conversion agency $25,000, includes franchise fee, leasehold improvements and signage.

Financial Assistance Available: Depends on region.

Training Provided: Uniglobe provides ongoing training both at the international headquarters and in each region. This consists of approximately 100 days per month of continual training courses for its owners, managers and consultants. Certain courses are mandatory for the owners and managers.

Managerial Assistance Available: The Uniglobe business development department works closely with agencies assisting, coaching and supporting new business development—much like an exclusive management consulting service. The department is made up of seasoned travel professionals whose only goal is to help the franchisee become more successful.

Information Submitted: June 1990

RETAILING—ART SUPPLIES/FRAMES

ART MANAGEMENT SERVICES, INC.
Franchisor of the KOENIG ART EMPORIUMS
265 Old Gate Lane
Milford, Connecticut 06460

Description of Operation: Koenig Art Emporiums are retail artists', drafting supply, picture frame stores selling to the creative person, amateur, professional, hobbyist, and the general public. Each Emporium's merchandise has a broad appeal to the general public through items such as fine writing instruments, framed posters and custom framing. Inventory is complemented by a full line catalogue. Average store size is 2,000 square feet.

Number of Franchisees: 86 in 21 States plus 30 company-owned stores.

In Business Since: 1933 (started franchising 1979).

Equity Capital Needed: Start-up franchises require a minimum cash investment of $50,000.

Financial Assistance Available: The total investment for a Koenig Art Emporium franchise is approximately $175,000-$225,000; included in the total investment is a franchise fee of $25,000. A.M.S. offers no financing arrangements directly to the franchisee, but will assist prospective franchisees with obtaining suitable financing from established lending institutions.

Training Provided: Training is of a minimum of 2 weeks' duration at A.M.S. headquarters, and will include familiarization with merchandise and its application, operating systems, do-it-yourself and custom picture framing techniques, computer reports, etc. In addition the franchisee will gain experience in store operations at an existing Koenig Art Emporium. Finally, A.M.S. will have a field representative on-site prior to and at the time of opening to instruct and assist the franchisee.

Managerial Assistance Available: A.M.S. provides a unique computerized inventory control system by interfacing its computer with the franchisee electric cash register. The computer will monitor inventory movement, generating orders automatically for timely stock replacement while providing meaningful reports to A.M.S. and the franchisee. A.M.S. also serves the franchisee as a continuing source of expertise in all facets of the store operation. The franchisee will also receive operations and employee manuals necessary for effective store procedures. A.M.S. will also offer advice with regard to the efficient and economical operation of the franchising Koenig Art Emporium.

Information Submitted: April 1990

CREATIVE WORLD MANAGEMENT SERVICES, INC.
13450 Farmington
Livonia, Michigan 48150
Dennis R. Kapp, President

Description of Operation: Retail art/drafting materials and equipment, custom framing and teach; painting classes.

Number of Franchisees: 5 in Michigan and Florida plus 11 company-owned.

In Business Since: 1946

Equity Capital Needed: $50,000 minimum investment

Financial Assistance Available: Will assist with bank presentation.

Training Provided: On location and classroom—30 days or as required.

Managerial Assistance Available: Site location, construction management, store design, product acquisition, advertising and on-site training and technical advisor for 3 weeks minimum.

Information Submitted: June 1990

*DECK THE WALLS
12450 Greenpoint Drive
Houston, Texas 77373
Steve Lowrey, Vice President

Description of Operation: Deck The Walls is the nation's largest chain of retail stores specializing in popularly priced prints, posters, frames and custom framing. Deck The Walls has tailored the art gallery concept to meet the tastes and needs of regional mall and shopping center shoppers. Many franchisees are involved in commercial art sales.

Number of Franchisees: 215 in 40 States plus 3 company-owned.

In Business Since: 1979

Equity Capital Needed: Cash and equity $150,000-$175,000

Financial Assistance Available: Will assist in seeking financing.

Training Provided: Extensive 10 day classroom training, including framing instruction, prepares franchisee for the daily operation of the store. Field staff continues training the franchisee and employees once the store is open, and ensures successful operation during the first critical weeks in business.

Managerial Assistance Available: Deck The Walls provides extensive assistance, including store construction specifications and plans; merchandise selection, pricing and visual presentation; national buying power; national and local marketing. Field staff make frequent store visits, supplemented by telecommunications, publications, regional meetings and an annual convention.

Information Submitted: June 1990

*FASTFRAME U.S.A., INC.
30495 Canwood Street
Agoura, California 91301
Mike Minihane, Vice President, Franchise Marketing

Description of Operation: High quality, custom picture framing and fine art sales.

Number of Franchisees: 106

In Business Since: 1987

Equity Capital Needed: Approximately $120,000

Financial Assistance Available: None

Training Provided: Complete training is provided.

Managerial Assistance Available: Continuous in all phases of operation.

Information Submitted: April 1990

FINE ART RENTALS FRANCHISING INC.
24321 La Hermosa
Laguna Niegel, California 92677

Description of Operation: Art work rented or leased to offices.

Number of Franchisees: 4

In Business Since: In business 31 years, started franchising 1987.

Equity Capital Needed: $30,000

Financial Assistance Available: None

Training Provided: 2 weeks full training program in all phases of operation.

Managerial Assistance Available: Provided on a continuing basis as needed.

Information Submitted: April 1990

FRAME AND SAVE
1126 Dixie Highway
Eranger, Kentucky 41018
Charles Karlosky, President

Description of Operation: Frame and Save offers to the public a "Do-It-Yourself and Custom Picture Framing Shop." Each store is approximately 1,600 square feet with a set-up of 8 individual working booths. Frame and Save has a line of quality moldings and mats.

Number of Franchisees: 40 in 7 States

In Business Since: 1973

Equity Capital Needed: $35,000

Financial Assistance Available: None

Training Provided: Intensive 2 weeks mandatory training course is scheduled for all new franchisees at one of our locations. This training involves learning the techniques of cutting and assembling molding, mats, glass, and conservation of valuable art work. Also, Frame and Save gives the franchisee one week of professional supervision at your location.

Managerial Assistance Available: Frame and Save provides continual contact with each individual franchisee with all update pricing and new techniques of the framing industry. District managers are available in all regions to work closely with the franchisees and visit the stores regularly to assist solving problems.

Information Submitted: June 1990

THE FRAMEWORKS FACTORY, INC.
190 Highway 18
East Brunswick, New Jersey 08816
Gary Nacht, President

Description of Operation: Retail custom picture framing shops and art galleries.

Number of Franchisees: 1 company-owned

In Business Since: 1989, franchising since 1990

Equity Capital Needed: $99,500-$115,600 total investment.

Financial Assistance Available: None

Training Provided: Complete training is provided.

Managerial Assistance Available: Continuous managerial assistance is provided.

Information Submitted: June 1990

FRAME WORLD
P. O. Box 762
Decatur, Alabama 35602
Ronald Clark, President

Description of Operation: Frame World picture frame stores are unique retail stores. We specialize in all phases of retail picture framing industry with emphasis on quality and volume.

Number of Franchisees: 5 in Alabama including 1 company-owned.

In Business Since: 1972

Equity Capital Needed: $32,500

Financial Assistance Available: None

Training Provided: 2 to 3 weeks in company-owned store, 2 to 3 weeks at franchisee store and assistance whenever needed.

Managerial Assistance Available: Managerial, technical and bookkeeping assistance provided in the above training period.

Information Submitted: May 1990

GRAPHICS GALLERY INTERNATIONAL FRANCHISE CORPORATION
219 Marine Avenue, P. O. Box J.J.
Balboa Island, California 92662
Rob Shively, Vice President

Description of Operation: Graphics Gallery is a marketing driven, full-service art and framing gallery franchise. We have developed a system that is designed to enhance our brand, ensure quality and consistency and ultimately to create and maintain customers. Our approach, our experience, our vision, our supplier discounts, our people and our success are unparalleled in this industry.

Number of Franchisees: 17

In Business Since: 1982

Equity Capital Needed: $30,000-$35,000

Financial Assistance Available: None

Training Provided: 7-10 days at corporate gallery featuring framing, design, purchasing, marketing and accounting; 7-10 days of intensive training in franchisee's gallery focusing on framing, operations and gallery systems.

Managerial Assistance Available: Assistance provided in framing, operations, purchasing, site location, lease negotiation, build out, accounting and ongoing field service.

Information Submitted: April 1990

*THE GREAT FRAME UP SYSTEMS, INC.
9335 Belmont Avenue
Franklin Park, Illinois 60131
Walter Wolnik, Director of Marketing

Description of Operation: Nation's largest do-it-yourself franchise frame shops; also include custom, commercial framing with art and preframed galleries.

Number of Franchisees: 110 in 25 States

In Business Since: 1975

Equity Capital Needed: $28,000-$33,000

Financial Assistance Available: Total investment is approximately $110,000 including a $19,500 franchise fee. The Great Frame Up will assist in obtaining suitable financing through SBA guaranteed loans or other institutions.

Training Provided: The training provides franchisee with complete working knowledge of framing techniques, customer service, business management and the Great Frame Up system. Hands-on, classroom and in-store training are part of the comprehensive program.

Managerial Assistance Available: In addition to site selection, design, layout and construction, the Great Frame Up provides advertising, field support and product, as well as vendor buying assistance, in addition to publications and an annual conference.

Information Submitted: April 1990

THE RINGGOLD CORPORATION
8705 Katy Freeway
Suite 105
Houston, Texas 77024
Thomas J. Devine, President

Description of Operation: The "frame factory" and "framing place" shops are retail picture framing and art shops. Each shop is designed to allow the customer to select how their "picture" is to be framed, and then to do all of the work themselves in the shop. The shop personnel cut and prepare all materials exactly as the customer chooses and then assist the customer in any way necessary to guarantee a professional job. All franchises offer custom framing.

Number of Franchisees: Approximately 100 in 28 States

In Business Since: 1971

Equity Capital Needed: Estimated maximum cost of $90,000. Equity of $30,000 required, balance financeable.

Financial Assistance Available: Assistance in arranging financing.

Training Provided: Not less than 3 weeks initially, 8 days immediately after the shop is opened. Regular seminars of shop owners are held for continuing education. Trade associations have regular local meetings and monthly periodicals.

Managerial Assistance Available: Managerial assistance is on a regular monthly basis. Technical assistance is provided on a group basis or when requested.

Information Submitted: June 1990

RETAILING—COMPUTER SALES/SERVICES

*CLASSIC CONFIGURATIONS, INC.
11011 South Wilcrest
Houston, Texas 77099
Glenn Kramer, President

Description of Operation: Full service retailer of microcomputers products and services.

Number of Franchisees: 4 plus 1 company-owned

In Business Since: 1987, franchising since 1989

Equity Capital Needed: $8,000-$121,000 total investment.

Financial Assistance Available: None

Training Provided: Training in operating a microcomputer retail store.

Managerial Assistance Available: Managerial assistance provided in all phases of operating a microcomputer retail center.

Information Submitted: June 1990

*COMPUTERLAND CORPORATION
5964 West Las Positas Boulevard
P. O. Box 9012
Pleasanton, California 94566-9012

Description of Operation: ComputerLand offers franchises for retail stores dealing in microcomputers, computer systems and related items, in a protected location, supported by marketing and purchasing services, under the name ComputerLand.

Number of Franchisees: 751 in 50 states and 30 countries.

In Business Since: 1976

Equity Capital Needed: $250,000 to $1,000,000, depending on market size and location.

Financial Assistance Available: Financing of franchise fee available to qualified applicants. Franchisor will assist franchisee in preparing a loan proposal package to present to a bank or other loaning institution.

Training Provided: There is an initial training program for franchisees. Subjects covered are product knowledge, sales training and management, accounting, merchandising, and general franchise operation management. Specific retail sales training classes are offered on an ongoing basis.

Managerial Assistance Available: Upon opening of the store, franchisor offers in-store aid. Franchisor develops advertising aids for the franchisee, makes available inventory for purchase by franchisee at cost and protects the ComputerLand name.

Information Submitted: April 1990

COMPUTERS UNLIMITED OF WISCONSIN
d/b/a COMPUTER BAY
4300 West Brown Deer Road
Suite 100
Milwaukee, Wisconsin 53223
Kailas Rao, President
Rob Howe, Director of Marketing and Communications
Susan Barber, Vice President of Finance

Description of Operation: Computers Unlimited of Wisconsin offers franchises of specialty retail computer centers and value-added resellers under the name Computer Bay. Computer Bay facilities offer business clients tailored solutions to their computing needs, through inside and outside sales consultants. Each center adds value to the products it sells with service and training support. IBM, Compaq, Hewlett-Packard, Epson and NEC.

Number of Franchisees: Over 100 locations in 26 States nationwide.

In Business Since: 1981

Equity Capital Needed: $100,000 liquid assets.

Financial Assistance Available: The franchisor does provide inventory financing programs assistance.

Training Provided: In addition to the training provided by each individual manufacturer, franchisor does provide a 1-day training program for its franchisees, at franchisor's corporate offices. Additional training is provided for those new franchisees who are brand new, start-up businesses.

Managerial Assistance Available: A complete and ongoing support program is provided for the duration of the franchise agreement in areas such as advertising, marketing, inventory management and distribution, forecasting, purchasing and information on new product announcements. Individual product marketing managers are available to work closely with franchisees at their locations.

Information Submitted: June 1990

CONNECTING POINT OF AMERICA, INC.
5240 South Quebec Street
Suite 300
Englewood, Colorado 80222
Peter Sherry

Description of Operation: The Connecting Point retail store is a single source for all computer hardware, software, training, and services.

Number of Franchisees: Over 300

In Business Since: 1982

Equity Capital Needed: At least $5,000 in liquid capital, plus $50,000 line of credit.

Financial Assistance Available: No direct financial assistance.

Training Provided: Customized sales and management training in all facets of store management, product knowledge, personnel management, inventory control, and sales techniques. All on-site.

Managerial Assistance Available: Pre-opening assistance includes site selection, lease negotiation, store design, construction management, staff recruitment, recommended inventory planning, and extensive training. Ongoing support includes monthly advertising and promotional planning, inventory recommendations, and new product awareness.

Information Submitted: June 1990

*INACOMP COMPUTER CENTERS
1800 West Maple Road
Troy, Michigan 48084
Richard Stopa, Vice President, National Franchising Department

Description of Operation: Inacomp Computer Centers are retailers of IBM, Apple and Compaq computers, and professional customer support services. Franchise stores are serviced by Regional Base/Distribution Centers that provide product and support programs to help franchisees maintain profitability and market control.

Number of Franchisees: 50 franchised outlets, 24 company-owned outlets, and 5 Regional Base/Distribution Centers.

In Business Since: 1976

Equity Capital Needed: Start-up investment required $215,000 to $300,000 plus approximately $100,000 in inventory (usually floorplanned).

Financial Assistance Available: No direct financial assistance. Floorplanning referrals only. We do provide leasing and credit programs for customer purchases.

Training Provided: Regional training centers provide the initial 2-week and ongoing owner/management team training in advertising, merchandising, market forecasting, staff productivity, and customer support services, as well as the initial 2-week and ongoing staff training for sales/customer management, consultation analysis, product knowledge, and technical proficiency.

Managerial Assistance Available: Regional Base/Distribution Centers provide localized franchise support programs for marketing, advertising, merchandising, inventory forecasting and staff training, and customer support programs for consultation and education, leasing and credit cards, technical support and product repair.

Information Submitted: April 1990

*INTELLIGENT ELECTRONICS, INC.
411 Eagleview Boulevard
Exton, Pennsylvania 19343
Joe de Simone, Franchise Development

Description of Operation: Intelligent Electronics is the parent franchisor for three chains of computer dealers: Connecting Point of America, Entre' Computer Centers, and Todays Computers Business Centers (TCBC). It is the largest network of computer dealers in North America.

Number of Franchisees: 850, in all States and throughout Canada.

In Business Since: 1982

Equity Capital Needed: Experienced dealers only, for conversion from independents, or purchase of available centers. Contact IE for more information.

Financial Assistance Available: None

Training Provided: Assistance in obtaining all authorizations and required staff training through manufacturers; headquarters orientation program.

Managerial Assistance Available: 1) Coordination of application for third party financing; 2) IE central electronic mail for ongoing PC product information; 3) IE technical support for on-demand product and installation support; 4) regional and conference meetings; 5) ongoing marketing programs and promotions; and 6) sales staff recruitment services.

Information Submitted: April 1990

*MICROAGE COMPUTER STORES, INC.
2308 South 55th Street
Tempe, Arizona 85282
Warren Mills

Description of Operation: A professional sales organization operation from a computer store front. Commercial quality service, support, hardware and software are offered for voice and data forecasting needs.

Number of Franchisees: 215 in the United States and worldwide.

In Business Since: 1980

Equity Capital Needed: Cash—$120,000-$140,000. Total investment—$275,000-$450,000 (includes above cash).

Financial Assistance Available: Franchisor does not make loans to franchisees. Extensive assistance is provided in the development by franchisee of a marketing and financial plan and bank presentation.

Training Provided: 2 weeks of training are provided prior to store opening. Ongoing training in the store as well as regional and home-office-located training is also provided.

Managerial Assistance Available: In-store sales, store management, marketing, product mix and business services support are provided on an ongoing basis. Software and hardware technical support are continually provided.

Information Submitted: June 1990

248

RICHARD YOUNG, INC.
508 S. Military Trail
Deerfield Beach, Florida 33442
Crawford Paton, Vice President, Franchise Sales

Description of Operation: The franchisor intends to offer franchises for the retail sale of computer accessories and supplies to businesses and individuals under the tradename Richard Young Products. A four color catalog will be used to help promote sales. Direct contact, telemarketing and customer mailings will be the main vehicles for selling product.

Number of Franchisees: 19 in continental United States and its territories.

In Business Since: 1985

Equity Capital Needed: Approximately $250,000.

Financial Assistance Available: In special cases the franchisor will consider financing up to one half of the franchise fee.

Training Provided: There will be a 1 week start-up training program followed by a 1 week on-site training and support program.

Managerial Assistance Available: Richard Young provides continual management service for the duration of the franchise agreement in such areas as sales advertising, inventory control, purchasing and product research. A complete operations and procedural manual will be provided to all franchisees. District managers are available to work closely with franchises at their locations.

Information Submitted: April 1990

SAC DISTRIBUTORS INTERNATIONAL, INC.
3491 Pall Mall Drive 101
Jacksonville, Florida 32257
Sarai Cook, Executive Vice President

Description of Operation: SAC Distributors franchises are regional value-added resellers of computer systems, peripherals, software, supplies, and data communications equipment. Drawing on its experience in the retail sector, SAC Distributors has been highly innovative in implementing marketing strategies that are unparalleled in the industry. However, more important than any individual program are the company's efforts to keep available to it an unprecedented variety of products to market at consistently competitive prices. This policy clearly aligns SAC Distributors' best interests with those of its customers by remaining responsive to industry changes and customer needs. In addition, we have computerized many of the marketing, office, and accounting procedures involved in running a SAC Distributors franchise.

Number of Franchisees: 4 in Florida and Georgia

In Business Since: 1985

Equity Capital Needed: $4000

Financial Assistance Available: An investment of $4000 is required to open a SAC Distributors franchise. This includes training, computer, software, working capital, franchisee fee, and the rights to a protected territory consisting of a 300,000 (approximately) population area.

Training Provided: We require all new franchisees to attend an intensive 2 week training program at our corporate office. Training includes business operations, product training, principles of selling, interfacing, and time management.

Managerial Assistance Available: SAC Distributors International, Inc., regularly provides franchisees with incentive programs and information on new vendors, marketing strategies, and management techniques. Negotiations with new and existing vendors are ongoing to ensure competitive pricing and service. An annual meeting is organized by SAC Distributors International, Inc., and on-site assistance at the franchisees' location is available.

Information Submitted: May 1990

*TODAYS COMPUTERS BUSINESS CENTERS
411 Eagleview Boulevard
Exton, Pennsylvania 19341
Mike Shabazian, President

Description of Operation: For already successful businesses that have an existing customer base and solid reputation under their own name, the opportunity to set up a "company within their company." A commercial and retail franchise for computers and other intelligent electronic products.

Number of Franchisees: 66 in 31 States

In Business Since: 1982

Equity Capital Needed: Approximately $105,000.

Financial Assistance Available: Franchisor will assist franchisee in preparing a loan proposal package to present to a bank or other loaning institution, and obtaining inventory financing (floorplanning).

Training Provided: Initial 2 week training covering integration of computer sales and service into an existing operation with a focus on product knowledge. Additional courses to be provided as necessary.

Managerial Assistance Available: Pre-opening consultation on cost-efficient methods of developing the business, site improvement and fixturization guidance as necessary. Ongoing support through technical hot-line, manuals, dealer account manager, and corporate marketing support staff.

Information Submitted: June 1990

VALCOM
10810 Farnam
Omaha, Nebraska 68154
Mike Steffan, Director of Channel Development

Description of Operation: ValCom Computer Center is a complete one source, one stop, hands on store, concentrating on the business markets in selected locations throughout the United States. At the core of each ValCom Computer Center is a learning center. Not just some place to hold classes, but an intregal part of the total concept—the driving force behind the ValCom Computer Center.

Number of Franchisees: 170 stores in 40 States including company-owned.

In Business Since: 1982

Equity Capital Needed: $125,000-$300,000

Financial Assistance Available: No direct financing available; however, franchisor does assist franchisee in preparing a business plan that can be presented to a bank or other loan institutions.

Training Provided: 1 week for the store manager and 1 week for the learning center manager. Subjects covered are product knowledge, sales training and management, accounting and merchandising. Updating and refresher courses are offered as need arises both at corporate headquarters and/or the franchisee's location. Currently no charge to franchisee.

Managerial Assistance Available: The franchisor provides continuing managerial and technical support services throughout the term of the franchise, through a field of regional managers that work with a group of 10 franchisees and live within their territories.

Information Submitted: June 1990

RETAILING—FLORIST

BUNNING THE FLORIST, INC.
P. O. Box 491950
Ft. Lauderdale, Florida 33309
Edward P. Thal, President
Arthur O. Stone, Chairman of the Board

Description of Operation: Bunning The Florist, Inc., offers unique retail florist shops throughout Florida and Western New York. Franchise package includes assistance in site selection and store layout, complete training program at headquarters in Ft. Lauderdale.

Number of Franchisees: 11 in Florida, 1 in New York plus 21 company-owned.

In Business Since: 1925 and began franchising in 1969.

Equity Capital Needed: $50,000

Financial Assistance Available: No financial assistance is provided by the franchisor.

Training Provided: 2 weeks provided at company headquarters in Ft. Lauderdale, Florida, plus continuing training in-store under company supervision.

Managerial Assistance Available: Franchisor assists franchisee in all aspects of shop operation, recordkeeping, advertising, promotion and selling techniques. Manuals of operation and counseling are provided. Home office personnel are available for periodic visits to stores.

Information Submitted: June 1990

*CONROY'S FLORISTS
6621 East Pacific Coast Highway
Suite 280
Long Beach, California 90803
Christopher Barr, Executive Vice President

Description of Operation: Conroy's, Inc., licenses individuals to operate under the Conroy's Flowers name and system as a full service florist and mass merchandiser of floral products. The stores average 2,000 square feet and are located on high exposure corners, either free-standing or in exceptionally visible end-line position. Conroy's assists with site acquisition and representatives coordinate initial set-up and grand opening, and assist in day-to-day operators. Conroy's provides complete computerized accounting services including monthly financial statements and the processing of accounts receivable billings. Through its advertising fund and national advertising agency, Conroy's also coordinates and manages local and regional advertising programs utilizing television, radio, newspaper and direct mail.

Number of Franchisees: 82, including 2 company operated stores.

In Business Since: 1960, franchising since 1974.

Equity Capital Needed: Minimum $100,000, in cash available.

Financial Assistance Available: Works with appropriate lenders.

Training Provided: 5 week program of classroom and on-the-job training in Southern California. Training encompasses all phases of retail operation including personnel recruitment and management, purchasing, basic floral design, holiday programs, marketing, sales and business management.

Managerial Assistance Available: Conroy's provides licensees with skilled and experienced personnel to assist in store opening and to support licensee's operation on an ongoing basis as needed. Continuing assistance in group purchase opportunities, bookkeeping, advertising and store operations is provided.

Information Submitted: May 1990

*FLOWERAMA OF AMERICA, INC.
3165 West Airline Highway
Waterloo, Iowa 50703
Chuck Nygren, Vice President

Description of Operation: Flowerama of America, Inc., offers a unique and innovative approach to retail floral merchandising. Flowerama offers prime regional mall locations consisting of 600-1,000 square feet and free-standing locations of between 2,000-3,000 square feet situated on high vehicular traffic sites. Flowerama offers fresh flowers, floral arrangements, green and blooming plants, silk product and related gift and accessory items at prices dramatically below conventional florist. Flowerama offers a comprehensive franchise package including site selection, lease negotiations, store design, training, supplier programs and continued operational support.

Number of Franchisees: 74 in 23 States plus 14 company-owned shops.

In Business Since: 1966

Equity Capital Needed: Mall locations: $20,000-$40,000. Free-standing: $50,000-$110,000

Financial Assistance Available: Assists franchisee in obtaining financing from local lending institutions; however, no direct funding is available.

Training Provided: Mall locations: 9 days training in classroom and on the job training. Free-standing: 4 weeks including classroom and on-the-job training.

Managerial Assistance Available: Flowerama provides continual management service for the life of the franchise in such areas as bookkeeping, advertising, store operations, and inventory control. Complete manuals of operations, forms, and directions are provided. Field representatives and staff personnel are continually available to provide franchise owners with assistance in the operation of their retail floral shop.

Information Submitted: April 1990

*SHE'S FLOWERS, INC.
740 South Olive Street
Los Angeles, California 90014
Marty Shih

Description of Operation: Full service retail florist.

Number of Franchisees: 5 in California

In Business Since: 1979

Equity Capital Needed: $103,000-$156,000

Financial Assistance Available: The company may assist a franchisee with arrangements for financing through third parties.

Training Provided: 7 weeks of training. The initial training program will include instruction in flower handling, design, and floral arrangements; care for perishable floral commodities; inventory controls, purchasing methods, and procedures; administrative recordkeeping and accounting controls; local merchandising techniques and obligations; gross sales reporting; employee and customer relations; delivery procedures; and other features of the She's Florists business system.

Managerial Assistance Available: Pre-opening assistance in site selection, design assistance, initial training program, operation manual and time to opening. Past opening assistance in inventory assistance, continuing supervision, accounting, promotion, updating of merchandising and supplier lists and computer networking.

Information Submitted: April 1990

*SILK PLANTS ETC.
1755 Butterfield Road
Libertyville, Illinois 60048
Steven E. Santos, Director of Franchising

Description of Operation: Full service specialty retailer of state-of-the-art artificial and preserved foliage. Store size varies from 1,500-2,500 square feet. Product is top quality and is highly competitive in price because of parent company's direct import program.

Number of Franchisees: 61 in 2 countries.

In Business Since: 1985

Equity Capital Needed: $75,000-$85,000

Financial Assistance Available: Development of business plan.

Training Provided: 7 days in classroom; 7-10 days in store pre-opening; 3-5 days in first 60 days.

Managerial Assistance Available: Merchandise presentation, retail disciplines, advertising programs, commercial sales training.

Information Submitted: April 1990

WESLEY BERRY FLOWERS
15305 Schoolcraft
Detroit, Michigan 48227
Wesley L. Berry III

Description of Operation: Wesley Berry Flowers is a full service floral shop that specializes in the sale of fresh cut as well as arranged flowers. The stores also carry green plants, silk flowers and plants, greeting cards, balloons, and an optional collectible package which consists of items such as Royal Doulton and Hummel figurines as well as fine leaded crystal. This franchise provides two avenues of business expansion. The prospective investor can own a single unit franchise or can purchase a master franchise that allows the franchisee to oversee the development of a chain of 30 to 50 locations and share in both the royalty and the franchise fee for each location that is opened. Investment range for a single unit is between $64,000-$88,000 and the investment for a master franchise is dependent on the size of the prospective territory.

Number of Franchisees: 22 in 4 States

In Business Since: 1946. Franchising began in late 1985.

Equity Capital Needed: $64,000-$88,000

Financial Assistance Available: From various financial institutions.

Training Provided: The training program begins with a set of video tapes and a library of 10 training manuals that are to be reviewed by the franchisee. After the completion of the review, the new owner is given 100 hours of in-store training that covers every phase of store operation from floral design to day-to-day store operation. Further support is provided in the form of telephone hot lines that can be called anytime the franchisee has questions or problems, monthly newsletters that cover important or timely information, and periodic seminars that will enhance previous training.

Managerial Assistance Available: Throughout the term of the agreement, the franchisor shall provide continuous sales, marketing and operational assistance by way of advice, consultations, periodic visits and telephone conferences.

Information Submitted: April 1990

RETAILING—NOT ELSEWHERE CLASSIFIED

AGWAY, INC.
P. O. Box 4933
Syracuse, New York 13221
Kenneth L. Gregg, Director of Representatives

Description of Operation: Agway, Inc., operates company-owned stores that distribute principally farm-input supplies to its farmer-members and other patrons. The company also franchises stores to independent operators that sell agriculturally related products to small farm operators and homeowners. The franchised product line consists primarily of animal feeds, lawn and garden supplies, hardware and outdoor living supplies.

Number of Franchisees: 363 franchises, 220 company-owned stores and 103 local cooperatives in 12 States.

In Business Since: 1964

Equity Capital Needed: The total cost of an Agway outlet is not ascertainable due to variables such as land cost, construction cost, lease costs, delays and contingencies. It can be assumed, however, that the total initial cost will exceed $150,000.

Financial Assistance Available: Agway's wholly owned subsidiary, Telmark, Inc., provides leasing services for equipment and buildings. Agway may provide for the purchase of inventory and supplies and may lease the premises. Terms and conditions vary with the need for credit and the creditworthiness of the franchisee.

Training Provided: The Agway training program covers all appropriate aspects of the operation of an Agway outlet. It is conducted in Syracuse, New York, for 1 week. The course is mandatory and must be successfully completed. The franchisee will also participate in 40 hours of continuing education per year.

Managerial Assistance Available: Agway provides a continual business advisory service through a staff of zone managers. Accounting services are provided the first year and are available at cost thereafter. Operations and identification manuals are provided. Advertising materials are provided at cost. An extensive staff of technicians and researchers is available to answer questions on a continual basis.

Information Submitted: April 1990

AMERICAN FAST PHOTO AND CAMERA, INC.
157 S. Pine Street
Spartanburg, South Carolina 29302
Diane Worman, Development Director

Description of Operation: American Fast Photo and Camera has established a unique niche in the photo finishing industry. Each center has 8 profit centers: color processing, black and white processing, enlargements (wallet to 20x30), slides, portrait studio, camera, film and retail accessories. All services are done in-house to insure maximum profitability.

Number of Franchisees: 20 in South Carolina, North Carolina, Georgia, Alabama, Michigan and Texas.

In Business Since: 1984

Equity Capital Needed: Franchise fee $27,000, leasehold improvements approximately $15,000, working capital minimum $25,000 and 2 equipment packages $22,000-$65,000.

Finacial Assistance Available: Equipment lease or financing.

Training Provided: 1 week sales training on-site, 1 week on-site training, 1 week equipment training by equipment manufacturer, and 1 week management training at the corporate headquarters.

Managerial Assistance Available: Site selection, lease negotiation, building layouts, 4 week training program, technical staff, operations staff, and accounting staff.

Information Submitted: April 1990

ANNIE'S BOOK STOP, INC.
15 Lackey Street
Westborough, Massachusetts 01581
Anne Adams

Description of Operation: Franchisor sells franchises to establish bookstore centers for the sale and exchange of pre-read paperback books, for the sale of new books, both paperback and hardcover editions, and for the sale of other book related or gift items.

Number of Franchisees: 95 in 23 States

In Business Since: 1981

Equity Capital Needed: $35,000-$50,000

Financial Assistance Available: None

Training Provided: On-hand training plus detailed manual, duration 2 weeks plus.

Managerial Assistance Available: Ongoing through phone and mail for life of franchise.

Information Submitted: May 1990

*APPLAUSE VIDEO
2622 South 156th Circle
Omaha, Nebraska 68130
Bruce Shackman, President

Description of Operation: Applause Video Corporation establishes a unique retail environment for the video industry. Each store is approximately 3,500 square feet with ample store front parking and is open 10 a.m. to 10 p.m. 7 days a week. An extensive inventory providing the proper selection as well as depth tailored to the individual community is part of what makes Applause so successful.

Number of Franchisees: 39 franchised outlets plus 19 company-owned outlets in Nebraska and Iowa.

In Business Since: 1983

Equity Capital Needed: $350,000 minimum.

Financial Assistance Available: Provide no financial assistance.

Training Provided: We provide an intensive 2 week mandatory training course with in-store training at one of our company-owned locations in Omaha, Nebraska. In addition, we provide on-premise management for the franchisee's store for the first week of operation.

Managerial Assistance Available: Applause Video provides continual management services for the life of the franchise in such areas as bookkeeping, advertising, promotion and inventory control. Field managers will work closely with franchisee and visit stores regularly to assist in solving problems.

Information Submitted: June 1990

*BATH & A-HALF FRANCHISE SYSTEMS, INC.
999 Elmhurst Road
Suite C-11
Mt. Prospect, Illinois 60056
Sandra K. Kreeger, President

Description of Operation: Retail stores specializing in bath accessories and bath related merchandise and gift lines, including towels, shower curtains, rugs, and coordinated bath accessories. Franchisor creates speciality merchandise and imports exclusive lines for Bath & A-Half stores only. Emphasis on coordinated ensembles and coordinates created for theme programs. Stores are located primarily in high traffic major enclosed mall shopping centers requiring approximately 1,200 square feet. Stores are inventoried according to market and varied according to income levels.

Number of Franchisees: 13 stores in Illinois, Texas, Wisconsin and Minnesota, including 7 company-owned stores.

In Business Since: 1985

Equity Capital Needed: $80,000 to $100,000

Financial Assistance Available: None. Franchisee must obtain own financing. Generally, the franchisee must have 50 percent of the needed capital to obtain an additional 50 percent bank financing.

Training Provided: Intensive 1 week mandatory training course is scheduled for all franchisees or their store managers or operators. Training held in home office and actually includes working in company-owned Bath & A-Half stores. A second week of training and assistance is provided in franchisee's outlet. An annual Managers Mart is held for special training and merchandise selection.

Managerial Assistance Available: Bath & A-Half has complete operating manuals, vendor catalogs for purchasing aids, accounting systems, monthly newsletters, window and theme decor planning aids, annual buying program for holiday planning and advertising assistance. Field supervisors will work closely with the franchisees and visit stores regularly to assist with any problems. Bath & A-Half will provide regular newsletters and special bulletins to advise of new product opportunities, special allowances, seasonal items and merchandise specials.

Information Submitted: June 1990

*BATHTIQUE INTERNATIONAL, LTD.
Carnegie Place—247 North Goodman Street
Rochester, New York 14607
Don A. Selpel, President

Description of Operation: A retail bath, bed and gift specialty shop offering the latest products and accessories.

Number of Franchisees: 67 in 30 States, Puerto Rico and the Virgin Islands including 16 company-owned shops.

In Business Since: 1969

Equity Capital Needed: $35,000. No direct financing, but assistance in acquiring funding through local banks.

Financial Assistance Available: No direct financing but assistance in acquiring financing through local banks.

Training Provided: A concentrated 1 week training period is conducted for all new franchisees. Individuals for each franchise participate in a 1 week manager training program. This program includes a classroom and on-the-job training under experienced managers. An additional 2 weeks of on-site location assistance is provided by the home office staff at the time the franchisee's shop opens. A follow-up briefing session is conducted on-site after opening.

Managerial Assistance Available: Bathtique International provides continuing review and feedback concerning shop operations in areas such as sales, purchasing, advertising, and labor schedule. Merchandising is recommended to franchisees after testing in company shop. Merchandise is bought directly from recommended suppliers; quantity discounts available. A continuous personnel training program is strongly emphasized. Advertising materials and co-op funds are provided regularly including direct mail books. Annual and regional conferences are offered throughout the country.

Information Submitted: April 1990

BIGHORN SHEEPSKIN COMPANY
11600 Manchaca Road
Austin, Texas 78748
Barry Silverman, President

Description of Operation: Bighorn Sheepskin Company franchises the operation of temporary retail locations in regional shopping malls during the Christmas season, selling genuine sheepskin gift items, apparel, and automotive accessories. Typical locations are 100 square foot kiosks located in the common areas of shopping malls and are open during November and December.

Number of Franchisees: 67 locations in 22 States

In Business Since: 1983

Equity Capital Needed: $2,500 plus $20,000 letter of credit.

Financial Assistance Available: None

Training Provided: 3 day seminar each October in Austin, Texas.

Managerial Assistance Available: Site selection, lease negotiation, comprehensive operations manual, computerized ordering system, and promotional materials.

Information Submitted: April 1990

BLACKBERRY COTTAGE
3107 Eubank NE
Albuquerque, New Mexico 87111
Jeffrey Goodman

Description of Operation: Extensive retail in dolls, plush animals, miniatures, doll houses and related items for the collector and non-collector alike. Magical displays for all ages in a place where enchantment is real called Blackberry Cottage.

Number of Franchisees: 4

In Business Since: 1987

Equity Capital Needed: $65,000-$150,000 (includes franchise fee of $81,500).

Financial Assistance Available: Available only on franchise fee.

Training Provided: At both headquarters and on-site locations and ongoing through first year of business.

Managerial Assistance Available: We provide complete and current handbook and work very closely with all our franchisees.

Information Submitted: June 1990

BLIND DESIGNS, INC.
5159 Seven Springs Boulevard
Newport Richey, Florida 34665
Michael J. Confronti, President

Description of Operation: Blind Designs is a specialty window treatment store offering a complete line of window coverings for both the commercial and residential customer. Our concept is unique, as we showcase them with lifesize displays. Our selling formula is to offer the consumer the best value, quality and service. As a franchise system of operation, Blind Designs stores are located in cities where there is immediate potential for further growth, and where the income and purchasing levels are in the middle to upper range. Our stores are conveniently located in strip centers of a modern type with a minimum suggested size of 600 square feet.

Number of Franchisees: 6 in Florida.

In Business Since: 1979, franchising since 1984

Equity Capital Needed: $15,000 franchise fee and up to $15,000 start-up expenses.

Financial Assistance Available: None

Training Provided: Training covers inside and outside sales, including soliciting and closing sales, management, hiring and firing of personnel, accounting and bookkeeping procedures, installing, product knowledge and pricing, advertising, and promotion, a 3 week training program and a representative for 1 week in store after opening.

Managerial Assistance Available: Our products are national brand products of the highest quality. Due to volume purchasing, the manufacturers we select will offer quick delivery, good service and competitive pricing. A representative will visit your location once every 2 months for a review and assist with any problems. Additional help will come in the way of a newsletter, pricing updates, sales techniques, new products and sales seminars.

Information Submitted: June 1990

BOOK RACK MANAGEMENT, INC.
2703 E. Commercial Boulevard
Ft. Lauderdale, Florida 33308
Fred M. Darnell

Description of Operation: Used paper back books and new books.

Number of Franchisees: 248 in 34 states

In Business Since: 1963

Equity Capital Needed: $12,000

Financial Assistance Available: None

Training Provided: 1 or 2 weeks training and site location. Help supply inventory, yearly meeting and monthly newsletter.

Managerial Assistance Available: Ongoing assistance

Information Submitted: April 1990

THE BOX SHOPPE, INC.
7165 East 87th Street
Indianapolis, Indiana 46256
Duke Smith

Description of Operation: We are a retail and wholesale business involved in the sale of gift boxes, moving boxes, storage boxes, bows, ribbons, gift wrap, etc.

Number of Franchisees: 63 in Indiana, Illinois, Kentucky, Ohio, North and South Carolina, and Michigan.

In Business Since: 1984

Equity Capital Needed: $30,700

Financial Assistance Available: Yes

Training Provided: Extensive 3 day training program at franchisor's headquarters, additional on-site assistance as necessary.

Managerial Assistance Available: None required.

Information Submitted: April 1990

BOXWORKS, INC.
1402 Donelson Pike
Suite A-3
Nashville, Tennessee 37217
Henry E. Zoller or Franchise Consultant

Description of Operation: An upscale operation selling greeting cards, gift wrap and bags, boxes, and many types of paper products, balloons and gifts. Also do expert shipping and packaging.

Number of Franchisees: 29

In Business Since: 1986

Equity Capital Needed: $72,000 to $122,000

Financial Assistance Available: None

Training Provided: 2 weeks

Managerial Assistance Available: Yes

Information Submitted: April 1990

*BUTTERFIELDS DEVELOPMENT, INC.
1250 Capitol of Texas Highway South
Suite 100, Building 2
Austin, Texas 78746

Description of Operation: Gourmet kitchen store featuring gadgets, accessories, decorator items, small appliances, and novelties. Locations are in regional shopping malls.

Number of Franchisees: 21

In Business Since: 1979, franchising since 1986

Equity Capital Needed: Total investment $120,000-$190,000

Financial Assistance Available: None

Training Provided: 2 weeks—1 week at headquarters and 1 week on-site at new store.

Managerial Assistance Available: Franchisor provides on-going supervision and purchasing aids, keeping franchisee informed on new items and trends in the business.

Information Submitted: June 1990

*CELLULAND
10717 Sorrento Valley Road
San Diego, California 92121

Description of Operation: Retail cellular car phone sales and service center offering a wide selection of cellular phones, products, installations, customer service, warranty work, cellular phone number activations and other communications products.

Number of Franchisees: 22 plus 2 company-owned in Arizona, California, Colorado, Minnesota and Nevada

In Business Since: 1985

Equity Capital Needed: $125,000 to $295,000 total investment.

Financial Assistance Available: Available through third parties.

Training Provided: 6 weeks at franchisor's location plus on-going support.

Managerial Assistance Available: Site selection assistance, store design, on-site support, cellular phone service contracts, central purchasing for products, computer software provided for lead tracking to customer cost of goods and profit reports.

Information Submitted: June 1990

CLEANING IDEAS, INC.
4219 Center Gate
San Antonio, Texas 78217
Attention: Franchise Director

Description of Operation: Cleaning Ideas is a unique retail/wholesale store operation. Cleaning Ideas stores sell over 1,600 items and chemicals to be used for cleaning. All chemical items are manufactured by Cleaning Ideas, thus gross profits run as high as 60 percent. All products are sold with a money back guarantee. Each store is 1,000 square feet.

Number of Franchisees: 12 in Texas

In Business Since: 1931

Equity Capital Needed: $6,000 minimum

Financial Assistance Available: A total investment of $15,000 is necessary to open a Cleaning Ideas franchise. The down payment of $6,000 pays for sign, shelving, 1/2 inventory, training. Cleaning Ideas will finance the balance with no interest (90 days).

Training Provided: Intensive 6 day mandatory training course is scheduled for all new franchisees. All training is performed in company-owned stores.

Managerial Assistance Available: Cleaning Ideas provides on-going managerial and technical assistance for the duration of the franchise agreement.

Information Submitted: June 1990

CLUBHOUSE GOLF LTD. PARTNERSHIP
7321 North Broadway Extension
Oklahoma City, Oklahoma 73116
Ted Smith

Description of Operation: Golf retail stores.

Number of Franchisees: 12

In Business Since: 1989

Equity Capital Needed: $200,000-$350,000

Financial Assistance Available: None

Training Provided: Yes

Managerial Assistance Available: Ongoing support.

Information Submitted: April 1990

COPY MAT
2000 Powell Street
Suite 1300
Emeryville, California 94608

Description of Operation: Copy Mat is a full service photo-copy center specializing in high-quality volume production (same day and overnight) and customer service. Store offers a whole range of ancillary services including stationery sales, self-service typing booths, postal boxes, spiral and velo-binding, cassette duplication, and full- and self-service desktop publishing services. Each distinctively designed Copy Mat is located in a highly visible, well lighted area and shops usually average approximately 2,000 square feet. Stores feature customer self-service on a walk-in basis on all equipment and can meet the needs of almost all types of businesses and personal use.

Number of Franchisees: 66 in California

In Business Since: 1973, franchising since 1986

Equity Capital Needed: $40,000 initial franchise fee; total investment from $225,000 to $350,000.

Financial Assistance Available: Franchisor will aid in securing outside financing in an advisory role.

Training Provided: Comprehensive training program for manager and assistant manager that includes up to 3 weeks at the franchisor's headquarters or store near their home. Program provides an operating manual, and hands-on experience and covers all the training phases of business including pre-opening checklist, marketing, operations, customer relations, staffing and training, budgeting, accounting, and purchasing.

Managerial Assistance Available: Franchisor aids in the purchase of equipment and supplies. Franchisee has access to company purchasing contracts and their discounts. Upon store opening, franchisor provides full-time assistance by the district manager for up to 30 days. A regional manager assists at the store at least 1 day monthly. There is continual marketing assistance at both regional and local levels. Management provides aid with business management, inventory control, bookkeeping, and customer relations. The firm also aids in site selection and leasehold arrangements, store design, grand opening, and technical assistance involving any phase of operations.

Information Submitted: May 1990

CREATE-A-BOOK
6380 Euclid Road
Cincinnati, Ohio 45236
Robert Young

Description of Operation: Create-A-Book is a company that prints and sells personalized children's books. Any child can have his/her name printed throughout colorful storybooks along with friends, relatives, pets, age, hometown, etc. It takes four minutes from start to finish to print, bind and place a book in a hard cover.

Franchisees have the equipment to completely print and bind the books. There are many, many different ways to sell and market the books. Training provided. Excellent home business.

Number of Franchisees: 400

In Business Since: 1980

Equity Capital Needed: $2,995 plus approximately $1,200 for equipment.

Financial Assistance Available: We do not offer any financial assistance.

Training Provided: Training is provided in Cincinnati, Ohio. For those people unable to attend the training, we provide a manual and video tape. Additional training is provided through seminars and meetings.

Managerial Assistance Available: Seminars and meetings are provided to update franchisees. Newsletters are sent to all franchisees throughout the year.

Information Submitted: April 1990

*CURTIS MATHES CORPORATION
One Curtis Mathes Parkway
Athens, Texas 75751
Ed McGuinness, Vice President, Development

Description of Operation: Curtis Mathes Corporation authorizes franchisees to operate businesses that sell, rent and lease a broad line of high quality Curtis Mathes brand electronic home entertainment products carrying extended warranties.

Number of Franchisees: 600 in 46 States

In Business Since: 1920

Equity Capital Needed: $50,000-$100,000

Financial Assistance Available: Neither the franchisor nor any affiliate directly offers financing to the franchisee. However, the franchisor indirectly offers inventory and consumer credit financing to the franchisee through third party lending institutions.

Training Provided: Curtis Mathes has initial and ongoing training programs.

Managerial Assistance Available: Continuing managerial and technical assistance are provided for the duration of the franchise in such areas as advertising and promotional materials, inventory and consumer credit financing, inventory control, etc. Complete manuals of operations, forms, and directions are provided. District and field managers are available to work closely with franchisees and visit stores regularly to assist in solving problems. Curtis Mathes sponsors meetings of franchisees on a national and regional basis.

Information Submitted: April 1990

CUT-UPS INTERNATIONAL, INC.
12212 Technology Boulevard
Austin, Texas 78727
Jerry Hofrock, Director of Marketing

Description of Operation: World leader, laser photo sculptures.

Number of Franchisees: Over 200 throughout the U.S.

In Business Since: 1987

Equity Capital Needed: $6,900 to $29,900

Financial Assistance Available: None

Training Provided: Training and support are provided plus all equipment.

Managerial Assistance Available: Continuous support by top professional staff plus 1-800 number.

Information Submitted: April 1990

DESCAMPS
A Division of THE DOLLFUS MIEG COMPANY, INC.
454 Columbus Avenue
New York, New York 10024

254

Description of Operation: Descamps franchise is in the business of linens, bath products and related items. The mother company is French and has at present 220 stores in 11 different countries. Each store has approximately 1,000 square feet, and operates using tradename, service marks, logos and designs summarized in a technical book provided by franchisor.

Number of Franchisees: 6 in California, Florida, Massachusetts and Texas, plus 4 company-owned stores.

In Business Since: 1980 in the USA

Equity Capital Needed: $130,000

Financial Assistance Available: Help in negotiating lease and most of time franchisor finds locations and in any case has to give his approbation. Measurements and supply of plans are provided to franchisee in a technical book. An experienced Descamps merchandiser is sent during construction, to decorate prior to opening (during different trips to the site), helps with the opening, and afterwards twice a year at least for guidance and animation. A credit for opening in 30 days was given to franchisees in 1981.

Training Provided: 2 weeks of training in our Madison Avenue, New York City store.

Managerial Assistance Available: Technical assistance is provided during term of franchise contract throughout our New York office to solve problems such as advertising, size of collection, and financial analysis.

Information Submitted: May 1990

*DOLLAR DISCOUNT STORES
7 Boulden Center
New Castle, Delaware 19720
Paul Cohen, President

Description of Operation: Dollar Discount Stores has developed a successful retail concept for the discount shopper market. Its stores offer a wide variety of low priced, high demand close-out and general merchandise.

Number of Franchisees: 38

In Business Since: 1982

Equity Capital Needed: $79,000-$109,000 total investment.

Financial Assistance Available: None

Training Provided: Initial training consists of 10 days in the classroom and in actual stores and covers all aspects of the business such as store management, merchandising, personnel management, policies and procedures, ordering, bookkeeping, hiring and training, theft prevention, etc. An experienced manager also will spend a minimum of 1 week on-site with each franchisee for the grand opening.

Managerial Assistance Available: Dollar Discount Stores assists its franchisees with site selection and development advice, lease negotiation, advertising and public relations, national and international product selection and purchasing, and ongoing operational support by a team of seasoned managers.

Information Submitted: April 1990

EXQUISITE CRAFTS
108 Gleneida Avenue
Carmel, New York 10512
Marianne Montagna

Description of Operation: Specialty craft retailer with over 30 departments including needlework, stenciling, paints, florals, ribbons, baskets, quilting, fabrics, art supplies, children's crafts, candymaking and miniatures. Each store requires at least 1,200 square feet and assistance with location and store layout is provided. At this time the only independent craft store to be franchised, we offer you unique designs as well as selected opening inventory. The stores also provide workshops in a variety of crafts and a line of handmade gifts.

Number of Franchisees: 1 in Vermont, 1 company-owned in New York.

In Business Since: 1973, franchising since 1989

Equity Capital Needed: $42,000-$55,000

Financial Assistance Available: None

Training Provided: Exquisite Crafts will provide 10 days of training that will cover hands-on experience with all of the craft products sold, how to order, inventory control, customer service programs, display, how to teach workshops, how to hire employees and how to hold an open house.

Managerial Assistance Available: The franchisor will offer ongoing assistance with products knowledge, new techniques, promotions, advertising and direct mail suggestions, assistance with any problems, and in-store visits.

Information Submitted: April 1990

FAN FAIR DEVELOPMENT CORPORATION
12425 Knoll Rd.
Elm Grove, Wisconsin 53122

Description of Operation: Fan Fair offers a unique retail store operation. Merle Harmon's Fan Fair is billed as the "Sports Fan's Gift Shop," featuring gifts and clothing bearing the team logos and colors from all professional teams and over 100 collegiate teams. Each store is about 1,000 square feet, located in a major regional shopping center, and merchandised according to local sports markets.

Number of Franchisees: 131

In Business Since: 1977

Equity Capital Needed: $90,000-$140,000

Financial Assistance Available: None. Franchisee must obtain own financing. Generally, the franchisee must have 50 percent of the needed capital to obtain an additional 50 percent bank financing.

Training Provided: Intensive 2-4 week mandatory training course is scheduled for all franchisees or their store operators. 10-14 days at the franchisee's outlet under the supervision of our training supervisors ongoing.

Managerial Assistance Available: Fan Fair has complete operating manuals, vendor catalogs for purchasing aids, accounting systems, forms, reports, co-op buying sessions, and a distribution center for store support on many items. Field supervisors will work closely with the franchisees and visit stores regularly to assist with problems. Fan Fair constantly advises franchisees of new product opportunities, special allowances, and seasonal merchandising ideas.

Information Submitted: May 1990

FRIEDMAN FRANCHISORS
2301 Broadway
Oakland, California 94612
Arthur Friedman, General Partner

Description of Operation: Friedman's Microwave Ovens, microwave specialty stores selling only microwave ovens and accessories enhanced by microwave cooking schools. A unique business with a focus on complete customer satisfaction by offering 60 day free exchange, competitive prices, free schools for life and discounts on accessories.

Number of Franchisees: 49 in 23 States

In Business Since: 1976, franchising since 1979

Equity Capital Needed: $25,000-$35,000

Financial Assistance Available: None

Training Provided: Week long training session held at Oakland, Calfiornia, headquarters, on-site training prior, during and after opening, telephone assistance always available.

Managerial Assistance Available: Included in the above.

Information Submitted: June 1990

GLITTER PHOTOGRAPHY INTERNATIONAL, LTD.
1655 Mesa Verde Avenue, Suite 230
Ventura, California 93003
Peggy Hatfield, Vice President, Administration

Description of Operation: Glitter Photography is a high quality upscale glamour photography salon. Each Glitter Salon has a makeup artist so all clients receive a complete makeover including hair enhancement. Glitter Photography Salons provide jewelry, furs, boas, and drapes to give the client 2 to 3 different clothing changes, and a 20 pose selection for the client to choose from.

Number of Franchisees: 1 in California and 1 sole proprietor also in California.

In Business Since: 1987, franchising since 1989.

Equity Capital Needed: $96,000 of total $213,000 total investment. Equity capital varies due to location and franchisee financial strength.

Financial Assistance Available: None

Training Provided: Franchisor trains franchisees 2 weeks at the corporate office in Ventura, California. Upon opening of franchisee's salon, franchisor trains 1 week in franchisee's salon. Additional training available as needed.

Managerial Assistance Available: Glitter Photography franchisees are given a confidential manual, which gives in detail the complete operations of Glitter Photography. There is also assistance provided in site selection, salon design, and equipment lists. Continuing assistance includes advertising, marketing, research and development of product and is available at all times to the franchisee to offer any assistance the franchisee may need.

Information Submitted: April 1990

GOODWILL CANDLE & INCENSE FRANCHISE CORP.
300 East Milwaukee
Detroit, Michigan 48202
Chester Flam

Description of Operation: Wholesale and retail sales of proprietary and non-proprietary religious goods including candles, incense, oils, statues, books, etc. Primarily to the Black and Spanish areas of cities.

Number of Franchisees: 2 in Michigan and Georgia

In Business Since: 1975

Equity Capital Needed: $13,500 to $20,000

Financial Assistance Available: None

Training Provided: 1 week in Detroit and on location.

Managerial Assistance Available: Unlimited and ongoing.

Information Submitted: June 1990

HAPPI-BATHER
c/o HAPPI-STORES, INC.
1225 Park Place Mall
Memphis, Tennessee 38119
J. Richard Holley, President

Description of Operation: A bath boutique featuring bath accessories and fragrances.

Number of Franchisees: 1 in 1 State

In Business Since: 1982

Equity Capital Needed: $50,000-$90,000

Financial Assistance Available: None

Training Provided: Total training program before and during installation, then ongoing as needed over entire period of franchise.

Managerial Assistance Available: Inventory control system, cash flow management and sales training.

Information Submitted: May 1990

HAPPI-COOK
c/o HAPPI-STORES, INC.
1225 Park Place Mall
Memphis, Tennessee 38119
J. Richard Holley, President

Description of Operation: Gourmet cook retail store featuring cookware, cook gadgets, books and accessories as well as homemade fudge, gourmet candies and other basket goods.

Number of Franchisees: 3 in 2 States

In Business Since: 1982

Equity Capital Needed: $70,000-$110,000

Financial Assistance Available: None

Training Provided: Total training program before and during installation, then ongoing as needed over entire period of franchise.

Managerial Assistance Available: Inventory control system, cash flow management and sales training.

Information Submitted: May 1990

HAPPI-NAMES
c/o HAPPI-STORES, INC.
1225 Park Place Mall
Memphis, Tennessee 38119
J. Richard Holley, President

Description of Operation: Personalized gift stores with demonstrating artist on premises at all times.

Number of Franchisees: 14 in 7 States

In Business Since: 1982

Equity Capital Needed: $50,000-$90,000

Financial Assistance Available: None

Training Provided: Total training program during installation, then ongoing as needed over entire period of franchise.

Managerial Assistance Available: Inventory control systems, cash flow management and sales training.

Information Submitted: May 1990

HEROES WORLD CENTERS, INC.
961 Rt. 10 E
Randolph, New Jersey 07069
Ivan Snyder

Description of Operation: Retail store located in regional malls catering to items relating to fictional and real-to-life super heroes, super stars, and cartoon characters. Featuring toys, books, novelties, plush items, T-shirts and wearing apparel, new and collector comics and books featuring Smurfs, Strawberry Shortcake, Snoopy, Spiderman, Batman, Star Wars, etc.

Number of Franchisees: 2 in 2 States plus 8 company-owned stores in 4 States

In Business Since: 1976

Equity Capital Needed: Minimum of $55,000 plus additional credit of $25,000-$40,000.

Financial Assistance Available: No financial assistance is provided.

Training Provided: Both classroom and on-the-job training required at company headquarters, plus on-the-job training in the franchisee's store.

Managerial Assistance Available: Operations manual and continuous managerial assistance from field personnel. Membership in Heroes World buying co-operative. Site evaluation and selection, lease negotiations.

Information Submitted: April 1990

HOBBYTOWN USA
5930 South 58th Street
Lincoln, Nebraska 68516
James E. Hogg, Franchise Operations Manager

Description of Operation: HobbyTown USA is America's largest chain of franchised hobby stores. HobbyTown USA stores are full-line retail hobby stores with product offerings in 8 to 10

hobby categories including model railroad supplies, radio controlled cars, trucks, airplanes, and helicopters, plastic model kits, games, sports cards, stamps and coins, and paints and tools.

Number of Franchisees: 25 franchise locations in 11 States.

In Business Since: 1969, franchising since 1985.

Equity Capital Needed: $25,000-$30,000 of total $80,000-$100,000 investment.

Financial Assistance Available: None

Training Provided: Franchisor trains and educates franchisees 1 to 2 weeks in its home office in Lincoln, Nebraska. Further training is provided at the franchisee's location during the first 1 to 2 weeks that the store is open.

Managerial Assistance Available: Full assistance is provided in site selection, lease negotiation, store layout and design, and all operational procedures of the store. Additionally, franchisor representatives visit each store 4 times a year, and the franchisor is available at all times to offer assistance to the franchisee.

Information Submitted: April 1990

THE HOUSE OF WATCH BANDS FRANCHISE CORPORATION
29205 Southfield Road
Southfield, Michigan 48076
Michael A. Max, President

Description of Operation: The House of Watch Bands Franchise Corporation offers a unique retail store operation. Each store is approximately 1,000 square feet with ample store-front parking and open 9 hours daily, 6 days a week, with one late night (9-9). An extensive inventory of House of Watch Bands products as well as brand name watch bands and accessories is maintained.

Number of Franchisees: 2 in Michigan

In Business Since: 1927

Equity Capital Needed: $67,200

Financial Assistance Available: A total investment of $67,500 is necessary to open a House of Watch Bands franchise. Franchisee has option to arrange own outside financing.

Training Provided: Intensive, 14 day, mandatory training course is scheduled for all new franchisees and their personnel. In addition to the 2 week training at headquarters, franchisees receive on-site training at franchisee's own store during the first few weeks of operation under the supervision of the franchise corporation's training staff.

Managerial Assistance Available: The House of Watch Bands Franchise Corporation provides continual management service for the life of the franchise in such areas as bookkeeping, advertising, personnel management, and inventory control. Complete manuals of operations, forms, and directions are provided. District and field managers are available in all regions to work closely with franchisees and visit stores regularly to assist in solving problems. The House of Watch Bands Franchise Corporation sponsors meetings of franchisees and conducts marketing and product research to maintain high House of Watch Bands consumer acceptance.

Information Submitted: June 1990

INTILE DESIGNS FRANCHISE SYSTEMS, INC.
9716 Old Katy Road
Suite 110
Houston, Texas 77055
C. William Cox, Chairman of the Board

Description of Operation: The sale of imported ceramic tiles and marble and the supplies necessary for their installation and cleaning, in addition to offering decorating suggestions for the use of tile. Intile Designs imports and warehouses the tile and marble and distributes for wholesale and retail sales to each franchisee.

Number of Franchisees: 6 franchisees plus 4 company-owned stores in 4 States: Texas, New Mexico, Arizona, and Florida.

In Business Since: 1976

Equity Capital Needed: $131,000-$168,000.

Financial Assistance Available: No financing offered by Intile Designs. We will assist franchisees in obtaining credit and equipment financing if necessary.

Training Provided: 1 week mandatory training at the corporate headquarters. One additional week optional at franchisee's location. Constant communication and assistance available from franchisor to franchisee. Routine visits to franchisee by franchisor.

Managerial Assistance Available: Because our franchisees do not maintain their own inventory, we assist in inventory purchasing and control. Each franchisee and the managers and sales staff are required to attend and complete our training courses.

Information Submitted: June 1990

ISLAND WATER SPORTS
10 Fairway Drive
Suite 302
Deerfield Beach, Florida 33441
Rick Englert

Description of Operation: Action sports (surfing, skateboarding, sailboating, etc.) is one of the nation's fastest growing industries and Island Water Sports is here to meet the nation's demand, not just in the equipment itself but also the unlimited area of apparel and accessories related to the image.

Number of Franchisees: 26 in Florida, Virginia, Missouri, Washington, D.C., and South Carolina.

In Business Since: 1978

Equity Capital Needed: $70,000

Financial Assistance Available: Franchisee must provide his own financing.

Training Provided: 4 weeks of training: 1 week in the office, 2 weeks in the corporate store and 1 week in the franchisee's store.

Managerial Assistance Available: Island Water Sports provides ongoing experienced staff and support in the area of financial planning, central purchasing and/or buying assistance, operations assistance, central computerization, local advertising assistance and national advertising. Complete manuals are provided. Corporate personnel visit the store regularly. Semi-annual franchise meetings are held.

Information Submitted: June 1990

JET PHOTO INTERNATIONAL, INC.
123 South Main Street
P.O. Box 1609
Minot, South Dakota 58702

Description of Operation: 1 hour photo processing.

Number of Franchisees: 11 in 5 states.

In Business Since: 1982

Equity Capital Needed: $95,000 to $112,000

Financial Assistance Available: None.

Training Provided: Technical, management, retailing, counter activities, plus comprehensive study and the processing of film through on-the-job training. Expert training in the fields of quality control, color analysis, primary and secondary systems, machine maintenance and operation of the processor and the printer.

Managerial Assistance Available: Regular contact with regard to management and technical assistance is available.

Information Submitted: June 1990

JEWELRY STORE FRANCHISES
339 Route 9 South
Summerton Plaza
Manalapan, New Jersey 07726
Burt Cowit, President

Description of Operation: Jewelry Store Franchises is a subsidiary of Jewelry Repairs by Us. Picture yourself in your own jewelry retail service business. A pre-selected inventory of 14Kt rings, bracelets, necklaces and diamonds is supplied to our stores. No experience is necessary. All jewelry repairs are performed by an accredited jeweler provided to you. That's what makes our jewelry retailing concept totally different. And that's why it works so well. The work environment is pleasant, in a carpeted, soft-lighted, air-conditioned store. Contrast that scene with the noises, odors, grime of certain other operations: fast food print shop auto repair services, etc. It's a clean business. Our jewelry stores are open 5 days a week 8 hours per day. You operate in 800 to 1,200 square feet. Your equipment and furnishings are standard.

Number of Franchisees: 10 stores in New Jersey, 2 stores in New York.

In Business Since: 1986

Equity Capital Needed: $85,000 to $125,000. This includes furnishings, equipment, site selection, lease agreement and 14kt gold merchandise.

Financial Assistance Available: Franchise fee $23,000.

Training Provided: Franchisee will train in our corporate store in New Jersey for 3 weeks.

Managerial Assistance Available: Retail sales/selling procedures/diamonds/advertising/bookkeeping etc. When your store opens, you will receive our ongoing support.

Information Submitted: April 1990

J. L. HAMMETT COMPANY
P. O. Box 9057
Braintree, Massachusetts 02184
Richard A. Krause, Vice President, Retail/Franchising

Description of Operation: As a part of the $60 million J. L. Hammett Co. business, the retail stores supply public and private school systems, businesses, hobbyists and "whiz kids" with educational supplies, office and art materials, games, toys and books. The complete line includes 7,000 items of retail stock supported by a catalog offering 14,000 additional items. Hammett's volume buying power provides a competitive pricing edge.

Number of Franchisees: 28, including company-owned, in 11 States

In Business Since: 1863. J. L. Hammett Co., the oldest school supply company in America, began when its founder invented the chalk-board eraser and manufactured the first kindergarten materials in the United States.

Equity Capital Needed: Franchise fee $25,000; leasehold improvements $10,000-$70,000; supplies and inventory $50,000-$75,000; working capital $5,000-$7,000.

Financial Assistance Available: No financial assistance is available from the franchisor; however, all necessary information for loan proposals is provided.

Training Provided: Intensive 2 week in-house, hands-on training stresses the areas crucial to the retail operation, including administrative systems, marketing, merchandising, site selection and opening assistance.

Managerial Assistance Available: Continuous operational and merchandising assistance provided by the corporate staff, plus on-site support by district managers. Also, direct mailings, seasonal advertising and special promotions for continued success.

Information Submitted: May 1990

JUST CHAIRS, INC.
446 Francisco Boulevard West
San Rafael, California 94901
Donald E. Sutton, President

Description of Operation: Business to business retail selling commercial seating to all sizes of end-users.

Number of Franchisees: 2 in California

In Business Since: 1984

Equity Capital Needed: $75,000-$125,000

Financial Assistance Available: None

Training Provided: 2 weeks, then ongoing assistance.

Managerial Assistance Available: Group purchasing, product evaluation, financial analysis, advertising materials, and advice hotline.

Information Submitted: May 1990

KIDS THINGS
3316 Governors Drive
San Diego, California 92122
Florence Kalanquin

Description of Operation: Consignment of children's clothing, furniture, toys and maternity wear.

Number of Franchisees: 2 in California

In Business Since: 1990

Equity Capital Needed: $20,000

Financial Assistance Available: None

Training Provided: Complete in-house training previous to opening at corporate office and store.

Managerial Assistance Available: Managerial skills will be presented in origination training and on-site assistance at store opening. Periodic meetings to present new ideas and systems on an ongoing basis. Corporate help is available any time upon request.

Information Submitted: June 1990

KITS CAMERAS, INC.
6051 South 194th
Kent, Washington 98032
Corporate Development Manager

Description of Operation: A Kits Camera franchise system offers a unique opportunity in the operation of a specialty photographic equipment, video and supplies store. Most stores are located in enclosed shopping centers. The store carries an extensive line of brand name and private label merchandise.

Number of Franchisees: 33 on the West Coast

In Business Since: 1975

Equity Capital Needed: Total investment of approximately $135,000 of which $50,000 has to be cash.

Financial Assistance Available: Franchisor will assist franchisee in arranging the balance from a commercial bank.

Training Provided: 4-6 week course at the home office and company stores. Successful completion of training course a prerequisite to obtaining a franchise.

Managerial Assistance Available: Kits Cameras provide continuous management service for the life of the franchise in areas of bookkeeping, advertising, merchandising and store operations. Coordinators visit stores regularly to provide assistance. Semi-annual conventions are sponsored by Kits Cameras.

Information Submitted: May 1990

LEMSTONE BOOKS
1123 Wheaton Oaks Ct.
Wheaton, Illinois 60187
Lynn P. Wheaton, Sales Manager

Description of Operation: Christian bookstores located in large regional shopping malls that stock a unique variety of books, Bibles, Bible study material, gifts, music, greeting cards designed to meet the needs of the family as well as the institutional church market. Telephone (708)682-1400.

Number of Franchisees: 37 in 14 States

In Business Since: 1981

Equity Capital Needed: Approximately $40,000.

Financial Assistance Available: Lemstone Books will assist franchisee in obtaining outside local financing if needed.

Training Provided: One week managers training class prior to opening at franchise headquarters. 400 page manual of operation detailing every aspect of store operations and procedure. On-site training during 5 days of new store set-up. Ongoing regular field visits throughout the year by member of franchise team. Regional advanced management seminars annually. Annual franchise convention in Chicago area.

Managerial Assistance Available: Will assist franchisee to hire sales staff. Regular field visits by franchise operations staff as well as regular franchise seminars. Comprehensive marketing and promotion program plus computerized inventory control and accounting systems provided. All aspects of financial accounting reviewed including monthly open to buy, cash flow projections, and actual to budget performance tracked monthly.

Information Submitted: April 1990

*LITTLE PROFESSOR BOOK CENTERS, INC.
110 North Fourth Avenue
Suite 400
Ann Arbor, Michigan 48104
Carla Garbin, Senior Vice President

Description of Operation: Little Professor Book Centers are full-line, full-service retail book stores. Each store (most are approximately 2,400 square feet) carries a complete selection of hardcover and papercover titles, magazines and newspapers. Franchisor provides complete assistance and counsel needed to open and operate a book store, from site selection to store opening and throughout the life of the franchise agreement.

Number of Franchisees: 135 stores in 35 States

In Business Since: 1969

Equity Capital Needed: $35,000 to $45,000 liquid, total investment $150,000 plus.

Financial Assistance Available: Little Professor Book Centers, Inc., will assist in the loan application process, but provide no direct financial assistance.

Training Provided: Little Professor Book Center franchise owners participate in an established training program to learn the important aspects of retailing including inventory control, general operations, financial management, advertising and other forms of sales promotion. The training program is conducted for 15 days: 10 days at company headquarters in Ann Arbor, Michigan, 5 days on-site in the new store.

Managerial Assistance Available: Little Professor Book Centers, Inc., provides continuous assistance and counsel in bookstore operation throughout the length of the franchise. Periodic visits are made by representatives of Little Professor Book Centers, Inc. Performance and results are evaluated and recommendations are offered on improving sales and profits. Experienced personnel are always available to assist in the solution of any problems. Comprehensive marketing and inventory management programs are provided.

Information Submitted: April 1990

MISS BOJANGLES, INC.
9711 Cortana Place
Baton Rouge, Louisiana 70815
G. Paul Smith

Description of Operation: Retail jewelry stores.

Number of Franchisees: 8 in 4 States

In Business Since: 1974

Equity Capital Needed: $20,000

Financial Assistance Available: Negotiable.

Training Provided: Complete training in all aspects of running a retail business, from ordering, to personnel, advertising techniques, etc. One week on-site training.

Managerial Assistance Available: Merchandising memos, feedback forum and convention.

Information Submitted: April 1990

MOBILITY CENTER, INC.
6693 Dixie
Bridgeport, Michigan 48722
Jay Redlin, Franchise Director

Description of Operation: Mobility Center retail stores sell a variety of contemporary mobility aids for those with walking disabilities, including the Amigo, the original 3 wheel, battery-powered wheelchair. Mobility Center, Inc., is a wholly owned subsidiary of Amigo Mobility International.

Number of Franchisees: 19 in 10 States

In Business Since: 1984

Equity Capital Needed: $71,000-$129,000

Financial Assistance Available: Financing provided by franchisor to qualified individuals.

Training Provided: 2 weeks intensive training course provided by franchisor, covering marketing, sales, administration and service.

Managerial Assistance Available: Continual support service provided for all areas of business operations.

Information Submitted: April 1990

MONOGRAMS PLUS, INC.
P. O. Box 20608
Waco, Texas 76702-0608

Description of Operation: Computerized "while you wait" monogramming stores operating in regional malls.

Number of Franchisees: 32

In Business Since: 1986

Equity Capital Needed: $45,000-$80,000 total investment.

Financial Assistance Available: Loan packaging and placement assistance available.

Training Provided: Complete training is provided.

Managerial Assistance Available: Ongoing in all phases of management.

Information Submitted: June 1990

MOVIES AND MORE FRANCHISE CORPORATION
1429 Warwick Avenue
Warwick, Rhode Island 02889
Arnold I. Kornstein, President

Description of Operation: We operate video specialty stores for the rental of pre-recorded movies, usually under a movie club plan; the sale of video cassette recorders, color television sets, camcorders, blank tapes, movies and video accessories; and the rental of video cassette recorders and television sets on a short-term or rental-to-own program. Franchises are being solicited in the continental United States.

Number of Franchisees: 36 in Rhode Island, Massachusetts, Connecticut, New Jersey, and Delaware.

In Business Since: 1981

Equity Capital Needed: $75,000

Financial Assistance Available: Franchisor extends credit to franchisee to secure as many VCRs as needed to operate short-term VCR rental program; generally ranges from $2,500-$10,000. Franchisor also assists in securing balance of financing needed.

Training Provided: Franchisor provides training in sales, movie club operation and the operation of the VCR rental programs, usually 1 week but longer if needed. Updated training provided on an ongoing basis as changes or new developments occur within the franchise system or in the video industry.

Managerial Assistance Available: Franchisor provides the systems for bookkeeping, inventory control, and the movie club program and for the VCR-TV rental programs, both short-term and rent-to-own. Franchisor also assists in personnel training, pricing of inventory and services, the buying and merchandising and the advertising and planning of promotions. This assistance is provided as needed both before the store opens for business and after the opening. Franchisor also arranges for franchisee to have his own direct accounts with suppliers and secures lines of credit for him. Franchisor provides store design and interior layout and assists in securing necessary fixtures and computer systems.

Information Submitted: June 1990

NEVADA BOB'S PRO SHOPS, INC.
3333 East Flamingo Road
Las Vegas, Nevada 89121
Mel Mead, President

Description of Operation: Selling discount golf equipment in an attractive atmosphere, specializing in top of the line golf clubs, golf bags and accessories from MacGregor, Spalding, Prima, Mizuno, Dunlop, etc. Also, professional advice on all golf equipment given by our professional staff.

Number of Franchisees: 216 located throughout the United States and Canada

In Business Since: 1974

Equity Capital Needed: $250,000 investment—$125,000 start-up cost and $125,000 credit line.

Financial Assistance Available: No financial assistance available at this time.

Training Provided: 1 week extensive training at the headquarters in Las Vegas. Training includes all aspects of the golf industry.

Managerial Assistance Available: Continuing assistance with all phases of operations. Annual convention sales seminars, weekly updating of product trends by phone and written correspondence.

Information Submitted: April 1990

*ONE HOUR MOTO PHOTO
4444 Lake Center Drive
Dayton, Ohio 45426
Michael Adler, President

Description of Operation: One Hour Moto-Photo is the world's largest franchisor of imaging services. A variety of imaging services is offered including on-site color negative film processing, color enlargements, portrait studios, video transfer, color copying and merchandising of frames, mats, and albums. The concept is expanding to include, among other things, video camera rental and commercial account development.

Number of Franchisees: 356 in the United States, Canada, Norway and Sweden.

In Business Since: 1981

Equity Capital Needed: $40,000

Financial Assistance Available: Franchisor assists in obtaining financing. Franchisor has secured various financing packages to assist qualified franchisees with their first store. Franchisor also offers a comprehensive financing package for additional stores.

Training Provided: Company provides up to 4 weeks of initial training. The training program includes 2 weeks in-store training and 2 weeks at franchisor's corporate training facility. A comprehensive on-site training program, including video tapes and manuals, is provided to franchisees to assist the ongoing training of their store associates.

Managerial Assistance Available: Moto Photo has over 100 corporate associates and a host of independent franchisees to assist a new franchisee with his/her business. Moto Photo offers support in training, marketing, business/operating systems, store design and construction, and real estate/site selection. Moto Photo provides franchisees with a proven marketing, promotion, in-store selling, and monitoring system. A Moto Photo marketing manager will work with you to develop a marketing and advertising plan tailored to your store and market area. Moto Photo will keep you up to date with the latest technology and trends so that you can take advantage of new profit opportunities. Moto Photo continues to develop complete training and marketing programs, not only for one hour processing, but also for portrait studios, merchandising, commercial account development and many other imaging products and services. Moto Photo's exclusive franchise accounting and point-of-sale system creates a data base with customer, marketing, and accounting information. The system provides all accounting functions, including inventory control, income and balance statements, invoicing, etc.

Information Submitted: May 1990

*PALMER VIDEO CORPORATION
1767 Morris Avenue
Union, New Jersey 07083
Dominick Romano, Franchise Sales

Description of Operation: Palmer Video has successfully established a rapidly growing chain of franchised Video Superstores based on sound operating principles and aggressive marketing concepts designed to increase market share.

Number of Franchisees: Over 100 in 11 States, including New Jersey, New York, Pennsylvania, Ohio, Illinois, Michigan, Alabama, Massachusetts and Colorado.

In Business Since: 1981, franchising since 1982.

Equity Capital Needed: $200,000-$300,000

Financial Assistance Available: No financial assistance available; however, franchisor will refer to appropriate lending agencies whenever possible, as well as be available for consultation with lenders.

Training Provided: Palmer Video will provide technical/management expertise, along with a state-of-the-art operating system, and ongoing support.

Managerial Assistance Available: Ongoing operational, promotional and advertising assistance, operations manual, monthly magazine, recommended purchases, and constant helpful comunications to franchisees.

Information Submitted: April 1990

PAPER WAREHOUSE, INC.
7120 Shady Oak Road
Eden Prairie, Minnesota 55344
William B. LaBelle, Director of Franchising

Description of Operation: Party and entertainment paper and plastic products plus home paper products and office products and supplies.

Number of Franchisees: 9 in 6 States plus 22 company-owned units.

In Business Since: 1983

Equity Capital Needed: $98,500

Financial Assistance Available: None

Training Provided: Training provided in all operations of the franchise.

Managerial Assistance Available: Ongoing with full support.

Information Submitted: April 1990

PARTY LAND, INC.
842 Red Lion Road
Philadelphia, Pennsylvania 19115
Todd Potter, Vice President

Description of Operation: Party supplies and balloons for all occasions.

Number of Franchisees: 10 units in Pennsylvania and New Jersey (1 company-owned).

In Business Since: 1986

Equity Capital Needed: $70,000

Financial Assistance Available: None

Training Provided: 2 weeks training for all new franchisees and management at a company-owned store.

Managerial Assistance Available: Monthly visits to update current trends and product information. Supervisors will also implement new advertising promotions and merchandising techniques.

Information Submitted: April 1990

260

PARTY WORLD FRANCHISE, INC.
10701 Vanowen Street
North Hollywood, California 91605
Stanley M. Tauber

Description of Operation: Party World is a company that specializes in the sale of party supplies, using a unique marketing strategy in the industry. By offering a large variety of selection, along with depth of merchandise and heavily discounted prices, we "bring the customer to us." In other words, the buying public seeks us out and we become the destination stop for party supplies.

Number of Franchisees: 4 franchise stores/3 more to open in 1990/10 stores. (All stores in Southern California.)

In Business Since: 1979

Equity Capital Needed: $250,000

Financial Assistance Available: Franchisor will assist franchisee in obtaining financing.

Training Provided: 3 weeks intensive training at headquarters store. Ongoing training and counseling at your store through our field representatives. Complete operations manual and hotline.

Managerial Assistance Available: Continual management service in such areas as site selection, lease negotiations, store design, national buying programs, recordkeeping, advertising, inventory control and store operations. A complete manual of operations, forms, directions, hotline, and advertising is provided. Field support managers are available to work closely with franchisees and visit stores regularly to assist in solving problems.

Information Submitted: April 1990

THE PERFUMERY, INC.
724 West 21st Street
Houston, Texas 77024
Beth Marshall, President

Description of Operation: Stores which average 300 square feet, are generally located in shopping malls but may be placed in strip shopping centers. Stores carry The Perfumery's line of approximately 110 reproduction and original fragrances. Stores also provide fragrance compatibility testing and custom blending of men's and women's fragrances.

Number of Franchisees: 13 in 3 States

In Business Since: 1983

Equity Capital Needed: Total investment required $50,000-$100,000. No minimum equity required.

Financial Assistance Available: The franchise fee ranges from $5,000 to $20,000 and averages $10,000. A total investment of $30,000 to $100,000 is required, of which $15,000 is inventory. No financing is currently provided by franchisor.

Training Provided: 6 days of training at company headquarters and company stores in Houston, Texas. Three days of training in franchisee's store at opening.

Managerial Assistance Available: Franchisor provides ongoing support in marketing, product development and training. Support includes periodic inspections of premises and evaluation of controls. A complete manual covering accounting controls, custom blending, fragrances and marketing is provided and video training on product knowledge.

Information Submitted: June 1990

PINCH A PENNY, INC.
14480 62nd Street North
Clearwater, Florida 33520
Fred A. Thomas, President

Description of Operation: Retail pool and patio supplies.

Number of Franchisees: 70 in Florida and Arizona

In Business Since: 1976

Equity Capital Needed: $90,000-$250,000

Financial Assistance Available: None

Training Provided: 4-6 weeks field training in retail stores and in the field doing service and repair. Regular calls on store by company representative. For advice/guidance on ordering, merchandising account and data processing, technical. Access to full service ad agency included in fees. Access to specialty promotion programs.

Managerial Assistance Available: Franchisor offers franchise owners an initial training program of up to 6 weeks duration at franchisor's headquarters or at such other sites as may be designated by franchisor. Offers ongoing management support, including current product information, marketing data, bookkeeping services, inventory control and advertising ideas ot its franchises.

Information Submitted: June 1990

PLAY IT AGAIN SPORTS
1550 Utica Avenue South
Suite 775
Minneapolis, Minnesota 55416
Craig Smock

Description of Operation: Retail sporting goods stores, new and used merchandise.

Number of Franchisees: 35

In Business Since: 1983, franchising since 1988

Equity Capital Needed: $30,000

Financial Assistance Available: None

Training Provided: 1 week of training provided in all operations of store.

Managerial Assistance Available: Ongoing support.

Information Submitted: April 1990

PORTRAIT AMERICA, INC.
22511 Telegraph Road
Suite 205
Southfield, Michigan 48034
Edward R. Schlager, Director of Franchise Development

Description of Operation: Full service professional photography specializing in children's and family portraits, weddings, executive portraits, sports teams, and special events. Excellent equipment and training allow franchisees to produce top quality work, resulting in referral and repeated business.

Number of Franchisees: 24 franchised locations, 2 company-owned locations.

In Business Since: 1987

Equity Capital Needed: Capital requirements are approximately $23,000.

Financial Assistance Available: Available for qualified franchisees.

Training Provided: An initial 1 week training in all areas of portrait photography and business operations including marketing, sales, pricing, bookkeeping, financial control, public relations and employee training provided. Ongoing training thereafter includes on-site, technical updates and seminars on various topics.

Managerial Assistance Available: The franchisor's department of operations provides ongoing managerial assistance in all technical and non-technical areas of the business.

Information Submitted: April 1990

PRO GOLF OF AMERICA, INC.
Tall Oaks Office Center
31884 Northwestern Highway
Farmington Hills, Michigan 48018
Bob Sage, President

Description of Operation: Golf equipment discount stores.

Number of Franchisees: 150 in 34 States and 4 countries.

In Business Since: 1961

Equity Capital Needed: $180,000-$225,000

Financial Assistance Available: Franchisor assists in opening credit with all major suppliers.

Training Provided: Initial 2 week training in Michigan. Assistance with grand opening on-site. Ongoing communications and training as long as franchise is owned.

Managerial Assistance Available: Continuous outgoing communications with regional co-ordinators and corporate advertising department. Monthly newsletter and news bulletins. Ordering, pricing and inventory assistance. Stores are visited regularly by field supervisors.

Information Submitted: April 1990

*THE PRO IMAGE
563 West 500 South
Suite 330
Bountiful, Utah 84010
Mark Gilleland, National Sales Director

Description of Operation: The Pro Image carries "Everything for the Sports Fan." These unique retail stores feature gifts and clothing that are licensed and approved by the professional and collegiate teams. The stores are generally 1,000 and 2,000 square feet in size and are located in regional shopping malls.

Number of Franchisees: 160 in 44 States, Canada and West Germany.

In Business Since: 1985

Equity Capital Needed: $85,000 to $125,000

Financial Assistance Available: None. The Pro Image assists in arranging third party financing.

Training Provided: The franchisee is trained in all phases of operations, merchandising, advertising, inventory control, management, bookkeeping, customer relations, and purchasing. Five to 10 days home office and field training.

Managerial Assistance Available: The Pro Image assists the franchisee in site selection and leasehold arrangements. The company provides complete operating manuals and accounting system. The Pro Image also allows the franchisee access to company purchasing system and its discounts. The company assists with grand opening and provides ongoing assistance for new products, promotions, and merchandising ideas.

Information Submitted: March 1990

PROJECT MULTIPLICATION INTERNATIONAL, INC.
7109 SW 117th Avenue
Miami, Florida 33183
Bruce F. Dales

Description of Operation: Retail concept featuring intercoordinated fashion accessories—jewelry, belts, hats, handbags, scarves. One of a kind PMI design group merchandise—accentuate and SKB originals and other name brand merchandise featured—emphasis on service and custom design plus wardrobe accessorizing.

Number of Franchisees: 4 in Florida and Georgia

In Business Since: 1981, retail stores and consulting, franchising 1986.

Equity Capital Needed: $65,000 to $85,000 includes inventory, fixtures, fee, sign, carpet and painting.

Financial Assistance Available: None, will assist in developing loan package.

Training Provided: 1 week at Miami training facility. 2 days (2 people) store set-up. 1 day (1 person) in store and ongoing helpline service.

Managerial Assistance Available: Full training and operations manual and systems linked to computer cash register, monthly report sales, cost/retail, percentage of gross profit, OTB by classifications, helpline, all operations forms, personnel package, monthly newsletter featuring merchandise, store promotions, and merchandise plans, marketing program for advertising and initial layout and real estate assistance.

Information Submitted: April 1990

*RADIO SHACK DIVISION
TANDY CORPORATION
1600 One Tandy Center
Fort Worth, Texas 76102
Robert Owens, Vice President

Description of Operation: Radio Shack presently offers a licensing program to established retailers in towns of 8,500 or less in population. The dealerships are called Authorized Sales Centers. Applicants must be already established in a retail business.

Number of Franchisees: 2,200 in all States, West Indies, Central America, South America, Guam, and American Samoa.

In Business Since: 1921

Equity Capital Needed: $40,000 to $60,000

Financial Assistance Available: Assist with bank presentation. No direct financial aid provided by franchisors.

Training Provided: Since dealerships are granted only to existing retailers, no formal training is provided. Procedures manual, display guide and miscellaneous instructional materials supplied upon approval of applicant.

Managerial Assistance Available: Weekly scheduled phone consultation, periodic visits (usually twice a year) for review of performance. Free ad mat service to introduce new lines and explain advertising and promotional plans. Provide technical manuals covering operations and servicing of consumer electronics merchandise.

Information Submitted: April 1990

RECEPTIONS PLUS, INC.
1970 Jerome Avenue
Bronx, New York 10453
David J. Lesser, President

Description of Operation: Receptions Plus offers a unique retail operation: a complete wedding service under one roof. Receptions Plus provides high quality products and services for low prices and offers the convenience of shop-at-home service. Products and services include catering, photography, video, cakes, flowers, limousines, tuxedos, invitations, souvenirs, travel, music, and jewelry.

Number of Franchisees: 1 in Massachusetts and 3 company-owned in New York and New Jersey.

In Business Since: 1969, franchising since September 1985.

Equity Capital Needed: Initial investments are available ranging from $61,000-$225,000.

Financial Assistance Available: The franchisor at the present time offers no financing assistance to franchisees.

Training Provided: Receptions Plus provides a comprehensive 3 week training program at its corporate headquarters. The training schedule accounts for every 15 minutes of each training day, and includes a 1,750 page operations manual and a complete set of 9 video training tapes covering every aspect of the operation. Training is also provided to operate and implement the Receptions Plus custom developed computer software programs. Additional training also includes 1 week on-site with an operations specialist from headquarters and extensive operations and follow-up support.

Managerial Assistance Available: Receptions Plus provides continual management service for the life of the franchise in such areas as bookkeeping, advertising, inventory, purchasing, and business relations. Complete manuals of operations, forms, and instructions are provided. Headquarters representatives are always available to work closely with franchisees and visit stores regularly. At headquarters there are always operations specialists to assist franchisees with problems. Headquarters is a perfect prototype of the operation and is always involved with the business and its day-to-day dealings with respect to research and development.

Information Submitted: May 1990

RE-SELL-IT SHOPS, INC.
3316 Governors Drive
San Diego, California 92122
Florence Kalanquin, President

Description of Operation: Sophisticated consignment stores: shops handle home furnishings and the boutique shops handle clothing.

Number of Franchisees: 3 in California plus 1 company-owned.

In Business Since: 1979, in California since 1981.

Equity Capital Needed: $20,000

Financial Assistance Available: 50 percent of franchise fee for 2 years. 50 percent of franchise fee over 2 years, amortized. Total amount financed $47.50. Interest 12 percent, payment $47.50 per month.

Training Provided: Complete in-house training previous to opening at corporate office and store. Assistance at store opening by corporation representative, then ongoing assistance whenever requested plus bi-monthly newsletter and advertising, including ad copy monthly. Periodic visits by corporation representative.

Managerial Assistance Available: Managerial skills will be presented in origination training and on-site assistance at store opening. Periodic meetings to present new ideas and systems on an ongoing basis. Corporate help is available any time upon request.

Information Submitted: June 1990

*RUSLAN DISCOUNT PETMART
(Lanrus, Inc.)
7390 Trade Street
San Diego, California 92121-9899
Russell N. Harris

Description of Operation: Ruslan Discount Petmart is a one-of-a-kind franchise opportunity offering turnkey retail pet supply stores. The stores offer only the highest quality foods and supplies for dogs, cats, birds, and fish without livestock. Stores are approximately 1,500 square feet and located in shopping centers with a supermarket anchor tenant.

Number of Franchisees: 23 in California

In Business Since: 1973

Equity Capital Needed: $61,000 to $77,000

Financial Assistance Available: Franchisor will assist in preparation of loan package for presentation to financial institution or SBA.

Training Provided: 1 week of classroom studies focused on pet care and product knowledge and 1 week in-store business management training. Training is conducted in San Diego, California.

Managerial Assistance Available: Complete ongoing managerial assistance is provided by field support staff and informational toll-free hotline. In-store signage, advertising campaigns, purchasing guidance, and business analysis are provided.

Information Submitted: June 1990

SILVER SCREEN VIDEO, INC.
1412B Baytree Road
P. O. Box 3724
Valdosta, Georgia 31604
L. L. Baggett, Jr., Franchise Marketing Manager

Description of Operation: Silver Screen Video grants franchises the right to operate retail video stores using its name, logo, decor, and operating procedures. Stores offer, for sale and rental, video tape cassettes, recorders and players, accessories, services and other video related products. Silver Screen Video offers its own computer and software packages using a bar code scanner at point-of-sale.

Number of Franchisees: 3 in Kansas, Georgia and Florida.

In Business Since: 1984

Equity Capital Needed: Varies.

Financial Assistance Available: An initial investment of $50,000 to $60,000 is required, which applies to the purchase of tapes, store fixtures, franchise fee and operating capital. Qualified franchisees may elect to lease machines and the computer package.

Training Provided: All franchisees and certain key employees are required to successfully complete a 2 day training course covering advertising, merchandising, product knowledge, store set-up, customer relations, selling, daily operations, management and employee relations, and computer training.

Managerial Assistance Available: Silver Screen Video offers ongoing management support, including current product information, marketing data, bookkeeping services, inventory control, and advertising ideas to its franchisees.

Information Submitted: May 1990

SOFTWARE CITY
111 Galway Place
Teaneck, New Jersey 07666
Shep Altshuler, President

Description of Operation: Leading chain of franchised software specialty stores. Discounted programs for recreation, education and business. Stores also carry a wide selection of books, magazines, peripherals, accessories, disks, etc.

Number of Franchisees: 85 stores throughout United States and overseas.

In Business Since: 1980

Equity Capital Needed: Approximately $150,000.

Financial Assistance Available: None

Training Provided: 1 week training in various phases of store operations is conducted at the home office in Teaneck, New Jersey, and in-store.

Managerial Assistance Available: Continual management assistance, group buying power, technical support, national advertising, in-store assistance, meetings and information bulletins.

Information Submitted: May 1990

SONMARK, INC.
184 Quigley Boulevard
New Castle, Delaware 19720
Gladys D. King

Description of Operation: Greeting card retail sales.

Number of Franchisees: 9

In Business Since: 1987

Equity Capital Needed: $14,500 and up

Financial Assistance Available: None

Training Provided: Complete training in various phases of store operation.

Managerial Assistance Available: Continuous management assistance.

Information Submitted: June 1990

SOUND FUTURE COMPACT DISC CENTERS
2315 Luna Road
Suite 136
Carrollton, Texas 75006
Walter Hawley, Vice President

Description of Operation: Compact disc and tapes retail operation offers a unique combination of full service, knowledgeable employees, great selection, separate listening rooms for rock/pop, jazz and classical music and all at competitive prices. Franchisees enjoy the exciting music industry first hand in stores averaging 2,400 square feet.

Number of Franchisees: 2 plus 4 company-owned

In Business Since: 1986, franchising since 1989.

Equity Capital Needed: $150,000 to $475,000

Financial Assistance Available: None

Training Provided: Sound Future Incorporated provides an intensive 5 day initial training and familiarization course as well as on-site training a few days before and after the store opening.

Managerial Assistance Available: Sound Future Incorporated provides continual management service for the life of the franchise in such areas as site selection, buying, advertising, promotion, accounting, policies and procedures and operations. A complete operations manual is available. A staff of dedicated professionals, as well as your own representative, are available to assist in solving problems at all times.

Information Submitted: July 1990

SPECIAL SELECTIONS
P. O. Box 3243
Boise, Idaho 83703
Roxanne Overton, President

Description of Operation: Special Selections is a personal shopping service that caters to gift buyers, both personal and business. We do not stock items, although we have vast and growing sources for unique, profitable gifts. Special Selections takes a fun creative career and shows you how to avoid costly mistakes and make money.

Number of Franchisees: 1 in 1 State

In Business Since: 1988

Equity Capital Needed: $5,000 plus

Financial Assistance Available: None

Training Provided: 4 day training class with complete operations manual.

Managerial Assistance Available: Yes

Information Submitted: April 1990

*ST. ANDREWS GOLF CORP.
(LAS VEGAS DISCOUNT GOLF & TENNIS)
5325 South Valley View Boulevard
Suite 10
Las Vegas, Nevada 89118

Description of Operation: St. Andrews Golf Corp., the exclusive franchisors of Las Vegas Discount Golf & Tennis, offers you a complete retail golf and tennis facility. Stores range in size from 3,500 square feet to 6,000 square feet. You will benefit from our enormous buying power in the industry as well as carry the exclusive St. Andrews brand of golf equipment. St. Andrews Golf Corp. provides you with all necessary training and assistance needed for a golf and tennis operation.

Number of Franchisees: 51 in 11 States, 4 in Canada, 2 in Spain, 1 in France and 1 in Japan.

In Business Since: 1984

Equity Capital Needed: Minimum of $150,000 cash—total investment of $300,000.

Financial Assistance Available: None provided by franchisor. However, all necessary information for loan applications is available.

Training Provided: Intensive classroom on-site training in the original Las Vegas store provided for all franchisees and their managerial staff. The course runs 14 days and covers every aspect of the golf and tennis retail industry. Refresher and new technique or product knowledge courses provided as needed.

Managerial Assistance Available: St. Andrews Golf Corp. provides complete site-selection and lease negotiating for all franchisees. Complete manuals of operations, forms and directions provided. New product and special purchase announcements provided on a continual basis. Field representatives to work closely with the franchisees and visit stores regularly to assist in any problem solving needed. Continual ongoing support and assistance for all franchisees.

Information Submitted: April 1990

THE TINDER BOX INTERNATIONAL, LTD.
Franchise Development Office
19060 Dominguez Hills Drive
Compton, California 90220
Wayne Best, Director, Franchise Development

Description of Operation: Specialty retail mall chain with product mix consisting of unique gifts as well as pipes, cigars, and tobaccos.

Number of Franchisees: 154 stores in 37 States plus 20 company-owned stores.

In Business Since: 1928

Equity Capital Needed: Minimum $50,000—total investment $135,000-$200,000 including inventory.

Financial Assistance Available: Financing assistance or direct financing available through company.

Training Provided: 5 day intensive training for franchisee and/or manager at franchisor's headquarters plus in-store set-up and training.

Managerial Assistance Available: Franchisor provides ongoing merchandising, advertising, marketing and accounting assistance. Also available are site selection, store design and lease assistance, operation manuals, training videos and various fliers and publications. Annual convention and/or regional seminars including a private gift and tobacco show.

Information Submitted: April 1990

USA DORACO CORP.
20 East Herman Street
Philadelphia, Pennsylvania 19144
J. Gary Fromm, C.E.O.

Description of Operation: Retail sales of residential custom doors and windows direct to the homeowner. Sales are made through retail showrooms. All products are custom-made; therefore there is virtually no inventory other than showroom displays. No inventory combined with the retail orientation means no cash tied up in slow moving products and no accounts receivable.

Number of Franchisees: None, 5 company-owned units in 3 States

In Business Since: 1987

Equity Capital Needed: $35,000 to $85,000

Financial Assistance Available: None; however, help is available for prospective franchises to prepare a loan proposal for their bank.

Training Provided: Intensive 1 week training program provided at company headquarters in Philadelphia, Pennsylvania, followed by 6 days of on-site assistance.

Managerial Assistance Available: At the franchisee's request, assistance in management, sales and accounting is available on a per diem basis.

Information Submitted: May 1990

VIDEO BIZ, INC.
2981 West S/R 434
Suite 100
Longwood FL 32779
Edward Fainelli

Description of Operation: Video movies and video equipment sales and rentals. Also film-to-tape transfer and accessories sale, special club member enrollments.

Number of Franchisees: 145 plus 75 affiliates in over 200 cities.

In Business Since: 1981

Equity Capital Needed: $59,950 plus construction costs.

Financial Assistance Available: None

Training Provided: Total training at franchisee's location 3 to 5 days, site selection assistance, and national and regional advertising.

Managerial Assistance Available: Complete operations manual including all printing forms required for operation; inventory control systems; company constantly available for consultation; technical assistance and opening manager provided. Computer store program provided.

Information Submitted: April 1990

VIDEO GALAXY FRANCHISE, INC.
P. O. Box 1033
East Granby, Connecticut 06026
William D. Corbin

Description of Operation: Video Galaxy Franchise began in the video rental and retail business in Connecticut in 1981 and has been franchising since 1985. Currently ranked number 8 in top 100 video companies in sales volume. Video Galaxy is actively seeking new franchisees in selected markets.

Number of Franchisees: 45

In Business Since: 1981

Equity Capital Needed: $50,000

Financial Assistance Available: None

Training Provided: Yes

Managerial Assistance Available: Yes

Information Submitted: April 1990

VIDEOMATIC INTERNATIONAL, INC.
1060 West Covina Parkway
West Covina, California 91790
Harold E. Brown, President

Description of Operation: Videomatic is a fully automated video store, operating 24 hours per day, with no employees and using an on-line computerized credit card system rather than cash to rent top hits and new releases. Requires only a few spare hours to operate. Seeking regional franchisors.

Number of Franchisees: 48 plus 1 company-owned in 10 States.

In Business Since: 1988

Equity Capital Needed: Approximately $40,000 of total investment of $160,000.

Financial Assistance Available: The company will assist franchisee in locating and applying for financing. The company does not make direct loans.

Training Provided: 2 days on-site.

Managerial Assistance Available: Continuous

Information Submitted: May 1990

*VIDEO UPDATE, INC.
World Headquarters
287 East 6th Street
St. Paul, Minnesota 55101
John Bedard

Description of Operation: A Video Update franchise enables franchisees to run a state-of-the-art video store while maximizing their independence and self-reward.

Number of Franchisees: 60 plus in 12 States

In Business Since: 1982

Equity Capital Needed: $73,250 to $228,100

Financial Assistance Available: Will help franchisee in obtaining financing, in some instances through the Small Business Administration.

Training Provided: Video Update provides ongoing educational services and support throughout the life of the franchise agreement.

Managerial Assistance Available: Video Update provides continual management assistance through its toll-free phone lines and maintains a highly trained staff to answer all questions and concerns that may arise. In addition, franchisees are provided with Video Update's pre-store opening manual and operations manual.

Information Submitted: April 1990

WEE WIN TOYS AND ACCESSORIES, INC.
15340 Vantage Parkway E.
Suite 250
Houston, Texas 77032
James D. Flanagan

Description of Operation: Wholesale 2 lines of toys, Christian toys and wholesome toys.

Number of Franchisees: 181 in entire U.S.A.

In Business Since: 1984

Equity Capital Needed: $9,500 initial investment.

Financial Assistance Available: None.

Training Provided: 3 day training meeting held once each month. We encourage distributors to come as often as possible.

Managerial Assistance Available: Continued, ongoing training by Wee Win managers.

Information Submitted: April 1990

*WEST COAST VIDEO
9990 Global Road
Philadelphia, Pennsylvania 19115
John L. Barry, Vice President, Franchise Development

Description of Operation: World's largest chain of franchised video stores.

Number of Franchisees: 600 plus 90 company operations in all 50 States, all 10 Canadian Provinces and the U.K.

In Business Since: 1983

Equity Capital Needed: $214,000

Financial Assistance Available: None

Training Provided: 1 week at West Coast College in Philadelphia, Pennsylvania.

Managerial Assistance Available: Ongoing consultation through field support, mini computer system, regional training, seminars and monthly analysis of operation.

Information Submitted: April 1990

*WICKS 'N' STICKS DIVISION
WNNS, INC.
P. O. Box 4586
Houston, Texas 77210-4586
Paul Klatsky, Senior Vice President

Description of Operation: Wicks 'N' Sticks is the nation's largest specialty retailer of candles, room fragrancing products and related home decorating accessories. Merchandise, including private label and exclusive products, comes from vendors worldwide. Stores are located in major regional malls, today's most desirable retail setting.

Number of Franchisees: 274 in 43 States

In Business Since: 1968

Equity Capital Needed: $65,000-$75,000

Financial Assistance Available: Some financing may be available.

Training Provided: Extensive 1-week classroom training prepares franchisee for the daily operation of the store. Field staff continues training the franchisee and employees once the store is open, and ensures successful operation during the first critical weeks in business.

Managerial Assistance Available: Wicks 'N' Sticks provides extensive assistance, including site selection guidelines, construction specifications and plans; merchandise selection, pricing guidelines and visual presentation recommendations; national buying power; marketing support materials. Field staff makes frequent store visits, supplemented by telecommunications, publications, regional meetings and an annual convention.

Information Submitted: June 1990

WILD BIRDS UNLIMITED, INC.
1430 Broad Ripple Avenue
Indianapolis, Indiana 46220
James R. Carpenter, President

Description of Operation: Wild Birds Unlimited, Inc., offers unique retail shops that specialize in supplying birdseed, feeders, and gift items for the popular hobby of backyard bird feeding. The franchise package includes assistance in site selection and store layout, and includes each store in a discount purchasing program for both feeders and birdseed. Franchises are currently available throughout the United States and Canada.

Number of Franchisees: 48 in 16 States and Canada

In Business Since: 1981

Equity Capital Needed: $35,000 to $50,000

Financial Assistance Available: No financial assistance is provided by the franchisor.

Training Provided: The franchisor provides 3 days of training at one of the company-owned stores and provides 2 training manuals, 1 for store operations, 1 for knowledge about bird feeding and sales techniques. Additional visits to the franchisee's store once opened will concentrate on displays, inventory and advertising techniques.

Managerial Assistance Available: Wild Birds Unlimited, Inc., provides continuing management assistance in areas such as group purchasing, advertising, new product information and help with any problems in the operation of the store.

Information Submitted: April 1990

WILLIAM ERNEST BROWN, LTD.
P. O. Box 153 (Sur House)
Big Sur, California 93920
James M. Josoff, Vice President

Description of Operation: Retail stationery shops, featuring very high quality custom designing of stationery and invitations.

Number of Franchisees: 11 plus 1 company-owned

In Business Since: 1970

Equity Capital Needed: Approximately $100,000.

Financial Assistance Available: None

Training Provided: Initial training and buying—3 to 4 weeks, continuing basis. Seminars, in-shop training, newsletters are provided on a continuing basis to all franchisees.

Managerial Assistance Available: As above.

Information Submitted: June 1990

WORLD BAZAAR FRANCHISE CORPORATION (WBFC)
4849 Massachusetts Boulevard
College Park, Georgia 30337-6605
Paul J. Modzelewski, Vice President Development

Description of Operation: We are the largest national franchising chain stores retailing wicker and rattan furniture, imported and domestic. We offer silk flowers, baskets, brass, glassware, plus a wide selection of home decor and gift items. Our stores range from the newest and most exciting malls and shopping centers to a stand-alone location.

Number of Franchisees: Our family of franchisees consists of 43 owners operating 108 stores plus 10 company-owned stores in 27 States across the United States.

In Business Since: The first World Bazaar was opened in 1965 and began franchising in 1968.

Equity Capital Needed: Approximately $140,000 to $225,000 to open your first store.

Financial Assistance Available: Franchise fee is $50,000, of which WBFC will finance $45,000 interest free for 5 years. We will also finance up to $50,000 to $55,000 on merchandise purchased from World Bazaar for 5 years at prime plus 1-1/2 percent.

Training Provided: 2 weeks in corporate office plus store opening assistance, usually consisting of 10 to 14 days.

Managerial Assistance Available: World Bazaar Franchise Corporation will work with or on behalf of the franchisee on lease negotiations and site selection. Our district managers will assist in all phases of training including personnel, merchandising, buying, display, accounting, and all other aspects of store management. Qualified district managers will work with you on promotions, especially those geared toward seasonal sales activities.

Information Submitted: April 1990

SECURITY SYSTEMS

CHAMBERS FRANCHISED SECURITY SYSTEMS, INC.
1103 Fredericksburg Road
San Antonio, Texas 78201
David Morris, President

Description of Operation: A high performance alarm signaling service primarily directed at high risk businesses and homeowners. Unique product utilizing an impact detection system with central station listen-in concept. The system detects burglars earlier than other systems. Central station listen-in verifies all alerts, thus reducing false alarms. Fully computerized. High recurring monthly revenue generation assures company stability after start-up. Franchisor company buy-back guarantee provided.

Number of Franchisees: Franchise operations starting in 1990. Lower cost "ground floor" opportunities available.

In Business Since: Founded in 1969 in Central Ohio by police officer John Chambers, who was seeking to offer his community a better security system. Texas operations began in 1979 as regional providers of the service. Franchising division activated in 1990.

Equity Capital Needed: Territorial variations. Start-up costs are dependent on degree of support needed.

Financial Assistance Available: Loan package assistance provided. We can lease major hardware items (computer, inventory, etc.).

Training Provided: 30 day start-up training program. Dealer must spend 2 weeks at national headquarters in San Antonio, Texas followed by a 2 week field training session in start-up city. Ongoing training in product marketing tips, technical updates and managerial style is provided on a continuing basis to the dealer.

Managerial Assistance Available: We train for turnkey operations. We provide assistance in employee selection and training, business site selection, competitor analysis and market potential.

Information Submitted: April 1990

DICTOGRAPH SECURITY SYSTEMS
21 Northfield Avenue
Edison, New Jersey 08818-3017
Myles C. Goldberg, Senior Vice President

Description of Operation: The first company in industry to franchise, with a 40-year history of assisting entrepreneurial businessmen and industry-experienced individuals alike in the sale, installation, maintenance and monitoring of security systems for the residential, commercial, industrial and institutional markets. Extensive line of proprietary and private labeled products, including automatic burglar, fire and smoke alarm systems, access control devices. Also a vast line of leading-edge closed circuit television systems for loss control and building management, including a unique transaction verification system particularly well-suited for the high large and small scale retail market of convenience stores, gas stations, liquor stores and the like. Fully computerized central monitoring station enables dealers to produce continuing monthly income.

Number of Franchisees: Over 50, several overseas.

In Business Since: Founding company since 1902; became affilate of Holmes Protection, established 1988.

Equity Capital Needed: Territorial variations based on population.

Financial Assistance Available: None

Training Provided: Dealer receives 2 weeks of intensive training in all facets of business at company's national headquarters training academy. Company provides dealer with opportunity to send sales, technical, installation and administrative personnel to headquarters training academy for specific classes held throughout the year. Periodic regional meetings held each year for attendance by dealer and key personnel. Yearly national convention features 3-5 days of important seminars, training courses and new product introductions.

Managerial Assistance Available: The company is constantly developing new material and programs including manuals, sales presentations, technical memorandums and marketing communications materials. Each dealer assigned a dealer advisor who remains a source of information and assistance regarding every facet of the business. Technical and field assistance available to help dealer with equipment applications and troubleshooting, sales development, recruiting and training. Monthly communications packets keep dealers apprised of business developments as they occur. Company coducts national sales contest as incentive for dealer's sales personnel. National and local advertising and public relations handled by in-house staff who will assist as needed in developing dealer's local marketing efforts through use of various media.

Information Submitted: April 1990

*DYNAMARK SECURITY CENTERS, INC.
P. O. Box 2068
Hagerstown, Maryland 21742-2068
Wayne E. Alter, Jr., President and Chief Executive Officer

Description of Operation: Dynamark Security Centers, over the past 13 years, has developed a unique program and method of marketing residential and light commercial security and fire protection devices. Using standardized trade names, service marks and trademarks, and advertising plus training and instructions in operating an exclusive DSC business, franchisees purchase from DSC at bonafide wholesale prices, then sell, install and service devices at retail prices in their marketing territories. Central station monitoring services are available through a DSC subsidiary, DynaWatch, Inc.

Number of Franchisees: Approximately 150 in 33 States.

In Business Since: 1977 as Amtronics, Inc.; in 1984 changed name to Dynamark Security Centers, Inc.

Equity Capital Needed: $50,000. This includes franchise fees, initial classroom and on-the-job training, opening inventory, working capital and miscellaneous costs.

Financial Assistance Available: DSC does not guarantee to obtain or provide financing for franchisee.

Training Provided: 5 day mandatory initial training course scheduled at national training center for all new franchisees and/or their operations managers. Ongoing advanced training conducted at national training center and at regional locations.

Managerial Assistance Available: DSC provides management services in such areas as marketing and sales, advertising and public relations, and bookkeeping. A complete manual of operations, forms, guidelines and directions is provided. Corporate staff as well as technical advisors work via phone in the field with franchise organizations for training and problem solving purposes. DSC sponsors national and regional meetings of franchisees in addition to conducting ongoing marketing research and development to maintain leadership position with the consumer public.

Information Submitted: April 1990

THE SECURITY ALLIANCE CORPORATION
1865 Miner Street
Des Plaines, Illinois 60016
Ron Davis, President

Description of Operation: Security Alliance Corporation is a franchisor of companies who wish to be in the residential and mini-commercial security systems business. Using state-of-the-art, supervised wireless systems, Security Alliance members are provided with a broad range of training, advertising and promotional support.

Number of Franchisees: 110 in 25 States

In Business Since: 1974

Equity Capital Needed: $15,000

Financial Assistance Available: Financing is available on a limited basis, although support is provided to obtain SBA assistance to qualified franchisees.

Training Provided: 1 week initial training, followed by 1 week of sales training plus quarterly regional training seminars plus monthly visitations.

Managerial Assistance Available: Franchisor provides on-going telephone, in-person support and managerial assistance through seminars. Three separate types of seminars are offered every 45 days, ranging from technical and sales support to sales management and management seminars. In addition, 5 field marketing people are available for in-field visitations, usually on a monthly basis.

Information Submitted: May 1990

SONITROL CORPORATION
424 North Washington Street
Alexandria, Virginia 22314

Description of Operation: Sonitrol Corporation is a manufacturer of audio intrusion detection alarm systems. A franchised Sonitrol dealer is granted a geographic area of primary responsibility where they are responsible for maintaining a sales effort of Sonitrol security alarm systems to businesses or residential end-users and monitoring those systems at a central monitoring station.

Number of Franchisees: 180 in 32 States

In Business Since: 1964

Equity Capital Needed: One-third of $100,000-$400,000 total capital required, which varies according to size of market and franchisee's business plan.

Financial Assistance Available: A subsidiary, Sonitrol Financial Corporation, can provide lease financing for central monitoring station equipment.

Training Provided: Each new franchisee is assigned a mentor to supervise the critical path events to organizing and opening the dealership. Classroom or on-site training is provided as appropriate for dealer/general manager, sales manager, sales persons, alarm installers, equipment technicians, and monitoring console operators.

Managerial Assistance Available: Assistance to the franchise network is provided in the areas of national sales and marketing programs; consultation from field sales representatives to address local dealership's needs; formal training programs for management, sales, installation and service, operators; and hot-line service engineering response for installers to monitor equipment technicians. Operating standards are published and periodic formal inspections are conducted to maintain a consistent level of service quality. Corporate product R&D is ongoing to maintain a differentiated technology edge in Sonitrol's audio listen-in security system.

Information Submitted: June 1990

SWIMMING POOLS

CARIBBEAN CLEAR, INC.
220 Executive Center Drive
Columbia, South Carolina 29210
Jerry Minchey, President

Description of Operation: Caribbean Clear offers a revolutionary new method of purifying swimming pools without chlorine using technology developed by NASA. Franchisee sells units directly to pool owners in his exclusive area.

Number of Franchisees: Over 100

In Business Since: 1977

Equity Capital Needed: $22,500 for initial inventory.

Financial Assistance Available: No financing provided at this time.

Training Provided: Intensive 2 day, mandatory training course for all new franchisees.

Managerial Assistance Available: Caribbean Clear provides continual management and technical consulting. A staff of engineers, chemist and managers are available to work directly with the franchisee as needed.

Information Submitted: June 1990

TOOLS, HARDWARE

AD A BOY TOOL RENTAL, INC.
6655 S. Sweetwater Road
Lithia Springs, Georgia 30057
Jimmy Sorrells, President

Description of Operation: Ad A Boy Tool Rental offers a small equipment and tool rental business with a broad range of items to serve the homeowner, contractor, party, and industrial customer. Store owners select their markets based on our feasibility study and their own personal preferences. Building required—1,800 to 3,200 square feet with outside storage and good traffic flow.

Number of Franchisees: 26 in Georgia, Florida, Idaho, Colorado, Louisiana, etc., and the Virgin Islands.

In Business Since: 1986

Equity Capital Needed: $24,000 plus $6,000 to $10,000 working capital. No franchise fee or royalty payments.

Financial Assistance Available: Your down payment of $24,000 is applied to the purchase of $85,000 of equipment, tools, and opening supplies. Balance can be financed with local banks. Guidance is provided in securing financing to qualified applicants.

Training Provided: Complete on-site training at the new store on a one-to-one basis for 2 full days. Training is very personalized to the individual store owner's requirements. Complete information on the equipment and how to run the rental business.

Managerial Assistance Available: Initial consultation covers market survey and feasibility study, site eveluation, lease negotiation, financing, insurance, advertising, bookkeeping, rental contracts, and rental rates. After the store is in operation consultation is provided in-store on an ongoing basis. Topics include operation and development of the rental business.

Information Submitted: April 1990

MAC TOOLS, INC.
P. O. Box 370
South Fayette Street
Washington Court House, Ohio 43160
Rick Cote, Vice President Sales

Description of Operation: Distributors carrying complete inventory of over 9,000 tools, calling directly on mechanics and light industry. These tools consist of a complete assortment of all small hand tools, sockets, wrenches, punches, chisels, screwdrivers, tool boxes, pneumatic tools, as well as special tools designed for the automotive market.

Number of Franchisees: Over 1,800 throughout the United States and Canada.

In Business Since: 1938

Equity Capital Needed: $45,000

Financial Assistance Available: The $45,000 starting amount includes a basic starting inventory, initial deposit on a new tool truck, business supplies, and backup capital. There are no franchise fees and the original investment is protected by a buy-back agreement. Financing for the starter inventory is available for qualified applicants.

Training Provided: After new distributor training in Ohio, each distributor is assigned to a district manager who lives in the local area and does all necessary follow-up training. He will aid in displaying the trucks, establishing bookkeeping systems, and technical knowledge, and spend approximately 3 weeks with any new distributor and then maintain a monthly contact. Also will continue to work with the distributor as he deems necessary.

Managerial Assistance Available: Same as above.

Information Submitted: April 1990

TOOL SHACK
TOOL STORES, INC.
19634 Ventura Boulevard
Suite 209
Tarzana, California 91356

Description of Operation: Tool stores retailing name brand tools at discount prices with full guarantees to professional tradesmen.

Number of Franchisees: 38 in California, Arizona, Texas, Oklahoma, and Maryland.

In Business Since: 1978, franchising since 1980.

Equity Capital Needed: Minimum $50,000 cash investment. Total package $120,000 including franchise fee $24,500; balance of investment used for inventory, deposits, working capital, etc.

Financial Assistance Available: SBA loans from $55,000 are available. Inventory of approximately $80,000 is provided at cost and financing available on balance.

Training Provided: Training in all phases of business conducted in actual operating store. One week to 10 days minimum duration, more if necessary. Additional days of training are provided during the grand opening of franchisee's store.

Managerial Assistance Available: The company provides a heavy concentration of radio and newspaper advertising on a consistent basis. Mass buying power is available to franchisees through tool distributors and factories. Site selection, lease negotiation and store set-up are also provided to franchisee.

Information Submitted: April 1990

VENDING

FORD GUM & MACHINE COMPANY, INC.
Division of LEAF, INC.
New and Hoag Streets
Akron, New York 14001
George H. Stege, Vice President

Description of Operation: Manufacturer and distributor of chewing gum, candy, and candy coated confections for sale through self-service vending machines, also manufactured and distrubuted to franchisees by the company.

Number of Franchisees: 183 in all States, Canada and Puerto Rico.

In Business Since: 1934 with manufacturing plant in Akron, New York.

Equity Capital Needed: $5,000-$30,000 depending on area.

Financial Assistance Available: Extended credit to new franchisees for, expansion of franchised territory, purchase of existing franchise from retiring franchisee, and purchase of equipment and supplies.

Training Provided: On-the-job training in machine and service operation in franchisee's area.

Managerial Assistance Available: See above.

Information Submitted: May 1990

UNITED SNACKS OF AMERICA, INC.
dba SNACKPACKER
P. O. Box 33488
Raleigh, North Carolina 27808
David A. Kachuck

Description of Operation: Snackpacker is an industrial snack food vending system. It provides a snack food service to small offices and shops.

Number of Franchisees: 5 in North Carolina, New Jersey and Georgia.

In Business Since: 1980

Equity Capital Needed: $75,000

Financial Assistance Available: None

Training Provided: Field training, classroom and on-site assistance as necessary, duration of training not guaranteed.

Managerial Assistance Available: Operating manual plus on-site assistance duration is not guaranteed. Periodic on-site and telephone consultation assistance for the life of the franchise.

Information Submitted: June 1990

WESTROCK VENDING VEHICLES CORP.
1565D 5th Industrial Court
Bayshore, New York 11706
Stephen L. Kronrad, President

Description of Operation: Westrock Vending Vehicles Corp. is offering a proven, highly respected franchise opportunity, mobile trailers and step vans for the selling of submarine sandwiches, hot food, soda and ice cream in industrial and high traffic areas. Operator works on high profit with very low overhead.

Number of Franchisees: 26 in New York.

In Business Since: 1970

Equity Capital Needed: Trailers start at $12,000 and trucks $30,000. As little as 10 percent down to qualified buyers of trucks or trailers with the balance financed.

Financial Assistance Available: A total investment of $116,000 is necessary to open a Master Distribution Center franchise; the down payment of $41,000 pays for 25 vehicles, freezer, tools, inventory and fees. Westrock can arrange to finance the balance for qualified individuals. Franchisee may arrange their own outside financing.

Training Provided: Westrock will assist in your training and any questions you might have.

Managerial Assistance Available: Westrock provides the most comprehensive managerial and technical assistance programs available in the industry. The franchisee is advised in the areas of managerial science and business administration, bookkeeping, advertising, inventory control, vehicles and equipment maintenance, and specific information related to the industry. Manuals of operation, forms, and directions are provided. Westrock executives are always available to assist in solving problems. Consulting expertise is available.

Information Submitted: April 1990

WATER CONDITIONING

CULLIGAN INTERNATIONAL COMPANY
One Culligan Parkway
Northbrook, Illinois 60062

Description of Operation: Parent company is supplier to franchisee for water treatment equipment. Franchisee sells, leases, maintains and repairs water treatment equipment for domestic, commercial, and industrial consumers.

Number of Franchisees: 835 in the United States and Canada.

In Business Since: 1936

Equity Capital Needed: $60,000-$150,000

Financial Assistance Available: Franchisor has various credit arrangements available for qualified franchisees with reference to the purchase of equipment from franchisor.

Training Provided: Franchisor provides training at Northbrook, Illinois, headquarters. Franchisor also provides management training, technical training and seminars.

Managerial Assistance Available: Franchisor has continuing managerial and technical assistance to franchisee through traveling district service training engineers, district managers, and industrial sales managers. This assistance is available to all franchisees as needed.

Information Submitted: April 1990

*RAINSOFT WATER CONDITIONING CO.
2080 Lunt Street
Elk Grove Village, Illinois 60007
John R. Grayson, President

Description of Operation: Sell, lease, and rent water treatment equipment to homes, businesses, and industry.

Number of Franchisees: Over 200 in most States

In Business Since: 1953

Equity Capital Needed: Varies from $15,000 minimum.

Financial Assistance Available: Assist in establishing retail financing. Financing of rental equipment to qualified dealers on selected basis.

Training Provided: On-plant and field training in sales, service, and operation.

Managerial Assistance Available: Continuing contact for training and assistance through national and regional seminars, plus regular person-to-person contact from regional field representatives.

Information Submitted: April 1990

WATERCARE CORPORATION
1520 North 24th Street
Manitowoc, Wisconsin 54220
William K. Granger, President

Description of Operation: Water conditioning sales and service, domestic, industrial, institutional and commercial. Method of service and sales is portable exchange water conditioners; permanently installed water conditioners on a rental basis and outright sales.

Number of Franchisees: 135 dealers in 35 States

In Business Since: 1946

Equity Capital Needed: $15,000

Financial Assistance Available: After initial financing Water-Care provides dealer growth money on plant equipment and rental water conditioners.

Training Provided: Includes techniques of water conditioning, water analysis, sales and service of equipment, office procedures, and management, all of which is done at our home office and plant in Manitowoc, Wisconsin, and our Dealer Lab company-owned retail operation at Green Bay, Wisconsin. Time is approximately 1 week in Wisconsin and 1 week by dealer counselor at the franchisee's place of operation. In addition, monthly call on franchisee by dealer counselor and semi-annual area work seminars.

Managerial Assistance Available: Same as above.

Information Submitted: April 1990

WATERMASTER AMERICA, INC.
1255 North High Street
Columbus, Ohio 43201
Jack W. Bernstein

Description of Operation: Water sub-metering for apartments, condos, office shopping centers and mobile home parks.

Number of Franchisees: 1 plus 1 company-owned.

In Business Since: 1983

Equity Capital Needed: Total investment $2,000-$5,000

Financial Assistance Available: Available

Training Provided: 1 week in Columbus, Ohio.

Managerial Assistance Available: Continuous.

Information Submitted: April 1990

WATER RESOURCES, INTERNATIONAL
2800 East Chambers Street
Phoenix, Arizona 85040
Chris Bower, Executive Vice President

Description of Operation: Manufacturing and distribution of water treatment and water purification equipment, both residential and commercial, to its nationwide network of franchisees who retail to the public.

Number of Franchisees: 100 franchise locations in the United States.

In Business Since: 1966

Equity Capital Needed: $20,000 plus start-up costs.

Financial Assistance Available: Franchisor will assist in securing consumer retail financing for franchisee.

Training Provided: 15 weeks of comprehensive training in all aspects of the business, including marketing, finance, installation, service, and administration.

Managerial Assistance Available: On-site training and ongoing supervision with a toll-free number to answer any questions that may arise.

Information Submitted: April 1990

MISCELLANEOUS WHOLESALE AND SERVICE BUSINESSES

ADS & TYPE EXPRESS
ADS & TYPE GRAPHICS, INC.
P. O. Box 133
Fairview, New Jersey 07022
Louis C. Fernandez, President

Description of Operation: State-of-the-art wholesale typesetting and graphics/art service without investing a cent on expensive typesetting equipment. No typesetting or art skills required whatsoever. We do all the production work for you. You wholesale to quick and commercial printers. You could operate this business at home with minimum overhead. Protected territory.

Number of Franchisees: 4 in 3 States.

In Business Since: 1985

Equity Capital Needed: Distributorship fee $1,500.

Financial Assistance Available: Credit-qualified individuals.

Training Provided: Complete training and continuous support. No typing, typesetting or art/graphics skills required.

Managerial Assistance Available: Continuous assistance via telephone hot line and periodic bulletins.

Information Submitted: May 1990

ALMOST HEAVEN HOT TUBS, LTD.
Route 1-F
Renick, West Virginia 24966
Barry Glick, Franchise Director

Description of Operation: Manufacture of hot tubs, spas, Jacuzzi whirlpool baths, sauna rooms, steam rooms and other leisure equipment.

Number of Franchisees: 1,493 in 50 States, Puerto Rico, Virgin Islands, and throughout the world.

In Business Since: 1968

Financial Assistance Available: Help in arranging financing through local banks.

Training Provided: Extensive training at manufacturing facility.

Managerial Assistance Available: Continual seminars, monthly bulletins, etc. 24-hour assistance, sales leads provided at no charge. Cooperative advertising program. Dealer territory protection.

Information Submitted: April 1990

THE ARMOLOY CORPORATION
1325 Sycamore Road
DeKalb, Illinois 60115
Jerome F. Bejbl, President

Description of Operation: Proprietary metal coating that is electrodeposited chromium, for wear and corrosion resistance of precision parts.

Number of Franchisees: 7 in 6 States, 1 in the United Kingdom, and 1 in West Germany.

In Business Since: 1955

Equity Capital Needed: $300,000-$400,000

Financial Assistance Available: None

Training Provided: Complete training period at corporate headquarters for key personnel. Continuing assistance in any phase of the business.

Managerial Assistance Available: Technical assistance is run by our quality control laboratory, and corporate provides any managerial help that is needed. We have advertising, administrative and sales help available.

Information Submitted: April 1990

ARMOR SHIELD, INC.
7685 Field Ertel Road
Cincinnati, Ohio 45241
Tony Rick

Description of Operation: Interior inspection, repair and coating of underground storage vessels containing petroleum products. Primary customers: major oil companies.

Number of Franchisees: 25 in 16 States

In Business Since: 1972

Equity Capital Needed: $80,000-$120,000

Financial Assistance Available: Very limited.

Training Provided: 3 weeks in field plus continual guidance.

Managerial Assistance Available: Annual seminar for managers and exchange of information. Technical assistance available.

Information Submitted: June 1990

BALLOON BOUQUETS, INC.
69 Kilburn Road
Belmont, Massachusetts 02178

Description of Operation: Balloon delivery and decorating and special events service.

Number of Franchisees: 16 in 12 States and Washington, D.C.

In Business Since: 1976

Equity Capital Needed: None

Financial Assistance Available: None

Training Provided: 2 days: business management, office operations, balloon delivery and balloon decorating.

Managerial Assistance Available: Continuing technical assistance. Advertising, purchasing, nationwide customer referrals to franchisees through toll-free 800 lines: 1-800-424-2323.

Information Submitted: April 1990

CHEMSTATION INTERNATIONAL, INC.
3201 Encrete Lane
Dayton, Ohio 45439
George F. Homan, President

Description of Operation: Chemical (cleaners) manufacturing and distribution to institutions and industry in unique bulk tanks tailored to the individual user's needs.

Number of Franchisees: 14 in Ohio, Michigan, Kentucky, Maryland, Wisconsin, Pennsylvania and Indiana

In Business Since: 1980

Equity Capital Needed: $50,000-$100,000

Financial Assistance Available: Help with third-party equipment leases, up to $30,000.

Training Provided: In field and equipment use training 5-10 days or as required up to 30 days.

Managerial Assistance Available: Ongoing managerial assistance throughout duration of 10 year agreement. Forecasting, sales analysis, product development, national account development, government supply development.

Information Submitted: April 1990

THE COMPLEAT ENGRAVER INTERNATIONAL, INC.
Plaza South, Suite 150-2
5850 Lakehurst Drive
Orlando, Florida 32819
Tom Foy, Sales Manager

Description of Operation: A perfected and proven system enables all franchisees to produce beautiful and very detailed engraved glassware. Coloration of the engraving is the latest technique added to the franchise; this allows our engravers to produce colored and engraved panels and mirrors to the highest standards. This is an exciting commercial business that appeals to both men and women seeking real job satisfaction. No artistic talent required.

Number of Franchisees: 16 in 4 countries.

In Business Since: 1974

Equity Capital Needed: $56,000

Financial Assistance Available: No direct financing but referral support provided.

Training Provided: 10 days at your location to set up workshop and classroom training.

Managerial Assistance Available: Up to 2 weeks at your location with a company representative assisting in marketing during your first month of operation. Ongoing seminars and regional meetings.

Information Submitted: June 1990

COMPOSIL NORTH AMERICA, INC.
6944 Sunbelt Drive South
San Antonio, Texas 78218
C. T. Amundsen, Director of Franchising

Description of Operation: Texile protection service for both commercial and residential accounts using an internationally proven product. Involves the marketing and application of the products for use on carpeting, wall fabric, upholstered fabric, and draperies.

Number of Franchisees: 22 in Texas, Kansas, Colorado, Arizona and Florida.

In Business Since: 1985

Equity Capital Needed: $1,500 to $2,500 depending on initial inventory desired.

Financial Assistance Available: None

Training Provided: Franchisee will take a mandatory one and one-half day training course that is scheduled for all new franchisees and key personnel. This one and one-half day process will be conducted at the corporate headquarters or franchise location.

Managerial Assistance Available: Composil provides continual management service for the life of the franchise. A complete manual covering all aspects of operations, forms, and advertising will be provided. Composil sponsors seminars for franchisees and conducts marketing and product research to maintain Composil consumer acceptance.

Information Submitted: April 1990

CROWN TROPHY, INC.
1 Odell Plaza
Yonkers, New York 10701
Chuck Wersenfeld, President

Description of Operation: Manufacturer of all types of awards, signs, trophies, plaques, medals, ribbons, desk accessories and advertising specialties.

Number of Franchisees: 13 in 4 States.

In Business Since: 1978

Equity Capital Needed: $48,000-$60,000

Financial Assistance Available: 100 percent financing for qualified buyers.

Training Provided: 2 weeks training: 1 week at home office and 1 week on-site.

Managerial Assistance Available: We will assist the buyer until he has enough knowledge on all the aspects of running his business.

Information Submitted: April 1990

FIRE DEFENSE CENTERS
3919 Morton Street
Jacksonville, Florida 32217

Description of Operation: Sale and service of fire extinguishers, sales and service of automatic fire extinguishing dry chemical restaurant systems, and sales plus service of first aid kits.

Number of Franchisees: 2 in Florida, 15 in other States.

In Business Since: 1973, franchising since 1985

Equity Capital Needed: $25,000-$29,500

Financial Assistance Available: Some

Training Provided: Sale, marketing, bookeeping, legal, service—complete turnkey operation, duration—7 days; followed by assistance at franchisee location—as needed.

Managerial Assistance Available: All managerial training in training, sales, marketing, bookkeeping, hiring, and servicing at regular intervals at home office and at franchisee's location.

Information Submitted: April 1990

FOLIAGE DESIGN SYSTEMS FRANCHISE CO.
1553 S.E. Fort King Avenue
Ocala, Florida 32671
John S. Hagood, C.E.O.

Description of Operation: The franchisor plans to authorize others to operate live foliage businesses, which sell foliage leasing and maintenance contracts to other businesses. The franchisee retains a contract from a business to provide and maintain live foliage plants on a lease basis or on a sale and maintenance basis. The plants are supplied to a business and are maintained by the franchisee, including replacing plants that need care in the greenhouse. The franchisee will also provide consultation with the businesses as to the number of live foliage plants, the types of plants, and the location within the business that plants are to be placed and can sell plants to the business, maintain them, or provide a guaranteed maintenance agreement, so that the business contracting with the franchisee would always maintain high grade foliage plants without having to be concerned with maintenance, replacement, greenhouse activities, and the like. The franchisee will maintain a local greenhouse, a van, and other facilities to properly maintain plants and to store an inventory of live foliage plants. The franchise businesses will be located mostly in urban or heavily populated suburban areas, where various types of businesses that might desire live foliage plants as part of the office decor can be found. The Foliage Design Systems Franchise Company makes no representation as to the amount of income the franchisee might expect from such franchise.

Number of Franchisees: 40 in 15 States.

In Business Since: 1971, franchising since 1980.

Equity Capital Needed: $20,000-$50,000

Financial Assistance Available: None

Training Provided: At least 10 days at franchise headquarters at Ocala, Florida, then 2 visits, each of which is 3-5 days to help with set-up of greenhouse and marketing help.

Managerial Assistance Available: Foliage Design Systems Franchise Company provides continual supervision of the life of the franchise. Manuals of operations, directories, and continued education are provided. The company makes available promotional advertising material and runs regional and national advertising for the benefit of the franchisees. In addition, the company publishes a newsletter quarterly that the franchisees can use for marketing.

Information Submitted: April 1990

*GREAT EXPECTATIONS CREATIVE MANAGEMENT, INC.
16830 Ventura Boulevard
Suite D
Encino, California 91436
Jeffrey Ullman, President

Description of Operation: Great Expectations is the oldest and largest singles introduction service in the world. In 1976 it created "video dating" so that singles could meet each offer for a committed romantic relationship. Currently, video dating is only one of several unique services offered to its singles membership.

Number of Franchisees: 39 in 18 States and Washington, D.C.

In Business Since: 1976

Equity Capital Needed: $175,000-$255,000

Financial Assistance Available: Negotiable

Training Provided: Intensive and comprehensive 2 week training at Los Angeles headquarters followed by a 1 month training visit to franchisee's centre. Additional training visits at franchisee's centre as well as at main headquarters are scheduled. Training includes a 500 page operations manual.

Managerial Assistance Available: Besides training at franchisee's home centre and franchisor's headquarters, frequent communication is maintained through telephone and letter correspondance. Franchisee is encouraged to pick up the phone and call franchisor or fellow franchisees. Each franchisee participates in the Great Expectations marketing group.

Information Submitted: May 1990

HAIR REPLACEMENT SYSTEMS (HRS)
dba HAIR ASSOCIATES, INC.
P. O. Box 939, Route 100
Old High School Building
Waitsfield, Vermont 05673
Leo Benjamin, Senior

Description of Operation: Sales and service of non-surgical men's and women's hair replacement procedures. Income from service is a major factor as well as repeat sales from existing clients.

Number of Franchisees: 51 in 19 States and 4 in Canada.

In Business Since: 1981

Equity Capital Needed: Franchise fee is $6,500 for the first 100,000 population. Capital requirements $25,000-$100,000.

Financial Assistance Available: Help in locating financing if collateral is available.

Training Provided: Franchisor will aid in location design. Pre-opening training includes sales and marketing training, technical training for hairstyling, and personnel and management training.

Training takes place in a working location as well as new franchised location. Ongoing sales training and technical training via regional workshops.

Managerial Assistance Available: Toll-free line into HRS administrative offices, support of administrative staff, professional consultants, plus other franchisees, annual national business meeting.

Information Submitted: April 1990

*HEEL/SEW QUIK!
1720 Cumberland Point Drive
Suite 15
Marietta, Georgia 30067

Description of Operation: Instant shoe repair, high-speed monogramming (computerized) and clothing alterations. Our objective is to create a one-stop service center to meet today's needs and demands. Hi-tech equipment and machinery means improved service/speed. Consistent quality work at very competitive prices. Specialty retail items related to all three services.

Number of Franchisees: 314 in 27 States and 5 countries.

In Business Since: 1984

Equity Capital Needed: $15,000-$25,000

Financial Assistance Available: None

Training Provided: 2 to 3 weeks training at company training center, operations manuals, video training tapes, continuing consulting support, in-the-field training, refresher and technical update sessions.

Managerial Assistance Available: In addition to training described above, licensor provides established total concept system of while-you-wait shoe repair methodology, sales, marketing techniques, trademarks and ongoing supervision and support, advertising package, training manuals and video tapes.

Information Submitted: April 1990

JEWELRY REPAIR ENTERPRISES, INC.
784 U.S. Highway 1, Suite 19
North Palm Beach, Florida 33408
Robert Goldstein

Description of Operation: Jewelry and watch repairs.

Number of Franchisees: 25

In Business Since: 1987

Equity Capital Needed: $65,000 depending on mall and location.

Financial Assistance Available: None

Training Provided: 1 week training.

Managerial Assistance Available: Yes, at all times.

Information Submitted: April 1990

MACHINERY WHOLESALERS CORP.
3510 Biscayne Boulevard
Miami, Florida 33137
Mark Fields, President

Description of Operation: Machinery Wholesalers is a totally unique industrial machinery brokerage network providing a computerized seller-to-buyer service through our computer center, with a data bank of more than 60,000 buyers, and offices coast to coast.

Number of Franchisees: Over 35 multiple territories in 32 States.

In Business Since: 1974

Equity Capital Needed: Territories $7,500 to $15,000.

Financial Assistance Available: Up to 50 percent, depending on amount of territories purchased by franchisee.

Training Provided: 3 working days of training from 8 am to 7 pm.

Managerial Assistance Available: Continuous supply of information; we are part of every sale.

Information Submitted: June 1990

MEISTERGRAM
3517 West Wendover Avenue
Greensboro, North Carolina 27407
Stephen R. Gluskin, Vice President/
General Manager

Description of Operation: Established in 1931, Meistergram, Inc., is the most comprehensive source of computerized, single-head monogramming and embroidery equipment. Meistergram owners include department stores, manufacturers, and entrepreneurs who establish a business in their home or storefront. New products include the Meistergram Embroidery Design System (MED), a computerized digitizing system for creating custom embroidery designs. Additional products include the ETCH-MASTER 2,000 and ETCH-MASTER 3,000, personalization equipment for glass and other hard-surfaced items including ceramics and acrylics. Comprehensive parts and supplies for monogramming/embroidery and etching systems, with a toll-free customer service hotline. Technical service in-house. On-site training by a certified Meistergram instructor.

Number of Franchisees: 8,000 in United States and overseas.

In Business Since: 1931

Equity Capital Needed: Monogramming/embroidery equipment: $19,750, ETCH-MASTER systems: $1,595-$1,995. MED equipment: $21,600-$27,400.

Financial Assistance Available: Leasing available to qualified U.S. applicants.

Training Provided: On-site, conducted by a trained Meistergram instructor.

Managerial Assistance Available: On-site training includes instruction in operation, techniques, and machine maintenance. Comprehensive manual includes marketing and promotional information.

Information Submitted: April 1990

MICROWAVE CLINIC
50 Budney Road
Newington, Connecticut 06111

Description of Operation: Microwave oven service center.

Number of Franchisees: 2 shops

In Business Since: 1987

Equity Capital Needed: $25,000-$40,000, includes franchise fee, equipment, tools, etc.

Financial Assistance Available: None

Training Provided: 2 weeks at home office location and continuing assistance at all times.

Managerial Assistance Available: Continuous as long as franchise is open.

Information Submitted: April 1990

NATURAL SETTINGS, INC.
Box 1277 - R.R. #3
Crete, Illinois 60417
Stan Woerner, Director of Franchising

Description of Operation: Natural Settings is an interior landscaping company specializing in a low overhead business concept that provides quality tropical plant lease and maintenance programs for offices, banks, restaurants, etc.

Number of Franchisees: 4 in 4 States

In Business Since: 1978, franchising since 1989.

Equity Capital Needed: $2,000-$5,000 working capital.

Financial Assistance Available: Financing is available and can be 100 percent depending on credit history.

Training Provided: An intensive 5 day training school is conducted using our Chicagoland accounts. The franchise owners will be trained in plant identification, bidding formulas, proper maintenance and technical assistance whenever needed.

Managerial Assistance Available: Ongoing.

Information Submitted: April 1990

OXYGEN THERAPY INSTITUTE, INC.
10656 Northend Avenue
Ferndale, Michigan 48220

Description of Operation: Manufacturer of portable emergency oxygen inhalators.

Number of Franchisees: 47 in 30 states and Canada

In Business Since: 1967

Financial Assistance Available: None

Training Provided: A training program is provided.

Managerial Assistance Available: Ongoing in all aspects of the operation.

Information Submitted: April 1990

*QUAL KROM FRANCHISING, INC.
301 Florida Avenue
Fort Pierce, Florida 33450
George W. Fluegel, President

Description of Operation: Restoration of chrome on antique automobiles, chrome plating marine, street rod parts, precious metal restoration, industrial plating and rechroming.

Number of Franchisees: 2 company-owned units in Florida and New York.

In Business Since: 1985

Equity Capital Needed: $50,000-$100,000

Financial Assistance Available: None

Training Provided: 6 weeks of initial training.

Managerial Assistance Available: Ongoing for term of agreement.

Information Submitted: June 1990

REDI NATIONAL PEST ELIMINATORS, INC.
4453 Aurora Avenue North
Seattle, Washington 98103-7376
Brett Lewis

Description of Operation: Redi National Pest Eliminator, Inc., offers a highly successful system for operating a pest control business including marketing programs and materials, technical methods and assistance and management systems.

Number of Franchisees: 11 in Alaska, Washington, Oregon and Arizona

In Business Since: 1980

Equity Capital Needed: $20,000

Financial Assistance Available: None

Training Provided: 15 day training program at the home office is mandatory. Follow-up training at franchisees location as necessary to meet minimum requirements.

Managerial Assistance Available: Ongoing support is provided to franchisee's including advertising, sales development programs, and field consultants to assist in all phases of operations. In addition, operations manuals, forms and materials are provided and continually updated.

Information Submitted: June 1990

SHOE FIXERS FRANCHISE SYSTEMS, INC.
3550 3 Mile Road
Grand Rapids, Michigan 49504
Sal Pierretta

Description of Operation: Instant shoe repair and shoe care stores.

Number of Franchisees: 33 in 13 States

In Business Since: 1987

Equity Capital Needed: $55,000-$120,000

Financial Assistance Available: Provides financing.

Training Provided: You receive 14 days of comprehensive instruction in store operation and management, from personnel to suggestive selling, at our franchise training center. Plus, upon opening you receive an additional 5 days of instruction and general assistance at your location.

Managerial Assistance Available: Our franchise development and support team possesses years of experience in the shoe care industry, retail management, franchise operations and marketing. You receive expert guidance in virtually every aspect of management, from business planning to personnel management to community relations.

Information Submitted: April 1990

SHOE STOP, INC.
13625 N.E. 165th Place
Suite 430
Kirkland, Washington 98034
Mike Pula, Manager, Franchise Sales

Description of Operation: Shoe Stop is an "instant" shoe-repair company that features quality repairs, outstanding customer service, and attractively designed stores. The outlets are located in shopping malls and other high-traffic sites; about 500 square feet of space is required.

Number of Franchisees: 20

In Business Since: 1984

Equity Capital Needed: $30,000 initial investment, total from $60,000 to $100,000.

Financial Assistance Available: Will work with franchisee to locate sources of capital.

Training Provided: Extensive training in shoe-repair skills and in the management of the business is provided. Shoe Stop has a training center and also uses company stores in the training process. The length of training is from 4-12 weeks, depending on the franchisee.

Managerial Assistance Available: Site selection, lease negotiations, turnkey store, operations manual, machine and equipment repairs, and promotion and sales support. Also able to purchase merchandise and materials directly from Shoe Stop.

Information Submitted: April 1990

THE SPORTS SECTION PHOTOGRAPHY, INC.
3120 Medlock Bridge Road
Norcross, Georgia 30071
R. Daniel Burgner, President

Description of Operation: TSS, a custom-color production facility, specializes in youth and youth sports photography. Franchisees with strengths in sales and marketing are trained in photography and become a part of our network of professionals offering unique photographic products and highly organized services to youth groups as a part- or full-time venture. Franchisees are encouraged to work from their homes. There is no merchandise to maintain; a protected territory of 500,000 to 1,000,000 population is worked year-round.

Number of Franchisees: 54 in 23 States including Canada and South Africa

In Business Since: 1983

Equity Capital Needed: Protected territories, $9,500-$25,000.

Financial Assistance Available: None

Training Provided: Sales and marketing training in territory for 1-2 days and complete photography training in territory. Additional training available according to size of territory and needed assistance.

Managerial Assistance Available: Turnkey operation provided, including all materials necessary for success. Sales and photography training provided in $20,000 franchise. Sales seminar in Atlanta headquarters for $7,900 franchise. Sales and photographic experts on call throughout United States.

Information Submitted: April 1990

*STAINED GLASS OVERLAY, INC.
2325 Morse Avenue
Irvine, California 92714
Peter Shea, President

Description of Operation: Franchisees are exclusive distributors of the patented "Overlay" process, which they apply to windows (without removing them from their mountings), mirrors, skylights, ceiling panels, etc. Just as beautiful as cut stained glass, Overlay has many benefits: it's seamless—no air or water leakage; it strengthens the glass; intricate designs are completed easily and quickly; over 200 colors coordinate with any decor; it can be used in residential and commercial markets anywhere—even where safety glass is specified. The corporation is continuously involved in market research and testing of new products and services. Complementary products available to franchisees now: oak doors and beveled glass, carved glass and designer rugs.

Number of Franchisees: 350 plus in United States, Australia, Canada, England, France, Germany, Switzerland, Japan and Israel.

In Business Since: 1974; franchising since 1981.

Equity Capital Needed: Franchise fee $34,000; start-up materials and supplies $11,000.

Financial Assistance Available: Initial cash investment required $45,000.

Training Provided: Minimum 40 hours training at corporate headquarters, including (but not limited to) Overlay application, marketing, and business administration. Ongoing updates and training through regional seminars and company newsletter.

Managerial Assistance Available: Corporate office provides continuous assistance in all phases of business operations and management, finances and recordkeeping, marketing and personnel. Upon request, a corporate representative will provide assistance at franchisee's location.

Information Submitted: June 1990

STARVING STUDENTS FRANCHISE CORPORATION
P. O. Box 351206
West Los Angeles, California 90035
Ethan H. Margalith, President

Description of Operation: Moving and storage—local, intrastate and interstate.

Number of Franchisees: 21

In Business Since: 1973

Equity Capital Needed: $16,950 to $40,000; $6,950 to $15,000 capital to begin business.

Financial Assistance Available: In some cases, for uniquely qualified individuals, franchisor will finance 100 percent under a partnership type arrangement! In some cases franchisor will accept a promissory note for $5,000 of the franchise fee.

Training Provided: Initial training lasts up to 8 weeks, depending on prior experience. Additionally, ongoing training is provided as necessary, for the duration of the franchise relationship.

Managerial Assistance Available: All phases of operations, moving company accounting, advertising and promotion, etc. Duration of assistance will vary with individual's experience and background.

Information Submitted: June 1990

SUNBANQUE ISLAND TANNING
2533 A Yonge Street
Toronto, M4P 2M9
Canada
Joel Giusto

Description of Operation: SunBanque has full service tanning salons with indoor and outdoor related products. State-of-the-art equipment. Full computerization with total inventory and sales control.

Number of Franchisees: 12 in Massachusetts and Canada

In Business Since: 1983

Equity Capital Needed: $40,000, depending on leasehold improvements.

Financial Assistance Available: Full financing.

Training Provided: Provided in advertising, public relations and merchandising techniques.

Managerial Assistance Available: Site selection, lease negotiations, training/operations manuals, supplies, advertising materials and ongoing support.

Information Submitted: April 1990

TEMPACO, INC.
1701 Alden Road
P. O. Box 547667
Orlando, Florida 32854-7667
Charles T. Clark, President

Description of Operation: Wholesale parts and controls for heating, air conditioning and refrigeration.

Number of Franchisees: 17 in 5 States

In Business Since: 1946

Equity Capital Needed: Approximately $60,000 to $75,000

Financial Assistance Available: None

Training Provided: 2 weeks introductory training, supplemental and retraining on a non-scheduled basis. Ongoing.

Managerial Assistance Available: Continuous management counsel in areas of bookkeeping, inventory control, accounts receivable, operational procedures, training, advertising and publicity, purchasing control, sales in accordance with the need of the franchisee.

Information Submitted: May 1990

TOGETHER DATING SERVICE
171 Main Street
Ashland, Massachusetts 01721
Brian J. Pappas

Description of Operation: Personal dating service.

Number of Franchisees: 62 offices nationwide; 17 company-owned offices.

In Business Since: 1974

Equity Capital Needed: Minimum $50,000.

Financial Assistance Available: Franchisor will finance up to 66-2/3 percent of initial franchise fee.

Training Provided: In our training offices and in the franchisee's office.

Managerial Assistance Available: Ongoing assistance in managerial and marketing especially—in the supply of new advertising materials, which include TV commercials, radio commercials, etc.

Information Submitted: June 1990

TRAILS END CREMAINS SCATTERING SERVICE, INC.
3279 Silverthorne Drive
Ft. Collins, Colorado 80526
Bonnie J. Harden

Description of Operation: Cremated remains scattered over a requested area by airplane.

Number of Franchisees: 2 company-owned, available in every state.

In Business Since: 1985

Equity Capital Needed: $8,000

Financial Assistance Available: None

Training Provided: Video instructional training course.

Managerial Assistance Available: Continuing support relating to the conduct of franchisee's business and interstate network.

Information Submitted: April 1990

NEW BUSINESS INVESTMENT CORPORATION
Franchisor of THE ULTIMATE TAN
408 Warren Avenue
Suite AA
Normal, Illinois 61761
Lawrence Pritts, President

Description of Operation: We plan 8 bed tanning salons. We are qualified in lease negotiations, site selection, decorating, floor plans, general contracting and all facets of the tanning business.

Number of Franchisees: 4 units including company-owned in Illinois.

In Business Since: 1984

Equity Capital Needed: Minimum cost: $100,000 and maximum cost: $150,000.

Financial Assistance Available: Yes

Training Provided: 2 weeks on-the-job training in one of franchisor's tanning salons plus ongoing assistance. This training will be received by the person who will manage franchisee store.

Managerial Assistance Available: Periodic inspections and ongoing managerial and technical assistance by telephone and mail will be provided for the duration of the agreement.

Information Submitted: June 1990

UNITED WORTH HYDROCHEM CORPORATION
P. O. Box 366
Fort Worth, Texas 76101
Roy Coleman, President

Description of Operation: Chemical water treating and chemical cleaning service for cooling towers, boilers, closed systems and heat exchangers. Program built around personal service. Start as one-person operation and grow from there. Territory is fully protected.

Number of Franchisees: 20 in 8 States

In Business Since: 1959

Equity Capital Needed: $1,500

Financial Assistance Available: Franchisee must have personal capital or income to support his family needs during first year.

Training Provided: Training school of 2 weeks at home office for theory. Close training in the field during first few months. Close technical support from there on.

Managerial Assistance Available: Worth provides continuous management, sales and technical service to all franchisers. Laboratory support is available on a no charge basis. Technical seminars are held on a semi-annual basis. Worth conducts continuous product research.

Information Submitted: May 1990

WATSCO, INC.
1943 Oakley
Topeka, Kansas 66604
Larry G. Waters, President

Description of Operation: Wat-A-Egg—Watsco, Inc., provides processing and marketing assistance to egg companies to enter the market of hard-cooked peeled egg processors. Wat-A-Heater—Wat-A-Heater is a waste heat water heater for residential use. Watsco, Inc., trains licensees to market and install these low cost units that reduce utility bills and increase volume of hot water. Licensees are in water softeners or plumbing.

Number of Franchisees: 31 in 12 States, Canada, United Kingdom, South Africa, Australia, the Netherlands, Belgium, Switzerland and Puerto Rico.

In Business Since: 1970

Equity Capital Needed: $5,000

Financial Assistance Available: None

Training Provided: 1 week at Watsco, Inc., home office.

Managerial Assistance Available: Initial training in installation and marketing at home office and continuous support in the field.

Information Submitted: April 1990

INDEX OF FRANCHISING PARTICIPANTS

Alphabetical

285

286

INDEX OF FRANCHISING PARTICIPANTS

By Category

BEAUTY SALONS/SUPPLIES

BUSINESS AIDS AND SERVICES

CAMPGROUNDS

CHILDRENS STORES/FURNITURE/PRODUCTS

CLOTHING/SHOES

CONSTRUCTION/REMODELING
MATERIALS/SERVICES

EQUIPMENT/RENTALS

FOOD—DONUTS

FOOD—GROCERY/SPECIALTY STORES

FOODS—ICE CREAM/YOGURT/CANDY/POPCORN/BEVERAGES

FOODS—PANCAKE/WAFFLE/PRETZEL

FOODS—RESTAURANTS/DRIVE-INS/CARRY-OUTS

295

GENERAL MERCHANDISING STORES

HEALTH AIDS/SERVICES

MAINTENANCE—CLEANING/SANITATION—SERVICES/SUPPLIES

MOTELS—HOTELS

OPTICAL PRODUCTS/SERVICES

PET SHOPS

PRINTING

REAL ESTATE

RECREATION/ENTERTAINMENT/ TRAVEL—SERVICES/SUPPLIES

RETAILING—ART SUPPLIES/FRAMES

RETAILING—COMPUTER SALES/SERVICES

RETAILING—FLORIST

RETAILING—NOT ELSEWHERE CLASSIFIED